Encyclopedia of

African~American

Culture *and* History

Editorial Board

second edition

THE BLACK EXPERIENCE
IN THE AMERICAS

ENCYCLOPEDIA of
AFRICAN~AMERICAN
CULTURE and HISTORY

published in association with
THE SCHOMBURG CENTER FOR RESEARCH IN BLACK CULTURE

COLIN A. PALMER
Editor in Chief

6

VOLUME

MACMILLAN REFERENCE USA
An imprint of Thomson Gale, a part of The Thomson Corporation

THOMSON

GALE

Detroit • New York • San Francisco • San Diego • New Haven, Conn. • Waterville, Maine • London • Munich

Encyclopedia of African-American Culture and History, Second Edition

Colin A. Palmer, Editor in Chief

LIBRARY OF CONGRESS CATALOGING-IN-PUBLICATION DATA

Encyclopedia of African-American culture and history : the Black experience in the Americas / Colin A. Palmer, editor in chief.— 2nd ed.
   p. cm.
     Includes bibliographical references and index.
     ISBN 0-02-865816-7 (set hardcover : alk. paper) —
     ISBN 0-02-865817-5 (v. 1) — ISBN 0-02-865818-3 (v. 2) —
     ISBN 0-02-865819-1 (v. 3) — ISBN 0-02-865820-5 (v. 4) —
     ISBN 0-02-865821-3 (v. 5) — ISBN 0-02-865822-1 (v. 6)
     1. African Americans—Encyclopedias. 2. African Americans—History—Encyclopedias. 3. Blacks—America—Encyclopedias. 4. Blacks—America—History—Encyclopedias. I. Palmer, Colin A., 1942-

E185.E54 2005
973'.0496073'003—dc22

2005013029

This title is also available as an e-book.
ISBN 0-02-866071-4

Contact your Thomson Gale representative for ordering information.

Printed in the United States of America
10 9 8 7 6 5 4 3 2 1

Editorial and Production Staff

PROJECT EDITORS
Christine Slovey
Jeffrey Lehman

CONTRIBUTING EDITORS
Shawn Corridor
Kristin Hart
Alan Hedblad
Jenai Mynatt

EDITORIAL TECHNICAL SUPPORT
Mark Springer

MANUSCRIPT EDITORS
Sheryl A. Ciccarelli
Judith Culligan
Andrew Cunningham
Peter Jaskowiak
Michael J. O'Neal

ADDITIONAL EDITORIAL SUPPORT
Jennifer Albers
Mark Drouillard
Anjanelle Klisz
Jaime E. Noce
Nicole Watkins

PROOFREADERS
Judith A. Clinebell
Amanda Quick

INDEXER
Laurie Andriot

PRODUCT DESIGN
Kate Scheible
Tracey Rowens

IMAGING
Dean Dauphinais
Leitha Etheridge-Sims
Lezlie Light
Christine O'Bryan

GRAPHIC ART
GGS Information Services
XNR Productions

RIGHTS ACQUISITION AND MANAGEMENT
Margaret Chamberlain-Gaston
Ronald Montgomery
Susan Rudolph

COMPOSITION
Evi Seoud
Mary Beth Trimper

COMPOSITOR
Datapage Technologies International, Inc.

MANUFACTURING
Wendy Blurton

DIRECTOR, NEW PRODUCT DEVELOPMENT
Hélène Potter

PUBLISHER
Frank Menchaca

Contents

Appendix Contents

Thematic Outline of Contents

This outline of contents provides an alphabetized list of the entries arranged by subject terms that are much broader than in the general index at the end of this volume. Any biographical entries related to the topic appear together at the end of the list. Most entries applied to more than one theme.

ASSOCIATIONS AND ORGANIZATIONS

Abakuá
African Blood Brotherhood
African Civilization Society (AfCS)
American Moral Reform Society
American Negro Academy (ANA)
American Tennis Association
Antebellum Convention Movement
Associated Publishers
Association for the Advancement of Creative Musicians
Association for the Study of African American Life and History
Black Academy of Arts and Letters
Black Panther Party for Self-Defense
Black Women's Club Movement
Brotherhood of Sleeping Car Porters
Brown Fellowship Society
Civil Rights Congress
Club Atenas
Colored Farmers Alliance
Congressional Black Caucus
Congress of National Black Churches, Inc.
Congress of Racial Equality (CORE)
Council on African Affairs
Farm Worker Program
Federal Writers' Project

Fraternal Orders
Fraternities, U.S.
Freedman's Bank
Freedmen's Hospital
Harlem Writers Guild
Institute of the Black World
Jack and Jill of America
League of Revolutionary Black Workers
Lowndes County Freedom Organization
Manumission Societies
Medical Associations
Mississippi Freedom Democratic Party
Montgomery Improvement Association
Mutual Aid Societies
NAACP Legal Defense and Educational Fund
National Afro-American League/ Afro-American Council
National Association for the Advancement of Colored People (NAACP)
National Association of Colored Women
National Association of Negro Musicians
National Bankers Association

National Baptist Convention, U.S.A., Inc.
National Black Evangelical Association
National Council of Negro Women
National Federation of Afro-American Women
National Hospital Association
National League for the Protection of Colored Women
National Negro Congress
National Negro Labor Council
National Urban League
National Welfare Rights Organization
Negro Sanhedrin
Niagara Movement
OBAC Writers' Workshop
Operation PUSH (People United to Serve Humanity)
Philanthropy and Foundations
Poor People's Campaign
Professional Organizations
Republic of New Africa
Sororities, U.S.
Southern Christian Leadership Conference (SCLC)
Spingarn Medal
Student Nonviolent Coordinating Committee (SNCC)

POLITICS

Popular, Visual, and Folk Culture

Turner, Henry McNeal

RELIGION AND SPIRITUALITY, TRADITIONAL/FOLK

Africanisms
Candomblé
Central African Religions and
    Culture in the Americas
Divination and Spirit Possession in
    the Americas
Folk Religion
Healing and the Arts in Afro-
    Caribbean Cultures
Kumina
Myal
Negros Brujos
Obeah
Orisha
Santería
Santería Aesthetics
Slave Religions
Voodoo
Winti in Suriname
Yoruba Religion and Culture in the
    Americas
Biographies
Kennedy, Imogene Queenie
Laveau, Marie

SCIENCES

African Burial Ground Project
African Diaspora
Anthropology and Anthropologists
Anti-Haitianism
Archaeology and Archaeologists
Archival Collections
Astronauts
Black Middle Class
Critical Mixed-Race Studies
Critical Race Theory
Demography
Educational Psychology and
    Psychologists
Environmental Racism
Ethnic Origins
Historians and Historiography,
    African-American
Inventors and Inventions
Mathematicians
Migration in the African Diaspora
Migration/Population, U.S.
Mortality and Morbidity in Latin
    America and the Caribbean
Mortality and Morbidity in the
    United States
Opportunity: Journal of Negro Life

Patents and Inventions
Phylon
Race, Scientific Theories of
Race and Science
Science
Skin Color
Social Psychology, Psychologists,
    and Race
Sociology
Biographies
Augier, Roy
Bailey, Beryl Loftman
Banneker, Benjamin
Brimmer, Andrew Felton
Brodber, Erna
Calloway, Nathaniel
Carneiro, Edison
Carver, George Washington
Cayton, Horace
Clark, Kenneth Bancroft
Clarke, John Henrik
Cox, Oliver Cromwell
Davis, Allison
Drake, St. Clair
Du Bois, W. E. B.
Franklin, John Hope
Frazier, Edward Franklin
Goveia, Elsa V.
Hancock, Gordon Blaine
Harris, Abram Lincoln, Jr.
Henson, Matthew A.
Hurston, Zora Neale
Hutson, Jean Blackwell
Jackson, Luther Porter
Johnson, Charles Spurgeon
Just, Ernest
Labov, William
Latimer, Lewis Howard
Logan, Rayford W.
Nethersole, Noel Newton
Ogbu, John
Painter, Nell Irvin
Quarles, Benjamin
Rebouças, André
Robeson, Eslanda
Schomburg, Arthur
Sherlock, Philip
Turner, Lorenzo Dow
Weaver, Robert Clifton
Wesley, Charles Harris
West, Cornel
Williams, George Washington
Wilson, William Julius
Woodson, Carter G.
Work, Monroe Nathan

Wynter, Sylvia

SLAVERY AND FREEDOM

Abolition
African Diaspora
Africanisms
Amelioration
Amistad Mutiny
Bureau of Refugees, Freedmen, and
    Abandoned Lands
Civil War, U.S.
Coartación
Congos of Panama
Declaration of Independence
Demerara Revolt
Domestic Workers
Dred Scott v. Sandford
Emancipation in Latin America and
    the Caribbean
Emancipation in the United States
Ethnic Origins
Frederick Douglass' Paper
Free Blacks, 1619–1860
Gracia Real de Santa Teresa de
    Mose
Gullah
Law and Liberty in England and
    America
Liberator, The
Manumission Societies
Maroon Societies in the Caribbean
Nat Turner's Rebellion
North Star
Palenque San Basilio
Palmares
Port Royal Experiment
Reparations
Runaway Slaves in Latin America
    and the Caribbean
Runaway Slaves in the United States
Slavery
Slavery and the Constitution
Slave Trade
Thirteenth Amendment
Underground Railroad
Biographies
Anastácia
Aponte, José Antonio
Bandera, Quintín
Barbadoes, James G.
Bibb, Henry Walton
Brown, Henry "Box"
Burns, Anthony
Carey, Lott
Celia
Clarke, Lewis G.
Coker, Daniel

Basquiat, Jean-Michel
Bearden, Romare
Blackburn, Robert
Burroughs, Margaret Taylor
Catlett, Elizabeth
DeCarava, Roy
Delaney, Joseph
Douglas, Aaron
Feelings, Thomas
Fuller, Meta Vaux Warrick
Hammons, David
Holder, Geoffrey
Huie, Albert
Johnson, Joshua

Jones, Philip Mallory
Lam, Wifredo
Lawrence, Jacob
Lewis, Edmonia
Ligon, Glenn
Lisboa, Antônio Francisco
Manley, Edna
Marshall, Kerry James
Motley, Archibald John, Jr.
Parks, Gordon
Piper, Adrian
Powers, Harriet
Puryear, Martin
Ringgold, Faith

Saar, Alison
Saar, Betye Irene
Savage, Augusta
Simpson, Lorna
Sleet, Moneta J., Jr.
Stout, Reneé
Tanner, Henry Ossawa
VanDerZee, James
Walker, Kara
Weems, Carrie Mae
Willis, Deborah
Wilson, Fred
Woodruff, Hale

PRIMARY SOURCE DOCUMENTS CONTENTS

The documents listed below and reprinted in chronological order in the following pages were selected by the editors of the Encyclopedia as important documents in the history and experience of Africans in the Americas.

THE BEGINNINGS OF THE PORTUGUESE-AFRICAN SLAVE TRADE IN THE FIFTEENTH CENTURY, AS DESCRIBED BY THE CHRONICLER GOMES EANNES DE AZURARA (C. 1450)

SOURCE: Conrad, Robert Edgar. *Children of God's Fire: A Documentary History of Black Slavery in Brazil.* Princeton, N.J.: Princeton University Press, 1984, pp. 5–11.

INTRODUCTION: *Portuguese historian Gomes Eannes de Azurara offers perhaps the earliest description of the onset of the Portuguese-African slave trade in the fifteenth century, commenting on the traders' motives and detailing the capture, treatment, and distribution of "Moorish captives."*

Since Prince [Henry the Navigator] was normally to be found in the Kingdom of the Algarve after his return from Tangier because of the town he was having built there, and since the prisoners whom [his captains] brought back were landed at Lagos [the town where Henry established his headquarters], it was the people of this place who first persuaded the Prince to grant them permission to go to that land from which the Moorish captives came. . . .

The most important captain was Lançarote, and the second Gil Eannes, who, as we have written, was the first to round Cape Bojador. Aside from these, there were Stevam Affonso, a nobleman who died later in the Canary Islands, Rodrigo Alvarez, Joham Dyaz, a shipowner, and Joham Bernaldez, all of whom were very well qualified. Setting out on their voyage, they arrived at the Island of Herons [Ilha das Garças] on the eve of Corpus Christi, where they rested for a time, living mainly from the many young birds they found there, since it was the breeding season. . . .

And so these two captains [Martim Vicente and Gil Vasquez] made preparations, and they took five boats manned by thirty men, six in each boat, and set out at about sunset. Rowing the entire night, they arrived about daybreak at the island they were looking for. And when they recognized it by signs the Moors had mentioned, they rowed for awhile close to the shore until, as it was getting light, they reached a Moorish village near the beach where all the island's inhabitants were gathered together. Seeing this, our men stopped for a time to discuss what they should do. . . . And after giving their opinions, they looked toward the village where they saw that the Moors, with their women and children, were leaving their houses as fast as they could, for they had seen their enemies. The latter, crying the names of St. James, St. George, and Portugal, attacked them, killing and seizing as many as they could. There you could have seen mothers forsaking their children, husbands abandoning their wives, each person trying to escape as best he could. And some drowned themselves in the water; others tried to hide in their huts; others, hoping they would escape, hid their children among the sea grasses where they were later discovered. And in the end our Lord God, who rewards every good deed, decided that, for their labors undertaken in His service, they should gain a victory over their enemies on that day, and a reward and payment for all their efforts and expenses. For on that day they captured 165 [Moors], including men, women, and the children, not counting those who died or were killed. When the battle was over, they praised God for the great favor He had shown them, in wishing to grant them such a victory, and with so little harm to themselves. After their captives had been put in the boats, with others securely tied up on land, since the boats were small and could not hold so many people, they ordered a man to go as far as he could along the coast to see if he could sight the caravels. He set out at once, and, going more than a league from where the others were waiting, he saw the caravels arriving, because, as he had promised, Lançarote had sailed at dawn.

And when Lançarote, with those squires and highborn men who accompanied him, heard of the good fortune which God had granted to that handful of men who had gone to the island, and saw that they had accomplished such a great deal, it pleasing God to bring the affair to such a conclusion, they were all very happy, praising God for wishing to aid those few Christians in this manner. . . .

On the next day, which was a Friday, they prepared their boats, since the caravels had to remain where they were, and loaded into them all the supplies needed for two days only, since they did not intend to stay away from their ships any longer than that. Some thirty men departed in the boats, namely Lancarote and the other captains of the caravels, and with them squires and highborn men who were there. And they took with them two of those Moors whom they had captured, because they had told them that on the island of Tiger, which was five leagues distant, there was a Moorish village of about 150 persons. And as soon as it was morning, they set out, all very devoutly commending themselves to God, and asking His help in guiding them so that He might be served and His Holy Catholic Faith exalted. And they rowed until they reached the said island of Tiger; and as soon as they had leaped upon the shore the Moor who was with them led them to a village, where all the Moors, or at least most of those on the island, had earlier assembled . . . ; and Lançarote, with fourteen or fifteen men, went toward the place where the Moor led them. And walking half a league . . . they saw nine Moors, both men and women, with ten or twelve asses loaded with turtles, who hoped to cross over to the island of Tiger, which would be a league from there, it being possible to cross from one island to the other on foot. And as soon as they saw them, they pursued them, and, offering no effective defense, they were all captured except one, who fled to inform the others in the village. And as soon as they had captured them, they sent them to the place where Gil Eannes was, Lançarote ordering him to place a guard over the Moors, and then to set out after them, using all the men he had, because he believed that they would find someone to fight with.

And as soon as the captives reached them, they bound them securely and put them in the boats, and leaving only one man with them, they set out at once behind Lançarote, following constantly in his footsteps until they reached the place where Lançarote and his followers were. After capturing the Moors whom they had sent to the boats, they followed the Moor to a village that its inhabitants had abandoned, having been warned by the Moor who had escaped when the others were taken prisoner.

And then they saw all the people of the island on a smaller island where they had gone in their canoes; and the Christians could not reach them except by swimming, nor did they dare to retreat for fear of encouraging their enemies, who were much more numerous than they were. And thus they remained until all the other men had reached them; and seeing that even when they were all together they could not do them any harm, because of the water that lay between them, they decided to return to their boats which were a good two leagues away.

And, upon their return, they entered the village and searched everything to see if they might find something in the houses. And, while searching, they found seven or eight Moorish women, whom they took with them, thanking God for their good fortune which they had received through His grace; and thus they returned to their boats, which they reached at about sunset, and they rested and enjoyed themselves that night like men who had toiled hard throughout the day. . . .

The needs of the night forced them to spend it mainly in sleep, but their minds were so fixed upon the tasks that lay before them that they could think of nothing else. And so they discussed what they would do the next day, and, after hearing many arguments, which I will omit in order not to make my story too long, they decided to go in their boats to attack the settlement before daybreak. . . . Having reached this decision, they set out in the dark, rowing their boats along the shore. And as the sun began to rise, they landed and attacked the village, but found no one in it, because the Moors, having seen their enemies leaving, had returned to the village, but, not wanting to sleep in it, they had gone to stay a quarter of a league away near a crossing point by which they went over to Tiger. And when the Christians recognized that they could find nothing in the village, they returned to their boats and coasted along that island on the other side of Tiger, and they sent fifteen men overland to see if they could find any Moors or any trace of them. And on their way they saw the Moors fleeing as fast as they could, for they had already observed them, and then all our men leaped out on land and began to pursue them. They were not able to reach the men, but they took seventeen or eighteen of the women and small children who could not run so fast. And one of the boats, in which Joham Bemaldez was traveling, one of the smallest, went along the coast of the island; and the men in the boat saw some twenty canoes which were moving toward Tiger, in which Moors of both sexes were traveling, both adults and children, four or five in each boat. And they were very pleased when they first saw this, but later greatly saddened. Their pleasure came from seeing the profit and honor that lay before them, which was their reason for going there; their sadness came when they recognized that their boat was so small that they could put only a very few aboard. And with their few oars, they pursued them as well as they could, until they were among the canoes; and, stirred by pity, even though the people in the canoes were heathens, they wished to kill very few of them. However, there is no reason not to believe that many of them, who in their terror abandoned the boats, did not perish in the sea.

And some of them were on the left and some on the right, and, going in among them, they selected the smallest, because this way they could load more into their boats, of which they took fourteen, so that those who were captured in those two days, not including some who died, totaled forty-eight. . . .

The caravels arrived at Lagos, from where they had set out, enjoying fine weather on the voyage, since fortune was no less generous in the mildness of the weather than it had been to them in the taking of their prizes. And from Lagos the news reached the Prince, who just hours before had arrived there from other places where he had spent some days. . . . And the next day, Lançarote, as the man who had had the main responsibility, said to the Prince: "Sir! Your Grace knows full well that you must accept the fifth of these Moors, and of everything which we took in that land, where you sent us in the service of God and yourself. And now these Moors, because of the long time we have been at sea, and because of the obvious sorrow in their hearts at finding themselves far from their birthplace and held in captivity, without possessing any knowledge of what their future will be; as well as because they are not used to sailing on ships; for all these reasons they are in a rather poor condition and sickly; and so it seems to me that it will be useful for you to order them removed from the caravels in the morning and taken to that field that lies outside the city gate, and there divided up into five parts, according to custom, and that Your Grace should go there and select one of the parts which best suits you." The Prince said that he was well pleased, and very early the next day Lançarote ordered the masters of the caravels to bring them outside and to take them to that field, where they were to be divided up, as stated before; but, before doing anything else, they took the best of the Moors as an offering to the church of that place, and another little one who later became a friar of St. Francis they sent to São Vicente do Cabo, where he always lived as a Catholic Christian, without any knowledge or feeling for any other law but the holy and true doctrine, in which all Christians await our salvation. And the Moors of that conquest numbered 235. . . .

On the next day, which was August 8, the seamen began to prepare their boats very early in the morning, because of the heat, and to bring out those captives so that they could be transferred as ordered. And the latter, placed together in that field, were a marvelous thing to behold, because among them there were some who were reasonably white, handsome, and genteel; others, not so white, who were like mulattoes; others as black as Ethiopians, so deformed both in their faces and bodies, that it seemed to those who guarded them that they were gazing upon images of the lowest hemisphere. But what human heart, no matter how hard, would not be stabbed by pious feelings when gazing upon such a company of people? For some had their heads held low and their faces bathed in tears, as they looked upon one another. Others were moaning most bitterly, gazing toward heaven, fixing their eyes upon it, as if they were asking for help from the father of nature. Others struck their faces with the palms of their hands, throwing themselves prostrate upon the ground; others performed their lamentations in the form of a chant, according to the custom of their country, and, although our people could not understand the words of their language, they were fully appropriate to the level of their sorrow. But to increase their suffering even more, those responsible for dividing them up arrived on the scene and began to separate one from another, in order to make an equal division of the fifths, from which arose the need to separate children from their parents, wives from their husbands, and brothers from their brothers. Neither friendship nor kinship was respected, but instead each one fell where fortune placed him! Oh powerful destiny, doing and undoing with your turning wheels, arranging the things of this world as you please! do you even disclose to those miserable people some knowledge of what is to become of them, so that they may receive some consolation in the midst of their tremendous sorrow? And you who labor so hard to divide them up, look with pity upon so much misery, and see how they cling to each other, so that you can hardly separate them! Who could accomplish that division without the greatest toil; because as soon as they had put the children in one place, seeing their parents in another, they rose up energetically and went over to them; mothers clasped their other children in their arms, and threw themselves face down upon the ground with them, receiving blows with little regard for their own flesh, if only they might not be parted from them!

And so with great effort they finished the dividing up, because, aside from the trouble they had with the captives, the field was quite full of people, both from the town and from the surrounding villages and districts, who for that day were taking time off from their work, which was the source of their earnings, for the sole purpose of observing this novelty. And seeing these things, while some wept, others took part in the separating, and they made such a commotion that they greatly confused those who were in charge of dividing them up.

The Prince was there mounted upon a powerful horse, accompanied by his retinue, distributing his favors, like a man who wished to derive little material advantage from his share; for of the forty-six souls who belonged to his fifth, he quickly divided them up among the rest, since his main source of wealth lay in his own purpose; for he reflected with great pleasure upon the salvation of those souls that before were lost.

And his thoughts were certainly not in vain, because, as we have said, as soon as they gained a knowledge of our language, they turned Christian without much difficulty; and I who have brought this history together in this volume saw boys and girls in the town of Lagos, the children and grandchildren of those people, born in this land, Christians as good and true as though they were descended from the beginnings of Christ's law, through the generation of those who were first baptized.

THE INTERESTING NARRATIVE OF THE LIFE OF OLAUDAH EQUIANO, OR GUSTAVUS VASSA, THE AFRICAN, WRITTEN BY HIMSELF (OLAUDAH EQUIANO, 1789)

■ ■ ■

SOURCE: Equiano, Olaudah. *The Interesting Narrative of the Life of Olaudah Equiano, or Gustavus Vassa, the African, Written by Himself.* Edited by Werner Sollors. New York: W. W. Norton & Company, 1991, pp. 38–43.

INTRODUCTION: *Born in 1745 in the region of Africa now known as Nigeria, Olaudah Equiano was sold into slavery in 1756 and transported with other slaves by ship to Barbadoes. He purchased his freedom a decade later and moved to England, where he penned his autobiography in 1789. The following excerpt from Equiano's narrative relates his experience of the "middle passage" from Africa to the West Indies.*

The first object which saluted my eyes when I arrived on the coast was the sea, and a slave ship, which was then riding at anchor, and waiting for its cargo. These filled me with astonishment, which was soon converted into terror when I was carried on board. I was immediately handled and tossed up to see if I were sound by some of the crew; and I was now persuaded that I had gotten into a world of bad spirits, and that they were going to kill me. Their complexions too differing so much from ours, their long hair, and the language they spoke, (which was very different from any I had ever heard) united to confirm me in this belief. Indeed such were the horrors of my views and fears at the moment, that, if ten thousand worlds had been my own, I would have freely parted with them all to have exchanged my condition with that of the meanest slave in my own country. When I looked round the ship too and saw a large furnace or copper boiling, and a multitude of black people of every description chained together, every one of their countenances expressing dejection and sorrow, I no longer doubted of my fate; and, quite overpowered with horror and anguish, I fell motionless on the deck and fainted. When I recovered a little I found some black people about me, who I believed were some of those who brought me on board, and had been receiving their pay; they talked to me in order to cheer me, but all in vain. I asked them if we were not to be eaten by those white men with horrible looks, red faces, and loose hair. They told me I was not; and one of the crew brought me a small portion of spirituous liquor in a wine glass; but, being afraid of him, I would not take it out of his hand. One of the blacks therefore took it from him and gave it to me, and I took a little down my palate, which, instead of reviving me, as they thought it would, threw me into the greatest consternation at the strange feeling it produced, having never tasted any such liquor before. Soon after this the blacks who brought me on board went off, and left me abandoned to despair. I now saw myself deprived of all chance of returning to my native country, or even the least glimpse of hope of gaining the shore, which I now considered as friendly; and I even wished for my former slavery in preference to my present situation, which was filled with horrors of every kind, still heightened by my ignorance of what I was to undergo. I was not long suffered to indulge my grief; I was soon put down under the decks, and there I received such a salutation in my nostrils as I had never experienced in my life: so that, with the loathsomeness of the stench, and crying together, I became so sick and low that I was not able to eat, nor had I the least desire to taste any thing. I now wished for the last friend, death, to relieve me; but soon, to my grief, two of the white men offered me eatables; and, on my refusing to eat, one of them held me fast by the hands, and laid me across I think the windlass, and tied my feet, while the other flogged me severely. I had never experienced any thing of this kind before; and although, not being used to the water, I naturally feared that element the first time I saw it, yet nevertheless, could I have got over the nettings, I would have jumped over the side, but I could not; and, besides, the crew used to watch us very closely who were not chained down to the decks, lest we should leap into the water: and I have seen some of these poor African prisoners most severely cut for attempting to do so, and hourly whipped for not eating. This indeed was often the case with myself. In a little time after, amongst the poor chained men, I found some of my own nation, which in a small degree gave ease to my mind. I inquired of these what was to be done with us; they gave me to understand we were to be carried to these white people's country to work for them. I then was a little revived, and thought, if it were no worse than working, my situation was not so desperate: but still I feared I should be put to death, the white people looked and acted, as I thought, in so savage a manner; for I had never seen among any people such instances of brutal cruelty; and this not only shewn towards us blacks, but also to some of the whites themselves. One white man in particular I saw, when we were permitted to be on deck, flogged so unmercifully with a large rope near the foremast, that he died in consequence of it; and they tossed him over the side as they would have done a brute. This made me fear these people the more; and I expected

nothing less than to be treated in the same manner. I could not help expressing my fears and apprehensions to some of my countrymen: I asked them if these people had no country, but lived in this hollow place (the ship): they told me they did not, but came from a distant one. "Then," said I, "how comes it in all our country we never heard of them?" They told me because they lived so very far off. I then asked where were their women? had they any like themselves? I was told they had: "and why," said I, "do we not see them?" they answered, because they were left behind. I asked how the vessel could go? they told me they could not tell; but that there were cloths put upon the masts by the help of the ropes I saw, and then the vessel went on; and the white men had some spell or magic they put in the water when they liked in order to stop the vessel. I was exceedingly amazed at this account, and really thought they were spirits. I therefore wished much to be from amongst them, for I expected they would sacrifice me: but my wishes were vain; for we were so quartered that it was impossible for any of us to make our escape. While we stayed on the coast I was mostly on deck; and one day, to my great astonishment, I saw one of those vessels coming in with the sails up. As soon as the whites saw it, they gave a great shout, at which we were amazed; and the more so as the vessel appeared larger by approaching nearer. At last she came to an anchor in my sight, and when the anchor was let go I and my countrymen who saw it were lost in astonishment to observe the vessel stop; and were now convinced it was done by magic. Soon after this the other ship got her boats out, and they came on board of us, and the people of both ships seemed very glad to see each other. Several of the strangers also shook hands with us black people, and made motions with their hands, signifying I suppose we were to go to their country; but we did not understand them. At last, when the ship we were in had got in all her cargo, they made ready with many fearful noises, and we were all put under deck, so that we could not see how they managed the vessel. But this disappointment was the least of my sorrow. The stench of the hold while we were on the coast was so intolerably loathsome, that it was dangerous to remain there for any time, and some of us had been permitted to stay on the deck for the fresh air; but now that the whole ship's cargo were confined together, it became absolutely pestilential. The closeness of the place, and the heat of the climate, added to the number in the ship, which was so crowded that each had scarcely room to turn himself, almost suffocated us. This produced copious perspirations, so that the air soon became unfit for respiration, from a variety of loathsome smells, and brought on a sickness among the slaves, of which many died, thus falling victims to the improvident avarice, as I may call it, of their purchasers. This wretched situation was again aggravated by the galling of the chains, now become insupportable; and the filth of the necessary tubs, into which the children often fell, and were almost suffocated. The shrieks of the women, and the groans of the dying, rendered the whole a scene of horror almost inconceivable. Happily perhaps for myself I was soon reduced so low here that it was thought necessary to keep me almost always on deck; and from my extreme youth I was not put in fetters. In this situation I expected every hour to share the fate of my companions, some of whom were almost daily brought upon deck at the point of death, which I began to hope would soon put an end to my miseries. Often did I think many of the inhabitants of the deep much more happy than myself. I envied them the freedom they enjoyed, and as often wished I could change my condition for theirs. Every circumstance I met with served only to render my state more painful, and heighten my apprehensions, and my opinion of the cruelty of the whites. One day they had taken a number of fishes; and when they had killed and satisfied themselves with as many as they thought fit, to our astonishment who were on the deck, rather than give any of them to us to eat as we expected, they tossed the remaining fish into the sea again, although we begged and prayed for some as well as we could, but in vain; and some of my countrymen, being pressed by hunger, took an opportunity, when they thought no one saw them, of trying to get a little privately; but they were discovered, and the attempt procured them some very severe floggings. One day, when we had a smooth sea and moderate wind, two of my wearied countrymen who were chained together (I was near them at the time), preferring death to such a life of misery, somehow made it through the nettings and jumped into the sea: immediately another quite dejected fellow, who, on one account of his illness, was suffered to be out of irons, also followed their example; and I believe many more would very soon have done the same if they had not been prevented by the ship's crew, who were instantly alarmed. Those of us that were the most active were in a moment put down under the deck, and here was such a noise and confusion amongst the people of the ship as I never heard before, to stop her, and get the boat out to go after the slaves. However two of the wretches were drowned, but they got the other, and afterwards flogged him unmercifully for thus attempting to prefer death to slavery. In this manner we continued to undergo more hardships than I can now relate, hardships which are inseparable from this accursed trade. Many a time we were near suffocation from the want of fresh air, which we were often without for whole days together. This, and the stench of the necessary tubs [latrines], carried off many. During our passage I first saw flying fishes, which surprised me very much: they used frequently to fly

across the ship, and many of them fell on the deck. I also now first saw the use of the quadrant; I had often with astonishment seen the mariners make observations with it, and I could not think what it meant. They at last took notice of my surprise; and one of them, willing to increase it, as well as to gratify my curiosity, made me one day look through it. The clouds appeared to me to be land, which disappeared as they passed along. This heightened my wonder; and I was now more persuaded than ever that I was in another world, and that every thing about me was magic. At last we came in sight of the island of Barbadoes, at which the whites on board gave a great shout, and made many signs of joy to us. We did not know what to think of this; but as the vessel drew nearer we plainly saw the harbour, and other ships of different kinds and sizes; and we soon anchored amongst them off Bridge Town. Many merchants and planters now came on board, though it was in the evening. They put us in separate parcels, and examined us attentively. They also made us jump, and pointed to the land, signifying we were to go there. We thought by this we should be eaten by these ugly men, as they appeared to us; and, when soon after we were all put down under the deck again, there was much dread and trembling among us, and nothing but bitter cries to be heard all the night from these apprehensions, insomuch that at last the white people got some old slaves from the land to pacify us. They told us we were not to be eaten, but to work, and were soon to go on land, where we should see many of our country people. This report eased us much; and sure enough, soon after we were landed, there came to us Africans of all languages. We were conducted immediately to the merchant's yard, where we were all pent up together like so many sheep in a fold, without regard to sex or age. As every object was new to me every thing I saw filled me with surprise. What struck me first was that the houses were built with stories, and in every other respect different from those in Africa: but I was still more astonished on seeing people on horseback. I did not know what this could mean; and indeed I thought these people were full of nothing but magical arts. While I was in this astonishment one of my fellow prisoners spoke to a countryman of his about the horses, who said they were the same kind they had in their country. I understood them, though they were from a distant part of Africa, and I thought it odd I had not seen any horses there; but afterwards, when I came to converse with different Africans, I found they had many horses amongst them, and much larger than those I then saw. We were not many days in the merchant's custody before we were sold after their usual manner, which is this:—On a signal given, (as the beat of a drum) the buyers rush at once into the yard where the slaves are confined, and make choice of that parcel they like best. The noise and clamour with which this is attended, and the eagerness visible in the countenances of the buyers, serve not a little to increase the apprehensions of the terrified Africans, who may well be supposed to consider them as the ministers of that destruction to which they think themselves devoted. In this manner, without scruple, are relations and friends separated, most of them never to see each other again. I remember in the vessel in which I was brought over, in the men's apartment, there were several brothers, who, in the sale, were sold in different lots; and it was very moving on this occasion to see and hear their cries at parting. O, ye nominal Christians! might not an African ask you, learned you this from your God, who says unto you, Do unto all men as you would men should do unto you? Is it not enough that we are torn from our country and friends to toil for your luxury and lust of gain? Must every tender feeling be likewise sacrificed to your avarice? Are the dearest friends and relations, now rendered more dear by their separation from their kindred, still to be parted from each other, and thus prevented from cheering the gloom of slavery with the small comfort of being together and mingling their sufferings and sorrows? Why are parents to lose their children, brothers their sisters, or husbands their wives? Surely this is a new refinement in cruelty, which, while it has no advantage to atone for it, thus aggravates distress, and adds fresh horrors even to the wretchedness of slavery.

AN APPEAL IN FOUR ARTICLES (DAVID WALKER, 1829)

SOURCE: Walker, David. *David Walker's Appeal, in Four Articles, Together with a Preamble, to the Coloured Citizens of the World, but in Particular, and Very Expressly, to Those of the United States of America.* 1829. Edited by Charles M. Wiltse. New York: Hill and Wang, 1965, pp. 19–33.

INTRODUCTION: *Born in the South in 1785, the son of a free black woman, David Walker traveled widely as a young man, eventually settling in Boston during the 1820s, where he began writing and lecturing on the abolition of slavery. His* Appeal, in Four Articles, *first published in 1829, constituted a fervent plea for slave rebellion, frightening many Southerners and causing rumors of a bounty for Walker's head. He died mysteriously in Boston the following year.*

Article II.

Our Wretchedness in Consequence of Ignorance.

Ignorance, my brethren, is a mist, low down into the very dark and almost impenetrable abyss in which, our fathers for many centuries have been plunged. The Christians, and enlightened of Europe, and some of Asia, seeing the ignorance and consequent degradation of our fathers, instead of trying to enlighten them, by teaching them that religion and light with which God had blessed them, they have plunged them into wretchedness ten thousand times more intolerable, than if they had left them entirely to the Lord, and to add to their miseries, deep down into which they have plunged them tell them, that they are an *inferior* and *distinct race* of beings, which they will be glad enough to recall and swallow by and by. Fortune and misfortune, two inseparable companions, lay rolled up in the wheel of events, which have from the creation of the world, and will continue to take place among men until God shall dash worlds together.

When we take a retrospective view of the arts and sciences—the wise legislators—the Pyramids, and other magnificent buildings—the turning of the channel of the river Nile, by the sons of Africa or of Ham, among whom learning originated, and was carried thence into Greece, where it was improved upon and refined. Thence among the Romans, and all over the then enlightened parts of the world, and it has been enlightening the dark and benighted minds of men from then, down to this day. I say, when I view retrospectively, the renown of that once mighty people, the children of our great progenitor I am indeed cheered. Yea further, when I view that mighty son of Africa, HANNIBAL, one of the greatest generals of antiquity, who defeated and cut off so many thousands of the white Romans or murderers, and who carried his victorious arms, to the very gate of Rome, and I give it as my candid opinion, that had Carthage been well united and had given him good support, he would have carried that cruel and barbarous city by storm. But they were dis-united, as the coloured people are now, in the United States of America, the reason our natural enemies are enabled to keep their feet on our throats.

Beloved brethren—here let me tell you, and believe it, that the Lord our God, as true as he sits on his throne in heaven, and as true as our Saviour died to redeem the world, will give you a Hannibal, and when the Lord shall have raised him up, and given him to you for your possession, O my suffering brethren! remember the divisions and consequent sufferings of *Carthage* and of *Hayti*. Read the history particularly of Hayti, and see how they were butchered by the whites, and do you take warning. The person whom God shall give you, give him your support and let him go his length, and behold in him the salvation of your God. God will indeed, deliver you through him from your deplorable and wretched condition under the Christians of America. I charge you this day before my God to lay no obstacle in his way, but let him go.

The whites want slaves, and want us for their slaves, but some of them will curse the day they ever saw us. As true as the sun ever shone in its meridian splendor, my colour will root some of them out of the very face of the earth. They shall have enough of making slaves of, and butchering, and murdering us in the manner which they have. No doubt some may say that I write with a bad spirit, and that I being a black, wish these things to occur. Whether I write with a bad or a good spirit, I say if these things do not occur in their proper time, it is because the world in which we live does not exist, and we are deceived with regard to its existence.—It is immaterial however to me, who believe, or who refuse—though I should like to see the whites repent peradventure God may have mercy on them, some however, have gone so far that their cup must be filled.

But what need have I to refer to antiquity, when Hayti, the glory of the blacks and terror of tyrants, is enough to convince the most avaricious and stupid of wretches—which is at this time, and I am sorry to say it, plagued with that scourge of nations, the Catholic religion; but I hope and pray God that she may yet rid herself of it, and adopt in its stead the Protestant faith; also, I hope that she may keep peace within her borders and be united, keeping a strict look out for tyrants, for if they get the least chance to injure her, they will avail themselves of it, as true as the Lord lives in heaven. But one thing which gives me joy is, that they are men who would be cut off to a man, before they would yield to the combined forces of the whole world—in fact, if the whole world was combined against them, it could not do any thing with them, unless the Lord delivers them up.

Ignorance and treachery one against the other—a grovelling servile and abject submission to the lash of tyrants, we see plainly, my brethren, are not the natural elements of the blacks, as the Americans try to make us believe; but these are misfortunes which God has suffered our fathers to be enveloped in for many ages, no doubt in consequence of their disobedience to their Maker, and which do, indeed, reign at this time among us, almost to the destruction of all other principles: for I must truly say, that ignorance, the mother of treachery and deceit, gnaws into our very vitals. Ignorance, as it now exists among us, produces a state of things, Oh my Lord! too horrible to present to the world. Any man who is curious to see the full force of ignorance developed among the coloured peo-

ple of the United States of America, has only to go into the southern and western states of this confederacy, where, if he is not a tyrant, but has the feelings of a human being, who can feel for a fellow creature, he may see enough to make his very heart bleed! He may see there, a son take his mother, who bore almost the pains of death to give him birth, and by the command of a tyrant, strip her as naked as she came into the world, and apply the cow-hide to her, until she falls a victim to death in the road! He may see a husband take his dear wife, not unfrequently in a pregnant state, and perhaps far advanced, and beat her for an unmerciful wretch, until his infant falls a lifeless lump at her feet! Can the Americans escape God Almighty? If they do, can he be to us a God of Justice? God is just, and I know it—for he has convinced me to my satisfaction—I cannot doubt him. My observer may see fathers beating their sons, mothers their daughters, and children their parents, all to pacify the passions of unrelenting tyrants. He may also, see them telling news and lies, making mischief one upon another. These are some of the productions of ignorance, which he will see practiced among my dear brethren, who are held in unjust slavery and wretchedness, by avaricious and unmerciful tyrants, to whom, and their hellish deeds, I would suffer my life to be taken before I would submit. And when my curious observer comes to take notice of those who are said to be free, (which assertion I deny) and who are making some frivolous pretentions to common sense, he will see that branch of ignorance among the slaves assuming a more cunning and deceitful course of procedure. —He may see some of my brethren in league with tyrants, selling their own brethren into *hell upon earth,* not dissimilar to the exhibitions in Africa, but in a more secret, servile and abject manner. Oh Heaven! I am full ! ! ! I can hardly move my pen ! ! ! ! and as I expect some will try to put me to death, to strike terror into others, and to obliterate from their minds the notion of freedom, so as to keep my brethren the more secure in wretchedness, where they will be permitted to stay but a short time (whether tyrants believe it or not)—I shall give the world a development of facts, which are already witnessed in the courts of heaven. My observer may see some of those ignorant and treacherous creatures (coloured people) sneaking about in the large cities, endeavouring to find out all strange coloured people, where they work and where they reside, asking them questions, and trying to ascertain whether they are runaways or not, telling them, at the same time, that they always have been, are, and always will be, friends to their brethren; and, perhaps, that they themselves are absconders, and a thousand such treacherous lies to get the better information of the more ignorant! ! ! There have been and are at this day in Boston, New-York, Philadelphia, and

Baltimore, coloured men, who are in league with tyrants, and who receive a great portion of their daily bread, of the moneys which they acquire from the blood and tears of their more miserable brethren, whom they scandalously delivered into the hands of our *natural enemies*! ! ! ! ! !

To show the force of degraded ignorance and deceit among us some farther, I will give here an extract from a paragraph, which may be found in the Columbian Centinel of this city, for September 9, 1829, on the first page of which, the curious may find an article, headed

"Affray and Murder."

"Portsmouth, (Ohio) Aug. 22, 1829.

"A most shocking outrage was committed in Kentucky, about eight miles from this place, on 14th inst. A negro driver, by the name of Gordon, who had purchased in Maryland about sixty negroes, was taking them, assisted by an associate named Allen, and the wagoner who conveyed the baggage, to the Mississippi. The men were hand-cuffed and chained together, in the usual manner for driving those poor wretches, while the women and children were suffered to proceed without incumbrance. It appears that, by means of a file the negroes, unobserved, had succeeded in separating the iron which bound their hands, in such a way as to be able to throw them off at any moment. About 8 o'clock in the morning, while proceeding on the state road leading from Greenup to Vanceburg, two of them dropped their shackles and commenced a fight, when the wagoner (Petit) rushed in with his whip to compel them to desist. At this moment, every negro was found to be perfectly at liberty; and one of them seizing a club, gave Petit a violent blow on the head, and laid him dead at his feet; and Allen, who came to his assistance, met a similar fate, from the contents of a pistol fired by another of the gang. Gordon was then attacked, seized and held by one of the negroes, whilst another fired twice at him with a pistol, the ball of which each time grazed his head, but not proving effectual, he was beaten with clubs, and left for dead. They then commenced pillaging the wagon, and with an axe split open the trunk of Gordon, and rifled it of the money, about $2,400. Sixteen of the negroes then took to the woods; Gordon, in the mean time, not being materially injured, was enabled, by the assistance of one of the women, to mount his horse and flee; pursued, however, by one of the gang on another horse, with a drawn pistol; fortunately he escaped with his life barely,

arriving at a plantation, as the negro came in sight; who then turned about and retreated.

"The neighbourhood was immediately rallied, and a hot pursuit given—which, we understand, has resulted in the capture of the whole gang and the recovery of the greatest part of the money. Seven of the negro men and one woman, it is said were engaged in the murders, and will be brought to trial at the next court in Greenupsburg."

Here my brethren, I want you to notice particularly in the above article, the *ignorant* and *deceitful actions* of this coloured woman. I beg you to view it candidly, as for ETERNITY! ! ! ! Here a *notorious wretch*, with two other confederates had SIXTY of them in a gang, driving them like *brutes*—the men all in chains and hand-cuffs, and by the help of God they got their chains and hand-cuffs thrown off, and caught two of the wretches and put them to death, and beat the other until they thought he was dead, and left him for dead; however, he deceived them, and rising from the ground, this *servile woman* helped him upon his horse, and he made his escape. Brethren, what do you think of this? Was it the natural *fine feelings* of this woman, to save such a wretch alive? I know that the blacks, take them half enlightened and ignorant, are more humane and merciful than the most enlightened and refined European that can be found in all the earth. Let no one say that I assert this because I am prejudiced on the side of my colour, and against the whites or Europeans. For what I write, I do it candidly, for my God and the good of both parties: Natural observations have taught me these things; there is a solemn awe in the hearts of the blacks, as it respects *murdering* men [footnoted: Which is the reason the whites take the advantage of us.]: whereas the whites, (though they are great cowards) where they have the advantage, or think that there are any prospects of getting it, they murder all before them, in order to subject men to wretchedness and degradation under them. This is the natural result of pride and avarice. But I declare, the actions of this black woman are really insupportable. For my own part, I cannot think it was any thing but servile deceit, combined with the most gross ignorance: for we must remember that *humanity, kindness* and the *fear of the Lord,* does not consist in protecting *devils.* Here is a set of wretches, who had SIXTY of them in a gang, driving them around the country like *brutes,* to dig up gold and silver for them, (which they will get enough of yet.) Should the lives of such creatures be spared? Are God and Mammon in league? What has the Lord to do with a gang of desperate wretches, who go *sneaking about the country like robbers*—light upon his people wherever they can get a chance, binding them with chains and hand-cuffs, beat and murder them as they would *rattle-snakes*? Are they not the Lord's enemies? Ought they not to be destroyed? Any person who will save such wretches from destruction, is fighting against the Lord, and will receive his just recompense. The black men acted like *blockheads*. Why did they not make sure of the wretch? He would have made sure of them, if he could. It is just the way with black men—eight white men can frighten fifty of them; whereas, if you can only get courage into the blacks, I do declare it, that one good black man can put to death six white men; and I give it as a fact, let twelve black men get well armed for battle, and they will kill and put to flight fifty whites. —The reason is, the blacks, once you get them started, they glory in death. The whites have had us under them for more than three centuries, murdering, and treating us like brutes; and, as Mr. Jefferson wisely said, they have never *found us out*—they do not know, indeed, that there is an unconquerable disposition in the breasts of the blacks, which, when it is fully awakened and put in motion, will be subdued, only with the destruction of the animal existence. Get the blacks started, and if you do not have a gang of tigers and lions to deal with, I am a deceiver of the blacks and of the whites. How sixty of them could let that wretch escape unkilled, I cannot conceive—they will have to suffer as much for the two whom, they secured, as if they had put one hundred to death: if you commence, make sure work—do not trifle, for they will not trifle with you—they want us for their slaves, and think nothing of murdering us in order to subject us to that wretched condition—therefore, if there is an *attempt* made by us, kill or be killed. Now, I ask you, had you not rather be killed than to be a slave to a tyrant, who takes the life of your mother, wife, and dear little children? Look upon your mother, wife and children, and answer God Almighty; and believe this, that it is no more harm for you to kill a man, who is trying to kill you, than it is for you to take a drink of water when thirsty; in fact, the man who will stand still and let another murder him, is worse than an infidel, and, if he has common sense, ought not to be pitied. The actions of this deceitful and ignorant coloured woman, in saving the life of a desperate wretch, whose avaricious and cruel object was to drive her, and her companions in miseries, through the country like cattle, to make his fortune on their carcasses, are but too much like that of thousands of our brethren in these states: if any thing is whispered by one, which has any allusion to the melioration of their dreadful condition, they run and tell tyrants, that they may be enabled to keep them the longer in wretchedness and miseries. Oh! coloured people of these United States, I ask you, in the name of that God who made us, have we, in consequence of oppression, nearly lost the spirit of man, and, in no very trifling degree,

adopted that of brutes? Do you answer, no? —I ask you, then, what set of men can you point me to, in all the world, who are so abjectly employed by their oppressors, as we are by our *natural enemies*? How can, Oh! how can those enemies but say that we and our children are not of the HUMAN FAMILY, but were made by our Creator to be an inheritance to them and theirs for ever? How can the slaveholders but say that they can bribe the best coloured person in the country, to sell his brethren for a trifling sum of money, and take that atrocity to confirm them in their avaricious opinion, that we were made to be slaves to them and their children? How could Mr. Jefferson but say, "I advance it therefore as a suspicion only, that the blacks, whether originally a distinct race, or made distinct by time and circumstances, are *inferior* to the whites in the endowments both of body and mind?" —"It," says he, "is not against experience to suppose, that different species of the same genius, or varieties of the same species, may possess different qualifications." [Here, my brethren, listen to him.] "Will not a lover of natural history, then, one who views the gradations in all the races of *animals* with the eye of philosophy, excuse an effort to keep those in the department of MAN as *distinct* as nature had formed them?" —I hope you will try to find out the meaning of this verse—its widest sense and all its bearings: whether you do or not, remember the whites do. This very verse, brethren, having emanated from Mr. Jefferson, a much greater philosopher the world never afforded, has in truth injured us more, and has been as great a barrier to our emancipation as any thing that has ever been advanced against us. I hope you will not let it pass unnoticed He goes on further, and says: "This *unfortunate* difference of colour, and *perhaps* of *faculty*, is a powerful obstacle to the emancipation of these people. Many of their advocates, while they wish to vindicate the liberty of human nature are anxious also to preserve its *dignity* and *beauty*. Some of these, embarrassed by the question, 'What further is to be done with them?' join themselves in opposition with those who are actuated by sordid avarice only." Now I ask you candidly, my suffering brethren in time, who are candidates for the eternal worlds, how could Mr. Jefferson but have given the world these remarks respecting us, when we are so submissive to them, and so much servile deceit prevail among ourselves—when we so *meanly* submit to their murderous lashes, to which neither the Indians nor any other people under Heaven would submit? No, they would die to a man, before they would suffer such things from men who are no better than themselves, and *perhaps not so good*. Yes, how can our friends but be embarrassed, as Mr. Jefferson says, by the question, "What further is to be done with these people?" For while they are working for our emancipation, we are, by our treachery, wickedness and deceit, working against ourselves and our children—helping ours, and the enemies of God, to keep us and our dear little children in their infernal chains of slavery! ! ! Indeed, our friends cannot but relapse and join themselves "with those who are actuated by *sordid avarice* only! ! ! !" For my own part, I am glad Mr. Jefferson has advanced his positions for your sake; for you will either have to contradict or confirm him by your own actions, and not by what our friends have said or done for us; for those things are other men's labours, and do not satisfy the Americans, who are waiting for us to prove to them ourselves, that we are MEN, before they will be willing to admit the fact; for I pledge you my sacred word of honour, that Mr. Jefferson's remarks respecting us, have sunk deep into the hearts of millions of the whites, and never will be removed this side of eternity. —For how can they, when we are confirming him every day, by our *groveling submissions* and *treachery*? I aver, that when I look over these United States of America, and the world, and see the ignorant deceptions and consequent wretchedness of my brethren, I am brought oftimes solemnly to a stand, and in the midst of my reflections I exclaim to my God, "Lord didst thou make us to be slaves to our brethren, the whites?" But when I reflect that God is just, and that millions of my wretched brethren would meet death with glory—yea, more, would plunge into the very mouths of cannons and be torn into particles as minute as the atoms which compose the elements of the earth, in preference to a mean submission to the lash of tyrants, I am with streaming eyes, compelled to shrink back into nothingness before my Maker, and exclaim again, thy will be done, O Lord God Almighty.

Men of colour, who are also of sense, for you particularly is my APPEAL designed. Our more ignorant brethren are not able to penetrate its value. I call upon you therefore to cast your eyes upon the wretchedness of your brethren, and to do your utmost to enlighten them—*go to work and enlighten your brethren!*—Let the Lord see you doing what you can to rescue them and yourselves from degradation. Do any of you say that you and your family are free and happy, and what have you to do with the wretched slaves and other people? So can I say, for I enjoy as much freedom as any of you, if I am not quite as well off as the best of you. Look into our freedom and happiness, and see of what kind they are composed! ! They are of the very lowest kind—they are the very *dregs*!—they are the most servile and abject kind, that ever a people was in possession of! If any of you wish to know how FREE you are, let one of you start and go through the southern and western States of this country, and unless you travel as a slave to a white man (a servant is a *slave* to the man whom he serves) or have your free papers, (which if you are not careful they will get from you) if they do not take you up and put you

in jail, and if you cannot give good evidence of your freedom, sell you into eternal slavery, I am not a living man: or any man of colour, immaterial who he is, or where he came from, if he is not *the fourth from the negro race*! ! (as we are called) the white Christians of America will serve him the same they will sink him into wretchedness and degradation for ever while he lives. And yet some of you have the hardihood to say that you are free and happy! May God have mercy on your freedom and happiness! ! I met a coloured man in the street a short time since, with a string of boots on his shoulders; we fell into conversation, and in course of which, I said to him, what a miserable set of people we are! He asked, why? —Said I, we are so subjected under the whites, that we cannot obtain the comforts of life, but by cleaning their boots and shoes, old clothes, waiting on them, shaving them &c. Said he, (with the boots on his shoulders) "I am completely happy! ! ! I never want to live any better or happier than when I can get a plenty of boots and shoes to clean! ! !" Oh! how can those who are actuated by avarice only, but think, that our Creator made us to be an inheritance to them for ever, when they see that our greatest glory is centered in such mean and low objects? Understand me, brethren, I do not mean to speak against the occupations by which we acquire enough and sometimes scarcely that, to render ourselves and families comfortable through life. I am subjected to the same inconvenience, as you all. —My objections are, to our *glorying* and being *happy* in such low employments; for if we are men, we ought to be thankful to the Lord for the past, and for the future. Be looking forward with thankful hearts to higher attainments than *wielding the razor* and *cleaning boots and shoes*. The man whose aspirations are not *above*, and even *below* these, is indeed, ignorant and wretched enough. I advanced it therefore to you, not as a *problematical*, but as an unshaken and for ever immovable *fact*, that your full glory and happiness, as well as all other coloured people under Heaven, shall never be fully consummated, but with the *entire emancipation of your enslaved brethren all over the world*. You may therefore, go to work and do what you can to rescue, or join in with tyrants to oppress them and yourselves, until the Lord shall come upon you all like a thief in the night. For I believe it is the will of the Lord that our greatest happiness shall consist in working for the salvation of our whole body. When this is accomplished a burst of glory will shine upon you, which will indeed astonish you and the world. Do any of you say this never will be done? I assure you that God will accomplish it—if nothing else will answer, he will hurl tyrants and devils into *atoms* and make way for his people. But O my brethren! I say unto you again, you must go to work and prepare the way of the Lord.

There is a great work for you to do, as trifling as some of you may think of it. You have to prove to the Americans and the world, that we are MEN, and not *brutes,* as we have been represented, and by millions treated. Remember, to let the aim of your labours among your brethren, and particularly the youths, be the dissemination of education and religion. [footnoted: Never mind what the ignorant ones among us may say, many of whom when you speak to them for their good, and try to enlighten their minds, laugh at you, and perhaps tell you plump to your face, that they want no instruction from you or any other Niger, and all such aggravating language. Now if you are a man of understanding and sound sense, I conjure you in the name of the Lord, and of all that is good, to impute their actions to ignorance, and wink at their follies, and do your very best to get around them some way or other, for remember they are your brethren; and I declare to you that it is for your interests to teach and enlighten them.] It is lamentable, that many of our children go to school, from four until they are eight or ten, and sometimes fifteen years of age, and leave school knowing but a little more about the grammar of their language than a horse does about handling a musket—and not a few of them are really so ignorant, that they are unable to answer a person correctly, general questions in geography, and to hear them read, would only be to disgust a man who has a taste for reading; which, to do well, as trifling as it may appear to some, (to the ignorant in particular) is a great part of learning. Some few of them, may make out to scribble tolerably well, over a half sheet of paper, which I believe has hitherto been a powerful obstacle in our way, to keep us from acquiring knowledge. An ignorant father, who knows no more than what nature has taught him, together with what little he acquires by the senses of hearing and seeing, finding his son able to write a neat hand, sets it down for granted that he has as good learning as any body; the young, ignorant gump, hearing his father or mother, who perhaps may be ten times more ignorant, in point of literature, than himself, extolling his learning, struts about, in the full assurance, that his attainments in literature are sufficient to take him through the world, when, in fact, he has scarcely any learning at all! ! ! !

I promiscuously fell in conversation once, with an elderly coloured man on the topics of education, and of the great prevalency of ignorance among us: Said he, "I know that our people are very ignorant but my son has a good education: I spent a great deal of money on his education: he can write as well as any white man, and I assure you that no one can fool him," &c. Said I, what else can your son do, besides writing a good hand? Can he post a set of books in a mercantile manner? Can he write a neat piece of composition in prose or in verse? To these interrogations he answered in the negative. Said I, did your son learn, while he was at school, the width and depth of English Grammar? To which he also replied in the negative, telling me his son did not learn those things. Your son, said I, then, has hardly any learning at all—he is almost as ignorant, and more so, than many of those who never went to school one day in all their lives. My friend got a little put out, and so walking off, said that his son could write as well as any white man. Most of the coloured people, when they speak of the education of one among us who can write a neat hand, and who perhaps knows nothing but to scribble and puff pretty fair on a small scrap of paper, immaterial whether his words are grammatical, or spelt correctly, or not; if it only looks beautiful, they say he has as good an education as any white man—he can write as well as any white man, &c. The poor, ignorant creature, hearing, this, he is ashamed, forever after, to let any person see him humbling himself to another for knowledge but going about trying to deceive those who are more ignorant than himself, he at last falls an ignorant victim to death in wretchedness. I pray that the Lord may undeceive my ignorant brethren, and permit them to throw away pretensions, and seek after the substance of learning. I would crawl on my hands and knees through mud and mire, to the feet of a learned man, where I would sit and humbly supplicate him to instil into me, that which neither devils nor tyrants could remove, only with my life—for coloured people to acquire learning in this country, makes tyrants quake and tremble on their sandy foundation. Why, what is the matter? Why, they know that their infernal deeds of cruelty will be made known to the world. Do you suppose one man of good sense and learning would submit himself, his father, mother, wife and children, to be slaves to a wretched man like himself, who, instead of compensating him for his labours, chains, handcuffs and beats him and family almost to death, leaving life enough in them, however, to work for, and call him master? No! no! he would cut his devilish throat from ear to ear, and well do slave-holders know it. The bare name of educating the coloured people, scares our cruel oppressors almost to death. But if they do not have enough to be frightened for yet, it will be, because they can always keep us ignorant, and because God approbates their cruelties, with which they have been for centuries murdering us. The whites shall have enough of the blacks, yet, as true as God sits on his throne in Heaven.

Some of our brethren are so very full of learning, that you cannot mention any thing to them which they do not know better than yourself! !—nothing is strange to them! !—they knew every thing years ago!—if any thing should be mentioned in company where they are, immaterial how important it is respecting us or the world, if they had not divulged it; they make light of it, and affect to have known it long before it was mentioned and try to make all in the room, or wherever you may be, believe that your conversation is nothing! !—not worth hearing! All this is the result of ignorance and ill-breeding; for a man of good-breeding, sense and penetration, if he had heard a subject told twenty times over, and should happen to be in company where one should commence telling it again, he would wait with patience on its narrator, and see if he would tell it as it was told in his presence before—paying the most strict attention to what is said, to see if any more light will be thrown on the subject: for all men are not gifted alike in telling, or even hearing the most simple narration. These ignorant, vicious, and wretched men, contribute almost as much injury to our body as tyrants themselves, by doing so much for the promotion of ignorance amongst us; for they, making such pretensions to knowledge, such of our youth as are seeking after knowledge, and can get access to them, take them as criterions to go by, who will lead them into a channel, where, unless the Lord blesses them with the privilege of seeing their folly, they will be irretrievably lost forever, while in time! ! !

I must close this article by relating the very heart-rending fact, that I have examined school-boys and young men of colour in different parts of the country, in the most simple parts of Murray's English Grammar, and not more than one in thirty was able to give a correct answer to my interrogations. If any one contradicts me, let him step out of his door into the streets of Boston, New-York, Philadelphia, or Baltimore, (no use to mention any other, for the Christians are too charitable further south or west!)—I say, let him who disputes me, step out of his door into the streets of either of those four cities, and promiscuously collect one hundred school-boys, or young men of colour, *who have been to school,* and who are considered by the coloured people to have received an excellent education, because, perhaps, some of them can write a good hand, but who, notwithstanding their neat writing, may be almost as ignorant, in comparison, as a horse. —And, I say it, he will hardly find (in this enlightened day, and in the midst of this *charitable* people) five in one hundred, who, are able to correct the false grammar of their language. —The cause of this almost universal ignorance among us, I appeal to our schoolmasters to declare. Here is a fact, which I this very minute take from the mouth of a young coloured man, who has been to school in this state (Massachusetts) nearly nine years, and who knows grammar this day, *nearly* as well as he did the day he first entered the schoolhouse, under a white master. This young man says: "My master would never allow me to study grammar." I asked him, why? "The school committee," said he

"forbid the coloured children learning grammar—they would not allow any but the white children to study grammar." It is a notorious fact, that the major part of the white Americans, have, ever since we have been among them, tried to keep us ignorant, and make us believe that God made us and our children to be slaves to them and theirs. *Oh! my God, have mercy on Christian Americans! ! !*

THE CONFESSIONS OF NAT TURNER (1831)

SOURCE: *The Nat Turner Rebellion.* Edited by John B. Duff and Peter M. Mitchell. New York: Harper & Row, 1971, pp. 11–28.

INTRODUCTION: *Nat Turner led a rebellion of slaves in Virginia in 1831, killing more than fifty whites. When the revolt was finally brought to an end by local militia, about twenty blacks were tried and executed, including Turner, and scores of others were put to death by bands of vengeful vigilantes in the weeks that followed. The text reprinted below is the entire confession of Nat Turner as recorded by white lawyer Thomas R. Gray just before Turner's trial.*

Agreeable to his own appointment, on the evening he was committed to prison, with permission of the jailer, I visited Nat on Tuesday the 1st November, when, without being questioned at all, he commenced his narrative in the following words:—

Sir,—You have asked me to give a history of the motives which induced me to undertake the late insurrection, as you call it—To do so I must go back to the days of my infancy, and even before I was born. I was thirty-one years of age the 2d of October last, and born the property of Benj. Turner, of this county. In my childhood a circumstance occurred which made an indelible impression on my mind, and laid the ground work of that enthusiasm, which has terminated so fatally to many, both white and black, and for which I am about to atone at the gallows. It is here necessary to relate this circumstance—trifling as it may seem, it was the commencement of that belief which has grown with time, and even now, sir, in this dungeon, helpless and forsaken as I am, I cannot divest myself of. Being at play with other children, when three or four years old, I was telling them something, which my mother overhearing, said it had happened before I was born—I stuck to my story, however, and related somethings which went, in her opinion, to confirm it—others being called on were greatly astonished, knowing that these things had happened, and caused them to say in my hearing, I surely would be a prophet, as the Lord had shewn me things that had happened before my birth. And my father and mother strengthened me in this my first impression, saying in my presence, I was intended for some great purpose, which they had always thought from certain marks on my head and breast—[a parcel of excrescences which I believe are not at all uncommon, particularly among negroes, as I have seen several with the same. In this case he has either cut them off or they have nearly disappeared] —My grand mother, who was very religious, and to whom I was much attached—my master, who belonged to the church, and other religious persons who visited the house, and whom I often saw at prayers, noticing the singularity of my manners, I suppose, and my uncommon intelligence for a child, remarked I had too much sense to be raised, and if I was, I would never be of any service to any one as a slave—To a mind like mine, restless, inquisitive and observant of every thing that was passing, it is easy to suppose that religion was the subject to which it would be directed, and although this subject principally occupied my thoughts—there was nothing that I saw or heard of to which my attention was not directed—The manner in which I learned to read and write, not only had great influence on my own mind, as I acquired it with the most perfect ease, so much so, that I have no recollection whatever of learning the alphabet—but to the astonishment of the family, one day, when a book was shewn me to keep me from crying, I began spelling the names of different objects—this was a source of wonder to all in the neighborhood, particularly the blacks—and this learning was constantly improved at all opportunities—when I got large enough to go to work, while employed, I was reflecting on many things that would present themselves to my imagination, and whenever an opportunity occurred of looking at a book, when the school children were getting their lessons, I would find many things that the fertility of my own imagination had depicted to me before; all my time, not devoted to my master's service, was spent either in prayer, or in making experiments in casting different things in moulds made of earth, in attempting to make paper, gunpowder, and many other experiments, that although I could not perfect, yet convinced me of its practicability if I had the means. I was not addicted to stealing in my youth, nor have ever been—Yet such was the confidence of the negroes in the neighborhood, even at this early period of my life, in my superior judgment, that they would often carry me with them when they were going on any roguery, to plan for them. Growing up among them, with this confidence in my superior judgment, and when this, in their opinions, was perfected by Divine inspiration, from the circumstances already alluded to in my infancy,

and which belief was ever afterwards zealously inculcated by the austerity of my life and manners, which became the subject of remark by white and black. —Having soon discovered to be great, I must appear so, and therefore studiously avoided mixing in society, and wrapped myself in mystery, devoting my time to fasting and prayer—By this time, having arrived to man's estate, and hearing the scriptures commented on at meetings, I was struck with that particular passage which says: "Seek ye the kingdom of Heaven and all things shall be added unto you." I reflected much on this passage, and prayed daily for light on this subject—As I was praying one day at my plough, the spirit spoke to me, saying "Seek ye the kingdom of Heaven and all things shall be added unto you." Question—what do you mean by the Spirit. Ans. The Spirit that spoke to the prophets in former days—and I was greatly astonished, and for two years prayed continually, whenever my duty would permit—and then again I had the same revelation, which fully confirmed me in the impression that I was ordained for some great purpose in the hands of the Almighty. Several years rolled round, in which many events occurred to strengthen me in this my belief. At this time I reverted in my mind to the remarks made of me in my childhood, and the things that had been shown me—and as it had been said of me in my childhood by those by whom I had been taught to pray, both white and black, and in whom I had the greatest confidence, that I had too much sense to be raised, and if I was, I would never be of any use to any one as a slave. Now finding I had arrived to man's estate, and was a slave, and these revelations being made known to me, I began to direct my attention to this great object, to fulfil the purpose for which, by this time, I felt assured I was intended. Knowing the influence I had obtained over the minds of my fellow servants, (not by the means of conjuring and such like tricks—for to them I always spoke of such things with contempt) but by the communion of the Spirit whose revelations I often communicated to them, and they believed and said my wisdom came from God. I now began to prepare them for my purpose, by telling them something was about to happen that would terminate in fulfilling the great promise that had been made to me—About this time I was placed under an overseer, from whom I ranaway—and after remaining in the woods thirty days, I returned, to the astonishment of the negroes on the plantation, who thought I had made my escape to some other part of the country, as my father had done before. But the reason of my return was, that the Spirit appeared to me and said I had my wishes directed to the things of this world, and not to the kingdom of Heaven, and that I should return to the service of my earthly master—"For he who knoweth his Master's will, and doeth it not, shall be beaten with many stripes, and thus have I chastened you." And the negroes found fault, and murmured against me, saying that if they had my sense they would not serve any master in the world. And about this time I had a vision—and I saw white spirits and black spirits engaged in battle, and the sun was darkened—the thunder rolled in the Heavens, and blood flowed in streams—and I heard a voice saying, "Such is your luck, such you are called to see, and let it come rough or smooth, you must surely bare it." I now withdrew myself as much as my situation would permit, from the intercourse of my fellow servants, for the avowed purpose of serving the Spirit more fully—and it appeared to me, and reminded me of the things it had already shown me, and that it would then reveal to me the knowledge of the elements, the revolution of the planets, the operation of tides, and changes of the seasons. After this revelation in the year 1825, and the knowledge of the elements being made known to me, I sought more than ever to obtain true holiness before the great day of judgment should appear, and then I began to receive the true knowledge of faith. And from the first steps of righteousness until the last, was I made perfect; and the Holy Ghost was with me, and said, "Behold me as I stand in the Heavens"—and I looked and saw the forms of men in different attitudes—and there were lights in the sky to which the children of darkness gave other names than what they really were—for they were the lights of the Saviour's hands, stretched forth from east to west, even as they were extended on the cross on Calvary for the redemption of sinners. And I wondered greatly at these miracles, and prayed to be informed of a certainty of the meaning thereof—and shortly afterwards, while laboring in the field, I discovered drops of blood on the corn as though it were dew from heaven—and I communicated it to many, both white and black, in the neighborhood—and I then found on the leaves in the woods hieroglyphic characters, and numbers, with the forms of men in different attitudes, portrayed in blood, and representing the figures I had seen before in the heavens. And now the Holy Ghost had revealed itself to me, and made plain the miracles it had shown me—For as the blood of Christ had been shed on this earth, and had ascended to heaven for the salvation of sinners, and was now returning to earth again in the form of dew—and as the leaves on the trees bore the impression of the figures I had seen in the heavens, it was plain to me that the Saviour was about to lay down the yoke he had borne for the sins of men, and the great day of judgment was at hand. About this time I told these things to a white man, (Etheldred T. Brantley) on whom it had a wonderful effect—and he ceased from his wickedness, and was attacked immediately with a cutaneous eruption, and blood oozed from the pores of his skin, and after praying and fasting nine days,

he was healed, and the Spirit appeared to me again, and said, as the Saviour had been baptised so should we be also—and when the white people would not let us be baptised by the church, we went down into the water together, in the sight of many who reviled us, and were baptised by the Spirit—After this I rejoiced greatly, and gave thanks to God. And on the 12th of May, 1828, I heard a loud noise in the heavens, and the Spirit instantly appeared to me and said the Serpent was loosened, and Christ had laid down the yoke he had borne for the sins of men, and that I should take it on and fight against the Serpent, for the time was fast approaching when the first should be last and the last should be first. Ques. Do you not find yourself mistaken now? Ans. Was not Christ crucified. And by signs in the heavens that it would make known to me when I should commence the great work—and until the first sign appeared, I should conceal it from the knowledge of men—And on the appearance of the sign, (the eclipse of the sun last February) I should arise and prepare myself, and slay my enemies with their own weapons. And immediately on the sign appearing in the heavens, the seal was removed from my lips, and I communicated the great work laid out for me to do, to four in whom I had the greatest confidence, (Henry, Hark, Nelson, and Sam)—it was intended by us to have begun the work of death on the 4th July last—Many were the plans formed and rejected by us, and it affected my mind to such a degree, that I fell sick, and the time passed without our coming to any determination how to commence—Still forming new schemes and rejecting them, when the sign appeared again, which determined me not to wait longer.

Since the commencement of 1830, I had been living with Mr. Joseph Travis, who was to me a kind master, and placed the greatest confidence in me; in fact, I had no cause to complain of his treatment to me. On Saturday evening, the 20th of August, it was agreed between Henry, Hark and myself, to prepare a dinner the next day for the men we expected, and then to concert a plan, as we had not yet determined on any. Hark, on the following morning, brought a pig, and Henry brandy, and being joined by Sam, Nelson, Will and Jack, they prepared in the woods a dinner, where, about three o'clock, I joined them.

Q. Why were you so backward in joining them.

A. The same reason that had caused me not to mix with them for years before.

I saluted them on coming up, and asked Will how came he there, he answered, his life was worth no more than others, and, his liberty as dear to him. I asked him if he thought to obtain it? He said he would, or loose his life. This was enough to put him in full confidence. Jack, I knew, was only a tool in the hands of Hark, it was quickly agreed we should commence at home (Mr. J. Travis') on that night, and until we had armed and equipped ourselves, and gathered sufficient force, neither age nor sex was to be spared, (which was invariably adhered to.) We remained at the feast, until about two hours in the night, when we went to the house and found Austin; they all went to the cider press and drank, except myself. On returning to the house, Hark went to the door with an axe, for the purpose of breaking it open, as we knew we were strong enough to murder the family, if they were awaked by the noise; but reflecting that it might create an alarm in the neighborhood, we determined to enter the house secretly, and murder them whilst sleeping. Hark got a ladder and set it against the chimney, on which I ascended, and hoisting a window, entered and came down stairs, unbarred the door, and removed the guns from their places. It was then observed that I must spill the first blood. On which, armed with a hatchet, and accompanied by Will, I entered my master's chamber, it being dark, I could not give a death blow, the hatchet glanced from his head, he sprang from the bed and called his wife, it was his last work, Will laid him dead, with a blow of his axe, and Mrs. Travis shared the same fate, as she lay in bed. The murder of this family, five in number, was the work of a moment, not one of them awoke; there was a little infant sleeping in a cradle, that was forgotten, until we had left the house and gone some distance, when Henry and Will returned and killed it; we got here, four guns that would shoot, and several old muskets, with a pound or two of powder. We remained some time at the barn, where we paraded; I formed them in a line as soldiers, and after carrying them through all the manoeuvres I was master of, marched them off to Mr. Salathul Francis', about six hundred yards distant. Sam and Will went to the door and knocked. Mr. Francis asked who was there, Sam replied it was him, and he had a letter for him, on which he got up and came to the door; they immediately seized him, and dragging him out a little from the door, he was dispatched by repeated blows on the head; there was no other white person in the family. We started from there for Mrs. Reese's, maintaining the most perfect silence on our march, where finding the door unlocked, we entered, and murdered Mrs. Reese in her bed, while sleeping; her son awoke, but it was only to sleep the sleep of death, he had only time to say who is that, and he was no more. From Mrs. Reese's we went to Mrs. Turner's, a mile distant, which we reached about sunrise, on Monday morning. Henry, Austin, and Sam, went to the still, where, finding Mr. Peebles, Austin shot him, and the rest of us went to the house; as we approached, the family discovered us, and shut the door. Vain hope! Will, with one stroke of his axe, opened it, and we entered and found Mrs. Turner and Mrs. Newsome in

the middle of a room, almost frightened to death. Will immediately killed Mrs. Turner, with one blow of his axe. I took Mrs. Newsome by the hand, and with the sword I had when I was apprehended, I struck her several blows over the head, but not being able to kill her, as the sword was dull. Will turning around and discovering it, despatched her also. A general destruction of property and search for money and ammunition, always succeeded the murders. By this time my company amounted to fifteen, and nine men mounted, who started for Mrs. Whitehead's, (the other six were to go through a by way to Mr. Bryant's, and rejoin us at Mrs. Whitehead's,) as we approached the house we discovered Mr. Richard Whitehead standing in the cotton patch, near the lane fence; we called him over into the lane, and Will, the executioner, was near at hand, with his fatal axe, to send him to an untimely grave. As we pushed on to the house, I discovered some one run round the garden, and thinking it was some of the white family, I pursued them, but finding it was a servant girl belonging to the house, I returned to commence the work of death, but they whom I left, had not been idle; all the family were already murdered, but Mrs. Whitehead and her daughter Margaret. As I came round to the door I saw Will pulling Mrs. Whitehead out of the house, and at the step he nearly severed her head from her body, with his broad axe. Miss Margaret, when I discovered her, had concealed herself in the corner, formed by the projection of the cellar cap from the house; on my approach she fled, but was soon overtaken, and after repeated blows with a sword, I killed her by a blow on the head, with a fence rail. By this time, the six who had gone by Mr. Bryant's, rejoined us, and informed me they had done the work of death assigned them. We again divided, part going to Mr. Richard Porter's, and from thence to Nathaniel Francis', the others to Mr. Howell Harris', and Mr. T. Doyles. On my reaching Mr. Porter's, he had escaped with his family. I understood there, that the alarm had already spread, and I immediately returned to bring up those sent to Mr. Doyles, and Mr. Howell Harris'; the party I left going on to Mr. Francis', having told them I would join them in that neighborhood. I met these sent to Mr. Doyles' and Mr. Harris' returning, having met Mr. Doyle on the road and killed him; and learning from some who joined them, that Mr. Harris was from home, I immediately pursued the course taken by the party gone on before; but knowing they would complete the work of death and pillage, at Mr. Francis' before I could get there, I went to Mr. Peter Edwards', expecting to find them there, but they had been here also. I then went to Mr. John T. Barrow's, they had been here and murdered him. I pursued on their track to Capt. Newit Harris', where I found the greater part mounted, and ready to start; the men now amounting to about forty, shouted and hurraed as I rode up, some were in the yard, loading their guns, others drinking. They said Captain Harris and his family had escaped, the property in the house they destroyed, robbing him of money and other valuables. I ordered them to mount and march instantly, this was about nine or ten o'clock, Monday morning. I proceeded to Mr. Levi Waller's, two or three miles distant. I took my station in the rear, and as it 'twas my object to carry terror and devastation wherever we went, I placed fifteen or twenty of the best armed and most to be relied on, in front, who generally approached the houses as fast as their horses could run; this was for two purposes, to prevent their escape and strike terror to the inhabitants—on this account I never got to the houses, after leaving Mrs. Whitehead's, until the murders were committed, except in one case. I sometimes got in sight in time to see the work of death completed, viewed the mangled bodies as they lay, in silent satisfaction, and immediately started in quest of other victims—Having murdered Mrs. Waller and ten children, we started for Mr. William Williams'—having killed him and two little boys that were there; while engaged in this, Mrs. Williams fled and got some distance from the house, but she was pursued, overtaken, and compelled to get up behind one of the company, who brought her back, and after showing her the mangled body of her lifeless husband, she was told to get down and lay by his side, where she was shot dead. I then started for Mr. Jacob Williams, where the family were murdered—Here we found a young man named Drury, who had come on business with Mr. Williams—he was pursued, overtaken and shot. Mrs. Vaughan was the next place we visited—and after murdering the family here, I determined on starting for Jerusalem—Our number amounted now to fifty or sixty, all mounted and armed with guns, axes, swords and clubs—On reaching Mr. James W. Parker's gate, immediately on the road leading to Jerusalem, and about three miles distant, it was proposed to me to call there, but I objected, as I knew he was gone to Jerusalem, and my object was to reach there as soon as possible; but some of the men having relations at Mr. Parker's it was agreed that they might call and get his people. I remained at the gate on the road, with seven or eight; the others going across the field to the house, about half a mile off. After waiting some time for them, I became impatient, and started to the house for them, and on our return we were met by a party of white men, who had pursued our blood-stained track, and who had fired on those at the gate, and dispersed them, which I knew nothing of, not having been at that time rejoined by any of them—Immediately on discovering the whites, I ordered my men to halt and form, as they appeared to be alarmed—The white men, eighteen in number, approached us in about

one hundred yards, when one of them fired, (this was against the positive orders of Captain Alexander P. Peete, who commanded, and who had directed the men to reserve their fire until within thirty paces) And I discovered about half of them retreating, I then ordered my men to fire and rush on them; the few remaining stood their ground until we approached within fifty yards, when they fired and retreated. We pursued and overtook some of them who we thought we left dead; (they were not killed) after pursuing them about two hundred yards, and rising a little hill, I discovered they were met by another party, and had halted, and were re-loading their guns, (this was a small party from Jerusalem who knew the negroes were in the field, and had just tied their horses to await their return to the road, knowing that Mr. Parker and family were in Jerusalem, but knew nothing of the party that had gone in with Captain Peete; on hearing the firing they immediately rushed to the spot and arrived just in time to arrest the progress of these barbarious villains, and save the lives of their friends and fellow citizens.) Thinking that those who retreated first, and the party who fired on us at fifty or sixty yards distant, had all only fallen back to meet others with ammunition. As I saw them re-loading their guns, and more coming up than I saw at first, and several of my bravest men being wounded, the others became panick struck and squandered over the field; the white men pursued and fired on us several times. Hark had his horse shot under him, and I caught another for him as it was running by me; five or six of my men were wounded, but none left on the field; finding myself defeated here I instantly determined to go through a private way, and cross the Nottoway river at the Cypress Bridge, three miles below Jerusalem, and attack that place in the rear, as I expected they would look for me on the other road, and I had a great desire to get there to procure arms and ammunition. After going a short distance in this private way, accompanied by about twenty men, I overtook two or three who told me the others were dispersed in every direction. After trying in vain to collect a sufficient force to proceed to Jerusalem, I determined to return, as I was sure they would make back to their old neighborhood, where they would rejoin me, make new recruits, and come down again. On my way back, I called at Mrs. Thomas's, Mrs. Spencer's, and several other places, the white families having fled, we found no more victims to gratify our thirst for blood, we stopped at Majr. Ridley's quarter for the night, and being joined by four of his men, with the recruits made since my defeat, we mustered now about forty strong. After placing out sentinels, I laid down to sleep, but was quickly roused by a great racket; starting up, I found some mounted, and others in great confusion; one of the sentinels having given the alarm that we were about to be attacked, I ordered some to ride round and reconnoitre, and on their return the others being more alarmed, not knowing who they were, fled in different ways, so that I was reduced to about twenty again, with this I determined to attempt to recruit, and proceed on to rally in the neighborhood, I had left. Dr. Blunt's was the nearest house, which we reached just before day; on riding up the yard, Hark fired a gun. We expected Dr. Blunt and his family were at Maj. Ridley's, as I knew there was a company of men there; the gun was fired to ascertain if any of the family were at home; we were immediately fired upon and retreated, leaving several of my men. I do not know what became of them, as I never saw them afterwards. Pursuing our course back and coming in sight of Captain Harris', where we had been the day before, we discovered a party of white men at the house, on which all deserted me but two, (Jacob and Nat,) we concealed ourselves in the woods until near night, when I sent them in search of Henry, Sam, Nelson, and Hark, and directed them to rally all they could, at the place we had had our dinner the Sunday before, where they would find me, and I accordingly returned there as soon as it was dark and remained until Wednesday evening, when discovering white men riding around the place as though they were looking for some one, and none of my men joining me, I concluded Jacob and Nat had been taken, and compelled to betray me. On this I gave up all hope for the present; and on Thursday night after having supplied myself with provisions from Mr. Travis's, I scratched a hole under a pile of fence rails in a field, where I concealed myself for six weeks, never leaving my hiding place but for a few minutes in the dead of night to get water which was very near; thinking by this time I could venture out, I began to go about in the night and eaves drop the houses in the neighborhood; pursuing this course for about a fortnight and gathering little or no intelligence, afraid of speaking to any human being, and returning every morning to my cave before the dawn of day. I know not how long I might have led this life, if accident had not betrayed me, a dog in the neighborhood passing by my hiding place one night while I was out, was attracted by some meat I had in my cave, and crawled in and stole it, and was coming out just as I returned. A few nights after, two negroes having started to go hunting with the same dog, and passed that way, the dog came again to the place, and having just gone out to walk about, discovered me and barked, on which thinking myself discovered, I spoke to them to beg concealment. On making myself known they fled from me. Knowing then they would betray me, I immediately left my hiding place, and was pursued almost incessantly until I was taken a fortnight afterwards by Mr. Benjamin Phipps, in a little hole I had dug out with my sword, for the purpose of concealment, under

the top of a fallen tree. On Mr. Phipps' discovering the place of my concealment, he cocked his gun and aimed at me. I requested him not to shoot and I would give up, upon which he demanded my sword. I delivered it to him, and he brought me to prison. During the time I was pursued, I had many hair breadth escapes, which your time will not permit you to relate. I am here loaded with chains, and willing to suffer the fate that awaits me.

I here proceeded to make some inquiries of him, after assuring him of the certain death that awaited him, and that concealment would only bring destruction on the innocent as well as guilty, of his own color, if he knew of any extensive or concerted plan. His answer was, I do not. When I questioned him as to the insurrection in North Carolina happening about the same time, he denied any knowledge of it; and when I looked him in the face as though I would search his inmost thoughts, he replied, "I see sir, you doubt my word; but can you not think the same ideas, and strange appearances about this time in the heaven's might prompt others, as well as myself, to this undertaking." I now had much conversation with and asked him many questions, having forborne to do so previously, except in the cases noted in parenthesis; but during his statement, I had, unnoticed by him, taken notes as to some particular circumstances, and having the advantage of his statement before me in writing, on the evening of the third day that I had been with him, I began a cross examination, and found his statement corroborated by every circumstance coming within my own knowledge or the confessions of others whom had been either killed or executed, and whom he had not seen nor had any knowledge since 22d of August last, he expressed himself fully satisfied as to the impracticability of his attempt. It has been said he was ignorant and cowardly, and that his object was to murder and rob for the purpose of obtaining money to make his escape. It is notorious, that he was never known to have a dollar in his life; to swear an oath, or drink a drop of spirits. As to his ignorance, he certainly never had the advantages of education, but he can read and write, (it was taught him by his parents,) and for natural intelligence and quickness of apprehension, is surpassed by few men I have ever seen. As to his being a coward, his reason as given for not resisting Mr. Phipps, shews the decision of his character. When he saw Mr. Phipps present his gun, he said he knew it was impossible for him to escape as the woods were full of men; he therefore thought it was better to surrender, and trust to fortune for his escape. He is a complete fanatic, or plays his part most admirably. On other subjects he possesses an uncommon share of intelligence, with a mind capable of attaining any thing; but warped and perverted by the influence of early impressions. He is below the ordinary stature, though strong and active, having the true negro face, every feature of which is strongly marked. I shall not attempt to describe the effect of his narrative, as told and commented on by himself, in the condemned hole of the prison. The calm, deliberate composure with which he spoke of his late deeds and intentions, the expression of his fiend-like face when excited by enthusiasm, still bearing the stains of the blood of helpless innocence about him; clothed with rags and covered with chains; yet daring to raise his manacled hands to heaven, with a spirit soaring above the attributes of man; I looked on him and my blood curdled in my veins.

I will not shock the feelings of humanity, nor wound afresh the bosoms of the disconsolate sufferers in this unparalleled and inhuman massacre, by detailing the deeds of their fiend-like barbarity. There were two or three who were in the power of these wretches, had they known it, and who escaped in the most providential manner. There were two whom they thought they left dead on the field at Mr. Parker's, but who were only stunned by the blows of their guns, as they did not take time to re-load when they charged on them. The escape of a little girl who went to school at Mr. Waller's, and where the children were collecting for that purpose. excited general sympathy. As their teacher had not arrived, they were at play in the yard, and seeing the negroes approach, she ran up on a dirt chimney, (such as are common to log houses,) and remained there unnoticed during the massacre of the eleven that were killed at this place. She remained on her hiding place till just before the arrival of a party, who were in pursuit of the murderers, when she came down and fled to a swamp, where, a mere child as she was, with the horrors of the late scene before her, she lay concealed until the next day, when seeing a party go up to the house, she came up, and on being asked how she escaped, replied with the utmost simplicity, "The Lord helped her." She was taken up behind a gentleman of the party, and returned to the arms of her weeping mother. Miss Whitehead concealed herself between the bed and the mat that supported it, while they murdered her sister in the same room, without discovering her. She was afterwards carried off, and concealed for protection by a slave of the family, who gave evidence against several of them on their trial. Mrs. Nathaniel Francis, while concealed in a closet heard their blows, and the shrieks of the victims of these ruthless savages; they then entered the closet where she was concealed, and went out without discovering her. While in this hiding place, she heard two of her women in a quarrel about the division of her clothes. Mr. John T. Barron, discovering them approaching his house, told his wife to make her escape, and scorning to fly, fell fighting on his own threshold. After firing his rifle, he discharged his gun at them, and then broke

it over the villain who first approached him, but he was overpowered, and slain. His bravery, however, saved from the hands of these monsters, his lovely and amiable wife, who will long lament a husband so deserving of her love. As directed by him, she attempted to escape through the garden, when she was caught and held by one of her servant girls, but another coming to her rescue, she fled to the woods, and concealed herself. Few indeed, were those who escaped their work of death. But fortunate for society, the hand of retributive justice has overtaken them; and not one that was known to be concerned has escaped.

THE LIFE EXPERIENCE AND GOSPEL LABORS OF THE RT. REV. RICHARD ALLEN (1833)

SOURCE: Allen, Richard. *The Life Experience and Gospel Labors of the Rt. Rev. Richard Allen.* Philadelphia: Lee and Yeocum, 1888, pp. 11–17.

INTRODUCTION: *From the posthumous autobiography of Richard Allen (1760–1831), founder of the African Methodist Episcopal Church.*

I was born in the year of our Lord 1760, on February 14th, a slave to Benjamin Chew, of Philadelphia. My mother and father and four children of us were sold into Delaware state, near Dover; and I was a child and lived with him until I was upwards of twenty years of age, during which time I was awakened and brought to see myself, poor, wretched and undone, and without the mercy of God must be lost. Shortly after, I obtained mercy through the blood of Christ, and was constrained to exhort my old companions to seek the Lord. I went rejoicing for several days and was happy in the Lord, in conversing with many old, experienced Christians. I was brought under doubts, and was tempted to believe I was deceived, and was constrained to seek the Lord a fresh. I went with my head bowed down for many days. My sins were a heavy burden. I was tempted to believe there was no mercy for me. I cried to the Lord both night and day. One night I thought hell would be my portion. I cried unto Him who delighteth to hear the prayers of a poor sinner, and all of a sudden my dungeon shook, my chains flew off, and, glory to God, I cried. My soul was filled. I cried, enough for me—the Saviour died. Now my confidence was strengthened that the Lord, for Christ's sake, had heard my prayers and pardoned all my sins. I was constrained to go from house to house, exhorting my old companions, and telling to all around what a dear Saviour I had found. I joined the Methodist Society and met in class at Benjamin Wells's, in the forest, Delaware state. John Gray was the class leader. I met in his class for several years.

My master was an unconverted man, and all the family, but he was what the world called a good master. He was more like a father to his slaves than anything else. He was a very tender, humane man. My mother and father lived with him for many years. He was brought into difficulty, not being able to pay for us, and mother having several children after he had bought us, he sold my mother and three children. My mother sought the Lord and found favor with him, and became a very pious woman. There were three children of us remained with our old master. My oldest brother embraced religion and my sister. Our neighbors, seeing that our master indulged us with the privilege of attending meeting once in two weeks, said that Stokeley's Negroes would soon ruin him; and so my brother and myself held a council together, that we would attend more faithfully to our master's business, so that it should not be said that religion made us worse servants; we would work night and day to get our crops forward, so that they should be disappointed. We frequently went to meeting on every other Thursday; but if we were likely to be backward with our crops we would refrain from going to meeting. When our master found we were making no provision to go to meeting, he would frequently ask us if it was not our meeting day, and if we were not going. We would frequently tell him: "No, sir, we would rather stay at home and get our work done." He would tell us: "Boys, I would rather you would go to your meeting; if I am not good myself, I like to see you striving yourselves to be good." Our reply would be: "Thank you, sir, but we would rather stay and get our crops forward." So we always continued to keep our crops more forward than our neighbors, and we would attend public preaching once in two weeks, and class meeting once a week. At length, our master said he was convinced that religion made slaves better and not worse, and often boasted of his slaves for their honesty and industry. Some time after, I asked him if I might ask the preachers to come and preach at his house. He being old and infirm, my master and mistress cheerfully agreed for me to ask some of the Methodist preachers to come and preach at his house. I asked him for a note. He replied, if my word was not sufficient, he should send no note. I accordingly asked the preacher. He seemed somewhat backward at first, as my master did not send a written request; but the class leader (John Gray) observed that my word was sufficient; so he preached at my old master's house on the next Wednesday. Preaching continued for some months; at length, Freeborn Garrettson preached from these words, "Thou art weighed in the balance, and art found wanting." In pointing out and weighing the different characters, and among the rest weighed the slaveholders, my master believed himself to be one of that number, and after that he could not be satisfied to hold slaves, believing it to be wrong. And after that he proposed to me and my brother buying our times, to pay him 60£ gold and silver, or $2000, Continental money, which we complied with in the year 17__.

We left our master's house, and I may truly say it was like leaving our father's house; for he was a kind, affectionate and tender-hearted master, and told us to make his house our home when we were out of a place or sick. While living with him we had family prayer in the kitchen, to which he frequently would come out himself at time of prayer, and my mistress with him. At length he invited us from the kitchen to the parlor to hold family prayer, which we attended to. We had our stated times to hold our prayer meetings and give exhortations at in the neighborhood.

I had it often impressed upon my mind that I should one day enjoy my freedom; for slavery is a bitter pill, notwithstanding we had a good master. But when we would think that our day's work was never done, we often thought that after our master's death we were liable to be sold to the highest bidder, as he was much in debt; and thus my troubles were increased, and I was often brought to weep between the porch and the altar. But I have had reason to bless my dear Lord that a door was opened unexpectedly for me to buy my time and enjoy my liberty. When I left my master's house I knew not what to do, not being used to hard work, what business I should follow to pay my master and get my living. I went to cutting of cord wood. The first day my hands were so blistered and sore, that it was with difficulty I could open or shut them. I kneeled down upon my knees and prayed that the Lord would open some way for me to get my living. In a few days, my hands recovered and became accustomed to cutting of wood and other hardships; so I soon became able to cut my cord and a half and two cords a day. After I was done cutting I was employed in a brickyard by one Robert Register, at $50 a month, Continental money. After I was done with the brickyard I went to days' work, but did not forget to serve my dear Lord. I used ofttimes to pray, sitting, standing or lying; and while my hands were employed to earn my bread, my heart was devoted to my dear Redeemer. Sometimes I would awake from my sleep, preaching and praying. I was after this employed in driving of wagon in time of the Continental war, in drawing salt from Rehoboth, Sussex County, in Delaware. I had my regular stops and preaching places on the road. I enjoyed many happy seasons in meditation and prayer while in this employment.

After peace was proclaimed, I then travelled extensively, striving to preach the Gospel. My lot was cast in Wilmington. Shortly after, I was taken sick with the fall fever and then the pleurisy. September the 3rd 1783, I left my native place. After leaving Wilmington, I went into New Jersey, and there traveled and strove to preach the Gospel until the spring of 1784. I then became acquainted with Benjamin Abbott, the great and good apostle. He was one of the greatest men that ever I was acquainted with. He seldom preached but what there were souls added to his labor. He was a man of as great faith as any that ever I saw. The Lord was with him, and blessed his labors abundantly. He was a friend and father to me. I was sorry when I had to leave West Jersey, knowing I had to leave a father. I was employed in cutting of wood for Captain Cruenkleton, although I preached the Gospel at nights and on Sundays. My dear Lord was with me, and blessed my labors—Glory to God—and gave me souls for my hire. I then visited East Jersey, and labored for my dear Lord, and became acquainted with Joseph Budd, and made my home with him, near the mills—a family, I trust, who loved and served the Lord. I labored some time there, but being much afflicted in body with the inflammatory rheumatism, was not so successful as in some other places. I went from there to Jonathan Bunn's near Bennington, East New Jersey. There I labored in that neighborhood for some time. I found him and his family kind and affectionate, and he and his dear wife were a father and mother of Israel. In the year 1784, I left East Jersey and labored in Pennsylvania. I waked until my feet became so sore and blistered the first day, that I scarcely could bear them to the ground. I found the people very humane and kind in Pennsylvania. I having but little money, I stopped at Caesar Waters's, at Radnor township, twelve miles from Philadelphia. I found him and his wife very kind and affectionate to me. In the evening they asked me if I would come and take tea with them; but after sitting awhile, my feet became so sore and painful that I could scarcely be able to put them to the floor. I told them that I would accept their kind invitation, but my feet pained me so that I could not come to the table. They brought the table to me. Never was I more kindly received by strangers that I had never before seen, than by them. She bathed my feet with warm water and bran; the next morning my feet were better and free from pain. They asked me if I would preach for them. I preached for them the next evening. We had a glorious meeting. They invited me to stay till Sabbath day, and preach for them. I agree to do so, and preached on Sabbath day to a large congregation of different persuasions, and my dear Lord was with me, and I believe there were many souls cut to the heart, and were added to the ministry. They insisted on me to stay longer with them. I stayed and

labored in Radnor several weeks. Many souls were awakened and cried aloud to the Lord to have mercy upon them. I was frequently called upon by many inquiring what they should do to be saved. I appointed them to prayer and supplication at the throne of grace, and to make use of all manner of prayer, and pointed them to the invitation of our Lord and Saviour, Jesus Christ, who has said: "Come unto me, all ye that are weary and heavy laden, and I will give you rest." Glory be to God! and I know he was a God at hand and not afar off. I preached my farewell sermon, and left these dear people. It was a time of visitation from above, many were the slain of the Lord. Seldom did I ever experience such a time of mourning and lamentation among a people. There were but few colored people in the neighborhood—the most of my congregation was white. Some said, "this man must be a man of God, I never heard such preaching before." We spent a greater part of the night in singing and prayer with the mourners. I expected I should have had to walk, as I had done before; but Mr. Davis had a creature that he made a present to me; but I intended to pay him for his horse if ever I got able. My dear Lord was kind and gracious to me. Some years after I got into business and thought myself able to pay for the horse. The horse was too light and small for me to travel on far. I traded it away with George Huftman for a blind horse but larger. I found my friend Huftman very kind and affectionate to me, and his family also. I preached several times at Huftman's meeting-house to a large and numerous congregation.

I proceeded on to Lancaster, Pennsylvania. I found the people in general dead to religion and scarcely a form of godliness. I went on to Little York, and put up at George Tess's, a sadler, and I believed him to be a man that loved and served the Lord. I had comfortable meetings with the Germans. I left Little York and proceeded on to the state of Maryland, and stopped at Mr. Benjamin Grover's; and I believed him to be a man that loved and served the Lord. I had many happy seasons with my dear friends. His wife was a very pious woman; but their dear children were strangers to vital religion. I preached in the neighborhood for some time, and travelled Hartford circuit with Mr. Porters, who travelled that circuit. I found him very useful to me. I also travelled with Jonathan Forest and Leari Coal.

December 1784, General Conference sat in Baltimore, the first General Conference ever held in America. The English preachers just arrived from Europe were, Rev. Dr. Coke, Richard Whatcoat and Thomas Vassey. This was the beginning of the Episcopal Church amongst the Methodists. Many of the ministers were set apart in holy orders at this conference, and were said to be entitled to the gown; and I have thought religion has been declining in the church ever since. There was a pamphlet published by some person which stated that when the Methodists were no people, then they were a people; and now they have become a people, they were no people, which had often serious weight upon my mind.

In 1785 the Rev. Richard Whatcoat was appointed on Baltimore circuit. He was, I believe, a man of God. I found great strength in travelling with him—a father in Israel. In his advice he was fatherly and friendly. He was of a mild and serene disposition. My lot was cast in Baltimore, in a small meeting-house called Methodist Alley. I stopped at Richard Mould's, and was sent to my lodgings, and lodged at Mr. McCannon's. I had some happy meetings in Baltimore. I was introduced to Richard Russell, who was very kind and affectionate to me, and attended several meetings. Rev. Bishop Asbury sent for me to meet him at Henry Gaff's. I did so. He told me he wished me to travel with him. He told me that in the slave countries, Carolina and other places, I must not intermix with the slaves, and I would frequently have to sleep in his carriage, and he would allow me my victuals and clothes. I told him I would not travel with him on these conditions. He asked me my reason. I told him if I was taken sick, who was to support me? and that I thought people ought to lay up something while they were able, to support themselves in time of sickness or old age. He said that was as much as he got, his victuals and clothes. I told him he would be taken care of, let his afflictions be as they were, or let him be taken sick where he would, he would be taken care of; but I doubted whether it would be the case with myself. He smiled, and told me he would give me from then until he returned from the eastward to make up my mind, which would be about three months. But I made up my mind that I would not accept of his proposals. Shortly after I left Hartford Circuit, and came to Pennsylvania, on Lancaster circuit. I travelled several months on Lancaster circuit with the Rev. Peter Morratte and Irie Ellis. They were very kind and affectionate to me in building me up; for I had many trials to pass through, and I received nothing from the Methodist connection. My usual method was, when I would get bare of clothes, to stop travelling and go to work, so that no man could say I was chargeable to the connection. My hands administered to my necessities. The autumn of 1785 I returned again to Radnor. I stopped at George Giger's, a man of God, and went to work. His family were all kind and affectionate to me. I killed seven beeves, and supplied the neighbors with meat; got myself pretty well clad through my own industry—thank God—and preached occasionally. The elder in charge in Philadelphia frequently sent for me to come to the city. February, 1786, I came to Philadelphia. Preaching was given out for me at five o'clock in the morning at St.

George church. I strove to preach as well as I could, but it was a great cross to me; but the Lord was with me. We had a good time, and several souls were awakened, and were earnestly seeking redemption in the blood of Christ. I thought I would stop in Philadelphia a week or two. I preached at different places in the city. My labor was much blessed. I soon saw a large field open in seeking and instructing my African brethren, who had been a long forgotten people and few of them attended public worship. I preached in the commons, in Southwark, Northern Liberties, and wherever I could find an opening. I frequently preached twice a day, at 5 o'clock in the morning and in the evening, and it was not uncommon for me to preach from four to five times a day. I established prayer meetings; I raised a society in 1786 for forty-two members. I saw the necessity of erecting a place of worship for the colored people. I proposed it to the most respectable people of color in this city; but here I met with opposition. I had but three colored brethren that united with me in erecting a place of worship—the Rev. Absalom Jones, William White and Dorus Ginnings. These united with me as soon as it became public and known by the elder who was stationed in the city. The Rev. C_____ B_____ opposed the plan, and would not submit to any argument we could raise; but he was shortly removed from the charge. The Rev. Mr. W_____ took the charge, and the Rev. L_____ G_____. Mr. W_____ was much opposed to an African church, and used very degrading and insulting language to us, to try and prevent us from going on. We all belonged to St. George's church—Rev. Absalom Jones, William White and Dorus Ginnings. We felt ourselves much cramped; but my dear Lord was with us, and we believed, if it was his will, the work would go on, and that we would be able to succeed in building the house of the Lord. We established prayer meetings and meetings of exhortation, and the Lord blessed our endeavors, and many souls were awakened; but the elder soon forbid us holding any such meetings; but we viewed the forlorn state of our colored brethren, and that they were destitute of a place of worship. They were considered as a nuisance.

A number of us usually attended St. George's church in Fourth street; and when the colored people began to get numerous in attending the church; they moved us from the seats we usually sat on, and placed us around the wall, and on Sabbath morning we went to church and the sexton stood at the door, and told us to go in the gallery. He told us to go, and we would see where to sit. We expected to take the seats over the ones we formerly occupied below, not knowing any better. We took those seats. Meeting had begun, and they were nearly done singing, and just as we got to the seats, the elder said, "Let us pray." We had not been long upon our knees before I heard considerable scuffling and low talking. I raised my head up and saw one of the trustees, H_____ M_____, having hold of the Rev. Absalom Jones, pulling him up off of his knees, and saying, "You must get up—you must not kneel here." Mr. Jones replied, "Wait until prayer is over." Mr. H_____ M_____ said, "No, you must get up now, or I will call for aid and force you away." Mr. Jones said, "Wait until prayer is over, and I will get up and trouble you no more." With that he beckoned to one of the other trustees. Mr. L_____ S_____ to come to his assistance. He came, and went to William White to pull him up. By this time prayer was over, and we all went out of the church in a body, and they were no more plagued with us in the church. This raised a great excitement and inquiry among the citizens, in so much that I believe they were ashamed of their conduct. But my dear Lord was with us, and we were filled with fresh vigor to get a house erected to worship God in. Seeing our forlorn and distressed situation, many of the hearts of our citizens were moved to urge us forward; notwithstanding we had subscribed largely towards finishing St. George's church, in building the gallery and laying new floors, and just as the house was made comfortable, we were turned out from enjoying the comforts of worshipping therein. We then hired a store-room, and held worship by ourselves. Here we were pursued with threats of being disowned, and read publicly out of meeting if we did continue worship in the place we had hired; but we believed the Lord would be our friend. We got subscription papers out to raise money to build the house of the Lord. By this time we had waited on Dr. Rush and Mr. Robert Ralston, and told them of our distressing situation. We considered it a blessing that the Lord had put it into our hearts to wait upon those gentlemen. They pitied our situation, and subscribed largely towards the church, and were very friendly towards us, and advised us how to go on. We appointed Mr. Ralston our treasurer. Dr. Rush did much for us in public by his influence. I hope the name of Dr. Benjamin Rush and Robert Ralston will never be forgotten among us. They were the first two gentlemen who espoused the cause of the oppressed, and aided us in building the house of the Lord for the poor Africans to worship in. Here was the beginning and rise of the first African church in America. But the elder of the Methodist Church still pursued us. Mr. John McClaskey called upon us and told us if we did not erase our names from the subscription paper, and give up the paper, we would be publicly turned out of meeting. We asked him if we had violated any rules of discipline by so doing. He replied, "I have the charge given to me by the Conference, and unless you submit I will read you publicly out of meeting." We told him we were willing to abide by the discipline of the Methodist Church, "And if you will show us where we have vio-

lated any law of discipline of the Methodist Church, we will submit; and if there is no rule violated in the discipline we will proceed on." He replied, "We will read you all out." We told him if he turned us out contrary to rule of discipline, we should seek further redress. We told him we were dragged off of our knees in St. George's church, and treated worse than heathens; and we were determined to seek out for ourselves, the Lord being our helper. He told us we were not Methodists, and left us. Finding we would go on in raising money to build the church, he called upon us again, and wished to see us all together. We met him. He told us that he wished us well, that he was a friend to us, and used many arguments to convince us that we were wrong in building a church. We told him we had no place of worship; and we did not mean to go to St. George's church any more, as we were so scandalously treated in the presence of all the congregation present; "and if you deny us your name, you cannot seal up the scriptures from us, and deny us a name in heaven. We believe heaven is free for all who worship in spirit and truth." And he said, "So you are determined to go on." We told him "Yes, God being our helper." He then replied, "We will disown you all from the Methodist connection." We believed if we put our trust in the Lord, he would stand by us. This was a trial that I never had to pass through before. I was confident that the great head of the church would support us. My dear Lord was with us. We went out with our subscription paper, and met with great success. We had no reason to complain of the liberality of the citizens. The first day the Rev. Absalom Jones and myself went out we collected three hundred and sixty dollars. This was the greatest day's collection that we met with. We appointed a committee to look out for a lot—the Rev. Absalom Jones, William Gray, William Wilcher and myself. We pitched upon a lot at the corner of Lombard and Sixth streets. They authorized me to go and agree for it. I did accordingly. The lot belonged to Mr. Mark Wilcox. We entered into articles of agreement for the lot. Afterwards the committee found a lot in Fifth street, in a more commodious part of the city, which we bought; and the first lot they threw upon my hands, and wished me to give it up. I told them they had authorized me to agree for the lot, and they were all well satisfied with the agreement I had made, and I thought it was hard that they would throw it upon my hands. I told them I would sooner keep it myself than to forfeit the agreement I had made. And so I did.

We bore much persecution from many of the Methodist connection; but we have reason to be thankful to Almighty God, who was our deliverer. The day was appointed to go and dig the cellar. I arose early in the morning and addressed the throne of grace, praying that the Lord would bless our endeavors. Having by this time two or three teams of my own—as I was the first proposer of the African church, I put the first spade in the ground to dig a cellar for the same. This was the first African Church or meetinghouse that was erected in the United States of America. We intended it for the African preaching-house or church; but finding that the elder stationed in this city was such an opposer to our proceedings of erecting a place of worship, though the principal part of the directors of this church belonged to the Methodist connection, the elder stationed here would neither preach for us, nor have anything to do with us. We then held an election, to know what religious denomination we should unite with. At the election it was determined—there were two in favor of the Methodist, the Rev. Absalom Jones and myself, and a large majority in favor of the Church of England. The majority carried. Notwithstanding we had been so violently persecuted by the elder, we were in favor of being attached to the Methodist connection; for I was confident that there was no religious sect or denomination would suit the capacity of the colored people as well as the Methodist; for the plain and simple gospel suits best for any people; for the unlearned can understand, and the learned are sure to understand; and the reason that the Methodist is so successful in the awakening and conversion of the colored people, the plain doctrine and having a good discipline. But in many cases the preachers would act to please their own fancy, without discipline, till some of them became such tyrants, and more especially to the colored people. They would turn them out of society, giving them no trial, for the smallest offense, perhaps only hearsay. They would frequently, in meeting the class, impeach some of the members of whom they had heard an ill report, and turn them out, saying, "I have heard thus and thus of you, and you are no more a member of society"—without witnesses on either side. This has been frequently done, notwithstanding in the first rise and progress in Delaware state, and elsewhere, the colored people were their greatest support; for there were but few of us free; but the slaves would toil in their little patches many a night until midnight to raise their little truck and sell to get something to support them more than what their masters gave them, but we used often to divide our little support among the white preachers of the Gospel. This was once a quarter. It was in the time of the old Revolutionary War between Great Britain and the United States. The Methodists were the first people that brought glad tidings to the colored people. I feel thankful that ever I heard a Methodist preach. We are beholden to the Methodists, under God, for the light of the Gospel we enjoy; for all other denominations preached so high-flown that we were not able to comprehend their doctrine. Sure am I that reading sermons will never prove so beneficial to the colored people as spiritual or extempore preaching. I am well convinced that the Methodist has proved beneficial to thousands and ten times thousands. It is to be awfully feared that the simplicity of the Gospel that was among them fifty years ago, and that they conform more to the world and the fashions thereof, they would fare very little better than the people of the world. The discipline is altered considerably from what it was. We would ask for the good old way, and desire to walk therein.

In 1793 a committee was appointed from the African Church to solicit me to be their minister, for there was no colored preacher in Philadelphia but myself. I told them I could not accept of their offer, as I was a Methodist. I was indebted to the Methodists, under God, for what little religion I had; being convinced that they were the people of God, I informed them that I could not be anything else but a Methodist, as I was both and awakened under them, and I could go no further with them, for I was a Methodist, and would leave you in peace and love. I would do nothing to retard them in building a church as it was an extensive building, neither would I go out with a subscription paper until they were done going out with their subscription. I bought an old frame that had been formerly occupied as a blacksmith shop, from Mr. Sims, and hauled it on the lot in Sixth near Lombard street, that had formely been taken for the Church of England. I employed carpenters to repair the old frame, and fit it for a place of worship. In July 1794, Bishop Asbury being in town I solicited him to open the church for us which he accepted. The Rev. John Dickins sung and prayed, and Bishop Asbury preached. The house was called Bethel, agreeable to the prayer that was made. Mr. Dickins prayed that it might be a bethel to the gathering in of thousands of souls. My dear Lord was with us, so that there were many hearty "amens" echoed through the house. This house of worship has been favored with the awakening of many souls, and I trust they are in the Kingdom, both white and colored. Our warfare and troubles now began afresh. Mr. C. proposed that we should make over the church to the Conference. This we objected to; he asserted that we could not be Methodists unless we did; we told him he might deny us their name, but they could not deny us a seat in Heaven. Finding that he could not prevail with us so to do, he observed that we had better be incorporated, then we could get any legacies that were left for us, if not, we could not. We agreed to be incorporated. He offered to draw the incorporation himself, that it would save us the trouble of paying for to get it drawn. We cheerfully submitted to his proposed plan. He drew the incorporation, but incorporated our church under the Conference, our property was then all consigned to the Conference for the present bishops, elders, ministers, etc., that belonged to the white Conference, and our property was gone. Being ignorant of incorporations we cheerfully agreed thereto. We labored about ten years under this incorporation, until James Smith was appointed to take the charge in Philadelphia; he soon waked us up by demanding the keys and books of the church, and forbid us holding any meetings except by orders from him; these propositions we told him we could not agree to. He observed he was elder, appointed to the charge, and unless we submitted to him, he would read us all out of meeting. We told him the house was ours, we had bought it, and paid for it. He said he would let us know it was not ours, it belonged to the Conference; we took counsel on it; counsel informed us we had been taken in; according to the incorporation it belonged to the white connection. We asked him if it couldn't be altered; he told us if two-thirds of the society agreed to have it altered, it could be altered. He gave me a transcript to lay before them; I called the society together and laid it before them. My dear Lord was with us. It was unanimously agreed to, by both male and female. We had another incorporation drawn that took the church from Conference, and got it passed, before the elder knew anything about it. This raised a considerable rumpus, for the elder contended that it would not be good unless he had signed it. The elder, with the trustees of St. George's, called us together, and said we must pay six hundred dollars a year for their services, or they could not serve us. We told them we were not able so to do. The trustees of St. George's insisted that we should or should not be supplied by their preachers. At last they made a move that they would take four hundred; we told them that our house was considerably in debt, and we were poor people, and we could not agree to pay four hundred, but we agreed to give them two hundred. It was moved by one of the trustees of St. George's that the money should be paid into their treasury; we refused paying it into their treasury, but we would pay it to the preacher that served; they made a move that the preacher should not receive the money from us. The Bethel trustees made a move that their funds should be shut and they would pay none; this caused a considerable contention. At length they withdrew their motion. The elder supplied us preaching five times in a year for two hundred dollars. Finding that they supplied us so seldom, the trustees of Bethel church passed a resolution that they would pay but one hundred dollars a year, as the elder only preached five times in a year for us; they called for the money, we paid him twenty-five dollars a quarter, but he being dissatisfied, returned the money back again, and would not have it unless we paid him fifty dollars. The trustees concluded it was enough for five sermons, and said they would pay no more; the elder of St. George's was determined to preach for us no more, unless we gave him

two hundred dollars, and we were left alone for upwards of one year.

Mr. Samuel Royal being appointed to the charge of Philadelphia, declared unless we should repeal the Supplement, neither he nor any white preacher, travelling or local, should preach any more for us; so we were left to ourselves. At length the preachers and stewards belonging to the Academy, proposed serving us on the same terms that we had offered to the St. George's preachers, and they preached for us better than twelve months, and then demanded $150 per year; this not being complied with, they declined preaching for us, and we were once more left to ourselves, as an edict was passed by the elder, that if any local preacher should serve us, he should be expelled from the connection. John Emory, then elder of the Academy, published a circular letter, in which we were disowned by the Methodists. A house was also hired and fitted up for worship, not far from Bethel, and an invitation given to all who desired to be Methodists to resort thither. But being disappointed in this plan, Robert R. Roberts, the resident elder, came to Bethel, insisted on preaching to us and taking the spiritual charge of the congregation, for we were Methodists he was told he should come on some terms with the trustees; his answer was that "He did not come to consult with Richard Allen or other trustees, but to inform the congregation, that on next Sunday afternoon, he would come and take the spiritual charge." We told him he could not preach for us under existing circumstances. However, at the appointed time he came, but having taken previous advice we had our preacher in the pulpit when he came, and the house was so fixed that he could not get but more than half way to the pulpit. Finding himself disappointed he appealed to those who came with him as witnesses, that "That man (meaning the preacher), had taken his appointment." Several respectable white citizens who knew the colored people had been ill-used, were present, and told us not to fear, for they would see us righted, and not suffer Roberts to preach in a forcible manner, after which Roberts went away.

The next elder stationed in Philadelphia was Robert Birch, who, following the example of his predecessor, came and published a meeting for himself. But the method just mentioned was adopted and he had to go away disappointed. In consequence of this, he applied to the Supreme Court for a writ of mandamus, to know why the pulpit was denied him. Being elder, this brought on a lawsuit, which ended in our favor. Thus by the Providence of God we were delivered from a long, distressing and expensive suit, which could not be resumed, being determined by the Supreme Court. For this mercy we desire to be unfeignedly thankful.

About this time, our colored friends in Baltimore were treated in a similar manner by the white preachers and trustees, and many of them driven away who were disposed to seek a place of worship, rather than go to law.

Many of the colored people in other places were in a situation nearly like those of Philadelphia and Baltimore, which induced us, in April 1816, to call a general meeting, by way of Conference. Delegates from Baltimore and other places which met those of Philadelphia, and taking into consideration their grievances, and in order to secure the privileges, promote union and harmony among themselves, it was resolved: "That the people of Philadelphia, Baltimore, etc., etc., should become one body, under the name of the African Methodist Episcopal Church." We deemed it expedient to have a form of discipline, whereby we may guide our people in the fear of God, in the unity of the Spirit, and in the bonds of peace, and preserve us from that spiritual despotism which we have so recently experienced—remembering that we are not to lord it over God's heritage, as greedy dogs that can never have enough. But with long suffering and bowels of compassion, to bear each other's burdens, and so fulfill the Law of Christ, praying that our mutual striving together for the promulgation of the Gospel may be crowned with abundant success.

The God of Bethel heard her cries,
He let his power be seen;
He stopp'd the proud oppressor's frown,
And proved himself a King.

Thou sav'd them in the trying hour,
Ministers and councils joined,
And all stood ready to retain
That helpless church of Thine.

Bethel surrounded by her foes,
But not yet in despair,
Christ heard her supplicating cries;
The God of Bethel heard.

ADDRESS AT THE AFRICAN MASONIC HALL (MARIA STEWART, 1833)

∎∎∎

SOURCE: Moses, Wilson Jeremiah, ed. *Classical Black Nationalism: From the American Revolution to Marcus Garvey.* New York: New York University Press, 1996, pp. 90–98.

INTRODUCTION: *Portraying African Americans as a people with a special God-given destiny, Stewart draws parallels from biblical references to Israel and Egypt in the Old Testament, and to Babylon in the Apocalypse, proclaiming her conviction that "many powerful sons and daughters of Africa will shortly arise, who will put down vice and immorality among us, and declare by Him that sitteth upon the throne, that they will have their rights. . . ." She concludes with a firm condemnation of the idea of African emigration.*

African rights and liberty is a subject that ought to fire the breast of every free man of color in these United States, and excite in his bosom a lively, deep, decided and heartfelt interest. When I cast my eyes on the long list of illustrious names that are enrolled on the bright annals of fame among the whites, I turn my eyes within, and ask my thoughts, "Where are the names of *our* illustrious ones?" It must certainly have been for the want of energy on the part of the free people of color, that they have been long willing to bear the yoke of oppression. It must have been the want of ambition and force that has given the whites occasion to say, that our natural abilities are not as good, and our capacities by nature inferior to theirs. They boldly assert, that, did we possess a natural independence of soul, and feel a love for liberty within our breasts, some one of our sable race, long before this, would have testified it, notwithstanding the disadvantages under which we labor. We have made ourselves appear altogether unqualified to speak in our own defence, and are therefore looked upon as objects of pity and commiseration. We have been imposed upon, insulted and derided on every side; and now, if we complain, it is considered as the height of impertinence. We have suffered ourselves to be considered as dastards, cowards, mean, faint-hearted wretches; and on this account, (not because of our complexion,) many despise us, and would gladly spurn us from their presence.

These things have fired my soul with a holy indignation, and compelled me thus to come forward, and endeavor to turn their attention to knowledge and improvement; for knowledge is power. I would ask, is it blindness of mind, or stupidity of soul, or the want of education, that has caused our men who are 60 or 70 years of age, never to let their voices be heard, nor their hands be raised in behalf of their color? Or has it been for the fear of offending the whites? If it has, O ye fearful ones, throw off your fearfulness, and come forth in the name of the Lord, and in the strength of the God of justice, and make yourselves useful and active members in society; for they admire a noble and patriotic spirit in others; and should they not admire it in us? If you are men, convince them that you possess the spirit of men; and as your day, so shall your strength be. Have the sons of Africa no souls? feel they no ambitious desires? shall the chains of ignorance forever confine them? shall the insipid appellation of "clever negroes," or "good creatures," any longer content them? Where can we find among ourselves the man of science, or a philosopher, or an able statesman, or a counsellor at law? Show me our fearless and brave, our noble and gallant ones. Where are our lecturers on natural history, and our critics in useful knowledge? There may be a few such men among us, but they are rare. It is true, our fathers bled and died in the revolutionary war, and others fought bravely under the command of Jackson, in defence of liberty. But where is the man that has distinguished himself in these modern days by acting wholly in the defence of African rights and liberty? There was one, although he sleeps, his memory lives.

I am sensible that there are many highly intelligent gentlemen of color in these United States, in the force of whose arguments, doubtless, I should discover my inferiority; but if they are blest with wit and talent, friends and fortune, why have they not made themselves men of eminence, by striving to take all the reproach that is cast upon the people of color, and in endeavoring to alleviate the woes of their brethren in bondage? Talk, without effort, is nothing; you are abundantly capable, gentlemen, of making yourselves selves men of distinction; and this gross neglect, on your part, causes my blood to boil within me. Here is the grand cause which hinders the rise and progress of the people of color. It is their want of laudable ambition and requisite courage.

Individuals have been distinguished according to their genius and talents, ever since the first formation of man, and will continue to be while the world stands. The different grades rise to honor and respectability as their merits may deserve. History informs us that we sprung from one of the most learned nations of the whole earth; from the seat, if not the parent of science; yes, poor, despised Africa was once the resort of sages and legislators of other nations, was esteemed the school for learning, and the most illustrious men in Greece flocked thither for instruction. But it was our gross sins and abominations that provoked the Almighty to frown thus heavily upon us, and give our glory unto others. Sin and prodigality have caused the downfall of nations, kings and emperors; and were it not that God in wrath remembers mercy, we might indeed despair; but a promise is left us; "Ethiopia shall again stretch forth her hands unto God."

But it is of no use for us to boast that we sprung from this learned and enlightened nation, for this day a thick mist of moral gloom hangs over millions of our race. Our condition as a people has been low for hundreds of years, and it will continue to be so, unless, by true piety and virtue, we strive to regain that which we have lost. White Americans, by their prudence, economy and exertions, have sprung up and become one of the most flourishing nations in the world, distinguished for their knowledge of the arts and sciences, for their polite literature. While our minds are vacant, and starving for want of knowledge, theirs are filled to overflowing. Most of our color have been taught to stand in fear of the white man, from their earliest infancy, to work as soon as they could walk, and call "master," before they scarce could lisp the name of *mother*. Continual fear and laborious servitude have in some degree lessened in us that natural force and energy which belong to man; or else, in defiance of opposition, our men, before this, would have nobly and boldly contended for their rights. But give the man of color an equal opportunity with the white from the cradle to manhood, and from manhood to the grave, and you would discover the dignified statesman, the man of science, and the philosopher. But there is no such opportunity for the sons of Africa, and I fear that our powerful ones are fully determined that there never shall be. Forbid, ye Powers on high, that it should any longer be said that our men possess no force. O ye sons of Africa, when will your voices be heard in our legislative halls, in defiance of your enemies, contending for equal rights and liberty? How can you, when you reflect from what you have fallen, refrain from crying mightily unto God, to turn away from us the fierceness of his anger, and remember our transgressions against us no more forever. But a God of infinite purity will not regard the prayers of those who hold religion in one hand, and prejudice, sin and pollution in the other; he will not regard the prayers of self-righteousness and hypocrisy. Is it possible, I exclaim, that for the want of knowledge, we have labored for hundreds of years to support others, and been content to receive what they chose to give us in return? Cast your eyes about, look as far as you can see; all, all is owned by the lordly white, except here and there a lowly dwelling which the man of color, midst deprivations, fraud and opposition, has been scarce able to procure. Like king Solomon, who put neither nail nor hammer to the temple, yet received the praise; so also have the white Americans gained themselves a name, like the names of the great men that are in the earth, while in reality we have been their principal foundation and support. We have pursued the shadow, they have obtained the substance; we have performed the labor, they have received the profits; we have planted the vines, they have eaten the fruits of them.

I would implore our men, and especially our rising youth, to flee from the gambling board and the dance-hall; for we are poor, and have no money to throw away. I do not consider dancing as criminal in itself, but it is astonishing to me that our young men are so blind to their own interest and the future welfare of their children, as to spend their hard earnings for this frivolous amusement; for it has been carried on among us to such an unbecoming extent, that it has became absolutely disgusting. "Faithful are the wounds of a friend, but the kisses of an enemy are deceitful." Had those men among us, who have had an opportunity, turned their attention as assiduously to mental and moral improvement as they have to gambling and dancing, I might have remained quietly at home, and they stood contending in my place. These polite accomplishments will never enrol your names on the bright annals of fame, who admire the belle void of intellectual knowledge, or applaud the dandy that talks largely on politics, without striving to assist his fellow in the revolution, when the nerves and muscles of every other man forced him into the field of action. You have a right to rejoice, and to let your hearts cheer you in the days of your youth; yet remember that for all these things, God will bring you into judgment. Then, O ye sons of Africa, turn your mind from these perishable objects, and contend for the cause of God and the rights of man. Form yourselves into temperance societies. There are temperate men among you; then why will you any longer neglect to strive, by your example, to suppress vice in all its abhorrent forms? You have been told repeatedly of the glorious results arising from temperance, and can you bear to see the whites arising in honor and respectability, without endeavoring to grasp after that honor and respectability also?

But I forbear. Let our money, instead of being thrown away as heretofore, be appropriated for schools and seminaries of learning for our children and youth. We ought to follow the example of the whites in this respect. Nothing would raise our respectability, add to our peace and happiness, and reflect so much honor upon us, as to be ourselves the promoters of temperance, and the supporters, as far as we are able, of useful and scientific knowledge. The rays of light and knowledge have been hid from our view; we have been taught to consider ourselves as scarce superior to the brute creation; and have performed the most laborious part of American drudgery. Had we as a people received one half the early advantages the whites have received, I would defy the government of these United States to deprive us any longer of our rights.

I am informed that the agent of the Colonization Society has recently formed an association of young men, for the purpose of influencing those of us to go to Liberia who may feel disposed. The colonizationists are blind to their own interest, for should the nations of the earth make war with America, they would find their forces much weakened by our absence; or should we remain here, can our "brave soldiers," and "fellow-citizens," as they were termed in time of calamity, condescend to defend the rights of the whites, and be again deprived of their own, or sent to Liberia in return? Or, if the colonizationists are real friends to Africa, let them expend the money which they collect, in erecting a college to educate her injured sons in this land of gospel light and liberty; for it would be most thankfully received on our part, and convince us of the truth of their professions, and save time, expense and anxiety. Let them place before us noble objects, worthy of pursuit, and see if we prove ourselves to be those unambitious negroes they term us. But ah! methinks their hearts are so frozen towards us, they had rather their money should be sunk in the ocean than to administer it to our relief; and I fear, if they dared, like Pharaoh, king of Egypt, they would order every male child among us to be drowned. But the most high God is still as able to subdue the lofty pride of these white Americans, as He was the heart of that ancient rebel. They say, though we are looked upon as *things,* yet we sprang from a scientific people. Had our men the requisite force and energy, they would soon convince them by their efforts both in public and private, that they were men, or things in the shape of men. Well may the colonizationists laugh us to scorn for our negligence; well may they cry, "Shame to the sons of Africa." As the burden of the Israelites was too great for Moses to bear, so also is our burden too great for our noble advocate to bear. You must feel interested, my brethren, in what he undertakes, and hold up his hands by your good works, or in spite of himself, his soul will become discouraged, and his heart will die within him; for he has, as it were, the strong bulls of Bashan to contend with.

It is of no use for us to wait any longer for a generation of well educated men to arise. We have slumbered and slept too long already; the day is far spent; the night of death approaches; and you have sound sense and good judgment sufficient to begin with, if you feel disposed to make a right use of it. Let every man of color throughout the United States, who possesses the spirit and principles of a man, sign a petition to Congress, to abolish slavery in the District of Columbia, and grant you the rights and privileges of common free citizens; for if you had had faith as a grain of mustard seed, long before this the mountains of prejudice might have been removed. We are all sensible that the Anti-Slavery Society has taken hold of the arm of our whole population, in order to raise them out of the mire. Now all we have to do is, by a spirit of virtuous ambition to strive to raise ourselves; and I am happy to have it in my power thus publicly to say, that the colored inhabitants of this city, in some respects, are beginning to improve. Had the free people of color in these United States nobly and boldly contended for their rights, and showed a natural genius and talent, although not so brilliant as some; had they held up, encouraged and patronized each other, nothing could have hindered us from being a thriving and flourishing people. There has been a fault among us. The reason why our distinguished men have not made themselves more influential is, because they fear that the strong current of opposition through which they must pass, would cause their downfall and prove their overthrow. And what gives rise to this opposition? Envy. And what has it amounted to? Nothing. And who are the cause of it? Our whited sepulchres, who want to be great, and don't know how; who love to be called of men "Rabbi, Rabbi," who put on false sanctity, and humble themselves to their brethren, for the sake of acquiring the highest place in the synagogue, and the uppermost seats at the feast. You, dearly beloved, who are the genuine followers of our Lord Jesus Christ, the salt of the earth and the light of the world, are not so culpable. As I told you, in the very first of my writing, I tell you again, I am but as a drop in the bucket—as one particle of the small dust of the earth. God will surely raise up those among us who will plead the cause of virtue, and the pure principles of morality, more eloquently than I am able to do.

It appears to me that America has become like the great city of Babylon, for she has boasted in her heart,—"I sit a queen, and am no widow, and shall see no sorrow"? She is indeed a seller of slaves and the souls of men; she has made the Africans drunk with the wine of her fornication; she has put them completely beneath her feet, and she means to keep them there; her right hand supports the reins of government, and her left hand the wheel of power, and she is determined not to let go her grasp. But many powerful sons and daughters of Africa will shortly arise, who will put down vice and immorality among us, and declare by Him that sitteth upon the throne, that they will have their rights; and if refused, I am afraid they will spread horror and devastation around. I believe that the oppression of injured Africa has come up before the Majesty of Heaven; and when our cries shall have reached the ears of the Most High, it will be a tremendous day for the people of this land; for strong is the arm of the Lord God Almighty.

Life has almost lost its charms for me; death has lost its sting and the grave its terrors; and at times I have a strong desire to depart and dwell with Christ, which is far better. Let me entreat my white brethren to awake and save our sons from dissipation, and our daughters from ruin. Lend the hand of assistance to feeble merit, plead the cause of virtue among our sable race; so shall our curses upon you be turned into blessings; and though you should endeavor to drive us from these shores, still we will cling to you the more firmly; nor will we attempt to rise above you: we will presume to be called your equals only.

The unfriendly whites first drove the native American from his much loved home. Then they stole our fathers from their peaceful and quiet dwellings, and brought them hither, and made bond-men and bond-women of them and their little ones; they have obliged our brethren to labor, kept them in utter ignorance, nourished them in vice, and raised them in degradation; and now that we have enriched their soil, and filled their coffers, they say that we are not capable of becoming like white men, and that we never can rise to respectability in this country. They would drive us to a strange land. But before I go, the bayonet shall pierce me through. African rights and liberty is a subject that ought to fire the breast of every free man of color in these United States, and excite in his bosom a lively, deep, decided and heart-felt interest.

An Address to Slaves of the United States of America (Henry Highland Garnet, 1843)

SOURCE: Bracey, John H. Jr., August Meier, and Elliott Rudwick, eds. *Black Nationalism in America.* Indianapolis: Bobbs-Merrill, 1970, pp. 67–76.

INTRODUCTION: *Addressing an abolitionist convention in Buffalo in 1843, Presbyterian minister Garnet advocated the violent overthrow of slave masters by slaves, declaring: "You had better all die— die immediately, than live slaves and entail your wretchedness upon your posterity."*

Brethren and Fellow Citizens:

Your brethren of the North, East, and West have been accustomed to meet together in National Conventions, to sympathize with each other, and to weep over your unhappy condition. In these meetings we have addressed all classes of the free, but we have never, until this time, sent a word of consolation and advice to you. We have been contented in sitting still and mourning over your sorrows, earnestly hoping that before this day your sacred liberty would have been restored. But, we have hoped in vain. Years have rolled on, and tens of thousands have been borne on streams of blood and tears, to the shores of eternity. While you have been oppressed, we have also been partakers with you; nor can we be free while you are enslaved. We, therefore, write to you as being bound with you.

Many of you are bound to us, not only by the ties of a common humanity, but we are connected by the more tender relations of parents, wives, husbands, children, brothers, and sisters, and friends. As such we most affectionately address you.

Slavery has fixed a deep gulf between you and us, and while it shuts out from you the relief and consolation which your friends would willingly render, it affects and persecutes you with a fierceness which we might not expect to see in the fiends of hell. But still the Almighty Father of mercies has left us to a glimmering ray of hope, which shines out like a lone star in a cloudy sky. Mankind are becoming wiser, and better—the oppressor's power is fading, and you, every day, are becoming better informed, and more numerous. Your grievances, brethren, are many. We shall not attempt, in this short address, to present to the world all the dark catalogue of this nation's sins, which have been committed upon an innocent people. Nor is it indeed necessary, for you to feel them from day to day, and all the civilized world look upon them with amazement.

Two hundred and twenty-seven years ago, the first of our injured race were brought to the shores of America. They came not with glad spirits to select their homes in the New World. They came not with their own consent, to find an unmolested enjoyment of the blessings of this fruitful soil. The first dealings they had with men calling themselves Christians, exhibited to them the worst features of corrupt and sordid hearts; and convinced them that no cruelty is too great, no villainy and no robbery too abhorrent for even enlightened men to perform, when influenced by avarice and lust. Neither did they come flying upon the wings of Liberty, to a land of freedom. But they came with broken hearts, from their beloved native land, and were doomed to unrequited toil and deep degradation. Nor did the evil of their bondage end at their emancipation by death. Succeeding generations inherited their chains, and millions have come from eternity into time, and have returned again to the world of spirits, cursed and ruined by American slavery.

The propagators of the system, or their immediate ancestors, very soon discovered its growing evil, and its tremendous wickedness, and secret promises were made to destroy it. The gross inconsistency of a people holding slaves, who had themselves "ferried o'er the wave" for freedom's sake, was too apparent to be entirely overlooked. The voice of Freedom cried, "Emancipate yourselves." Humanity supplicated with tears for the deliverance of the children of Africa. Wisdom urged her solemn plea. The bleeding captive plead his innocence, and pointed to Christianity who stood weeping at the cross. Jehovah frowned upon the nefarious institution, and thunderbolts, red with vengeance, struggled to leap forth to blast the

guilty wretches who maintained it. But all was in vain. Slavery had stretched its dark wings of death over the land, the Church stood silently by—the priests prophesied falsely, and the people loved to have it so. Its throne is established, and now it reigns triumphant.

Nearly three million of your fellow citizens are prohibited by law and public opinion (which in this country is stronger than law) from reading the Book of Life. Your intellect has been destroyed as much as possible, and every ray of light they have attempted to shut out from your minds. The oppressors themselves have become involved in the ruin. They have become weak, sensual, and rapacious—they have cursed you—they have cursed themselves—they have cursed the earth which they have trod.

The colonists threw the blame upon England. They said that the mother country entailed the evil upon them, and that they would rid themselves of it if they could. The world thought they were sincere, and the philanthropic pitied them. But time soon tested their sincerity.

In a few years the colonists grew strong, and severed themselves from the British Government. Their independence was declared, and they took their station among the sovereign powers of the earth. The declaration was a glorious document. Sages admired it, and the patriotic of every nation reverenced the God-like sentiments which it contained. When the power of Government returned to their hands, did they emancipate the slaves? No; they rather added new links to our chains. Were they ignorant of the principles of Liberty? Certainly they were not. The sentiments of their revolutionary orators fell in burning eloquence upon their hearts, and with one voice they cried, Liberty or Death. Oh what a sentence was that! It ran from soul to soul like electric fire, and nerved the arm of thousands to fight in the holy cause of Freedom. Among the diversity of opinions that are entertained in regard to physical resistance, there are but a few found to gainsay that stern declaration. We are among those who do not. Slavery! How much misery is comprehended in that single word. What mind is there that does not shrink from its direful effects? Unless the image of God be obliterated from the soul, all men cherish the love of Liberty. The nice discerning political economist does not regard the sacred right more than the untutored African who roams in the wilds of Congo. Nor has the one more right to the full enjoyment of his freedom than the other. In every man's mind the good seeds of liberty are planted, and he who brings his fellow down so low, as to make him contented with a condition of slavery, commits the highest crime against God and man. Brethren, your oppressors aim to do this. They endeavor to make you as much like brutes as possible. When they have blinded the eyes of your mind—when they have embittered the sweet waters of life—then, and not till then, has American slavery done its perfect work.

TO SUCH DEGRADATION IT IS SINFUL IN THE EXTREME FOR YOU TO MAKE VOLUNTARY SUBMISSION. The divine commandments you are in duty bound to reverence and obey. If you do not obey them, you will surely meet with the displeasure of the Almighty. He requires you to love him supremely, and your neighbor as yourself—to keep the Sabbath day holy—to search the Scriptures—and bring up your children with respect for his laws, and to worship no other God but him. But slavery sets all these at nought, and hurls defiance in the face of Jehovah. The forlorn condition in which you are placed, does not destroy your moral obligation to God. You are not certain of heaven, because you suffer yourselves to remain in a state of slavery, where you cannot obey the commandments of the Sovereign of the universe. If the ignorance of slavery is a passport to heaven, then it is a blessing, and no curse, and you should rather desire its perpetuity than its abolition. God will not receive slavery, nor ignorance, nor any other state of mind, for love and obedience to him. Your condition does not absolve you from your moral obligation. The diabolical injustice by which your liberties are cloven down, NEITHER GOD, NOR ANGELS, OR JUST MEN, COMMAND YOU TO SUFFER FOR A SINGLE MOMENT. THEREFORE IT IS YOUR SOLEMN AND IMPERATIVE DUTY TO USE EVERY MEANS, BOTH MORAL, INTELLECTUAL, AND PHYSICAL THAT PROMISES SUCCESS. If a band of heathen men should attempt to enslave a race of Christians, and to place their children under the influence of some false religion, surely Heaven would frown upon the men who would not resist such aggression, even to death. If, on the other hand, a band of Christians should attempt to enslave a race of heathen men, and to entail slavery upon them, and to keep them in heathenism in the midst of Christianity, the God of heaven would smile upon every effort which the injured might make to disenthral themselves.

Brethren, it is as wrong for your lordly oppressors to keep you in slavery, as it was for the man thief to steal our ancestors from the coast of Africa. You should therefore now use the same manner of resistance, as would have been just in our ancestors when the bloody foot-prints of the first remorseless soul-thief was placed upon the shores of our fatherland. The humblest peasant is as free in the sight of God as the proudest monarch that ever swayed a sceptre. Liberty is a spirit sent out from God, and like its great Author, is no respecter of persons.

Brethren, the time has come when you must act for yourselves. It is an old and true saying that, "if hereditary bondmen would be free, they must themselves strike the blow." You can plead your own cause, and do the work of emancipation better than any others. The nations of the world are moving in the great cause of universal freedom, and some of them at least will, ere long, do you justice. The combined powers of Europe have placed their broad seal of disapprobation upon the African slave-trade. But in the slave-holding parts of the United States, the trade is as brisk as ever. They buy and sell you as though you were brute beasts. The North has done much—her opinion of slavery in the abstract is known. But in regard to the South, we adopt the opinion of the *New York Evangelist*—We have advanced so far, that the cause apparently waits for a more effectual door to be thrown open than has been yet. We are about to point out that more effectual door. Look around you, and behold the bosoms of your loving wives heaving with untold agonies! Hear the cries of your poor children! Remember the stripes your fathers bore. Think of the torture and disgrace of your noble mothers. Think of your wretched sisters, loving virtues and purity, as they are driven into concubinage and are exposed to the unbridled lusts of incarnate devils. Think of the undying glory that hangs around the ancient name of Africa—and forget not that you are native born American citizens, and as such, you are justly entitled to all the rights that are granted to the freest. Think how many tears you have poured out upon the soil which you have cultivated with unrequited toil and enriched with your blood; and then go to your lordly enslavers and tell them plainly, that you *are determined to be free.* Appeal to their sense of justice, and tell them that they have no more right to oppress you, than you have to enslave them. Entreat them to remove the grievous burdens which they have imposed upon you, and to remunerate you for your labor. Promise them renewed diligence in the cultivation of the soil, if they will render to you an equivalent for your services. Point them to the increase of happiness and prosperity in the British West Indies since the Act of Emancipation.

Tell them in language which they cannot misunderstand, of the exceeding sinfulness of slavery, and of a future judgment, and of the righteous retributions of an indignant God. Inform them that all you desire is FREEDOM, and that nothing else will suffice. Do this, and for ever after cease to toil for the heartless tyrants, who give you no other reward but stripes and abuse. If they then commence the work of death, they, and not you, will be responsible for the consequences. You had better all die—*die immediately,* than live slaves and entail your wretchedness upon your posterity. If you would be free in this generation, here is your only hope. However much you and all of us may desire it, there is not much hope of redemption without the shedding of blood. If you must bleed, let it all come at once—rather *die freemen, than live to be slaves.* It is impossible like the children of Israel, to make a grand exodus from the land of bondage. The Pharaohs are on both sides of the blood-red waters! You cannot move *en masse,* to the dominions of the British Queen—nor can you pass through Florida and overrun Texas, and at last find peace in Mexico. The propagators of American slavery are spending their blood and treasure, that they may plant the black flag in the heart of Mexico and riot in the halls of the Montezumas. In the language of the Rev. Robert Hall, when addressing the volunteers of Bristol, who were rushing forth to repel the invasion of Napoleon, who threatened to lay waste the fair homes of England, "Religion is too much interested in your behalf, not to shed over you her most gracious influences."

You will not be compelled to spend much time in order to become inured to hardships. From the first moment that you breathed the air of heaven, you have been accustomed to nothing else but hardships. The heroes of the American Revolution were never put upon harder fare than a peck of corn and a few herrings per week. You have not become enervated by the luxuries of life. Your sternest energies have been beaten out upon the anvil of severe trial. Slavery has done this, to make you subservient, to its own purposes; but it has done more than this, it has prepared you for any emergency. If you receive good treatment, it is what you could hardly expect; if you meet with pain, sorrow, and even death, these are the common lot of slaves.

Fellow men! Patient sufferers! behold your dearest rights crushed to the earth! See your sons murdered, and your wives, mothers and sisters doomed to prostitution. In the name of the merciful God, and by all that life is worth, let it no longer be a debatable question whether it is better to choose *liberty* or *death.*

In 1822, Denmark Veazie, of South Carolina, formed a plan for the liberation of his fellow men. In the whole history of human efforts to overthrow slavery, a more complicated and tremendous plan was never formed. He was betrayed by the treachery of his own people, and died a martyr to freedom. Many a brave hero fell, but history, faithful to her high trust, will transcribe his name on the same monument with Moses, Hampden, Tell, Bruce and Wallace, Toussaint L'Ouverture, Lafayette and Washington. That tremendous movement shook the whole empire of slavery. The guilty soul-thieves were overwhelmed with fear. It is a matter of fact, that at that time, and in consequence of the threatened revolution, the slave States talked strongly of emancipation. But they blew but one blast of the trumpet of freedom and then laid it aside. As these men became quiet, the slaveholders ceased to talk about emancipation; and now behold your condition today! An-

gels sigh over it, and humanity has long since exhausted her tears in weeping on your account!

The patriotic Nathaniel Turner followed Denmark Veazie. He was goaded to desperation by wrong and injustice. By despotism, his name has been recorded on the list of infamy, and future generations will remember him among the noble and brave.

Next arose the immortal Joseph Cinque, the hero of the *Amistad.* He was a native African, and by the help of God he emancipated a whole ship-load of his fellow men on the high seas. And now he sings of liberty on the sunny hills of Africa and beneath his native palm-trees, where he hears the lion roar and feels himself as free as that king of the forest.

Next arose Madison Washington that bright star of freedom, and took his station in the constellation of true heroism. He was a slave on board the brig *Creole,* of Richmond, bound to New Orleans, that great slave mart, with a hundred and four others. Nineteen struck for liberty or death. But one life was taken, and the whole were emancipated, and the vessel was carried into Nassau, New Providence.

Noble men! Those who have fallen in freedom's conflict, their memories will be cherished by the true-hearted and the God-fearing in all future generations; those who are living, their names are surrounded by a halo of glory.

Brethren, arise, arise! Strike for your lives and liberties. Now is the day and the hour. Let every slave throughout the land do this, and the days of slavery are numbered. You cannot be more oppressed than you have been—you cannot suffer greater cruelties than you have already. *Rather die freemen than live to be slaves.* Remember that you are FOUR MILLIONS!

It is in your power so to torment the God-cursed slaveholders that they will be glad to let you go free. If the scale was turned, and black men were the masters and white men the slaves, every destructive agent and element would be employed to lay the oppressor low. Danger and death would hang over their heads day and night. Yes, the tyrants would meet with plagues more terrible than those of Pharaoh. But you are a patient people. You act as though you were made for the special use of these devils. You act as though your daughters were born to pamper the lusts of your masters and overseers. And worse than all, you tamely submit while your lords tear your wives from your embraces and defile them before your eyes. In the name of God, we ask, are you men? Where is the blood of your fathers? Has it all run out of your veins? Awake, awake; millions of voices are calling you! Your dead fathers speak to you from their graves. Heaven, as with a voice of thunder, calls on you to arise from the dust.

Let your motto be resistance! *resistance!* RESISTANCE! No oppressed people have ever secured their liberty without resistance. What kind of resistance you had better make, you must decide by the circumstances that surround you, and according to the suggestion of expediency. Brethren, adieu! Trust in the living God. Labor for the peace of the human race, and remember that you are FOUR MILLIONS.

WHAT TO THE SLAVE IS THE FOURTH OF JULY? (FREDERICK DOUGLASS, 1852)

SOURCE: Douglass, Frederick. *Narrative of the Life of Frederick Douglass, an American Slave.* Edited by David W. Blight. Boston: Bedford Books of St. Martin's Press, 1993, pp. 141–145.

INTRODUCTION: *Frederick Douglass, a powerful and popular abolitionist orator, delivered the following address in Rochester, New York, on July 5, 1852. Douglass reflects on the hypocrisy of whites who celebrate their ancestors' successful struggle for liberty, while denying freedom to millions of African Americans dwelling among them.*

Fellow Citizens:

Pardon me, and allow me to ask, why am I called upon to speak here to-day? What have I or those I represent to do with your national independence? Are the great principles of political freedom and of natural justice, embodied in that Declaration of Independence, extended to us? and am I, therefore, called upon to bring our humble offering to the national altar, and to confess the benefits, and express devout gratitude for the blessings resulting from your independence to us?

Would to God, both for your sakes and ours, that an affirmative answer could be truthfully returned to these questions. Then would my task be light, and my burden easy and delightful. For who is there so cold that a nation's sympathy could not warm him? Who so obdurate and dead to the claims of gratitude, that would not thankfully acknowledge such priceless benefits? Who so stolid and selfish that would not give his voice to swell the hallelujahs of a nation's jubilee, when the chains of servitude had been torn from his limbs? I am not that man. In a case like that, the dumb might eloquently speak, and the "lame man leap like a hart."

But such is not the state of the case. I say it with a sad sense of disparity between us. I am not included within the pale of this glorious anniversary! Your high independence only reveals the immeasurable distance between us. The blessings in which you this day rejoice are not enjoyed in common. The rich inheritance of justice, liberty, prosperity, and independence bequeathed by your fathers is shared by you, not by me. The sunlight that brought life and healing to you has brought stripes and death to me. This Fourth of July is yours, not mine. You may rejoice, I must mourn. To drag a man in fetters into the grand illuminated temple of liberty, and call upon him to join you in joyous anthems, were inhuman mockery and sacrilegious irony. Do you mean, citizens, to mock me, by asking me to speak to-day? If so, there is a parallel to your conduct. And let me warn you, that it is dangerous to copy the example of a nation whose crimes, towering up to heaven, were thrown down by the breath of the Almighty, burying that nation in irrevocable ruin. I can to-day take up the lament of a peeled and woe-smitten people.

"By the rivers of Babylon, there we sat down. Yes! We wept when we remembered Zion. We hanged our harps upon the willows in the midst thereof. For there they that carried us away captive, required of us a song; and they who wasted us, required of us mirth, saying, Sing us one of the songs of Zion. How can we sing the Lord's song in a strange land? If I forget thee, O Jerusalem, let my right hand forget her cunning. If I do not remember thee, let my tongue cleave to the roof of my mouth."

Fellow citizens, above your national, tumultuous joy, I hear the mournful wail of millions, whose chains, heavy and grievous yesterday, are to-day rendered more intolerable by the jubilant shouts that reach them. If I do forget, if I do not remember those bleeding children of sorrow this day, "may my right hand forget her cunning, and may my tongue cleave to the roof of my mouth!" To forget them, to pass lightly over their wrongs, and to chime in with the popular theme, would be treason most scandalous and shocking, and would make me a reproach before God and the world. My subject, then, fellow citizens, is "American Slavery." I shall see this day and its popular characteristics from the slave's point of view. Standing here, identified with the American bondman, making his wrongs mine, I do not hesitate to declare, with all my soul, that the character and conduct of this nation never looked blacker to me than on this Fourth of July. Whether we turn to the declarations of the past, or to the professions of the present, the conduct of the nation seems equally hideous and revolting. America is false to the past, false to the present, and solemnly binds herself to be false to the future. Standing with God and the crushed and bleeding slave on this occasion, I will, in the name of humanity, which is outraged, in the name of liberty, which is fettered, in the name of the Constitution and the Bible, which are disregarded and trampled upon, dare to call in question and to denounce, with all the emphasis I can command, everything that serves to perpetuate slavery—the great sin and shame of America! "I will not equivocate; I will not excuse;" I will use the severest language I can command, and yet not one word shall escape me that any man, whose judgment is not blinded by prejudice, or who is not at heart a slave-holder, shall not confess to be right and just.

But I fancy I hear some one of my audience say it is just in this circumstance that you and your brother abolitionists fail to make a favorable impression on the public mind. Would you argue more and denounce less, would you persuade more and rebuke less, your cause would be much more likely to succeed. But, I submit, where all is plain there is nothing to be argued. What point in the anti-slavery creed would you have me argue? On what branch of the subject do the people of this country need light? Must I undertake to prove that the slave is man? That point is conceded already. Nobody doubts it. The slave-holders themselves acknowledge it in the enactment of laws for their government. They acknowledge it when they punish disobedience on the part of the slave. There are seventy-two crimes in the State of Virginia, which, if committed by a black man (no matter how ignorant he be), subject him to the punishment of death; while only two of these same crimes will subject a white man to like punishment. What is this but the acknowledgment that the slave is a moral, intellectual, and responsible being? The manhood of the slave is conceded. It is admitted in the fact that Southern statute-books are covered with enactments, forbidding, under severe fines and penalties, the teaching of the slave to read or write. When you can point to any such laws in reference to the beasts of the field, then I may consent to argue the manhood of the slave. When the dogs in your streets, when the fowls of the air, when the cattle on your hills, when the fish of the sea, and the reptiles that crawl, shall be unable to distinguish the slave from a brute, then will I argue with you that the slave is a man!

For the present it is enough to affirm the equal manhood of the Negro race. Is it not astonishing that, while we are plowing, planting, and reaping, using all kinds of mechanical tools, erecting houses, constructing bridges, building ships, working in metals of brass, iron, copper, silver, and gold; that while we are reading, writing, and cyphering, acting as clerks, merchants, and secretaries, having among us lawyers, doctors, ministers, poets, authors, editors, orators, and teachers; that while we are engaged in all manner of enterprises common to other men— digging gold in California, capturing the whale in the Pacific, feeding sheep and cattle on the hillside, living, mov-

ing, acting, thinking, planning, living in families as husbands, wives, and children, and above all, confessing and worshiping the Christian God, and looking hopefully for life and immortality beyond the grave—we are called upon to prove that we are men?

Would you have me argue that man is entitled to liberty? That he is the rightful owner of his own body? You have already declared it. Must I argue the wrongfulness of slavery? Is that a question for republicans? Is it to be settled by the rules of logic and argumentation, as a matter beset with great difficulty, involving a doubtful application of the principle of justice, hard to be understood? How should I look to-day in the presence of Americans, dividing and subdividing a discourse, to show that men have a natural right to freedom, speaking of it relatively and positively, negatively and affirmatively? To do so would be to make myself ridiculous, and to offer an insult to your understanding. There is not a man beneath the canopy of heaven who does not know that slavery is wrong for him.

What! Am I to argue that it is wrong to make men brutes, to rob them of their liberty, to work them without wages, to keep them ignorant of their relations to their fellow men, to beat them with sticks, to flay their flesh with the lash, to load their limbs with irons, to hunt them with dogs, to sell them at auction, to sunder their families, to knock out their teeth, to burn their flesh, to starve them into obedience and submission to their masters? Must I argue that a system thus marked with blood and stained with pollution is wrong? No; I will not. I have better employment for my time and strength that such arguments would imply.

What, then, remains to be argued? Is it that slavery is not divine; that God did not establish it; that our doctors of divinity are mistaken? There is blasphemy in the thought. That which is inhuman cannot be divine. Who can reason on such a proposition? They that can, may; I cannot. The time for such argument is past.

At a time like this, scorching irony, not convincing argument, is needed. Oh! had I the ability, and could I reach the nation's ear, I would to-day pour out a fiery streak of biting ridicule, blasting reproach, withering sarcasm, and stern rebuke. For it is not light that is needed, but fire; it is not the gentle shower, but thunder. We need the storm, the whirlwind, and the earthquake. The feeling of the nation must be quickened; the conscience of the nation must be roused; the propriety of the nation must be startled; the hypocrisy of the nation must be exposed; and its crimes against God and man must be denounced.

What to the American slave is your Fourth of July? I answer, a day that reveals to him, more than all other days of the year, the gross injustice and cruelty to which he is the constant victim. To him your celebration is a sham; you boasted liberty an unholy license; your national greatness, swelling vanity; your sounds of rejoicing are empty and heartless; your denunciations of tyrants, brass-fronted impudence; your shouts of liberty and equality, hollow mockery; your prayers and hymns, your sermons and thanksgivings, with all your religious parade and solemnity, are to him mere bombast, fraud, deception, impiety, and hypocrisy—a thin veil to cover up crimes which would disgrace a nation of savages. There is not a nation on the earth guilty of practises more shocking and bloody than are the people of these United States at this very hour.

Go where you may, search where you will, roam through all the monarchies and despotisms of the Old World, travel through South America, search out every abuse and when you have found the last, lay your facts by the side of the every-day practises of this nation, and you will say with me that, for revolting barbarity and shameless hypocrisy, America reigns without a rival.

While we recognize that school officials will have certain administrative problems in transferring from a segregated to a nonsegregated system, we will resist the use of any tactics contrived for the sole purpose of delaying desegregation. . . .

We insist that there should be integration at all levels, including the assignment of teacher-personnel on a nondiscriminatory basis. . . .

We look upon this memorable decision not as a victory for Negroes alone, but for the whole American people and as a vindication of America's leadership of the free world.

Lest there be any misunderstanding of our position, we here rededicate ourselves to the removal of all racial segregation in public education and reiterate our determination to achieve this goal without compromise of principle.

THE ATLANTA DECLARATION (NATIONAL ASSOCIATION FOR THE ADVANCEMENT OF COLORED PEOPLE, 1854)

▪▪▪

SOURCE: Carson, Clayborne, et al, eds. *The Eyes on the Prize: Civil Rights Reader.* New York: Viking, 1991, p. 82.

INTRODUCTION: *In May 1954, shortly after the Supreme Court reached its unanimous decision in* Brown v. Board of Education of Topeka, Kansas, *an NAACP press conference was held in Atlanta, Georgia. The organization urged rapid compliance with court-ordered desegregation.*

All Americans are now relieved to have the law of the land declare in the clearest language: ". . . in the field of public education the doctrine of 'separate but equal' has no place. Separate educational facilities are inherently unequal." Segregation in public education is now not only unlawful; it is un-American. True Americans are grateful for this decision. Now that the law is made clear, we look to the future. Having canvassed the situation in each of our states, we approach the future with the utmost confidence. . . .

We stand ready to work with other law abiding citizens who are anxious to translate this decision into a program of action to eradicate racial segregation in public education as speedily as possible. . . .

THE CALL OF PROVIDENCE TO THE DESCENDANTS OF AFRICA IN AMERICA (EDWARD WILMOT BLYDEN, 1862)

▪▪▪

SOURCE: Moses, Wilson Jeremiah. *Classical Black Nationalism: From the American Revolution to Marcus Garvey.* New York: New York University Press, 1996, pp. 188–208.

INTRODUCTION: *Born on the Caribbean island of St. Thomas to free black parents in 1832, Blyden traveled to the United States at the age of seventeen, seeking admission to Rutgers Theological College. Turned down because of his race, he left the United States in January 1851 for Liberia, aided by the support of members of the American Colonization Society (ACS). In Liberia, Blyden resumed his education, becoming an educator, statesman, and Presbyterian minister, eventually holding many academic and governmental offices. Blyden also became a vocal proponent of pan-Africanism, with a major portion of his writings focusing on a call for blacks to colonize in Liberia.*

Among the descendants of Africa in this country the persuasion seems to prevail, though not now to the same extent as formerly, that they owe no special duty to the land of their forefathers; that their ancestors having been brought to this country against their will, and themselves having been born in the land, they are in duty bound to remain here and give their attention exclusively to the acquiring for themselves, and perpetuating to their posterity, social and political rights, notwithstanding the urgency of the call which their fatherland, by its forlorn and degraded moral condition, makes upon them for their assistance.

All other people feel a pride in their ancestral land, and do everything in their power to create for it, if it has not already, an honorable name. But many of the descendants of Africa, on the contrary, speak disparagingly of their country; are ashamed to acknowledge any connection with that land, and would turn indignantly upon any who would bid them go up and take possession of the land of their fathers.

It is a sad feature in the residence of Africans in this country, that it has begotten in them a forgetfulness of Africa—a want of sympathy with her in her moral and intellectual desolation, and a clinging to the land which for centuries has been the scene of their thralldom. A shrewd European observer of American society, says of the Negro in this country, that he "makes a thousand fruitless efforts to insinuate himself among men who repulse him; he conforms to the taste of his oppressors, adopts their opinions, and hopes by imitating them to form a part of their community. Having been told from infancy that his race is naturally inferior to that of the whites, he assents to the proposition, and is ashamed of his own nature. In each of his features he discovers a trace of slavery, and, if it were in his power, he would willingly rid himself of everything that makes him what he is."

It can not be denied that some very important advantages have accrued to the black man from his deportation to this land, but it has been at the expense of his manhood. Our nature in this country is not the same as it appears among the lordly natives of the interior of Africa, who have never felt the trammels of a foreign yoke. We have been dragged into depths of degradation. We have been taught a cringing servility. We have been drilled into contentment with the most undignified circumstances. Our finer sensibilities have been blunted. There has been an almost utter extinction of all that delicacy of feeling and sentiment which adorns character. The temperament of our souls has become harder or coarser, so that we can walk forth here, in this land of indignities, in ease and in complacency, while our complexion furnishes ground for every species of social insult which an intolerant prejudice may choose to inflict.

But a change is coming over us. The tendency of events is directing the attention of the colored people to some other scene, and Africa is beginning to receive the attention, which has so long been turned away from her; and as she throws open her portals and shows the inex-

haustible means of comfort and independence within, the black man begins to feel dissatisfied with the annoyances by which he is here surrounded, and looks with longing eyes to his fatherland. I venture to predict that, within a very brief period, that down-trodden land instead of being regarded with prejudice and distaste, will largely attract the attention and engage the warmest interest of every man of color. A few have always sympathized with Africa, but it has been an indolent and unmeaning sympathy—a sympathy which put forth no effort, made no sacrifices, endured no self-denial, braved no obloquy for the sake of advancing African interests. But the scale is turning, and Africa is becoming the all-absorbing topic.

It is my desire, on the present occasion, to endeavor to set before you the work which, it is becoming more and more apparent, devolves upon the black men of the United States; and to guide my thoughts, I have chosen the words of the text: "Behold, the Lord thy God hath set the land before thee: go up and possess it, as the Lord God of thy fathers hath said unto thee; fear not, neither be discouraged."

You will at once perceive that I do not believe that the work to be done by black men is in this country. I believe that their field of operation is in some other and distant scene. Their work is far nobler and loftier than that which they are now doing in this country. It is theirs to betake themselves to injured Africa, and bless those outraged shores, and quiet those distracted families with the blessings of Christianity and civilization. It is theirs to bear with them to that land the arts of industry and peace, and counteract the influence of those horrid abominations which an inhuman avarice as introduced—to roll back the appalling cloud of ignorance and superstition which wherever found. This is the work to which Providence is obviously calling the black men of this country.

I am aware that some, against all experience, are hoping for the day when they will enjoy equal social and political rights in this land. We do not blame them for so believing and trusting. But we would remind them that there is a faith against reason, against experience, which consists in believing or pretending to believe very important propositions upon very slender proofs, and in maintaining opinions without any proper grounds. It ought to be clear to every thinking and impartial mind, that there can never occur in this country an equality, social or political, between whites and blacks. The whites have for a long time had the advantage. All the affairs of the country are in their hands. They make and administer the laws; they teach the schools; here, in the North, they ply all the trades, they own all the stores, they have possession of all the banks, they own all the ships and navigate them; they are the printers, proprietors, and editors of the leading newspapers, and they shape public opinion. Having always had the lead, they have acquired an ascendency they will ever maintain. The blacks have very few or no agencies in operation to counteract the ascendant influence of the Europeans. And instead of employing what little they have by a unity of effort to alleviate their condition, they turn all their power against themselves by their endless jealousies, and rivalries, and competition; everyone who is able to "pass" being emulous of a place among Europeans or Indians. This is the effect of their circumstances. It is the influence of the dominant class upon them. It argues no essential inferiority in them—no more than the disadvantages of the Israelites in Egypt argued their essential inferiority to the Egyptians. They are the weaker class overshadowed and depressed by the stronger. They are the feeble oak dwarfed by the overspreadings of a large tree, having not the advantage overspreads the land, and to rear on those shores an asylum of liberty for the down-trodden sons of Africa of rain, and sunshine, and fertilizing dews.

Before the weaker people God has set the land of their forefathers, and bids them go up and possess it without fear or discouragement. Before the tender plant he sets an open field, where, in the unobstructed air and sunshine, it may grow and flourish in all its native luxuriance.

There are two ways in which God speaks to men: one is by his word and the other by his providence. He has not sent any Moses, with signs and wonders, to cause an exodus of the descendants of Africa to their fatherland, yet he has loudly spoken to them as to their duty in the matter. He has spoken by his providence. First; By suffering them to be brought here and placed in circumstances where they could receive a training fitting them for the work of civilizing and evangelizing the land whence they were torn, and by preserving them under the severest trials and afflictions. Secondly; By allowing them, notwithstanding all the services they have rendered to this country, to be treated as strangers and aliens, so as to cause them to have anguish of spirit, as was the case with the Jews in Egypt, and to make them long for some refuge from their social and civil deprivations. Thirdly; By bearing a portion of them across the tempestuous seas back to Africa, by preserving them through the process of acclimation, and by establishing them in the land, despite the attempts of misguided men to drive them away. Fourthly; By keeping their fatherland in reserve for them in their absence.

The manner in which Africa has been kept from invasion is truly astounding. Known for ages, it is yet unknown. For centuries its inhabitants have been the victims of the cupidity of foreigners. The country has been rifled of its population. It has been left in some portions almost wholly unoccupied, but it has remained unmolested by foreigners. It has been very near the crowded countries of the world, yet none has relieved itself to any great extent of its overflowing population by seizing upon its domains. Europe, from the North, looks wishfully and with longing eyes across the narrow straits of Gilbraltar. Asia, with its teeming millions, is connected with us by an isthmus wide enough to admit of her throwing thousands into the country. But, notwithstanding the known wealth of the resources of the land, of which the report has gone into all the earth, there is still a terrible veil between us and our neighbors, the all-conquering Europeans, which they are only now essaying to lift; while the teeming millions of Asia have not even attempted to leave their boundaries to penetrate our borders. Neither alluring visions of glorious conquests, nor brilliant hopes of rapid enrichment, could induce them to invade the country. It has been preserved alike from the boastful civilization of Europe, and the effete and barbarous institutions of Asia. We call it, then, a Providential interposition, that while the owners of the soil have been abroad, passing through the fearful ordeal of a most grinding oppression, the land, though entirely unprotected, has lain uninvaded. We regard it as a providential call to Africans every where, to "go up and possess the land"; so that in a sense that is not merely constructive and figurative, but truly literal, God says to the black men of this country, with reference to Africa: "Behold, I set the land before you, go up and possess it."

Of course it can not be expected that this subject of the duty of colored men to go up and take possession of their fatherland, will be at once clear to every mind. Men look at objects from different points of view, and form their opinions according to the points from which they look, and are guided in their actions according to the opinions they form. As I have already said, the majority of exiled Africans do not seem to appreciate the great privilege of going and taking possession of the land. They seem to have lost all interest in that land, and to prefer living in subordinate and inferior positions in a strange land among oppressors, to encountering the risks involved in emigrating to a distant country. As I walk the streets of these cities, visit the hotels, go on board the steamboats, I am grieved to notice how much intelligence, how much strength and energy is frittered away in those trifling employments, which, if thrown into Africa, might elevate the millions of that land from their degradation, tribes at a time, and create an African power which would command the respect of the world, and place in the possession of Africans, its rightful owners, the wealth which is now diverted to other quarters. Most of the wealth that could be drawn from that land, during the last six centuries, has passed into the hands of Europeans, while many of Africa's own sons, sufficiently intelligent to control those immense resources, are sitting down in poverty and dependence in the land of strangers—exiles when they have so rich a domain from which they have never been expatriated, but which is willing, nay, anxious to welcome them home again.

We need some African power, some great center of the race where our physical, pecuniary, and intellectual strength may be collected. We need some spot whence such an influence may go forth in behalf of the race as shall be felt by the nations. We are now so scattered and divided that we can do nothing. The imposition begun last year by a foreign power upon Hayti, and which is still persisted in, fills every black man who has heard of it with indignation, but we are not strong enough to speak out effectually for that land. When the same power attempted an outrage upon the Liberians, there was no African power strong enough to interpose. So long as we remain thus divided, we may expect impositions. So long as we live simply by the sufferance of the nations, we must expect to be subject to their caprices.

Among the free portion of the descendants of Africa, numbering about four or five millions, there is enough talent, wealth, and enterprise, to form a respectable nationality on the continent of Africa. For nigh three hundred years their skill and industry have been expended in building up the southern countries of the New World, the poor, frail constitution of the Caucasian not allowing him to endure the fatigue and toil involved in such labors. Africans and their descendants have been the laborers, and the mechanics, and the artisans in the greater portion of this hemisphere. By the results of their labor the European countries have been sustained and enriched. All the cotton, coffee, indigo, sugar, tobacco, etc., which have formed the most important articles of European commerce, have been raised and prepared for market by the labor of the black man. Dr. Palmer of New-Orleans, bears the same testimony. And all this labor they have done, for the most part not only without compensation, but with abuse, and contempt, and insult, as their reward.

Now, while Europeans are looking to our fatherland with such eagerness of desire, and are hastening to explore and take away its riches, ought not Africans in the Western hemisphere to turn their regards, thither also? We need to collect the scattered forces of the race, and there is no rallying-ground more favorable than Africa. There

"No pent-up Utica contracts our powers,

The whole boundless continent is ours."

Ours as a gift from the Almighty when he drove asunder the nations and assigned them their boundaries; and ours by peculiar physical adaptation.

An African nationality is our great need, and God tells us by his providence that he has set the land before us, and bids us go up and possess it. We shall never receive the respect of other races until we establish a powerful nationality. We should not content ourselves with living among other races, simply by their permission or their endurance, as Africans live in this country. We must build up Negro states; we must establish and maintain the various institutions; we must make and administer laws, erect and preserve churches, and support the worship of God; we must have governments; we must have legislation of our own; we must build ships and navigate them; we must ply the trades, instruct the schools, control the press, and thus aid in shaping the opinions and guiding the destinies of mankind. Nationality is an ordinance of Nature. The heart of every true Negro yearns after a distinct and separate nationality.

Impoverished, feeble, and alone, Liberia is striving to establish and build up such a nationality in the home of the race. Can any descendant of Africa turn contemptuously upon a scene where such efforts are making? Would not every right-thinking Negro rather lift up his voice and direct the attention of his brethren to that land? Liberia, with outstretched arms, earnestly invites all to come. We call them forth out of all nations; we bid them take up their all and leave the countries of their exile, as of old the Israelites went forth from Egypt, taking with them their trades and their treasures, their intelligence, their mastery of arts, their knowledge of the sciences, their practical wisdom, and every thing that will render them useful in building up a nationality. We summon them from these States, from the Canadas, from the East and West-Indies, from South-America, from every where, to come and take part with us in our great work.

But those whom we call are under the influence of various opinions, having different and conflicting views of their relations and duty to Africa, according to the different stand-points they occupy. So it was with another people who, like ourselves, were suffering from the effects of protracted thralldom, when on the borders of the land to which God was leading them. When Moses sent out spies to search the land of Canaan, every man, on his return, seemed to be influenced in his report by his peculiar temperament, previous habits of thought, by the degree of his physical courage, or by something peculiar in his point of observation. All agreed, indeed, that it was an exceedingly rich land, "flowing with milk and honey," for they carried with them on their return, a proof of its amazing fertility. But a part, and a larger part, too, saw only giants and walled towns, and barbarians and cannibals. "Surely," said they, "it floweth with milk and honey. Nevertheless the people be strong that dwell in the land, and the cities are walled, and very great; and moreover we saw the children of Anak there. The land through which we have gone to search it, is a land that eateth up the inhabitants thereof; and all the people that we saw in it are men of a great stature. And there we saw the giants, the sons of Anak, which come of the giants: and we were in our own sight as grasshoppers, and so we were in their sight." It was only a small minority of that company that saw things in a more favorable light. "Caleb stilled the people, before Moses, and said, Let us go up at once and possess it; for we be well able to overcome it." (Numbers 13.)

In like manner there is division among the colored people of this country with regard to Africa, that land which the providence of God is bidding them go up and possess. Spies sent from different sections of this country by the colored people—and many a spy not commissioned—have gone to that land, and have returned and reported. Like the Hebrew spies, they have put forth diverse views. Most believe Africa to be a fertile and rich country, and an African nationality a desirable thing. But some affirm that the land is not fit to dwell in, for "it is a land that eateth up the inhabitants thereof," notwithstanding the millions of strong and vigorous aborigines who throng all parts of the country, and the thousands of colonists who are settled along the coast; some see in the inhabitants incorrigible barbarism, degradation, and superstition, and insuperable hostility to civilization; others suggest that the dangers and risks to be encountered, and the self-denial to be endured, are too great for the slender advantages which, as it appears to them, will accrue from immigration. A few only report that the land is open to us on every hand—that "every prospect pleases," and that the natives are so tractable that it would be a comparatively easy matter for civilized and Christianized black men to secure all the land to Christian law, liberty, and civilization.

I come to-day to defend the report of the minority. The thousands of our own race, emigrants from this country, settled for more than forty years in that land, agree with the minority report. Dr. Barth, and other travelers to the east and south-east of Liberia, indorse the sentiment of the minority, and testify to the beauty, and healthfulness, and productiveness of the country, and to the mildness and hospitality of its inhabitants. In Liberia we hear from natives, who are constantly coming to our settlements from the far interior, of land exuberantly fertile, of large, numerous, and wealthy tribes, athletic and industrious; not the descendants of Europeans—according to Bowen's insane theory—but *black* men, pure Negroes, who live in large towns, cultivate the soil, and carry on extensive traffic, maintaining amicable relations with each other and with men from a distance.

The ideas that formerly prevailed of the interior of Africa, which suited the purposes of poetry and sensation writing, have been proved entirely erroneous. Poets may no longer sing with impunity of Africa:

"A region of drought, where no river glides,
Nor rippling brook with osiered sides;
Where sedgy pool, nor bubbling fount,
Nor tree, nor cloud, nor misty mount,
Appears to refresh the aching eye,
But barren earth and the burning sky
And the blank horizon round and round."

No; missionary and scientific enterprises have disproved such fallacies. The land possesses every possible inducement. That extensive and beauteous domain which God has given us appeals to us and to black men every where, by its many blissful and benignant aspects; by its flowery landscapes, its beautiful rivers, its serene and peaceful skies; by all that attractive and perennial verdure which overspreads the hills and valleys; by its every prospect lighted up by delightful sunshine; by all its natural charms, it calls upon us to rescue it from the grasp of remorseless superstition, and introduce the blessings of the Gospel.

But there are some among the intelligent colored people of this country who, while they profess to have great love for Africa, and tell us that their souls are kindled when they hear of their fatherland, yet object to going themselves, because, as they affirm, the black man has a work to accomplish in this land-he has a destiny to fulfill. He, the representative of Africa, like the representatives from various parts of Europe, must act his part in building up this great composite nation. It is not difficult to see what the work of the black man is in this land. The most inexperienced observer may at once read his destiny. Look at the various departments of society here in the *free* North; look at the different branches of industry, and see how the black man is aiding to build up this nation. Look at the hotels, the saloons, the steamboats, the barbershops, and see how successfully he is carrying out his destiny! And there is an extreme likelihood that such are forever to be the exploits which he is destined to achieve in this country until he merges his African peculiarities in the Caucasian.

Others object to the *climate* of Africa, first, that it is unhealthy, and secondly, that it is not favorable to intellectual progress. To the first, we reply that it is not more insalubrious than other new countries. Persons going to Africa, who have not been broken down as to their constitutions in this country, stand as fair a chance of successful acclimation as in any other country of large, unbroken forests and extensively uncleared lands. In all new countries there are sufferings and privations. All those countries which have grown up during the last two centuries, in this hemisphere, have had as a foundation the groans, and tears, and blood of the pioneers. But what are the sufferings of pioneers, compared with the greatness of the results they accomplish for succeeding generations? Scarcely any great step in human progress is made without multitudes of victims. Every revolution that has been effected, every nationality that has been established, every country that has been rescued from the abominations of savagism, every colony that has been planted, has involved perplexities and sufferings to the generation who undertook it. In the evangelization of Africa, in the erection of African nationalities, we can expect no exceptions. The man, then, who is not able to suffer and to die for his fellows when necessity requires it, is not fit to be a pioneer in this great work.

We believe, as we have said, that the establishment of an African nationality in Africa is the great need of the African race; and the men who have gone, or may hereafter go to assist in laying the foundations of empire, so far from being dupes, or cowards, or traitors, as some have ignorantly called them, are the truest heroes of the race. They are the soldiers rushing first into the breach physicians who at the risk of their own lives are first to explore an infectious disease. How much more nobly do they act than those who have held for years that it is nobler to sit here and patiently suffer with our brethren! Such sentimental inactivity finds no respect in these days of rapid movement. The world sees no merit in mere innocence. The man who contents himself to sit down and exemplify the virtue of patience and endurance will find no sympathy from the busy, restless crowd that rush by him. Even the "sick man" must get out of the way when he hears the tramp of the approaching host, or be crushed by the heedless and massive car of progress. Blind Bartimeuses are silenced by the crowd. The world requires active service; it respects only productive workers. The days of hermits and monks have passed away. Action—work, work—is the order of the day. Heroes in the strife and struggle of humanity are the demand of the age.

"They who would be free, themselves *must* strike
the blow."

With regard to the objection founded upon the unfavorableness of the climate to intellectual progress, I have only to say, that proper moral agencies, when set in operation, can not be overborne by physical causes. "We continually behold lower laws held in restraint by higher; mechanic by dynamic; chemical by vital; physical by moral." It has not yet been proved that with the proper influences, the tropics will not produce men of "cerebral activity." Those races which have degenerated by a removal from the North to the tropics did not possess the proper moral

power. They had in themselves the seed of degeneracy, and would have degenerated any where. It was not Anglo-Saxon blood, nor a temperate climate, that kept the first emigrants to this land from falling into the same indolence and inefficiency which have overtaken the European settlers in South-America, but the Anglo-Saxon Bible—the principles contained in that book, are the great conservative and elevating power. Man is the same, and the human mind is the same, whether existing beneath African suns or Arctic frosts. I can conceive of no difference. It is the moral influences brought to bear upon the man that make the difference in his progress.

"High degrees of moral sentiment," says a distinguished American writer, "control the unfavorable influences of climate; and some of our grandest examples of men and of races come from the equatorial regions." Man is elevated by taking hold of that which is higher than himself. Unless this is done, climate, color, race, will avail nothing.

"—unless above himself he can

Erect himself, how poor a thing is man!"

For my own part, I believe that the brilliant world of the tropics, with its marvels of nature, must of necessity give to mankind a new career of letters, and new forms in the various arts, whenever the millions of men at present uncultivated shall enjoy the advantages of civilization.

Africa will furnish a development of civilization which the world has never yet witnessed. Its great peculiarity will be its moral element. The Gospel is to achieve some of its most beautiful triumphs in that land. "God shall enlarge Japheth, and he shall dwell in the tents of Shem," was the blessing upon the European and Asiatic races. Wonderfully have these predictions been fulfilled. The all-conquering descendants of Japheth have gone to every clime, and have planted themselves on almost every shore. By means fair and unfair, they have spread themselves, have grown wealthy and powerful. They have been truly "enlarged." God has "dwelt in the tents of Shem," for so some understand the passage. The Messiah—God manifest in the flesh—was of the tribe of Judah. He was born and dwelt in the tents of Shem. The promise to Ethiopia, or Ham, is like that to Shem, of a spiritual kind. It refers not to physical strength, not to large and extensive domains, not to foreign conquests, not to wide-spread domination, but to the possession of spiritual qualities, to the elevation of the soul heavenward, to spiritual aspirations and divine communications. "Ethiopia shall stretch forth her hands unto God." Blessed, glorious promise! Our trust is not to be in chariots or horses, not in our own skill or power, but our help is to be in the name of the Lord. And surely, in reviewing our history as a people, whether we consider our preservation in the lands of our exile, or the preservation of fatherland from invasion, we are compelled to exclaim: "Hitherto hath the Lord helped us!" Let us, then, fear not the influence climate. Let us go forth stretching out our hands to God, and be as hot as Nebuchadnezzar's furnace, there will be one in midst like unto the Son of God, counteracting its deleterious influences.

Behold, then, the Lord our God has set the land before us, with its burning climate, with its privations, with its moral, intellect and political needs, and by his providence he bids us go up possess it without fear or discouragement. Shall we go up at bidding? If the black men of this country, through unbelief indolence, or for any other cause, fail to lay hold of the blessings which God is proffering to them, and neglect to accomplish work which devolves upon them, the work will be done, but others will be brought in to do it, and to take possession of the country.

For while the colored people here are tossed about by various and conflicting opinions as to their duty to that land, men are going thither from other quarters of the globe. They are entering the land from various quarters with various motives and designs, and may eventually so preoccupy the land as to cut us off from the fair inheritance which lies before us, unless we go forth without further delay and establish ourselves.

The enterprise and energy manifested by white men who, with uncongenial constitutions, go from a distance to endeavor to open up that land to the world, are far from creditable to the civilized and enlightened colored men of the United States, when contrasted with their indifference in the matter. A noble army of self-expatriated evangelists have gone to that land from Europe and America and, while anxious to extend the blessings of true religion, they have in no slight degree promoted the cause of science and commerce. Many have fallen, either from the effects of the climate or the hands of violence; still the interest in the land is by no means diminished. The enamored worshiper of science, and the Christian philanthropist, are still laboring to solve the problem of African geography, and to elevate its benighted tribes. They are not only disclosing to the world the mysteries of regions hitherto unexplored, but tribes whose very existence had not before been known to the civilized world have been brought, through their instrumentality, into contact with civilization and Christianity. They have discovered in the distant portions of that land countries as productive as any in Europe and America. They have informed the world of bold and lofty mountains, extensive lakes, noble rivers, falls rivaling Niagara, so that, as a result of their arduous, difficult, and philanthropic labors of exploration, the cause of Chris-

tianity, ethnology, geography, and commerce has been, in a very important degree, subserved.

Dr. Livingstone, the indefatigable African explorer, who, it is estimated, has passed over not less than eleven thousand miles of African ground, speaking of the motives which led him to those shores, and still keep him there in spite of privations and severe afflictions, says:

> "I expect to find for myself no large fortune in that country; nor do I expect to explore any large portions of a new country; but I do hope to find a pathway, by means of the river Zambesi, which may lead to highlands, where Europeans may form a settlement, and where, by opening up communication and establishing commercial intercourse with the natives of Africa, they may slowly, but not the less surely, impart to the people of that country the knowledge and inestimable blessings of Christianity."

The recently formed Oxford, Cambridge, and Dublin Missionary Society state their object to be to spread Christianity among the untaught people of Central Africa, "so to operate among them as by mere teaching and influence to help *to build up native Christian states.*" The idea of building up "native Christian states" is a very important one, and is exactly such an idea as would be carried out if there were a large influx of civilized blacks from abroad.

I am sorry to find that among some in this country, the opinion prevails that in Liberia a distinction is maintained between the colonists and the aborigines, so that the latter are shut out from the social and political privileges of the former. No candid person who has read the laws of Liberia, or who has visited that country, can affirm or believe such a thing. The idea no doubt arises from the fact that the aborigines of a country generally suffer from the settling of colonists among them. But the work of Liberia is somewhat different from that of other colonies which have been planted on foreign shores. The work achieved by other emigrants has usually been—the enhancement of their own immediate interests; the increase of their physical comforts and conveniences; the enlargement of their borders by the most speedy and available methods, without regard to the effect such a course might have upon the aborigines. Their interests sometimes coming into direct contact with those of the owners of the soil, they have not unfrequently, by their superior skill and power, reduced the poor native to servitude or complete annihilation. The Israelites could live in peace in the land of Canaan only by exterminating the indigenous inhabitants. The colony that went out from Phenicia, and that laid the foundations of empire on the northern shores of Africa, at first paid a yearly tax to the natives; with the increasing wealth and power of Carthage, however, the respective conditions of the Carthaginians and the natives were changed, and the Phenician adventurers assumed and maintained a dominion over the Lybians. The colonies from Europe which landed at Plymouth Rock, at Boston, and at Jamestown—which took possession of the West-India islands and of Mexico, treated the aborigines in the same manner. The natives of India, Australia, and New-Zealand are experiencing a similar treatment under the overpowering and domineering rule of the Anglo-Saxons. Eagerness for gain and the passion for territorial aggrandisement have appeared to the colonists necessary to their growth and progress.

The work of Liberia, as I have said, is different and far nobler. We, on the borders of our fatherland, can not, as the framers of our Constitution wisely intimated, allow ourselves to be influenced by "avaricious speculations," or by desires for "territorial aggrandisement." Our work there is moral and intellectual as well as physical. We have to work upon the *people,* as well as upon the *land*—upon *mind* as well as upon *matter.* Our prosperity depends as much upon the wholesome and elevating influence we exert upon the native population, as upon the progress we make in agriculture, commerce, and manufacture. Indeed the conviction prevails in Liberia among the thinking people that we can make no important progress in these things without the cooperation of thez aborigines. We believe that no policy can be more suicidal in Liberia than that which would keep aloof from the natives around us. We believe that our life and strength will be to elevate and incorporate them among us as speedily as possible.

And, then, the aborigines are not a race alien from the colonists. We are a part of them. When alien and hostile races have come together, as we have just seen, one has had to succumb to the other; but when different peoples of the same family have been brought together, there has invariably been a fusion, and the result has been an improved and powerful class. When three branches of the great Teutonic family met on the soil of England, they united. It is true that at first there was a distinction of caste among them in consequence of the superiority in every respect of the great Norman people; but, as the others came up to their level, the distinctions were quietly effaced, and Norman, Saxon, and Dane easily amalgamated. Thus, "a people inferior to none existing in the world was formed by the mixture of three branches of the great Teutonic family with each other and the aboriginal Britons."

In America we see how readily persons from all parts of Europe assimilate; but what great difficulty the Negro, the Chinese, and the Indian experience! We find here representatives from all the nations of Europe easily blending with each other. But we find elements that will not assimilate. The Negro, the Indian, and the Chinese, who do not belong to the same family, repel each other, and are repelled by the Europeans. "The antagonistic elements are in contact, but refuse to unite, and as yet no agent has been found sufficiently potent to reduce them to unity."

But the case with Americo-Liberians and the aborigines is quite different. We are all descendants of Africa. In Liberia there may be Mend persons of almost every tribe in West-Africa, from Senegal Congo. And not only do we and the natives belong to the same ice, but we are also of the same family. The two peoples can no lore be kept from assimilating and blending than water can be kept from mingling with its kindred elements. The policy of Liberia is to diffuse among them as rapidly as possible the principles of Christianity and civilization, to prepare them to take an active part in the duties of the nationality which we are endeavoring to erect. Whence, then, comes the slander which represents Liberians as "maintaining a distance from the aborigines—a constant and uniform separation"?

To take part in the noble work in which they are engaged on that coast, the government and people of Liberia earnestly invite the descendants of Africa in this country. In all our feebleness, we have already accomplished something; but very little in comparison of what has to be done. A beginning has been made, however—a great deal of preparatory work accomplished. And if the intelligent and enterprising colored people of this country would emigrate in large numbers, an important work would be done in a short time. And we know exactly the kind of work that would be done. We know that where now stand unbroken forests would spring up towns and villages, with their schools and churches—that the natives would be taught the arts of civilization—that their energies would be properly directed—that their prejudices would disappear—that there would be a rapid and important revulsion from the practices of heathenism, and a radical change in their social condition—that the glorious principles of a Christian civilization would diffuse themselves throughout those benighted communities. Oh! that our people would take this matter into serious consideration, and think of the great privilege of kindling in the depths of the moral and spiritual gloom of Africa a glorious light—of causing the wilderness and the solitary place to be glad—the desert to bloom and blossom as the rose—and the whole land to be converted into a garden of the Lord.

Liberia, then, appeals to the colored men of this country for assistance in the noble work which she has begun. She appeals to those who believe that the descendants of Africa live in the serious neglect of their duty if they fail to help to raise the land of their forefathers from her degradation. She appeals to those who believe that a well-established African nationality is the most direct and efficient means of securing respectability and independence for the African race. She appeals to those who believe that a rich and fertile country, like Africa, which has lain so long under the cheerless gloom of ignorance, should not be left any longer without the influence of Christian civilization—to those who deem it a far more glorious work to save extensive tracts of country from barbarism and continued degradation than to amass for themselves the means of individual comfort and aggrandizement—to those who believe that there was a providence in the deportation of our forefathers from the land of their birth, and that that same providence now points to a work in Africa to be done by us their descendants. Finally, Liberia appeals to all African patriots and Christians-to all lovers of order and refinement—to lovers of industry and enterprise—of peace, comfort, and happiness—to those who having felt the power of the Gospel in opening up to them life and immortality, are desirous that their benighted kindred should share in the same blessings. "Behold, the Lord thy God hath set the land before thee: go up and possess it, as the Lord God of thy fathers hath said unto thee; fear not, neither be discouraged."

THE EMANCIPATION PROCLAMATION (1863)

∎∎∎

SOURCE: Franklin, John Hope. *The Emancipation Proclamation.* Garden City, N.Y.: Doubleday, 1963.

INTRODUCTION: *On September 22, 1862, in an attempt to bring an end to the Civil War, President Abraham Lincoln, acting on his authority as commander-in-chief, issued a warning that slavery would be abolished in any state that continued to rebel. With the war still raging, Lincoln issued the Emancipation Proclamation on January 1, 1863, freeing slaves in those states that had seceded from the Union.*

January 1, 1863

By the President of the United States of America: A Proclamation

Whereas on the 22d day of September, A.D. 1862, a proclamation was issued by the President of the United States, containing, among other things, the following, to wit:

"That on the 1st day of January, A.D. 1863, all persons held as slaves within any State or desig-

nated part of a State the people whereof shall then, be in rebellion against the United States shall be thenceforward, and forever free; and the executive government of the United States, including the military and naval authority thereof, will recognize and maintain the freedom of such persons and will do no act or acts to repress such persons, or any of them, in any efforts they may make for their actual freedom.

"That the executive will on the 1st day of January aforesaid, by proclamation, designate the States and parts of States, if any, in which the people thereof, respectively, shall then be in rebellion against the United States; and the fact that any State or the people thereof shall on that day be in good faith represented in the Congress of the United States by members chosen thereto at elections wherein a majority of the qualified voters of such States shall have participated shall, in the absence of strong countervailing testimony, be deemed conclusive evidence that such State and the people thereof are not then in rebellion against the United States."

Now, therefore, I, Abraham Lincoln, President of the United States, by virtue of the power in me vested as Commander-in-Chief of the Army and Navy of the United States in time of actual armed rebellion against the authority and government of the United States, and as a fit and necessary war measure for suppressing said rebellion, do, on this 1st day of January, A.D. 1863, and in accordance with my purpose so to do, publicly proclaimed for the full period of one hundred days from the first day above mentioned, order and designate as the States and parts of States wherein the people thereof, respectively, are this day in rebellion against the United States the following, to wit:

Arkansas, Texas, Louisiana (except the parishes of St. Bernard, Plaquemines, Jefferson, St. John, St. Charles, St. James, Ascension, Assumption, Terrebonne, Lafourche, St. Mary, St. Martin, and Orleans, including the city of New Orleans), Mississippi, Alabama, Florida, Georgia, South Carolina, North Carolina, and Virginia (except the forty-eight counties designated as West Virginia, and also the counties of Berkeley, Accomac, Northampton, Elizabeth City, York, Princess Anne, and Norfolk, including the cities of Norfolk and Portsmouth), and which excepted parts are for the present left precisely as if this proclamation were not issued.

And by virtue of the power and for the purpose aforesaid, I do order and declare that all persons held as slaves within said designated States and parts of States are, and henceforward shall be, free; and that the Executive Government of the United States, including the military and naval authorities thereof, will recognize and maintain the freedom of said persons.

And I hereby enjoin upon the people so declared to be free to abstain from all violence, unless in necessary self-defense; and I recommend to them that, in all cases when allowed, they labor faithfully for reasonable wages.

And I further declare and make known that such persons of suitable condition will be received into the armed service of the United States to garrison forts, positions, stations, and other places, and to man vessels of all sorts in said service.

And upon this act, sincerely believed to be an act of justice, warranted by the Constitution upon military necessity, I invoke the considerate judgment of mankind and the gracious favor of Almighty God.

ADDRESS TO THE FIRST ANNUAL MEETING OF THE EQUAL RIGHTS ASSOCIATION (SOJOURNER TRUTH, 1867)

▪▪▪

SOURCE: Hill, Patricia Liggins, ed. *Call and Response: The Riverside Anthology of the African American Literary Tradition.* New York: Houghton Mifflin, 1998, pp. 263–264.

"My friends, I am rejoiced that you are glad, but I don't know how you will feel when I get through. I come from another field—the country of the slave. They have got their liberty—so much good luck to have slavery partly destroyed; not entirely. I want it root and branch destroyed. Then we will all be free indeed. I feel that if I have to answer for the deeds done in my body just as much as a man, I have a right to have just as much as a man. There is a great stir about colored men getting their rights, but not a word about the colored women; and if colored men get their rights, and not colored women theirs, you see the colored men will be masters over the women, and it will be just as bad as it was before. So I am for keeping the thing going while things are stirring; because if we wait till it is still, it will take a great while to get it going again. White women are a great deal smarter, and know more than colored women, while colored women do not know

scarcely anything. They go out washing, which is about as high as a colored woman gets, and their men go about idle, strutting up and down; and when the women come home, they ask for their money and take it all, and then scold because there is no food. I want you to consider on that, chil'n. I call you chil'n; you are somebody's chil'n, and I am old enough to be mother of all that is here. I want women to have their rights. In the courts women have no right, no voice; nobody speaks for them. I wish woman to have her voice there among the pettifoggers. If it is not a fit place for women, it is unfit for men to be there.

"I am above eighty years old; it is about time for me to be going. I have been forty years a slave and forty years free, and would be here forty years more to have equal rights for all. I suppose I am kept here because something remains for me to do; I suppose I am yet to help to break the chain. I have done a great deal of work; as much as a man, but did not get so much pay. I used to work in the field and bind grain, keeping up with the cradler; but men doing no more, got twice as much pay, so with the German women. They work in the field and do as much work, but do not get the pay. We do as much, we eat as much, we want as much. I suppose I am about the only colored woman that goes about to speak for the rights of the colored women. I want to keep the thing stirring, now that the ice is cracked. What we want is a little money. You men know that you get as much again as women when you write, or for what you do. When we get our rights we shall not have to come to you for money, for then we shall have money enough in our own pockets; and may be you will ask us for money. But help us now until we get it. It is a good consolation to know that when we have got this battle once fought we shall not be coming to you any more. You have been having our rights so long, that you think, like a slave-holder, that you own us. I know that it is hard for one who has held the reins for so long to give up; it cuts like a knife. It will feel all the better when it closes up again. I have been in Washington about three years, seeing about these colored people. Now colored men have the right to vote. There ought to be equal rights now more than ever, since colored people have got their freedom. I am going to talk several times while I am here; so now I will do a little singing. I have not heard any singing since I came here."

Accordingly, suiting the action to the word, Sojourner sang, "We are going home." "There, children," said she, "in heaven we shall rest from all our labors; first do all we have to do here. There I am determined to go, not to stop short of that beautiful place, and I do not mean to stop till I get there, and meet you there, too."

THANKSGIVING DAY SERMON: THE SOCIAL PRINCIPLE AMONG A PEOPLE AND ITS BEARING ON THEIR PROGRESS AND DEVELOPMENT (ALEXANDER CRUMMELL, 1875)

▐ ▌ ▐

SOURCE: Oldfield, J.R., ed. *Civilization and Black Progress: Selected Writings of Alexander Crummell on the South.* Charlottesville: University Press of Virginia, 1995, pp. 29–42.

INTRODUCTION: *In 1875, Crummell devoted his annual Thanksgiving Day sermon in Washington, D.C., to themes of self-help and racial solidarity. Citing a scripture from the Bible book of* Isaiah (They helped every one his neighbor, and every one said to his neighbor, Be of good courage—Isa. 41:8), *Crummell declared:* "[This] principle of united effort, and of generous concord, is worthy of the imitation of the colored people of this country, if they would fain rise to superiority and achievement."

More than a month has passed away since we received the proclamation of our Chief Magistrate, appointing the 25th of November a day of public thanksgiving to Almighty God.

And, in accordance with this pious custom, we, in common with millions of our fellow-citizens, have met together this morning, to offer up our tribute of praise and thankfulness to our common Parent in heaven, for all the gifts, favors, blessings, and benefactions, civil, domestic, religious, and educational, which have been bestowed upon us during the year; for the blessings of heaven above; for the precious fruits brought forth by the sun; for the precious things of the earth and the fullness thereof; for the golden harvests of peace, unstained by blood, and unbroken by strife; for the constant stream of health which has flowed through our veins and households, untainted by plague or pestilence; for the babes whom the Lord has laid upon your arms and given to your hearts; for the plentiful supply of food which has been granted us from the fields, and which has laden our boards; for the goodly instruction which trains the mind and corrects the hearts of our children, and prepares them for responsibility, for duty, and eternity; for the civil privileges and the national freedom, in which we are permitted to participate; for the measure of success which God has given His Gospel, and for the hope that is ours that the Cross shall yet conquer everywhere beneath the sun, and that JESUS shall rule and reign through all the world. For these and all other gifts and blessings we render our tribute of praise and gratitude to the Lord, our Maker, Preserver, and Benefactor, through JESUS CHRIST our Lord!

Grateful as is this theme of gratitude, and inviting as it is for thought and further expression, it is not my purpose to pursue it to-day. I feel that we should turn the occasion into an opportunity for improvement and progress.

Especially is this the duty of a people situated as we are in this country; cut loose, blessed be GOD, for evermore, from the dark moorings of servitude and oppression; but not fully arrived at—only drifting towards, the deep, quiet waters of fullest freedom and equality. Few, comparatively, in numbers; limited in resources; the inheritors of prodigious disasters; the heirs of ancestral woes and sorrows; burdened with most manifest duties and destinies; anxious for our children; thoughtful for our race; culpability and guilt of the deepest dye will be ours, if we do not most seriously consider the means and instruments by which we shall be enabled to go forward, and to rise upward. It is peculiarly a duty at this time when there is evidently an ebb-tide of indifference in the country, with regard to our race; and when the anxiety for union neutralizes the interest in the black man.

The agencies to the high ends I have referred to are various; but the text I have chosen suggests a train of thought, in a distinct and peculiar line. It shews us that spirit of unity which the world exhibits, when it would fain accomplish its great, commanding ends.

The prophet shews us here the notable sight, that is, that GOD comes down from heaven to put an end to the devices of the wicked. Whatever discord and strife may have before existed among them, at once it comes to an end. A common danger awaits them; a common peril menaces. At once they join hands; immediately their hearts are united. "They helped every one his neighbor, and every one said to his neighbor, be of good courage."

The lesson is one which we shall do well to learn with diligence; that it comes from the wicked, does not detract from its value. The world acts on many a principle which Christians would do well to lay to heart. Our Saviour tells us that "the children of this world are wiser in their generation than the children of light." So here, this principle of united effort, and of generous concord, is worthy of the imitation of the colored people of this country, if they would fain rise to superiority of both character and achievement. I shall speak, therefore, of the "*Social principle among a people; and its bearing on their progress and development.*"

What I mean by the social principle, is the disposition which leads men to associate and join together for specific purposes; the principle which makes families and societies, and which binds men in unity and brotherhood, in races and churches and nations.

For man, you will observe, is a social being. In his mental and moral constitution God has planted certain sympathies and affections, from which spring the desire for companionship. It is with reference to these principles that God declared of the single and solitary Adam, "It is not good for the man to live alone."' It was no newly-discovered affinity of the Maker, no after-thought of the Almighty. He had *formed* His creature with a fitness and proclivity for association. He had made him with a nature that demanded society. And from this principle flows, as from a fountain, the loves, friendships, families, and combinations which tie men together, in union and concord. A wider and more imposing result of this principle is the welding of men in races and nationalities. All the fruit and flower of these organisms come from the coalescence of divers faculties and powers, tending to specific ends. For no one man can effect anything important alone. There never was a great building, a magnificent city, a noble temple, a grand cathedral, a stately senate-house which was the work of one single individual. We know of no important event in history, no imposing scheme, no great and notable occurrence which stands as an epoch in the annals of the race, which was accomplished by a single, isolated individual. Whether it is the upbuilding of Imperial Rome; or the retreat of the Ten Thousand; or the discovery of America; or Cook's or Anson's voyages around the globe; or the conquest of India; or the battle of Waterloo; everywhere we find that the great things of history have been accomplished by the combination of men.

Not less is this the case in those more humane and genial endeavors which have been for the moral good of men, and wherein the individuality of eminent leaders has been more conspicuous. We read of the evangelization of Europe, from the confines of Asia to Britain; and, in more modern times, we have the abolition of the Slave Trade and Slavery, the grand efforts for the relief of prisoners, the Temperance Reformation, the Sunday-school system. These were noble schemes, which originated in the fruitful brains and sprung from the generous hearts of single individuals, and which, in their gracious results, have made the names of Howard and Wilberforce, of Clarkson and Robert Raikes, bright and conspicuous. But yet we know that even they of themselves did not achieve the victories which are associated with their names. Thousands, nay, tens of thousands of the good and pious were aroused by their passionate appeals to stirring energy; and only when the masses of the godly were marshalled to earnest warfare, were those evils doomed; and they fell, never to rise again!

The application of this truth to the interests and the destiny of the colored race of America is manifest. We are living in this country, a part of its population, and yet, in divers respects, we are as foreign to its inhabitants as though we were living in the Sandwich Islands. It is this our actual separation from the real life of the nation, which constitutes us "a nation within a nation:" thrown very considerably upon ourselves for many of the largest interests of life, and for nearly all our social and religious advantages. As a consequence on this state of things, all the stimulants of ambition and self-love should lead this people to united effort for personal superiority and the uplifting of the race; but, instead thereof, overshadowed by a more powerful race of people; wanting in the cohesion which comes from racial enthusiasm; lacking in the confidence which is the root of a people's stability; disintegration, doubt, and distrust almost universally prevail, and distract all their business and policies.

Among a people, as in a nation, we find farmers, mechanics, sailors, servants, business men, trades. For life, energy, and progress in a people, it is necessary that all these various departments of activity should be carried on with spirit, skill, and unity. It is the cooperative principle, working in trades, business, and manufacturing, which is the great lever that is lifting up the million masses in great nations, and giving those nations themselves a more masterly superiority than they have ever known, in all their past histories. No people can discard this principle, and achieve greatness. Already I have shown that it cannot be done in the confined sphere of individual, personal effort. The social principle prevails in the uprearing of a nation, as in the establishing of a family. Men must associate and combine energies in order to produce large results. In the same way that a family becomes strong, influential, and wealthy by uniting the energies of parents and children, so a people go on to honor and glory, in the proportion and extent that they combine their powers to definite and productive ends.

Two principles are implied in the remarks I have made, that is, the *one* of mutuality, and the *other* of dependence.

By *mutuality* I mean the reciprocal tendencies and desires which interact between large bodies of men, aiming at single and definite ends. I mean the several sentiments of sympathy, cheer, encouragement, and combination, among any special body of people; which are needed and required in distinct departments of labor. Solitude, in any matter, is alien to the human heart. We need, we call for the aid of our fellow-creatures. The beating heart of man waits for the answering heart of his brother.

It is the courageous voice of the venturesome soldier that leads on a whole column to the heart of the fray. It is the cheering song of the hardy sailor as he hangs upon the shrouds, amid the fierceness of the tempest, that lifts up the heart of his timid messmates, and stimulates to boldness and noble daring. On the broad fields of labor, where the scythe, the plough, and the spade work out those wondrous transformations which change the wild face of nature to order and beauty, and in the end, bring forth those mighty cargoes of grain which gladden the hearts and sustain the frames of millions; there the anthems of toil invigorate the brawny arms of labor; while the sun pours down its fiery rays, and the midday heat allures in vain to the shade and to rest. Deep down in the dark caves of earth, where the light of the sun never enters, tens of thousands of men and children delve away in the coal beds, or iron mines, buried in the bowels of the earth; cheered on in their toilsome labor by the joyous voices and the gladdening songs of their companions. What is it, in these several cases, that serves at once to lighten toil, and to stimulate to hardier effort? Several principles indeed concur; but it is evident that what I call mutuality, *i.e.,* sympathy and unison of feeling, act upon the hearts of soldiers, sailors, laborers, and miners, and spur them on to duty and endurance.

So, likewise, we may not pass by the other motive, *i.e.,* the feeling of *dependence.* We need the skill, the energy, the achievement of our fellow-creatures. No man stands up entirely alone, self-sufficient in the entire circle of human needs. Even in a state of barbarism the rude native man feels the need of the right arm of his brother. How much more with those who are civilized and enlightened! If you or I determine upon absolute independency of life and action, rejecting the arm and the aid of all other men, into how many departments of labor should we not at once have to multiply ourselves?

It is the recognition of this principle of association, which has made Great Britain, France, the United States, Holland, and Belgium the greatest nations of the earth. There are more partnerships, combinations; trades-unions, banking-houses, and insurance companies in those countries than in all the rest of the world together. The mere handful of men in these nations, numbering but one hundred millions, sway and dominate all the other nine hundred millions of men on the globe. Or just look at one single instance in our own day: here are England and France—fifty-eight millions of men—who, united, only a few years ago, humbled the vast empire of China, with its three hundred millions of semi-civilized inhabitants.

The principles of growth and mastery in a race, a nation, or people, are the same all over the globe. The same great agencies which are needed to make a people in one quarter of the globe and in one period of time are needed here, at this time, in this American nationality. We children of Africa in this land are no way different from any other people in these respects. Many of the differences of races are slight and incidental, and oftentimes become obliterated by circumstances, position, and religion. I can take you back to a period in the history of England when its rude inhabitants lived in caves and huts, when they fed on bark and roots, when their dress was the skins of animals. When you next look at some eminent Englishman, the personification, perchance, of everything cultivated, graceful, and refined, you may remember that his distant ancestors were wild and bloody savages, and that it has taken ten centuries to change him from the rudeness of his brutalized forefathers into an enlightened and civilized human being.

The great general laws of growth and superiority are unchangeable. The Almighty neither relaxes nor alters them for the convenience of any people. Conformity, then, to this demand for combination of forces is a necessity which we, as a people, cannot resist without loss and ruin. We cannot pay heed to it too soon; for if there has been anything for which the colored people of this country have been and now are noted, it is for disseverance, the segregation of their forces, the lack of the co-operative spirit. Neither in farming operations, nor trades, nor business, nor in mechanical employment, nor marketing, nor in attempts at grocery-keeping, do we find attempts at combination of their forces. No one hears anywhere of a company of fifty men to start a farm, to manufacture bricks, to begin a great trading business, to run a mill, or to ply a set of vessels in the coasting trade. No one sees a spontaneous movement of thirty or forty families to take possession of a tract of land for a specific monetary venture. Nowhere do we see a united movement in any State for general moral and educational improvement, whereby the masses may be delivered from inferiority and degradation. The people, as a body, seem delivered over to the same humble, servile occupations of life in which their fathers trod, because, from a lack of co-operation they are unable to step into the higher callings of business; and hence penury, poverty, inferiority, dependence, and even servility is their one general characteristic throughout the country, along with a dreadful state of mortality.

And the cause of this inferiority of purpose and of action is two-fold, and both the fault, to some extent, of unwise and unphilosophic leaders. For, since, especially emancipation, *two* special heresies have influenced and governed the minds of colored men in this nation: (I) The one is the dogma which I have heard frequently from the lips of leaders, personal and dear, but mistaken, friends, *that the colored people of this country should forget, as soon as possible, that they* ARE *colored people:*—a fact, in the first place, which is an impossibility. Forget it, forsooth, when you enter a saloon and are repulsed on account of your color! Forget it when you enter a car, South or West, and are denied a decent seat! Forget it when you enter the Church of God, and are driven to a hole in the gallery! Forget it when every child of yours would be driven ignominiously from four-fifths of the common schools of the country! Forget it, when thousands of mechanics in the large cities would make a "strike" rather than work at the same bench, in the same yard, with a black carpenter or brick-maker! Forget it, when the boyhood of our race is almost universally deprived of the opportunity of learning trades, through prejudice! Forget it, when, in one single State, twenty thousand men dare not go to the polls on election-day, through the tyranny of caste! Forget it, when one great commonwealth offers a new constitution for adoption, by which a man like *Dumas* the younger, if he were a North Carolinian, could be indicted for marrying the foulest white woman in that State, and merely because she was white! Forget that you are colored, in these United States! Turn madman, and go into a lunatic asylum, and then, perchance, you may forget it! But, if you have any sense or sensibility, how is it possible for you, or me, or any other colored man, to live oblivious of a fact of so much significance in a land like this! The only place I know of in this land where you can "forget you are colored" is the grave!

But not only is this dogma folly, it is disintegrating and socially destructive. For shut out, for instance, as I am and you are from the cultivated sociaII life of the superior classes of this country, if I forget that I am a black man, if you ignore the fact of race, and we both, ostrich-like, stick our heads in the sand, or stalk along, high-headed, oblivious of the actual distinctions which *do* exist in American society, what are you or I to do for our social nature? What will become of the measure of social life among ourselves which we now possess? Where are we to find our friends? Where find the circles for society and cheerful intercourse?

Why, my friends, the only way you, and I, and thousands of our people get domestic relations, marry wives and husbands, secure social relations, form good neighborhood and companionship, is by the very remembrance which we are told to scout and forswear.

2. The other dogma is the demand *that colored men should give up all distinctive effort, as colored men, in schools, churches, associations, and friendly societies.* But this, you will observe, is equivalent to a demand to the race to give up all civilization in this land and to submit to bar-

barism. The cry is: "Give up your special organization." "Mix in with your white fellow-citizens."

Now I waive, for the present, all discussion of abstract questions of rights and prerogatives. I direct my attention to the simple point of practicality; and I beg to say, that this is a thing which cannot be forced. Grieved, wearied and worried as humanity has been with the absurd, factitious arrangements of society in every quarter of the globe, yet men everywhere have had to wait. You can batter down oppression and tyranny with forceful implements; not so social disabilities and the exclusiveness of caste. The Saxon could not force it upon the Norman. Upon this point, if everything is not voluntary, generous, gracious, and spontaneous, the repulsive will is as icy, and as obstinate too, as Mt. Blanc. I wonder that the men who talk in the style I have referred to, forget that nine-tenths of the American people have become so poisoned and stimulated by the noxious influence of caste, that, in the present day, they would resist to the utmost before they would allow the affiliations, however remote, that implied the social or domestic principle.

Nay, more than this: not only would they reject your advances, but, after they had repelled you, they would leave you to reap the fruits of your own Folly in breaking up your own distinctive and productive organisms, under the flighty stimulants of imaginative conceit.

And the disaster, undoubtedly, would be deserved; not, indeed, morally, for the inflictions of caste are unjust and cruel; but because of your unwisdom; for it is the office of common sense to see, as well the exact situation, to comprehend the real condition of things as they exist in this nation; as well as to take cognizance of the pernicious and atrocious virulence of caste!

Few things in policy are more calamitous in result than mere conceit. An unbalanced and blind imagination is one of the most destructive, most disastrous of all guides. Such I believe to be the nature of the suggestion which I reprobate. But remember, I do not condemn the men who hold them. Oppression and caste are responsible for many worse things than unwisdom, or blind speculation. How intolerable are the distinctions which hedge up our ardent, ambitious minds, on every side, I thoroughly apprehend! How the excited mind turns passionately to every fancied and plausible mode of escape, I can easily understand! But remember that the pilotage of a whole people, of an entire race, through the quicksands and the breakers of civil and social degradation, up to the plane of manly freedom and equality, while it is, by its very hazards, calculated to heighten the pulse, and to quicken the activity of the brain, is, nevertheless, just that sort of work which calls for the coolest head, and the hardest, most downright reasonableness. When you are pleading for natural rights, when men are endeavoring to throw off the yoke of oppression, you may indeed

—imitate the action of the tiger,
Stiffen the sinews, summon up the blood.

But a war against a gross public sentiment, a contest with prejudices and repulsions, is a thing of a different kind, and calls for a warfare of an opposite character. You cannot destroy caste with a ten pounder! You cannot sweep away a prejudice with a park of artillery!

I know, to use the words of another, "how difficult it is to silence imagination enough to make the voice of Reason even distinctly heard in this case; as we are accustomed from our youth up to indulge that forward and delusive faculty ever obtruding beyond its sphere; of some assistance indeed to apprehension, but the author of all error; as we plainly lose ourselves in gross and crude conception of things, taking for granted that we are acquainted with what indeed we are wholly ignorant of"; so it seems to me the gravest of all duties to get rid of all delusions upon this subject; and to learn to look at it in the light of hard, serious, long-continued, painful, plodding work. It is *work,* you will observe, not abnormal disturbances, not excitement; but a mighty effort of moral and mental reconstruction, reaching over to a majestic end. And then when that is reached and secured, then all the hindrances of caste will be forever broken down!

Nothing is more idle than to talk of the invincibility of prejudice. The Gospel is sure to work out all the issues and results of brotherhood, everywhere under the sun, and in this land; but, until that day arrives, we are a nation, set apart, in this country. As such, we have got to strive—not to get rid of ourselves; not to agonize over our distinctive peculiarities; but to accept the situation as Providence allows it, and to quit "ourselves as men," in, if you say so, painful and embarrassing circumstances; determined to shift the groove of circumstance, and to reverse it.

The special duty before us is to strive for footing and for superiority in this land, *on the line of race,* as a temporary but needed expedient, for the ultimate extinction of caste, and all race distinctions. For if *we* do not look after our own interests, as a people, and strive for advantage, no other people will. It is folly for mere idealists to content themselves with the notion that "we are American citizens;" that, "as American citizens, ours is the common heritage and destiny of the nation;" that "special solicitude for the colored people is a superfluity;" that "there is but one tide in this land; and we shall flow with all others on it."

On the contrary, I assert, we are just now a "peculiar people" in this land; looked at, repulsed, kept apart, legislated for, criticised in journals, magazines, and scientific societies, at an insulting and intolerable distance, as a peculiar people; with the doubt against us whether or not we can hold on to vital power on this soil; or whether we have capacity to rise to manhood and superiority.

And hence I maintain that there is the greatest need for us all to hold on to the remembrance that *we* are "colored men," and not to forget it!

While one remnant of disadvantage abides in this land, stand by one another! While proscription in any quarter exists, maintain intact all your phalanxes! While antagonism confronts your foremost men, hold on to all the instincts of race for the support of your leaders, and the elevation of your people! While the imputation of inferiority, justly or unjustly, is cast upon you, combine for all the elements of culture, wealth, and power! While any sensitiveness or repulsion discovers itself at your approach or presence, hold on to your own self-respect, keep up, *and be satisfied with,* your own distinctive circles!

And then the "poor, forsaken ones," in the lanes and alleys and cellars of the great cities; in remote villages and hamlets; on old plantations which their fathers' blood has moistened from generation to generation; ignorant, unkempt, dirty, animal-like, repulsive, and half heathen—brutal and degraded; in some States, tens and hundreds of thousands, not slaves, indeed, according to the letter of the law, but the tools and *serfs* of would-be oppressors: stand by THEM until the school-master and preacher reach them as well as us; and the noble Christian civilization of the land transforms their features and their forms, and changes their rude huts into homes of beauty; and lifts them up into such grand superiority, that no one in the land will associate the word "Negro" with inferiority and degradation; but the whole land, yea, the whole world shall look upon them by-and-by, multitudinous in their brooding, clustered masses, "redeemed, regenerated, disenthralled," and exclaim, "Black, but comely!" But, while they are low, degraded, miserable, almost beastly, don't forget that you are colored men, as well as they; "your brothers' keepers."

Do not blink at the charge of inferiority. It is not a race peculiarity; and whatever its measure or extent in this country, it has been forced upon you. Do not deny it, but neutralize and destroy it, not by shrieks, or agonies, or foolish pretense; but by culture, by probity, and industry.

I know the natural resource of some minds, under these painful circumstances, to cry out, "Agitates agitate!" But *cui bono?* What advantage will agitation bring? Everything has a value, according to its relation to its own natural and specific end. But what is the bearing of agitation to a purpose which is almost entirely subjective in its nature. For, as I take it, the object we must needs have in view, in the face of the disabilities which confront our race in this land, is the attainment of such general superiority that prejudice must decline. But agitation has no such force, possesses no such value. Agitation is the expenditure of force: our end and aim is the husbandry of all our vital resources.

Character, my friends, is the grand, effective instrument which we are to use for, the destruction of caste: Character, in its broad, wide, deep, and high significance; character, as evidenced in high moral and intellectual attainments; as significant of general probity, honor, honesty, and self-restraint; as inclusive of inward might and power; as comprehending the attainments of culture, refinement, and enlightenment; as comprising the substantial results of thrift, economy, and enterprise; and as involving the forces of combined energies and enlightened cooperation. Make this, *not* the exceptional, but the common, general reality, amid the diverse, widespread populations of the colored people in this country; and then all the theories of inferiority, all the assumptions of your native and invincible degradation will pass, with wonderful rapidity, into endless forgetfulness; and the people of the very *next*, nay, multitudes, in the decline of *this* generation, when they look upon us, will wonder at the degrading facts of a past and wretched history. Only secure high, commanding, and masterly Character; and then all the problems of caste, all the enigmas of prejudice, all unreasonable and all unreasoning repulsion, will be settled forever, though you were ten times blacker than midnight! Then all false ideas concerning your nature and your qualities, all absurd notions relative to your capacity, shall vanish! Then every contemptuous fling shall be hushed, every insulting epithet be forgotten! Then, also, all the remembrances of a servile heritage, of ancestral degradation, shall be obliterated! Then all repulsive feelings, all evil dislikes shall fly away! Then, too, all timid disconcert shall depart from us, and all cramped and hesitant manhood shall die!

Dear brethren and friends, let there be but the clear demonstration of manly power and grand capacity in our race, in general, in this country; let there only be the wide out-flashings of art and genius, from their brains; and caste will slink, at once, oblivious to the shades. But no mere self-assertion, no strong, vociferous claims and clamor, can ever secure recognition and equality, so long as inferiority and degradation, if even cruelly entailed, abide as a heritage and a cancer. And I maintain we must *organize,* to the end that we may attain such character. The whole of our future on this soil depends upon that single fact of magnitude-character. Race, color, and all the incidents thereof have but little to do with the matter; and

men talk idly when they say "we must forget that we are colored men." What is needed is not that we should forget this fact, but that we should rise to such elevation that the *people of the land* be forced to forget all the facts and theories of race, when they behold our thorough equality with them, in all the lines of activity and attainment, of culture and moral grandeur. The great necessity in this and is that its *white* population should forget, be made to forget, that we are *colored* men! Hence there is a work ahead of us, for the overthrow of caste, which will consume the best part of a century. He, whoever he may be, commits the greatest blunder, who advises you to disband your forces, until that work is brought to its end. It was only *after* the battle of Waterloo that England and her allies broke up their armies, and scattered their huge battalions. Not until we, as a people, have fully vindicated our race; not until we have achieved to the full their rights and prerogatives; not until, by character, we challenge universal respect and consideration in the land, can we sing the song:

—Come to the sunset tree,
The day is past and gone,
The woodman's axe lies free,
And the reaper's work is done.

Until that time, far distant from to-day, should the cry be everywhere among us: "Combine and marshal, for all the highest achievements in industry, social progress, literature, and religion!"

I hasten to conclude with two brief remarks:

First, then, let me remind and warn you, my friends, that we, as colored men, have no superfluity of powers or faculties in the work which is before as, as a race, in this country. First of all, we all start with maimed and stunted powers. And next, the work before us is so distinct, definite, and, withal, so immense, that it tolerates no erratic wanderings to out-of-the-way and foreign fields.

And yet there are men who tell us that much of our work of the day is objective, that it lies among another people. But I beg to say that we have more than we are equal to in the needs of the six millions of our ignorant and benighted people, yet crippled and paralyzed by the lingering maladies of slavery. If we address ourselves strenuously and unitedly to *their* elevation and improvement we shall have our hands full for more than one generation, without flowing over with zeal and offices to a masterful people, laden with the enlightenment of centuries.

For one, I say very candidly that I do not feel it *my* special calling to wage war with and to extirpate caste. I am no way responsible for its existence. I abominate it as an enormity. *Theirs* is the responsibility who uphold it, and theirs is the obligation to destroy it. My work is special to my own people, and it is constructive. I beg leave to differ from that class of colored men who think that ours is a special mission, to leave our camp and to go over, as it were, among the Philistines, and to destroy their idols.

For my part, I am satisfied that my field of labor is with my own race in these times. I feel I have no exuberance of powers or ability to spend in any other field, or to bestow upon any other people. I say, as said the Shunamite woman, "I DWELL AMONG MY OWN PEOPLE" (2 Kings: IV, 13); not, indeed, as mindless of the brotherhood of the entire species, not as forgetful of the sentiment of fellowship with disciples of every name and blood; but as urged by the feeling of kinship, to bind myself as "with hooks of steel" to the most degraded class in the land, my own "kinsmen according to the flesh." I have the most thorough and radical conviction that the very first duty of colored men, in this our day and generation, is in the large field of effort which requires the regeneration and enlightenment of the colored race in these United States.

And second, from this comes the legitimate inference suggested by the text, i.e., of union and co-operation through all our ranks for effective action and for the noblest ends. Everywhere throughout the Union wide and thorough organization of the people should be made, not for idle political logomachy, but for industrial effort, for securing trades for youth, for joint-stock companies, for manufacturing, for the production of the great staples of the land, and likewise for the higher purposes of life, *i.e.*, for mental and moral improvement, and raising the plane of social and domestic life among us.

In every possible way these needs and duties should be pressed upon their attention, by sermons, by lectures, by organized societies, by state and national conventions; the *latter not* for political objects, but for social, industrial ends and attainments. I see nought in the future but that we shall be scattered like chaff before the wind before the organized labor of the land, the great power of capital, and the tremendous tide of emigration, unless, as a people, we fall back upon the might and mastery which come from the combination of forces and the principle of industrial co-operation. Most of your political agitation is but wind and vanity. *What* this *race needs in this coun*try is POWER—*the forces that may be felt.* And that comes from character, and character is the product of religion, intelligence, virtue, family order, superiority, wealth, and the show of industrial forces. THESE ARE FORCES WHICH WE DO NOT POSSESS. *We are the only class which, as a class,* IN THIS COUNTRY, IS WANTING IN THESE GRAND ELEMENTS. The very first effort of the colored people should be to lay hold of them; and then they will take such root in this American soil that only the convulsive upheaving of the judgement-day can throw them out!

And therefore I close, as I began, with the admonitory tones of the text. God grant they may be heeded at least by You who form this congregation, in your sacred work *here,* and in all your other relations: "They helped every one his neighbor, and every one said to his brother, Be of good courage. So the carpenter encouraged the goldsmith, and he that smootheth with the hammer him that smote the anvil, saying, It is ready for the soldering; and he fastened it with nails, that it SHOULD NOT BE MOVED!"

Guerilla Warfare, A Bush Negro View (Johannes King, 1885)

■ ■ ■

SOURCE: Price, Richard, ed. *Maroon Societies: Rebel Slave Communities in the Americas.* Baltimore: Johns Hopkins University Press, 1979, pp. 298–304.

Here is the story of our ancestors and of their difficulties while they were at war with the bakra ["whites"]. At that time they suffered severe shortages and were living under dreadful conditions, but the lack of food was their worst problem. They didn't even have time to clear and plant gardens to produce food. The whites were always pursuing them and attacking. Whenever they did manage with great difficulty to clear an area, they would fell the trees; then, when they planted food and it began to ripen, the whites would always be on them again with more fighting. Whenever the soldiers arrived in one of the camps, some of the women, frightened by the noise of battle, would run and take a rice mortar, heft it onto their shoulders, and flee with it into the forest. They would run on until the crisis subsided a little, when their heads would clear and they would realize that instead of their children they had brought with them nothing but pieces of wood. Well, listen to this: As soon as those soldiers got into one of our ancestors' camps and saw some young child, they would take that child, put him in a mortar and beat him with pestles, just as people mash bananas. That child would be completely crushed. And then they would burn the whole settlement and cut down all the banana trees and throw away any other food they saw. They slashed the crops to bits, ruining everything that they saw. They set fire to everything they found that they didn't want to carry off with them. Well, that enraged our early ancestors against the whites. And they swore a blood oath, vowing to take proper revenge against those whites for the blood of the slaves that the whites had spilled on their plantations, at the time when there were still no Bush Negroes.

. . . Well, by the time the war had dragged on for five years [sic; actually more than a half century], this strenuous life had begun to wear very heavily on our ancestors. There was no food to eat. But some of the seeds that God had put in the forest helped them, and they ate many of these sweet seeds of the forest instead of regular food [rice]. But there was no lack of game and fish, not at all. Animals and birds were not scarce; these were very abundant, and there were many fish too. This helped them greatly, because these things were not difficult to find. But there was a real shortage of salt. They were even forced to make "bush salt" with the various kinds of trees whose trunks contain salt.

. . . The women made giant clay pots to cook things in. Likewise, they made big clay pans and big tubs that could hold a lot of water. . . . And they made water jugs, big ones and little ones. As for iron pots, large or small, these our ancestors had to capture from the enemy. And when the fighting got hard, sometimes the soldiers saw that the bush people were killing too many of them and ran back to save their lives. Then they could not carry all their big pots back with them. Often they ran off and abandoned everything. Our ancestors would sometimes take these and wipe out the entire detachment of soldiers. They would spare only two soldiers so that they could carry the message back to the city to tell the government, to let them know that all the soldiers in that detachment were gone, that it was all over for them, that they had all been killed. In this way our ancestors would obtain more iron pots as well as guns and machetes, gun powder, bullets, everything. And some of the rest of them would go sack a plantation, taking away many Negroes and all kinds of goods. They took men and women, children and adults, and killed any slaves who refused to go off to the bush. Then they would take all that they could carry and go back with it into the forest. In this way our ancestors got things in the bush to help them survive during those five [sic] years while the fighting was going on, until the whites finally made peace with them.

. . . [In the course of the wars] when the Bush Negroes had killed too many whites and destroyed plantations one after another, and when the whites saw that they were losing even more slaves over and above the original ones and that the government soldiers were dying in vain, they decided to send a white to the Matawai tribe to make a truce with the Matawai people. When the whites arrived, those people replied to the whites that it was good, that they would make peace with them just as the whites suggested, and that they would put an end to the fighting. They said, yes, that was good for them too. And they discussed the whole thing together. Then the whites gave the Bush Negroes presents.

They brought lots of cloths and many other things to give them as presents. Well, the Bush Negroes took all the presents. But then they did not do the right thing. Those people acted dishonorably and tricked the whites. At this first treaty, they thought that the whites were coming to deceive them and that the treaty that the whites were offering could not be in good faith. And that is why the Bush Negroes tricked the whites at the outset. Each one took a soldier as his mati, to sleep in his own hut. This is how they divided up the soldiers, but some of the blacks were left over because there were more of them than whites. Well, during the night, each one killed his mati. And that is how they killed all the soldiers; they spared just two of the whites to send them to the city to bring the news to the government.

Well, after that the government tried sending another detachment to the Djuka people to ask them if they wanted to make a treaty with the whites. But how did they make that request? A house slave who knew how to write a little had run away to the forest. The whites wrote a letter and left it on one of the Bush Negroes' paths. When they found the letter, they had the man read it. That is how they learned that the whites wanted to come make peace with them. And then the Djukas said yes, they wanted it. So the Djukas went to meet the whites and told them everything that they needed in order to live. Then they swore an oath with the whites; they made peace together; they made an agreement. With that, they drank a blood oath. The whites said they would not go shoot the Negroes or fight with them anymore. But they too must cease their fighting with the whites and must no longer raid plantations or take more of the whites' slaves back to the bush. And whenever a plantation slave ran off to join them, they must not harbor him; they must bring him back to the whites. And if a slave from the city ran off to them, they must return him to the whites and the whites would pay them for that. The government's forests were all open to them, and the Bush Negroes along the upper courses of the rivers could do whatever they wanted. In other words, they were free to clear the underbrush, cut lumber, fell trees, make horticultural camps, clear gardens, and plant crops. They could do any work they were able to do and bring things to sell in the city. The government allowed them to do all these things. But the government did not give the Bush Negroes permission to do as they liked along the lower course of the rivers, where the tide was still visible and where the whites themselves worked. Upstream, from where the rapids begin, the government has continued to allow them a free hand to this very day.

. . . The government closed this treaty with a solemn oath, requiring the Bush Negroes to renew the oath every three years. They would bring lots of goods to distribute among them.

That is: salt and cloth, guns, powder, bullets, shot, beads, pots, knives, cutlasses, axes, grindstones, two types of adzes, razors, shovels, scissors, mirrors, and nails to nail things, screwdrivers, tinderboxes and flintstones, large griddles for making cassava cakes and pans for cooking fish, cloth to make hammocks, hammers, cowrie shells, bells, cockle shells, barrels of rum, barrels of salt meat, barrels of bacon, and barrels of salt cod. Well, such was the agreement the early whites made with our early ancestors in the bush. The Bush Negroes were satisfied with the agreement and the whites were satisfied too. It was good for them all. The whites took a knife and cut their hands, drawing a little blood. They wiped it onto the inside of a glass. And then the blacks took a little blood the same way and put it in the glass. The whites then swore upon the blood of the blacks, and the blacks swore upon the blood of the whites. Then they mixed a little wine with the blood and "drank the oath." Well that's how the whites and the Bush Negroes made the very first peace treaty.

[King here recounts the similar stories of how the government made peace with the Saramakas and then with the Matawais.]

. . . The government said that if they honored the agreements, every three years they would send many goods to distribute among the three tribes. . . . Every three years they had to drink an oath all over again. The whites did indeed hold to the agreement and the oath. For more than a hundred years they kept giving goods. And they drank a blood oath every three years, for more than a hundred years. Even up to my, Johannes King's, lifetime when I was a little boy, the government kept sending presents to give to the three tribes of Djuka, Saramaka, and Matawai. But by the time I saw the distribution of presents for the second time, I was already pretty big. They again drank an oath. That was the last time whites and Bush Negroes ever drank a blood oath. After that, the government sent goods again to distribute to the three Bush Negro tribes. By then I, Johannes King, had already become a young man. I could already do everything like a man. After that, whites and Bush Negroes never drank a blood oath again. The whites and the Bush Negro chiefs gave each other their hand; they shook hands together to make peace; it was over. And the whites gave presents, which the Bush Negroes received with joy.

. . . The story of how our forefathers honored God and their early ancestors when they came to receive the presents and then returned to their villages:

When they got back safely to their villages, they fired many salutes for the people who had waited at home.

These people came to the bank of the river singing, to escort them to shore. They played drums, danced, blew African trumpets, and sang, danced and celebrated the whole afternoon until nighttime and the whole night until morning. In the morning, they took a piece of white cloth and they raised a white flag to Gran Gado or Masra Gado [the supreme deity] in the heavens. Then *they* all touched their knees to the ground and gave Masra Gado thanks for all that he had done for them and for the strength that he had given them against the many hardships they encountered in the bush. Moreover, Masra Gado had helped them and given them strength in the forest to fight and win a major war against the whites. Now the whites themselves were bringing them peace and many goods. And for that, everyone knelt down on the ground and to give Masra Gado thanks. They put all their children with their bellies to the ground, and even many of the adults threw themselves with their bellies to the ground to show Masra Gado respect and to give him thanks for the good things that he had done for them. Then they got up, took their guns, and shot many salutes for Masra Gado, to honor him. And finally they were finished.

Then they raised another flag with a black cloth. This they did to honor the former warriors, those who had fought and won against the whites. Then they all came together under the flag; this was also to give thanks to the warriors and to honor their name and to blow African trumpets, which the Africans had made out of wood in Africa, and which they loved to blow whenever they went off to battle and with which they talked to one another. These early people who lived in the bush really loved to blow those trumpets Whenever they blew such a trumpet, they would shoot many salutes, play drums, sing, dance, and play *sanga* drums. And the adults would *sanga* all over the place. That word, "*sanga*," means many people with guns, machetes, and spears in their hands running all over the place exactly the way that the warriors used to fight in Africa itself, and with many war cries. And the older men showed the youths and young girls how they fought with the whites and how the warriors raided and destroyed white plantations, carrying off people to the forest. While they were running around like this, they would shoot many, many salutes, just like the [government] soldiers do in the city square. Then many people would shout together. "Battle! Battle! The battle's on!" And then they would fire guns, play drums, and blow horns, like warriors going off to raid a plantation. And if someone were far off who didn't know about this, he would think that a real battle was taking place on a plantation, there were so many cries and guns shooting. And they played drums so! When they were finished, they would bring a bush drink that they made from sugar cane juice, and which is called bush rum.

They would pour a libation on the ground. That was in order to give thanks to God and the ancestors. After that they would play for the *obeahs* and for the other gods who had helped them fight.

A VOICE FROM THE SOUTH (ANNA JULIA COOPER, 1892)

SOURCE: Cooper, Anna Julia. *A Voice from the South.* Xenia, Ohio: Aldine Printing House, 1892, pp. 24–31. Available online via the University of North Carolina Library's *Documenting the American South* website at <http://docsouth.unc.edu/church/cooper/cooper.html> UNC Library requests that this acknowledgement be cited if using this text: © This work is the property of the University of North Carolina at Chapel Hill. It may be used freely by individuals for research, teaching and personal use as long as this statement of availability is included in the text.

I would beg, however, with the Doctor's permission, to add my plea for the *Colored Girls* of the South:—that large, bright, promising fatally beautiful class that stand shivering like a delicate plantlet before the fury of tempestuous elements, so full of promise and possibilities, yet so sure of destruction; often without a father to whom they dare apply the loving term, often without a stronger brother to espouse their cause and defend their honor with his life's blood; in the midst of pitfalls and snares, waylaid by the lower classes of white men, with no shelter, no protection nearer than the great blue vault above, which half conceals and half reveals the one Care-Taker they know so little of. Oh, save them, help them, shield, train, develop, teach, inspire them! Snatch them, in God's name, as brands from the burning! There is material in them well worth your while, the hope in germ of a staunch, helpful, regenerating womanhood on which, primarily, rests the foundation stones of our future as a race.

It is absurd to quote statistics showing the Negro's bank account and rent rolls, to point to the hundreds of newspapers edited by colored men and lists of lawyers, doctors, professors, D.D's, LL D's, etc., etc., etc., while the source from which the life-blood of the race is to flow is subject to taint and corruption in the enemy's camp.

True progress is never made by spasms. Real progress is growth. It must begin in the seed. Then, "first the blade, then the ear, after that the full corn in the ear." There is something to encourage and inspire us in the advancement of individuals since their emancipation from slavery.

It at least proves that there is nothing irretrievably wrong in the shape of the black man's skull, and that under given circumstances his development, downward or upward, will be similar to that of other average human beings.

But there is no time to be wasted in mere felicitation. That the Negro has his niche in the infinite purposes of the Eternal, no one who has studied the history of the last fifty years in America will deny. That much depends on his own right comprehension of his responsibility and rising to the demands of the hour, it will be good for him to see; and how best to use his present so that the structure of the future shall be stronger and higher and brighter and nobler and holier than that of the past, is a question to be decided each day by every one of us.

The race is just twenty-one years removed from the conception and experience of a chattel, just at the age of ruddy manhood. It is well enough to pause a moment for retrospection, introspection, and prospection. We look back, not to become inflated with conceit because of the depths from which we have arisen, but that we may learn wisdom from experience. We look within that we may gather together once more our forces, and, by improved and more practical methods, address ourselves to the tasks before us. We look forward with hope and trust that the same God whose guiding hand led our fathers through and out of the gall and bitterness of oppression, will still lead and direct their children, to the honor of His name, and for their ultimate salvation.

But this survey of the failures or achievments of the past, the difficulties and embarrassments of the present, and the mingled hopes and fears for the future, must not degenerate into mere dreaming nor consume the time which belongs to the practical and effective handling of the crucial questions of the hour; and there can be no issue more vital and momentous than this of the womanhood of the race.

Here is the vulnerable point, not in the heel, but at the heart of the young Achilles; and here must the defenses be strengthened and the watch redoubled.

We are the heirs of a past which was not our fathers' moulding. "Every man the arbiter of his own destiny" was not true for the American Negro of the past: and it is no fault of his that he finds himself to-day the inheritor of a manhood and womanhood impoverished and debased by two centuries and more of compression and degradation.

But weaknesses and malformations, which to-day are attributable to a vicious schoolmaster and a pernicious system, will a century hence be rightly regarded as proofs of innate corruptness and radical incurability.

Now the fundamental agency under God in the regeneration, the re-training of the race, as well as the ground work and starting point of its progress upward, must be the *black woman.*

With all the wrongs and neglects of her past, with all the weakness, the debasement, the moral thralldom of her present, the black woman of to-day stands mute and wondering at the Herculean task devolving around her. But the cycles wait for her. No other hand can move the lever. She must be loosed from her bands and set to work.

Our meager and superficial results from past efforts prove their futility; and every attempt to elevate the Negro, whether undertaken by himself or through the philanthropy of others, cannot but prove abortive unless so directed as to utilize the indispensable agency of an elevated and trained womanhood.

A race cannot be purified from without. Preachers and teachers are helps, and stimulants and conditions as necessary as the gracious rain and sunshine are to plant growth. But what are rain and dew and sunshine and cloud if there be no life in the plant germ? We must go to the root and see that it is sound and healthy and vigorous; and not deceive ourselves with waxen flowers and painted leaves of mock chlorophyll.

We too often mistake individuals' honor for race development and so are ready to substitute pretty accomplishments for sound sense and earnest purpose.

A stream cannot rise higher than its source. The atmosphere of homes is no rarer and purer and sweeter than are the mothers in those homes. A race is but a total of families. The nation is the aggregate of its homes. As the whole is sum of all its parts, so the character of the parts will determine the characteristics of the whole. These are all axioms and so evident that it seems gratuitous to remark it; and yet, unless I am greatly mistaken, most of the unsatisfaction from our past results arises from just such a radical and palpable error, as much almost on our own part as on that of our benevolent white friends.

The Negro is constitutionally hopeful and proverbially irrepressible; and naturally stands in danger of being dazzled by the shimmer and tinsel of superficials. We often mistake foliage for fruit and overestimate or wrongly estimate brilliant results.

The late Martin R. Delany, who was an unadulterated black man, used to say when honors of state fell upon him, that when he entered the council of kings the black race entered with him; meaning, I suppose, that there was no discounting his race identity and attributing his achievements to some admixture of Saxon blood. But our present record of eminent men, when placed beside the actual status of the race in America to-day, proves that no man can represent the race. Whatever the attainments of the individual may be, unless his home has moved on *pari passu,*

he can never be regarded as identical with or representative of the whole.

Not by pointing to sun-bathed mountain tops do we prove that Phoebus warms the valleys.

We must point to homes, average homes, homes of the rank and file of horny handed toiling men and women of the South (where the masses are) lighted and cheered by the good, the beautiful, and the true,—then and not till then will the whole plateau be lifted into the sunlight.

Only the BLACK WOMAN can say "when and where I enter, in the quiet, undisputed dignity of my womanhood, without violence and without suing or special patronage, then and there the whole *Negro race enters with me.*" Is it not evident then that as individual workers for this race we must address ourselves with no half-hearted zeal to this feature of our mission. The need is felt and must be recognized by all. There is a call for workers, for missionaries, for men and women with the double consecration of a fundamental love of humanity and a desire for its melioration through the Gospel; but superadded to this we demand an intelligent and sympathetic comprehension of the interests and special needs of the Negro.

THE AMERICAN NEGRO AND HIS FATHERLAND (HENRY McNEAL TURNER, 1895)

SOURCE: Congress on Africa, Atlanta, 1895. *Africa and the American Negro.* Edited by J. W. E. Bowen. Gammon Theological Seminary, 1896. Reprinted. Miami: Mnemosyne Publishing, 1969, pp. 195–197.

It would be a waste of time to expend much labor, the few moments I have to devote to this subject, upon the present status of the Negroid race in the United States. It is too well known already. However, I believe that the Negro was brought to this country in the providence of God to a heaven permitted if not a divine-sanctioned manual laboring school, that he might have direct contact with the mightiest race that ever trod the face of the globe.

The heathen African, to my certain knowledge, I care not what others may say, eagerly yearn for that civilization which they believe will elevate them and make them potential for good. The African was not sent and brought to this country by chance, or by the avarice of the white man, single and alone. The white slave purchaser went to the shores of that continent and bought our ancestors from their African masters. The bulk who were brought to this country were the children of parents who had been in slavery a thousand years. Yet hereditary slavery is not universal among the African slaveholders. So that the argument often advanced, that the white man went to Africa and stole us, is not true. They bought us out of a slavery that still exists over a large portion of that continent. For there are millions and millions of slaves in Africa to-day. Thus the superior African sent us, and the white man brought us, and we remained in slavery as long as it was necessary to learn that a God, who is a spirit, made the world and controls it, and that that Supreme Being could be sought and found by the exercise of faith in His only begotten Son. Slavery then went down, and the colored man was thrown upon his own responsibility, and here he is today, in the providence of God, cultivating self-reliance and imbibing a knowledge of civil law in contra-distinction to the dictum of one man, which was the law of the black man until slavery was overthrown. I believe that the Negroid race has been free long enough now to begin to think for himself and plan for better conditions than he can lay claim to in this country or ever will. *There is no manhood future in the United States for the Negro.* He may eke out an existence for generations to come, but he can never be a man—full, symmetrical and undwarfed. Upon this point I know thousands who make pretensions to scholarship, white and colored, will differ and may charge me with folly, while I in turn pity their ignorance of history and political and civil sociology. We beg here to itemize and give a cursory glance at a few facts calculated to convince any man who is not biased or lamentably ignorant. Let us note a few of them.

1. There is a great chasm between the white and black, not only in this country, but in the West India Islands, South America, and as much as has been said to the contrary, I have seen inklings of it in Ireland, in England, in France, in Germany, and even away down in southern Spain in sight of Morocco in Africa. We will not however deal with foreign nations, but let us note a few facts connected with the United States.

I repeat that a great chasm exists between the two race varieties in this country. The white people, neither North nor South, will have social contact as a mass between themselves and any portion of the Negroid race. Although they may be as white in appearance as themselves, yet a drop of African blood imparts a taint, and the talk about two races remaining in the same country with mutual interest and responsibility in its institutions and progress, with no social contact, is the jargon of folly, and no man who has read the history of nations and the development of countries, and the agencies which have culminated in the homogeneity of racial variations, will proclaim such a

docrine. Senator Morgan, of Alabama, tells the truth when he says that the Negro has nothing to expect without social equality with the whites, and that the whites will never grant it.

This question must be examined and opinions reached in the light of history and sociological philosophy, and not by a mere think-so on the part of men devoid of learning. When I use the term learning, I do not refer to men who have graduated from some college and have a smattering knowledge of Greek, Latin, mathematics and a few school books, and have done nothing since but read the trashy articles of newspapers. That is not scholarship. Scholarship consists in wading through dusty volumes for forty and fifty years. That class of men would not dare to predict symmetrical manhood for the Negroid race in this or any other country, without social equality. The colored man who will stand up and in one breath say, that the Negroid race does not want social equality and in the next predict a great future in the face of all the proscription of which the colored man is the victim, is either an ignoramus, or is an advocate of the perpetual servility and degradation of his race variety. I know, as Senator Morgan says, and as every white man in the land will say, that the whites will not grant social equality to the Negroid race, nor am I certain that God wants them to do it. And as such, I believe that two or three millions of us should return to the land of our ancestors, and establish our own nation, civilization, laws, customs, style of manufacture, and not only give the world, like other race varieties, the benefit of our individuality, but build up social conditions peculiarly our own, and cease to be grumblers, chronic complainers and a menace to the white man's country, or the country he claims and is bound to dominate.

The civil status of the Negro is simply what the white man grants of his own free will and accord. The black man can demand nothing. He is deposed from the jury and tried, convicted and sentenced by men who do not claim to be his peers. On the railroads, where the colored race is found in the largest numbers, he is the victim of proscription, and he must ride in the Jim Crow car or walk. The Supreme Court of the United States decided, October 15th, 1882, that the colored man had no civil rights under the general government, and the several States, from then until now, have been enacting laws which limit, curtail and deprive him of his civil rights, immunities and privileges, until he is now being disfranchised, and where it will end no one can divine.

They told me in the Geographical Institute in Paris, France, that according to their calculation there are not less than 400,000,000 of Africans and their descendants on the globe, so that we are not lacking in numbers to form a nationality of our own.

2. The environments of the Negroid race variety in this country tend to the inferiority of them, even if the argument can be established that we are equals with the white man in the aggregate, notwithstanding the same opportunities may be enjoyed in the schools. Let us note a few facts.

The discriminating laws, all will concede, are degrading to those against whom they operate, and the degrader will be degraded also. "For all acts are reactionary, and will return in curses upon those who curse," said Stephen A. Douglass, the great competitor of President Lincoln. Neither does it require a philosopher to inform you that degradation begets degradation. Any people oppressed, proscribed, belied, slandered, burned, flayed and lynched will not only become cowardly and servile, but will transmit that same servility to their posterity, and continue to do so *ad infinitum,* and as such will never make a bold and courageous people. The condition of the Negro in the United States is so repugnant to the instincts of respected manhood that thousands, yea hundreds of thousands, of miscegenated will pass for white, and snub the people with whom they are identified at every opportunity, thus destroying themselves, or at least *unracing* themselves. They do not want to be black because of its ignoble condition, and they cannot be white, thus they become monstrosities. Thousands of young men who are even educated by white teachers never have any respect for people of their own color and spend their days as devotees of white gods. Hundreds, if not thousands, of the terms employed by the white race in the English language are also degrading to the black man. Everything that is satanic, corrupt, base and infamous is denominated *black,* and all that constitutes virtue, purity, innocence, religion, and that which is divine and heavenly, is represented as white. Our Sabbath-school children, by the time they reach proper consciousness, are taught to sing to the laudation of white and to the contempt of black. Can any one with an ounce of common sense expect that these children, when they reach maturity, will ever have any respect for their black or colored faces, or the faces of their associates? But, without multiplying words, the terns used in our religious experience, and the hymns we sing in many instances, are degrading, and will be as long as the black man is surrounded by the idea that *white* represents God and black represents the devil. The Negro should, therefore, build up a nation of his own, and create a language in keeping with his color, as the whites have done. Nor will he ever respect himself until he does it.

3. In this country the colored man, with a few honorable exceptions, folds his arms and waits for the white man to propose, project, erect, invent, discover, combine, plan and execute everything connected with civilization, including machinery, finance, and indeed everything. This, in the nature of things, dwarfs the colored man and allows his great faculties to slumber from the cradle to the grave. Yet he possesses mechanical and inventive genius, I believe, equal to any race on earth. Much has been said about the natural inability of the colored race to engage in the professions of skilled labor. Yet before the war, right here in this Southland, he erected and completed all of the fine edifices in which the lords of the land luxuriated. It is idle talk to speak of a colored man not being a success in skilled labor or the fine arts. What the black man needs is a country and surroundings in harmony with his color and with respect for his manhood. Upon this point I would delight to dwell longer if I had time. Thousands of white people in this country are ever and anon advising the colored people to keep out of politics, but they do not advise themselves. If the Negro is a man in keeping with other men, why should he be less concerned about politics than any one else? Strange, too, that a number of would-be colored leaders are ignorant and debased enough to proclaim the same foolish jargon. For the Negro to stay out of politics is to level himself with a horse or a cow, which is no politician, and the Negro who does it proclaims his inability to take part in political affairs. If the Negro is to be a man, full and complete, he must take part in everything that belongs to manhood. If he omits a single duty, responsibility or privilege, to that extent he is limited and incomplete.

Time, however, forbids my continuing the discussion of this subject, roughly and hastily as these thoughts have been thrown together. Not being able to present a dozen or two more phases, which I would cheerfully and gladly do if opportunity permitted, I conclude by saying the argument that it would be impossible to transport the colored people of the United States back to Africa is an advertisement of folly. Two hundred millions of dollars would rid this country of the last member of the Negroid race, if such a thing was desirable, and two hundred and fifty millions would give every man, woman and child excellent fare, and the general government could furnish that amount and never miss it, and that would only be the pitiful sum of a million dollars a year for the time we labored for nothing, and for which somebody or some power is responsible. The emigrant agents at New York, Boston, Philadelphia, St. John, N. B., and Halifax, N. S., with whom I have talked, establish beyond contradiction, that over a million, and from that to twelve hundred thousand persons, come to this country every year, and yet there is no public stir about it. But in the case of African emigration, two or three millions only of self-reliant men and women would be necessary to establish the conditions we are advocating in Africa.

The Atlanta Exposition Address (Booker T. Washington, 1895)

▪ ▪ ▪

SOURCE: *Up from Slavery.* New York: Doubleday, Page & Company, 1901, pp. 217–225.

INTRODUCTION: *Invited to offer one of the opening addresses at the Cotton States and International Exposition in Atlanta in 1895, Booker T. Washington sought "to say something that would cement the friendship of the races and bring about hearty cooperation between them." Rejecting legislated equality in favor of progress and an equality that he felt blacks could eventually earn, Washington made the proposal that came to be known as the Atlanta Compromise. The following excerpt, from Washington's autobiography,* Up from Slavery, *includes the address as well as the author's recollections about the response it drew.*

The Atlanta Exposition, at which I had been asked to make an address as a representative of the Negro race . . . was opened with a short address from Governor Bullock. After other interesting exercises, including an invocation from Bishop Nelson, of Georgia, a dedicatory ode by Albert Howell, Jr., and addresses by the President of the Exposition and Mrs. Joseph Thompson, the President of the Woman's Board, Governor Bullock introduced me with the words, "We have with us to-day a representative of Negro enterprise and Negro civilization."

When I arose to speak, there was considerable cheering, especially from the coloured people. As I remember it now, the thing that was uppermost in my mind was the desire to say something that would cement the friendship of the races and bring about hearty cooperation between them. So far as my outward surroundings were concerned, the only thing that I recall distinctly now is that when I got up, I saw thousands of eyes looking intently into my face. The following is the address which I delivered:—

Mr. President and Gentlemen of the Board of Directors and Citizens:

One-third of the population of the South is of the Negro race. No enterprise seeking the material, civil, or moral welfare of this section can disregard this element of our population and reach the highest success. I but convey to you, Mr. President and Directors, the sentiment of the masses of my race when I say that in no way have the value and manhood of the American Negro been more fittingly and generously recognized than by the managers of this magnificent Exposition at every stage of its progress. It is a recognition that will do more to cement the friendship of the two races than any occurrence since the dawn of our freedom.

Not only this, but the opportunity here afforded will awaken among us a new era of industrial progress. Ignorant and inexperienced, it is not strange that in the first years of our new life we began at the top instead of at the bottom; that a seat in Congress or the state legislature was more sought than real estate or industrial skill; that the political convention of stump speaking had more attractions than starting a dairy farm or truck garden.

A ship lost at sea for many days suddenly sighted a friendly vessel. From the mast of the unfortunate vessel was seen a signal, "Water, water; we die of thirst!" The answer from the friendly vessel at once came back, "Cast down your bucket where you are." A second time the signal, "Water, water; send us water!" ran up from the distressed vessel, and was answered, "Cast down your bucket where you are." And a third and fourth signal for water was answered, "Cast down your bucket where you are." The captain of the distressed vessel, at last heeding the injunction, cast down his bucket, and it came up full of fresh, sparkling water from the mouth of the Amazon River. To those of my race who depend on bettering their condition in a foreign land or who underestimate the importance of cultivating friendly relations with the Southern white man, who is their next-door neighbour, I would say: "Cast down your bucket where you are"—cast it down in making friends in every manly way of the people of all races by whom we are surrounded.

Cast it down in agriculture, mechanics, in commerce, in domestic service, and in the professions. And in this connection it is well to bear in mind that whatever other sins the South may be called to bear, when it comes to business, pure and simple, it is in the South that the Negro is given a man's chance in the commercial world, and in nothing is this Exposition more eloquent than in emphasizing this chance. Our greatest danger is that in the great leap from slavery to freedom we may overlook the fact that the masses of us are to live by the productions of our hands, and fail to keep in mind that we shall prosper in proportion as we learn to dignify and glorify common labour and put brains and skill into the common occupations of life; shall prosper in proportion as we learn to draw the line between the superficial and the substantial, the ornamental gewgaws of life and the useful. No race can prosper till it learns that there is as much dignity in tilling a field as in writing a poem. It is at the bottom of life we must begin, and not at the top. Nor should we permit our grievances to overshadow our opportunities.

To those of the white race who look to the incoming of those of foreign birth and strange tongue and habits for the prosperity of the South, were I permitted I would repeat what I say to my own race, "Cast down your bucket where you are." Cast it down among the eight millions of Negroes whose habits you know, whose fidelity and love you have tested in days when to have proved treacherous meant the ruin of your firesides. Cast down your bucket among these people who have, without strikes and labour wars, tilled your fields, cleared your forests, builded your railroads and cities, and brought forth treasures from the bowels of the earth, and helped make possible this magnificent representation of the progress of the South. Casting down your bucket among my people, helping and encouraging them as you are doing on these grounds, and to education of head, hand, and heart, you will find that they will buy your surplus land, make blossom the waste places in your fields, and run your factories. While doing this, you can be sure in the future, as in the past, that you and your families will be surrounded by the most patient, faithful, law-abiding, and unresentful people that the world has seen. As we have proved our loyalty to you in the past, in nursing your children, watching by the sickbed of your mothers and fathers, and often following them with tear-dimmed eyes to their graves, so in the future, in our humble way, we shall stand by you with a devotion that no foreigner can approach, ready to lay down our lives, if need be, in defence of yours, interlacing our industrial, commercial, civil, and religious life with yours in a way that shall make the interests of both races one. In all things that are purely social we can be as separate as the fingers, yet one as the hand in all things essential to mutual progress.

There is no defence or security for any of us except in the highest intelligence and development of all. If anywhere there are efforts tending to curtail the fullest growth of the Negro, let these efforts be turned into stimulating, encouraging, and making him the most useful and intelligent citizen. Effort or means so invested will pay a thousand per cent interest. These efforts will be twice blessed—"blessing him that gives and him that takes."

There is no escape through law of man or God from the inevitable:—

The laws of changeless justice bind
Oppressor with oppressed;
And close as sin and suffering joined
We march to fate abreast.

Nearly sixteen millions of hands will aid you in pulling the load upward, or they will pull against you the load down-ward. We shall constitute one-third and more of the ignorance and crime of the South, or one-third its intelligence and progress; we shall contribute one-third to the business and industrial prosperity of the South, or we shall prove a veritable body of death, stagnating, depressing, retarding every effort to advance the body politic.

Gentlemen of the Exposition, as we present to you our humble effort at an exhibition of our progress, you must not expect overmuch. Starting thirty years ago with ownership here and there in a few quilts and pumpkins and chickens (gathered from miscellaneous sources), remember the path that has led from these to the inventions and production of agricultural implements, buggies, steam-engines, newspapers, books, statuary, carving, paintings, the management of drug-stores and banks, has not been trodden without contact with thorns and thistles. While we take pride in what we exhibit as a result of our independent efforts, we do not for a moment forget that our part in this exhibition would fall far short of your expectations but for the constant help that has come to our educational life, not only from the Southern states, but especially from Northern philanthropists, who have made their gifts a constant stream of blessing and encouragement.

The wisest among my race understand that the agitation of questions of social equality is the extremest folly, and that progress in the enjoyment of all the privileges that will come to us must be the result of severe and constant struggle rather than of artificial forcing. No race that has anything to contribute to the markets of the world is long in any degree ostracized. It is important and right that all privileges of the law be ours, but it is vastly more important that we be prepared for the exercises of these privileges. The opportunity to earn a dollar in a factory just now is worth infinitely more than the opportunity to spend a dollar in an opera-house.

In conclusion, may I repeat that nothing in thirty years has given us more hope and encouragement, and drawn us so near to you of the white race, as this opportunity offered by the Exposition; and here bending, as it were, over the altar that represents the results of the struggles of your race and mine, both starting practically empty-handed three decades ago. I pledge that in your effort to work out the great and intricate problem which God has laid at the doors of the South, you shall have at all times the patient, sympathetic help of my race; only let this be constantly in mind, that, while from representations in these buildings of the product of field, of forest, of mine, of factory, letters, and art, much good will come, yet far above and beyond material benefits will be that higher good, that, let us pray God, will come, in a blotting out of sectional differences and racial animosities and suspicions, in a determination to administer absolute justice, in a willing obedience among all classes to the mandates of law. This, then, coupled with our material prosperity, will bring into our beloved South a new heaven and a new earth.

The first thing that I remember, after I had finished speaking, was that Governor Bullock rushed across the platform and took me by the hand, and that others did the same. I received so many and such hearty congratulations that I found it difficult to get out of the building. I did not appreciate to any degree, however, the impression which my address seemed to have made, until the next morning, when I went into the business part of the city. As soon as I was recognized, I was surprised to find myself pointed out and surrounded by a crowd of men who wished to shake hands with me. This was kept up on every street on to which I went, to an extent which embarrassed me so much that I went back to my boarding place. The next morning I returned to Tuskegee. At the station in Atlanta, and at almost all of the stations at which the train stopped between that city and Tuskegee, I found a crowd of people anxious to shake hands with me.

The papers in all parts of the United States published the address in full, and for months afterward there were complimentary editorial references to it. Mr. Clark Howell, the editor of the Atlanta *Constitution,* telegraphed to a New York paper, among other words, the following, "I do not exaggerate when I say that Professor Booker T. Washington's address yesterday was one of the most notable speeches, both as to character and as to the warmth of its reception, ever delivered to a Southern audience. The address was a revelation. The whole speech is a platform upon which blacks and whites can stand with full justice to each other."

The Boston *Transcript* said editorially: "The speech of Booker T. Washington at the Atlanta Exposition, this week, seems to have dwarfed all the other proceedings and the Exposition itself. The sensation that it has caused in the press has never been equalled."

I very soon began receiving all kinds of propositions from lecture bureaus, and editors of magazines and papers, to take the lecture platform, and to write articles. One lecture bureau offered me fifty thousand dollars, or two hundred dollars a night and expenses, if I would place my services at its disposal for a given period. To all these communications I replied that my life-work was at Tuskegee; and that whenever I spoke it must be in the interests of the Tuskegee school and my race, and that I would enter into no arrangements that seemed to place a mere commercial value upon my services.

PLESSY V. FERGUSON

INTRODUCTION: *At issue in* Plessy v. Ferguson *was an 1890 Louisiana law that required passenger trains operating within the state to provide "equal but separate" accommodations for "white and colored races." The Supreme Court upheld the law by a 7–1 vote, in the process putting a stamp of approval on all laws that mandated racial segregation. In his majority opinion, Justice Henry Billings Brown concluded that the Fourteenth Amendment "could not have intended to abolish distinctions based upon color, or to enforce social, as distinguished from political, equality, or a commingling of the two races upon terms unsatisfactory to either."*

Justice John M. Harlan, the lone dissenter, responded that the "arbitrary separation of citizens on the basis of race" was equivalent to imposing a "badge of servitude" on African Americans. He contended that the real intent of the law was not to provide equal accommodations but to compel African Americans "to keep to themselves." This was intolerable because "our Constitution is color-blind, and neither knows nor tolerates classes among citizens." Nevertheless, Plessy *was the law of the land until 1954.*

Plessy v. Ferguson

(May 18, 1896.)

No. 210.

1. An act requiring white and colored persons to be furnished with separate accommodations on railway trains does not violate Const. Amend. 13, abolishing slavery and involuntary servitude. 11 South. 948, affirmed.

2. A state statute requiring railway companies to provide separate accommodations for white and colored persons, and making a passenger insisting on occupying a coach or compartment other than the one set apart for his race liable to fine or imprisonment, does not violate Const. Amend. 14, by a abridging the privileges or immunities of United States citizens, or depriving persons of liberty or property without due process of law, or by denying them the equal protection of the laws. 11 South. 948. affirmed.

Mr. Justice Harlan dissenting.

In Error to the Supreme Court of the State of Louisiana.

This was a petition for writs of prohibition and certiorari originally filed in the supreme court of the state by Plessy, the plaintiff in error, against the Hon. John H. Ferguson, judge of the criminal district court for the parish of Orleans, and setting forth, in substance, the following facts:

That petitioner was a citizen of the United States and a resident of the state of Louisiana, of mixed descent, in the proportion of seven-eighths Caucasian and one-eighth African blood; that the mixture of colored blood was not discernible in him, and that he was entitled to every recognition, right, privilege, and immunity secured to the citizens of the United States of the white race by its constitution and laws; that on June 7, 1892, he engaged and paid for a first-class passage on the East Louisiana Railway, from New Orleans to Covington, in the same state, and thereupon entered a passenger train, and took possession of a vacant seat in a coach where passengers of the white race were accommodated; that such railroad company was incorporated by the laws of Louisiana as a common carrier, and was not authorized to distinguish between citizens according to their race, but, withstanding this, petitioner was required by the conductor, under penalty of ejection from said train and imprisonment, to vacate said coach, and occupy another seat, in a coach assigned by said company for persons not of the white race, and for no other reason than that petitioner was of the colored race; that, upon petitioner's refusal to comply with such order, he was, with the aid of a police officer, forcibly ejected from said coach, and hurried off to, and imprisoned in, the parish jail of New Orleans, and there held to answer a charge made by such officer to the effect that he was guilty of having criminally violated an act of the general assembly of the state, approved July 10, 1890, in such case made and provided.

The petitioner was subsequently brought before the recorder of the city of preliminary examination, and committed for trial to the criminal district court for the parish of Orleans, where an information was filed against him in the matter above set forth, for a violation of the above act, which act the petitioner affirmed to be null and void, because in conflict with the constitution of the United States; that petitioner interposed a plea to such information, based upon the unconstitutionality of the act of the general assembly, to which the district attorney, on behalf of the state, filed a demurrer; that, upon issue being joined upon such demurrer and plea, the court sustained the demurrer, overruled the plea, and ordered petitioner to plead over to the facts set forth in the information, and that, unless the judge of the said court be enjoined by a writ of prohibition from further proceeding in such case, the court will proceed to fine and sentence petitioner to imprisonment, and thus deprive him of his constitutional rights set forth in his said plea, notwithstanding the unconstitutionality of the act under which was being prosecuted; that no appeal lay from such sentence, and petitioner was without relief or remedy except by writs of prohibition and certiorari. Copies of the information and other proceedings in the criminal district court were annexed to the petition as an exhibit.

Upon the filing of this petition, an order was issued upon the respondent to show cause why a writ of prohibition should not issue, and be made perpetual, and further order that the record of the proceedings had in the criminal cause be certified and transmitted to the supreme court.

To this order the respondent made answer, transmitting a certified copy of the proceedings, asserting the constitutionality of the law, and averring that, instead of pleading or admitting that he belonged to the colored race, the said Plessy declined and refused, either by pleading or otherwise, to admit that he was in any sense or in any proportion a colored man.

The case coming on for hearing before the supreme court, that court was of opinion that the law under which the prosecution was had was constitutional and denied the relief prayed for by the petitioner (*Ex parte Plessy*, 45 La. Ann. 80, 11 South. 948); whereupon petitioner prayed for a writ of error from this court, which was allowed by the chief justice of the Supreme Court of Louisiana.

A.W. Tourgee and S. F. Phillips, for plaintiff in error. Alex. Porter Morse, for defendant in error.

Mr. Justice Brown, after stating the facts in the foregoing language, delivered the opinion of the court.

This case turns upon the constitutionality of an act of the general assembly of the state of Louisiana, passed in 1890, providing for separate railway carriages for the white and colored races. Acts 1890, No. 111, p. 152.

The first section of the statute enacts

"that all railway companies in this state, shall provide equal but separate accommodations for the white, and colored races, by providing two or more passenger coaches for each passenger train, or by dividing the passenger coaches by a partition so as to secure separate accommodations: provided, that this section shall not be construed to apply to street railroads. No person or persons shall be permitted to occupy seats in coaches, other than the ones assigned to them, on account of the race they belong to."

By the second section it was enacted

"that the officers of such passenger trains shall have power and are hereby required to assign each passenger to the coach or compartment used for the race to which such passenger belongs; any passenger insisting on going into a coach or compartment to which by race he does not belong, shall be liable to a fine of twenty-five dollars, or in lieu thereof to imprisonment for a period of not more than twenty days in the parish prison, and any officer of any railroad insisting on assigning a passenger to a coach or compartment other than the one set aside for the race to which said passenger belongs, shall be liable to a fine of twenty-five dollars, or in lieu thereof to imprisonment for a period of not more than twenty days in the parish prison; and should any passenger refuse to occupy the coach or compartment to which he or she is assigned by the officer of such railway, said officer shall have power to refuse to carry such passenger on his train, and for such refusal neither he nor the railway company which he represents shall be liable for damages in any of the courts of this state."

The third section provides penalties for the refusal or neglect of the officers, directors, conductors, and employes of railway companies to comply with the act, with a proviso that "nothing in this act shall be construed as applying to nurses attending children of the other race." The fourth section is immaterial.

The information filed in the criminal district court charged, in substance, that Plessy, being a passenger between two stations within the state of Louisiana, was assigned by officers of the company to the coach used for the race to which he belonged, but he insisted upon going into a coach used by the race to which he did not belong. Neither in the information nor plea was his particular race or color averred.

The petition for the writ of prohibition averred that petitioner was seven-eighths Caucasian and one-eighth African blood; that the mixture of colored blood was not discernible in him; and that he was entitled to every right, privilege, and immunity secured to citizens of the United States of the white race; and that, upon such theory, he took possession of a vacant seat in a coach where passengers of the white race were accommodated, and was ordered by the conductor to vacate said coach, and take a seat in another, assigned to persons of the colored race, and, having refused to comply with such demand he was forcibly ejected with the aid of a police officer and imprisoned in the parish jail to answer a charge of having violated the above act.

The constitutionality of this act is attacked upon the ground that it conflicts both with the Thirteenth Amendment of the Constitution, abolishing slavery and the Fourteenth Amendment, which prohibits certain restrictive legislation on the part of the states.

1. That is does not conflict with the Thirteenth Amendment, which abolished slavery and involuntary servitude, except as a punishment for crime, is too clear for argument. Slavery implies involuntary servitude—a state of bondage; the ownership of mankind as a chattel, or, at least, the control of the labor and services of one man for the benefit of another, and the absence of a legal right to the disposal of his own person, property, and services. This amendment was said in the *Slaughter-House Cases*, 16 Wall. 36, to have been intended primarily to abolish slavery, as it had been previously known in this country, and that it equally forbade Mexican peonage or the Chinese coolie trade, when they amounted to slavery or involuntary servitude, and that the use of the word "servitude" was intended to prohibit the use of all forms of involuntary slavery, of whatever class or name. It was intimated, however, in that case, that this amendment was regarded by the statesmen of that day as insufficient to protect the colored race from certain laws which had been enacted in the Southern states, imposing upon the colored race onerous disabilities and burdens, and curtailing their rights in the pursuit of life, liberty, and property to such an extent that their freedom was of little value; and that the Fourteenth Amendment was devised to meet this exigency

So, too, in the *Civil Rights Cases*, 100 U.S. 3, 3 Sup. Ct. 18, it was said that the act of a mere individual, the owner of an inn, a public conveyance or place of amusement, refusing accommodations to colored people, cannot be justly regarded as imposing any badge of slavery or servitude upon the applicant, but only as involving an ordinary civil injury, properly cognizable by the laws of the state, and presumably subject to redress by those laws until the contrary appears. "It would be running the slavery question into the ground," said Mr. Justice Bradley,

"to make it apply to every act of discrimination which a person may see fit to make as to the guests he will entertain, or as to the people he will take into his coach or cab or car, or admit to his concert or theater, or deal with in other matters of intercourse or business."

A statute which implies merely a legal distinction between the white and colored races—a distinction which is found in the color of the two races, and which must always exist so long as white men are distinguished from the other race by color—has no tendency to destroy the legal equality of the two races, or re-establish a state of involuntary servitude. Indeed, we do not understand that the Thirteenth Amendment is strenuously relied upon by the plaintiff in error in this connection.

2. By the Fourteenth Amendment, all persons born or naturalized in the United States, and subject to the jurisdiction thereof, are made citizens of the United States and of the state wherein they reside; and the states are forbidden from making or enforcing any law which shall abridge the privileges or immunities of citizens of the United

States, or shall deprive any person of life, liberty or property without due process of law, or deny to any person within their jurisdiction the equal protection of the laws.

The proper construction of this amendment was first called to the attention of this court in the *Slaughter-House Cases,* 16 Wall. 36, which involved, however, not a question of race, but one of exclusive privileges. The case did not call for any expression of opinion as to the exact rights it was intended to secure to the colored race, but it was said generally that its main purpose was to establish the citizenship of the negro, to give definitions of citizenship of the United States and of the states, and to protect from the hostile legislation of the states the privileges and immunities of citizens of the United States, as distinguished from those of citizens of the states.

The object of the amendment was undoubtedly to enforce the absolute equality of the two races before the law, but, in the nature of things, it could not have been intended to abolish distinctions based upon color, or to enforce social, as distinguished from political, equality, or a commingling of the two races upon terms unsatisfactory to either. Laws permitting, and even requiring, their separation, in places where they are liable to be brought into contact, do not necessarily imply the inferiority of either race to the other, and have been generally, if not universally, recognized as within the competency of the state legislatures in the exercise of their police power. The most common instance of this is connected with the establishment of separate schools for white and colored children, which have been held to be a valid exercise of the legislative power even by courts of states where the political rights of the colored race have been longest and most earnestly enforced.

One of the earliest of these cases is that of *Roberts v. City of Boston,* 5 Cush. 198, in which the supreme judicial court of Massachusetts held that the general school committee of Boston had power to make provision for the instruction of colored children in separate schools established exclusively for them, and to prohibit their attendance upon the other schools. "The great principle," said Chief Justice Shaw,

> "advanced by the learned and eloquent advocate for the plaintiff [Mr. Charles Sumner], is that, by the constitution and laws of Massachusetts, all persons, without distinction of age or sex, birth or color, origin or condition, are equal before the law. * * * But, when this great principle comes to be applied to the actual and various conditions of persons in society, it will not warrant the assertion that men and women are legally clothed with the same civil and political powers, and that

> children and adults are legally to have the same functions and be subject to the same treatment; but only that the rights of all, as they are settled and regulated by law, are equally entitled to the paternal consideration and protection of the law for their maintenance and security."

It was held that the powers of the committee extended to the establishment of separate schools for children of different ages, sexes, and colors, and that they might also establish special schools for poor and neglected children, who have become too old to attend the primary school, and yet not acquired the rudiments of learning, to enable them to enter the ordinary schools. Similar laws have been enacted by Congress under its general power of legislation over the District of Columbia (sections 281–283, 310, 319, Rev. St. D. C.), as well as by the legislatures of many of the states, and have been generally, if not uniformly, sustained by the courts. *State v. McCann* 21 Ohio St. 210; *Lehew v. Brummell* (Mo. Sup.) 15 S. W. 705; *Ward v. Flood,* 48 Cal. 36; *Bertonneau v. Directors of City Schools,*3 Woods, 177 Fed. Cas. No. 1,361; *People v. Gallagher,* 93 N. Y. 438; *Cory v. Carter,* 48 Ind. 337; *Dawson v. Lee,* 83 Ky. 49.

Laws forbidding the intermarriage of the two races may be said in a technical sense to interfere with the freedom of contract, and yet have been universally recognized as within the police power of the state. *State v. Gibson,* 36 Ind. 389.

The distinction between laws interfering with the political equality of the negro and those requiring the separation of two races in schools, theaters, and railway carriages has been frequently drawn by this court. Thus, in *Strauder v. West Virginia,* 100 U.S. 303, it was held that a law of West Virginia limiting to white male persons 21 years of age, and citizens of the state the right to sit upon juries, was a discrimination which implied a legal inferiority in civil society, which lessened the security of the right of the colored race, and was a step towards reducing them to a condition of servility. Indeed, the right of a colored man that in the selection of jurors to pass upon his life, liberty, and property there shall be no exclusion of his race, and no discrimination against them because of color, has been asserted in a number of cases. *Virginia v. Rives,* 100 U. S. 313; *Neal v. Delaware,* 103 U.S. 370; *Bush v. Com,* 107 U.S. 110, 1 Sup. Ct. 625; *Gibson v. Mississippi,* 162 U.S. 565, 16 Sup. Ct 904. So, where the laws of a particular locality or the charter of a particular railway corporation has provided that no person shall be excluded from the cars on account of color, we have held that this meant that persons of color should travel in the same car as white ones, and that the enactment was not satisfied by the company providing cars assigned exclusively to white persons. *Railroad Co. v. Brown,* 17 Wall. 445.

Upon the other hand, where a statute of Louisiana required those engaged in the transportation of passengers among the states to give to all persons traveling within that state, upon vessels employed in that business, equal rights and privileges in all parts of the vessel, without distinction on account of race or color, and subjected to an action for damages the owner of such a vessel who excluded colored passengers on account of their color from the cabins set aside by him for the use of whites, it was held to be, so far as it applied to interstate commerce, unconstitutional and void. *Hall v. De Cuir,* 95 U. S. 485. The court in this case, however, expressly disclaimed that it had anything whatever to do with the statute as a regulation of internal commerce, or affecting anything else that commerce among the states.

In the *Civil Rights Cases,* 109 U. S. 3, 3 Sup. Ct. 18, it was held that an act of Congress entitling all persons within the jurisdiction of the United States to the full and equal enjoyment of the accommodations, advantages, facilities, and privileges of inns, public conveyances, on land or water, theaters, and other places of public amusement, and made applicable to citizens of every race and color, regardless of any previous condition of servitude, was unconstitutional and void, upon the ground that the Fourteenth Amendment was prohibitory upon the states only, and the legislation authorized to be adopted by Congress for enforcing it was not direct legislation on matters respecting which the states were prohibited from making or enforcing certain laws, or doing certain acts, but was corrective legislation, such as might be necessary or proper for counteracting and redressing the effect of such laws or acts. In delivering the opinion of the court, Mr. Justice Bradley observed that the Fourteenth Amendment

"does not invest Congress with power to legislate upon subjects that are within the domain of state legislation, but to provide modes of relief against state legislation or state action of the kind referred to. It does not authorize Congress to create a code of municipal law for the regulation of private rights, but to provide modes to redress against the operation of state laws, and the action of state officers, executive or judicial, when these are subversive of the fundamental rights specified in the amendment. Positive rights and privileges are undoubtedly secured by the Fourteenth Amendment; but they are secured by way of prohibition against state laws and state proceedings affecting those rights and privileges, and by power given to Congress to legislate for the purpose of carrying such prohibition into effect; and such legislation must necessarily be predicated

upon such supposed state laws or state proceedings, and be directed to the correction of their operation and effect."

Much nearer, and, indeed, almost directly in point, is the case of the *Louisville, N. O. & T. Ry Co. v. State,* 133 U.S. 587, 10 Sup. Ct. 348, wherein the railway company was indicted for a violation of a statute of Mississippi, enacting that all railroads carrying passengers should provide equal, but separate, accommodations for the white and colored races, by providing two or more passenger cars for each passenger train, or by dividing the passenger cars by a petition, so as to secure separate accommodations. The case was presented in a different aspect from the one under consideration, inasmuch as it was an indictment against the railway company for failing to provide the separate accommodations, but the question considered was the constitutionality of the law. In that case, the Supreme Court of Mississippi (66 Miss. 662, 6 South. 203) had held that the statute applied solely to commerce within the state, and that being the construction of the state statute by its highest court, was accepted as conclusive. "If it be a matter," said the court (page 591, 133 U.S., and page 348, 10 Sup. Ct.),

"respecting commerce wholly within a state, and not interfering with commerce between the states, then, obviously, there is no violation of the commerce clause of the federal constitution. * * * No question arises under this section as to the power of the state to separate in different compartments interstate passengers, or affect, in any manner, the privileges and rights of such passengers. All that we can consider is whether the state has the power to require that railroad trains within her limits shall have separate accommodations for the two races. That affecting only commerce within the state is no invasion of the power given to Congress by the commerce clause"

A like course of reasoning applies to the case under consideration, since the Supreme Court of Louisiana, in the case of *State v. Judge,* 44 La. Ann. 770, 11 South, 74, held that the statute in question did not apply to interstate passengers, but was confined in its application to passengers traveling exclusively within the borders of the state. The case was decided largely upon the authority of *Louisville, N. O. & T. Ry. Co. v. State,* 66 Miss. 662, 6 South. 203, and affirmed by this court in 133 U.S. 587, 10 Sup. Ct. 348. In the present case no question of interference with interstate commerce can possibly arise, since the East Louisiana Railway appears to have been purely a local line, with both its termini within the state of Louisiana. Similar statutes for the separation of the two races upon public conveyances were held to be constitutional in *Railroad v. Miles,* 55 Pa. St. 209; *Day v. Owen,* 5 Mich. 520; *Railway Co. v. Williams,* 55 Ill. 185; *Railroad Co. v. Wells,* 85 Tenn. 613; 4 S. W. 5; *Railroad Co. v. Benson,* 85 Tenn. 627, 4 S. W. 5; *The Sue,* 22 Fed. 843; *Logwood v. Railroad Co.,* 23 Fed. 318; *McGuinn v. Forbes,* 37 Fed. 639; *People v. King* (N. Y. App.) 18 N. E. 245; *Houck v. Railway Co.,* 38 Fed. 226; *Heard v. Railroad Co.,* 3 Inter St. Commerce Com. R. 111, 1 Inter St. Commerce Com. R. 428.

While we think the enforced separation of the races, as applied to the internal commerce of the state, neither abridges the privileges or immunities of the colored man, deprives him of his property without due process of law, nor denies him the equal protection of the laws, within the meaning of the Fourteenth Amendment, we are not prepared to say that the conductor, in assigning passengers to the coaches according to their race, does not act at his peril, or that the provision of the second section of the act that denies to the passenger compensation in damages for a refusal to receive him into the coach in which he properly belongs is a valid exercise of the legislative power. Indeed, we understand it to be conceded by the state's attorney that such part of the act as exempts from liability the railway company and its officers is unconstitutional. The power to assign to a particular coach obviously implies the power to determine to which race the passenger belongs, as well as the power to determine who, under the laws of the particular state is to be deemed a white, and who a colored person. This question, though indicated in the brief of the plaintiff in error, does not properly arise upon the record in this case, since the only issue made is as to the unconstitutionality of the act, so far as it requires the railway to provide separate accommodations, and the conductor to assign passengers according to their race.

It is claimed by the plaintiff in error that, in any mixed community, the reputation of belonging to the dominant race, in this instance the white race, is "property," in the same sense that a right of action or of inheritance is property. Conceding this to be so, for the purposes of this case, we are unable to see how this statute deprives him of, or in any way affects his right to, such property. If he be a white man, and assigned to a colored coach, he may have his action for damages against the company for being deprived of his so-called "property." Upon the other hand, if he be a colored man, and be so assigned, he has been deprived of no property, since he is not lawfully entitled to the reputation of being a white man.

In this connection, it is also suggested by the learned counsel for the plaintiff in error that the same argument that will justify the state legislature in requiring railways to provide separate accommodations for the two races will also authorize them to require separate cars to be provided for people whose hair is of a certain color, or who are aliens, or who belong to certain nationalities, or to enact laws requiring colored people to walk upon one side of the street, and white people upon the other, or requiring white men's houses to be painted white, and colored men's black, or their vehicles or business signs to be of different colors, upon the theory that one side of the street is as good as the other, or that a house or vehicle of one color is as good as one of another color. The reply to all this is that every exercise of the police power must be reasonable, and extend only to such laws as are enacted in good faith for the promotion of the public good, and not for the annoyance or oppression of a particular class. Thus, in *Yick Wo v. Hopkins,* 118 U. S. 356, 6 Sup. Ct. 1064, it was held by this court that a municipal ordinance of the city of San Francisco: to regulate the carrying on of public laundries within the limits of the municipality, violated the provisions of the constitution of the United States, if it conferred upon the municipal authorities arbitrary power, at their own will, and without regard to discretion, in the legal sense of the term, to give or withhold consent as to persons or places, without regard to the competency of the persons applying or the propriety of the places selected for the carrying on of the business. It was held to be a covert attempt on the part of the municipality to make an arbitrary and unjust discrimination against the Chinese race. While this was the case of a municipal ordinance, a like principle has been held to apply to acts of a state legislature passed in the exercise of the police power. *Railroad Co. v. Husen,* 95 U. S. 465; *Louisville & N. R. Co. v. Kentucky,* 161 U. S. 677, 16 Sup. Ct. 714, and cases cited on page 700, 161 U. S., and page 714, 16 Sup. Ct.; *Daggett v. Hudson,* 43 Ohio St. 548, 3 N. E. 538; *Capen v. Foster,* 12 Pick. 485; *State v. Baker,* 38 Wis. 71; *Monroe v. Collins,* 17 Ohio St. 665; *Hulseman v. Gems,* 41 Pa. St. 396; *Osman v. Riley,* 15 Cal. 48

So far, then, as a conflict with the Fourteenth Amendment is concerned, the case reduces itself to the question whether the statute of Louisiana is a reasonable regulation, and with respect to this there must necessarily be a large discretion on the part of the legislature. In determining the question of reasonableness, it is at liberty to act with reference to the established usages, customs, and traditions of the people, and with a view to the promotion of their comfort, and the preservation of the public peace and good order. Gauged by this standard, we cannot say that a law which authorizes or even requires the separation of the two races in public conveyances is unreasonable, or more obnoxious to the Fourteenth Amendment than the acts of Congress requiring separate schools for colored children in the District of Columbia, the constitutionality of which does not seem to have been questioned, or the corresponding acts of state legislatures.

We consider the underlying fallacy of the plaintiff's argument to consist in the assumption that the enforced separation of the two races stamps the colored race with a badge of inferiority. If this be so, it is not by reason of anything found in the act, but solely because the colored race chooses to put that construction upon it. The argument necessarily assumes that if, as has been more than once the case, and is not unlikely to be so again, the colored race should become the dominant power in the state legislature, and should enact a law in precisely similar terms, it would thereby relegate the white race to an inferior position. We imagine that the white race, at least, would not acquiesce in this assumption. The argument also assumes that social prejudices may be overcome by legislation, and that equal rights cannot be secured to the negro except by an enforced commingling of the two races. We cannot accept this proposition. If the two races are to meet upon terms of social equality, it must be the result of natural affinities, a mutual appreciation of each other's merits, and a voluntary consent of individuals. As was said by the court of appeals of New York in *People v. Gallagher,* 93 N. Y. 438, 448:

> "This end can neither be accomplished nor promoted by laws which conflict with the general sentiment of the community upon whom they are designed to operate. When the government, therefore, has secured to each of its citizens equal rights before the law, and equal opportunities for improvement and progress, it has accomplished the end for which it was organized, and performed all of the functions respecting social advantages with which it is endowed."

Legislation is powerless to eradicate racial instincts, or to abolish distinctions based upon physical differences, and the attempt to do so can only result in accentuating the difficulties of the present situation. If the civil and political rights of both races be equal, one cannot be inferior to the other socially, the constitution of the United States cannot put them upon the same plane.

It is true that the question of the proportion of colored blood necessary to constitute a colored person, as distinguished from a white person, is one upon which there is a difference of opinion in the different states; some holding that any visible admixture of black blood stamps the person as belonging to the colored race (*State v. Chavers,* 5 Jones [N. C.] 1); others, that it depends upon the preponderance of blood (*Gray v. State,* 4 Ohio, 354; *Monroe v. Collins,* 17 Ohio St. 665); and still others, that

the predominance of white blood must only be in the proportion of three-fourths (*People v. Dean,* 14 Mich. 406; *Jones v. Com.,* 80 Va. 544). But these are questions to be determined under the laws of each state, and are not properly put in issue in this case. Under the allegations of his petition, it may undoubtedly become a question of importance whether, under the laws of Louisiana, the petitioner belongs to the white or colored race.

The judgment of the court below is therefore affirmed.

Mr. Justice BREWER did not hear the argument or participate in the decision of this case.

Mr. Justice HARLAN dissenting.

By the Louisiana statute the validity of which is here involved, all railway companies (other than street-railroad companies) carrying passengers in that state are required to have separate but equal accommodations for white and colored persons, "by providing two or more passenger coaches for each passenger train or by dividing the passenger coaches by a partition so as to secure separate accommodations." Under this statute, no colored person is permitted to occupy a seat in a coach assigned to white persons; nor any white person to occupy a seat in a coach assigned to a colored persons. The managers of the railroad are not allowed to exercise any discretion in the premises, buy are required to assign each passenger to some coach or compartment set apart for the exclusive use of his race. If a passenger insists upon going into a coach or compartment not set apart for persons of his race, he is subject to be fined, or to be imprisoned in the parish jail. Penalties are prescribed for the refusal or neglect of the officers, directors, conductors, and employes of railroad companies to comply with the provisions of the act.

Only "nurses attending children of the other race" are excepted from the operation of the statute. No exception is made of colored attendants traveling with adults. A white man is not permitted to have his colored servant with him in the same coach, even if his condition of health requires the constant personal assistance of such servant. If a colored maid insists upon riding in the same coach with a white woman whom she has been employed to serve, and who may need her personal attention while traveling, she is subject to be fined or imprisoned for such an exhibition of zeal in the discharge of duty.

While there may be in Louisiana person of different races who are not citizens of the United States, the words in the act "white and colored races" necessarily include all citizens of the United States of both races residing in the state. So that we have before us a state enactment that compels, under penalties, the separation of the two races in railroad passenger coaches, and makes it a crime for a citizen of either race to enter a coach that has been assigned to citizens of the other race.

Thus, the state regulates the use of a public highway by citizens of the United States solely upon the basis of race.

However apparent the injustice of such legislation may be, we have only to consider whether it is consistent with the Constitution of the United States.

That a railroad is a public highway, and that the corporation which owns or operates it is in the exercise of public functions, is not, at this day, to be disputed. Mr. Justice Nelson, speaking for this court in *New Jersey Steam Nav. Co. v. Merchants' Bank,* 6 How. 344, 382, said that a common carrier was in the exercise "of a sort of public office, and has public duties to perform, from which he should not be permitted to exonerate himself without the assent of the parties concerned." Mr. Justice Strong, delivering the judgment of this court in *Olcott v. Supervisors,* 16 Wall. 678, 694, said

> "That railroads, though constructed by private corporations, and owned by them, are public highways, has been the doctrine of nearly all the courts ever since such conveniences for passage and transportation have had any existence. Very early the question arose whether a state's right of eminent domain could be exercised by a private corporation created for the purpose of constructing a railroad. Clearly, it could not, unless taking land for such a purpose by such an agency is taking land for public use. The right of eminent domain nowhere justifies taking property for a private use. Yet it is a doctrine universally accepted that a state legislature may authorize a private corporation to take land for the construction of such a road, making compensation to the owner. What else does this doctrine mean if not that building a railroad, though it be built by a private corporation, is an act done for a public use?"

So, in *Township of Pine Grove v. Talcott,* 19 Wall. 666, 676: "Though the corporation [a railroad company] was private, its work was public, as much so as if it were to be constructed by the state." So, in *Inhabitants of Worcester v. Western R. Corp.,* 4 Metc. (Mass.) 564:

> "The establishment of that great thoroughfare is regarded as a public work, established by public authority, intended for the public use and benefit the use of which is secured to the whole community, and constitutes, therefore, like a canal, turnpike, or highway, a public easement."

> "It is true that the real and personal property, necessary to the establishment and management of the railroad, is vested in the corporation; but it is in trust for the public."

In respect of civil rights, common to all citizens, the constitution of the United States does not, I think, permit any public authority to know the race of those entitled to be protected in the enjoyment of such rights. Every true man has pride of race, and under appropriate circumstances, when the rights of others, his equals before the law, are not to be affected, it is his privilege to express such pride and take such action based upon it as to him seems proper. But I can deny that any legislative body or judicial tribunal may have regard to the race of citizens when the civil rights of those citizens are involved. Indeed, such legislation as that here in question is inconsistent not only with that equality of rights which pertains to citizenship, national and state, but with the personal liberty enjoyed by every one within the United States.

The Thirteenth Amendment does not permit the withholding or the deprivation of any right necessarily inhering in freedom. It not only struck down the institution of slavery as previously existing in the United States, but it prevents the imposition of any burdens or disabilities that constitute badges of slavery or servitude. It decreed universal civil freedom in this country. This court has so adjudged. But, that amendment having been found inadequate to the protection of the rights of those who had been in slavery, it was followed by the Fourteenth Amendment, which added greatly to the dignity and glory of American citizenship, and to the security of personal liberty, by declaring that

> "all persons born or naturalized in the United States, and subject to the jurisdiction thereof, are citizens of the United States and of the sate wherein they reside,"

and that

> "no state shall make or enforce any law which shall abridge the privileges or immunities of citizens of the United States; not shall any state deprive any person of life, liberty or property without due process of law, nor deny to any person within its jurisdiction the equal protection of the laws."

These two amendments, if enforced according to their true intent and meaning, will protect all the civil rights that pertain to freedom and citizenship. Finally, and to the end that no citizen should be denied, on account of his race, the privilege of participating in the political control of his country, it was declared by the Fifteenth Amendment that "the right of citizens of the United States to vote shall not be denied or abridged by the United States or by any state on account of race, color or previous condition of servitude."

These notable additions to the fundamental law were welcomed by the friends of liberty throughout the world. They removed the race line from our governmental systems. They had, as this court has said, a common purpose, namely, to secure "to a race recently emancipated, a race that through many generations have been held in slavery, all the civil rights that the superior race enjoy." They declared, in legal effect, this court has further said

"that the law in the states shall be the same for the black as for the white; that all persons, whether colored or white, shall stand equal before the laws of the states; and in regard to the colored race, for whose protection the amendment was primarily designed, that no discrimination shall be made against them by law because of their color."

We also said:

"The words of the amendment, is true, are prohibitory, but they contain a necessary implication of a positive immunity or right, most valuable to the colored—race the right to exemption from unfriendly legislation against them distinctively as colored; exemption from legal discriminations, implying inferiority in civil society, lessening the security of their enjoyment of the rights which others enjoy; and discriminations which are steps towards reducing them to the condition of a subject."

It was, consequently, adjudged that a state law that excluded citizens of the colored race from juries, because of their race, however well qualified in other respects to discharge the duties of jurymen, was repugnant to the Fourteenth Amendment. *Strauder v. West Virginia,* 100 U.S. 303, 306, 307; *Virginia v. Rives,* Id. 313; *Ex parte Virginia,* Id. 339: *Neal v. Delaware,* 103 U.S. 370, 386; *Bush v. Com.,* 107 U.S. 110, 116, 1 Sup. Ct. 625. At the present term referring to the previous adjudications, this court declared that

"underlying all of those decisions is the principle that the constitution of the United States, in its present form, forbids, so far as civil and political rights are concerned, discrimination by the general government or the states against any citizen because of his race. All citizens are equal before the law. *Gibson v. State,* 162 U.S. 565, 16 Sup. Ct. 904."

The decisions referred to show the scope of the recent amendments of the constitution. They also show that it is not within the power of a state to prohibit colored citizens, because of their race, from participating as jurors in the administration of justice.

It was said in argument that the statute of Louisiana does not discriminate against either race, but prescribes a rule applicable alike to white and colored citizens. But this argument does not meet the difficulty. Every one knows that the statute in question had its origin in the purpose, not so much to exclude white persons from railroad cars occupied by blacks, as to exclude colored people from coaches occupied by or assigned to white persons. Railroad corporations of Louisiana did not make discrimination among whites in the matter of accommodation for travelers. The thing to accomplish was, under the guise of giving equal accommodation for whites and blacks, to compel the latter to keep to themselves while traveling in railroad passenger coaches. No one would be so wanting in candor as to assert the contrary. The fundamental objection, therefore, to the statute, is that it interferes with the personal freedom of citizens. "Personal liberty," it has been well said, "consists in the power of locomotion, of changing situation, or removing one's person to whatsoever places one's own inclination may direct, without imprisonment or restraint, unless by due course of law." 1. Bl. Comm. *134. If a white man and a black man choose to occupy the same public conveyance on a public highway, it is their right to do so; and no government, proceeding alone on grounds of race, can prevent it without infringing the personal liberty of each.

It is one thing for railroad carriers to furnish, or to be required by law to furnish, equal accommodations for all whom they are under a legal duty to carry. It is quite another thing for government to forbid citizens of the white and black races from traveling in the same public conveyance, and to punish officers of railroad companies for permitting persons of the two races to occupy the same passenger coach. If a state can prescribe, as a rule of civil conduct, that whites and blacks shall not travel as passengers in the same railroad coach, why may it not so regulate the use of the streets of its cities and towns as to compel white citizens to keep on one side of a street, and black citizens to keep on the other? Why may it not, upon like grounds, punish whites and blacks who ride together in street cars or in open vehicles on a public road or street? Why may it not require sheriffs to assign whites to one side of a court room, and blacks to the other? And why may it not also prohibit the commingling of the two races in the galleries of legislative halls or in public assemblages convened for the consideration of the political questions of the day? Furthermore, if this statute of Louisiana is consistent with the personal liberty of citizens, why may not the state require the separation in railroad coaches of native and naturalized citizens of the United States, or of Protestants and Roman Catholics?

The answer given at the argument to these question was that regulations of the kind they suggest would be unreasonable, and could not, therefore, stand before the law. Is it meant that the determination of questions of legislative power depends upon the inquiry whether the statute whose validity is questions is, in the judgment of the courts, a reasonable one, taking all the circumstances into consideration? A statute may be unreasonable merely because a sound public policy forbade its enactment. But I do not understand that the courts have anything to do with the policy or expediency of legislation. A statute may be valid, and yet, upon grounds of public policy, may well be characterized as unreasonable. Mr. Sedgwick correctly states the rule when he says that, the legislative intention being clearly ascertained "the courts have no other duty to perform than to execute the legislative will, without any regard to their views as to the wisdom or justice of the particular enactment." Sedg. St. & Const. Law, 324. There is a dangerous tendency in these latter days to enlarge the functions of the courts, by means of judicial interference with the will of the people as expressed by the legislature. Our institutions have the distinguishing characteristic that the three departments of government are co-ordinate and separate. Each must keep within the limits defined by the constitution. And the courts best discharge their duty by executing the will of the lawmaking power, constitutionally expressed, leaving the results of legislation to be dealt with by the people through their representatives. Statutes must always have a reasonable construction. Sometimes they are to be construed strictly, sometimes literally, in order to carry out the legislative will. But, however construed, the intent of the legislature is to be respected if the particular statute in question is valid, although the courts, looking at the public interests, may conceive the statute to be both unreasonable and impolitic. If the power exists to enact a statute, that ends the matter so far as the courts are concerned. The adjudged cases in which statutes have been held to be void, because unreasonable, are those in which the means employed by the legislature were not at all germane to the end to which the legislature was competent.

The white race deems itself to be the dominant race in this country. And so it is, in prestige, in achievements, in education, in wealth, and in power. So, I doubt not, it will continue to be for all time, if it remains true to its great heritage, and holds fast to the principles of constitutional liberty. But in view of the constitution, in the eye of the law, there is in this country no superior, dominant, ruling class of citizens. There is no caste here. Our constitution is color-blind and neither knows nor tolerates classes among citizens. In respect of civil rights, all citizens are equal before the law. The humblest is the peer of the most powerful. The law regards man as man, and takes no account of his surroundings or of his color when his civil rights as guarantied by the supreme law of the land are involved. It is therefore to be regretted that this high tribunal, the final expositor of the fundamental law of the land, has reached the conclusion that it is competent for a state to regulate the enjoyment by citizens of their civil rights solely upon the basis of race.

In my opinion, the judgment this day rendered will, in time, prove to be quite as pernicious as the decision made by this tribunal in the *Dred Scott Case*.

It was adjudged in that case that the descendants of Africans who were imported into this country, and sold as slaves, were not included nor intended to be included under the word "citizens" in the constitution, and could not claim any of the rights and privileges which that instrument provided for and secured to citizens of the United States; that, at the time of the adoption of the constitution, they were

> "considered as a subordinate and inferior class of beings, who had been subjugated by the dominant race, and, whether emancipated or not, yet remained subject to their authority, and had no rights or privileges but such as those who held the power and the government might choose to grant them." 17 How. 393, 404.

The recent amendments of the constitution, it was supposed, had eradicated these principles from our institutions. But it seems that we have yet, in some of the states, a dominant race—a superior class of citizens—which assumes to regulate the enjoyment of civil rights, common to all citizens, upon the basis of race. The present decision, it may well be apprehended, will not only stimulate aggressions, more or less brutal and irritating, upon the admitted rights of colored citizens, but will encourage the belief that it is possible, by means of state enactments, to defeat the beneficent purposes which the people of the United States had in view when they adopted the recent amendments of the constitution, by one of which the blacks of this country were made citizens of the United States and of the states in which they respectively reside, and whose privileges and immunities, as citizens, the states are forbidden to abridge. Sixty millions of whites are in no danger from the presence here of eight million of blacks. The destinies of the two races, in this country, are indissolubly linked together, and the interests of both require that the common government of all shall not permit the seeds of race hate to be planted under the sanction of law. What can more certainly arouse race hate, what more certainly create and perpetuate a feeling of distrust between these races, than state enactments which, in fact, proceed on the ground that colored citizens are so inferior and degraded that they cannot be allowed to sit in public coaches occupied by white citizens? That, as all will admit, is the real meaning of such legislation as was enacted in Louisiana.

The sure guaranty of the peace and security of each race is the clear, distinct, unconditional recognition by our governments, national and state, of every right that inheres in civil freedom, and of the equality before the law of all citizens of the United States, without regard to race. State enactments regulating the enjoyment of civil rights upon the basis of race, and cunningly devised to defeat legitimate results of the war, under the pretense of recognizing equality of rights, can have no other result than to render permanent peace impossible, and to keep alive a conflict of races, the continuance of which must do harm to all concerned. This question is not met by the suggestion that social equality cannot exist between the white and black races in this country. That argument, if it can be properly regarded as one, is scarcely worthy of consideration; for social equality no more exists between two races when traveling in a passenger coach or a public highway than when members of the same races sit by each other in a street car or in the jury box, or stand or sit with each other in a political assembly, or when they use in common the streets of a city or town, or when they are in the same room for the purpose of having their names placed on the registry of voters, or when they approach the ballot box in order to exercise the high privilege of voting.

There is a race so different from our own that we do not permit those belonging to it to become citizens of the United States. Persons belonging to it are, with few exceptions, absolutely excluded from our country. I allude to the Chinese race. But, by the statute in question, a Chinaman can ride in the same passenger coach with white citizens of the United States, while citizens of the black race in Louisiana, many of whom, perhaps, risked their lives for the preservation of the Union, who are entitled, by law, to participate in the political control of the state and nation, who are not excluded, by law or by reason of their race, from public stations from public stations of any kind, and who have all the legal rights that belong to white citizens, are yet declared to be criminals, liable to imprisonment, if they ride in a public coach occupied by citizens of the white race. It is scarcely just to say that a colored citizen should not object to occupying a public coach assigned to his own race. He does not object, nor, perhaps,

would he object to separate coaches for his race if his rights under the law were recognized. But he does object, and he ought never to cease objecting, that citizens of the white and black races can be adjudged criminals because they sit, or claim the right to sit, in the same public coach on a public highway.

The arbitrary separation of citizens, on the basis of race, while they are on a public highway, is a badge of servitude wholly inconsistent with the civil freedom and the equality before the law established by the constitution. It cannot be justified upon any legal grounds.

If evils will result from the commingling of the two races upon public highways established for the benefit of all, they will be infinitely less than those that will surely come from state legislation regulating the enjoyment of civil rights upon the basis of race. We boast of the freedom enjoyed by our people above all other peoples. But it is difficult to reconcile that boast with a state of the law which, practically, puts the brand of servitude and degradation upon a large class of our fellow citizens—our equals before the law. The thin disguise of "equal" accommodations for passengers in railroad coaches will not mislead any one, nor atone for the wrong this day done.

The result of the whole matter is that while this court has frequently adjudged, and at the present term has recognized the doctrine, that a state cannot, consistently with the constitution of the United States, prevent white and black citizens, having the required qualifications for jury service, from sitting in the same jury box, it is now solemnly held that a state may prohibit white and black citizens from sitting in the same passenger coach on a public highway, or may require that they be separated by a "partition" when in the same passenger coach. May it not now be reasonably expected that astute men of the dominant race, who affect to be disturbed at the possibility that the integrity of the white race may be corrupted, or that its supremacy will be imperiled by contact on public highways with black people, will endeavor to procure statutes requiring white and black jurors to be separated in the jury box by a "partition," and that, upon retiring from the court room to consult as to their verdict, such partition, if it be a movable one, shall be taken to their consultation room, and set up in such was as to prevent black jurors from coming too close to their brother jurors of the white race. If the "partition" used in the court room happens to be stationary, provision could be made for screens with openings through which jurors of the two races could confer as to their verdict without coming into personal contact with each other. I cannot see but that, according to the principles this day announced, such state legislation, although conceived in hostility to, and enacted for the purpose of humiliating, citizens of the United States of a particular race, would be held to be consistent with the constitution.

I do deem it necessary to review the decisions of state courts to which reference was made in argument. Some, and the most important, of them, are wholly inapplicable, because rendered prior to the adoption of the last amendments of the Constitution, when colored people had very few rights which the dominant race felt obliged to respect. Others were made at a time when public opinion, in many localities, was dominated by the institution of slavery; when it would not have been safe to do justice to the black man; and when, so far as the rights of blacks were concerned, race prejudice was, practically, the supreme law of the land. Those decisions cannot be guides in the era introduced by the recent amendments of the supreme law, which established universal civil freedom, gave citizenship to all born or naturalized in the United States, and residing here, obliterated the race line from our systems of governments, national and state, and placed our free institutions upon the broad and sure foundation of the equality of all men before the law.

I am of opinion that the statute of Louisiana is inconsistent with the personal liberty of citizens, white and black, in that state, and hostile to both the spirit and letter of the constitution of the United States. If laws of like character should be enacted in the several states of the Union, the effect would be in the highest degree mischievous. Slavery, as an institution tolerated by law, would, it is true, have disappeared from our country; but there would remain a power in the states, by sinister legislation, to interfere with the full enjoyment of the blessings of freedom, to regulate civil rights, common to all citizens, upon the basis of race, and to place in a condition of legal inferiority a large body of American citizens, now constituting a part of the political community, called the "People of the United States," for whom, and by whom through representatives, our government is administered. Such a system is inconsistent with the guaranty given by the Constitution to each state of a republican form of government, and may be stricken down by congressional action, or by the courts in the discharge of their solemn duty to maintain the supreme law of the land, anything in the constitution or laws of any state to the contrary notwithstanding.

For the reason stated, I am constrained to withhold my assent from the opinion and judgment of the majority.

Mr. Justice Brewer did not hear the argument or participate in the decision of this case.

God is a Negro (Bishop Henry M. Turner, 1898)

▪ ▪ ▪

SOURCE: *Black Nationalism in America.* Edited by John H. Bracey Jr., August Meier, and Elliott Rudwick. Indianapolis: Bobbs-Merrill, 1970, pp. 154–155.

Bishop Turner of the African Methodist Church says, "that God is a Negro." The good Bishop has been represented as one of the ablest men of his race and we thought justly so, for he is not only an intelligent thinker, but upon all subjects connected with his people his reasoning is profound, and in most instances unanswerable, but he is evidently becoming demented if he used the language attributed to him.

—Observer.

The Observer has our thanks for the compliment tendered in respect to our thinking faculties, notwithstanding our demented condition when we understand God to be a Negro. We have as much right biblically and otherwise to believe that God is a Negro, as you buckra or white people have to believe that God is a fine looking, symmetrical and ornamented white man. For the bulk of you and all the fool Negroes of the country believe that God is a white-skinned, blue-eyed, straight-haired, projecting nosed, compressed lipped and finely robed *white* gentleman, sitting upon a throne somewhere in the heavens. Every race of people since time began who have attempted to describe their God by words, or by paintings, or by carvings, or by any other form or figure, have conveyed the idea that the God who made them and shaped their destinies was symbolized in themselves, and why should not the Negro believe that he resembles God as much so as other people? We do not believe that there is any hope for a race of people who do not believe they look like God.

Demented though we be, whenever we reach the conclusion that God, or even that Jesus Christ, while in the flesh, was a white man, we shall hang our gospel trumpet upon the willow and cease to preach.

We had rather be an atheist and believe in no God, or a pantheist and believe that all nature is God, than to believe in the personality of a God, and not to believe that He is a Negro. Blackness is much older than whiteness, for black was here before white, if the Hebrew word, coshach, or chashach, has *any* meaning. We do not believe in the eternity of matter, but we do believe that chaos floated in infinite darkness or blackness millions, billions, quintillions and eons of years before God said, "Let there be light," and that during that time God had no material light Himself and was shrouded in darkness, so far as *human* comprehension is able to grasp the situation.

Yet we are no stickler as to God's color, anyway, but if He has any we would prefer to believe that it is nearer symbolized in the blue sky above us and the blue water of the seas and oceans; but we certainly protest against God being a white man or against God being white *at all;* abstract as this theme must forever remain while we are in the flesh. This is one of the reasons we favor African emigration, or Negro naturalization, wherever we can find a domain, for, as long as we remain among the whites, the Negro will believe that the devil is black and that he (the Negro) favors the devil, and that God is white and that he (the Negro) bears no resemblance to Him, and the effects of such a sentiment is contemptuous and degrading, and one-half of the Negro race will be trying to get white and the other half will spend their days in trying to be white men's scullions in order to please the whites; and the time they should be giving to the study of such things as will dignify and make our race great will be devoted to studying about how unfortunate they are in not being white.

We conclude these remarks by repeating for the information of the Observer what it adjudged us, demented, for *"God is a Negro."*

OF OUR SPIRITUAL STRIVINGS (W. E. B. DU BOIS, 1903)

■ ■ ■

SOURCE: Du Bois, W. E. B. "Of Our Spiritual Strivings." In *The Souls of Black Folk.* 1903. New edition, with introductions by Nathan Hare and Alvin F. Poussaint. New York: The New American Library, 1969, pp. 43–53.

Between me and the other world there is ever an unasked question: unasked by some through feelings of delicacy; by others through the difficulty of rightly framing it. All, nevertheless, flutter round it. They approach me in a half-hesitant sort of way, eye me curiously or compassionately, and then, instead of saying directly, How does it feel to be a problem? they say, I know an excellent colored man in my town; or, I fought at Mechanicsville; or, Do not these Southern outrages make your blood boil? At these I smile, or am interested, or reduce the boiling to a simmer, as the occasion may require. To the real question, How does it feel to be a problem? I answer seldom a word.

And yet, being a problem is a strange experience,—peculiar even for one who has never been anything else, save perhaps in babyhood and in Europe. It is in the early days of rollicking boyhood that the revelation first bursts upon one, all in a day, as it were. I remember well when the shadow swept across me. I was a little thing, away up in the hills of New England, where the dark Housatonic winds between Hoosac and Taghkanic to the sea. In a wee wooden schoolhouse, something put it into the boys' and girls' heads to buy gorgeous visiting-cards—ten cents a package—and exchange. The exchange was merry, till one girl, a tall newcomer, refused my card,—refused it peremptorily, with a glance. Then it dawned upon me with a certain suddenness that I was different from the others; or like, mayhap, in heart and life and longing, but shut out from their world by a vast veil. I had thereafter no desire to tear down that veil, to creep through; I held all beyond it in common contempt, and lived above it in a region of blue sky and great wandering shadows. That sky was bluest when I could beat my mates at examination-time, or beat them at a foot-race, or even beat their stringy heads. Alas, with the years all this fine contempt began to fade; for the words I longed for, and all their dazzling opportunities, were theirs, not mine. But they should not keep these prizes, I said: some, all, I would wrest from them. Just how I would do it I could never decide: by reading law, by healing the sick, by telling the wonderful tales that swam in my head,—some way. With other black boys the strife was not so fiercely sunny: their youth shrunk into tasteless sycophancy, or into silent hatred of the pale world about them and mocking distrust of everything white; or wasted itself in a bitter cry, Why did God make me an outcast and a stranger in mine own house? The shades of the prison-house closed round about us all: walls strait and stubborn to the whitest, but relentlessly narrow, tall, and unscalable to sons of night who must plod darkly on in resignation, or beat unavailing palms against the stone, or steadily, half hopelessly, watch the streak of blue above.

After the Egyptian and Indian, the Greek and Roman, the Teuton and Mongolian, the Negro is a sort of seventh son, born with a veil, and gifted with second-sight in this American world,—a world which yields him no true self-consciousness, but only lets him see himself through the revelation of the other world. It is a peculiar sensation, this double-consciousness, this sense of always looking at one's self through the eyes of others, of measuring one's soul by the tape of a world that looks on in amused contempt and pity. One ever feels his twoness,—an American, a Negro; two souls, two thoughts, two unreconciled strivings; two warring ideals in one dark body, whose dogged strength alone keeps it from being torn asunder.

The history of the American Negro is the history of this strife,—this longing to attain self-conscious manhood, to merge his double self into a better and truer self.

In this merging he wishes neither of the older selves to be lost. He would not Africanize America, for America has too much to teach the world and Africa. He would not bleach his Negro soul in a flood of white Americanism, for he knows that Negro blood has a message for the world. He simply wishes to make it possible for a man to be both a Negro and an American, without being cursed and spit upon by his fellows, without having the doors of Opportunity closed roughly in his face.

This, then, is the end of his striving: to be a coworker in the kingdom of culture, to escape both death and isolation, to husband and use his best powers and his latent genius. These powers of body and mind have in the past been strangely wasted, dispersed, or forgotten. The shadow of a mighty Negro past flits through the tale of Ethiopia the Shadowy and of Egypt the Sphinx. Through history, the powers of single black men flash here and there like falling stars, and die sometimes before the world has rightly gauged their brightness. Here in America, in the few days since Emancipation, the black man's turning hither and thither in hesitant and doubtful striving has often made his very strength to lose effectiveness, to seem like absence of power, like weakness. And yet it is not weakness,—it is the contradiction of double aims. The double-aimed struggle of the black artisan—on the one hand to escape white contempt for a nation of mere hewers of wood and drawers of water, and on the other hand to plough and nail and dig for a poverty-stricken horde—could only result in making him a poor craftsman, for he had but half a heart in either cause. By the poverty and ignorance of his people, the Negro minister or doctor was tempted toward quackery and demagogy; and by the criticism of the other world, toward ideals that made him ashamed of his lowly tasks. The would-be black *savant* was confronted by the paradox that the knowledge his people needed was a twice-told tale to his white neighbors, while the knowledge which would teach the white world was Greek to his own flesh and blood. The innate love of harmony and beauty that set the ruder souls of his people a-dancing and a-singing raised but confusion and doubt in the soul of the black artist; for the beauty revealed to him was the soul-beauty of a race which his larger audience despised, and he could not articulate the message of another people. This waste of double aims, this seeking to satisfy two unreconciled ideals, has wrought sad havoc with the courage and faith and deeds of ten thousand thousand people,—has sent them often wooing false gods and invoking false means of salvation, and at times has even seemed about to make them ashamed of themselves.

Away back in the days of bondage they thought to see in one divine event the end of all doubt and disappointment; few men ever worshipped Freedom with half such unquestioning faith as did the American Negro for two centuries. To him, so far as he thought and dreamed, slavery was indeed the sum of all villainies, the cause of all sorrow, the root of all prejudice; Emancipation was the key to a promised land of sweeter beauty than ever stretched before the eyes of wearied Israelites. In song and exhortation swelled one refrain—Liberty; in his tears and curses the God he implored had Freedom in his right hand. At last it came,—suddenly, fearfully, like a dream. With one wild carnival of blood and passion came the message in his own plaintive cadences:—

"Shout, O children!
Shout, you're free!
For God has bought your liberty!"

Years have passed away since then,—ten, twenty, forty; forty years of national life, forty years of renewal and development, and yet the swarthy spectre sits in its accustomed seat at the Nation's feast. In vain do we cry to this our vastest social problem:—

"Take any shape but that, and my firm nerves
Shall never tremble!"

The Nation has not yet found peace from its sins; the freedman has not yet found in freedom his promised land. Whatever of good may have come in these years of change, the shadow of a deep disappointment rests upon the Negro people,—a disappointment all the more bitter because the unattained ideal was unbounded save by the simple ignorance of a lowly people.

The first decade was merely a prolongation of the vain search for freedom, the boon that seemed ever barely to elude their grasp,—like a tantalizing will-o'-the-wisp, maddening and misleading the headless host. The holocaust of war, the terrors of the Ku-Klux Klan, the lies of carpet-baggers, the disorganization of industry, and the contradictory advice of friends and foes, left the bewildered serf with no new watchword beyond the old cry for freedom. As the time flew, however, he began to grasp a new idea. The ideal flow of liberty demanded for its attainment powerful means, and these the Fifteenth Amendment gave him. The ballot, which before he had looked upon as a visible sign of freedom, he now regarded as the chief means of gaining and perfecting the liberty with which war had partially endowed him. And why not? Had not votes made war and emancipated millions? Had not votes enfranchised the freedmen? Was anything impossible to a power that had done all this? A million black men started with renewed zeal to vote themselves into the kingdom. So the decade flew away, the revolution of 1876 came, and left the half-free serf weary, wondering, but still inspired. Slowly but steadily, in the following years, a new vision began gradually to replace the dream of political power,—a powerful movement, the rise of another ideal to guide the unguided, another pillar of fire by night after a clouded day. It was the ideal of "book-learning"; the curiosity, born of compulsory ignorance, to know and test the power of the cabalistic letters of the white man, the longing to know. Here at last seemed to have been discovered the mountain path to Canaan; longer than the highway of Emancipation and law, steep and rugged, but straight, leading to heights high enough to overlook life.

Up the new path the advance guard toiled, slowly, heavily, doggedly; only those who have watched and guided the faltering feet, the misty minds, the dull understandings, of the dark pupils of these schools know how faithfully, how piteously, this people strove to learn. It was weary work. The old statistician wrote down the inches of progress here and there, noted also where here and there a foot had slipped or some one had fallen. To the tired climbers, the horizon was ever dark, the mists were often cold, the Canaan was always dim and far away. If, however, the vistas disclosed as yet no goal, no resting-place, little but flattery and criticism, the journey at least gave leisure for reflection and self-examination; it changed the child of Emancipation to the youth with dawning self-consciousness, self-realization, self-respect. In those sombre forests of his striving his own soul rose before him, and he saw himself,—darkly as through a veil; and yet he saw in himself some faint revelation of his power, of his mission. He began to have a dim feeling that, to attain his place in the world, he must be himself, and not another. For the first time he sought to analyze the burden he bore upon his back, that dead-weight of social degradation partially masked behind a half-named Negro problem. He felt his poverty; without a cent, without a home, without land, tools, or savings, he had entered into competition with rich, landed, skilled neighbors. To be a poor man is hard, but to be a poor race in a land of dollars is the very bottom of hardships. He felt the weight of his ignorance,—not simply of letters, but of life, of business, of the humanities; the accumulated sloth and shirking and awkwardness of decades and centuries shackled his hands and feet. Nor was his burden all poverty and ignorance. The red stain of bastardy, which two centuries of systematic legal defilement of Negro women had stamped upon his race, meant not only the loss of ancient African chastity, but also the hereditary weight of a mass of corruption from white adulterers, threatening almost the obliteration of the Negro home.

A people thus handicapped ought not to be asked to race with the world, but rather allowed to give all its time and thought to its own social problems. But alas! while so-ciologists gleefully count his bastards and his prostitutes, the very soul of the toiling, sweating black man is darkened by the shadow of a vast despair. Men call the shadow prejudice, and learnedly explain it as the natural defence of culture against barbarism, learning against ignorance, purity against crime, the "higher" against the "lower" races. To which the Negro cries Amen! and swears that to so much of this strange prejudice as is founded on just homage to civilization, culture, righteousness, and progress, he humbly bows and meekly does obeisance. But before that nameless prejudice that leaps beyond all this he stands helpless, dismayed, and well-nigh speechless; before that personal disrespect and mockery, the ridicule and systematic humiliation, the distortion of fact and wanton license of fancy, the cynical ignoring of the better and the boisterous welcoming of the worse, the all-pervading desire to inculcate disdain for everything black, from Toussaint to the devil,—before this there rises a sickening despair that would disarm and discourage any nation save that black host to whom "discouragement" is an unwritten word.

But the facing of so vast a prejudice could not but bring the inevitable self-questioning, self-disparagement, and lowering of ideals which ever accompany repression and breed in an atmosphere of contempt and hate. Whisperings and portents came borne upon the four winds: Lo! we are diseased and dying, cried the dark hosts; we cannot write, our voting is vain; what need of education, since we must always cook and serve? And the Nation echoed and enforced this self-criticism, saying: Be content to be servants, and nothing more; what need of higher culture for half-men? Away with the black man's ballot, by force or fraud,—and behold the suicide of a race! Nevertheless, out of the evil came something of good,—the more careful adjustment of education to real life, the clearer perception of the Negroes' social responsibilities, and the sobering realization of the meaning of progress.

So dawned the time of *Sturm und Drang*: storm and stress to-day rocks our little boat on the mad waters of the world-sea; there is within and without the sound of conflict, the burning of body and rending of soul; inspiration strives with doubt, and faith with vain questionings. The bright ideals of the past,—physical freedom, political power, the training of brains and the training of hands,—all these in turn have waxed and waned, until even the last grows dim and overcast. Are they all wrong,—all false? No, not that, but each alone was over-simple and incomplete,—the dreams of a credulous race-childhood, or the fond imaginings of the other world which does not know and does not want to know our power. To be really true, all these ideas must be melted and welded into one. The training of the schools we need to-day more than ever,—the training of deft hands, quick eyes and ears, and above all the broader, deeper, higher culture of gifted minds and pure hearts. The power of the ballot we need in sheer self-defence,—else what shall save us from a second slavery? Freedom, too, the long-sought, we still seek,—the freedom of life and limb, the freedom to work and think, the freedom to love and aspire. Work, culture, liberty,—all these we need, not singly but together, not successively but together, each growing and aiding each, and all striving toward that vaster ideal that swims before the Negro people, the ideal of human brotherhood, gained through the unifying ideal of Race; the ideal of fostering and developing the traits and talents of the Negro, not in opposition to or contempt for other races, but rather in large conformity to the greater ideals of the American Republic, in order that some day on American soil two world-races may give each to each those characteristics both so sadly lack. We the darker ones come even now not altogether empty-handed: there are to-day no truer exponents of the pure human spirit of the Declaration of Independence than the American Negroes; there is no true American music but the wild sweet melodies of the Negro slave; the American fairy tales and folklore are Indian and African; and, all in all, we black men seem the sole oasis of simple faith and reverence in a dusty desert of dollars and smartness. Will America be poorer if she replace her brutal dyspeptic blundering with light-hearted but determined Negro humility? or her coarse and cruel wit with loving jovial good-humor? or her vulgar music with the soul of the Sorrow Songs?

Merely a concrete test of the underlying principles of the great republic is the Negro Problem, and the spiritual striving of the freedmen's sons is the travail of souls whose burden is almost beyond the measure of their strength, but who bear it in the name of an historic race, in the name of this the land of their fathers' fathers, and in the name of human opportunity.

And now what I have briefly sketched in large outline let me on coming pages tell again in many ways, with loving emphasis and deeper detail, that men may listen to the striving in the souls of black folk.

THE TALENTED TENTH
(W. E. B. DU BOIS, 1903)

▮▮▮

SOURCE: *The Negro Problem: A Series of Articles by Representative American Negroes of Today.* New York: J. Pott & Company, 1903. (This text is available online at <http://douglassarchives.org>.)

The Negro race, like all races, is going to be saved by its exceptional men. The problem of education, then, among Negroes must first of all deal with the Talented Tenth; it is the problem of developing the Best of this race that they may guide the Mass away from the contamination and death of the Worst, in their own and other races. Now the training of men is a difficult and intricate task. Its technique is a matter for educational experts, but its object is for the vision of seers. If we make money the object of man-training, we shall develop money-makers but not necessarily men; if we make technical skill the object of education, we may possess artisans but not, in nature, men. Men we shall have only as we make manhood the object of the work of the schools—intelligence, broad sympathy, knowledge of the world that was and is, and of the relation of men to it—this is the curriculum of that Higher Education which must underlie true life. On this foundation we may build bread winning, skill of hand and quickness of brain, with never a fear lest the child and man mistake the means of living for the object of life. . . .

If this be true—and who can deny it—three tasks lay before me; first to show from the past that the Talented Tenth as they have risen among American Negroes have been worthy of leadership; secondly, to show how these men may be educated and developed; and thirdly, to show their relation to the Negro problem. . . .

From the very first it has, been the educated and intelligent of the Negro people that have led and elevated the mass, and the sole obstacles that nullified and retarded their efforts were slavery and race prejudice; . . .

And so we come to the present—a day of cowardice and vacillation, of strident wide-voiced wrong and faint hearted compromise; of double-faced dallying with Truth and Right. Who are to-day guiding the work of the Negro people? The "exceptions" of course. And yet so sure as this Talented Tenth is pointed out, the blind worshippers of the Average cry out in alarm; "These are exceptions, look here at death, disease and crime—these are the happy rule." Of course they are the rule, because a silly nation made them the rule: Because for three long centuries this people lynched Negroes who dared to be brave, raped black women who dared to be virtuous, crushed dark-hued youth who dared to be ambitious, and encouraged and made to flourish servility and lewdness and apathy. But not even this was able to crush all manhood and chastity and aspiration from black folk. A saving remnant continually survives and persists, continually aspires, continually shows itself in thrift and ability and character. Exceptional it is to be sure, but this is its chiefest promise; it shows the capability of Negro blood, the promise of black men . . . . Is it fair, is it decent, is it Christian to ignore these facts of the Negro problem, to belittle such aspiration, to nullify such leadership and seek to crush these people back into the mass out of which by toil and travail, they and their fathers have raised themselves?

Can the masses of the Negro people be in any possible way more quickly raised than by the effort and example of this aristocracy of talent and character? Was there ever a nation on God's fair earth civilized from the bottom upward? Never; it is, ever was and ever will be from the top downward that culture filters. The Talented Tenth rises and pulls all that are worth the saving up to their vantage ground. This is the history of human progress; . . .

How then shall the leaders of a struggling people be trained and the hands of the risen few strengthened? There can be but one answer: The best and most capable of their youth must be schooled in the colleges and universities of the land. . . . All men cannot go to college but some men must; every isolated group or nation must have its yeast, must have for the talented few centers of training where men are not so mystified and befuddled by the hard and necessary toil of earning a living, as to have no aims higher than their bellies, and no God greater than Gold. This is true training, and thus in the beginning were the favored sons of the freedom trained. Out of the colleges of the North came, after the blood of war, Ware, Cravath, Chase, Andrews, Bumstead and Spence to build the foundations of knowledge and civilization in the black South. Where ought they to have begun to build? At the bottom, of course, quibbles the mole with his eyes in the earth. Aye! truly at the bottom, at the very bottom; at the bottom of knowledge, down in the very depth of knowledge there where the roots of justice strike into the lowest soil of Truth. And so they did begin; they founded colleges, and up from the colleges shot normal schools, and out from the normal schools went teachers, and around the normal teachers clustered other teachers to teach the public schools; the college trained in Greek and Latin and mathematics, 2,000 men; and these men trained full 50,000 others in morals and manners, and they in turn taught thrift and the alphabet to nine millions of men who to-day hold $300,000,000 of property. If was a miracle—the most wonderful peace-battle of the 19th century, and yet to-day men smile at it, and in fine superiority tell us that it was all a strange mistake; that a proper way to found a system of education is first to gather the children and buy them spelling books and hoes; afterward men may look about for teachers, if haply they may find them; or again they would teach men Work, but as for Life—why, what has Work to do with Life, they ask vacantly. . . .

These figures illustrate vividly the function of the college-bred Negro. He is, as he ought to be, the group leader, the man who sets the ideals of the community where he lives, directs its thoughts and heads its social movements. It need hardly be argued that the Negro people need social leadership more than most groups; that they have no traditions to fall back upon, no long established customs, no strong family ties, no well defined social classes. All these things must be slowly and painfully evolved. The preacher was, even before the war, the group leader of the Negroes, and the church their greatest social institution. Naturally this preacher was ignorant and often immoral, and the problem of replacing the older type by better educated men has been a difficult one. Both by direct work and by direct influence on other preachers, and on congregations, the college-bred preacher has an opportunity for reformatory work and moral inspiration, the value of which cannot be overestimated.

It has, however, been in the furnishing of teachers that the Negro college has found its peculiar function. Few persons realize how vast a work, how mighty a revolution has been thus accomplished. To furnish five millions and more of ignorant people with teachers of their own race and blood, in one generation, was not only a very difficult undertaking, but a very important one, in that it placed before the eyes of almost every Negro child an attainable ideal. It brought the masses of the blacks in contact with modern civilization, made black men the leaders of their communities and trainers of the new generation. In this work college-bred Negroes were first teachers, and then teachers of teachers. And here it is that the broad culture of college work has been of peculiar value. Knowledge of life and its wider meaning, has been the point of the Negro's deepest ignorance, and the sending out of teachers whose training has not been simply for bread winning, but also for human culture, has been of inestimable value in the training of these men. . . .

The main question, so far as the Southern Negro is concerned, is: What under the present circumstance, must a system of education do in order to raise the Negro as quickly as possible in the scale of civilization? The answer to this question seems to me clear: It must strengthen the Negro's character, increase his knowledge and teach him to earn a living. Now it goes without saying, that it is hard to do all these things simultaneously or suddenly, and that at the same time it will not do to give all the attention to one and neglect the others; we could give black boys trades, but that alone will not civilize a race of ex-slaves; we might simply increase their knowledge of the world, but this would not necessarily make them wish to use this knowledge honestly; we might seek to strengthen character and purpose, but to what end if this people have nothing to eat or to wear? . . . . If then we start out to train an ignorant and unskilled people with a heritage of bad habits, our system of training must set before itself two great aims—the one dealing with knowledge and character, the other part seeking to give the child the technical knowledge necessary for him to earn a living under the present circumstances. These objects are accomplished in part by the opening of the common schools on the one, and of the industrial schools on the other. But only in part, for there must also be trained those who are to teach these schools—men and women of knowledge and culture and technical skill who understand modern civilization, and have the training and aptitude to impart it to the children under them. There must be teachers, and teachers of teachers, and to attempt to establish any sort of a system of common and industrial school training, without *first* (and I say *first* advisedly) without *first* providing for the higher training of the very best teachers, is simply throwing your money to the winds. . . . Nothing, in these latter days, has so dampened the faith of thinking Negroes in recent educational movements, as the fact that such movements have been accompanied by ridicule and denouncement and decrying of those very institutions of higher training which made the Negro public school possible, and make Negro industrial schools thinkable . . . .

I would not deny, or for a moment seem to deny, the paramount necessity of teaching the Negro to work, and to work steadily and skillfully; or seem to depreciate in the slightest degree the important part industrial schools must play in the accomplishment of these ends, but I *do* say, and insist upon it, that it is industrialism drunk, with its vision of success, to imagine that its own work can be accomplished without providing for the training of broadly cultured men and women to teach its own teachers, and to teach the teachers of the public schools.

But I have already said that human education is not simply a matter of schools; it is much more a matter of family and group life—the training of one's home, of one's daily companions, of one's social class. Now the black boy of the South moves in a black world—a world with its own leaders, its own thoughts, its own ideals. In this world he gets by far the larger part of his life training, and through the eyes of this dark world he peers into the veiled world beyond. Who guides and determines the education which he receives in his world? His teachers here are the group-leaders of the Negro people—the physicians and clergymen, the trained fathers and mothers, the influential and forceful men about him of all kinds; here it is, if at all, that all culture of the surrounding world trickles through and is handed on by the graduates of the higher schools. Can such culture training of group leaders be neglected? Can we afford to ignore it? . . . You have no choice; either you

must help furnish this race from within its own ranks with thoughtful men of trained leadership, or you must suffer the evil consequences of a headless misguided rabble.

I am an earnest advocate of manual training and trade teaching for black boys, and for white boys, too. I believe that next to the founding of Negro colleges the most valuable addition to Negro education since the war, has been industrial training for black boys. Nevertheless, I insist that the object of all true education is not to make men carpenters, it is to make carpenters men; there are two means of making the carpenter a man, each equally important: the first is to give the group and community in which he works, liberally trained teachers and leaders to teach him and his family what life means; the second is to give him sufficient intelligence and technical skill to make him an efficient workman; the first object demands the Negro college and college-bred men—not a quantity of such colleges, but a few of excellent quality; not too many college-bred men, but enough to leaven the lump, to inspire the masses, to raise the Talented Tenth to leadership; the second object demands a good system of common schools, well-taught, conventionally located and properly equipped . . . .

Further than this, after being provided with group leaders of civilization, and a foundation of intelligence in the public schools, the carpenter, in order to be a man, needs technical skill. This calls for trade schools. . . .

Even at this point, however, the difficulties were not surmounted. In the first place modern industry has taken great strides since the war, and the teaching of trades is no longer a simple matter. Machinery and long processes of work have greatly changed the work of the carpenter, the ironworker and the shoemaker. A really efficient workman must be to-day an intelligent man who has had good technical training in addition to thorough common school, and perhaps even higher training. . . .

Thus, again, in the manning of trade schools and manual training schools we are thrown back upon the higher training as its source and chief support. There was a time when any aged and worn-out carpenter could teach in a trade school. But not so to-day. Indeed the demand for college-bred men by a school like Tuskegee, ought to make Mr. Booker T. Washington the firmest friend of higher training. Here he has as helpers the son of a Negro senator, trained in Greek and the humanities, and graduated at Harvard; the son of a Negro congressman and lawyer, trained in Latin and mathematics, and graduated at Oberlin; he has as his wife, a woman who read Virgil and Homer in the same class room with me; he has as college chaplain, a classical graduate of Atlanta University; as teacher of science, a graduate of Fisk; as teacher of history, a graduate of Smith,—indeed some thirty of his chief teachers are college graduates, and instead of studying French grammars in the midst of weeds, or buying pianos for dirty cabins, they are at Mr. Washington's right hand helping him in a noble work. And yet one of the effects of Mr. Washington's propaganda has been to throw doubt upon the expediency of such training for Negroes, as these persons have had.

Men of America, the problem is plain before you. Here is a race transplanted through the criminal foolishness of your fathers. Whether you like it or not the millions are here, and here they will remain. If you do not lift them up, they will pull you down. Education and work are the levers to uplift a people. Work alone will not do it unless inspired by the right ideals and guided by intelligence. Education must not simply teach work—it must teach Life. The Talented Tenth of the Negro race must be made leaders of thought and missionaries of culture among their people. No others can do this and Negro colleges must train men for it. The Negro race, like all other races, is going to be saved by its exceptional men.

THE NIAGARA MOVEMENT: DECLARATION OF PRINCIPLES (1905)

▮▮▮

SOURCE: *Black Protest Thought in the Twentieth Century.* Edited by August Meier, Elliott Rudwick, and Francis L. Broderick. 2d ed. Indianapolis: Bobbs-Merrill, 1971, pp. 59–62.

INTRODUCTION: *In 1905, W. E. B. Du Bois assembled a group of black civil rights advocates to demand full civil liberties for African Americans. With the manifesto that is reprinted here, the group provided vocal opposition to the accommodationist philosophy of Booker T. Washington, who argued for a gradual attainment of social equality through industry and economic advancement. Generally considered the first significant African-American protest movement of the twentieth century, the Niagara Movement convened near Niagara Falls in Canada after conference members met with opposition in Buffalo, New York.*

The members of the conference, known as the Niagara Movement, assembled in annual meeting at Buffalo, July 11th, 12th and 13th, 1905, congratulate the Negro-Americans on certain undoubted evidences of progress in the last decade, particularly the increase of intelligence, the buying of property, the checking of crime, and uplift in home life, the advance in literature and art, and the demonstration of constructive and executive ability in the conduct of great religious, economic and educational institutions.

At the same time, we believe that this class of American citizens should protest emphatically and continually against the curtailment of their political rights. We believe in manhood suffrage; we believe that no man is so good, intelligent or wealthy as to be entrusted wholly with the welfare of his neighbor.

We believe also in protest against the curtailment of our civil rights. All American citizens have the right to equal treatment in places of public accommodation according to their behavior and deserts.

We especially complain against the denial of equal opportunities to us in economic life; in the rural districts of the South this I amounts to peonage and virtual slavery; all over the South it tends to crush labor and small business enterprises; and every-where American prejudice, helped often by iniquitous laws, is making it more difficult for Negro-Americans to earn a decent living.

Common school education should be free to all American children and compulsory. High school training should be adequately provided for all, and college training should be the monopoly of I no class or race in any section of our common country. We believe that, in defense of our own institutions, the United States should aid common school education, particularly in the South, and we especially recommend concerted agitation to this end. We urge an increase in public high school facilities in the South, where Negro-Americans are almost wholly without such provisions. We favor well-equipped trade and technical schools for the training of artisans, and the need of adequate and liberal endowment for a few institutions of higher education must be patent to sincere well-wishers of the race.

We demand upright judges in courts, juries selected without discrimination on account of color and the same measure of punishment and the same efforts at reformation for black as for white offenders. We need orphanages and farm schools for dependent children, juvenile reformatories for delinquents, and the abolition of the dehumanizing convict-lease system.

We note with alarm the evident retrogression in this land of sound public opinion on the subject of manhood rights, republican government and human brotherhood, and we pray God that this nation will not degenerate into a mob of boasters and oppressors, but rather will return to the faith of the fathers, that all men were created free and equal, with certain unalienable rights.

We plead for health—for an opportunity to live in decent houses and localities, for a chance to rear our children in physical and moral cleanliness.

We hold up for public execration the conduct of two opposite classes of men: The practice among employers of importing ignorant Negro-American laborers in emergencies, and then affording them neither protection nor permanent employment; and the practice of labor unions in proscribing and boycotting and oppressing thousands of their fellow-toilers, simply because they are black. These methods have accentuated and will accentuate the war of labor and capital, and they are disgraceful to both sides.

We refuse to allow the impression to remain that the Negro-American assents to inferiority, is submissive under oppression and apologetic before insults. Through helplessness we may submit, but the voice of protest of ten million Americans must never cease to assail the ears of their fellows, so long as America is unjust.

Any discrimination based simply on race or color is barbarous, we care not how hallowed it be by custom, expediency, or prejudice. Differences made on account of ignorance, immorality, or disease are legitimate methods of fighting evil, and against them we have no word of protest; but discrimination based simply and solely on physical peculiarities, place of birth, color of skin, are relics of that unreasoning human savagery of which the world is and ought to be thoroughly ashamed.

We protest against the "Jim Crow" car, since its effect is and must be, to make us pay first-class fare for third-class accommodations, render us open to insults and discomfort and to crucify wantonly our manhood, womanhood and self-respect.

We regret that this nation has never seen fit adequately to reward the black soldiers who, in its five wars, have defended their country with their blood, and *yet* have been systematically denied the promotions which their abilities deserve. And we regard as unjust, the exclusion of black boys from the military and navy training schools.

We urge upon Congress the enactment of appropriate legislation for securing the proper enforcement of those articles of freedom, the thirteenth, fourteenth and fifteenth amendments of the Constitution of the United States.

We repudiate the monstrous doctrine that the oppressor should be the sole authority as to the rights of the oppressed.

The Negro race in America, stolen, ravished and degraded, struggling up through difficulties and oppression, needs sympathy and receives criticism; needs help and is given hindrance, needs protection and is given mob-violence, needs justice and is given charity, needs leadership and is given cowardice and apology, needs bread and is given a stone. This nation will never stand justified before God until these things are changed.

Especially are we surprised and astonished at the recent attitude of the church of Christ—on the increase of a desire to bow to racial prejudice, to narrow the bounds of human brotherhood, and to segregate black men in some outer sanctuary. This is wrong, unchristian and disgraceful to the twentieth century civilization.

Of the above grievances we do not hesitate to complain, and to complain loudly and insistently. To ignore, overlook, or apologize for these wrongs is to prove ourselves unworthy of freedom. Persistent manly agitation is the way to liberty, and toward this goal the Niagara Movement has started and asks the cooperation of all men of all races.

At the same time we want to acknowledge with deep thankfulness the help of our fellowmen from the abolitionist down to those who to-day still stand for equal opportunity and who have given and still give of their wealth and of their poverty for our advancement.

And while we are demanding, and ought to demand, and will continue to demand the rights enumerated above, God forbid that we should ever forget to urge corresponding duties upon our people:

—The duty to vote.

—The duty to respect the rights of others.

—The duty to work.

—The duty to obey the laws.

—The duty to be clean and orderly.

—The duty to send our children to school.

—The duty to respect ourselves, even as we respect others.

This statement, complaint and prayer we submit to the American people, and Almighty God.

Poems of the Harlem Renaissance (1919–1931)

If We Must Die (Claude McKay, 1919)

SOURCE: Johnson, James Weldon, ed. *The Book of American Negro Poetry*. New York: Harcourt, Brace & World, 1922.

If we must die—let it not be like hogs
Hunted and penned in an inglorious spot,
While round us bark the mad and hungry dogs,
Making their mock at our accursed lot.
If we must die—oh, let us nobly die,

So that our precious blood may not be shed
In vain; then even the monsters we defy
Shall be constrained to honor us though dead!
Oh, Kinsmen! We must meet the common foe;
Though far outnumbered, let us show us brave,
And for their thousand blows deal one deathblow!
What though before us lies the open grave?
Like men we'll face the murderous, cowardly pack,
Pressed to the wall, dying, but fighting back!

The Negro Speaks of Rivers (Langston Hughes, 1921)

> SOURCE: Hughes, Langston. *Collected Poems.* New York: Alfred A. Knopf, 1994.

I've known rivers:
I've known rivers ancient as the world and older than
  the flow
of human blood in human veins.

My soul has grown deep like the rivers.

I bathed in the Euphrates when dawns were young.
I built my hut near the Congo and it lulled me to sleep.
I looked upon the Nile and raised the pyramids above
  it.
I heard the singing of the Mississippi when Abe Lincoln
  went
down to New Orleans, and I've seen its muddy bosom
  turn
all golden in the sunset.

I've known rivers:
Ancient, dusky rivers.

My soul has grown deep like rivers.

Heritage (Countee Cullen, 1925)

> SOURCE: Cullen, Countee. *Color.* New York: Harper & Bros, 1925.

> —For Harold Jackman

What is Africa to me:
Copper sun or scarlet sea,
Jungle star or jungle track,
Strong bronzed men, or regal black
Women from whose loins I sprang
When the birds of Eden sang?
One three centuries removed
From the scenes his fathers loved,
Spicy grove, cinnamon tree,
What is Africa to me?

So I lie, who all day long
Want no sound except the song
Sung by wild barbaric birds
Goading massive jungle herds,
Juggernauts of flesh that pass

Trampling tall defiant grass
Where young forest lovers lie,
Plighting troth beneath the sky.
So I lie, who always hear,
Though I cram against my ear
Both my thumbs, and keep them there,
Great drums throbbing through the air.
So I lie, whose fount of pride,
Dear distress, and joy allied,
Is my somber flesh and skin,
With the dark blood dammed within
Like great pulsing tides of wine
That, I fear, must burst the fine
Channels of the chafing net
Where they surge and foam and fret.

Africa? A book one thumbs
Listlessly, till slumber comes.
Unremembered are her bats
Circling through the night, her cats
Crouching in the river reeds,
Stalking gentle flesh that feeds
By the river brink; no more
Does the bugle-throated roar
Cry that monarch claws have leapt
From the scabbards where they slept.
Silver snakes that once a year
Doff the lovely coats you wear,
Seek no covert in your fear
Lest a mortal eye should see
What's your nakedness to me?
Here no leprous flowers rear
Fierce corollas in the air;
Here no bodies sleek and wet,
Dripping mingled rain and sweat,
Tread the savage measures of
Jungle boys and girls in love.
What is last year's snow to me,
Last year's anything? The tree
Budding yearly must forget
How its past arose or set—
Bough and blossom, flower, fruit,
Even what shy bird with mute
Wonder at her travail there,
Meekly labored in its hair.
One three centuries removed
From the scenes his fathers loved,
Spicy grove, cinnamon tree,
What is Africa to me?
So I lie, who find no peace
Night or day, no slight release
From the unremittent beat
Made by cruel padded feet

Walking through my body's street.
Up and down they go, and back,
Treading out a jungle track.
So I lie, who never quite
Safely sleep from rain at night—
I can never rest at all
When the rain begins to fall;
Like a soul gone mad with pain
I must match its weird refrain;
Ever must I twist and squirm,
Writhing like a baited worm,
While its primal measures drip
Through my body, crying, "Strip!
Doff this new exuberance.
Come and dance the Lover's Dance!"
In an old remembered way
Rain works on me night and day.
Quaint, outlandish heathen gods
Black men fashion out of rods,
Clay, and brittle bits of stone,
In a likeness like their own,
My conversion came high-priced;
I belong to Jesus Christ,
Preacher of Humility;
Heathen gods are naught to me.
Father, Son, and Holy Ghost,
So I make an idle boast;
Jesus of the twice-turned cheek,
Lamb of God, although I speak
With my mouth thus, in my heart
Do I play a double part.
Ever at Thy glowing altar
Must my heart grow sick and falter,
Wishing He I served were black,
Thinking then it would not lack
Precedent of pain to guide it,
Let who would or might deride it;
Surely then this flesh would know
Yours had borne a kindred woe.
Lord, I fashion dark gods, too,
Daring even to give You
Dark despairing features where,
Crowned with dark rebellious hair,
Patience wavers just so much as
Mortal grief compels, while touches
Quick and hot, of anger, rise
To smitten cheek and weary eyes.
Lord, forgive me if my need
Sometimes shapes a human creed.
All day long and all night through,
One thing only must I do:
Quench my pride and cool my blood,

Lest I perish in the flood,
Lest a hidden ember set
Timber that I thought was wet
Burning like the dryest fax,
Melting like the merest wax,
Lest the grave restore its dead.
Not yet has my heart or head
In the least way realized
They and I are civilized.

Strong Men (Sterling Brown, 1931)

SOURCE: Johnson, James Weldon, ed. *The Poetry of Black America: Anthology of the Twentieth Century.* New York: Harper & Row, 1973.

They dragged you from homeland,
They chained you in coffles,
They huddled you spoon-fashion in filthy hatches,
They sold you to give a few gentlemen ease.

They broke you in like oxen, They scourged you,
They branded you,
They made your women breeders,
They swelled your numbers with bastards. . . .
They taught you the religion they disgraced.

You sang:

> *Keep a-inchin' along*
> *Lak a po' inch worm. . . .*

You sang:

> *Bye and bye*
> *I'm gonna lay down dis heaby load. . .*

You sang:

> *Walk togedder, chillen,*
> *Dontcha git weary. . . .*

>> *The strong men keep a-comin' on*
>> *The strong men git stronger.*

They point with pride to the roads you built for them
They ride in comfort over the rails you laid for them
They put hammers in your hands
And said—Drive so much before sundown.

You sang:

> *Ain't no hammah*
> *In dis lan',*
> *Strikes lak mine, bebby,*
> *Strikes lak mine.*

They cooped you in their kitchens,
They penned you in their factories,
They gave you the jobs that they were too good for,
They tried to guarantee happiness to themselves
By shunting dirt and misery to you.

You sang:

> *Me an' muh baby gonna shine, shine*
> *Me an' muh baby gonna shine.*

The strong men keep a-comin' on
The strong men git stronger. . . .

They bought off some of your leaders
You stumbled, as blind men will. . . .
They coaxed you, unwontedly soft voiced. . . .
You followed a way.
Then laughed as usual.
They heard the laugh and wondered;
Uncomfortable;
Unadmitting a deeper terror. . . .
     The strong men keep a-comin' on
     Gittin' stronger. . . .

What, from the slums
Where they have hemmed you,
What, from the tiny huts
They could not keep from you—
What reaches them
Making them ill at ease, fearful?
Today they shout prohibition at you
"Thou shalt not this."
"Thou shalt not that."
"Reserved for whites only"
You laugh.

One thing they cannot prohibit —
     The strong men . . . coming on
     The strong men gittin' stronger.
     Strong men. . .
     Stronger. . . .

OUR WOMEN GETTING INTO THE LARGER LIFE (AMY JACQUES GARVEY, C. 1925)

▪▪▪

SOURCE: Guy-Sheftall, Beverly. *Words of Fire: An Anthology of African-American Feminist Thought.* New York: The New Press, 1995, pp. 91–92.

The worldwide movement for the enlargement of woman's sphere of usefulness is one of the most remarkable of the ages. In all countries and in all ages, men have arrogated to themselves the prerogative of regulating not only the domestic, but also the civic and economic life of women. In many countries, women were subject entirely to the whims and legislation of men. It is that way now in most Asiatic countries and among some of the tribes in Africa.

The recent upheaval in Turkey has carried with it condemnation of harem relations and the sanction of the family life as it has developed in Christian countries. Madam Kemal is the leader of the Turkish women for larger freedom in the ordering of their lives, but the innovation, which is bound to work for the betterment of men as well as women as the harem life is a blight on womanhood which degrades manhood as well, could only have been accomplished by the separation of Church and State, the Sultanate and the Caliphate, which amounts to negating the hitherto predominating influence of the Mohammedan religion in the affairs of State as of Church. However far the innovation will extend to other Moslem countries, and what influence, if any, it will have on the domestic life of the people of Asia and Africa, where the Mohammedan religion is strong, remains to be seen.

In Europe, average womanhood has been held at a very low valuation until it got into the recently developed currents of modern innovation, and the average still remains low, peasant life for the man and the woman and their children being of the lowest and hardest. Only in Great Britain has the movement for the larger and better life for women, by allowing them reasonable voice in making and enforcing the laws, made any appreciable headway.

The United States has gone further than any other nation in giving woman a share in making and enforcing the laws and in regulating her economic life to her advantage and not entirely to the advantage of man. She is now given an equal part in political matters, and she is allowed a freedom in earning and controlling her earnings, which is a great improvement upon the former of old things. In social and personal matters, the American woman has attained to an independence and freedom which it will take centuries for the women of other nations to attain to.

Negro women of the United States share equally in the larger life which has come to women of other race groups, and she has met every test in the home, in bread winning, in church and social upbuilding, in charitable uplift work, and in the school room which could have been expected of her reasonably. She has yet to develop as active an interest in political affairs as the women of other race groups, but she is bound to grow in this as in other matters in which her interests are involved.

The women of the Universal Negro Improvement Association have shown an interest and a helpfulness so far-flung as to make it doubtful if the organization could have reached the high point of strength and effectiveness it has without them. To take woman and her sympathies and work out of the association would be like taking the wife out of the home of the husband. The women of the association are a tower of strength. They know it and glory in the fact, and their men are proud of them, and justly. The success of the Negro race thus far has been largely due to the sympathy and support which our women have given to the cause.

Our women are getting into the larger life, which has the womanhood of the world in its sweep. We are sure they will be equal to all of the demands made upon them in the future as in the past, and the demands are going to increase in volume and importance as we go along. It stands to reason.

Black Skin, White Masks (Frantz Fanon, excerpts, 1952)

—■—■—■—

SOURCE: Bolland, O. Nigel, ed. *The Birth of Caribbean Civilization: A Century of Ideas about Culture and Identity, Nation and Society.* Kingston: Ian Randle, 2004, pp. 228–235.

INTRODUCTION: *Born in Martinique in 1925, Fanon journeyed to France to study medicine at the age of 22. He became a psychiatrist, later drawing on the experiences of his youth in the Caribbean to formulate two ground-breaking analyses of the black experience in the colonial world:* Peau Noire, Masques Blancs *(Black Skin, White Masks), 1952, and* Les damnés de la terre *(The Wretched of the Earth), 1961.*

I propose nothing short of the liberation of the man of color from himself. We shall go very slowly, for there are two camps: the white and the black. . . .

We shall have no mercy for the former governors, the former missionaries. To us, the man who adores the Negro is as "sick" as the man who abominates him.

Conversely, the black man who wants to turn his race white is as miserable as he who preaches hatred for the whites. . . .

The white man is sealed in his whiteness.

The black man in his blackness. . . .

Concern with the elimination of a vicious circle has been the only guide-line for my efforts.

There is a fact: White men consider themselves superior to black men.

There is another fact: Black men want to prove to white men, at all costs, the richness of their thought, the equal value of their intellect.

How do we extricate ourselves? . . .

The analysis that I am undertaking is psychological. In spite of this it is apparent to me that the effective disa-

lienation of the black man entails an immediate recognition of social and economic realities. If there is an inferiority complex, it is the outcome of a double process:

–primarily, economic;

–subsequently, the internalization—or, better, the epidermalization—of this inferiority. . . .

It will be seen that the black man's alienation is not an individual question . . .

The black man has two dimensions. One with his fellows, the other with the white man. A Negro behaves differently with a white man and with another Negro. That this self-division is a direct result of colonist subjugation is beyond question. . . .

Every colonized people—in other words, every people in whose soul an inferiority complex has been created by the death and burial of its local cultural originality—finds itself face to face with the language of the civilizing nation; that is, with the culture of the mother country. . . .

In any group of young men in the Antilles, the one who expresses himself well, who has mastered the language, is inordinately feared; keep an eye on that one, he is almost white. In France one says, "He talks like a book". In Martinique, "He talks like a white man" . . . .

And the fact that the newly returned Negro adopts a language different from that of the group into which he was born is evidence of a dislocation, a separation. . . .

In every country of the world there are climbers, "the ones who forget who they are", and, in contrast to them, "the ones who remember where they came from". The Antilles Negro who goes home from France expresses himself in dialect if he wants to make it plain that nothing has changed. . . .

To speak a language is to take on a world, a culture. The Antilles Negro who wants to be white will be the whiter as he gains greater mastery of the cultural tool that language is. . . .

Historically, it must be understood that the Negro wants to speak French because it is the key that can open doors which were still barred to him fifty years ago. . . .

There was a myth of the Negro that had to be destroyed at all costs. . . .

I was hated, despised, detested, not by the neighbor across the street or my cousin on my mother's side, but by an entire race. . . .

A feeling of inferiority? No, a feeling of nonexistence. Sin is Negro as virtue is white. All those white men in a group, guns in their hands, cannot be wrong. I am guilty. I do not know of what, but I know that I am no good. . . .

The Negro is a toy in the white man's hands; so, in order to shatter the hellish cycle, he explodes. . . .

Nevertheless . . . I feel in myself a soul as immense as the world, truly a soul as deep as the deepest of rivers, my chest has the power to expand without limit. I am a master and I am advised to adopt the humility of the cripple. . . .

The black schoolboy in the Antilles, who in his lessons is forever talking about "our ancestors, the Gauls," identifies himself with the explorer, the bringer of civilisation, the white man who carries truth to savages—an all-white truth. There is identification—that is, the young Negro subjectively adopts a white man's attitude. He invests the hero, who is white, with all his own aggression. . . .

Little by little, one can observe in the young Antillean the formation and crystallization of an attitude and a way of thinking and seeing that are essentially white. When in school he has to read stories of savages told by white men, he always thinks of the Senegalese. As a schoolboy, I had many occasions to spend whole hours talking about the supposed customs of the savage Senegalese. In what was said there was a lack of awareness that was at the least very paradoxical. Because the Antillean does not think of himself as a black man; he thinks of himself as an Antillean. The Negro lives in Africa. Subjectively, intellectually, the Antillean conducts himself like a white man. But he is a Negro. That he will learn once he goes to Europe; and when he hears Negroes mentioned he will recognize that the word includes himself as well as the Senegalese. . . .

As long as he remains among his own people, the little black follows very nearly the same course as the little white. But if he goes to Europe, he will have to reappraise his lot. For the Negro in France, which is his country, will feel different from other people. One can hear the glib remark: The Negro makes himself inferior. But the truth is that he is made inferior. The young Antillean is a Frenchman called upon constantly to live with white compatriots. Now, the Antillean family has for all practical purposes no connection with the national—that is, the French, or European—structure. The Antillean has therefore to choose between his family and European society; in other words, the individual who *climbs up* into society—white and civilized—tends to reject his family—black and savage—on the plane of imagination. . . .

I have just shown that for the Negro there is a myth to be faced. A solidly established myth. The Negro is unaware of it as long as his existence is limited to his own environment; but the first encounter with a white man oppresses him with the whole weight of his blackness. . . .

The civilized white man retains an irrational longing for unusual eras of sexual license, of orgiastic scenes, of unpunished rapes, of unrepressed incest. . . . Projecting his own desires onto the Negro, the white man behaves "as

if" the Negro really had them. When it is a question of the Jew, the problem is clear: He is suspect because he wants to own the wealth or take over the positions of power. But the Negro is fixated at the genital; or at any rate he has been fixated there. Two realms: the intellectual and the sexual. . . . The Negro symbolizes the biological danger; the Jew, the intellectual danger.

To suffer from a phobia of Negroes is to be afraid of the biological. For the Negro is only biological. The Negroes are animals. . . .

In the beginning I wanted to confine myself to the Antilles. But . . . I was compelled to *see* that the Antillean is first of all a Negro. Nevertheless, it would be impossible to overlook the fact that there are Negroes whose nationality is Belgian, French, English; there are also Negro republics. . . . The truth is that the Negro race has been scattered, that it can no longer claim unity. When Il Duce's troops invaded Ethiopia, a movement of solidarity arose among men of color. . . .

Wherever he goes, the Negro remains a Negro. . . .

Is not whiteness in symbols always ascribed in French to Justice, Truth, Virginity? I knew an Antillean who said of another Antillean, "His body is black, his language is black, his soul must be black too." This logic is put into daily practice by the white man. The black man is the symbol of Evil and Ugliness. . . .

European civilization is characterized by the presence, at the heart of what [Carl Gustav] Jung calls the collective unconscious, of an archetype: an expression of the bad instincts, of the darkness inherent in every ego, of the uncivilized savage, the Negro who slumbers in every white man. And Jung claims to have found in uncivilized peoples the same psychic structure that his diagram portrays. Personally, I think that Jung has deceived himself. . . .

Jung locates the collective unconscious in the inherited cerebral matter. But the collective unconscious, without our having to fall back on the genes, is purely and simply the sum of prejudices, myths, collective attitudes of a given group. . . .

I hope I have shown that . . . the collective unconscious is cultural, which means acquired. . . . *In Europe, the black man is the symbol of Evil.* . . . Satan is black, one talks of shadow, when one is dirty one is black—whether one is thinking of physical dirtiness or of moral dirtiness. It would be astonishing, if the trouble were taken to bring them all together, to see the vast number of expressions that make the black man the equivalent of sin. In Europe, whether concretely or symbolically, the black man stands for the bad side of the character. As long as one cannot understand this fact, one is doomed to talk in circles about the "black problem". . . . In Europe, that is to say, in every civilized and civilizing country, the Negro is the symbol of sin. The archetype of the lowest values is represented by the Negro. . . .

In Europe the Negro has one function: that of symbolizing the lower emotions, the baser inclinations, the dark side of the soul. In the collective unconscious of *homo occidentalis,* the Negro—or, if one prefers, the color black—symbolizes evil, sin, wretchedness, death, war, famine. . . .

The collective unconscious is not dependent on cerebral heredity; it is the result of what I shall call the unreflected imposition of a culture. Hence there is no reason to be surprised when an Antillean exposed to waking-dream therapy relives the same fantasies as a European. It is because the Antillean partakes of the same collective unconscious as the European.

If what has been said thus far is grasped, this conclusion may be stated: It is normal for the Antillean to be anti-Negro. Through the collective unconscious the Antillean has taken over all the archetypes belonging to the European. But I too am guilty, ... There is no help for it: I am a white man. For unconsciously I distrust what is black in me, that is, the whole of my being. . . .

[W]ithout thinking, the Negro selects himself as an object capable of carrying the burden of original sin. The white man chooses the black man for this function, and the black man who is white also chooses the black man. The black Antillean is the slave of this cultural imposition. After having been the slave of the white man, he enslaves himself. The Negro is in every sense of the word a victim of white civilization. . . .

Hence a Negro is forever in combat with his own image. . . .

[E]ach individual has to charge the blame for his baser drives, his impulses, to the account of an evil genius, which is that of the culture to which he belongs (we have seen that this is the Negro). This collective guilt is borne by what is conventionally called the scapegoat. Now the scapegoat for white society—which is based on myths of progress, civilization, liberalism, education, enlightenment, refinement—will be precisely the force that opposes the expansion and the triumph of these myths. This brutal opposing force is supplied by the Negro.

In the society of the Antilles, where the myths are identical with those of the society of Dijon or Nice, the young Negro, identifying himself with the civilizing power, will make the nigger the scapegoat of his moral life. . . .

As I begin to recognize that the Negro is the symbol of sin, I catch myself hating the Negro. But then I recognize that I am a Negro. . . .

[A]t its extreme, the myth of the Negro, the idea of the Negro, can become the decisive factor of an authentic alienation. . . .

I wonder sometimes whether school inspectors and government functionaries are aware of the role they play in the colonies. For twenty years they poured every effort into programs that would make the Negro a white man. In the end, they dropped him and told him, "You have an indisputable complex of dependence on the white man". . . .

I said in my introduction that man is a *yes.* I will never stop reiterating that.

Yes to life. *Yes* to love. *Yes* to generosity.

But man is also a *no. No* to scorn of man. *No* to degradation of man. *No* to exploitation of man. *No* to the butchery of what is most human in man: freedom . . . .

I do not carry innocence to the point of believing that appeals to reason or to respect for human dignity can alter reality. For the Negro who works on a sugar plantation in Le Robert, there is only one solution: to fight. He will embark on this struggle, and he will pursue it, not as the result of a Marxist or idealistic analysis but quite simply because he cannot conceive of life otherwise than in the form of a battle against exploitation, misery, and hunger. . . .

Those Negroes and white men will be disalienated who refuse to let themselves be sealed away in the materialized Tower of the Past. For many other Negroes, in other ways, disalienation will come into being through their refusal to accept the present as definitive.

I am a man, and what I have to recapture is the whole past of the world. I am not responsible solely for the revolt in Santo Domingo.

Every time a man has contributed to the victory of the dignity of the spirit, every time a man has said no to an attempt to subjugate his fellows, I have felt solidarity with his act.

In no way should I derive my basic purpose from the past of the peoples of color.

In no way should I dedicate myself to the revival of an unjustly unrecognized Negro civilization. I will not make myself the man of any past. I do not want to exalt the past at the expense of my present and of my future. . . .

If the question of practical solidarity with a given past ever arose for me, it did so only to the extent to which I was committed to myself and to my neighbor to fight for all my life and with all my strength so that never again would a people on the earth be subjugated. It was not the black world that laid down my course of conduct. My black skin is not the wrapping of specific values. . . .

I find myself suddenly in the world and I recognize that I have one right alone: That of demanding human behavior from the other.

One duty alone: That of not renouncing my freedom through my choices. . . .

I am a Negro, and tons of chains, storms of blows, rivers of expectoration flow down my shoulders.

But I do not have the right to allow myself to bog down. I do not have the right to allow the slightest fragment to remain in my existence. I do not have the right to allow myself to be mired in what the past has determined.

I am not the slave of the Slavery that dehumanized my ancestors. . . .

Let us be clearly understood. I am convinced that it would be of the greatest interest to be able to have contact with a Negro literature or architecture of the third century before Christ. I should be very happy to know that a correspondence had flourished between some Negro philosopher and Plato. But I can absolutely not see how this fact would change anything in the lives of the eight-year-old children who labor in the cane fields of Martinique or Guadeloupe.

No attempt must be made to encase man, for it is his destiny to be set free.

The body of history does not determine a single one of my actions.

I am my own foundation. . . .

The Negro is not. Any more than the white man.

Both must turn their backs on the inhuman voices which were those of their respective ancestors in order that authentic communication be possible. Before it can adopt a positive voice, freedom requires an effort at disalienation. . . .

It is through the effort to recapture the self and to scrutinize the self, it is through the lasting tension of their freedom that men will be able to create the ideal conditions of existence for a human world.

Superiority? Inferiority?

Why not the quite simple attempt to touch the other, to feel the other, to explain the other to myself?

▪▪▪ WE SHALL OVERCOME (1960)

SOURCE: Musical and lyrical adaptation by Zilphia Horton, Frank Hamilton, Guy Carawan, and Pete Seeger. Inspired by African American Gospel Singing, members of the Food & Tobacco Workers Union, Charleston, SC, and the southern Civil Rights Movement. TRO Songways, Ludlow Music, Inc., 1960.

INTRODUCTION: *"We Shall Overcome" was the unofficial theme song of the freedom movement, adapted from a union version of an old spiritual.*

We shall overcome, we shall overcome,
We shall overcome someday.
Oh, deep in my heart, I do believe,
We shall overcome someday.

We'll walk hand in hand, we'll walk hand in hand,
We'll walk hand in hand someday.
Oh, deep in my heart, I do believe,
We shall overcome someday.

We are not afraid, we are not afraid,
We are not afraid today.
Oh, deep in my heart, I do believe,
We shall overcome someday.

We shall stand together, we shall stand together,
We shall stand together—now.
Oh, deep in my heart, I do believe,
We shall overcome someday.

The truth will make us free, the truth will make us free,
The truth will make us free someday.
Oh, deep in my heart, I do believe,
We shall overcome someday.

The Lord will see us through, the Lord will see us through,
The Lord will see us through someday.
Oh, deep in my heart, I do believe,
We shall overcome someday.

We shall be like Him, we shall be like Him,
We shall be like Him someday.
Oh, deep in my heart, I do believe,
We shall overcome someday.

We shall live in peace, we shall live in peace,
We shall live in peace someday.
Oh, deep in my heart, I do believe,
We shall overcome someday.

The whole wide world around, the whole wide world around,
The whole wide world around someday.
Oh, deep in my heart, I do believe,
We shall overcome someday.

We shall overcome, we shall overcome,
We shall overcome someday.
Oh, deep in my heart, I do believe,
We shall overcome someday.

The African Presence
(George Lamming, 1960)

SOURCE: Lamming, George. *The Pleasures of Exile.* London and New York: Allison & Busby, 1960, pp. 160–165.

I shall no longer graze the donkey
Now my camel is full grown
—*Jolof folk poem*

GHANA

An American tourist in Europe is often in search of monuments cathedrals and palaces, important graves, the whole kingdom of names and faces that are kept alive by the architecture of history. He rummages through his reading to pay homage, in person, to those streets, and rooms and restaurants that have survived the men who made them famous. He claims some share in this heritage, and long before he arrives, his responses are, in some way, determined by this sense of expectation. He is a descendant of men whose migration from this continent was a freely chosen act, and whose memory is kept alive today by his own way of looking at the world. Europe does not add to his problem of identifying himself.

The West Indian Negro who sets out on a similar journey to Africa is less secure. His relation to that continent is more personal and more problematic. It is more personal because the conditions of his life today, his status as a man, are a clear indication of the reasons which led to the departure of his ancestors from that continent. That migration was not a freely chosen act; it was a commercial deportation which has left its consequences heavily marked on every level of his life in the West Indies. Consequences which are most deeply felt in his personal life and relations with his environment: the politics of colour and colonialism that are the very foundation as well as the landmarks of his voyage from childhood to adolescence. His relation to Africa is more problematic because he has not, like the American, been introduced to it through history. His education did not provide him with any reading to rummage through as a guide to the lost kingdoms of names and places which give geography a human significance. He knows it through rumour and myth which is made sinister by a foreign tutelage, and he becomes, through the gradual conditioning of his education, identified with fear: fear of that continent as a world beyond human intervention. Part product of that world, and living still under the shadow of its past disfigurement, he appears reluctant to acknowledge his share of the legacy which is part of his heritage.

So throughout that flight from London to Accra I was trying to put together the fragments of my early education; trying to recall when I had first heard the word Africa, what emotions it had registered. I recalled that at the age of eight or nine I had heard the headmaster of my primary school making some noise about Ethiopia. He seemed angry; for it was the 24th of May, and the English inspector of schools had come to distribute prizes. No one really told us what Ethiopia was. There were no maps in that room to indicate its position in the world. Some of us thought it might have been the Christian name of a lion whose surname was Judah. The name Judah made more sense since the Bible was a part of our alphabet.

Such were the fragments of rumour and fantasy which I was trying to put together during that flight. But planes leave little time for this kind of reflection, and when the land appeared, flat, scorched and empty, I found that I was even without any preconceptions. Nor was I prepared, on leaving the airport, for my first shock of familiarity.

At midday, indifferent to the stupefying heat of Accra, a loyal procession of Boy Scouts had arrived to welcome some dignitary from England. Incredibly correct in their stance, they went through the role of welcome. It was exactly like a West Indian village migrating its children in order to celebrate some important occasion. Neither waiters nor my friends could now distract my attention from the efficient soldiery of those little boys. Their limbs were tight as wire, now supple as water, according to the orders which their training had taught them to follow. Their faces split wide with laughter when a voice allowed them to stand at ease. But in a matter of seconds their muscles were like stone, the smiles rubbed out, and their eyes turned still and sinister as knives. The sun could set no mark on their complexion. When the wind came, the green and yellow scarves ran like flames around their necks, raving like a prisoner to be released.

They were completely identified with the role which they had rehearsed for today. It was a profound experience, for I was seeing myself in every detail which they lived. So I remembered again the old primary school headmaster reminding the English inspector about the name of the lion which was somewhere on this land mass. This experience was deeper and more resonant than the impression left by the phrase: "we used to be like that." It was not just a question of me and my village when I was the age of these boys. Like the funeral ceremony of the King, it was an example of habits and history reincarnated in this moment. It was as though the Haitian ceremony of the Souls had come real: a resurrection of voices at once familiar and unknown had taken place.

The English Scoutmaster was a fragile man, lean, amiable, and full of wonder. I hadn't noticed him on the 'plane; for in that roaring kennel we were all anonymous cargo. But it was impossible to avoid him now. He tried to support a smile; but always the sun closed his teeth, reminding him that this heat was no laughing matter. He looked quite startled; and one wondered whether it was his recognition of the boys' imperviousness to the weather, or the stupendous shock of his own importance in their presence.

Soon it was all over: a brief speech of welcome and reply, a final salute, and the ceremony was dead. The boys forgot their uniform and turned the whole place into their own jamboree. They ran in all directions towards the buses where the village spectators, aunts and cousins, presumably, had watched them perform. They were all talking at the same time. The voices clashed like steel; and their hands were like batons conducting the wild cacophany of their argument. It was impossible to understand how so harmless a ritual as meeting that English Scoutmaster could now lead to such a terrifying chorus of discord.

What were they quarrelling about? Or what were they rejoicing about? For it was difficult to distinguish which noise was war and which was peace. I turned to ask my West Indian friend what it was all about. He smiled; and suddenly I realised the meaning of that smile and the fact about that invading noise. Neither of us could understand a word of what those boys were saying. Nor could the English Scoutmaster. It was at this point that the difference between my childhood and theirs broke wide open. They owed Prospero no debt of vocabulary. English was a way of thinking which they would achieve when the situation required it. But their passions were poured through another rhythm of speed.

"They are speaking Fanti and Ga," said N.

"And if you know Fanti, does it mean that you also know Ga?"

I was getting my first lesson in speech magic.

"Not necessarily," said N., "but what often happens is this: when I speak to you in Fanti you will reply in Ga, and although I can't speak Ga and you can't speak Fanti, somewhere in between the meaning is clear."

Sitting on the terrace of the airport hotel I had lived through again, and forgotten as quickly, all the trouble I had had with school uniforms. I found that I was soon talking, unheard, to myself; and instinctively the same delight kept revealing itself: "But Ghana is free," I was thinking, "a free independent State." And the implication of that silence was an acute awareness that the West Indies were not. And as we had our first drink, both N. and I agreed that it was Ghana which helped to reduce our feeling of disgrace.

The afternoon was, in its way, a kind of emergency. Accra had the look of a place unfinished: there was scaffolding everywhere, the open spaces where demolition had recently taken place, roads under repair, the brand-new building on the eve of opening. You could not detect the precise form of the town; you could not guess its centre, because the town itself was in the process of going up. It was a workshop whose centre was activity. You had the impression that it would change face every day. A year from now you would not know it. Ghana was in a fever of building: roads, schools, harbours and hospitals. It was, I felt, part of the freedom feeling.

And the names, not a day older than the present Government, were still fresh with the echo of an historic moment: Nkrumah Circle, Independence Avenue. And the life-size bust of the Prime Minister dominating the entrance to the House of Assembly with its urgent inscription: "Seek Ye first the political Kingdom."

But behind all this, there is the Ghana of mud-hut villages and an ancient communal living, impenetrable vegetation, the declining magic of chieftancy. As you come, so to speak, to the heart of the soil, the traditional belly and life-blood of the country, you realise that this is not only a country in a state of peaceful emergency; it is a country in a state of transition. The splendour of African dress comes first as a shock; but the shock is too frequent, and soon you are beyond surprise. Green and gold, orange and purple, night blue and lily white. Natural as grass, they are simply there, at once an ordinary and intoxicating part of the street, crowded with cars, pavement traders, cattle, and an occasional madman. Or a Hausa is seen making ready to meet his God. He unfolds his mat, squats and worships with his brow in the dust, unnoticed, as though he were an inanimate part of the pavement.

It is this amalgamation of the various styles of living, this feeling of ambiguity towards the future that gives the country its special quality of excitement. But what is even more striking is the overwhelming sense of confidence.

Some weeks later I witnessed an example of this confidence. I was sitting with a group of Ashantis in one of the popular hotels of Kumasi. We were talking about various aspects of Ashanti culture, and in particular the custom whereby the nephew and not the son is regarded as the heir. I had now grown used to the kind of variety in this place: a few Europeans, meaning white, jawing away over beer, the Ashanti girls looking magnificent in their cloth. One will never forget the rhythm of their bodies moving with an almost insolent casualness across the floor; some of the men in shirt and pants, others in N.T. smocks.

Suddenly A. left the table and walked up to two old women who were standing at the door. They were, one felt, the embodiment of all that is meant by Ashanti. The expression of the faces was male with the hair cropped close to the skull, and the fine, razor line making a complete circle round the base and brow of the skull. A. was also Ashanti, but the old women belonged to another world of intercourse. He sat them at a table, ordered their drinks, and returned to us.

"They came in from the village for a funeral," he said, "and felt like a drink before going back."

Funerals, I should say, are an expensive business in this part of the world. Until you get to know the continuity of relations between the living and the dead, you can't help thinking of funerals as a kind of expensive bacchanal. The occasion surpasses Christmas for drinking; and once when my friend Kufuor suggested that I should get a lift into Accra with a driver who was thought very erratic, I had the distinct suspicion that it was some funeral drinking he was getting at.

A. was looking to see that all was well with the old women. We talked about their dress, the purple cloth drawn easily round the body, and tucked under the arm: the grave, silent concentration of the faces as though they were trying to read the meaning, of this place, the intentions of the young, or the motives of those who, were obviously foreign. When they finished their beer, they walked over to our table. Instinctively, everyone stood, and we shook hands all round, each man bowing to the brief curtsy of the old women. They were leaving. And what one was struck by was the formality of it all; as though each Ashanti understood by instinct his relation to those women within the context of a single and unified culture. They did not know each other; but they knew the meaning of age in their world of morality.

Then A. said: "Five years ago they wouldn't have come in here."

"But of course they could have come?" I suggested.

"They could have come," said A., "but they would not have had any desire to do so. It was not their sort of place." And then he continued: "And five years ago I might not have made it my business to remind them that it belongs to them."

This is not just a change which denotes increase of privileges. It is a fundamental change of attitude even to privileges which could have been claimed five years before. It permeates everything that Ghanians do or say. And here one saw the psychological significance of freedom. It does something to a man's way of seeing the world. It is an experience which is not gained by education or money, but by an instinctive re-evaluation of your place in the world, an attitude that is the logical by-product of political action. And again one felt the full meaning, the full desecra-

tion of human personality which is contained in the word: colonial. One felt that the West Indian of my generation was truly backward, in this sense. For he was not only without this experience of freedom won; it was not even a vital force or need in his way of seeing himself and the world which imprisoned him.

I Have A Dream (Martin Luther King Jr., 1963)

—▪▪▪—————————

SOURCE: Washington, James Melvin, ed. *A Testament of Hope: The Essential Writings of Martin Luther King, Jr.* New York: Harper & Row, 1986, pp. 217–220.

INTRODUCTION: *Highlighting the civil rights movement's March on Washington, August 28, 1963, Martin Luther King delivered the following address on the steps at the Lincoln Memorial.*

I am happy to join with you today in what will go down in history as the greatest demonstration for freedom in the history of our nation.

Five score years ago, a great American, in whose symbolic shadow we stand signed the Emancipation Proclamation. This momentous decree came as a great beacon light of hope to millions of Negro slaves who had been seared in the flames of withering injustice. It came as a joyous daybreak to end the long night of captivity. But one hundred years later, we must face the tragic fact that the Negro is still not free.

One hundred years later, the life of the Negro is still sadly crippled by the manacles of segregation and the chains of discrimination. One hundred years later, the Negro lives on a lonely island of poverty in the midst of a vast ocean of material prosperity. One hundred years later, the Negro is still languishing in the corners of American society and finds himself an exile in his own land.

So we have come here today to dramatize an appalling condition. In a sense we have come to our nation's capital to cash a check. When the architects of our republic wrote the magnificent words of the Constitution and the Declaration of Independence, they were signing a promissory note to which every American was to fall heir.

This note was a promise that all men would be guaranteed the inalienable rights of life, liberty, and the pursuit of happiness. It is obvious today that America has defaulted on this promissory note insofar as her citizens of color are concerned. Instead of honoring this sacred obligation, America has given the Negro people a bad check which has come back marked "insufficient funds." But we refuse to believe that the bank of justice is bankrupt. We refuse to believe that there are insufficient funds in the great vaults of opportunity of this nation.

So we have come to cash this check—a check that will give us upon demand the riches of freedom and the security of justice. We have also come to this hallowed spot to remind America of the fierce urgency of now. This is no time to engage in the luxury of cooling off or to take the tranquilizing drug of gradualism. Now is the time to rise from the dark and desolate valley of segregation to the sunlit path of racial justice. Now is the time to open the doors of opportunity to all of God's children. Now is the time to lift our nation from the quicksands of racial injustice to the solid rock of brotherhood.

It would be fatal for the nation to overlook the urgency of the moment and to underestimate the determination of the Negro. This sweltering summer of the Negro's legitimate discontent will not pass until there is an invigorating autumn of freedom and equality. Nineteen sixty-three is not an end, but a beginning. Those who hope that the Negro needed to blow off steam and will now be content will have a rude awakening if the nation returns to business as usual. There will be neither rest nor tranquility in America until the Negro is granted his citizenship rights.

The whirlwinds of revolt will continue to shake the foundations of our nation until the bright day of justice emerges. But there is something that I must say to my people who stand on the warm threshold which leads into the palace of justice. In the process of gaining our rightful place we must not be guilty of wrongful deeds. Let us not seek to satisfy our thirst for freedom by drinking from the cup of bitterness and hatred.

We must forever conduct our struggle on the high plane of dignity and discipline. We must not allow our creative protest to degenerate into physical violence. Again and again we must rise to the majestic heights of meeting physical force with soul force.

The marvelous new militancy which has engulfed the Negro community must not lead us to distrust of all white people, for many of our white brothers, as evidenced by their presence here today, have come to realize that their destiny is tied up with our destiny and their freedom is inextricably bound to our freedom.

We cannot walk alone. And as we walk, we must make the pledge that we shall march ahead. We cannot turn back. There are those who are asking the devotees of civil rights, "When will you be satisfied?" We can never be satisfied as long as our bodies, heavy with the fatigue of travel, cannot gain lodging in the motels of the highways and the hotels of the cities. We cannot be satisfied as long as

the Negro's basic mobility is from a smaller ghetto to a larger one. We can never be satisfied as long as a Negro in Mississippi cannot vote and a Negro in New York believes he has nothing for which to vote. No, no, we are not satisfied, and we will not be satisfied until justice rolls down like waters and righteousness like a mighty stream.

I am not unmindful that some of you have come here out of great trials and tribulations. Some of you have come fresh from narrow cells. Some of you have come from areas where your quest for freedom left you battered by the storms of persecution and staggered by the winds of police brutality. You have been the veterans of creative suffering. Continue to work with the faith that unearned suffering is redemptive.

Go back to Mississippi, go back to Alabama, go back to Georgia, go back to Louisiana, go back to the slums and ghettos of our northern cities, knowing that somehow this situation can and will be changed. Let us not wallow in the valley of despair. I say to you today, my friends, that in spite of the difficulties and frustrations of the moment, I still have a dream. It is a dream deeply rooted in the American dream.

I have a dream that one day this nation will rise up and live out the true meaning of its creed: "We hold these truths to be self-evident: that all men are created equal." I have a dream that one day on the red hills of Georgia the sons of former slaves and the sons of former slaveowners will be able to sit down together at a table of brotherhood. I have a dream that one day even the state of Mississippi, a desert state, sweltering with the heat of injustice and oppression, will be transformed into an oasis of freedom and justice. I have a dream that my four children will one day live in a nation where they will not be judged by the color of their skin but by the content of their character. I have a dream today.

I have a dream that one day the state of Alabama, whose governor's lips are presently dripping with the words of interposition and nullification, will be transformed into a situation where little black boys and black girls will be able to join hands with little white boys and white girls and walk together as sisters and brothers. I have a dream today. I have a dream that one day every valley shall be exalted, every hill and mountain shall be made low, the rough places will be made plain, and the crooked places will be made straight, and the glory of the Lord shall be revealed, and all flesh shall see it together. This is our hope. This is the faith with which I return to the South. With this faith we will be able to hew out of the mountain of despair a stone of hope. With this faith we will be able to transform the jangling discords of our nation into a beautiful symphony of brotherhood. With this faith we will be able to work together, to pray together, to struggle together, to go to jail together, to stand up for freedom together, knowing that we will be free one day.

This will be the day when all of God's children will be able to sing with a new meaning, "My country, 'tis of thee, sweet land of liberty, of thee I sing. Land where my fathers died, land of the pilgrim's pride, from every mountainside, let freedom ring." And if America is to be a great nation, this must become true. So let freedom ring from the prodigious hilltops of New Hampshire. Let freedom ring from the mighty mountains of New York. Let freedom ring from the heightening Alleghenies of Pennsylvania! Let freedom ring from the snowcapped Rockies of Colorado! Let freedom ring from the curvaceous peaks of California! But not only that; let freedom ring from Stone Mountain of Georgia! Let freedom ring from Lookout Mountain of Tennessee! Let freedom ring from every hill and every molehill of Mississippi. From every mountainside, let freedom ring.

When we let freedom ring, when we let it ring from every village and every hamlet, from every state and every city, we will be able to speed up that day when all of God's children, black men and white men, Jews and Gentiles, Protestants and Catholics, will be able to join hands and sing in the words of the old Negro spiritual, "Free at last! free at last! thank God Almighty, we are free at last!"

Letter from Birmingham Jail (Martin Luther King Jr., 1963)

SOURCE: Carson, Clayborne, et al, eds. *The Eyes on the Prize: Civil Rights Reader.* New York: Viking, 1991, pp. 153–158.

INTRODUCTION: *In the spring of 1963, Martin Luther King was arrested and jailed for leading a protest march in Birmingham, Alabama. A group of Alabama clergymen wrote him a letter while he was imprisoned, criticizing his activities and accusing him of being an outside agitator stirring up trouble and violence in the city. King responded to their charges in the letter reprinted below.*

April 16, 1963

MY DEAR FELLOW CLERGYMEN:
While confined here in the Birmingham city jail, I came across your recent statement calling my present activities

"unwise and untimely." Seldom do I pause to answer criticism of my work and ideas. If I sought to answer all the criticisms that cross my desk, my secretaries would have little time for anything other than such correspondence in the course of the day, and I would have no time for constructive work. But since I feel that you are men of genuine good will and that your criticisms are sincerely set forth, I want to try to answer your statements in what I hope will be patient and reasonable terms.

I think I should indicate why I am here in Birmingham, since you have been influenced by the view which argues against "outsiders coming in." I have the honor of serving as president of the Southern Christian Leadership Conference, an organization operating in every southern state, with headquarters in Atlanta, Georgia. We have some eighty-five affiliated organizations across the South, and one of them is the Alabama Christian Movement for Human Rights. Frequently we share staff, educational and financial resources with our affiliates. Several months ago the affiliate here in Birmingham asked us to be on call to engage in a nonviolent direct-action program if such were deemed necessary. We readily consented, and when the hour came we lived up to our promise. So I, along with several members of my staff, am here because I was invited here I am here because I have organizational ties here.

But more basically, I am in Birmingham because injustice is here. Just as the prophets of the eighth century B.C. left their villages and carried their "thus saith the Lord" far beyond the boundaries of their home towns, and just as the Apostle Paul left his village of Tarsus and carried the gospel of Jesus Christ to the far corners of the Greco-Roman world, so am I compelled to carry the gospel of freedom beyond my own home town. Like Paul, I must constantly respond to the Macedonian call for aid.

Moreover, I am cognizant of the interrelatedness of all communities and states. I cannot sit idly by in Atlanta and not be concerned about what happens in Birmingham. Injustice anywhere is a threat to justice everywhere. We are caught in an inescapable network of mutuality, tied in a single garment of destiny. Whatever affects one directly, affects all indirectly. Never again can we afford to live with the narrow, provincial "outside agitator" idea. Anyone who lives inside the United States can never be considered an outsider anywhere within its bounds.

You deplore the demonstrations taking place in Birmingham. But your statement, I am sorry to say, fails to express a similar concern for the conditions that brought about the demonstrations. I am sure that none of you would want to rest content with the superficial kind of social analysis that deals merely with effects and does not grapple with underlying causes. It is unfortunate that demonstrations are taking place in Birmingham, but it is even more unfortunate that the city's white power structure left the Negro community with no alternative.

In any nonviolent campaign there are four basic steps: collection of the facts to determine whether injustices exist; negotiation; self-purification; and direct action. We have gone through an these steps in Birmingham. There can be no gainsaying the fact that racial injustice engulfs this community. Birmingham is probably the most thoroughly segregated city in the United States. Its ugly record of brutality is widely known. Negroes have experienced grossly unjust treatment in the courts. There have been more unsolved bombings of Negro homes and churches in Birmingham than in any other city in the nation. These are the hard, brutal facts of the case. On the basis of these conditions, Negro leaders sought to negotiate with the city fathers. But the latter consistently refused to engage in good-faith negotiation.

Then, last September, came the opportunity to talk with leaders of Birmingham's economic community. In the course of the negotiations, certain promises were made by the merchants—for example, to remove the stores' humiliating racial signs. On the basis of these promises, the Reverend Fred Shuttlesworth and the leaders of the Alabama Christian Movement for Human Rights agreed to a moratorium on all demonstrations. As the weeks and months went by, we realized that we were the victims of a broken promise. A few signs, briefly removed, returned; the others remained.

As in so many past experiences, our hopes bad been blasted, and the shadow of deep disappointment settled upon us. We had no alternative except to prepare for direct action, whereby we would present our very bodies as a means of laying our case before the conscience of the local and the national community. Mindful of the difficulties involved, we decided to undertake a process of self-purification. We began a series of workshops on nonviolence, and we repeatedly asked ourselves: "Are you able to accept blows without retaliating?" "Are you able to endure the ordeal of jail?" We decided to schedule our direct-action program for the Easter season, realizing that except for Christmas, this is the main shopping period of the year. Knowing that a strong economic withdrawal program would be the by-product of direct action, we felt that this would be the best time to bring pressure to bear on the merchants for the needed change.

Then it occurred to us that Birmingham's mayoralty election was coming up in March, and we speedily decided to postpone action until after election day. When we discovered that the Commissioner of Public Safety, Eugene "Bull" Connor, had piled up enough votes to be in the run-off, we decided again to postpone action until the day after the run-off so that the demonstrations could not be used to cloud the issues. Like many others, we waited to see Mr. Connor defeated, and to this end we endured postponement after postponement. Having aided in this community need, we felt that our direct-action program could be delayed no longer.

You may well ask: "Why direct action? Why sit-ins, marches and so forth? Isn't negotiation a better path?" You are quite right in calling for negotiation. Indeed, this is the very purpose of direct action. Nonviolent direct action seeks to create such a crisis and foster such a tension that a community which has constantly refused to negotiate is forced to confront the issue. It seeks so to dramatize the issue that it can no longer be ignored. My citing the creation of tension as part of the work of the nonviolent-resister may sound rather shocking. But I must confess that I am not afraid of the word "tension." I have earnestly opposed violent tension, but there is a type of constructive, nonviolent tension which is necessary for growth. Just as Socrates felt that it was necessary to create a tension in the mind so that individuals could rise from the bondage of myths and half-truths to the unfettered realm of creative analysis and objective appraisal, we must we see the need for nonviolent gadflies to create the kind of tension in society that will help men rise from the dark depths of prejudice and racism to the majestic heights of understanding and brotherhood.

The purpose of our direct-action program is to create a situation so crisis-packed that it will inevitably open the door to negotiation. I therefore concur with you in your call for negotiation. Too long has our beloved Southland been bogged down in a tragic effort to live in monologue rather than dialogue.

One of the basic points in your statement is that the action that I and my associates have taken in Birmingham is untimely. Some have asked: "Why didn't you give the new city administration time to act?" The only answer that I can give to this query is that the new Birmingham administration must be prodded about as much as the outgoing one, before it will act. We are sadly mistaken if we feel that the election of Albert Boutwell as mayor will bring the millennium to Birmingham. While Mr. Boutwell is a much more gentle person than Mr. Connor, they are both segregationists, dedicated to maintenance of the status quo. I have hope that Mr. Boutwell will be reasonable enough to see the futility of massive resistance to desegregation. But he will not see this without pressure from devotees of civil rights. My friends, I must say to you that we have not made a single gain civil rights without determined legal and nonviolent pressure. Lamentably, it is an historical fact that privileged groups seldom give up their privileges voluntarily. Individuals may see the moral light and voluntarily give up their unjust posture; but, as Reinhold Niebuhr has reminded us, groups tend to be more immoral than individuals.

We know through painful experience that freedom is never voluntarily given by the oppressor; it must be demanded by the oppressed. Frankly, I have yet to engage in a direct-action campaign that was "well timed" in the view of those who have not suffered unduly from the disease of segregation. For years now I have heard the word "Wait!" It rings in the ear of every Negro with piercing familiarity. This "Wait" has almost always meant "Never." We must come to see, with one of our distinguished jurists, that "justice too long delayed is justice denied."

We have waited for more than 340 years for our constitutional and God-given rights. The nations of Asia and Africa are moving with jetlike speed toward gaining political independence, but we stiff creep at horse-and-buggy pace toward gaining a cup of coffee at a lunch counter. Perhaps it is easy for those who have never felt the stinging dark of segregation to say, "Wait." But when you have seen vicious mobs lynch your mothers and fathers at will and drown your sisters and brothers at whim; when you have seen hate-filled policemen curse, kick and even kill your black brothers and sisters; when you see the vast majority of your twenty million Negro brothers smothering in an airtight cage of poverty in the midst of an affluent society; when you suddenly find your tongue twisted and your speech stammering as you seek to explain to your six-year-old daughter why she can't go to the public amusement park that has just been advertised on television, and see tears welling up in her eyes when she is told that Funtown is closed to colored children, and see ominous clouds of inferiority beginning to form in her little mental sky, and see her beginning to distort her personality by developing an unconscious bitterness toward white people; when you have to concoct an answer for a five-year-old son who is asking: "Daddy, why do white people treat colored people so mean?"; when you take a cross-county drive and find it necessary to sleep night after night in the uncomfortable corners of your automobile because no motel will accept you; when you are humiliated day in and day out by nagging signs reading "white" and "colored"; when your first name becomes "nigger," your middle name becomes "boy" (however old you are) and your last name becomes "John," and your wife and mother are never given the respected title "Mrs."; when you are harried by day and haunted by night by the fact that you are a Negro, living constantly at tiptoe stance, never quite knowing what to expect next, and are plagued with inner fears and outer resentments; when you no forever fighting a degenerating sense of "nobodiness" then you will understand why we find it difficult to wait. There comes a time when the cup of endurance runs over, and men are no longer willing to be plunged into the abyss of despair. I hope, sirs, you can understand our legitimate and unavoidable impatience.

You express a great deal of anxiety over our willingness to break laws. This is certainly a legitimate concern. Since we so diligently urge people to obey the Supreme Court's decision of 1954 outlawing segregation in the public schools, at first glance it may seem rather paradoxical for us consciously to break laws. One may well ask: "How can you advocate breaking some laws and obeying others?" The answer lies in the fact that there fire two types of laws: just and unjust. I would be the first to advocate obeying just laws. One has not only a legal but a moral responsibility to obey just laws. Conversely, one has a moral responsibility to disobey unjust laws. I would agree with St. Augustine that "an unjust law is no law at all."

Now, what is the difference between the two? How does one determine whether a law is just or unjust? A just law is a man-made code that squares with the moral law or the law of God. An unjust law is a code that is out of harmony with the moral law. To put it in the terms of St. Thomas Aquinas: An unjust law is a human law that is not rooted in eternal law and natural law. Any law that uplifts human personality is just. Any law that degrades human personality is unjust. All segregation statutes are unjust because segregation distorts the soul and damages the personality. It gives the segregator a false sense of superiority and the segregated a false sense of inferiority. Segregation, to use the terminology of the Jewish philosopher Martin Buber, substitutes an "I-it" relationship for an "I-thou" relationship and ends up relegating persons to the status of things. Hence segregation is not only politically, economically and sociologically unsound, it is morally wrong and awful. Paul Tillich said that sin is separation. Is not segregation an existential expression of man's tragic separation, his awful estrangement, his terrible sinfulness? Thus it is that I can urge men to obey the 1954 decision of the Supreme Court, for it is morally right; and I can urge them to disobey segregation ordinances, for they are morally wrong.

Let us consider a more concrete example of just and unjust laws. An unjust law is a code that a numerical or power majority group compels a minority group to obey but does not make binding on itself. This is difference made legal. By the same token, a just law is a code that a majority compels a minority to follow and that it is willing to follow itself. This is sameness made legal.

Let me give another explanation. A law is unjust if it is inflicted on a minority that, as a result of being denied the right to vote, had no part in enacting or devising the law. Who can say that the legislature of Alabama which set up that state's segregation laws was democratically elected? Throughout Alabama all sorts of devious methods are used to prevent Negroes from becoming registered voters, and there are some counties in which, even though Negroes constitute a majority of the population, not a single Negro is registered. Can any law enacted under such circumstances be considered democratically structured?

Sometimes a law is just on its face and unjust in its application. For instance, I have been arrested on a charge of parading without a permit. Now, there is nothing wrong in having an ordinance which requires a permit for a parade. But such an ordinance becomes unjust when it is used to maintain segregation and to deny citizens the First Amendment privilege of peaceful assembly and protest.

I hope you are able to see the distinction I am trying to point out. In no sense do I advocate evading or defying the law, as would the rabid segregationist. That would lead to anarchy. One who breaks an unjust law must do so openly, lovingly, and with a willingness to accept the penalty. I submit that an individual who breaks a law that conscience tells him is unjust and who willingly accepts the penalty of imprisonment in order to arouse the conscience of the community over its injustice, is in reality expressing the highest respect for law.

Of course, there is nothing new about this kind of civil disobedience. It was evidenced sublimely in the refusal of Shadrach, Meshach and Abednego to obey the laws of Nebuchadnezzar, on the ground that a higher moral law was at stake. It was practiced superbly by the early Christians, who were willing to face hungry lions and the excruciating pain of chopping blocks rather than submit to certain unjust laws of the Roman Empire. To a degree, academic freedom is a reality today because Socrates practiced civil disobedience. In our own nation, the Boston Tea Party represented a massive act of civil disobedience.

We should never forget that everything Adolf Hitler did in Germany was "legal" and everything the Hungarian freedom fighters did in Hungary was "illegal." It was "illegal" to aid and comfort a Jew in Hitler's Germany. Even so, I am sure that, had I lived in Germany at the time, I would have aided and comforted my Jewish brothers. If today I lived in a Communist country where certain principles dear to the Christian faith are suppressed, I would openly advocate disobeying that country's antireligious laws.

I must make two honest confessions to you, my Christian and Jewish brothers. First, I must confess that over the past few years I have been gravely disappointed

with the white moderate. I have almost reached the regrettable conclusion that the Negro's great stumbling block in his stride toward freedom is not the White Citizen's Counciler or the Ku Klux Klanner, but the white moderate, who is more devoted to "order" than to justice; who prefers a negative peace which is the absence of tension to a positive peace which is the presence of justice; who constantly says: "I agree with you in the goal you seek, but I cannot agree with your methods of direct action"; who paternalistically believes he can set the timetable for another man's freedom; who lives by a mythical concept of time and who constantly advises the Negro to wait for a "more convenient season." Shallow understanding from people of good will is more frustrating than absolute misunderstanding from people of ill will. Lukewarm acceptance is much more bewildering than outright rejection.

I had hoped that the white moderate would understand that law and order exist for the purpose of establishing justice and that when they fail in this purpose they become the dangerously structured dams that block the flow of social progress. I had hoped that the white moderate would understand that the present tension in the South is a necessary phase of the transition from an obnoxious negative peace, in which the Negro passively accepted his unjust plight, to a substantive and positive peace, in which all men will respect the dignity and worth of human personality. Actually, we who engage in nonviolent direct action are not the creators of tension. We merely bring to the surface the hidden tension that is already alive. We bring it out in the open, where it can be seen and dealt with. Like a boil that can never be cured so long as it is covered up but must be opened with an its ugliness to the natural medicines of air and light, injustice must be exposed, with all the tension its exposure creates, to the light of human conscience and the air of national opinion before it can be cured.

In your statement you assert that our actions, even though peaceful, must be condemned because they precipitate violence. But is this a logical assertion? Isn't this like condemning a robbed man because his possession of money precipitated the evil act of robbery? Isn't this like condemning Socrates because his unswerving commitment to truth and his philosophical inquiries precipitated the act by the misguided populace in which they made him drink hemlock? Isn't this like condemning Jesus because his unique God-consciousness and never-ceasing devotion to God's will precipitated the evil act of crucifixion? We must come to see that, as the federal courts have consistently affirmed, it is wrong to urge an individual to cease his efforts to gain his basic constitutional rights because the quest may precipitate violence. Society must protect the robbed and punish the robber.

I had also hoped that the white moderate would reject the myth concerning time in relation to the struggle for freedom. I have just received a letter from a white brother in Texas. He writes: "All Christians know that the colored people will receive equal rights eventually, but it is possible that you are in too great a religious hurry. It has taken Christianity almost two thousand years to accomplish what it has. The teachings of Christ take time to come to earth." Such an attitude stems from a tragic misconception of time, from the strangely rational notion that there is something in the very flow of time that will inevitably cure all ills. Actually, time itself is neutral; it can be used either destructively or constructively. More and more I feel that the people of ill will have used time much more effectively than have the people of good will. We will have to repent in this generation not merely for the hateful words and actions of the bad people but for the appalling silence of the good people. Human progress never rolls in on wheels of inevitability; it comes through the tireless efforts of men willing to be co-workers with God, and without this hard work, time itself becomes an ally of the forces of social stagnation. We must use time creatively, in the knowledge that the time is always ripe to do right. Now is the time to make real the promise of democracy and transform our pending national elegy into a creative psalm of brotherhood. Now is the time to lift our national policy from the quicksand of racial injustice to the solid rock of human dignity.

You speak of our activity in Birmingham as extreme. At fist I was rather disappointed that fellow clergymen would see my nonviolent efforts as those of an extremist. I began thinking about the fact that I stand in the middle of two opposing forces in the Negro community. One is a force of complacency, made up in part of Negroes who, as a result of long years of oppression, are so drained of self-respect and a sense of "somebodiness" that they have adjusted to segregation; and in part of a few middle class Negroes who, because of a degree of academic and economic security and because in some ways they profit by segregation, have become insensitive to the problems of the masses. The other force is one of bitterness and hatred, and it comes perilously close to advocating violence. It is expressed in the various black nationalist groups that are springing up across the nation, the largest and best-known being Elijah Muhammad's Muslim movement. Nourished by the Negro's frustration over the continued existence of racial discrimination, this movement is made up of people who have lost faith in America, who have absolutely repudiated Christianity, and who have concluded that the white man is an incorrigible "devil."

I have tried to stand between these two forces, saying that we need emulate neither the "do-nothingism" of the complacent nor the hatred and despair of the black nationalist. For there is the more excellent way of love and nonviolent protest. I am grateful to God that, through the influence of the Negro church, the way of nonviolence became an integral part of our struggle.

If this philosophy had not emerged, by now many streets of the South would, I am convinced, be flowing with blood. And I am further convinced that if our white brothers dismiss as "rabble-rousers" and "outside agitators" those of us who employ nonviolent direct action, and if they refuse to support our nonviolent efforts, millions of Negroes will, out of frustration and despair, seek solace and security in black-nationalist ideologies a development that would inevitably lead to a frightening racial nightmare.

Oppressed people cannot remain oppressed forever. The yearning for freedom eventually manifests itself, and that is what has happened to the American Negro. Something within has reminded him of his birthright of freedom, and something without has reminded him that it can be gained. Consciously or unconsciously, he has been caught up by the Zeitgeist, and with his black brothers of Africa and his brown and yellow brothers of Asia, South America and the Caribbean, the United States Negro is moving with a sense of great urgency toward the promised land of racial justice. If one recognizes this vital urge that has engulfed the Negro community, one should readily understand why public demonstrations are taking place. The Negro has many pent-up resentments and latent frustrations, and he must release them. So let him march; let him make prayer pilgrimages to the city hall; let him go on freedom rides—and try to understand why he must do so. If his repressed emotions are not released in nonviolent ways, they will seek expression through violence; this is not a threat but a fact of history. So I have not said to my people: "Get rid of your discontent." Rather, I have tried to say that this normal and healthy discontent can be channeled into the creative outlet of nonviolent direct action. And now this approach is being termed extremist.

But though I was initially disappointed at being categorized as an extremist, as I continued to think about the matter I gradually gained a measure of satisfaction from the label. Was not Jesus an extremist for love: "Love your enemies, bless them that curse you, do good to them that hate you, and pray for them which despitefully use you, and persecute you." Was not Amos an extremist for justice: "Let justice roll down like waters and righteousness like an ever-flowing stream." Was not Paul an extremist for the Christian gospel: "I bear in my body the marks of the Lord Jesus." Was not Martin Luther an extremist: "Here I stand; I cannot do otherwise, so help me God."

And John Bunyan: "I will stay in jail to the end of my days before I make a butchery of my conscience." And Abraham Lincoln: "This nation cannot survive half slave and half free." And Thomas Jefferson: "We hold these truths to be self-evident, that all men are created equal. . . ." So the question is not whether we will be extremists, but what kind of extremists we will be. Will we be extremists for hate or for love? Will we be extremists for the preservation of injustice or for the extension of justice? In that dramatic scene on Calvary's hill three men were crucified. We must never forget that all three were crucified for the same crime—the crime of extremism. Two were extremists for immorality, and thus fell below their environment. The other, Jeans Christ, was an extremist for love, truth and goodness, and thereby rose above his environment. Perhaps the South, the nation and the world are in dire need of creative extremists.

I had hoped that the white moderate would see this need. Perhaps I was too optimistic; perhaps I expected too much. I suppose I should have realized that few members of the oppressor race can understand the deep groans and passionate yearnings of the oppressed race, and still fewer have the vision to see that injustice must be rooted out by strong, persistent and determined action. I am thankful, however, that some of our white brothers in the South have grasped the meaning of this social revolution and committed themselves to it. They are still too few in quantity, but they are big in quality. Some-such as Ralph McGill, Lillian Smith, Harry Golden, James McBride Dabbs, Ann Braden and Sarah Patton Boyle—have written about our struggle in eloquent and prophetic terms. Others have marched with us down nameless streets of the South. They have languished in filthy, roach-infested jails, suffering the abuse and brutality of policemen who view them as "dirty nigger lovers." Unlike so many of their moderate brothers and sisters, they have recognized the urgency of the moment and sensed the need for powerful "action" antidotes to combat the disease of segregation.

Let me take note of my other major disappointment. I have been so greatly disappointed with the white church and its leadership. Of course, there are some notable exceptions. I am not unmindful of the fact that each of you has taken some significant stands on this issue. I commend you, Reverend Stallings, for your Christian stand on this past Sunday, in welcoming Negroes to your worship service on a nonsegregated basis. I commend the Catholic leaders of this state for integrating Spring Hill College several years ago.

But despite these notable exceptions, I must honestly reiterate that I have been disappointed with the church. I do not say this as one of those negative critics who can always find something wrong with the church. I say this as a minister of the gospel, who loves the church; who was nurtured in its bosom; who has been sustained by its spiritual blessings and who will remain true to it as long as the cord of life shall lengthen.

When I was suddenly catapulted into the leadership of the bus protest in Montgomery, Alabama, a few years ago, I felt we would be supported by the white church. I felt that the white ministers, priests and rabbis of the South would be among our strongest allies. Instead, some have been outright opponents, refusing to understand the freedom movement and misrepresenting its leaders; all too many others have been more cautious than courageous and have remained silent behind the anesthetizing security of stained-glass windows.

In spite of my shattered dreams, I came to Birmingham with the hope that the white religious leadership of this community would see the justice of our cause and, with deep moral concern, would serve as the channel through which our just grievances could reach the power structure. I had hoped that each of you would understand. But again I have been disappointed.

I have heard numerous southern religious leaders admonish their worshipers to comply with a desegregation decision because it is the law, but I have longed to hear white ministers declare: "Follow this decree because integration is morally right and because the Negro is your brother." In the midst of blatant injustices inflicted upon the Negro, I have watched white churchmen stand on the sideline and mouth pious irrelevancies and sanctimonious trivialities. In the midst of a mighty struggle to rid our nation of racial and economic injustice, I have heard many ministers say: "Those are social issues, with which the gospel has no real concern." And I have watched many churches commit themselves to a completely other worldly religion which makes a strange, un-Biblical distinction between body and soul, between the sacred and the secular.

I have traveled the length and breadth of Alabama, Mississippi and all the other southern states. On sweltering summer days and crisp autumn mornings I have looked at the South's beautiful churches with their lofty spires pointing heavenward. I have beheld the impressive outlines of her massive religious-education buildings. Over and over I have found myself asking: "What kind of people worship here? Who is their God? Where were their voices when the lips of Governor Barnett dripped with words of interposition and nullification? Where were they when Governor Wallace gave a clarion call for defiance and hatred? Where were their voices of support when bruised and weary Negro men and women decided to rise from the dark dungeons of complacency to the bright hills of creative protest?"

Yes, these questions are still in my mind. In deep disappointment I have wept over the laxity of the church. But be assured that my tears have been tears of love. There can be no deep disappointment where there is not deep love. Yes, I love the church. How could I do otherwise? I am in the rather unique position of being the son, the grandson and the great-grandson of preachers. Yes, I see the church as the body of Christ. But, oh! How we have blemished and scarred that body through social neglect and through fear of being nonconformists.

There was a time when the church was very powerful in the time when the early Christians rejoiced at being deemed worthy to suffer for what they believed. In those days the church was not merely a thermometer that recorded the ideas and principles of popular opinion; it was a thermostat that transformed the mores of society. Whenever the early Christians entered a town, the people in power became disturbed and immediately sought to convict the Christians for being "disturbers of the peace" and "outside agitators"' But the Christians pressed on, in the conviction that they were "a colony of heaven," called to obey God rather than man. Small in number, they were big in commitment. They were too God intoxicated to be "astronomically intimidated." By their effort and example they brought an end to such ancient evils as infanticide and gladiatorial contests.

Things are different now. So often the contemporary church is a weak, ineffectual voice with an uncertain sound. So often it is an archdefender of the status quo. Far from being disturbed by the presence of the church, the power structure of the average community is consoled by the church's silent and often even vocal sanction of things as they are.

But the judgment of God is upon the church as never before. If today's church does not recapture the sacrificial spirit of the early church, it will lose its authenticity, forfeit the loyalty of millions, and be dismissed as an irrelevant social club with no meaning for the twentieth century. Every day I meet young people whose disappointment with the church has turned into outright disgust.

Perhaps I have once again been too optimistic. Is organized religion too inextricably bound to the status quo to save our nation and the world? Perhaps I must turn my faith to the inner spiritual church, the church within the church, as the true ekklesia and the hope of the world. But again I am thankful to God that some noble souls from the ranks of organized religion have broken loose from the paralyzing chains of conformity and joined us as active partners in the struggle for freedom, They have left their secure congregations and walked the streets of Albany, Georgia, with us. They have gone down the highways of the South on tortuous rides for freedom. Yes, they have gone to jail with us. Some have been dismissed from their churches, have lost the support of their bishops and fellow ministers. But they have acted in the faith that right defeated is stronger than evil triumphant. Their witness has been the spiritual salt that has preserved the true meaning of the gospel in these troubled times. They have carved a tunnel of hope through the dark mountain of disappointment.

I hope the church as a whole will meet the challenge of this decisive hour. But even if the church does not come to the aid of justice, I have no despair about the future. I have no fear about the outcome of our struggle in Birmingham, even if our motives are at present misunderstood. We will reach the goal of freedom in Birmingham and all over the nation, because the goal of America is freedom. Abused and scorned though we may be, our destiny is tied up with America's destiny. Before the pilgrims landed at Plymouth, we were here. Before the pen of Jefferson etched the majestic words of the Declaration of Independence across the pages of history, we were here. For more than two centuries our forebears labored in this country without wages; they made cotton king; they built the homes of their masters while suffering gross injustice and shameful humiliation—and yet out of a bottomless vitality they continued to thrive and develop. If the inexpressible cruelties of slavery could not stop us, the opposition we now face will surely fail. We will win our freedom because the sacred heritage of our nation and the eternal will of God are embodied in our echoing demands.

Before closing I feel impelled to mention one other point in your statement that has troubled me profoundly. You warmly commended the Birmingham police force for keeping "order" and "preventing violence." I doubt that you would have so warmly commended the police force if you had seen its dogs sinking their teeth into unarmed, nonviolent Negroes. I doubt that you would so quickly commend the policemen if you were to observe their ugly and inhumane treatment of Negroes here in the city jail; if you were to watch them push and curse old Negro women and young Negro girls; if you were to see them slap and kick old Negro men and young boys; if you were to observe them, as they did on two occasions, refuse to give us food because we wanted to sing our grace together. I cannot join you in your praise of the Birmingham police department.

It is true that the police have exercised a degree of discipline in handling the demonstrators. In this sense they have conducted themselves rather "nonviolently" in public. But for what purpose? To preserve the evil system of segregation. Over the past few years I have consistently preached that nonviolence demands that the means we use must be as pure as the ends we seek. I have tried to make clear that it is wrong to use immoral means to attain moral ends. But now I must affirm that it is just as wrong, or perhaps even more so, to use moral means to preserve immoral ends. Perhaps Mr. Connor and his policemen have been rather nonviolent in public, as was Chief Pritchett in Albany, Georgia, but they have used the moral means of nonviolence to maintain the immoral end of racial injustice. As T. S. Eliot has said: "The last temptation is the greatest treason: To do the right deed for the wrong reason."

I wish you had commended the Negro sit-inners and demonstrators of Birmingham for their sublime courage, their willingness to suffer and their amazing discipline in the midst of great provocation. One day the South will recognize its real heroes. They will be the James Merediths, with the noble sense of purpose that enables them to face jeering, and hostile mobs, and with the agonizing loneliness that characterizes the life of the pioneer. They will be old, oppressed, battered Negro women, symbolized in a seventy-two-year-old woman in Montgomery, Alabama, who rose up with a sense of dignity and with her people decided not to ride segregated buses, and who responded with ungrammatical profundity to one who inquired about her weariness: "My feets is tired, but my soul is at rest." They will be the young high school and college students, the young ministers of the gospel and a host of their elders, courageously and nonviolently sitting in at lunch counters and willingly going to jail for conscience's sake. One day the South will know that when these disinherited children of God sat down at lunch counters, they were in reality standing up for what is best in the American dream and for the most sacred values in our Judaeo-Christian heritage, thereby bringing our nation back to those great wells of democracy which were dug deep by the founding fathers in their formulation of the Constitution and the Declaration of Independence.

Never before have I written so long a letter. I'm afraid it is much too long to take your precious time. I can assure you that it would have been much shorter if I had been writing from a comfortable desk, but what else can one do when he is alone in a narrow jail cell, other than write long letters, think long thoughts and pray long prayers?

If I have said anything in this letter that overstates the truth and indicates an unreasonable impatience, I beg you to forgive me. If I have said anything that understates the truth and indicates my having a patience that allows me to settle for anything less than brotherhood, I beg God to forgive me.

I hope this letter finds you strong in the faith. I also hope that circumstances will soon make it possible for me to meet each of you, not as an integrationist or a civil rights leader but as a fellow clergyman and a Christian brother. Let us all hope that the dark clouds of racial prejudice will soon pass away and the deep fog of misunderstanding will be lifted from our fear-drenched communities, and in some not too distant tomorrow the radiant stars of love and brotherhood will shine over our great nation with all their scintillating beauty.

Yours for the cause of Peace and Brotherhood,

MARTIN LUTHER KING JR.

THE BALLOT OR THE BULLET (MALCOLM X, 1964)

SOURCE: Frazier, Thomas R., ed. *Readings in African-American History*, 3d edition. Belmont, Calif.: Wadsworth/Thomson Learning, 2001, pp. 374–388.

INTRODUCTION: *On April 3, 1964, Malcolm X appeared with journalist Louis Lomax at a symposium sponsored by the Congress of Racial Equality (CORE) in Cleveland. Lomax supported CORE's philosophy of nonviolence in the pursuit of civil liberties for black Americans. Malcolm X advocated "action on all fronts by whatever means necessary."*

Mr. Moderator, Brother Lomax, brothers and sisters, friends and enemies: I just can't believe everyone in here is a friend and I don't want to leave anybody out. The question tonight, as I understand it, is "The Negro Revolt, and Where Do We Go From Here?" or "What Next?" In my little humble way of understanding it, it points toward either the ballot or the bullet.

Before we try and explain what is meant by the ballot or the bullet, I would like to clarify something concerning myself. I'm still a Muslim, my religion is still Islam. That's my personal belief. Just as Adam Clayton Powell is a Christian minister who heads the Abyssinian Baptist Church in New York, but at the same time takes part in the political struggles to try and bring about rights to the black people in this country; and Dr. Martin Luther King is a Christian minister down in Atlanta, Georgia, who heads another organization fighting for the civil rights of black people in this country; and Rev. Galamison, I guess you've heard of him, is another Christian minister in New York who has been deeply involved in the school boycotts to eliminate segregated education; well, I myself am a minister, not a Christian minister, but a Muslim minister; and I believe in action on all fronts by whatever means necessary.

Although I'm still a Muslim, I'm not here tonight to discuss my religion. I'm not here to try and change your religion. I'm not here to argue or discuss anything that we differ about, because it's time for us to submerge our differences and realize that it is best for us to first see that we have the same problem, a common problem—a problem that will make you catch hell whether you're a Baptist, or a Methodist, or a Muslim, or a nationalist. Whether you're educated or illiterate, whether you live on the boulevard or in the alley, you're going to catch hell just like I am. We're all in the same boat and we all are going to catch the same hell from the same man. He just happens to be a white man. All of us have suffered here, in this country, political oppression at the hands of the white man, economic exploitation at the hands of the white man, and social degradation at the hands of the white man.

Now in speaking like this, it doesn't mean that we're anti-white, but it does mean we're anti-exploitation, we're anti-degradation, we're anti-oppression. And if the white man doesn't want us to be anti-him, let him stop oppressing and exploiting and degrading us. Whether we are Christians or Muslims or nationalists or agnostics or atheists, we must first learn to forget our differences. If we have differences, let us differ in the closet; when we come out in front, let us not have anything to argue about until we get finished arguing with the man. If the late President Kennedy could get together with Khrushchev and exchange some wheat, we certainly have more in common with each other than Kennedy and Khrushchev had with each other.

If we don't do something real soon, I think you'll have to agree that we're going to be forced either to use the ballot or the bullet. It's one or the other in 1964. It isn't that time is running out—time has run out! 1964 threatens to be the most explosive year America has ever witnessed. The most explosive year. Why? It's also a political year. It's the year when all of the white politicians will be back in the so-called Negro community jiving you and me for some votes. The year when all of the white political crooks will be right back in your and my community with their false promises, building up our hopes for a letdown, with their trickery and their treachery, with their false promises which they don't intend to keep. As they nourish these dissatisfactions, it can only lead to one thing, an explosion; and now we have the type of black man on the scene in America today—I'm sorry, Brother Lomax—who just doesn't intend to turn the other cheek any longer.

Don't let anybody tell you anything about the odds are against you. If they draft you, they send you to Korea and make you face 800 million Chinese. If you can be brave over there, you can be brave right here. These odds aren't as great as those odds. And if you fight here, you will at least know what you're fighting for.

I'm not a politician, not even a student of politics; in fact, I'm not a student of much of anything. I'm not a Democrat, I'm not a Republican, and I don't even consider myself an American. If you and I were Americans, there'd be no problem. Those Hunkies that just got off the boat, they're already Americans; Polacks are already Americans; the Italian refugees are already Americans. Everything that came out of Europe, every blue-eyed thing, is already an American. And as long as you and I have been over here, we aren't Americans yet.

Well, I am one who doesn't believe in deluding myself. I'm not going to sit at your table and watch you eat, with nothing on my plate, and call myself a diner. Sitting at the table doesn't make you a diner, unless you eat some of what's on that plate. Being here in America doesn't make you an American. Being born here in America doesn't make you an American. Why, if birth made you American, you wouldn't need any legislation, you wouldn't need any amendments to the Constitution, you wouldn't be faced with civil-rights filibustering in Washington, D.C., right now. They don't have to pass civil-rights legislation to make a Polack an American.

No, I'm not an American. I'm one of the 22 million black people who are the victims of Americanism. One of the 22 million black people who are the victims of democracy, nothing but disguised hypocrisy. So, I'm not standing here speaking to you as an American, or a patriot, or a flag-saluter, or a flag-waver—no, not I. I'm speaking as a victim of this American system. And I see America through the eyes of the victim. I don't see any American dream; I see an American nightmare.

These 22 million victims are waking up. Their eyes are coming open. They're beginning to see what they used to only look at. They're becoming politically mature. They are realizing that there are new political trends from coast to coast. As they see these new political trends, it's possible for them to see that every time there's an election the races are so close that they have to have a recount. They had to recount in Massachusetts to see who was going to be governor, it was so close. It was the same way in Rhode Island, in Minnesota, and in many other parts of the country. And the same with Kennedy and Nixon when they ran for president. It was so close they had to count all over again. Well, what does this mean? It means that when white people are evenly divided, and black people have a bloc of votes of their own, it is left up to them to determine who's going to sit in the White House and who's going to be in the dog house.

It was the black man's vote that put the present administration in Washington, D.C. Your vote, your dumb vote, your ignorant vote, your wasted vote put in an administration in Washington, D.C., that has seen fit to pass every kind of legislation imaginable, saving you until last, then filibustering on top of that. And your and my leaders have the audacity to run around clapping their hands and talk about how much progress we're making. And what a good president we have. If he wasn't good in Texas, he sure can't be good in Washington, D.C. Because Texas is a lynch state. It is in the same breath as Mississippi, no different; only they lynch you in Texas with a Texas accent and lynch you in Mississippi with a Mississippi accent. And these Negro leaders have the audacity to go and have some coffee in the White House with a Texan, a Southern cracker—that's all he is—and then come out and tell you and me that he's going to be better for us because, since he's from the South, he knows how to deal with the Southerners. What kind of logic is that? Let Eastland be president, he's from the South too. He should be better able to deal with them than Johnson.

In this present administration they have in the House of Representatives 257 Democrats to only 177 Republicans. They control two-thirds of the House vote. Why can't they pass something that will help you and me? In the Senate, there are 67 senators who are of the Democratic Party. Only 22 of them are Republicans. Why, the Democrats have got the government sewed up, and you're the one who sewed it up for them. And what have they given you for it? Four years in office, and just now getting around to some civil-rights legislation. Just now, after everything else is gone, out of the way, they're going to sit down now and play with you all summer long—the same old giant con game that they call filibuster. All those are in cahoots together. Don't you ever think they're not in cahoots together, for the man that is heading the civil-rights filibuster is a man from Georgia named Richard Russell. When Johnson became president, the first man he asked for when he got back to Washington, D.C., was "Dicky"—that's how tight they are. That's his boy, that's his pal, that's his buddy. But they're playing that old con game. One of them makes believe he's for you, and he's got it fixed where the other one is so tight against you, he never has to keep his promise.

So it's time in 1964 to wake up. And when you see them coming up with that kind of conspiracy, let them know your eyes are open. And let them know you got something else that's wide open too. It's got to be the bal-

lot or the bullet. The ballot or the bullet. If you're afraid to use an expression like that, you should get on out of the country, you should get back in the cotton patch, you should get back in the alley. They get all the Negro vote, and after they get it, the Negro gets nothing in return. All they did when they got to Washington was give a few big Negroes big jobs. Those big Negroes didn't need big jobs, they already had jobs. That's camouflage, that's trickery, that's treachery, window-dressing. I'm not trying to knock out the Democrats for the Republicans, we'll get to them in a minute. But it is true—you put the Democrats first and the Democrats put you last.

Look at it the way it is. What alibis do they use, since they control Congress and the Senate? What alibi do they use when you and I ask, "Well, when are you going to keep your promise?" They blame the Dixiecrats. What is a Dixiecrat? A Democrat. A Dixiecrat is nothing but a Democrat in disguise. The titular head of the Democrats is also the head of the Dixiecrats, because the Dixiecrats are a part of the Democratic Party. The Democrats have never kicked the Dixiecrats out of the party. The Dixiecrats bolted themselves once, but the Democrats didn't put them out. Imagine, these lowdown Southern segregationists put the Northern Democrats down. But the Northern Democrats have never put the Dixiecrats down. No, look at that thing the way it is. They have got a con game going on, a political con game, and you and I are in the middle. It's time for you and me to wake up and start looking at it like it is, and trying to understand it like it is; and then we can deal with it like it is.

The Dixiecrats in Washington, D.C., control the key committees that run the government. The only reason the Dixiecrats control these committees is because they have seniority. The only reason they have seniority is because they come from states where Negroes can't vote. This is not even a government that's based on democracy. It is not a government that is made up of representatives of the people. Half of the people in the South can't even vote. Eastland is not even supposed to be in Washington. Half of the senators and congressmen who occupy these key positions in Washington, D.C., are there illegally, are there unconstitutionally.

I was in Washington, D.C., a week ago Thursday, when they were debating whether or not they should let the bill come onto the floor. And in the back of the room where the Senate meets, there's a huge map of the United States, and on that map it shows the location of Negroes throughout the country. And it shows that the Southern section of the country, the states that are most heavily concentrated with Negroes, are the ones that have senators and congressmen standing up filibustering and doing all other kinds of trickery to keep the Negro from being able to vote. This is pitiful. But it's not pitiful for us any longer; it's actually pitiful for the white man, because soon now, as the Negro awakens a little more and sees the vise that he's in, sees the bag that he's in, sees the real game that he's in, then the Negro's going to develop a new tactic.

These senators and congressmen actually violate the constitutional amendments that guarantee the people of that particular state or county the right to vote. And the Constitution itself has within it the machinery to expel any representative from a state where the voting rights of the people are violated. You don't even need new legislation. Any person in Congress right now, who is there from a state or a district where the voting rights of the people are violated, that particular person should be expelled from Congress. And when you expel him, you've removed one of the obstacles in the path of any real meaningful legislation in this country. In fact, when you expel them, you don't need new legislation, because they will be replaced by black representatives from counties and districts where the black man is in the majority, not in the minority.

If the black man in these Southern states had his full voting rights, the key Dixiecrats in Washington, D.C., which means the key Democrats in Washington, D.C., would lose their seats. The Democratic Party itself would lose its power. It would cease to be powerful as a party. When you see the amount of power that would be lost by the Democratic Party if it were to lose the Dixiecrat wing, or branch, or element, you can see where it's against the interests of the Democrats to give voting rights to Negroes in states where the Democrats have been in complete power and authority ever since the Civil War. You just can't belong to that party without analyzing it.

I say again, I'm not anti-Democrat, I'm not anti-Republican, I'm not anti-anything. I'm just questioning their sincerity, and some of the strategy that they've been using on our people by promising them promises that they don't intend to keep. When you keep the Democrats in power, you're keeping the Dixiecrats in power. I doubt that my good Brother Lomax will deny that. A vote for a Democrat is a vote for a Dixiecrat. That's why, in 1964, it's time now for you and me to become more politically mature and realize what the ballot is for; what we're supposed to get when we cast a ballot; and that if we don't cast a ballot, it's going to end up in a situation where we're going to have to cast a bullet. It's either a ballot or a bullet.

In the North, they do it a different way. They have a system that's known as gerrymandering, whatever that means. It means when Negroes become too heavily concentrated in a certain area, and begin to gain too much political power, the white man comes along and changes the district lines. You may say, "Why do you keep saying white man?" Because it's the white man who does it. I haven't ever seen any Negro changing any lines. They don't let him get near the line. It's the white man who does this. And usually, it's the white man who grins at you the most, and pats you on the back, and is supposed to be your friend. He may be friendly, but he's not your friend.

So, what I'm trying to impress upon you, in essence, is this: You and I in America are faced not with a segregationist conspiracy, we're faced with a government conspiracy. Everyone who's filibustering is a senator—that's the government. Everyone who's finagling in Washington, D.C., is a congressman—that's the government. You don't have anybody putting blocks in your path but people who are a part of the government. The same government that you go abroad to fight for and die for is the government that is in a conspiracy to deprive you of your voting rights, deprive you of your economic opportunities, deprive you of decent housing, deprive you of decent education. You don't need to go to the employer alone, it is the government itself, the government of America, that is responsible for the oppression and exploitation and degradation of black people in this country. And you should drop it in their lap. This government has failed the Negro. This so-called democracy has failed the Negro. And all these white liberals have definitely failed the Negro.

So, where do we go from here? First, we need some friends. We need some new allies. The entire civil-rights struggle needs a new interpretation, a broader interpretation. We need to look at this civil-rights thing from another angle—from the inside as well as from the outside. To those of us whose philosophy is black nationalism, the only way you can get involved in the civil-rights struggle is give it a new interpretation. That old interpretation excluded us. It kept us out. So, we're giving a new interpretation to the civil-rights struggle, an interpretation that will enable us to come into it, take part in it. And these hand-kerchief-heads who have been dillydallying and pussyfooting and compromising—we don't intend to let them pussyfoot and dillydally and compromise any longer.

How can you thank a man for giving you what's already yours? How then can you thank him for giving you only part of what's already yours? You haven't even made progress, if what's being given to you, you should have had already. That's not progress. And I love my Brother Lomax, the way he pointed out we're right back where we were in 1954. We're not even as far up as we were in 1954. We're behind where we were in 1954. There's more segregation now than there was in 1954. There's more racial animosity, more racial hatred, more racial violence today in 1964, than there was in 1954. Where is the progress?

And now you're facing a situation where the young Negro's coming up. They don't want to hear that "turn-the-other-cheek" stuff, no. In Jacksonville, those were teenagers, they were throwing Molotov cocktails. Negroes have never done that before. But it shows you there's a new deal coming in. There's new thinking coming in. There's new strategy coming in. It'll be Molotov cocktails this month, hand grenades next month, and something else next month. It'll be ballots, or it'll be bullets. It'll be liberty, or it will be death. The only difference about this kind of death—it'll be reciprocal. You know what is meant by "reciprocal"? That's one of Brother Lomax's words, I stole it from him. I don't usually deal with those big words because I don't usually deal with big people. I deal with small people. I find you can get a whole lot of small people and whip hell out of a whole lot of big people. They haven't got anything to lose, and they've got everything to gain. And they'll let you know in a minute: "It takes two to tango; when I go, you go."

The black nationalists, those whose philosophy is black nationalism, in bringing about this new interpretation of the entire meaning of civil rights, look upon it as meaning, as Brother Lomax has pointed out, equality of opportunity. Well, we're justified in seeking civil rights, if it means equality of opportunity, because all we're doing there is trying to collect for our investment. Our mothers and fathers invested sweat and blood. Three hundred and ten years we worked in this country without a dime in return—I mean without a *dime* in return. You let the white man walk around here talking about how rich this country is, but you never stop to think how it got rich so quick. It got rich because you made it rich.

You take the people who are in this audience right now. They're poor, we're all poor as individuals. Our weekly salary individually amounts to hardly anything. But if you take the salary of everyone in here collectively it'll fill up a whole lot of baskets. It's a lot of wealth. If you can collect the wages of just these people right here for a year, you'll be rich—richer than rich. When you look at it like that, think how rich Uncle Sam had to become, not with this handful, but millions of black people. Your and my mother and father, who didn't work an eight-hour shift, but worked from "can't see" in the morning until "can't see" at night, and worked for nothing, making the white man rich, making Uncle Sam rich.

This is our investment. This is our contribution—our blood. Not only did we give of our free labor, we gave of our blood. Every time he had a call to arms, we were the first ones in uniform. We died on every battlefield the white man had. We have made a greater sacrifice than anybody who's standing up in America today. We have made

a greater contribution and have collected less. Civil rights, for those of us whose philosophy is black nationalism, means: "Give it to us now. Don't wait for next year. Give it to us yesterday, and that's not fast enough."

I might stop right here to point out one thing. Whenever you're going after something that belongs to you, anyone who's depriving you of the right to have it is a criminal. Understand that. Whenever you are going after something that is yours, you are within your legal rights to lay claim to it. And anyone who puts forth any effort to deprive you of that which is yours, is breaking the law, is a criminal. And this was pointed out by the Supreme Court decision. It outlawed segregation. Which means segregation is against the law. Which means a segregationist is breaking the law. A segregationist is a criminal. You can't label him as anything other than that. And when you demonstrate against segregation, the law is on your side. The Supreme Court is on your side.

Now, who is it that opposes you in carrying out the law? The police department itself. With police dogs and clubs. Whenever you demonstrate against segregation, whether it is segregated education, segregated housing, or anything else, the law is on your side, and anyone who stands in the way is not the law any longer. They are breaking the law, they are not representatives of the law. Any time you demonstrate against segregation and a man has the audacity to put a police dog on you, kill that dog, kill him, I'm telling you, kill that dog. I say it, if they put me in jail tomorrow, kill—that—dog. Then you'll put a stop to it. Now, if these white people in here don't want to see that kind of action, get down and tell the mayor to tell the police department to pull the dogs in. That's all you have to do. If you don't do it, someone else will.

If you don't take this kind of stand, your little children will grow up and look at you and think "shame." If you don't take an uncompromising stand—I don't mean go out and get violent; but at the same time you should never be nonviolent unless you run into some nonviolence. I'm nonviolent with those who are nonviolent with me. But when you drop that violence on me, then you've made me go insane, and I'm not responsible for what I do. And that's the way every Negro should get. Any time you know you're within the law, within your legal rights, within your moral rights, in accord with justice, then die for what you believe in. But don't die alone. Let your dying be reciprocal. This is what is meant by equality. What's good for the goose is good for the gander.

When we begin to get in this area, we need new friends, we need new allies. We need to expand the civil-rights struggle to a higher level—to the level of human rights. Whenever you are in a civil-rights struggle, whether you know it or not, you are confining yourself to the jurisdiction of Uncle Sam. No one from the outside world can speak out in your behalf as long as your struggle is a civil-rights struggle. Civil rights comes within the domestic affairs of this country. All of our African brothers and our Asian brothers and our Latin-American brothers cannot open their mouths and interfere in the domestic affairs of the United States. And as long as it's civil rights, this comes under the jurisdiction of Uncle Sam.

But the United Nations has what's known as the charter of human rights, it has a committee that deals in human rights. You may wonder why all of the atrocities that have been committed in Africa and in Hungary and in Asia and in Latin America are brought before the UN, and the Negro problem is never brought before the UN. This is part of the conspiracy. This old, tricky, blue-eyed liberal who is supposed to be your and my friend, supposed to be in our corner, supposed to be subsidizing our struggle, and supposed to be acting in the capacity of an adviser, never tells you anything about human rights. They keep you wrapped up in civil rights. And you spend so much time barking up the civil-rights tree, you don't even know there's a human-rights tree on the same floor.

When you expand the civil-rights struggle to the level of human rights, you can then take the case of the black man in this country before the nations in the UN. You can take it before the General Assembly. You can take Uncle Sam before a world court. But the only level you can do it on is the level of human rights. Civil rights keeps you under his restrictions, under his jurisdiction. Civil rights keeps you in his pocket. Civil rights means you're asking Uncle Sam to treat you right. Human rights are something you were born with. Human rights are your God-given rights. Human rights are the rights that are recognized by all nations of this earth. And any time any one violates your human rights, you can take them to the world court. Uncle Sam's hands are dripping with blood, dripping with the blood of the black man in this country. He's the earth's number-one hypocrite. He has the audacity—yes, he has—imagine him posing as the leader of the free world. The free world!—and you over here singing "We Shall Overcome." Expand the civil-rights struggle to the level of human rights, take it into the United Nations, where our African brothers can throw their weight on our side, where our Asian brothers can throw their weight on our side, where our Latin-American brothers can throw their weight on our side, and where 800 million Chinamen are sitting there waiting to throw their weight on our side.

Let the world know how bloody his hands are. Let the world know the hypocrisy that's practiced over here. Let it be the ballot or the bullet. Let him know that it must be the ballot or the bullet.

When you take your case to Washington, D.C., you're taking it to the criminal who's responsible; it's like running from the wolf to the fox. They're all in cahoots together. They all work political chicanery and make you look like a chump before the eyes of the world. Here you are walking around in America, getting ready to be drafted and sent abroad, like a tin soldier, and when you get over there, people ask you what are you fighting for, and you have to stick your tongue in your cheek. No, take Uncle Sam to court, take him before the world.

By ballot I only mean freedom. Don't you know—I disagree with Lomax on this issue—that the ballot is more important than the dollar? Can I prove it? Yes. Look in the UN. There are poor nations in the UN; yet those poor nations can get together with their voting power and keep the rich nations from making a move. They have one nation—one vote, everyone has an equal vote. And when those brothers from Asia, and Africa and the darker parts of this earth get together, their voting power is sufficient to hold Sam in check. Or Russia in check. Or some other section of the earth in check. So, the ballot is most important.

Right now, in this country, if you and I, 22 million African-Americans—that's what we are—Africans who are in America. You're nothing but Africans. Nothing but Africans. In fact, you'd get farther calling yourself African instead of Negro. Africans don't catch hell. You're the only one catching hell. They don't have to pass civil-rights bills for Africans. An African can go anywhere he wants right now. All you've got to do is tie your head up. That's right, go anywhere you want. Just stop being a Negro. Change your name to Hoogagagooba. That'll show you how silly the white man is. You're dealing with a silly man. A friend of mine who's very dark put a turban on his head and went into a restaurant in Atlanta before they called themselves desegregated. He went into a white restaurant, he sat down, they served him, and he said, "What would happen if a Negro came in here?" And there he's sitting, black as night, but because he had his head wrapped up the waitress looked back at him and says, "Why, there wouldn't no nigger dare come in here."

So, you're dealing with a man whose bias and prejudice are making him lose his mind, his intelligence, every day. He's frightened. He looks around and sees what's taking place on this earth, and he sees that the pendulum of time is swinging in your direction. The dark people are waking up. They're losing their fear of the white man. No place where he's fighting right now is he winning. Everywhere he's fighting, he's fighting someone your and my complexion. And they're beating him. He can't win any more. He's won his last battle. He failed to win the Korean

War. He couldn't win it. He had to sign a truce. That's a loss. Any time Uncle Sam, with all his machinery for warfare, is held to a draw by some rice-eaters, he's lost the battle. He had to sign a truce. America's not supposed to sign a truce. She's supposed to be bad. But she's not bad any more. She's bad as long as she can use her hydrogen bomb, but she can't use hers for fear Russia might use hers. Russia can't use hers, for fear that Sam might use his. So, both of them are weaponless. They can't use the weapon because each's weapon nullifies the other's. So the only place where action can take place is on the ground. And the white man can't win another war fighting on the ground. Those days are over. The black man knows it, the brown man knows it, the red man knows it, and the yellow man knows it. So they engage him in guerilla warfare. That's not his style. You've got to have heart to be a guerilla warrior, and he hasn't got any heart. I'm telling you now.

I just want to give you a little briefing on guerilla warfare because, before you know it, before you know it—It takes heart to be a guerilla warrior because you're on your own. In conventional warfare you have tanks and a whole lot of other people with you to back you up, planes over your head and all that kind of stuff. But a guerilla is on his own. All you have is a rifle, some sneakers and a bowl of rice, and that's all you need—and a lot of heart. The Japanese on some of those islands in the Pacific, when the American soldiers landed, one Japanese sometimes could hold the whole army off. He'd just wait until the sun went down, and when the sun went down they were all equal. He would take his little blade and slip from bush to bush, and from American to American. The white soldiers couldn't cope with that. Whenever you see a white solider that fought in the Pacific, he has the shakes, he has a nervous condition, because they scared him to death.

The same thing happened to the French up in French Indochina. People who just a few years previously were rice farmers got together and ran the heavily-mechanized French army out of Indochina. You don't need it—modern warfare today won't work. This is the day of the guerillas. They did the same thing in Algeria. Algerians, who were nothing but Bedouins, took a rifle and sneaked off to the hills, and de Gaulle and all of his highfalutin' war machinery couldn't defeat those guerillas. Nowhere on this earth does the white man win in a guerilla warfare. It's not his speed. Just as guerilla warfare is prevailing in Asia and in parts of Africa and in parts of Latin America, you've got to be mighty naive, or you've got to play the black man cheap, if you don't think some day he's going to wake up and find that it's got to be the ballot or the bullet.

I would like to say, in closing, a few things concerning the Muslim Mosque, Inc., which we established recently in New York City. It's true we're Muslims and our religion is Islam, but we don't mix our religion with our politics and our economics and our social and civil activities—not any more. We keep our religion in our mosque. After our religious services are over, then as Muslims we become involved in political action, economic action and social and civic action. We become involved with anybody, anywhere, any time and in any manner that's designed to eliminate the evils, the political, economic and social evils that are afflicting the people of our community.

The political philosophy of black nationalism means that the black man should control the politics and the politicians in his own community; no more. The black man in the black community has to be re-educated into the science of politics so he will know what politics is supposed to bring him in return. Don't be throwing out any ballots. A ballot is like a bullet. You don't throw your ballots until you see a target, and if that target is not within your reach, keep your ballot in your pocket. The political philosophy of black nationalism is being taught in the Christian church. It's being taught in the NAACP. It's being taught in CORE meetings. It's being taught in SNCC [Student Nonviolent Coordinating Committee] meetings. It's being taught in Muslim meetings. It's being taught where nothing but atheists and agnostics come together. It's being taught everywhere. Black people are fed up with the dilly-dallying, pussyfooting, compromising approach that we've been using toward getting our freedom. We want freedom *now*, but we're not going to get it saying "We Shall Overcome." We've got to fight until we overcome.

The economic philosophy of black nationalism is pure and simple. It only means that we should control the economy of our community. Why should white people be running all the stores in our community? Why should white people be running the banks of our community? Why should the economy of our community be in the hands of the white man? Why? If a black man can't move his store into a white community, you tell me why a white man should move his store into a black community. The philosophy of black nationalism involves a re-education program in the black community in regards to economics. Our people have to be made to see that any time you take your dollar out of your community and spend it in a community where you don't live, the community where you live will get poorer and poorer, and the community where you spend your money will get richer and richer. Then you wonder why where you live is always a ghetto or a slum area. And where you and I are concerned, not only do we lose it when we spend it out of the community, but the white man has got all our stores in the community tied up; so that though we spend it in the community, at sundown the man who runs the store takes it over across town somewhere. He's got us in a vise.

So the economic philosophy of black nationalism means in every church, in every civic organization, in every fraternal order, it's time now for our people to become conscious of the importance of controlling the economy of our community. If we own the stores, if we operate the businesses, if we try and establish some industry in our own community, then we're developing to the position where we are creating employment for our own kind. Once you gain control of the economy of your own community, then you don't have to picket and boycott and beg some cracker downtown for a job in his business.

The social philosophy of black nationalism only means that we have to get together and remove the evils, the vices, alcoholism, drug addiction, and other evils that are destroying the moral fiber of our community. We ourselves have to lift the level of our community, the standard of our community to a higher level, make our own society beautiful so that we will be satisfied in our own social circles and won't be running around here trying to knock our way into a social circle where we're not wanted.

So I say, in spreading a gospel such as black nationalism, it is not designed to make the black man re-evaluate the white man—you know him already—but to make the black man re-evaluate himself. Don't change the white man's mind—you can't change his mind, and that whole thing about appealing to the moral conscience of America—America's conscience is bankrupt. She lost all conscience a long time ago. Uncle Sam has no conscience. They don't know what morals are. They don't try and eliminate an evil because it's evil, or because it's illegal, or because it's immoral; they eliminate it only when it threatens their existence. So you're wasting your time appealing to the moral conscience of a bankrupt man like Uncle Sam. If he had a conscience, he'd straighten this thing out with no more pressure being put upon him. So it is not necessary to change the white man's mind. We have to change our own mind. You can't change his mind about us. We've got to change our own minds about each other. We have to see each other with new eyes. We have to see each other as brothers and sisters. We have to come together with warmth so we can develop unity and harmony that's necessary to get this problem solved ourselves. How can we do this? How can we avoid jealousy? How can we avoid the suspicion and the divisions that exist in the community? I'll tell you how.

I have watched how Billy Graham comes into a city, spreading what he calls the gospel of Christ, which is only white nationalism. That's what he is. Billy Graham is a white nationalist; I'm a black nationalist. But since it's the natural tendency for leaders to be jealous and look upon a powerful figure like Graham with suspicion and envy, how is it possible for him to come into a city and get all the cooperation of the church leaders? Don't think because they're church leaders that they don't have weaknesses that make them envious and jealous—no, everybody's got it. It's not an accident that when they want to choose a cardinal [as Pope] over there in Rome, they get in a closet so you can't hear them cursing and fighting and carrying on.

Billy Graham comes in preaching the gospel of Christ, he evangelizes the gospel, he stirs everybody up, but he never tries to start a church. If he came in trying to start a church, all the churches would be against him. So, he just comes in talking about Christ and tells everybody who gets Christ to go to any church where Christ is; and in this way the church cooperates with him. So we're going to take a page from his book.

Our gospel is black nationalism. We're not trying to threaten the existence of any organization, but we're spreading the gospel of black nationalism. Anywhere there's a church that is also preaching and practicing the gospel of black nationalism, join that church. If the NAACP is preaching and practicing the gospel of black nationalism, join the NAACP. If CORE is spreading and practicing the gospel of black nationalism, join CORE. Join any organization that has a gospel that's for the uplift of the black man. And when you get into it and see them pussyfooting or compromising, pull out of there because that's not black nationalism. We'll find another one.

And in this manner, the organizations will increase in number and in quantity and in quality, and by August, it is then our intention to have a black nationalist convention which will consist of delegates from all over the country who are interested in the political, economic and social philosophy of black nationalism. After these delegates convene, we will hold a seminar, we will hold discussions, we will listen to everyone. We want to hear new ideas and new solutions and new answers. And at that time, if we see fit then to form a black nationalist party, we'll form a black nationalist party. If it's necessary to form a black nationalist army, we'll form a black nationalist army. It'll be the ballot or the bullet. It'll be liberty or it'll be death.

It's time for you and me to stop sitting in this country, letting some cracker senators, Northern crackers and Southern crackers, sit there in Washington, D.C., and come to a conclusion in their mind that you and I are supposed to have civil rights. There's no white man going to tell me anything about *my* rights. Brothers and sisters, always remember, if it doesn't take senators and congressmen and presidential proclamations to give freedom to the white man, it is not necessary for legislation or proclamation or Supreme Court decisions to give freedom to the black man. You let that white man know, if this is a country of freedom, let it be a country of freedom; and if it's not a country of freedom, change it.

We will work with anybody, anywhere, at any time, who is genuinely interested in tackling the problem head-on, nonviolently as long as the enemy is nonviolent, but violent when the enemy gets violent. We'll work with you on the voter-registration drive, we'll work with you on rent strikes, we'll work with you on school boycotts—I don't believe in any kind of integration; I'm not even worried about it because I know you're not going to get it anyway; you're not going to get it because you're afraid to die; you've got to be ready to die if you try and force yourself on the white man, because he'll get just as violent as those crackers in Mississippi, right here in Cleveland. But we will still work with you on the school boycotts because we're against a segregated school system. A segregated school system produces children who, when they graduate, graduate with crippled minds. But this does not mean that a school is segregated because it's all black. A segregated school means a school that is controlled by people who have no real interest in it whatsoever.

Let me explain what I mean. A segregated district or community is a community in which people live, but outsiders control the politics and the economy of that community. They never refer to the white section as a segregated community. It's the all-Negro section that's a segregated community. Why? The white man controls his own school, his own bank, his own economy, his own politics, his own everything, his own community—but he also controls yours. When you're under someone else's control, you're segregated. They'll always give you the lowest or the worst that there is to offer, but it doesn't mean you're segregated just because you have your own. You've got to *control* your own. Just like the white man has control of his, you need to control yours.

You know the best way to get rid of segregation? The white man is more afraid of separation than he is of integration. Segregation means that he puts you away from him, but not far enough for you to be out of his jurisdiction; separation means you're gone. And the white man will integrate faster than he'll let you separate. So we will work with you against the segregated school system because it's criminal, because it is absolutely destructive, in every way imaginable, to the minds of the children who have to be exposed to that type of crippling education.

Last but not least, I must say this concerning the great controversy over rifles and shotguns. The only thing that I've ever said is that in areas where the government has proven itself either unwilling or unable to defend the lives and the property of Negroes, it's time for Negroes to defend themselves. Article number two of the constitutional amendments provides you and me the right to own a rifle or a shotgun. It is constitutionally legal to own a shotgun or a rifle. This doesn't mean you're going to get a rifle and form battalions and go out looking for white folks, although you'd be within your rights—I mean, you'd be justified; but that would be illegal and we don't do anything illegal. If the white man doesn't want the black man buying rifles and shotguns, then let the government do its job. That's all. And don't let the white man come to you and ask you what you think about what Malcolm says—why, you old Uncle Tom. He would never ask you if he thought you were going to say, "Amen!" No, he is making a Tom out of you.

So this doesn't mean forming rifle clubs and going out looking for people, but it is time, in 1964, if you are a man, to let that man know. If he's not going to do his job in running the government and providing you and me with the protection that our taxes are supposed to be for, since he spends all those billions for his defense budget, he certainly can't begrudge you and me spending $12 or $15 for a single-shot, or double-action. I hope you understand. Don't go out shooting people, but any time, brothers and sisters, and especially the men in this audience—some of you wearing Congressional Medals of Honor, with shoulders this wide, chests this big, muscles that big—any time you and I sit around and read where they bomb a church and murder in cold blood, not some grownups, but four little girls while they were praying to the same god the white man taught them to pray to, and you and I see the government go down and can't find who did it.

Why, this man—he can find Eichmann hiding down in Argentina somewhere. Let two or three American soldiers, who are minding somebody else's business way over in South Vietnam, get killed, and he'll send battleships, sticking his nose in their business. He wanted to send troops down to Cuba and make them have what he calls free elections—this old cracker who doesn't' have free elections in his own country. No, if you never see me another time in your life, if I die in the morning, I'll die saying one thing: the ballot or the bullet, the ballot or the bullet.

If a Negro in 1964 has to sit around and wait for some cracker senator to filibuster when it comes to the rights of black people, why, you and I should hang our heads in shame. You talk about a march on Washington in 1963, you haven't seen anything. There's some more going down in '64. And this time they're not going like they went last year. They're not going singing "We Shall Overcome." They're not going with white friends. They're not going with placards already painted for them. They're not going with round-trip tickets. They're going with one-way tickets.

And if they don't want that non-nonviolent army going down there, tell them to bring the filibuster to a halt. The black nationalists aren't going to wait. Lyndon B. Johnson is the head of the Democratic Party. If he's for civil rights, let him go into the Senate next week and declare himself. Let him go in there right now and declare himself. Let him go in there and denounce the Southern branch of his party. Let him go in there right now and take a moral stand—right now, not later. Tell him, don't wait until election time. If he waits too long, brothers and sisters, he will be responsible for letting a condition develop in this country which will create a climate that will bring seeds up out of the ground with vegetation on the end of them looking like something these people never dreamed of. In 1964, it's the ballot or the bullet. Thank you.

LIFE IN MISSISSIPPI: AN INTERVIEW WITH FANNIE LOU HAMER (1965)

SOURCE: Frazier, Thomas R., ed. *Readings in African-American History.* 3d edition. Belmont, Calif.: Wadsworth/Thomson Learning, 2001, pp. 348–357.

INTRODUCTION: *Civil rights activist Fannie Lou Hamer was one of the delegates of the Mississippi Freedom Democratic Party to the National Democratic Convention in 1964. The following year, in an interview first published in the civil rights journal* Freedomways, *Hamer reflected on her childhood and later life in Mississippi.*

O'DELL:

Mrs. Hamer, it's good to see you again. I understand you have been to Africa since we last talked? I would like for you to talk about your African trip today.

HAMER:

It was one of the proudest moments in my life.

O'DELL:

That is a marvelous experience for any black American, particularly for anyone who has lived here all of his life. Then, too, we want to talk about some of your early childhood experiences which helped to make you the kind of person you are and provided the basis for your becoming so active in the Freedom Movement.

HAMER:

I would like to talk about some of the things that happened that made me know that there was something wrong in the South from a child. My parents moved to Sunflower County when I was two years old. I remember, and I will never forget, one day—I was six years old and I was playing beside the road and this plantation owner drove up to me and stopped and asked me "could I pick cotton." I told him I didn't know and he said, "Yes, you can. I will give you things that you want from the commissary store," and he named things like crackerjacks and sardines—and it was a huge list that he called off. So I picked the 30 pounds of cotton that week, but I found out what actually happened was he was trapping me into beginning the work I was to keep doing and I never did get out of his debt again. My parents tried so hard to do what they could to keep us in school, but school didn't last but four months out of the year and most of the time we didn't have clothes to wear. My parents would make huge crops of sometimes 55 to 60 bales of cotton. Being from a big family where there were 20 children, it wasn't too hard to pick that much cotton. But my father, year after year, didn't get too much money and I remember he just kept going. Later on he did get enough money to buy mules. We didn't have tractors, but he bought mules, wagons, cultivators and some farming equipment. As soon as he bought that and decided to rent some land, because it was always better if you rent the land, but as soon as he got the mules and wagons and everything, somebody went to our trough—a white man who didn't live very far from us—and he fed the mules Paris Green, put it in their food and it killed the mules and our cows. That knocked us right back down. And things got so tough then I began to wish I was white. We worked all the time, just worked and then we would be hungry and my mother was clearing up a new ground trying to help to feed us for $1.25 a day. She was using an axe, just like a man, and something flew up and hit her in the eye. It eventually caused her to lose both her eyes and I began to get sicker and sicker of the system there. I used to see my mother wear clothes that would have so many patches on them, they had been done over and over and over again. She would do that but she would try to keep us decent. She still would be ragged and I always said if I lived to get grown and had a chance, I was going to try to get something for my mother and I was going to do something for the black man of the South if it would cost my life; I was determined to see that things were changed. My mother got down sick in '53 and she lived with me, an invalid, until she passed away in 1961. And during the time she was staying with me sometime I would be worked so hard I couldn't sleep at night. . . .

O'DELL:

What kind of work were you doing?

HAMER:

I was a timekeeper and sharecropper on the same plantation I was fired from. During the time she was with me, if there was something I had to do without, I was determined to see that she did have something in her last few years. I went almost naked to see that my mother was kept decent and treated as a human being for the first time in all of her life. My mother was a great woman. To look at her from the suffering she had gone through to bring us up—20 children: 6 girls and 14 boys, but she still taught us to be decent and to respect ourselves, and that is one of the things that has kept me going, even after she passed. She tried so hard to make life easy for us. Those are the things that forced me to try to do something different and when this Movement came to Mississippi I still feel it is one of the greatest things that ever happened because only a person living in the State of Mississippi knows what it is like to suffer; knows what it is like to be hungry; knows what it is like to have no clothing to wear. And these people in Mississippi State, they are not "down"; all they need is a chance. And I am determined to give my part not for what the Movement can do for me, but what I can do for the Movement to bring about a change in the State of Mississippi. Actually, some of the things I experienced as a child still linger on; what the white man has done to the black people in the South!

One of the things I remember as a child: There was a man named Joe Pulliam. He was a great Christian man; but one time, he was living with a white family and this white family robbed him of what he earned. They didn't pay him anything. This white man gave him $150 to go to the hill (you see, I lived in the Black Belt of Mississippi) . . . to get another Negro family. Joe Pulliam knew what this white man had been doing to him so he kept the $150 and didn't go. This white man talked with him then shot him in the shoulder and Joe Pulliam went back into the house and got a Winchester and killed this white man. The other white fellow that was with him he "outrun the word of God" back to town. That gave this Negro a chance to go down on the bayou that was called Powers Bayou and he got in a hollowed-out stump where there was enough room for a person. He got in there and he stayed and was tracked there, but they couldn't see him and every time a white man would peep out, he busted him. He killed 13 white men and wounded 26 and Mississippi was a quiet place for a long time. I remember that until this day and I won't forget it. After they couldn't get him, they took gas—one man from Clarksdale used a machine gun—(Bud Doggins)—they used a machine gun and they tried

to get him like that and then they took gas and poured it on Powers Bayou. Thousands of gallons of gas and they lit it and when it burned up to the hollowed-out stump, he crawled out. When they found him, he was unconscious and he was lying with his head on his gun but the last bullet in the gun had been snapped twice. They dragged him by his heels on the back of a car and they paraded about with that man and they cut his ears off and put them in a showcase and it stayed there a long, long time—in Drew, Mississippi. All of those things, when they would happen, would make me sick in the pit of my stomach and year after year, everytime something would happen it would make me more and more aware of what would have to be done in the State of Mississippi.

O'DELL:

What do you think will have to be done?

HAMER:

The only thing I really feel is necessary is that the black people, not only in Mississippi, will have to actually upset this applecart. What I mean by that is, so many things are under the cover that will have to be swept out and shown to this whole world, not just to America. There is so much hypocrisy in America. This thing they say of "the land of the free and the home of the brave" is all on paper. It doesn't mean anything to us. The only way we can make this thing a reality in America is to do all we can to destroy this system and bring this thing out to the light that has been under the cover all these years. That's why I believe in Christianity because the Scriptures said: "The things that have been done in the dark will be known on the house tops."

Now many things are beginning to come out and it was truly a reality to me when I went to Africa, to Guinea. The little things that had been taught to me about the African people, that they were "heathens," "savages," and they were just downright stupid people. But when I got to Guinea, we were greeted by the Government of Guinea, which is *Black People*—and we stayed at a place that was the government building, because we were the guests of the Government. You don't know what that meant to me when I got to Guinea on the 12th of September. The President of Guinea, Sekou Touré, came to see us on the 13th. Now you know, I don't know how you can compare this by me being able to see a President of a country, when I have just been there two days; and here I have been in America, born in America, and I am 46 years pleading with the President for the last two to three years to just give us a chance—and this President in Guinea recognized us enough to talk to us.

O'DELL:

How many were in your delegation?

HAMER:

It was eleven of us during that time, and I could get a clear picture of actually what had happened to the black people of America. Our foreparents were mostly brought from West Africa, the same place that we visited in Africa. We were brought to America and our foreparents were sold; white people bought them; white people changed their names . . . and actually . . . here, my maiden name is supposed to be Townsend; but really, what is my maiden name. . . ? What is my name? This white man who is saying "it takes time." For three hundred and more years they have had "time," and now it is time for them to listen. We have been listening year after year to them and what have we got? We are not even allowed to think for ourselves. "I know what is best for you," but they don't know what is best for us! It is time now to let them know what they owe us, and they owe us a great deal. Not only have we paid the price with our names in ink, but we have also paid in blood. And they can't say that black people can't be intelligent, because going back to Africa, in Guinea, there are almost 4 million people there and what he, President Touré, is doing to educate the people: as long as the French people had it they weren't doing a thing that is being done now. I met one child there eleven years old, speaking three languages. He could speak English, French and Malinke. Speaking my language actually better than I could. And this hypocrisy—they tell us here in America. People should go there and see. It would bring tears in your eyes to make you think of all those years, the type of brain-washing that this man will use in America to keep us separated from our own people. When I got on that plane, it was loaded with white people going to Africa for the Peace Corps. I got there and met a lot of them, and actually they had more peace there in Guinea than I have here. I talked to some of them. I told them before they would be able to clean up somebody else's house you would have to clean up yours; before they can tell somebody else how to run their country, why don't they do something here. This problem is not only in Mississippi. During the time I was in the Convention in Atlantic City, I didn't get any threats from Mississippi. The threatening letters were from Philadelphia, Chicago and other big cities.

O'DELL:

You received threatening letters while you were at the Convention?

HAMER:

Yes. I got pictures of us and they would draw big red rings around us and tell what they thought of us. I got a letter said, "I have been shot three times through the heart. I hope I see your second act." But this white man who wants to stay *white*, and to think for the Negro, he is not only destroying the Negro, he is destroying himself, because a house divided against itself cannot stand and that same thing applies to America. America that is divided against itself cannot stand, and we cannot say we have all this unity they say we have when black people are being discriminated against in every city in America I have visited.

I was in jail when Medgar Evers was murdered and *nothing*, I mean *nothing* has been done about that. You know what really made me sick? I was in Washington, D.C., at another time reading in a paper where the U.S. gives Byron de la Beckwith—the man who is charged with murdering Medgar Evers—they were giving him so much money for some land and I ask "Is this America?" We can no longer ignore the fact that America is NOT the "land of the free and the home of the brave." I used to question this for years—what did our kids actually fight for? They would go in the service and go through all of that and come right out to be drowned in a river in Mississippi. I found this hypocrisy is all over America.

The 20th of March in 1964, I went before the Secretary of State to qualify to run as an official candidate for Congress from the 2nd Congressional District, and it was easier for me to qualify to run than it was for me to pass the literacy test to be a registered voter. And we had four people to qualify and run in the June primary election but we didn't have enough Negroes registered in Mississippi. The 2nd Congressional District where I ran, against Jamie Whitten, is made up of 24 counties. Sixty-eight percent of the people are Negroes, only 6–8 percent are registered. And it is not because Negroes don't want to register. They try and they try and they try. That's why it was important for us to set up the "Freedom Registration" to help us in the Freedom Democratic Party.

O'DELL:

This was a registration drive organized by the Movement?

HAMER:

Yes. The only thing we took out was the Constitution of the State of Mississippi and the interpretation of the Constitution. We had 63,000 people registered on the Freedom Registration form. And we tried from every level to go into the regular Democratic Party medium. We tried from the precinct level. The 16th of June when they were holding precinct meetings all across the state, I was there and there was eight of us there to attend the meeting, and they had the door locked at 10 o'clock in the morning. So we had our own meeting and elected our permanent chairman and secretary and regulars and alternates and we passed a resolution as the law requires and then mailed it to Oscar Townsend, our permanent chairman. This is what's happening in the State of Mississippi. We had hoped for a change, but these people (Congressmen) go to Washington and stay there 25 and 30 years and more without representing the people of Mississippi. We have never been represented in Washington. You can tell this by the program the federal government had to train 2,400 tractor drivers. They would have trained Negro and white together, but this man, Congressman Jamie Whitten, voted against it and everything that was decent. So we've got to have somebody in Washington who is concerned about the people of Mississippi.

After we testified before the Credentials Committee in Atlantic City, their Mississippi representative testified also. He said I got 600 votes but when they made the count in Mississippi, I was told I had 388 votes. So actually it is no telling how many votes I actually got.

O'DELL:

In other words, a Mr. Collins came before the Credentials Committee of the Democratic National Convention and actually gave away the secret in a sense, because the figure he gave was not the same figure he gave to you as an official candidate?

HAMER:

That's right. He also said I had been allowed to attend the precinct meeting which was true. But he didn't say we were locked out of the polling place there and had to hold our meeting on the lawn.

O'DELL:

So now you have a situation where you had the basis for a Freedom Democratic Party. You have had four candidates to run for Congress. You had a community election where 63,000 of our folk showed their interest in the election. How do you size up the situation coming out of Atlantic City? What impressions did you get from your effort in Atlantic City to be seated, and how do you feel the people back home are going to react to this next period you are going into?

HAMER:

The people at home will work hard and actually all of them think it was important that we made the decision that we did make *not to compromise*; because we didn't have anything to *compromise* for. Some things I found out in the National Convention I wasn't too glad I did find out. But we will work hard, and it was important to actually really bring this out to the open, the things I will say some people knew about and some people didn't; this stuff that has been kept under the cover for so many years. Actually, the world and America is upset and the only way to bring about a change is to upset it more.

O'DELL:

What was done about the beating you and Miss Annelle Ponder, your colleague in the citizenship school program, experienced while in jail? Was any action taken at all?

HAMER:

The Justice Department filed a suit against the brutality of the five law officials and they had this trial. The trial began the 2nd of December 1963 and they had white jurors from the State of Mississippi, and the Federal Judge Clayton made it plain to the jurors that they were dealing with "nigras" and that "who would actually accuse such upstanding people like those law officials"—be careful what they was doing because they are law-abiding citizens and were dealing with agitators and niggers. It was as simple as that. And those police were cleared. They were on the loose for about a week before I left for Atlantic City. One of those men was driving a truck from the State Penitentiary. One night he passed my house and pointed me out to one of the other men in the State Penitentiary truck and that same night I got a threat: "We got you located Fannie Lou and we going to put you in the Mississippi River." A lot of people say why do they let the *hoodlums* do that? But it is those people supposed to have class that are doing the damage in Mississippi. You know there was a time, in different places, when people felt safe going to a law official. But I called them that day and got the answer back, "You know you don't look to us for help."

O'DELL:

This threat: the man called you up and said "we've got you spotted"; I gather from that that the river has some special meaning to us living there in Mississippi?

HAMER:

Yes. So many people have been killed and put in the Mississippi River. Like when they began to drag the river for Mickey and Chaney and Andy. Before he was to go to Oxford, Ohio, Mickey was telling me his life had been threatened and a taxi driver had told him to be careful because they was out to get him.

When they (the sailors) began to drag the river they found other people and I actually feel like they stopped because they would have been shook up to find so many if they had just been fishing for bodies. The Mississippi is not the only river. There's the Tallahatchie and the Big Black. People have been put in the river year after year, these things *been* happening.

O'DELL:

The general policy of striking fear in people's hearts. In other words, it's like lynching used to be. They used to night ride. . . .

HAMER:

They still night ride. The exact count was 32 churches they had burned in the State of Mississippi and they still ride at night, and throw bombs at night. You would think they would cut down with Mrs. Chaney. But since they murdered James Chaney, they have shot buckshot at his mother's house. And hate won't only destroy us. It will destroy these people that's hating as well. And one of the things is, they are afraid of getting back what they have been putting out all of these years. You know the Scripture says "be not deceived for God is not mocked; whatsoever a man sow that shall he also reap." And *one day,* I don't know how they're going to get it, but they're going to get some of it back. They are scared to death and are more afraid now than we are.

O'DELL:

How active is the White Citizen's Council? Has it the kind of outlet through TV and radio and so forth that Negroes are aware of its presence?

HAMER:

They announce their programs. In fact, one day I was going to Jackson and I saw a huge sign that U.S. Senator John Stennis was speaking that night for the White Citizens Council in Yazoo City and they also have a State Charter that they may set up for "private schools." It is no secret.

O'DELL:

Does it seem to be growing? Is the white community undergoing any change as a result of all the pressure that has been put now with the Mississippi Summer Project and the killing of the three civil rights workers? What effect is it having on the white community?

HAMER:

You can't ever tell. I have talked to two or three whites that's decent in the State of Mississippi, but you know, just two or three speaking out. I do remember, one time, a man came to me after the students began to work in Mississippi and he said the white people were getting tired and they were getting tense and anything might happen. Well, I asked him "how long he thinks *we* had been getting tired"? I had been *tired* for 46 years and my parents were *tired* before me and their parents were *tired*; and I have always wanted to do something that would help some of the things I would see going on among Negroes that I didn't like and I don't like now.

O'DELL:

Getting back just for a minute to Atlantic City. You all were in the national spotlight because there was nothing else happening in the Democratic National Convention other than your challenge to the Mississippi delegation and I would like to go back to that and pull together some of the conclusions you might have drawn from that experience.

HAMER:

In coming to Atlantic City, we believed strongly that we were right. In fact, it was just right for us to come to chal-

lenge the seating of the regular Democratic Party from Mississippi. But we didn't think when we got there that we would meet people, that actually the other leaders of the Movement would differ with what we felt was right. We would have accepted the Green proposal. But, when we couldn't get that, it didn't make any sense for us to take "two votes at large." What would that mean to Mississippi? What would it have meant to us to go back and tell the Mississippi people? And actually, I think there will be great leaders emerging from the State of Mississippi. The people that have the experience to know and the people not interested in letting somebody pat you on the back and tell us "I think it is right." And it was very important for us not to accept a compromise and after I got back to Mississippi, people there said it was the most important step that had been taken. We figured it was right and it was right, and if we had accepted that compromise, then we would have been letting the people down in Mississippi. Regardless of leadership, *we have to think for ourselves!*

O'DELL:

In other words, you had two battles on your hands when you went to Atlantic City?

HAMER:

Yes. I was in one of the meetings when they spoke about accepting two votes and I said I wouldn't dare think about anything like this. So, I wasn't allowed to attend the other meetings. It was quite an experience.

O'DELL:

There will be other elections and other conventions and the people in Mississippi should be a little stronger.

HAMER:

I think so.

O'DELL:

Well, it's good to know that the people you have to work with every day are with *you.*

HAMER:

Yes, they are with us one hundred percent.

O'DELL:

That's encouraging because it makes the work that much easier. Is there any final thing you want to say that is part of this historic statement of life in Mississippi for yourself as a person who lives there?

HAMER:

Nothing other than we will be working. When I go back to Mississippi we will be working as hard or harder to bring about a change, but things are not always pleasant there.

O'DELL:

You will probably have the support of more people than you have ever had, all around the country.

HAMER:

Yes, actually since the Convention I have gotten so many letters that I have tried to answer but every letter said they thought this decision, not to accept the compromise, was so important. There wasn't one letter I have gotten so far that said we should have accepted the compromise—not one.

O'DELL:

So, those are the people who are interested in your work, and as you get back into the main swing of things you will be keeping in touch with those people so that they should be asked to help in any way they can regardless of where they live. It is national and international public pressure that is needed.

Are you aware that there has been any coverage of the African trip by the Mississippi press? Have they made any comments on it?

HAMER:

I don't know about the press, but I know in the town where I live everybody was aware that I was in Africa, because I remember after I got back some of the people told me that Mayor Durr of our town said he just wished they would boil me in tar. But, that just shows how ignorant he is, I didn't see any tar over there. But I was treated much better in Africa than I was treated in America. And you see, often I get letters like this: "Go back to Africa."

Now I have just as much right to stay in America—in fact, the black people have contributed more to America than any other race, because our kids have fought here for what was called "democracy"; our mothers and fathers were sold and brought here for a price. So all I can say when they say "go back to Africa," I say "when you send the Chinese back to China, the Italians back to Italy, etc., and you get on that Mayflower from whence you came, and give the Indians their land back, who really would be here at home?" It is our right to stay here and we will stay and stand up for what belongs to us as American citizens, because they can't say that we haven't had patience.

O'DELL:

Was there a lot of interest in your trip among the African people that you met?

HAMER:

Yes. I saw how the Government was run there and I saw where black people were running the banks. I saw, for the first time in my life, a black stewardess walking through a plane and that was quite an inspiration for me. It shows what black people can do if we only get the chance in America. It is there within us. We can do things if we only get the chance. I see so many ways America uses to rob Negroes and it is sinful and America can't keep holding on, and doing these things. I saw in Chicago, on the street where I was visiting my sister-in-law, this "Urban Renewal" and it means one thing: "Negro removal." But they want to tear the homes down and put a parking lot there. Where are those people going? Where will they go? And as soon as Negroes take to the street demonstrating, one hears people say, "they shouldn't have done it." The world is looking at America and it is really beginning to show up for what it is really like. "Go Tell It on the Mountain." We can no longer ignore this, that America is not "the land of the free and the home of the brave."

O'DELL:

Thank you, Mrs. Fannie Lou Hamer, Vice-Chairman of the Freedom Democratic Party of Mississippi; courageous fighter for human rights.

PLATFORM AND PROGRAM OF THE BLACK PANTHER PARTY (1966)

▪▪▪

SOURCE: Frazier, Thomas R., ed. *Afro-American History: Primary Sources.* New York: Harcourt, Brace & World, 1970, pp. 467–470.

INTRODUCTION: *Founded in Oakland, California, by Huey Newton and Bobby Seale in 1966, the Black Panthers vocally affirmed Black Power and black pride and took an uncompromising stance on civil liberties for black Americans. The ten points outlined in the party's Platform and Program itemize their demands for justice and for an equal share in the protection and benefits of American citizenship.*

What We Want, What We Believe

1. We want freedom. We want power to determine the destiny of our Black Community.

We believe that black people will not be free until we are able to determine our destiny.

2. We want full employment for our people.

We believe that the federal government is responsible and obligated to give every man employment or a guaranteed income. We believe that if the white American businessmen will not give full employment, then the means of production should be taken from the businessmen and placed in the community so that the people of the community can organize and employ all of its people and give a high standard of living.

3. We want an end to the robbery by the white man of our Black Community.

We believe that this racist government has robbed us and now we are demanding the overdue debt of forty acres and two mules. Forty acres and two mules was promised 100 years ago as restitution for slave labor and mass murder of black people. We will accept the payment as currency which will be distributed to our many communities. The Germans are now aiding the Jews in Israel for the genocide of the Jewish people. The Germans murdered six million Jews. The American racist has taken part in the slaughter of over twenty million black people; therefore, we feel that this is a modest demand that we make.

4. We want decent housing, fit for shelter of human beings.

We believe that if the white landlords will not give decent housing to our black community, then the housing and the land should be made into cooperatives so that our community, with government aid, can build and make decent housing for its people.

5. We want education for our people that exposes the true nature of this decadent American society. We want education that teaches us our true history and our role in the present-day society.

We believe in an educational system that will give to our people a knowledge of self. If a man does not have knowledge of himself and his position in society and the world, then he has little chance to relate to anything else.

6. We want all black men to be exempt from military service.

We believe that Black people should not be forced to fight in the military service to defend a racist government that does not protect us. We will not fight and kill other people of color in the world who, like black people, are being victimized by the white racist government of America. We will protect ourselves from the force and violence of the racist police and the racist military, by whatever means necessary.

7. We want an immediate end to POLICE BRUTALITY and MURDER of black people.

We believe we can end police brutality in our black community by organizing black self-defense groups that are dedicated to defending our black community from racist police oppression and brutality. The Second Amendment to the Constitution of the United States gives a right to bear arms. We therefore believe that all black people should arm themselves for self defense.

8. We want freedom for all black men held in federal, state, county and city prisons and jails.

We believe that all black people should be released from the many jails and prisons because they have not received a fair and impartial trial.

9. We want all black people when brought to trial to be tried in court by a jury of their peer group or people from their black communities, as defined by the Constitution of the United States.

We believe that the courts should follow the United States Constitution so that black people will receive fair trials. The 14th Amendment of the U.S. Constitution gives a man a right to be tried by his peer group. A peer is a person from a similar economic, social, religious, geographical, environmental, historical and racial background. To do this the court will be forced to select a jury from the black community from which the black defendant came. We have been, and are being tried by all-white juries that have no understanding of the "average reasoning man" of the black community.

10. We want land, bread, housing, education, clothing, justice and peace. And as our major political objective, a United Nations-supervised plebiscite to be held throughout the black colony in which only black colonial subjects will be allowed to participate for the purpose of determining the will of black people as to their national destiny.

When in the course of human events, it becomes necessary for one people to dissolve the political bands which have connected them with another, and to assume, among the powers of the earth, the separate and equal station to which the laws of nature and nature's God entitle them, a decent respect to the opinions of mankind requires that they should declare the causes which impel them to the separation.

We hold these truths to be self evident, that all men are created equal; that they are endowed by their Creator with certain unalienable rights; that among these are life, liberty, and the pursuit of happiness. That, to secure these rights, governments are instituted among men, deriving their just powers from the consent of the governed; that, whenever any form of government becomes destructive of these ends, it is the right of the people to alter or to abolish it, and to institute a new government, laying its foundation on such principles, and organizing its powers in such form, as to them shall seem most likely to effect their safety and happiness. Prudence, indeed, will dictate that governments long established should not be changed for light and transient causes; and accordingly, all experience hath shown, that mankind are more disposed to suffer, while evils are sufferable, than to right themselves by abolishing the forms to which they are accustomed. But, when a long train of abuses and usurpations, pursuing invariable the same object, evinces a design to reduce them under absolute despotism, it is their right, it is their duty, to throw off such government, and to provide new guards for their future security.

Toward Black Liberation (Stokely Carmichael, 1966)

▐▐▐

SOURCE: Frazier, Thomas R., ed. *Readings in African-American History*. 3d edition. Belmont, Calif.: Wadsworth/Thomson Learning, 2001, pp. 402–410.

INTRODUCTION: *In the fall of 1966, Carmichael published the following article in* The Massachusetts Review, *articulating the concept of black power while insisting that the black community must organize more effectively to gain political power and bring an end to civil rights abuses.*

One of the most pointed illustrations of the need for Black Power, as a positive and redemptive force in a society degenerating into a form of totalitarianism, is to be made by examining the history of distortion that the concept has received in national media of publicity. In this "debate," as in everything else that affects our lives, Negroes are dependent on, and at the discretion of, forces and institutions within the white society which have little interest in representing us honestly. Our experience with the national press has been that where they have managed to escape a meretricious special interest in "Git Whitey" sensationalism and race-war mongering, individual reporters and commentators have been conditioned by the enveloping racism of the society to the point where they are incapable even of objective observation and reporting of racial *incidents*, much less the analysis of *ideas*. But this limitation of vision and perceptions is an inevitable consequence of the dictatorship of definition, interpretation, and consciousness, along with the censorship of history that the society has inflicted upon the Negro—and itself.

Our concern for black power addresses itself directly to this problem, the necessity to reclaim our history and our identity from the cultural terrorism and depredation of self-justifying white guilt.

To do this we shall have to struggle for the right to create our own terms through which to define ourselves and our relationship to the society, and to have these terms recognized. This is the first necessity of a free people, and the first right that any oppressor must suspend. The white fathers of American racism knew this—instinctively it seems—as is indicated by the continuous record of the distortion and omission in their dealings with the red and black men. In the same way that southern apologists for the "Jim Crow" society have so obscured, muddied and misrepresented the record of the reconstruction period, until it is almost impossible to tell what really happened, their contemporary counterparts are busy doing the same thing with the recent history of the civil rights movement.

In 1964, for example, the National Democratic Party, led by L. B. Johnson and Hubert H. Humphrey, cynically undermined the efforts of Mississippi's Black population to achieve some degree of political representation. Yet, whenever the events of that convention are recalled by the press, one sees only that version fabricated by the press agents of the Democratic Party. A year later the House of Representatives in an even more vulgar display of political racism made a mockery of the political rights of Mississippi's Negroes when it failed to unseat the Mississippi Delegation to the House which had been elected through a process which methodically and systematically excluded over 450,000 voting age Negroes, almost one half of the total electorate of the state. Whenever this event is mentioned in print it is in terms which leaves one with the rather curious impression that somehow the oppressed Negro people of Mississippi are at fault for confronting the Congress with a situation in which they had no alternative but to endorse Mississippi's racist political practices.

I mention these two examples because, having been directly involved in them, I can see very clearly the discrepancies between what happened, and the versions that are finding their way into general acceptance as a kind of popular mythology. Thus the victimization of the Negro takes place in two phases—first it occurs in fact and deed, then, and this is equally sinister, in the official recording of those facts.

The "Black Power" program and concept which is being articulated by SNCC, CORE, and a host of community organizations in the ghettoes of the North and South has not escaped that process. The white press has been busy articulating their own analyses, their own interpretations, and criticisms of their own creations. For example, while the press had given wide and sensational dissemination to attacks made by figures in the Civil Rights movement—foremost among which are Roy Wilkins of the NAACP and Whitney Young of the Urban League—and to the hysterical ranting about black racism made by the political chameleon that now serves as Vice-President, it has generally failed to give accounts of the reasonable and productive dialogue which is taking place in the Negro community, and in certain important areas in the white religious and intellectual community. A national committee of influential Negro Churchmen affiliated with the National Council of Churches, despite their oblivious respectability and responsibility, had to resort to a paid advertisement to articulate their position, while anyone shouting the hysterical yappings of "Black Racism" got ample space. Thus the American people have gotten at best a superficial and misleading account of the very terms and tenor of this debate. I wish to quote briefly from the statement by the national committee of Churchmen which I suspect that the majority of Americans will not have seen. This statement appeared in the *New York Times* of July 31, 1966.

We an informal group of Negro Churchmen in America are deeply disturbed about the crisis brought upon our country by historic distortions of important human realities in the controversy about "black power." What we see shining through the variety of rhetoric is not anything new but the same old problem of power and race which has faced our beloved country since 1619.

. . . The conscience of black men is corrupted because, having no power to implement the demands of conscience, the concern for justice in the absence of justice becomes a chaotic self-surrender. Powerlessness breeds a race of beggars. We are faced now with a situation where powerless conscience meets conscienceless power, threatening the very foundations of our Nation.

. . . We deplore the overt violence of riots, but we feel it is more important to focus on the real sources of these eruptions. These sources may be abetted inside the Ghetto, but their basic cause lies in the silent and covert violence which white middleclass America inflicts upon the victims of the inner city.

. . . In short the failure of American leaders to use American power to create equal opportunity in life as well as law, this is the real problem and not the anguished cry for black power.

. . . Without the capacity to participate with power, i.e., to have some organized political and economic strength to really influence people with whom one interacts—integration is not meaningful.

. . . America has asked its Negro citizens to fight for opportunity as individuals, whereas at certain points in our history what we have needed most has been opportunity for the whole group, not just for selected and approved Negroes.

. . . We must not apologize for the existence of this form of group power, for we have been oppressed as a group and not as individuals. We will not find our way out of that oppression until both we and America accept the need for Negro Americans, as well as for Jews, Italians, Poles, and white Anglosaxon Protestants, among others, to have and to wield group power. [©1966 by The New York Times Company.]

Traditionally, for each new ethnic group, the route to social and political integration into America's pluralistic society, has been through the organization of their own institutions with which to represent their communal needs within the larger society. This is simply stating what the advocates of black power are saying. The strident outcry, *particularly* from the liberal community, that has been evoked by this proposal can only be understood by examining the historic relationship between Negro and White power in this country.

Negroes are defined by two forces, their blackness and their powerlessness. There have been traditionally two communities in America. The White community, which controlled and defined the forms that all institutions within the society would take, and the Negro community which has been excluded from participation in the power decisions that shaped the society, and has traditionally been dependent upon, and subservient to the White community.

This has not been accidental. The history of every institution of this society indicates that a major concern in the ordering and structuring of the society has been the maintaining of the Negro community in its condition of dependence and oppression. This has not been on the level of individual acts of discrimination between individual whites against individual Negroes, but as total acts by the White community against the Negro community. This fact cannot be too strongly emphasized—the racist assumptions of white superiority have been so deeply ingrained in the structure of the society that it infuses its entire functioning, and is so much a part of the national subconscious that it is taken for granted and is frequently not even recognized.

Let me give an example of the difference between individual racism and institutionalized racism, and the society's response to both. When unidentified white terrorists bomb a Negro Church and kill five children, that is an act of individual racism, widely deplored by most segments of the society. But when in that same city, Birmingham, Alabama, not five but 500 Negro babies die each year because of a lack of proper food, shelter and medical facilities, and thousands more are destroyed and maimed physically, emotionally and intellectually because of conditions of poverty and deprivation in the ghetto, that is a function of institutionalized racism. But the society either pretends it doesn't know of this situation, or is incapable of doing anything meaningful about it. And this resistance to doing anything meaningful about conditions in that ghetto comes from the fact that the ghetto is itself a product of a combination of forces and special interests in the white community, and the groups that have access to the resources and power to change that situation benefit, politically and economically, from the existence of that ghetto.

It is more than a figure of speech to say that the Negro community in America is the victim of white imperialism and colonial exploitation. This is in practical economic and political terms true. There are over 20 million black people comprising ten percent of this nation. They for the most part live in well-defined areas of the country—in the shanty-towns and rural black belt areas of the South, and increasingly in the slums of northern and western industrial cities. If one goes into any Negro community, whether it be in Jackson, Miss., Cambridge, Md., or Harlem, N.Y., one will find that the same combination of political, economic, and social forces are at work. The people in the Negro community do not control the resources of that community, its political decisions, its law enforcement, its housing standards; and even the physical ownership of the land, houses, and stores *lie outside that community.*

It is white power that makes the laws, and it is violent white power in the form of armed white cops that enforces those laws with guns and nightsticks. The vast majority of Negroes in this country live in these captive communities and must endure these conditions of oppression because, and only because, *they are black and powerless.* I do not suppose that at any point the men who control the power and resources of this country ever sat down and designed these black enclaves, and formally articulated the terms of their colonial and dependent status, as was done, for example, by the Apartheid government of South Africa. Yet, one can not distinguish between one ghetto and another. As one moves from city to city it is as though some malignant racist planning-unit had done precisely this—designed each one from the same master blueprint. And indeed, if the ghetto had been formally and deliberately planned, instead of growing spontaneously and inevitably from the racist functioning of the various institutions that combine to make the society, it would be somehow less frightening. The situation would be less frightening because, if these ghettoes were the result of design and conspiracy, one could understand their similarity as being artificial and consciously imposed, rather than the result of identical patterns of white racism which repeat themselves in cities as distant as Boston and Birmingham. Without bothering to list the historic factors which contribute to this pattern—economic exploitation, political impotence, discrimination in employment and education—one can see that to correct this pattern will require far-reaching changes in the basic power-relationship and the ingrained

social patterns within the society. The question is, of course, what kinds of changes are necessary, and how is it possible to bring them about?

In recent years the answer to these questions which has been given by most articulate groups of Negroes and their white allies, the "liberals" of all stripes, has been in terms of something called "integration." According to the advocates of integration, social justice will be accomplished by "integrating the Negro into the mainstream institutions of the society from which he has been traditionally excluded." It is very significant that each time I have heard this formulation it has been in terms of "the Negro," the individual Negro, rather than in terms of the community.

The concept of integration had to be based on the assumption that there was nothing of value in the Negro community and that little of value could be created among Negroes, so the thing to do was to siphon off the "acceptable" Negroes into the surrounding middle-class white community. Thus the goal of the movement for integration was simply to loosen up the restrictions barring the entry of Negroes into the white community. Goals around which the struggle took place, such as public accommodation, open housing, job opportunity on the executive level (which is easier to deal with than the problem of semi-skilled and blue collar jobs which involve more far-reaching economic adjustments), are quite simply middle-class goals, articulated by a tiny group of Negroes who had middle-class aspirations. It is true that the student demonstrations in the South during the early sixties, out of which SNCC came, had a similar orientation. But while it is hardly a concern of a black sharecropper, dishwasher, or welfare recipient whether a certain fifteen-dollar-a-day motel offers accommodations to Negroes, the overt symbols of white superiority and the imposed limitations on the Negro community had to be destroyed. Now, black people must look beyond these goals, to the issue of collective power.

Such a limited class orientation was reflected not only in the program and goals of the civil rights movement, but in its tactics and organization. It is very significant that the two oldest and most "respectable" civil rights organizations have constitutions which *specifically* prohibit partisan political activity. CORE once did, but changed that clause when it changed its orientation toward black power. But this is perfectly understandable in terms of the strategy and goals of the older organizations. The civil rights movement saw its role as a kind of liaison between the powerful white community and the dependent Negro one. The dependent status of the black community apparently was unimportant since—if the movement were successful—it was going to blend into the white community anyway. We made no pretense of organizing and developing institutions of community power in the Negro community, but appealed to the conscience of white institutions of power. The posture of the civil rights movement was that of the dependent, the suppliant. The theory was that without attempting to create any organized base of political strength itself, the civil rights movement could, by forming coalitions with various "liberal" pressure organizations in the white community—liberal reform clubs, labor unions, church groups, progressive civic groups—and at times one or other of the major political parties—influence national legislation and national social patterns.

I think we all have seen the limitations of this approach. We have repeatedly seen that political alliances based on appeals to conscience and decency are chancy things, simply because institutions and political organizations have no consciences outside their own special interests. The political and social rights of Negroes have been and always will be negotiable and expendable the moment they conflict with the interests of our "allies." If we do not learn from history, we are doomed to repeat it, and that is precisely the lesson of the Reconstruction. Black people were allowed to register, vote and participate in politics because it was to the advantage of powerful white allies to promote this. But this was the result of white decision, and it was ended by other white men's decision before any political base powerful enough to challenge that decision could be established in the southern Negro community. (Thus at this point in the struggle Negroes have no assurance—save a kind of idiot optimism and faith in a society whose history is one of racism—that if it were to become necessary, even the painfully limited gains thrown to the civil rights movement by the Congress will not be revoked as soon as a shift in political sentiments should occur.)

The major limitation of this approach was that it tended to maintain the traditional dependence of Negroes, and of the movement. We depended upon the good-will and support of various groups within the white community whose interests were not always compatible with ours. To the extent that we depended on the financial support of other groups, we were vulnerable to their influence and domination.

Also the program that evolved out of this coalition was really limited and inadequate in the long term and one which affected only a small select group of Negroes. Its goal was to make the white community accessible to "qualified" Negroes and presumably each year a few more Negroes armed with their passport—a couple of university degrees—would escape into middle-class America and adopt the attitudes and life styles of that group; and one

day the Harlems and the Watts would stand empty, a tribute to the success of integration. This is simply neither realistic nor particularly desirable. You can integrate communities, but you assimilate individuals. Even if such a program were possible its result would be, not to develop the black community as a functional and honorable segment of the total society, with its own cultural identity, life patterns, and institutions, but to abolish it—the final solution to the Negro problem. Marx said that the working class is the first class in history that ever wanted to abolish itself. If one listens to some of our "moderate" Negro leaders it appears that the American Negro is the first race that ever wished to abolish itself. The fact is that what must be abolished is not the black community, but the dependent colonial status that has been inflicted upon it. The racial and cultural personality of the black community must be preserved and the community must win its freedom while preserving its cultural integrity. This is the essential difference between integration as it is currently practiced and the concept of black power.

What has the movement for integration accomplished to date? The Negro graduating from M.I.T. with a doctorate will have better job opportunities available to him than to Lynda Bird Johnson. But the rate of unemployment in the Negro community is steadily increasing, while that in the white community decreases. More educated Negroes hold executive jobs in major corporations and federal agencies than ever before, but the gap between white income and Negro income has almost doubled in the last twenty years. More suburban housing is available to Negroes, but housing conditions in the ghetto are steadily declining. While the infant mortality rate of New York City is at its lowest rate ever in the city's history, the infant mortality rate of Harlem is steadily climbing. There has been an organized national resistance to the Supreme Court's order to integrate the schools, and the federal government has not acted to enforce that order. Less than 15 percent of black children in the South attend integrated schools; and Negro schools, which the vast majority of black children still attend, are increasingly decrepit, overcrowded, under-staffed, inadequately equipped and funded.

This explains why the rate of school dropouts is increasing among Negro teenagers, who then express their bitterness, hopelessness, and alienation by the only means they have—rebellion. As long as people in the ghettoes of our large cities feel that they are victims of the misuse of white power without any way to have their needs represented—and these are frequently simple needs: to get the welfare inspectors to stop kicking down your doors in the middle of the night, the cops from beating your children, the landlord to exterminate the vermin in your home, the city to collect your garbage—we will continue to have riots. These are not the products of "black power," but of the absence of any organization capable of giving the community the power, the black power, to deal with its problems.

SNCC proposes that it is now time for the black freedom movement to stop pandering to the fears and anxieties of the white middle class in the attempt to earn its "good-will," and to return to the ghetto to organize these communities to control themselves. This organization must be attempted in northern and southern urban areas as well as in the rural black belt counties of the South. The chief antagonist to this organization is, in the South, the overtly racist Democratic party, and in the North the equally corrupt big city machines.

The standard argument presented against independent political organization is "But you are only 10 percent." I cannot see the relevance of this observation, since no one is talking about taking over the country, but taking control over our own communities.

The fact is that the Negro population, 10 percent or not, is very strategically placed because—ironically—of segregation. What is also true is that Negroes have never been able to utilize the full voting potential of our numbers. Where we could vote, the case has always been that the white political machine stacks and gerrymanders the political subdivisions in Negro neighborhoods so the true voting strength is never reflected in political strength. Would anyone looking at the distribution of political power in Manhattan, ever think that Negroes represented 60 percent of the population there?

Just as often the effective political organization in Negro communities is absorbed by tokenism and patronage—the time honored practice of "giving" certain offices to selected Negroes. The machine thus creates a "little machine," which is subordinate and responsive to it, in the Negro community. These Negro political "leaders" are really vote deliverers, more responsible to the white machine and the white power structure, than to the community they allegedly represent. Thus the white community is able to substitute patronage control for audacious black power in the Negro community. This is precisely what Johnson tried to do even before the Voting Rights Act of 1966 was passed. The National Democrats made it very clear that the measure was intended to register Democrats, not Negroes. The President and top officials of the Democratic Party called in about almost 100 selected Negro "leaders" from the Deep South. Nothing was said about changing the policies of the racist state parties, nothing was said about repudiating such leadership figures as East-

land and Ross Barnett in Mississippi or George Wallace in Alabama. What was said was simply "Go home and organize your people into the local Democratic Party—*then* we'll see about poverty money and appointments." (Incidentally, for the most part the War on Poverty in the South is controlled by local Democratic ward heelers—and outspoken racists who have used the program to change the form of the Negroes' dependence. People who were afraid to register for fear of being thrown off the farm are now afraid to register for fear of losing their Head-Start jobs.)

We must organize black community power to end these abuses, and to give the Negro community a chance to have its needs expressed. A leadership which is truly "responsible"—not to the white press and power structure, but to the community—must be developed. Such leadership will recognize that its power lies in the unified and collective strength of that community. This will make it difficult for the white leadership group to conduct its dialogue with individuals in terms of patronage and prestige, and will force them to talk to the community's representatives in terms of real power.

The single aspect of the black power program that has encountered most criticism is this concept of independent organization. This is presented as third-partyism which has never worked, or a withdrawal into black nationalism and isolationism. If such a program is developed it will not have the effect of isolating the Negro community but the reverse. When the Negro community is able to control local office, and negotiate with other groups from a position of organized strength, the possibility of meaningful political alliances on specific issues will be increased. That is a rule of politics and there is no reason why it should not operate here. The only difference is that we will have the power to define the terms of these alliances.

The next question usually is, "So—can it work, can the ghettoes in fact be organized?" The answer is that this organization must be successful, because there are no viable alternatives—not the War on Poverty, which was at its inception limited to dealing with effects rather than causes, and has become simply another source of machine patronage. And "Integration" is meaningful only to a small chosen class within the community.

The revolution in agricultural technology in the South is displacing the rural Negro community into northern urban areas. Both Washington, D.C. and Newark, N.J. have Negro majorities. One third of Philadelphia's population of two million people is black. "Inner city" in most major urban areas is already predominantly Negro, and with the white rush to suburbia, Negroes will in the next three decades control the heart of our great cities. These areas can become either concentration camps with a bitter and volatile population whose only power is the power to destroy, or organized and powerful communities able to make constructive contributions to the total society. Without the power to control their lives and their communities, without effective political institutions through which to relate to the total society, these communities will exist in a constant state of insurrection. This is a choice that the country will have to make.

BLACK POWER—ITS RELEVANCE TO THE WEST INDIES (WALTER RODNEY, 1968)

SOURCE: Bolland, O. Nigel, ed. *The Birth of Caribbean Civilization: A Century of Ideas about Culture and Identity, Nation and Society.* Kingston: Ian Randle, 2004, pp. 476–491.

INTRODUCTION: *Guyanese historian Walter Rodney received his Ph.D. from the School of Oriental and African Studies at the University of London in 1966. An activist and advocate of the politics of Black Power, he taught at a university in Tanzania before returning to the Caribbean in 1968 to lecture on African History at the University of the West Indies in Jamaica. Rodney's popular lectures drew the attention of the Jamaican government, who expelled him as a dangerous influence, leading to widespread rioting in Kingston and a temporary closing of the university. Before that time, Rodney spoke to an audience assembled at the UWI campus at Mona on the subject of Black Power and its relevance to the West Indies.*

About a fortnight ago I had the opportunity of speaking on Black Power to an audience on this campus. At that time, the consciousness among students as far as the racial question is concerned had been heightened by several incidents on the world scene—notably, the hangings in Rhodesia and the murder of Dr. Martin Luther King. Indeed, it has been heightened to such an extent that some individuals have started to organize a Black Power movement. My presence here attests to my full sympathy with their objectives.

The topic on this occasion is no longer just "Black Power" but "Black Power and You." Black Power can be seen as a movement and an ideology springing from the reality of oppression of black peoples by whites within the imperialist world as a whole. Now we need to be specific in defining the West Indian scene and our own particular roles in the society. You and I have to decide whether we want to think black or to *remain* as a dirty version of white. (I shall indicate the full significance of this later.)

Recently there was a public statement in *Scope* where Black Power was referred to as "Black supremacy." This may have been a genuine error or a deliberate falsification. Black Power is a call to black peoples to throw off white domination and resume the handling of their own destinies. It means that blacks would enjoy power commensurate with their numbers in the world and in particular localities. Whenever an oppressed black man shouts for equality he is called a racist. This was said of Marcus Garvey in his day. Imagine that! We are so inferior that if we demand equality of opportunity and power that is outrageously racist! Black people who speak up for their rights must beware of this device of false accusations. Is it intended to place you on the defensive and if possible embarrass you into silence. How can we be both oppressed and embarrassed? Is it that our major concern is not to hurt the feelings of the oppressor? Black people must now take the offensive—if it is anyone who should suffer embarrassment it is the whites. Did black people roast six million Jews? Who exterminated millions of indigenous inhabitants in the Americas and Australia? Who enslaved countless millions of Africans? The white capitalist cannibal has always fed on the world's black peoples. White capitalist imperialist society is profoundly and unmistakably racist.

The West Indies have always been a part of white capitalist society. We have been the most oppressed section because we were a slave society and the legacy of slavery still rests heavily upon the West Indian black man. I will briefly point to five highlights of our social development: (1) the development of racialism under slavery; (2) emancipation; (3) Indian indentured labour; (4) the year 1865 in Jamaica; (5) the year 1938 in the West Indies.

Slavery.

As C.L.R. James, Eric Williams and other W.I. scholars have pointed out, slavery in the West Indies started as an economic phenomenon rather than a racial one. But it rapidly became racist as all white labour was withdrawn from the fields, leaving black to be identified with slave labour and white to be linked with property and domination. Out of this situation where blacks had an inferior status in practice, there grew social and scientific theories relating to the supposed inherent inferiority of the black man, who was considered as having been created to bring water and hew wood for the white man. This theory then served to rationalise white exploitation of blacks all over Africa and Asia. The West Indies and the American South share the dubious distinction of being the breeding ground for world racialism. Even the blacks became convinced of their own inferiority, though fortunately we are capable of the most intense expressions when we recognise that we have been duped by the white men. Black power recognises both the reality of the black oppression and self-negation as well as the potential for revolt.

Emancipation.

By the end of the 18th century, Britain had got most of what it wanted from black labour in the West Indies. Slavery and the slave trade had made Britain strong and now stood in the way of new developments, so it was time to abandon those systems. The Slave Trade and Slavery were thus ended; but Britain had to consider how to squeeze what little remained in the territories and *how to maintain the local whites in power.* They therefore decided to give the planters £20 million compensation and to guarantee their black labour supplies for the next six years through a system called apprenticeship. In that period, white society consolidated its position to ensure that slave relations should persist in our society. The Rastafari Brethren have always insisted that the black people were promised £20 million at emancipation. In reality, by any normal standards of justice, we black people should have got the £20 million compensation money. We were the ones who had been abused and wronged, hunted in Africa and brutalised on the plantations. In Europe, when serfdom was abolished, the serfs usually inherited the land as compensation and by right. In the West Indies, the exploiters were compensated because they could no longer exploit us in the same way as before. White property was of greater value than black humanity. It still is—white property is of greater value than black humanity in the British West Indies today, especially here in Jamaica.

Indian Indentured Labour.

Britain and the white West Indians had to maintain the plantation system in order to keep whites supreme. When Africans started leaving the plantations to set up as independent peasants they threatened the plantation structure and therefore Indians were imported under the indenture arrangements. That was possible because white power controlled most of the world and could move non-white peoples around as they wished. It was from British-controlled India that the indentured labour was obtained. It was the impact of British commercial, military and political policies that was destroying the life and culture of 19th century India and forcing people to flee to other parts of the world to earn bread. Look where Indians fled—to the West Indies! The West Indies is a place black people want to leave, not to come to. One must therefore appreciate the pressure of white power on India which gave rise

to migration to the West Indies. Indians were brought here solely in the interest of white society—at the expense of Africans already in the West Indies and often against their own best interests, for Indians perceived indentured labour to be a form of slavery and it was eventually terminated through the pressure of Indian opinion in the homeland. The West Indies has made a unique contribution to the history of suffering in the world, and Indians have provided part of that contribution since indentures were first introduced. This is another aspect of the historical situation which is still with us.

1865.

In that year Britain found a way of perpetuating White Power in the West Indies after ruthlessly crushing the revolt of our black brothers led by Paul Bogle. The British Government took away the Constitution of Jamaica and placed the island under the complete control of the Colonial Office, a manoeuvre that was racially motivated. The Jamaican legislature was then largely in the hands of the local whites with a mulatto minority, but if the gradual changes continued the mulattoes would have taken control—and the blacks were next in line. Consequently, the British Government put a stop to the process of the gradual takeover of political power by blacks. When we look at the British Empire in the 19th century, we see a clear difference between white colonies and black colonies. In the white colonies like Canada and Australia the British were giving white people their freedom and self-rule. In the black colonies of the West Indies, Africa and Asia, the British were busy taking away the political freedom of the inhabitants. Actually, on the constitutional level, Britain had already displayed its racialism in the West Indies in the early 19th century when it refused to give mulattoes the power of Government in Trinidad, although they were the majority of free citizens. In 1865 in Jamaica it was not the first nor the last time on which Britain made it clear that its white "kith and kin" would be supported to hold dominion over blacks.

1938.

Slavery ended in various islands of the West Indies between 1834 and 1838. Exactly 100 years later (between 1934–38) the black people in the West Indies revolted against the hypocritical freedom of the society. The British were very surprised—they had long forgotten all about the blacks in the British West Indies and they sent a Royal Commission to find out what it was all about. The report of the conditions was so shocking that the British government did not release it until after the war, because they wanted black colonials to fight the white man's battles. By the time the war ended it was clear in the West Indies and throughout Asia and Africa that some concessions would have to be made to black peoples. In general, the problem as seen by white imperialists was to give enough power to certain groups in colonial society to keep the whole society from exploding and to maintain the essentials of the imperialist structure. In the British West Indies, they had to take into account the question of military strategy because we lie under the belly of the world's imperialist giant, the U.S.A. Besides, there was the new and vital mineral bauxite, which had to be protected. The British solution was to pull out wherever possible and leave the imperial government in the hands of the U.S.A., while the local government was given to a white, brown and black petty-bourgeoisie who were culturally the creations of white capitalist society and who therefore support the white imperialist system because they gain personally and because they have been brainwashed into aiding the oppression of black people.

Black Power in the West Indies means three closely related things: (i) the break with imperialism which is historically white racist; (ii) the assumption of power by the black masses in the islands; (iii) the cultural reconstruction of the society in the image of the blacks.

I shall anticipate certain questions on who are the blacks in the West Indies since they are in fact questions which have been posed to me elsewhere. I maintain that it is the white world which has defined who are blacks—if you are not white then you are black. However, it is obvious that the West Indian situation is complicated by factors such as the variety of racial types and racial mixtures and by the process of class formation. We have, therefore, to note not simply what the white world says but also how individuals perceive each other. Nevertheless, we can talk of the mass of the West Indian population as being black—either African or Indian. There seems to have been some doubts on the last point, and some fear that Black Power is aimed against the Indian. This would be a flagrant denial of both the historical experience of the West Indies and the reality of the contemporary scene.

When the Indian was brought to the West Indies, he met the same racial contempt which whites applied to Africans. The Indian, too, was reduced to a single stereotype—the coolie or labourer. He too was a hewer of wood and a bringer of water. I spoke earlier of the revolt of the blacks in the West Indies in 1938. That revolt involved Africans in Jamaica, Africans and Indians in Trinidad and Guyana. The uprisings in Guyana were actually led by Indian sugar workers. Today, some Indians (like some Africans) have joined the white power structure in terms of economic activity and culture; but the underlying reality is that poverty resides among Africans and Indians in the West Indies and that power is denied them. Black Power

in the West Indies, therefore, refers primarily to people who are recognisably African or Indian.

The Chinese, on the other hand, are a former labouring group who have now become bastions of white West Indian social structure. The Chinese of the People's Republic of China have long broken with and are fighting against white imperialism, but *our* Chinese have nothing to do with that movement. They are to be identified with Chiang-Kai-Shek and not Chairman Mao Tse-tung. They are to be put in the same bracket as the lackeys of capitalism and imperialism who are to be found in Hong Kong and Taiwan. Whatever the circumstances in which the Chinese came to the West Indies, they soon became (as a group) members of the exploiting class. They will have either to relinquish or be deprived of that function before they can be re-integrated into a West Indian society where the black man walks in dignity.

The same applies to the mulattoes, another group about whom I have been questioned. The West Indian brown man is characterised by ambiguity and ambivalence. He has in the past identified with the black masses when it suited his interests, and at the present time some browns are in the forefront of the movement towards black consciousness; but the vast majority have fallen to the bribes of white imperialism, often outdoing the whites in their hatred and oppression of blacks. Garvey wrote of the Jamaican mulattoes—"I was openly hated and persecuted by some of these coloured men of the island who did not want to be classified as Negroes but as white." Naturally, conscious West Indian blacks like Garvey have in turn expressed their dislike for the browns, but there is nothing in the West Indian experience which suggests that browns are unacceptable when they choose to identify with blacks. The post–1938 developments in fact showed exactly the opposite. It seems to me, therefore, that it is not for the Black Power movement to determine the position of the browns, reds and so-called West Indian whites—the movement can only keep the door open and leave it to those groups to make their choice.

Black Power is not racially intolerant. It is the hope of the black man that he should have power over his own destinies. This is not incompatible with a multiracial society where each individual counts equally. Because the moment that power is equitably distributed among several ethnic groups then the very relevance of making the distinction between groups will be lost. What we must object to is the current image of a multi-racial society living in harmony—that is a myth designed to justify the exploitation suffered by the blackest of our population, at the hands of the lighter-skinned groups. Let us look at the figures for the racial composition of the Jamaican population. Of every 100 Jamaicans,

76.8% are visibly African

0.8% European

1.1% Indian

0.6% Chinese

91% have African blood

0.1% Syrian

14.6% Afro-European

5.4% other mixtures

This is a black society where Africans preponderate. Apart from the mulatto mixture all other groups are numerically insignificant and yet the society seeks to give them equal weight and indeed more weight than the Africans. If we went to Britain we could easily find non-white groups in the above proportions—Africans and West Indians, Indians and Pakistanis, Turks, Arabs and other Easterners—but Britain is not called a multi-racial society. When we go to Britain we don't expect to take over all of the British real estate business, all their cinemas and most of their commerce as the European, Chinese and Syrian have done here. All we ask for there is some work and shelter, and we can't even get that. Black Power must proclaim that Jamaica is a black society—we should fly Garvey's Black Star banner and we will treat all other groups in the society on that understanding—they can have *the basic right of all individuals* but *no privileges to exploit Africans* as has been the pattern during slavery and ever since.

The present government knows that Jamaica is a black man's country. That is why Garvey has been made a national hero, for they are trying to deceive black people into thinking that the government is with them. The government of Jamaica recognises black power—it is afraid of the potential wrath of Jamaica's black and largely African population. It is that same fear which forced them to declare mourning when black men are murdered in Rhodesia, and when Martin Luther King was murdered in the U.S.A. But the black people don't need to be told that Garvey is a national hero—they know that. Nor do they need to be told to mourn when blacks are murdered by White Power, because they mourn every day right here in Jamaica where white power keeps them ignorant, unemployed, ill-clothed and ill-fed. They will stop mourning when things change—and that means a revolution, for the first essential is to break the chains which bind us to white imperialists, and that is a very revolutionary step. Cuba is the only country in the West Indies and in this hemisphere which has broken with white power. That is why Stokely Carmichael can visit Cuba but he can't visit Trinidad or Jamaica. That is why Stokely can call Fidel "one of the blackest men in the Americas" and that is why our leaders in contrast qualify as "white."

Here I'm not just playing with words—I'm extending the definition of Black Power by indicating the nature of its opposite, "White Power," and I'm providing a practical illustration of what Black Power means in one particular West Indian community where it had already occurred. White power is the power of whites over blacks without any participation of the blacks. White power rules the imperialist world as a whole. In Cuba the blacks and mulattoes numbered 1,585,073 out of a population of 5,829,029 in 1953—i.e., about one quarter of the population. Like Jamaica's black people today, they were the poorest and most depressed people on the island. Lighter-skinned Cubans held local power, while real power was in the hands of the U.S. imperialists. Black Cubans fought alongside white Cuban workers and peasants because they were all oppressed. Major Juan Almeida, one of the outstanding leaders of Cuba today, was one of the original guerillas in the Sierra Maestra, and he is black. Black Cubans today enjoy political, economic and social rights and opportunities of exactly the same kind as white Cubans. They too bear arms in the Cuban Militia as an expression of their basic rights. In other words, White Power in Cuba is ended. The majority of the white population naturally predominates numerically in most spheres of activity but they do not hold dominion over blacks without regard to the latter's interests. The blacks have achieved power commensurate with their own numbers by their heroic self-efforts during the days of slavery, in fighting against the Spanish and in fighting against imperialism. Having achieved their rights they can in fact afford to forget the category "black" and think simply as Cuban citizens, as Socialist equals and as men. In Jamaica, where blacks are far greater in numbers and have no whites alongside them as oppressed workers and peasants, it will be the black people who alone can bear the brunt of revolutionary fighting.

Trotsky once wrote that Revolution is the carnival of the masses. When we have that carnival in the West Indies, are people like us here at the university going to join the bacchanal?

Let us have a look at our present position. Most of us who have studied at the U.W.I. are discernibly black, and yet we are undeniably part of the white imperialist system. A few are actively pro-imperialist. They have no confidence in anything that is not white—they talk nonsense about black people being lazy—the same nonsense which was said about the Jamaican black man after emancipation, although he went to Panama and performed the giant task of building the Panama Canal—the same nonsense which is said about W.I. unemployed today, and yet they proceed to England to run the whole transport system. Most of us do not go to quite the same extremes in denigrating ourselves and our black brothers, but we say nothing against the system, and that means that we are acquiescing in the exploitation of our brethren. One of the ways that the situation has persisted especially in recent times is that it has given a few individuals like you and . . . [me] . . . a vision of personal progress measured in terms of front lawn and the latest model of a huge American car. This has recruited us into their ranks and deprived the black masses of articulate leadership. That is why at the outset I stressed that our choice was to *remain* as part of the white system or to break with it. There is no other alternative.

Black Power in the W.I. must aim at transforming the Black intelligensia into the servants of the black masses. Black Power, within the university and without must aim at overcoming white cultural imperialism. Whites have dominated us both physically and mentally. This fact is brought out in virtually any serious sociological study of the region—the brainwashing process has been so stupendous that it has convinced so many black men of their inferiority. I will simply draw a few illustrations to remind you of this fact which blacks like us at Mona prefer to forget.

The adult black in our West Indian society is fully conditioned to thinking white, because that is the training we are given from childhood. The little black girl plays with a white doll, identifying with it as she combs its flaxen hair. Asked to sketch the figure of a man or woman, the black schoolboy instinctively produces a white man or a white woman. This is not surprising, since until recently the illustrations in our textbooks were all figures of Europeans. The few changes which have taken place have barely scratched the surface of the problem. West Indians of every colour still aspire to European standards of dress and beauty. The language which is used by black people in describing ourselves shows how we despise our African appearance. "Good hair" means European hair, "good nose" means a straight nose, "good complexion" means a light complexion. Everybody recognises how incongruous and ridiculous such terms are, but we continue to use them and to express our support of the assumption that white Europeans have the monopoly of beauty, and that black is the incarnation of ugliness. That is why Black Power advocates find it necessary to assert that BLACK IS BEAUTIFUL.

The most profound revelation of the sickness of our society on the question of race is our respect for all the white symbols of the Christian religion. God the Father is white, God the Son is white, and presumably God the Holy Ghost is white also. The disciples and saints are white, all the Cherubim, Seraphim and angels are white—except Lucifer, of course, who was black, being the embodiment

of evil. When one calls upon black people to reject these things, this is not an attack on the teachings of Christ or the ideals of Christianity. What we have to ask is "Why should Christianity come to us all wrapped up in white?" The white race constitute about 20 per cent of the world's population, and yet non-white peoples are supposed to accept that all who inhabit the heavens are white. There are 650 million Chinese, so why shouldn't God and most of the angels be Chinese? The truth is that there is absolutely no reason why different racial groups should not provide themselves with their own religious symbols. A picture of Christ could be red, white or black, depending upon the people who are involved. When Africans adopt the European concept that purity and goodness must be painted white and all that is evil and damned is to be painted black then we are flagrantly self-insulting.

Through the manipulation of this media of education and communication, white people have produced black people who administer the system and perpetuate the white values—"white-hearted black men," as they are called by conscious elements. This is as true of the Indians as it is true of the Africans in our West Indian society. Indeed, the basic explanation of the tragedy of African/Indian confrontation in Guyana and Trinidad is the fact that both groups are held captive by the European way of seeing things. When an African abuses an Indian he repeats all that the white men said about Indian indentured "coolies"; and in turn the Indian has borrowed from the whites the stereotype of the "lazy nigger" to apply to the African beside him. It is as though no black man can see another black man except by looking through a white person. It is time we started seeing through our own eyes. The road to Black Power here in the West Indies and everywhere else must begin with a revaluation of ourselves as blacks and with a redefinition of the world from our own standpoint.

A Black Feminist Statement (The Combahee River Collective, 1977)

SOURCE: Guy-Sheftall, Beverly. *Words of Fire: An Anthology of African-American Feminist Thought.* New York: The New Press, 1995, pp. 232–240.

INTRODUCTION: *Taking their name from the name of a river in South Carolina where Harriet Tubman organized a campaign to free hundreds of slaves during the Civil War, the Combahee River Collective was an important black feminist group of the 1970s. The group formed in 1974 as the Boston chapter of the National Black Feminist Organization, founded the previous year. In 1977, the Collective published a statement discussing their activities and articulating their philosophy.*

We are a collective of black feminists who have been meeting together since 1974. During that time we have been involved in the process of defining and clarifying our politics, while at the same time doing political work within our own group and in coalition with other progressive organizations and movements. The most general statement of our politics at the present time would be that we are actively committed to struggling against racial, sexual, heterosexual, and class oppression and see as our particular task the development of integrated analysis and practice based upon the fact that the major systems of oppression are interlocking. The synthesis of these oppressions creates the conditions of our lives. As black women we see black feminism as the logical political movement to combat the manifold and simultaneous oppressions that all women of color face.

We will discuss four major topics in the paper that follows: (1) The genesis of contemporary black feminism; (2) what we believe, i.e., the specific province of our politics; (3) the problems in organizing black feminists, including a brief herstory of our collective; and (4) black feminist issues and practice.

1. The Genesis of Contemporary Black Feminism

Before looking at the recent development of black feminism, we would like to affirm that we find our origins in the historical reality of Afro-American women's continuous life-and-death struggle for survival and liberation. Black women's extremely negative relationship to the American political system (a system of white male rule) has always been determined by our membership in two oppressed racial and sexual castes. As Angela Davis points out in "Reflections on the Black Woman's Role in the Community of Slaves," black women have always embodied, if only in their physical manifestation, an adversary stance to white male rule and have actively resisted its inroads upon them and their communities in both dramatic and subtle ways. There have always been black women activists—some known, like Sojourner Truth, Harriet Tubman, Frances E. W. Harper, Ida B. Wells-Barnett, and Mary Church Terrell, and thousands upon thousands unknown—who had a shared awareness of how their sexual identity combined with their racial identity to make their whole life situation and the focus of their political struggles unique. Contemporary black feminism is the

outgrowth of countless generations of personal sacrifice, militancy, and work by our mothers and sisters.

A black feminist presence has evolved most obviously in connection with the second wave of the American women's movement beginning in the late 1960s. Black, other Third World, and working women have been involved in the feminist movement from its start, but both outside reactionary forces and racism and elitism within the movement itself have served to obscure our participation. In 1973 black feminists, primarily located in New York, felt the necessity of forming a separate black feminist group. This became the National Black Feminist Organization (NBFO).

Black feminist politics also have an obvious connection to movements for black liberation, particularly those of the 1960s and 1970s. Many of us were active in those movements (civil rights, black nationalism, the Black Panthers), and all of our lives were greatly affected and changed by their ideology, their goals, and the tactics used to achieve their goals. It was our experience and disillusionment within these liberation movements, as well as experience on the periphery of the white male left, that led to the need to develop a politics that was antiracist, unlike those of white women, and antisexist, unlike those of black and white men.

There is also undeniably a personal genesis for black feminism, that is, the political realization that comes from the seemingly personal experiences of individual black women's lives. Black feminists and many more black women who do not define themselves as feminists have all experienced sexual oppression as a constant factor in our day-to-day existence.

Black feminists often talk about their feelings of craziness before becoming conscious of the concepts of sexual politics, patriarchal rule, and, most importantly, feminism, the political analysis and practice that we women use to struggle against our oppression. The fact that racial politics and indeed racism are pervasive factors in our lives did not allow us, and still does not allow most black women, to look more deeply into our own experiences and define those things that make our lives what they are and our oppression specific to us. In the process of consciousness-raising, actually life-sharing, we began to recognize the commonality of our experience and, from that sharing and growing consciousness, to build a politics that will change our lives and inevitably end our oppression.

Our development also must be tied to the contemporary economic and political position of black people. The post-World War II generation of black youth was the first to be able to minimally partake of certain educational and employment options, previously closed completely to black people. Although our economic position is still at the very bottom of the American capitalist economy, a handful of us have been able to gain certain tools as a result of tokenism in education and employment that potentially enable us to more effectively fight our oppression.

A combined antiracist and antisexist position drew us together initially, and as we developed politically we addressed ourselves to heterosexism and economic oppression under capitalism.

2. What We Believe

Above all else, our politics initially sprang from the shared belief that black women are inherently valuable, that our liberation is a necessity not as an adjunct to somebody else's but because of our need as human persons for autonomy. This may seem so obvious as to sound simplistic, but it is apparent that no other ostensibly progressive movement has ever considered our specific oppression a priority or worked seriously for the ending of that oppression. Merely naming the pejorative stereotypes attributed to black women (e.g., mammy, matriarch, Sapphire, whore, bulldagger), let alone cataloguing the cruel, often murderous, treatment we receive, indicates how little value has been placed upon our lives during four centuries of bondage in the Western Hemisphere. We realize that the only people who care enough about us to work consistently for our liberation is us. Our politics evolve from a healthy love for ourselves, our sisters, and our community, which allows us to continue our struggle and work.

This focusing upon our own oppression is embodied in the concept of identity politics. We believe that the most profound and potentially the most radical politics come directly out of our own identity, as opposed to working to end somebody else's oppression. In the case of black women this is a particularly repugnant, dangerous, threatening, and therefore revolutionary concept because it is obvious from looking at all the political movements that have preceded us that anyone is more worthy of liberation than ourselves. We reject pedestals, queenhood, and walking ten paces behind. To be recognized as human, levelly human, is enough.

We believe that sexual politics under patriarchy is as pervasive in black women's lives as are the politics of class and race. We also often find it difficult to separate race from class from sex oppression because in our lives they are most often experienced simultaneously. We know that there is such a thing as racial-sexual oppression that is neither solely racial nor solely sexual, e.g., the history of rape of black women by white men as a weapon of political repression.

Although we are feminists and lesbians, we feel solidarity with progressive black men and do not advocate the fractionalization that white women who are separatists demand. Our situation as black people necessitates that we have solidarity around the fact of race, which white women of course do not need to have with white men, unless it is their negative solidarity as racial oppressors. We struggle together with black men against racism, while we also struggle with black men about sexism.

We realize that the liberation of all oppressed peoples necessitates the destruction of the political-economic systems of capitalism and imperialism as well as patriarchy. We are socialists because we believe the work must be organized for the collective benefit of those who do the work and create the products and not for the profit of the bosses. Material resources must be equally distributed among those who create these resources. We are not convinced, however, that a socialist revolution that is not also a feminist and antiracist revolution will guarantee our liberation. We have arrived at the necessity for developing an understanding of class relationships that takes into account the specific class position of black women who are generally marginal in the labor force, while at this particular time some of us are temporarily viewed as doubly desirable tokens at white-collar and professional levels. We need to articulate the real class situation of persons who are not merely raceless, sexless workers, but for whom racial and sexual oppression are significant determinants in their working-economic lives. Although we are in essential agreement with Marx's theory as it applied to the very specific economic relationships he analyzed, we know that this analysis must be extended further in order for us to understand our specific economic situation as black women.

A political contribution that we feel we have already made is the expansion of the feminist principle that the personal is political. In our consciousness-raising sessions, for example, we have in many ways gone beyond white women's revelations because we are dealing with the implications of race and class as well as sex. Even our black women's style of talking/testifying in black language about what we have experienced has a resonance that is both cultural and political. We have spent a great deal of energy delving into the cultural and experiential nature of our oppression out of necessity because none of these matters have ever been looked at before. No one before has ever examined the multilayered texture of black women's lives.

As we have already stated, we reject the stance of lesbian separatism because it is not a viable political analysis or strategy for us. It leaves out far too much and far too many people, particularly black men, women, and children. We have a great deal of criticism and loathing for what men have been socialized to be in this society: what they support, how they act, and how they oppress. But we do not have the misguided notion that it is their maleness, per se—i.e., their biological maleness—that makes them what they are. As black women we find any type of biological determinism a particularly dangerous and reactionary basis upon which to build a politic. We must also question whether lesbian separatism is an adequate and progressive political analysis and strategy, even for those who practice it, since it so completely denies any but the sexual sources of women's oppression, negating the facts of class and race.

3. Problems in Organizing Black Feminists

During our years together as a black feminist collective we have experienced success and defeat, joy and pain, victory and failure. We have found that it is very difficult to organize around black feminist issues, difficult even to announce in certain contexts that we are black feminists. We have tried to think about the reasons for our difficulties, particularly since the white women's movement continues to be strong and to grow in many directions. In this section we will discuss some of the general reasons for the organizing problems we face and also talk specifically about the stages in organizing our own collective.

The major source of difficulty in our political work is that we are not just trying to fight oppression on one front or even two, but instead to address a whole range of oppressions. We do not have racial, sexual, heterosexual, or class privilege to rely upon, nor do we have even the minimal access to resources and power that groups who possess any one of these types of privilege have.

The psychological toll of being a black woman and the difficulties this presents in reaching political consciousness and doing political work can never be underestimated. There is a very low value placed upon black women's psyches in this society, which is both racist and sexist. As an early group member once said, "We are all damaged people merely by virtue of being black women." We are dispossessed psychologically and on every other level, and yet we feel the necessity to struggle to change our condition and the condition of all black women. In "A Black Feminist's Search for Sisterhood," Michele Wallace arrives at this conclusion:

> We exist as women who are black who are feminists, each stranded for the moment, working independently because there is not yet an environment in this society remotely congenial to our struggle—because, being on the bottom, we would have to do what no one else has done: we would have to fight the world. (Michele Wallace. "A Black Feminist's Search for Sisterhood," *Village Voice*, July 28, 1975, 6–7.)

Wallace is not pessimistic but realistic in her assessment of black feminists' position, particularly in her allusion to the nearly classic isolation most of us face. We might use our position at the bottom, however, to make a clear leap into revolutionary action. If black women were free, it would mean that everyone else would have to be free since our freedom would necessitate the destruction of all the systems of oppression.

Feminism is, nevertheless, very threatening to the majority of black people because it calls into question some of the most basic assumptions about our existence, i.e., that gender should be a determinant of power relationships. Here is the way male and female roles were defined in a black nationalist pamphlet from the early 1970s.

> We understand that it is and has been traditional that the man is the head of the house. He is the leader of the house/nation because his knowledge of the world is broader, his awareness is greater, his understanding is fuller and his application of this information is wiser. . . . After all, it is only reasonable that the man be the head of the house because he is able to defend and protect the development of his home. . . . Women cannot do the same things as men—they are made by nature to function differently. Equality of men and women is something that cannot happen even in the abstract world. Men are not equal to other men, i.e., ability, experience, or even understanding. The value of men and women can be seen as in the value of gold and silver—they are not equal but both have great value. We must realize that men and women are a complement to each other because there is no house/family without a man and his wife. Both are essential to the development of any life. (Mumininas of Committee for Unified Newark, *Mwanamke Mwananchi [The Nationalist Woman]*, Newark, N.J., c. 1971, 4–5.)

The material conditions of most black women would hardly lead them to upset both economic and sexual arrangements that seem to represent some stability in their lives. Many black women have a good understanding of both sexism and racism, but because of the everyday constrictions of their lives cannot risk struggling against them both.

The reaction of black men to feminism has been notoriously negative. They are, of course, even more threatened than black women by the possibility that black feminists might organize around our own needs. They realize that they might not only lose valuable and hard-working allies in their struggles, but that they might also be forced to change their habitually sexist ways of interacting with and oppressing black women. Accusations that black feminism divides the black struggle are powerful deterrents to the growth of an autonomous black women's movement.

Still, hundreds of women have been active at different times during the three-year existence of our group. And every black woman who came came out of a strongly felt need for some level of possibility that did not previously exist in her life.

When we first started meeting early in 1974 after the NBFO first eastern regional conference, we did not have a strategy for organizing, or even focus. We just wanted to see what we had. After a period of months of not meeting, we began to meet again late in the year and started doing an intense variety of consciousness-raising. The overwhelming feeling that we had is that after years and years we had finally found each other. Although we were not doing political work as a group, individuals continued their involvement in lesbian politics, sterilization abuse, and abortion rights work, Third World Women's International Women's Day activities, and support activity for the trials of Dr. Kenneth Edelin, Joan Little, and Inez Garcia. During our first summer, when membership had dropped off considerably, those of us remaining devoted serious discussion to the possibility of opening a refuge for battered women in a black community. (There was no refuge in Boston at that time.) We also decided around that time to become an independent collective since we had serious disagreements with NBFO's bourgeois-feminist stance and their lack of a clear political focus.

We also were contacted at that time by socialist feminists, with whom we had worked on abortion rights activities, who wanted to encourage us to attend the National Socialist Feminist Conference in Yellow Springs. One of our members did attend and despite the narrowness of the ideology that was promoted at that particular conference, we became more aware of the need for us to understand our own economic situation and to make our own economic analysis.

In the fall, when some members returned, we experienced several months of comparative inactivity and internal disagreements which were first conceptualized as a lesbian-straight split but which were also the result of class and political differences. During the summer those of us who were still meeting had determined the need to do political work and to move beyond consciousness-raising and serving exclusively as an emotional support group. At the beginning of 1976, when some of the women who had not wanted to do political work and who also had voiced disagreements stopped attending of their own accord, we again looked for a focus. We decided at that time, with the

addition of new members, to become a study group. We had always shared our reading with each other, and some of us had written papers on black feminism for group discussion a few months before this decision was made. We began functioning as a study group and also began discussing the possibility of starting a black feminist publication. We had a retreat in the late spring, which provided a time for both political discussion and working out interpersonal issues. Currently we are planning to gather together a collection of black feminist writing. We feel that it is absolutely essential to demonstrate the reality of our politics to other black women and believe that we can do this through writing and distributing our work. The fact that individual black feminists are living in isolation all over the country, that our own numbers are small, and that we have some skills in writing, printing, and publishing makes us want to carry out these kinds of projects as a means of organizing black feminists as we continue to do political work in coalition with other groups.

4. Black Feminist Issues and Practice

During our time together we have identified and worked on many issues of particular relevance to black women. The inclusiveness of our politics makes us concerned with any situation that impinges upon the lives of women, Third World, and working people. We are of course particularly committed to working on those struggles in which race, sex, and class are simultaneous factors in oppression. We might, for example, become involved in workplace organizing at a factory that employs Third-World women or picket a hospital that is cutting back on already inadequate health care to a Third World community, or set up a rape crisis center in a black neighborhood. Organizing around welfare or day-care concerns might also be a focus. The work to be done and the countless issues that this work represents merely reflect the pervasiveness of our oppression.

Issues and projects that collective members have actually worked on are sterilization abuse, abortion rights, battered women, rape, and health care. We have also done many workshops and educationals on black feminism on college campuses, at women's conferences, and most recently for high school women.

One issue that is of major concern to us and that we have begun to publicly address is racism in the white women's movement. As black feminists we are made constantly and painfully aware of how little effort white women have made to understand and combat their racism, which requires among other things that they have a more than superficial comprehension of race, color, and black history and culture. Eliminating racism in the white women's movement is by definition work for white women to do, but we will continue to speak to and demand accountability on this issue.

In the practice of our politics we do not believe that the end always justifies the means. Many reactionary and destructive acts have been done in the name of achieving "correct" political goals. As feminists we do not want to mess over people in the name of politics. We believe in collective process and a nonhierarchical distribution of power within our own group and in our vision of a revolutionary society. We are committed to a continual examination of our politics as they develop through criticism and self-criticism as an essential aspect of our practice. As black feminists and lesbians we know that we have a very definite revolutionary task to perform, and we are ready for the lifetime of work and struggle before us.

THE AFROCENTRIC IDEA IN EDUCATION (MOLEFI KETE ASANTE, 1991)

SOURCE: Asante, Molefi Kete. "The Afrocentric Idea in Education." *Journal of Negro Education* v. 60, no. 2 (Spring 1991): 170–180.

INTRODUCTION: *Creator of the first Ph.D. program for African American Studies in 1987, Asante is also credited as the founder of the theory of Afrocentricity in education, which calls for students to study peoples, places, ideas, and history from an African, rather than Eurocentric, perspective.*

Introduction

Many of the principles that govern the development of the Afrocentric idea in education were first established by Carter G. Woodson in *The Mis-education of the Negro* (1933). Indeed, Woodson's classic reveals the fundamental problems pertaining to the education of the African person in America. As Woodson contends, African Americans have been educated away from their own culture and traditions and attached to the fringes of European culture; thus dislocated from themselves, Woodson asserts that African Americans often valorize European culture to the detriment of their own heritage (p. 7). Although Woodson does not advocate rejection of American citizenship or nationality, he believed that assuming African Americans hold the same position as European Americans vis-à-vis the realities of America would lead to the psychological and cultural death of the African American population. Furthermore, if education is ever to be substantive and

meaningful within the context of American society, Woodson argues, it must first address the African's historical experiences, both in Africa and America (p. 7). That is why he places on education, and particularly on the traditionally African American colleges, the burden of teaching the African American to be responsive to the long traditions and history of Africa as well as America. Woodson's alert recognition, more than 50 years ago, that something is severely wrong with the way African Americans are educated provides the principal impetus for the Afrocentric approach to American education.

In this article I will examine the nature and scope of this approach, establish its necessity, and suggest ways to develop and disseminate it throughout all levels of education. Two propositions stand in the background of the theoretical and philosophical issues I will present. These ideas represent the core presuppositions on which I have based most of my work in the field of education, and they suggest the direction of my own thinking about what education is capable of doing to and for an already politically and economically marginalized people—African Americans:

(1) Education is fundamentally a social phenomenon whose ultimate purpose is to socialize the learner; to send a child to school is to prepare that child to become part of a social group.

(2) Schools are reflective of the societies that develop them (i.e., a White supremacist-dominated society will develop a White supremacist educational system).

Definitions

An alternative framework suggests that other definitional assumptions can provide a new paradigm for the examination of education within the American society. For example, in education, *centricity* refers to a perspective that involves locating students within the context of their own cultural references so that they can relate socially and psychologically to other cultural perspectives. Centricity is a concept that can be applied to any culture. The centrist paradigm is supported by research showing that the most productive method of teaching any student is to place his or her group within the center of the context of knowledge (Asante, 1990). For White students in America this is easy because almost all the experiences discussed in American classrooms are approached from the standpoint of White perspectives and history. American education, however, is not centric; it is Eurocentric. Consequently, non-White students are also made to see themselves and their groups as the "acted upon." Only rarely do they read or hear of non-White people as active participants in history. This is as true for a discussion of the American Revolution as it is for a discussion of Dante's *Inferno*; for instance, most classroom discussions of the European slave trade concentrate on the activities of Whites rather than on the resistance efforts of Africans. A person educated in a truly centric fashion comes to view all groups' contributions as significant and useful. Even a White person educated in such a system does not assume superiority based upon racist notions. Thus, a truly centric education is different from a Eurocentric, racist (that is, White supremacist) education.

Afrocentricity is a frame of reference wherein phenomena are viewed from the perspective of the African person. The Afrocentric approach seeks in every situation the appropriate centrality of the African person (Asante, 1987). In education this means that teachers provide students the opportunity to study the world and its people, concepts, and history from an African world view. In most classrooms, whatever the subject, Whites are located in the center perspective position. How alien the African American child must feel, how like an outsider! The little African American child who sits in a classroom and is taught to accept as heroes and heroines individuals who defamed African people is being actively de-centered, dislocated, and made into a nonperson, one whose aim in life might be to one day shed that "badge of inferiority": his or her Blackness. In Afrocentric educational settings, however, teachers do not marginalize African American children by causing them to question their own self-worth because their people's story is seldom told. By seeing themselves as the subjects rather than the objects of education—be the discipline biology, medicine, literature, or social studies—African American students come to see themselves not merely as seekers of knowledge but as integral participants in it. Because all content areas are adaptable to an Afrocentric approach, African American students can be made to see themselves as centered in the reality of any discipline.

It must be emphasized that Afrocentricity is *not* a Black version of Eurocentricity (Asante, 1987). Eurocentricity is based on White supremacist notions whose purposes are to protect White privilege and advantage in education, economics, politics, and so forth. Unlike Eurocentricity, Afrocentricity does not condone ethnocentric valorization at the expense of degrading other groups' perspectives. Moreover, Eurocentricity presents the particular historical reality of Europeans as the sum total of the human experience (Asante, 1987). It imposes Eurocentric realities as "universal"; i.e., that which is White is presented as applying to the human condition in general, while that which is non-White is viewed as group-specific and

therefore not "human." This explains why some scholars and artists of African descent rush to deny their Blackness; they believe that to exist as a Black person is not to exist as a universal human being. They are the individuals Woodson identified as preferring European art, language, and culture over African art, language, and culture; they believe that anything of European origin is inherently better than anything produced by or issuing from their own people. Naturally, the person of African descent should be centered in his or her historical experiences as an African, but Eurocentric curricula produce such aberrations of perspective among persons of color.

Multiculturalism in education is a nonhierarchical approach that respects and celebrates a variety of cultural perspectives on world phenomena (Asante, 1991). The multicultural approach holds that although European culture is the majority culture in the United States, that is not sufficient reason for it to be imposed on diverse student populations as "universal." Multiculturalists assert that education, to have integrity, must begin with the proposition that all humans have contributed to world development and the flow of knowledge and information, and that most human achievements are the result of mutually interactive, international effort. Without a multicultural education, students remain essentially ignorant of the contributions of a major portion of the world's people. A multicultural education is thus a fundamental necessity for anyone who wishes to achieve competency in almost any subject.

The Afrocentric idea must be the stepping-stone from which the multicultural idea is launched. A truly authentic multicultural education, therefore, must be based upon the Afrocentric initiative. If this step is skipped, multicultural curricula, as they are increasingly being defined by White "resisters" (to be discussed below) will evolve without any substantive infusion of African American content, and the African American child will continue to be lost in the Eurocentric framework of education. In other words, the African American child will neither be confirmed nor affirmed in his or her own cultural information. For the mutual benefit of all Americans, this tragedy, which leads to the psychological and cultural dislocation of African American children, can and should be avoided.

The Revolutionary Challenge

Because it centers African American students inside history, culture, science, and so forth rather than outside these subjects, the Afrocentric idea presents the most revolutionary challenge to the ideology of White supremacy in education during the past decade. No other theoretical position stated by African Americans has ever captured the imagination of such a wide range of scholars and students of history, sociology, communications, anthropology, and psychology. The Afrocentric challenge has been posed in three critical ways:

(1) It questions the imposition of the White supremacist view as universal and/or classical (Asante, 1990).

(2) It demonstrates the indefensibility of racist theories that assault multiculturalism and pluralism.

(3) It projects a humanistic and pluralistic viewpoint by articulating Afrocentricity as a valid, nonhegemonic perspective.

Suppression and Distortion: Symbols of Resistance

The forces of resistance to the Afrocentric, multicultural transformation of the curriculum and teaching practices began to assemble their wagons almost as quickly as word got out about the need for equality in education (Ravitch, 1990). Recently, the renowned historian Arthur Schlesinger and others formed a group called the Committee for the Defense of History. This is a paradoxical development because only lies, untruths, and inaccurate information need defending. In their arguments against the Afrocentric perspective, these proponents of Eurocentrism often clothe their arguments in false categories and fake terms (i.e., "pluralistic" and "particularistic" multiculturalism) (Keto, 1990; Asante, 1991). Besides, as the late African scholar Cheikh Anta Diop (1980) maintained: "African history and Africa need no defense." Afrocentric education is not against history. It is *for* history—correct, accurate history—and if it is against anything, it is against the marginalization of African American, Hispanic American, Asian American, Native American, and other non-White children. The Committee for the Defense of History is nothing more than a futile attempt to buttress the crumbling pillars of a White supremacist system that conceals its true motives behind the cloak of American liberalism. It was created in the same spirit that generated Bloom's *The Closing of the American Mind* (1987) and Hirsch's *Cultural Literacy: What Every American Needs to Know* (1987), both of which were placed at the service of the White hegemony in education, particularly its curricular hegemony. This committee and other evidences of White backlash are a predictable challenge to the contemporary thrust for an Afrocentric, multicultural approach to education.

Naturally, different adherents to a theory will have different views on its meaning. While two discourses presently are circulating about multiculturalism, only one is relevant to the liberation of the minds of African and White people in the United States. That discourse is Afrocentricity: the acceptance of Africa as central to African

people. Yet, rather than getting on board with Afrocentrists to fight against White hegemonic education, some Whites (and some Blacks as well) have opted to plead for a return to the educational plantation. Unfortunately for them, however, those days are gone, and such misinformation can never be packaged as accurate, correct education again.

Ravitch (1990), who argues that there are two kinds of multiculturalism—*pluralist multiculturalism* and *particularist multiculturalism*—is the leader of those professors whom I call "resisters" or opponents to Afrocentricity and multiculturalism. Indeed, Ravitch advances the imaginary divisions in multicultural perspectives to conceal her true identity as a defender of White supremacy. Her tactics are the tactics of those who prefer Africans and other non-Whites to remain on the mental and psychological plantation of Western civilization. In their arrogance the resisters accuse Afrocentrists and multiculturalists of creating "fantasy history" and "bizarre theories" of non-White people's contributions to civilization. What they prove, however, is their own ignorance. Additionally, Ravitch and others (Nicholson, 1990) assert that multiculturalism will bring about the "tribalization" of America, but in reality America has always been a nation of ethnic diversity. When one reads their works on multiculturalism, one realizes that they are really advocating the imposition of a White perspective on everybody else's culture. Believing that the Eurocentric position is indisputable, they attempt to resist and impede the progressive transformation of the monoethnic curriculum. Indeed, the closets of bigotry have opened to reveal various attempts by White scholars (joined by some Blacks) to defend White privilege in the curriculum in much the same way as it has been so staunchly defended in the larger society. It was perhaps inevitable that the introduction of the Afrocentric idea would open up the discussion of the American school curriculum in a profound way.

Why has Afrocentricity created so much of a controversy in educational circles? The idea that an African American child is placed in a stronger position to learn if he or she is centered—that is, if the child sees himself or herself within the content of the curriculum rather than at its margins—is not novel (Asante, 1980). What is revolutionary is the movement from the idea (conceptual stage) to its implementation in practice, when we begin to teach teachers how to put African American youth at the center of instruction. In effect, students are shown how to see with new eyes and hear with new ears. African American children learn to interpret and center phenomena in the context of African heritage, while White students are taught to see that their own centers are not threatened by the presence or contributions of African Americans and others.

The Condition of Eurocentric Education

Institutions such as schools are conditioned by the character of the nation in which they are developed. Just as crime and politics are different in different nations, so, too, is education. In the United States a "Whites-only" orientation has predominated in education. This has had a profound impact on the quality of education for children of all races and ethnic groups. The African American child has suffered disproportionately, but White children are also the victims of monoculturally diseased curricula.

The Tragedy of Ignorance

During the past five years many White students and parents have approached me after presentations with tears in their eyes or expressing their anger about the absence of information about African Americans in the schools. A recent comment from a young White man at a major university in the Northeast was especially striking. As he said to me: "My teacher told us that Martin Luther King was a commie and went on with the class." Because this student's teacher made no effort to discuss King's ideas, the student maliciously had been kept ignorant. The vast majority of White Americans are likewise ignorant about the bountiful reservoirs of African and African American history, culture, and contributions. For example, few Americans of any color have heard the names of Cheikh Anta Diop, Anna Julia Cooper, C. L. R. James, or J. A. Rogers. All were historians who contributed greatly to our understanding of the African world. Indeed, very few teachers have ever taken a course in African American Studies; therefore, most are unable to provide systematic information about African Americans.

Afrocentricity and History

Most of America's teaching force are victims of the same system that victimizes today's young. Thus, American children are not taught the names of the African ethnic groups from which the majority of the African American population are derived; few are taught the names of any of the sacred sites in Africa. Few teachers can discuss with their students the significance of the Middle Passage or describe what it meant or means to Africans. Little mention is made in American classrooms of either the brutality of slavery or the ex-slaves' celebration of freedom. American children have little or no understanding of the nature of the capture, transport, and enslavement of Africans. Few have been taught the true horrors of being taken, shipped naked across 25 days of ocean, broken by abuse and indignities of all kinds, and dehumanized into a beast of burden, a thing without a name. If our students only knew

the truth, if they were taught the Afrocentric perspective on the Great Enslavement, and if they knew the full story about the events since slavery that have served to constantly dislocate African Americans, their behavior would perhaps be different. Among these events are: the infamous constitutional compromise of 1787, which decreed that African Americans were, by law, the equivalent of but three-fifths of a person (see Franklin, 1974); the 1857 Dred Scott decision in which the Supreme Court avowed that African Americans had no rights Whites were obliged to respect (Howard, 1857); the complete dismissal and non-enforcement of Section 2 of the Fourteenth Amendment to the Constitution (this amendment, passed in 1868, stipulated as one of its provisions a penalty against any state that denied African Americans the right to vote, and called for the reduction of a state's delegates to the House of Representatives in proportion to the number of disenfranchised African American males therein); and the much-mentioned, as-yet-unreceived 40 acres and a mule, reparation for enslavement, promised to each African American family after the Civil War by Union General William T. Sherman and Secretary of War Edwin Stanton (Oubre, 1978, pp. 18-19, 182-183; see also Smith, 1987, pp. 106-107). If the curriculum were enhanced to include readings from the slave narratives; the diaries of slave ship captains; the journals of slaveowners; the abolitionist newspapers; the writings of the freedmen and freedwomen; the accounts of African American civil rights, civic, and social organizations; and numerous others, African American children would be different, White children would be different—indeed, America would be a different nation today.

America's classrooms should resound with the story of the barbaric treatment of the Africans, of how their dignity was stolen and their cultures destroyed. The recorded experiences of escaped slaves provide the substance for such learning units. For example, the narrative of Jacob and Ruth Weldon presents a detailed account of the Middle Passage (Feldstein, 1971). The Weldons noted the Africans, having been captured and brought onto the slave ships, were chained to the deck, made to bend over, and "branded with a red hot iron in the form of letters or signs dipped in an oily preparation and pressed against the naked flesh till it burnt a deep and ineffaceable scar, to show who was the owner" (pp. 33–37). They also recalled that those who screamed were lashed on the face, breast, thighs, and backs with a "cat-o'-nine tails" wielded by White sailors: "Every blow brought the returning lash pieces of grieving flesh" (p. 44). They saw "mothers with babies at their breasts basely branded and lashed, hewed and scarred, till it would seem as if the very heavens must smite the infernal tormentors with the doom they so richly merited" (p. 44). Children and infants were not spared from this terror. The Weldons tell of a nine-month-old baby on board a slave ship being flogged because it would not eat. The ship's captain ordered the child's feet placed in boiling water, which dissolved the skin and nails, then ordered the child whipped again; still the child refused to eat. Eventually the captain killed the baby with his own hands and commanded the child's mother to throw the dead baby overboard. When the mother refused, she, too, was beaten, then forced to the ship's side, where "with her head averted so she might not see it, she dropped the body into the sea" (p. 44). In a similar vein a captain of a ship with 440 Africans on board noted that 132 had to be thrown overboard to save water (Feldstein, 1971, p. 47). As another wrote, the "groans and soffocating [*sic*] cries for air and water coming from below the deck sickened the soul of humanity" (Feldstein, 1971, p. 44).

Upon landing in America the situation was often worse. The brutality of the slavocracy is unequalled for the psychological and spiritual destruction it wrought upon African Americans. Slave mothers were often forced to leave their children unattended while they worked in the fields. Unable to nurse their children or properly care for them, they often returned from work at night to find their children dead (Feldstein, 1971, p. 49). The testimony of Henry Bibb also sheds light on the bleakness of the slave experience:

> I was born May 1815, of a slave mother. . .and was claimed as the property of David White, Esq. . . . I was flogged up; for where I should have received moral, mental, and religious instructions, I received stripes without number, the object of which was to degrade and keep me in subordination. I can truly say that I drank deeply of the bitter cup of suffering and woe. I have been dragged down to the lowest depths of human degradation and wretchedness, by slaveholders. (Feldstein, 1971, p. 60)

Enslavement was truly a living death. While the ontological onslaught caused some Africans to opt for suicide, the most widespread results were dislocation, disorientation, and misorientation—all of which are the consequences of the African person being actively de-centered. The "Jim Crow" period of second-class citizenship, from 1877 to 1954, saw only slight improvement in the lot of African Americans. This era was characterized by the sharecropper system, disenfranchisement, enforced segregation, internal migration, lynchings, unemployment, poor housing conditions, and separate and unequal educational facilities. Inequitable policies and practices veritably plagued the race.

No wonder many persons of African descent attempt to shed their race and become "raceless." One's basic identity is one's self-identity, which is ultimately one's cultural identity; without a strong cultural identity, one is lost. Black children do not know their people's story and White children do not know the story, but remembrance is a vital requisite for understanding and humility. This is why the Jews have campaigned (and rightly so) to have the story of the European Holocaust taught in schools and colleges. Teaching about such a monstrous human brutality should forever remind the world of the ways in which humans have often violated each other. Teaching about the African Holocaust is just as important for many of the same reasons. Additionally, it underscores the enormity of the effects of physical, psychological, and economic dislocation in the African population in America and throughout the African diaspora. Without an understanding of the historical experiences of African people, American children cannot make any real headway in addressing the problems of the present.

Certainly, if African American children were taught to be fully aware of the struggles of our African forebears they would find a renewed sense of purpose and vision in their own lives. They would cease acting as if they have no past and no future. For instance, if they were taught about the historical relationship of Africans to the cotton industry—how African American men, women, and children were forced to pick cotton from "can't see in the morning 'till can't see at night," until the blood ran from the tips of their fingers where they were pricked by the hard boll; or if they were made to visualize their ancestors in the burning sun, bent double with constant stooping, and dragging rough, heavy croaker sacks behind them—or picture them bringing those sacks trembling to the scale, fearful of a sure flogging if they did not pick enough, perhaps our African American youth would develop a stronger entrepreneurial spirit. If White children were taught the same information rather than that normally fed them about American slavery, they would probably view our society differently and work to transform it into a better place.

Correcting Distorted Information

Hegemonic education can exist only so long as true and accurate information is withheld. Hegemonic Eurocentric education can exist only so long as Whites maintain that Africans and other non-Whites have never contributed to world civilization. It is largely upon such false ideas that invidious distinctions are made. The truth, however, gives one insight into the real reasons behind human actions, whether one chooses to follow the paths of others or not. For example, one cannot remain comfortable teaching that art and philosophy originated in Greece if one learns that the Greeks themselves taught that the study of these subjects originated in Africa, specifically ancient Kemet (Herodotus, 1987). The first philosophers were the Egyptians Kagemni, Khun-anup, Ptahhotep, Kete, and Seti; but Eurocentric education is so disjointed that students have no way of discovering this and other knowledge of the organic relationship of Africa to the rest of human history. Not only did Africa contribute to human history, African civilizations predate all other civilizations. Indeed, the human species originated on the continent of Africa—this is true whether one looks at either archaeological or biological evidence.

Two other notions must be refuted. There are those who say that African American history should begin with the arrival of Africans as slaves in 1619, but it has been shown that Africans visited and inhabited North and South America long before European settlers "discovered" the "New World" (Van Sertima, 1976). Secondly, although America became something of a home for those Africans who survived the horrors of the Middle Passage, their experiences on the slave ships and during slavery resulted in their having an entirely different (and often tainted) perspective about America from that of the Europeans and others who came, for the most part, of their own free will seeking opportunities not available to them in their native lands. Afrocentricity therefore seeks to recognize this divergence in perspective and create centeredness for African American students.

Conclusion

The reigning initiative for total curricular change is the movement that is being proposed and led by Africans, namely, the Afrocentric idea. When I wrote the first book on Afrocentricity (Asante, 1980), now in its fifth printing, I had no idea that in 10 years the idea would both shake up and shape discussions in education, art, fashion, and politics. Since the publication of my subsequent works, *The Afrocentric Idea* (Asante, 1987) and *Kemet, Afrocentricity, and Knowledge* (Asante, 1990), the debate has been joined in earnest. Still, for many White Americans (and some African Americans) the most unsettling aspect of the discussion about Afrocentricity is that its intellectual source lies in the research and writings of African American scholars. Whites are accustomed to being in charge of the major ideas circulating in the American academy. Deconstructionism, Gestalt psychology, Marxism, structuralism, Piagetian theory, and so forth have all been developed, articulated, and elaborated upon at length, generally by White scholars. On the other hand, Afrocentricity is the product of scholars such as Nobles (1986), Hilliard (1978), Karenga (1986), Keto (1990), Richards (1991), and Myers

(1989). There are also increasing numbers of young, impressively credentialled African American scholars who have begun to write in the Afrocentric vein (Jean, 1991). They, and even some young White scholars, have emerged with ideas about how to change the curriculum Afrocentrically.

Afrocentricity provides all Americans an opportunity to examine the perspective of the African person in this society and the world. The registers claim that Afrocentricity is anti-White; yet, if Afrocentricity as a theory is against anything it is against racism, ignorance, and monoethnic hegemony in the curriculum. Afrocentricity is not anti-White; it is, however, pro-human. Further, the aim of the Afrocentric curriculum is not to divide America, it is to make America flourish as it ought to flourish. This nation has long been divided with regard to the educational opportunities afforded to children. By virtue of the protection provided by society and reinforced by the Eurocentric curriculum, the White child is already ahead of the African American child by first grade. Our efforts thus must concentrate on giving the African American child greater opportunities for learning at the kindergarten level. However, the kind of assistance the African American child needs is as much cultural as it is academic. If the proper cultural information is provided, the academic performance will surely follow suit.

When it comes to educating African American children, the American educational system does not need a tune-up, it needs an overhaul. Black children have been maligned by this system. Black teachers have been maligned. Black history has been maligned. Africa has been maligned. Nonetheless, two truisms can be stated about education in America. First, some teachers *can and do* effectively teach African American children; secondly, if some teachers can do it, others can, too. We must learn all we can about what makes these teachers' attitudes and approaches successful, and then work diligently to see that their successes are replicated on a broad scale. By raising the same questions that Woodson posed more than 50 years ago, Afrocentric education, along with a significant reorientation of the American educational enterprise, seeks to respond to the African person's psychological and cultural dislocation. By providing philosophical and theoretical guidelines and criteria that are centered in an African perception of reality and by placing the African American child in his or her proper historical context and setting, Afrocentricity may be just the "escape hatch" African Americans so desperately need to facilitate academic success and "steal away" from the cycle of miseducation and dislocation.

■ ■ *Bibliography*

Asante, M. K. *Afrocentricity: The Theory of Social Change.* Buffalo, N.Y.: Amulefi, 1980.

Asante, M. K. *The Afrocentric Idea.* Philadelphia: Temple University Press, 1987.

Asante, M. K. *Kemet, Afrocentricity, and Knowledge.* Trenton, N.J.: Africa World Press, 1990.

Bloom, A. *The Closing of the American Mind.* New York: Simon & Schuster, 1987.

Feldstein, S. *Once a Slave: The Slave's View of Slavery.* New York: William Morrow, 1971.

Franklin, J. H. *From Slavery to Freedom.* New York: Knopf, 1974.

Herodotus. *The History.* Chicago: University of Illinois Press, 1987.

Hilliard, A. G., III. *Anatomy and Dynamics of Oppression.* Speech delivered at the National Conference on Human Relations in Education, Minneapolis, Minn., June 20, 1978.

Hirsch, E. D. *Cultural Literacy: What Every American Needs to Know.* New York: Houghton Mifflin, 1987.

Howard, B. C. *Report of the Decision of the Supreme Court of the United States and the Opinions of the Justices Thereof in the Case of Dred Scott versus John F. A. Sandford, December Term, 1856.* New York: D. Appleton & Co., 1857.

Jean, C. *Beyond the Eurocentric Veils.* Amherst: University of Massachusetts Press, 1991.

Karenga, M. R. *Introduction to Black Studies.* Los Angeles: University of Sankore Press, 1986.

Keto, C. T. *Africa-centered Perspective of History.* Blackwood, N.J.: C. A. Associates, 1990.

Nicholson, D. "Afrocentrism and the Tribalization of America." *The Washington Post* (September 23, 1990): B-1.

Nobles, W. *African Psychology.* Oakland, Calif.: Black Family Institute, 1986.

Oubre, C. F. *Forty Acres and a Mule: The Freedman's Bureau and Black Land Ownership.* Baton Rouge: Louisiana State University Press, 1978.

Ravitch, D. "Multiculturalism: E Pluribus Plures." *The American Scholar* (Summer 1990): 337–354.

Richards, D. *Let the Circle be Unbroken.* Trenton, N.J.: Africa World Press, 1991.

Smith, J. O. *The Politics of Racial Inequality: A Systematic Comparative Macro-analysis from the Colonial Period to 1970.* New York: Greenwood Press, 1987.

Van Sertima, I. *They Came Before Columbus.* New York: Random House, 1976.

Woodson, C. G. *The Education of the Negro Prior to 1861: A History of the Education of the Colored People of the U.S. from the Beginning of Slavery.* New York: G. P. Putnam's Sons, 1915.

Woodson, C. G. *The Mis-education of the Negro.* Washington, D.C.: Associated Publishers, 1933.

Woodson, C. G. *African Background Outlined.* Washington, D.C.: Association for the Study of Afro-American Life and History, 1936.

Statistics and Lists Contents

FIGURE 1.1

Black Enterprise's top 10 U.S. asset managers, 2005

2005	2004	Company name	Location	Chief Executive	Began	Staff	Assets under management*
1	1	Ariel Capital Management L.L.C.	Chicago, IL	John W. Rogers, Jr.	1983	88	21,433.000
2	2	Earnest Partners L.L.C.	Atlanta, GA	Paul E. Viera	1998	35	13,934.000
3	3	Rhumbline Advisers	Boston, MA	J. D. Nelson	1990	15	10,307.000
4	4	Brown Capital Management Inc.	Baltimore, MD	Eddie C. Brown	1983	24	5,279.000
5	6	Advent Capital Management L.L.C.	New York, NY	Tracy V. Maitland	1995	40	3,848.000
6	5	MDL Capital Management Inc.	Pittsburgh, PA	Mark D. Lay	1992	32	2,821.000
7	10	Holland Capital Management L.P.	Chicago, IL	Louis A. Holland	1991	24	2,628.000
8	7	NCM Capital Management Group Inc.	Durham, NC	Maceo K. Sloan	1986	25	2,145.000
9	9	The Edgar Lomax Group	Springfield, VA	Randall R. Eley	1986	12	1,962.000
10	8	Smith Graham & Co. Investment Advisors L.P.	Houston, TX	Gerald B. Smith	1990	25	1,958.000

* In Millions of Dollars to the nearest thousand. As of Dec. 31, 2004. Prepared by B.E. Research. Verified by Barge Consulting & the Securities and Exchange Commission. Reviewed by the certified public accounting firm Edwards & Co.

SOURCE: Securities and Exchange Commission.

FIGURE 1.2

Black Enterprise's top 10 U.S. private equity companies, 2005

2005	2004	Company name	Location	Chief Executive	Began	Staff	Capital under management*
1	1	Fairview Capital Partners Inc.	Farmington, CT	Laurence C. Morse/ JoAnn H. Price	1994	16	1,600.000
2	4	Pharos Capital Group L.L.C.	Dallas, TX	Dale LeFebvre	1998	14	350.000
3	5	SYNCOM	Silver Spring, MD	Herbert P. Wilkins, Sr.	1977	8	250.000
4	3	Smith Whiley & Co.	Hartford, CT	Gwendolyn Smith Iloani	1994	12	222.000
5	6	Quetzal/J.P Morgan Partners	New York, NY	Reginald J. Hollinger/ Lauren M. Tyler	2000	4	170.000
6	7	Provender Capital Group L.L.C.	New York, NY	Frederick O. Terrell	1997	5	145.000
7	8	Opportunity Capital Partners	Fremont, CA	J. Peter Thompson	1993	8	135.000
8	9	ICV Capital Partners L.L.C.	New York, NY	Willie Woods	1999	10	130.000
9	10	Black Enterprise Greenwich Street Corporate Growth Management L.L.C.	New York, NY	Ed A. Williams	1998	8	91.000
10	—	United Enterprise Fund L.P.	New York, NY	John O. Utendahl/ Jeffery Keys/Daniel Dean	2000	5	41.000

* In Millions of Dollars to the nearest thousand. As of Dec. 31, 2004 Prepared by B.E. Research. Reviewed by the certified public accounting firm Edwards & Co.

FIGURE 1.3

Black Enterprise's top 10 U.S. auto dealers, 2005

2005	2004	Company name	Location	Chief Executive	Began	Staff	Sales*	Type of business
1	1	Prestige Automotive	Detroit, MI	Gregory Jackson	1989	400	1,066.597	Chevrolet, Pontiac, Ford, Saturn, Lincoln-Mercury, Buick, GMC Truck
2	2	March/Hodge Automotive Group	Hartford, CT	Tony March/ Ernest M. Hodge	1998	800	558.383	GM, Toyota, Lexus, Honda, Infiniti, Volkswagen, Jaguar, Volvo
3	3	Martin Automotive Group	Bowling Green, KY	Cornelius A. Martin	1985	706	382.445	Cadillac, Dodge, Jeep, Chrysler, Kia
4	4	S. Woods Enterprises Inc.	Tampa, FL	Sanford L. Woods	1989	354	343.556	Dodge, Chrysler, Jeep, Toyota, Lexus, Honda, Hyundai, Chevrolet, Ford, Hummer, Saab
5	5	The Harrell Companies	Atlanta, GA	H. Steve Harrell	1987	412	287.791	Lexus, Nissan, Honda, Volvo, Kia, Hyundai
6	7	Boyland Auto Group	Orlando, FL	Dorian S. Boyland	1987	380	241.630	Dodge, Nissan, Ford, Honda, Mercedes-Benz
7	6	Family Automotive Group	San Juan Capistrano, CA	Raymond Dixon	1993	320	206.518	Ford, Toyota, Honda
8	11	Winston Pittman Enterprise	Louisville, KY	Winston R. Pittman, Sr.	1988	235	167.578	Dodge, Chrysler, Jeep, Toyota, Lexus, Scion, Nissan
9	9	Legacy Automotive Group	McDonough, GA	Emanuel D. Jones	1992	220	162.000	Ford, Toyota, Scion, Mercury
10	10	32 Ford Mercury Inc.	Batavia, OH	Clarence F. Warren	1990	130	161.388	Ford, Lincoln-Mercury

* In Millions of Dollars to the nearest thousand. As of Dec. 31, 2004. Prepared by B.E. Research. Reviewed by the certified public accounting firm Edwards & Co.Black Enterprise Top 10 Auto

FIGURE 1.4

Black Enterprise's top 10 U.S. advertising companies, 2005

2005	2004	Company name	Location	Chief Executive	Began	Staff	Billings*
1	1	Globalhue	Southfield, MI	Donald A. Coleman	1988	180	400.000
2	2	Carol H. Williams Advertising	Oakland, CA	Carol H. Williams	1986	165	350.000
3	4	UniWorld Group Inc.	New York, NY	Byron E. Lewis	1969	117	220.798
4	3	Burrell	Chicago, IL	Fay Ferguson/McGhee Williams	1971	131	190.000
5	5	Compas Inc.	Cherry Hill, NJ	Stanley R. Woodland	1991	54	170.000
6	6	Muse Communications	Los Angeles, CA	Jo Muse	1995	50	60.000
7	—	Fuse Inc.	St. Louis, MO	Clifford Franklin	1997	22	53.396
8	7	Equals Three Communications Inc.	Bethesda, MD	Eugene M. Faison, Jr.	1984	40	50.000
9	10	Matlock Advertising & Public Relations	Atlanta, GA	Kent Matlock	1986	30	48.700
10	8	Spike DDB	New York, NY	Dana Wade	1997	45	45.000

* In Millions of Dollars to the nearest thousand. As of Dec. 31, 2004. Prepared by B.E. Research. Reviewed by the certified public accounting firm Edwards & Co.

FIGURE 1.5

Black Enterprise's top 10 U.S. banks, 2005

2005	2004	Company name	Location	Chief Executive	Began	Staff	Assets*	Capital*	Deposits*	Loans*
1	1	Carver Federal Savings Bank	New York, NY	Deborah C. Wright	1948	137	616.415	56.893	443.316	411.462
2	2	OneUnited Bank	Boston, MA	Kevin Cohee	1982	126	478.590	30.214	329.229	391.430
3	6	Liberty Bank and Trust Company	New Orleans, LA	Alden J. McDonald, Jr.	1972	160	348.175	24.589	293.835	219.999
4	5	Industrial Bank NA	Washington, DC	B. Doyle Mitchell, Jr.	1934	165	333.496	25.816	274.387	157.890
5	3	Citizens Trust Bank	Atlanta, GA	James E. Young	1921	164	330.833	31.025	266.564	261.406
6	7	City National	Newark, NJ	Louis E. Prezeau	1973	96	325.103	20.080	280.863	159.359
7	4	Seaway National Bank	Chicago, IL	Walter E. Grady	1965	250	322.144	30.230	276.476	163.602
8	8	Broadway Federal Bank FSB	Los Angeles, CA	Paul C. Hudson	1947	61	276.067	19.444	197.184	252.518
9	10	The Harbor Bank of Maryland	Baltimore, MD	Joseph Haskins, Jr.	1982	82	234.979	23.029	210.224	172.205
10	9	M&F Bank	Durham, NC	Lee Johnson, Jr.	1907	97	230.541	20.340	189.059	170.779

* In Millions of Dollars to the nearest thousand. As of Dec. 31, 2004. Prepared by B.E. Research. Reviewed by the certified public accounting firm Edwards & Co.

FIGURE 1.6

Black Enterprise's top U.S. insurance companies, 2005

2005	2004	Company name	Location	Chief Executive	Began	Staff	Assets*	Insurance in force*
1	1	North Carolina Mutual Life Insurance Co.	Durham, NC	James H. Speed, Jr.	1898	147	161.207	14,372.304
2	2	Golden State Mutual Life Insurance Co.	Los Angeles, CA	Larkin Teasley	1925	250	112.836	2,842.000
3	3	Atlanta Life Financial Group	Atlanta, GA	Ronald D. Brown	1905	30	76.389	11,809.837
4	4	Booker T. Washington Insurance Co.	Birmingham, AL	Walter Howlett, Jr.	1931	85	56.209	1,382.784
5	—	Williams-Progressive Life & Accident Insurance Co.	Opelousas, LA	Patrick Fontenot	1947	44	10.366	35.158

* In Millions of Dollars to the nearest thousand. As of Dec. 31, 2004. Prepared by B.E. Research. Reviewed by the certified public accounting firm Edwards & Co.

FIGURE 1.7

Black Enterprise's top 10 U.S. investment banks, 2005

2005	2004	Company name	Location	Chief Executive	Began	Staff	Total managed issues*
1	1	The Williams Capital Group L.P.	New York, NY	Christopher J. Williams	1994	58	122.318
2	2	Blaylock & Partners L.P.	New York, NY	Ronald E. Blaylock	1993	70	109.329
3	3	Loop Capital Markets L.L.P.	Chicago, IL	James Reynolds, Jr.	1997	80	83.753
4	5	Utendahl Capital Partners L.P.	New York, NY	John Oscar Utendahl	1992	29	29.299
5	4	Siebert Brandford Shank & Co. L.L.C.	Oakland, CA	Suzanne Shank	1996	45	50.957
6	6	M. R. Beal & Co.	New York, NY	Bernard B. Beal	1988	35	45.325
7	7	Jackson Securities L.L.C.	Atlanta, GA	Reuben R. McDaniel III	1987	30	36.425
8	9	SBK-Brooks Investment Corp.	Cleveland, OH	Eric L. Small	1993	20	14.500
9	10	Rice Financial Products Co.	New York, NY	J. Donald Rice, Jr.	1987	26	12.388
10	—	Powell Capital Markets Inc.	Roseland, NJ	Arthur F. Powell	1990	5	2.982

* In Billions of Dollars to the nearest thousand. As of Dec. 31, 2004. Prepared by B.E. Research. Reviewed by the certified public accounting firm Edwards & Co.

FIGURE 1.8

Black Enterprise's top 10 U.S. industrial/service companies, 2005

2005	2004	Company name	Location	Chief Executive	Began	Staff	Sales*	Type of business
1	1	World Wide Technology Inc.	St. Louis, MO	David Steward	1990	620	1,400.00	IT systems integrator, supply chain services of IT products
2	2	CAMAC International Inc.	Houston, TX	Kase Lawal	1986	1,300	987.000	Crude oil and gas exploration, production, and trading
3	22	Bridgewater Interiors L.L.C.	Detroit, MI	Ronald E. Hall	1998	1,100	645.309	Car seat and overhead systems manufacturer
4	3	Act-1 Group	Torrance, CA	Janice Bryant Howroyd	1978	300	622,729	Staffing and professional services
5	4	Johnson Publishing Co.	Chicago, IL	Linda Johnson Rice/ John H. Johnson	1942	1,699	498.224	Publishing, TV productions, and cosmetics
6	5	The Philadelphia Coca-Cola Bottling Co.	Philadelphia, PA	L. Bruce Llewellyn	1985	1,900	450.000	Bottling and distributing soft drinks
7	10	Converge	Peabody, MA	Dale LeFebvre/ Frank Cavallaro	2002	283	390.000	Distributor of semiconductors and computer products
8	6	Barden Cos. Inc.	Detroit, MI	Don H. Barden	1981	4,055	372.000	Casino gaming, real estate development, and international trade
8	7	The Bing Group	Detroit, MI	Dave Bing	1980	1,414	372.000	Steel processing, steel stamping, full seat assembly, mirror assembly
10	8	Radio One Inc.[1]	Lanham, MD	Alfred C. Liggins III	1980	1,750	363.982	Radio broadcasting and other media businesses

* In Millions of Dollars to the nearest thousand. As of Dec. 31, 2004. Prepared by B.E. Research. Reviewed by the certified public accounting firm Edwards & Co. (1) Publicly traded company. Majority ownership of voting class stock is held by African Americans.

FIGURE 2.1

Children living below the poverty level in the U.S., 1970–2000*

Year	Total (All races, in thousands)	%	Blacks (in thousands)	%
1970	10,235	14.9	3,922	41.5
1980	11,114	17.9	3,906	42.1
1985	12,483	20.1	4,057	43.1
1990	12,715	19.9	4,412	44.2
1995	13,999	20.2	4,644	41.5
2000	11,005	15.6	3,495	30.9

* Persons are classified as being above or below the poverty level using the poverty index, based on the Department of Agriculture's 1961 Economy Food Plan. Poverty thresholds are updated every year. In 1990 the weighted average poverty threshold for a family of four was $13,359; in 2000 it was $17,604. These statistics cover only children under 18 years of age living in families.

SOURCE: *Statistical Abstract, 1992, 2004–2005.*

FIGURE 2.3

Persons living below the poverty level in the U.S., 1959–2000*

Year	Total (in millions)	%	Blacks (in millions)	%
1959	39.5	22.4	9.9	55.1
1970	25.4	12.6	7.5	33.5
1980	29.3	13.0	8.6	32.5
1990	33.6	13.5	9.8	31.9
2000	31.6	11.3	8.0	22.5

* Persons are classified as being above or below the poverty level using the poverty index, based on the Department of Agriculture's 1961 Economy Food Plan. Poverty thresholds are updated every year. In 1990 the weighted average poverty threshold for a family of four was $13,359; in 2000 it was $17,604.

SOURCE: *Statistical Abstract, 1992,* and *Statistical Abstract, 2004–2005* using information from the 2000 U.S. Census.

FIGURE 2.2

Median money income of families in the U.S, 1980–2002[1]

	Black	White	All races
1980	12,674	21,904	21,023
1985	16,786	29,152	27,735
1990	21,423	36,915	35,353
1995	25,970	42,646	40,611
2000	33,676	53,029	50,732
2002	33,525	54,633	51,680

(1) In current dollars.

SOURCE: *Statistical Abstracts of the United States, 2004–2005.*

FIGURE 3.1

Bachelor's degrees conferred in the U.S., 1976–1977 to 2001–2002

Year	All			Black			% Black		
	Total	Male	Female	Total	Male	Female	Total	Male	Female
1976–1977[1]	917,900	494,424	423,476	58,636	25,147	33,489	6.6	5.1	7.9
1978–1979[2]	919,540	476,065	443,475	60,246	24,659	35,587	6.6	5.2	8.0
1980–1981[3]	934,800	469,625	465,175	60,673	24,511	36,162	6.5	5.2	7.8
1984–1985[4]*	968,311	476,148	492,163	57,473	23,018	34,455	5.9	4.8	7.0
1986–1987	991,264	480,782	510,482	56,560	22,501	34,059	5.7	4.7	6.7
1988–1989[5]	1,016,350	481,946	534,404	58,078	22,370	35,708	5.7	4.6	6.7
1989–1990	1,051,344	491,696	559,648	61,046	23,257	37,789	5.8	4.7	6.8
1990–1991	1,094,538	504,045	590,493	66,375	24,800	41,575	6.1	4.9	7.0
1991–1992	1,136,553	520,811	615,742	72,680	27,092	45,588	6.4	5.2	7.4
1992–1993	1,165,178	532,881	632,297	78,099	28,962	49,137	6.7	5.4	7.8
1993–1994	1,169,275	532,422	636,853	83,909	30,766	53,143	7.2	5.8	8.3
1994–1995	1,160,134	526,131	634,003	87,236	31,793	55,443	7.5	6.0	8.7
1995–1996	1,164,792	522,454	642,338	91,496	32,974	58,522	7.9	6.3	9.1
1996–1997	1,172,879	520,515	652,264	94,349	33,616	60,733	8.0	6.5	9.3
1997–1998	1,184,406	519,956	664,450	98,251	34,510	63,741	8.3	6.6	9.6
1998–1999	1,200,303	518,746	681,557	102,214	34,876	67,338	8.5	6.7	9.9
1999–2000	1,237,875	530,367	707,508	108,013	37,024	70,989	8.7	7.0	10.0
2000–2001	1,244,171	531,840	712,331	111,307	38,103	73,204	8.9	7.2	10.3
2001–2002	1,291,900	549,816	742,084	116,624	39,194	77,430	9.0	7.1	10.4

(1) Excludes 1,121 men and 528 women whose racial/ethnic group was not available.
(2) Excludes 1,279 men and 571 women whose racial/ethnic group was not available.
(3) Excludes 258 men and 82 women whose racial/ethnic group was not available.
(4) Excludes 6,380 men and 4,786 women whose racial/ethnic group was not available.
(5) Excludes 1,400 men and 1,005 women whose racial/ethnic group was not available.

* For years 1984–85 to 2001–02, reported racial/ethnic distributions of students by level of degree, field of degree, and sex were used to estimate race/ethnicity for students whose race/ethnicity was not reported. Data for 1998–99 were imputed using alternative procedures. Detail may not sum to totals due to rounding.

SOURCE: U.S. Department of Education, National Center for Education Statistics, Higher Education General Information Survey (HEGIS), "Degrees and Other Formal Awards Conferred" surveys 1976–77 through 1984–85, and Integrated Postsecondary Education Data System (IPEDS), "Completions" surveys, 1986–87 through 1998–99, and Fall 2000 through Fall 2002 surveys. (This table was prepared August 2003.)

FIGURE 3.2

Doctoral degrees conferred in the U.S, by major field of study, 2001–2002*

Major field of study	Total	Total black**	Black men	Black women
All fields, total	44,160	2,397	921	1,476
Agriculture and natural resources	1,166	19	12	7
Architecture and related programs	183	8	0	8
Area, ethnic, and cultural studies	216	33	14	19
Biological sciences/ life sciences	4,489	117	54	63
Business	1,158	71	42	29
Communications	374	33	10	23
Communications technologies	9	0	0	0
Computer and information sciences	750	22	14	8
Education	6,967	900	252	648
Engineering	5,195	86	60	26
Engineering-related technologies	15	0	0	0
English language and literature/letters	1,446	74	24	50
Foreign languages and literature	843	17	7	10
Health professions and related sciences	3,523	124	32	92
Home economics and vocational home economics	355	32	6	26
Law and legal studies	79	1	0	1
Liberal arts and sciences, general studies, and humanities	113	6	1	5
Library science	45	5	0	5
Mathematics	958	16	7	9
Multi/interdisciplinary studies	384	18	11	7
Parks, recreation, leisure and fitness studies	151	5	2	3
Philosophy and religion	606	17	6	11
Physical sciences and science technologies	3,803	77	44	33
Protective services	49	3	2	1
Psychology	4,341	257	52	205
Public administration and services	571	75	31	44
[continued]				

Doctoral degrees conferred in the U.S., by major field of study, 2001–2002*[CONTINUED]

Major field of study	Total	Total black**	Black men	Black women
Social sciences and history	3,902	206	107	99
Theological studies and religious vocations	1,355	150	115	9
Visual and performing arts	1,114	25	16	9

* Includes Ph.D., Ed.D, and comparable degrees at the doctoral level. Excludes first-professional degrees, such as M.D., D.D.S., and law degrees.

** Reported racial/ethnic distributions of students by level of degree, field of degree, and sex were used to estimate race/ethnicity for students whose race/ethnicity was not reported. To facilitate trend comparisons, certain aggregations have been made of the degree fields as reported in the IPEDS "Completions" survey: "Agriculture and natural resources" includes Agricultural business and production, Agricultural sciences, and Conservation and renewable natural resources; and "Business" includes Business management and administrative services, Marketing operations/marketing and distribution, and Consumer and personal services.

SOURCE: U.S. Department of Education, National Center for Education Statistics, Integrated Postsecondary Education Data System (IPEDS), Fall 2002 survey. (This table was prepared August 2003.)

FIGURE 3.3

First professional degrees conferred in the U.S., by major field of study, 2001–2002

Major field of study	Total	Total black*	Black men	Black women
All fields, total	n.a.	5,811	2,223	3,588
Dentistry (D.D.S. or D.M.D.)	4,239	155	63	92
Medicine (M.D)	n.a.	1,104	407	697
Optometry (O.D)	1,280	22	10	12
Osteopathic medicine (D.O.)	2,416	97	39	58
Pharmacy (Pharm.D.)	7,076	570	190	380
Podiatry (Pod.D. or D.P.) or podiatric medicine (D.P.M.)	474	38	16	22
Veterinary medicine (D.V.M)	2,289	67	17	50
Chiropractic medicine (D.C. or D.C.M)	3,284	116	63	53
Law (LL.B. or J.D.)	n.a.	3,002	1,092	1,910
Theology (M.Div., M.H.L., B.D., or Ord.)	5,195	636	324	312

* Reported racial/ethnic distributions of students by level of degree, field of study, and sex were used to estimate race/ethnicity for students whose race/ethnicity was not reported.

SOURCE: U.S. Department of Education, National Center for Education Statistics, Integrated Postsecondary Education Data System (IPEDS), Fall 2002 survey. (This table was prepared August 2003.)

FIGURE 3.4

Master's degrees conferred in the U.S., 1976–1977 to 2001–2002*

Year	All			Black			% Black		
	Total	Male	Female	Total	Male	Female	Total	Male	Female
1976–1977[1]	316,602	167,396	149,206	21,037	7,781	13,256	6.6	4.6	8.9
1978–1979[2]	300,255	152,637	147,618	19,418	7,070	12,348	6.5	4.6	8.4
1980–1981[3]	294,183	145,666	148,517	17,133	6,158	10,975	5.8	4.2	7.4
1984–1985[4]**	280,421	139,417	140,004	13,939	5,200	8,739	5.0	3.7	6.2
1986–1987	289,349	141,269	148,080	13,873	5,153	8,720	4.8	3.6	5.9
1988–1989[5]	309,770	148,872	160,898	14,095	5,175	8,920	4.6	3.5	5.5
1989–1990	324,301	153,653	170,648	15,336	5,474	9,862	4.7	3.6	5.8
1990–1991	337,168	156,482	180,686	16,616	5,916	10,700	4.9	3.8	5.9
1991–1992	352,838	161,842	190,996	18,256	6,112	12,144	5.2	3.8	6.4
1992–1993	369,585	169,258	200,327	19,744	6,803	12,941	5.3	4.0	6.5
1993–1994	387,070	176,085	210,985	21,986	7,424	14,562	5.7	4.2	6.9
1994–1995	397,629	178,598	219,031	24,166	8,097	16,069	6.1	4.5	7.3
1995–1996	406,301	179,081	227,220	25,822	8,445	17,377	6.4	4.7	7.6
1996–1997	419,401	180,947	238,454	28,403	8,960	19,443	6.8	5.0	8.2
1997–1998	430,164	184,375	245,789	30,155	9,652	20,503	7.0	5.2	8.3
1998–1999	439,986	186,148	253,838	32,541	10,058	22,483	7.4	5.4	8.9
1999–2000	457,056	191,792	265,264	35,874	11,212	24,662	7.8	5.8	9.3
2000–2001	468,476	194,351	274,125	38,265	11,568	26,697	8.2	6.0	9.7
2001–2002	482,118	199,120	282,998	40,373	11,796	28,577	8.4	5.9	10.1

* Areas of study included agriculture, architecture and environmental design, area and ethnic studies, biological sciences, business, communications, computer science, construction trades, education, engineering, English language and literature, foreign languages, health, home economics, law, letters, liberal/general studies,library and archival sciences, life sciences, mathematics, multi/interdisciplinary studies, philosophy and religion, theology, physical sciences, protective services and public affairs, psychology, public administration, social sciences, visual and performing arts, other.

(1) Excludes 387 men and 175 women whose racial/ethnic group was not available.

(2) Excludes 733 men and 91 women whose racial/ethnic group was not available.

(3) Excludes 1,377 men and 179 women whose racial/ethnic group was not available.

(4) Excludes 3,973 men and 1,857 women whose racial/ethnic group was not available.

(5) Excludes 482 men and 369 women whose racial/ethnic group was not available.

** For years 1984–85 to 2001–02, reported racial/ethnic distributions of students by level of degree, field of degree, and sex were used to estimate race/ethnicity for students whose race/ethnicity was not reported. Data for 1998–99 were imputed using alternative procedures. Detail may not sum to totals due to rounding.

SOURCE: U.S. Department of Education, National Center for Education Statistics, Higher Education General Information Survey (HEGIS), "Degrees and Other Formal Awards Conferred" surveys 1976–77 through 1984–85, and Integrated Postsecondary Education Data System (IPEDS), "Completions" surveys, 1986–87 through 1998–99, and Fall 2000 through Fall 2002 surveys. (This table was prepared August 2003.)

FIGURE 3.5

Bachelor's degrees conferred in the U.S., by major field of study, 2001–2002

Major field of study	Total	Total black*	Black men	Black women
All fields, total	1,291,900	116,624	39,194	77,430
Agriculture and natural resources	23,353	653	281	372
Architecture and related programs	8,808	348	203	145
Area, ethnic, and cultural studies	6,557	881	290	591
Biological sciences/life sciences	60,256	4,807	1,329	3,478
Business	281,330	28,153	10,088	18,065
Communications	62,791	5,540	1,873	3,667
Communications technologies	1,110	149	76	73
Computer and information sciences	47,299	5,030	2,670	2,360
Construction trades	202	6	4	2
Education	106,383	6,976	1,822	5,154
Engineering	59,481	3,099	1,966	1,133
Engineering-related technologies[1]	14,117	1,387	1,077	310
English language and literature/letters	53,162	4,049	1,029	3,020
Foreign languages and literature	15,318	622	153	469
Health professions and related sciences	70,517	8,011	1,041	6,970
Home economics and vocational home economics	18,153	1,659	235	1,424
Law and legal studies	1,971	303	58	245
Liberal arts and sciences, general studies, and humanities	39,333	4,688	1,399	3,289
Library science	74	0	0	0
Mathematics	12,395	935	417	518
Mechanics and repairers	164	18	17	1
Multi/interdisciplinary studies	27,629	2,739	824	1,915
Parks, recreation, leisure and fitness studies	20,554	1,751	951	800
Philosophy and religion	9,306	481	273	208
Physical sciences and science technologies	17,851	1,142	463	679
Precision production trade	468	25	21	4
Protective services	25,536	4,484	1,812	2,672
Psychology	76,671	8,107	1,614	6,493
Public administration and services	19,392	4,036	757	3,279
R.O.T.C. and military sciences	3	0	0	0
Social sciences and history	132,874	12,530	4,493	8,037
Theological studies and religious vocations	7,785	411	247	164
Transportation and material moving workers	4,020	220	197	23
Visual and performing arts	66,773	3,373	1,506	1,867
Not classified by field or study	264	11	8	3

* Reported racial/ethnic distributions of students by level of degree, field of degree, and sex were used to estimate race/ethnicity for students whose race/ethnicity was not reported. To facilitate trend comparisons, certain aggregations have been made of the degree fields as reported in the IPEDS "Completions" survey: "Agriculture and natural resources" includes Agricultural business and production, Agricultural sciences, and Conservation and renewable natural resources; and "Business" includes Business management and administrative services, Marketing operations/marketing and distribution, and Consumer and personal services.

(1) Excludes "Construction trades" and "Mechanics and repairers," which are listed separately.

SOURCE: U.S. Department of Education, National Center for Education Statistics, Integrated Postsecondary Education Data System (IPEDS), Fall 2002 survey. (This table was prepared August 2003.)

FIGURE 3.6

First professional degrees conferred in the U.S., 1976–1977 to 2001–2002

Year	Total			Black			% Black		
	Total	Male	Female	Total	Male	Female	Total	Male	Female
1976–1977[1]	63,953	51,980	11,973	2,537	1,761	776	4.0	3.4	6.5
1978–1979[2]	68,611	52,425	16,186	2,836	1,783	1,053	4.1	3.4	6.5
1980–1981[3]	71,340	52,194	19,146	2,931	1,772	1,159	4.1	3.4	6.1
1984–1985[4]*	71,057	47,501	23,556	3,029	1,623	1,406	4.3	3.4	6.0
1986–1987	71,617	46,523	25,094	3,420	1,835	1,585	4.8	3.9	6.3
1988–1989	70,856	45,046	25,810	3,148	1,618	1,530	4.4	3.6	5.9
1989–1990	70,988	43,961	27,027	3,409	1,671	1,738	4.8	3.8	6.4
1990–1991	71,948	43,846	28,102	3,588	1,679	1,909	5.0	3.8	6.8
1991–1992	74,146	45,071	29,075	3,628	1,645	1,983	4.9	3.6	6.8
1992–1993	75,387	45,153	30,234	4,132	1,801	2,331	5.5	4.0	7.7
1993–1994	75,418	44,707	30,711	4,444	1,902	2,542	5.9	4.3	8.3
1994–1995	75,800	44,853	30,947	4,747	2,077	2,670	6.3	4.6	8.6
1995–1996	76,734	44,748	31,986	5,022	2,112	2,910	6.5	4.7	9.1
1996–1997	78,730	45,564	33,166	5,301	2,201	3,100	6.7	4.8	9.3
1997–1998	78,598	44,911	33,687	5,499	2,310	3,189	7.0	5.1	9.5
1998–1999	78,439	44,339	34,100	5,333	2,197	3,136	6.8	5.0	9.2
1999–2000	80,057	44,239	35,818	5,555	2,313	3,242	6.9	5.2	9.1
2000–2001	79,707	42,862	36,845	5,416	2,110	3,306	6.8	4.9	9.0
2001–2002	80,698	42,507	38,191	5,811	2,223	3,588	7.2	5.2	9.4

(1) Excludes 394 men and 12 women whose racial/ethnic group was not available.

(2) Excludes 227 men and 10 women whose racial/ethnic group was not available.

(3) Excludes 598 men and 18 women whose racial/ethnic group was not available.

(4) Excludes 2,954 men and 1,052 women whose racial/ethnic group was not available.

* For years 1984–85 to 2001–02, reported racial/ethnic distributions of students by level of degree, field of degree, and sex were used to estimate race/ethnicity for students whose race/ethnicity was not reported. Data for 1998–99 were imputed using alternative procedures. Detail may not sum to totals due to rounding.

SOURCE: U.S. Department of Education, National Center for Education Statistics, Higher Education General Information Survey (HEGIS), "Degrees and Other Formal Awards Conferred" surveys 1976–77 through 1984–85, and Integrated Postsecondary Education Data System (IPEDS), "Completions" surveys, 1986–87 through 1998–99, and Fall 2000 through Fall 2002 surveys. (This table was prepared August 2003.)

FIGURE 3.7

Doctoral degrees conferred in the U.S., 1976–1977 to 2001–2002*

Year	Total			Black			% Black		
	Both	**Male**	**Female**	**Both**	**Male**	**Female**	**Both**	**Male**	**Female**
1976-1977[1]	33,126	25,036	8,090	1,253	766	487	3.8	3.1	6.0
1978-1979[2]	32,675	23,488	9,187	1,268	734	534	3.9	3.1	5.8
1980-1981[3]	32,839	22,595	10,244	1,265	694	571	3.9	3.1	5.6
1984-1985[4]**	32,307	21,296	11,011	1,154	561	593	3.6	2.6	5.4
1986-1987	34,041	22,061	11,980	1,057	485	572	3.1	2.2	4.8
1988-1989[5]	35,659	22,597	13,062	1,066	491	575	3.0	2.2	4.4
1989-1990	38,371	24,401	13,970	1,149	531	618	3.0	2.2	4.4
1990-1991	39,294	24,756	14,538	1,248	597	651	3.2	2.4	4.5
1991-1992	40,659	25,557	15,102	1,239	584	655	3.0	2.3	4.3
1992-1993	42,132	26,073	16,059	1,350	617	733	3.2	2.4	4.6
1993-1994	43,185	26,552	16,633	1,385	627	758	3.2	2.4	4.6
1994-1995	44,446	26,916	17,530	1,667	730	937	3.8	2.7	5.3
1995-1996	44,652	26,841	17,811	1,632	727	905	3.7	2.7	5.1
1996-1997	45,876	27,146	18,730	1,865	795	1,070	4.1	2.9	5.7
1997-1998	46,010	26,664	19,346	2,067	824	1,243	4.5	3.1	6.4
1998-1999	44,077	25,146	18,931	2,136	873	1,263	4.8	3.5	6.7
1999-2000	44,808	25,028	19,780	2,246	876	1,370	5.0	3.5	6.9
2000-2001	44,904	24,728	20,176	2,207	855	1,352	4.9	3.5	6.7
2001-2002	44,160	23,708	20,452	2,397	921	1,476	5.4	3.9	7.2

* Includes Ph.D., Ed.D., and comparable degrees at the doctoral level. Excludes first professional degrees, such as M.D., D.D.S., and law degrees.

(1) Excludes 106 men whose racial/ethnic group was not available.

(2) Excludes 53 men and 2 women whose racial/ethnic group was not available.

(3) Excludes 116 men and 3 women whose racial/ethnic group was not available.

(4) Excludes 404 men and 232 women whose racial/ethnic group was not available.

(5) Excludes 51 men and 10 women whose racial/ethnic group and field of study were not available.

** For years 1984–85 to 2001– 02, reported racial/ethnic distributions of students by level of degree, field of degree, and sex were used to estimate race/ethnicity for students whose race/ethnicity was not reported. Data for 1998–99 were imputed using alternative procedures. Detail may not sum to totals due to rounding.

SOURCE: U.S. Department of Education, National Center for Education Statistics, Higher Education General Information Survey (HEGIS), "Degrees and Other Formal Awards Conferred" surveys 1976–77 through 1984–85, and Integrated Postsecondary Education Data System (IPEDS), "Completions" surveys, 1986–87 through 1998–99, and Fall 2000 through Fall 2002 surveys. (This table was prepared August 2003.)

FIGURE 3.8

Master's degrees conferred in the U.S., by major field of study, 2001–2002

Major field of study	Total	Total black*	Black men	Black women
All fields, total	482,118	40,373	11,796	28,577
Agriculture and natural resources	4,519	122	61	61
Architecture and related programs	4,566	164	76	88
Area, ethnic, and cultural studies	1,578	130	36	94
Biological sciences/ life sciences	6,205	303	92	211
Business	120,785	10,434	3,962	6,472
Communications	5,510	532	116	416
Communications technologies	549	36	14	22
Computer and information sciences	16,113	745	403	342
Construction trades	9	1	1	0
Education	136,579	13,069	2,829	10,240
Engineering	26,015	794	512	282
Engineering-related technologies[1]	896	75	49	26
English language and literature/letters	7,268	349	74	275
Foreign languages and literature	2,861	55	17	38
Health professions and related sciences	43,644	3,249	568	2,681
Home economics and vocational home economics	2,616	270	36	234
Law and legal studies	4,053	176	82	94
Liberal arts and sciences, general studies, and humanities	2,754	214	66	148
Library science	5,113	259	35	224
Mathematics	3,487	126	55	71
Multi/interdisciplinary studies	3,211	250	63	187
Parks, recreation, leisure and fitness studies	2,754	210	102	108
Philosophy and religion	1,334	60	37	23
Physical sciences and science technologies	5,034	149	74	75
Precision production trades	2	0	0	0
Protective services	2,935	482	205	277
Psychology	14,888	1,837	381	1,456
Public administration and services	25,448	4,386	1,010	3,376
Social sciences and history	14,112	1,022	403	619
[continued]				

Master's degrees conferred in the U.S., by major field of study, 2001–2002 [CONTINUED]

Major field of study	Total	Total black*	Black men	Black women
Theological studies and religious vocations	4,952	334	178	156
Transportation and material moving workers	709	32	29	3
Visual and performing arts	11,595	508	230	278
Not classified by study	24	0	0	0

* Reported racial/ethnic distributions of students by level of degree, field of degree, and sex were used to estimate race/ethnicity for students whose race/ethnicity was not reported. To facilitate trend comparisons, certain aggregations have been made of the degree fields as reported in the IPEDS "Completions" survey: "Agriculture and natural resources" includes Agricultural business and production, Agricultural sciences, and Conservation and renewable natural resources; and "Business" includes Business management and administrative services, Marketing operations/marketing and distribution, and Consumer and personal services.

(1) Excludes "Construction trades" which is listed separately.

SOURCE: U.S. Department of Education, National Center for Education Statistics, Integrated Postsecondary Education Data System (IPEDS), Fall 2002 survey. (This table was prepared August 2003.)

FIGURE 3.9

Enrollment in undergraduate degree-granting institutions in the U.S., 1976–2001*

Year	Total			Black		
	Both	Male	Female	Both**	Male	Female
1976[1]	9,419.0	4,896.8	4,522.1	943.4	430.7	512.7
1980[1]	10,469.1	4,997.4	5,471.7	1,018.8	428.2	590.6
1990[1]	11,959.1	5,379.8	6,579.3	1,147.2	448.0	699.2
1996[2]	12,326.9	5,420.7	6,906.3	1,358.6	513.6	845.0
1998[2]	12,436.9	5,446.1	6,990.8	1,421.7	530.2	891.5
1999[2]	12,681.2	5,559.5	7,121.8	1,471.9	548.4	923.5
2000[2]	13,155.4	5,778.3	7,377.1	1,548.9	577.0	971.9
2001[2]	13,715.6	6,004.4	7,711.2	1,657.1	611.7	1,045.4

* In thousands.

** Because of underreporting and nonreporting of racial/ethnic data, some figures are slightly lower than corresponding data in other tables. Data for 1999 were imputed using alternative procedures. Detail may not sum to totals due to rounding.

(1) Institutions that were accredited by an agency or association that was recognized by the U.S. Department of Education, or recognized directly by the Secretary of Education.

(2) Data are for 4-year and 2-year degree-granting higher education institutions that participated in Title IV federal financial aid programs.

SOURCE: U.S. Department of Education, National Center for Education Statistics, Higher Education General Information Survey (HEGIS), "Fall Enrollment in Colleges and Universities" surveys, 1976 and 1980; and Integrated Postsecondary Education Data System (IPEDS), "Fall Enrollment" surveys, 1990 through 1999, and Spring 2001 and Spring 2002 surveys. (This table was prepared September 2003.)

FIGURE 3.10

Years of school completed by persons twenty-five and over in the U.S., 1940–2002

Date	Less than 5 yrs. of elementary school (%)		4 yrs. of high school or more (%)		4 years of college or more (%)	
	Total	Black	Total	Black	Total	Black
April 1940	13.7	41.8	24.5	7.7	4.6	1.3
April 1950	11.1	32.6	34.3	13.7	6.2	2.2
April 1960	8.3	23.5	41.1	21.7	7.7	3.5
March 1970	5.3	14.7	55.2	36.1	11.0	6.1
March 1975	4.2	12.3	62.5	42.6	13.9	6.4
March 1980	3.4	9.1	68.6	51.4	17.0	7.9
March 1985	2.7	6.1	73.9	59.9	19.4	11.1
March 1990	2.4	5.1	77.6	66.1	21.3	11.3
March 1995	1.8	2.5	81.7	73.8	23.0	13.3
March 2000	1.6	1.6	84.1	78.9	25.6	16.6
March 2002	1.6	1.6	84.1	79.2	26.7	17.2

SOURCE: U.S. Department of Commerce, Bureau of the Census, *U.S. Census of Population*, 1960, Volume 1, part 1; Current Population Reports, Series P-20 and previously unpublished tabulations; and 1960 Census Monograph, "Education of the American Population," by John K. Folger and Charles B. Nam. (This table was prepared October 2003.)

FIGURE 4.1

Emmy Award winners

Year	Performer	Category	Performance
1959	Harry Belafonte	Outstanding Performance in a Variety or Musical Program Series	"Tonight with Belafonte," *Revlon Revue*
1966	Bill Cosby	Outstanding Continued Performance by an Actor in a Leading Role in a Dramatic Series	*I Spy*
1967	Bill Cosby	Outstanding Continued Performance by an Actor in a Leading Role in a Dramatic Series	*I Spy*
1968	Bill Cosby	Outstanding Variety or Musical Program	*The Bill Cosby Special*
1970	Flip Wilson	Outstanding Writing Achievement in Variety or Music Series	*The Flip Wilson Show*
1973	Cicely Tyson	Best Lead Actress in a Drama—Special Program	*The Autobiography of Miss Jane Pittman*
1973	Cicely Tyson	Actress of the Year—Special Program	*The Autobiography of Miss Jane Pittman*
1976	Olivia Cole	Outstanding Single Performance by a Supporting Actress in a Drama or Comedy Series	*Roots, Part 8*
1976	Louis Gossett, Jr	Outstanding Lead Actor for a Single Appearance in a Drama or Comedy Series	*Roots, Part 2*
1976	Quincy Jones	Outstanding Music Series Composition	*Roots, Part 1*
1978	Robert Guillaume	Outstanding Supporting Actor in a Comedy or Music Series	*Soap*
1978	Esther Rolle	Outstanding Supporting Actress in a Limited Series	*Summer of My German Soldier*
1980	Isabel Sanford	Outstanding Lead Actress in a Comedy Series	*The Jeffersons*
1981	Debbie Allen	Outstanding Choreography	"Come One, Come All," *Fame*
1981	Nell Carter	Outstanding Individual Achievement—Special Class	"Ain't Misbehavin'"
1982	Debbie Allen	Outstanding Choreography	"Class Act," *Fame*
1982	Leontyne Price	Outstanding Individual Performance in a Variety or Music Program	*From Lincoln Center*
1982	Leslie Uggams	Outstanding Host/Hostess in a Variety Series	*Fantasy*
1983	Suzanne de Passe	Outstanding Producing	*Motown 25: Yesterday, Today, Forever*
1984	Robert Guillaume	Outstanding Lead Actor in a Comedy Series	*Benson*
1985	Alfre Woodard	Outstanding Supporting Actress in a Drama Series	"Doris in Wonderland," *Hill Street Blues*
1985	George Stanford Brown	Outstanding Directing in a Drama Series	"Parting Shots," *Cagney & Lacey*
1985	Roscoe Lee Browne	Outstanding Guest Performer in a Comedy Series	*The Cosby Show*
1985	Suzanne de Passe	Outstanding Producing	*Motown at the Apollo*
1985	Whitney Houston	Outstanding Performance in a Variety or Music Program	*The 28th Annual Grammy Awards*
1986	Alfre Woodard	Outstanding Guest Performer in a Drama Series	*L.A. Law*
1987	Jackée (Harry)	Outstanding Supporting Actress in a Comedy Series	*227*
1988	Beah Richards	Outstanding Guest Performer in a Comedy Series	*Frank's Place*
1989	Suzanne de Passe	Outstanding Producing	*Lonesome Dove*
1991	Debbie Allen	Outstanding Choreography	*Motown 30: What's Goin' On!*
1991	Ruby Dee	Outstanding Supporting Actress in a Miniseries or Special	"Decoration Day," *Hallmark Hall of Fame*
1991	James Earl Jones	Outstanding Lead Actor in a Drama Series	*Gabriel's Fire*
1991	James Earl Jones	Outstanding Supporting Actor in a Miniseries or Special	*Heat Wave*
1991	Madge Sinclair	Outstanding Supporting Actress in a Drama Series	*Gabriel's Fire*
1991	Lynn Whitfield	Outstanding Lead Actress in a Miniseries or Special	*The Josephine Baker Story*
1992	Eric Laneuville	Outstanding Individual Achievement in Directing in a Drama Series	"All God's Children," *I'll Fly Away*
1993	Mary Alice	Outstanding Supporting Actress in a Drama Series	*I'll Fly Away*
1993	Laurence Fishburne	Outstanding Guest Actor in a Drama Series	"The Box," *Tribeca*
1994	Oprah Winfrey	Best Talk Show	*The Oprah Winfrey Show*
1994	Oprah Winfrey	Best Talk Show Host	*The Oprah Winfrey Show*
1994	Dianne Hudson	Outstanding Producing	*The Oprah Winfrey Show*
1994	Legrande Green	Outstanding Producing	*The Oprah Winfrey Show*
1995	Paul Winfield	Best Guest Actor in a Drama Series	*NYPD Blue*
1996	Robi Reed-Humes	Casting For A Miniseries or A Special	*The Tuskegee Airmen*
1997	Chris Rock	Best Writing of a Variety or Music Program	*Chris Rock: Bring the Pain*
		Best Variety, Music, or Comedy Special	*Chris Rock: Bring the Pain*

[continued]

Emmy Award winners [CONTINUED]

Year	Performer	Category	Performance
1997	Alfre Woodard	Best Lead Actress for a Miniseries or Special	*Miss Evers' Boys*
1998	Andre Baugher	Outstanding Actor in a Drama Series	*Homicide: Life on the Street*
1998	Paris Barclay	Outstanding Director for a Drama Series	*NYPD Blue*
1998	Thomas Carter	Outstanding Made for Television Movie	*Don King: Only in America*
1999	Chris Rock	Best Writing, Variety or Music Show	*The Chris Rock Show*
1999	Ali LeRoi	Best Writing, Variety or Music Show	*The Chris Rock Show*
1999	Wanda Sykes-Hall	Best Writing, Variety or Music Show	*The Chris Rock Show*
1999	Lance Crouther	Best Writing, Variety or Music Show	*The Chris Rock Show*
1999		Best Television Movie	*A Lesson Before Dying*
1999	Paris Barclay	Best Directing for a Drama Series	"Hearts and Souls," *NYPD Blue*
1999	Ja'Net DuBois	Outstanding Voice-Over Performance	*The PJs*
1999	Judith Jamison	Outstanding Choreography	*Dance In America: A Hymn for Alvin Ailey (Great Performances)*
1999	Donald A. Morgan	Outstanding Lighting Direction "Electronic" For a Comedy Series	*Home Improvement*
2000	Halle Berry	Best Actress in a Television Movie	*Introducing Dorothy Dandridge*
2000	Charles S. Dutton	Outstanding Directing for a Miniseries, Movie, or Special	*The Corner*
2000		Best Miniseries	*The Corner*
2001	Ja'Net DuBois	Outstanding Voice-Over Performance	"Let's Get Ready to Rumba" *The PJs*
2003	Bill Cosby	Bob Hope Humanitarian Award	
2003	Wayne Brady	Best Individual Performance in a Variety or Music Program	*Whose Line Is It Anyway?*
2003	Alfre Woodard	Outstanding Guest Actress in a Drama Series	*The Practice*
2003	Charles S. Dutton	Outstanding Guest Actor in a Drama Series	*Without A Trace*
2004	Jeffrey Wright	Best Supporting Actor in a Miniseries	*Angels in America*

FIGURE 4.2

Academy Award/Oscar winners

Year	Performer	Category	Performance
1939	Hattie McDaniel	Best Supporting Actress	*Gone With the Wind*
1947	James Baskett	Special Award	*Song of the South*
1963	Sidney Poitier	Best Actor	*Lilies of the Field*
1971	Isaac Hayes	Best Song (from film)	"Theme from *Shaft*" —*Shaft*
1978	Paul Jabara	Best Song (from film)	"Last Dance"—*Thank God It's Friday*
1982	Louis Gossett, Jr.	Best Supporting Actor	*An Officer and a Gentleman*
1984	Stevie Wonder	Best Song (from film)	"I Just Called to Say I Love You" — *The Woman in Red*
1985	Lionel Ritchie	Best Song (from film)	"Say You, Say Me"— *White Nights*
1986	Herbie Hancock	Original Score	*'Round Midnight*
1989	Denzel Washington	Best Supporting Actor	*Glory*
1990	Whoopi Goldberg	Best Supporting Actress	*Ghost*
1996	Cuba Gooding, Jr.	Best Supporting Actor	*Jerry Maguire*
2001	Halle Berry	Best Actress	*Monster's Ball*
2001	Denzel Washington	Best Actor	*Training Day*
2004	Jamie Foxx	Best Actor	*Ray*
2004	Morgan Freeman	Best Supporting Actor	*Million Dollar Baby*

FIGURE 4.3

Rock and Roll Hall of Fame inductees

Year	Inductee	Category
1986	Robert Johnson	Early Influences
	Jimmy Yancey	Early Influences
	Chuck Berry	Performers
	James Brown	Performers
	Ray Charles	Performers
	Sam Cooke	Performers
	Fats Domino	Performers
	Little Richard	Performers
1987	Louis Jordan	Early Influences
	T-Bone Walker	Early Influences
	The Coasters	Performers
	Bo Diddley	Performers
	Aretha Franklin	Performers
	Marvin Gaye	Performers
	B.B. King	Performers
	Clyde McPhatter	Performers
	Smokey Robinson	Performers
	Big Joe Turner	Performers
	Muddy Waters	Performers
	Jackie Wilson	Performers
1988	Berry Gordy, Jr.	Nonperformers
	Leadbelly	Early Influences
	The Drifters	Performers
	The Supremes	Performers
1989	The Ink Spots	Early Influences
	Bessie Smith	Early Influences
	The Soul Stirrers	Early Influences
	Otis Redding	Performers
	The Temptations	Performers
	Stevie Wonder	Performers
1990	Lamont Dozier, Brian Holland & Eddie Holland	Nonperformers
	Hank Ballard	Early Influences
	The Platters	Performers
1991	Dave Bartholomew	Nonperformers
	Howlin' Wolf	Early Influences
	La Vern Baker	Performers
	John Lee Hooker	Performers
	The Impressions	Performers
	Wilson Pickett	Performers
	Jimmy Reed	Performers
	Ike & Tina Turner	Performers
1992	Elmore James	Early Influences
	Professor Longhair	Early Influences
	Bobby "Blue" Bland	Performers
	Booker T. & the MG's	Performers
	The Jimi Hendrix Experience	Performers
	The Isley Brothers	Performers
	Sam & Dave	Performers
1993	Dinah Washington	Early Influences
	Ruth Brown	Performers
	Etta James	Performers
	Frankie Lymon & the Teenagers	Performers
	Sly & the Family Stone	Performers
1994	Willie Dixon	Early Influences
	Bob Marley	Performers
1995	The Orioles	Early Influences
	Al Green	Performers
	Martha & the Vandellas	Performers
1996	Gladys Knight & the Pips	Performers
	Little Willie John	Performers
	The Shirelles	Performers
1997	Mahalia Jackson	Early Influences
	The Jackson Five	Performers
	Parliament-Funkadelic	Performers

[continued]

Rock and Roll Hall of Fame inductees [CONTINUED]

Year	Inductee	Category
1998	Allen Toussaint	Early Influences
	Lloyd Price	Performers
1999	Charles Brown	Early Influences
	Curtis Mayfield	Performers
	The Staple Singers	Performers
2000	Nat "King" Cole	Early Influences
	Billie Holiday	Early Influences
	King Curtis	Sidemen
	James Jamerson	Sidemen
	Earl Palmer	Sidemen
	Earth, Wind & Fire	Performers
	The Moonglows	Performers
2001	Johnnie Johnson	Sidemen
	Solomon Burke	Performers
	The Flamingos	Performers
	Michael Jackson	Performers
2002	Isaac Hayes	Performers
2003	Benny Benjamin	Sidemen
2004	The Dells	Performers
	Prince	Performers
2005	Buddy Guy	Performers
	The O'Jays	Performers
	Percy Sledge	Performers

FIGURE 4.4

Tony Award winners

Date	Performer	Category	Performance
1962	Diahann Carroll	Best Actress in a Musical	*No Strings*
1968	Leslie Uggams	Best Actress in a Musical	*Hallelujah, Baby!*
1968	Lillian Hayman	Best Supporting Actress in a Musical	*Hallelujah, Baby!*
1968	Pearl Bailey	Special Award	
1969	James Earl Jones	Best Actor in a Dramatic Play	*The Great White Hope*
1969	The Negro Ensemble Company	Special Award	
1970	Cleavon Little	Best Actor in a Musical	*Purlie*
1970	Melba Moore	Best Supporting Actress in a Musical	*Purlie*
1974	Virginia Capers	Best Actress in a Musical	*Raisin*
1974	Producer: The Negro Ensemble Company	Best Play	*The River Niger*
1974		Best Musical	*Raisin*
1975	John Kani & Winston Ntshona	Best Actor in a Dramatic Play	*Sizwe Banzi Is Dead & The Island*
1975	Dee Dee Bridgewater	Best Supporting Actress in a Musical	*The Wiz*
1975	Ted Ross	Best Supporting Actor in a Musical	*The Wiz*
1975		Best Musical	*The Wiz*
1977	Trazana Beverley	Best Actress in a Featured Role in a Dramatic Play	*For Colored Girls Who Have Considered Suicide...*
1977		Most Innovative Production of a Musical	*Porgy and Bess*
1977	Diana Ross	Special Award	
1978		Best Musical	*Ain't Misbehavin'*
1978	Nell Carter	Outstanding Performance by an Actress in a Featured Role in a Musical	*Ain't Misbehavin'*
1982	Jennifer Holliday	Outstanding Performance by an Actress in a Musical	*Dreamgirls*
1982	Cleavant Derricks	Outstanding Performance by a Featured Actor in a Musical	*Dreamgirls*
1982	Ben Harney	Outstanding Performance by an Actor in a Musical	*Dreamgirls*
1983	Charles "Honi" Coles	Outstanding Performance by a Featured Actor in a Musical	*My One and Only*
1987	James Earl Jones	Best Actor in a Play	*Fences*
1989	Ruth Brown	Best Actress in a Musical	*Black and Blue*
1991	Hinton Battle	Outstanding Actor in a Featured Role in a Musical	*Miss Saigon*
1992	Gregory Hines	Best Actor in a Musical	*Jelly's Last Jam*
1992	Laurence Fishburne	Outstanding Featured Actor in a Play	*Two Trains Running*
1992	Tonya Pinkins	Outstanding Featured Actress in a Musical	*Jelly's Last Jam*
1993	Jeffrey Wright	Best Actor in a Featured Role, Play	*Angels in America: Millennium Approaching*
1994	Audra McDonald	Best Actress in a Featured Role, Musical	*Carousel*
1996	Ruben Santiago-Hudson	Best Actor in a Featured Role, Play	*Seven Guitars*
1996	Audra McDonald	Best Actress in a Featured Role, Play	*Master Class*
1996	Ann Duquesnay	Best Actress in a Featured Role, Musical	*Bring in 'da Noise, Bring in 'da Funk*
1996	George C. Wolfe	Best Director	*Bring in 'da Noise, Bring in 'da Funk*
1996	Savion Glover	Best Choreographer	*Bring in 'da Noise, Bring in 'da Funk*
1997	Lynne Thigpen	Best Actress in a Featured Role, Play	*An American Daugher*
1997	Chuck Cooper	Best Actor in a Featured Role, Musical	*The Life*
1997	Lillian White	Best Actress in a Featured Role, Musical	*The Life*
1998	Audra McDonald	Best Actress in Featured Role, Musical	*Ragtime*
1998		Best Musical	*The Lion King*
1998	Garth Fagan	Best Choreographer	*The Lion King*
1999	Crossroads Theatre Company	Best Regional Theatre Award	
2000	Brian Stokes Mitchell	Best Actor in a Musical	*Kiss Me, Kate*
2000	Heather Headley	Best Actress in a Musical	*Aida*
2000		Best Revival of a Musical	*Aida*
2001	Viola Davis	Best Actress in a Featured Role, Play	*King Hedley II*
2002		Best Revival of a Musical	*Into the Woods*
2003	Russell Simmons	Best Special Theatrical Event	*Russell Simmons' Def Poetry Jam on Broadway*
2004	Phylicia Rashad	Best Actress in a Play	*A Raisin in the Sun*
2004	Audra McDonald	Best Actress in a Featured Role, Play	*A Raisin in the Sun*
2004	Anika Noni Rose	Best Actress in a Featured Role, Musical	*Caroline, or Change*
2005	Adriane Lenox	Best Performance by a Featured Actress	*Doubt*

FIGURE 4.5

Grammy Award winners

Year	Category	Performance	Performer
1958	Best Vocal Performance, Female	*The Irving Berlin Song Book*	Ella Fitzgerald
	Best Performance by a Dance Band	*Basie*	Count Basie
	Best Jazz Performance, Individual	*The Duke Ellington Song Book*	Ella Fitzgerald
	Best Jazz Performance, Group	*Basie*	Count Basie
1959	Best Vocal Performance, Female	"But Not for Me"	Ella Fitzgerald
	Best Performance by a Dance Band	*Anatomy of a Murder*	Duke Ellington
	Best Jazz Performance, Soloist	*Ella Swings Lightly*	Ella Fitzgerald
	Best Jazz Performance, Group	"I Dig Chicks"	Jonah Jones
	Best Musical Composition	*Anatomy of a Murder*	Duke Ellington
	Best Performance by "Top 40" Artist	"Midnight Flyer"	Nat "King" Cole
	Best Rhythm & Blues Performance	"What a Diff'rence a Day Makes"	Dinah Washington
1960	Best Vocal Performance—Single, Female	"Mack the Knife"	Ella Fitzgerald
	Best Vocal Performance—Album, Female	*Mack the Knife—Ella in Berlin*	Ella Fitzgerald
	Best Vocal Performance—Single, Male	"Georgia On My Mind"	Ray Charles
	Best Vocal Performance—Album, Male	*Genius of Ray Charles*	Ray Charles
	Best Performance by a Band for Dancing	*Dance with Basie*	Count Basie
	Best Classical Performance Vocal Soloist	*A Program of Song*	Leontyne Price
	Best Performance by a Pop Artist	"Georgia On My Mind"	Ray Charles
	Best Rhythm & Blues Performance	"Let the Good Times Roll"	Ray Charles
	Best Performance—Folk	"Swing Dat Hammer"	Harry Belafonte
	Best Jazz Composition of More Than Five Minutes	*Sketches of Spain*	Miles Davis & Gil Evans
1961	Best Rock and Roll Recording	"Let's Twist Again"	Chubby Checker
	Best Rhythm & Blues Recording	"Hit the Road Jack"	Ray Charles
	Best Gospel Recording	"Everytime I Feel the Spirit"	Mahalia Jackson
1962	Best Solo Vocal Performance—Female	*Ella Swings Brightly with Nelson Riddle*	Ella Fitzgerald
	Best Rhythm & Blues Recording	"I Can't Stop Loving You"	Ray Charles
	Best Gospel Recording	*Great Songs of Love and Faith*	Mahalia Jackson
1963	Best Performance by an Orchestra for Dancing	*This Time by Basie!*	Count Basie
	Best Instrumental Arrangement	"I Can't Stop Loving You"	Quincy Jones
	Best Classical Performance	*Scenes from "Porgy and Bess"*	Leontyne Price
	Most Promising New Classical Recording Artist	*André Watts*	André Watts
	Best Rhythm & Blues Recording	"Busted"	Ray Charles
	Best Comedy Performance	*Bill Cosby Is a Very Funny Fellow…Right!*	Bill Cosby
1964	Best Vocal Performance, Male	"Hello, Dolly!"	Louis Armstrong
	Best Comedy Performance	*I Started Out As a Child*	Bill Cosby
	Best Rhythm & Blues Recording	*How Glad I Am*	Nancy Wilson
	Best Classical Vocal Soloist	*Berlioz: Nuits d'été*	Leontyne Price
1965	Best Comedy Performance	*Why Is There Air?*	Bill Cosby
	Best Instrumental Jazz Performance, Small Group	*The "In" Crowd*	Ramsey Lewis Trio
	Best Instrumental Jazz Performance, Large Group	*Ellington '66*	Duke Ellington
	Best Rhythm & Blues Recording	"Papa's Got a Brand New Bag"	James Brown
	Best Folk Recording	*An Evening With Belafonte*	Harry Belafonte
	Best Classical Vocal Performance	*Strauss: Salomé*	Leontyne Price
1966	Best Comedy Performance	*Wonderfulness*	Bill Cosby
	Best Original Jazz Composition	*In the Beginning God*	Duke Ellington
	Best Rhythm & Blues Recording	"Crying Time"	Ray Charles
	Best Rhythm & Blues Solo Vocal Performance	"Crying Time"	Ray Charles
	Best Rhythm & Blues Group Performance	"Hold It Right There"	Ramsey Lewis
	Best Classical Vocal Soloist	*Prima Donna*	Leontyne Price
1967	Record of the Year	"Up, Up, and Away"	The 5th Dimension
	Best Performance by a Vocal Group	"Up, Up, and Away"	The 5th Dimension
	Best Performance by a Chorus	"Up, Up, and Away"	Johnny Mann Singers
	Best Comedy Recording	*Revenge*	Bill Cosby
	Best Instrumental Jazz Performance, Small Group	*Mercy, Mercy, Mercy*	Cannonball Adderly Quintet
	Best Instrumental Jazz Performance, Large Group	*Far East Suite*	Duke Ellington
	Best Contemporary Single	"Up, Up, and Away"	The 5th Dimension
	Best Contemporary Group Performance	"Up, Up, and Away"	The 5th Dimension
	Best Rhythm & Blues Recording	"Respect"	Aretha Franklin
	Best Rhythm & Blues Solo Vocal Performance, Female	"Respect"	Aretha Franklin
	Best Rhythm & Blues Solo Vocal Performance, Male	"Dead End Street"	Lou Rawls
	Best Rhythm & Blues Group Performance	"Soul Man"	Sam & Dave
	Best Classical Vocal Soloist Performance	*Prima Donna, Vol. 2*	Leontyne Price

[continued]

Grammy Award winners [CONTINUED]

Year	Category	Performance	Performer
1968	Best Contemporary Pop Vocal Performance, Female	"Do You Know the Way to San José?"	Dionne Warwick
	Best Rhythm & Blues Vocal Performance, Female	"Chain of Fools"	Aretha Franklin
	Best Rhythm & Blues Vocal Performance, Male	"(Sittin' on) the Dock of the Bay"	Otis Redding
	Best Rhythm & Blues Performance by a Duo or Group	*Cloud Nine*	The Temptations
	Best Rhythm & Blues Song	"(Sittin' on) The Dock of the Bay"	Otis Redding
	Best Comedy Recording	*To Russell, My Brother, Whom I Slept With*	Bill Cosby
	Best Instrumental Jazz Performance, Large Group	*And His Mother Called Him Bill*	Duke Ellington
1969	Record of the Year	"Aquarius/Let the Sunshine In"	The 5th Dimension
	Best Contemporary Vocal Performance by a Group	"Aquarius/Let the Sunshine In"	The 5th Dimension
	Best Rhythm & Blues Vocal Performance, Female	"Share Your Love with Me"	Aretha Franklin
	Best Rhythm & Blues Vocal Performance, Male	"The Chokin' Kind"	Joe Simon
	Best Rhythm & Blues Vocal Performance by a Group	*It's Your Thing*	The Isley Brothers
	Best Rhythm & Blues Song	"Color Him Father"	The Winstons
	Best Rhythm & Blues Instrumental Performance	*Games People Play*	King Curtis
	Best Soul Gospel Performance	*Oh Happy Day*	Edwin Hawkins Singers
	Best Comedy Recording	*Bill Cosby*	Bill Cosby
	Best Instrumental Jazz Performance, Small Group	*Willow Weep for Me*	Wes Montgomery
	Best Instrumental Jazz Performance, Large Group	*Walking in Space*	Quincy Jones
	Best Vocal Soloist Performance, Classical	*Barber: Two Scenes from "Antony & Cleopatra"*	Leontyne Price
1970	Best Contemporary Vocal Performance, Female	*I'll Never Fall in Love Again*	Dionne Warwick
	Best Rhythm & Blues Vocal Performance, Female	"Don't Play That Song"	Aretha Franklin
	Best Rhythm & Blues Vocal Performance, Male	"The Thrill Is Gone"	B.B. King
	Best Rhythm & Blues Vocal Performance, Group	"Didn't I (Blow Your Mind This Time)?"	The Delfonics
	Best Soul Gospel Performance	"Every Man Wants to Be Free"	Edwin Hawkins Singers
	Best Ethnic or Traditional Recording	*Good Feelin'*	T-Bone Walker
	Best Comedy Recording	*The Devil Made Me Buy This Dress*	Flip Wilson
	Best Spoken Word Performance	*Why I Oppose the War in Vietnam*	Dr. Martin Luther King, Jr.
	Best Jazz Performance, Large Group	*Bitches Brew*	Miles Davis
1971	Best Instrumental Arrangement	*Shaft*	Isaac Hayes, Johnny Allen
	Best Pop Instrumental Performance	*Smackwater Jack*	Quincy Jones
	Best Rhythm & Blues Vocal Performance, Female	"Bridge Over Troubled Water"	Aretha Franklin
	Best Rhythm & Blues Vocal Performance, Male	"A Natural Man"	Lou Rawls
	Best Rhythm & Blues Vocal Performance, Group	"Proud Mary"	Ike & Tina Turner
	Best Rhythm & Blues Song	"Ain't No Sunshine"	Bill Withers
	Best Soul Gospel Performance	*Put Your Hand in the Hand of the Man from Galilee*	Shirley Caesar
	Best Sacred Performance	*Did You Think to Pray?*	Charley Pride
	Best Gospel Performance	*Let Me Live*	Charley Pride
	Best Ethnic or Traditional Recording	*They Call Me Muddy Waters*	Muddy Waters
	Best Original Film Score	*Shaft*	Isaac Hayes
	Best Recording for Children	*Bill Cosby Talks to Kids About Drugs*	Bill Cosby
	Best Jazz Performance by a Big Band	*New Orleans Suite*	Duke Ellington
	Best Classical Vocal Soloist Performance	*Leontyne Price Sings Robert Schumann*	Leontyne Price
1972	Record of the Year	"The First Time Ever I Saw Your Face"	Roberta Flack
	Best Jazz Performance by a Group	*First Light*	Freddie Hubbard
	Best Jazz Performance by a Big Band	*Toga Brava Suite*	Duke Ellington
	Best Pop Vocal Performance by a Duo	"Where Is the Love?"	Roberta Flack, Donny Hathaway
	Best Pop Instrumental Performance by an Instrumental Performer	"Outa-Space"	Billy Preston
	Best Pop Instrumental Performance with Vocal Coloring	*Black Moses*	Isaac Hayes
	Best Rhythm & Blues Vocal Performance, Female	*Young, Gifted & Black*	Aretha Franklin
	Best Rhythm & Blues Vocal Performance, Male	"Me & Mrs. Jones"	Billy Paul
	Best Rhythm & Blues Vocal Performance, Group	"Papa Was a Rollin' Stone"	The Temptations
	Best Rhythm & Blues Song	"Papa Was a Rollin' Stone"	The Temptations
	Best Soul Gospel Performance	"Amazing Grace"	Aretha Franklin
	Best Country Vocal Performance, Male	*Charley Pride Sings Heart Songs*	Charley Pride
	Best Ethnic or Traditional Recording	*The London Muddy Waters Session*	Muddy Waters
1973	Record of the Year	*Killing Me Softly With His Song*	Roberta Flack
	Album of the Year	*Innervisions*	Stevie Wonder
	Best Instrumental Arrangement	"Summer in the City"	Quincy Jones
	Best Jazz Performance by a Soloist	*God Is in the House*	Art Tatum
	Best Pop Vocal Performance, Female	"Killing Me Softly with His Song"	Roberta Flack
	Best Pop Vocal Performance, Male	"You Are the Sunshine of My Life"	Stevie Wonder
	Best Pop Vocal Performance, Group	"Neither One of Us"	Gladys Knight & The Pips
	Best Rhythm & Blues Vocal Performance, Female	"Master of Eyes"	Aretha Franklin
	Best Rhythm & Blues Vocal Performance, Male	"Superstition"	Stevie Wonder
	Best Rhythm & Blues Vocal Performance by a Group	"Midnight Train to Georgia"	Gladys Knight & The Pips

[continued]

Grammy Award winners [CONTINUED]

Year	Category	Performance	Performer
	Best Rhythm & Blues Instrumental Performance	"Hang On, Sloopy"	Ramsey Lewis
	Best Rhythm & Blues Song	"Superstition"	Stevie Wonder
	Best Country Vocal Performance, Male	"Behind Closed Doors"	Charley Pride
	Best Classical Vocal Soloist Performance	*Puccini: Heroines*	Leontyne Price
1974	Album of the Year	*Fulfillingness' First Finale*	Stevie Wonder
	Best Jazz Performance by a Soloist	*First Recordings!*	Charlie Parker
	Best Jazz Performance by a Group	*The Trio*	Joe Pass, Niels Pedersen & Oscar Peterson
	Best Pop Vocal Performance, Male	*Fulfillingness' First Finale*	Stevie Wonder
	Best Rhythm & Blues Vocal Performance, Female	"Ain't Nothing Like the Real Thing"	Aretha Franklin
	Best Rhythm & Blues Vocal Performance, Male	"Boogie On, Reggae Woman"	Stevie Wonder
	Best Rhythm & Blues Vocal Performance, Group	"Tell Me Something Good"	Rufus
	Best Rhythm & Blues Instrumental Performance	"TSOP (The Sound of Philadelphia)"	MFSB
	Best Rhythm & Blues Song	"Living for the City"	Stevie Wonder
	Best Comedy Recording	*The Nigger's Crazy*	Richard Pryor
	Best Score From the Original Cast Show	*Raisin*	Judd Woldin & Robert Britton
	Best Classical Vocal Soloist Performance	*Leontyne Price Sings Richard Strauss*	Leontyne Price
1975	Best New Artist of the Year		Natalie Cole
	Best Jazz Performance by a Soloist	*Oscar Peterson & Dizzy Gillespie*	Dizzy Gillespie
	Best Rhythm & Blues Vocal Performance, Female	"This Will Be"	Natalie Cole
	Best Rhythm & Blues Vocal Performance, Male	"Living for the City"	Ray Charles
	Best Rhythm & Blues Vocal Performance, Group	"Shining Star"	Earth, Wind & Fire
	Best Rhythm & Blues Instrumental Performance	"Fly, Robin, Fly"	Silver Convention
	Best Rhythm & Blues Song	"Where Is the Love"	Betty Wright
	Best Ethnic or Traditional Recording	*The Muddy Waters Woodstock Album*	Muddy Waters
1976	Best Jazz Vocal Performance	*Fitzgerald & Pass … Again*	Ella Fitzgerald
	Best Jazz Performance by a Soloist	*Basie & Zoot*	Count Basie
	Best Jazz Performance by a Big Band	*The Ellington Suites*	Duke Ellington
	Best Pop Vocal Performance, Male	*Songs in the Key of Life*	Stevie Wonder
	Best Pop Instrumental Performance	*Breezin'*	George Benson
	Best Rhythm & Blues Vocal Performance, Female	"Sophisticated Lady"	Natalie Cole
	Best Rhythm & Blues Vocal Performance, Male	"I Wish"	Stevie Wonder
	Best Rhythm & Blues Instrumental Performance	"Theme from Good King Bad"	George Benson
	Best Comedy Recording	*Bicentennial Nigger*	Richard Pryor
	Album of Best Original Score for Film or TV	*Car Wash*	Norman Whitfield
	Best Cast Show Album	*Bubbling Brown Sugar*	Producers: Luigi Creatore & Hugo Peretti
1977	Best Jazz Vocal Performance	*Look to the Rainbow*	Al Jarreau
	Best Jazz Performance by a Soloist	*The Giants*	Oscar Peterson
	Best Jazz Performance by a Big Band	*Prime Time*	Count Basie & Orchestra
	Best Rhythm & Blues Vocal Performance, Female	"Don't Leave Me This Way"	Thelma Houston
	Best Rhythm & Blues Vocal Performance, Male	*Unmistakably Lou*	Lou Rawls
	Best Rhythm & Blues Vocal Performance by Group	"Best of My Love"	The Emotions
	Best Rhythm & Blues Instrumental Performance	"Q"	Brothers Johnson
	Best Soul Gospel Performance Traditional	*James Cleveland Live at Carnegie Hall*	James Cleveland
	Best Ethnic or Traditional Recordings	*Hard Again*	Muddy Waters
	Best Opera Recording	*Gershwin: Porgy & Bess*	John De Main conducting Houston Grand Opera Production
1978	Best Rhythm & Blues Vocal Performance, Female	"Last Dance"	Donna Summer
	Best Rhythm & Blues Vocal Performance, Male	"On Broadway"	George Benson
	Best Rhythm & Blues Vocal Performance by a Group	*All 'n All*	Earth, Wind & Fire
	Best Rhythm & Blues Instrumental Performance	"Runnin'"	Earth, Wind & Fire
	Best Soul Gospel Performance, Traditional	*Live and Direct*	Mighty Clouds of Joy
	Best Ethnic or Traditional Recording	*I'm Ready*	Muddy Waters
	Best Cast Show Album	*Ain't Misbehavin'*	Composer: Fats Waller; Producer: Thomas Z. Shepard
	Best Jazz Vocal Performance	*All Fly Home*	Al Jarreau
	Best Jazz Instrumental Performance, Soloist	*Montreuz '77 Oscar Peterson Jam*	Oscar Peterson
	Best Instrumental Arrangement	*The Wiz (Original Soundtrack)*	Quincy Jones & Robert Freedman
1979	Best Pop Vocal Performance, Female	"I'll Never Love This Way Again"	Dionne Warwick
	Best Rock Vocal Performance, Female	"Hot Stuff"	Donna Summer
	Best Rhythm & Blues Vocal Performance, Female	"Déjà Vu"	Dionne Warwick
	Best Rhythm & Blues Vocal Performance, Male	"Don't Stop 'Til You Get Enough"	Michael Jackson
	Best Rhythm & Blues Vocal Performance by a Group	"After the Love Has Gone"	Earth, Wind & Fire

[continued]

Grammy Award winners [CONTINUED]

Year	Category	Performance	Performer
	Best Rhythm & Blues Instrumental Performance	"Boogie Wonderland"	Earth, Wind & Fire
	Best Disco Recording	"I Will Survive"	Gloria Gaynor
	Best Soul Gospel Performance, Contemporary	*I'll Be Thinking of You*	Andrae Crouch
	Best Soul Gospel Performance, Traditional	*Changing Times*	Mighty Clouds of Joy
	Best Ethnic of Traditional Recording	*Muddy "Mississippi" Waters Live*	Muddy Waters
	Best Ethnic of Traditional Recording	*Muddy "Mississippi" Waters Live*	Muddy Waters
	Best Jazz Fusion Performance	*8:30*	Weather Report
	Best Jazz Vocal Performance	*Fine and Mellow*	Ella Fitzgerald
	Best Jazz Instrumental Performance, Soloist	*Jousts*	Oscar Peterson
	Best Jazz Instrumental Performance, Big Band	*At Fargo, 1940 Live*	Duke Ellington
	Best Historic Reissue	*Billie Holiday (Giants of Jazz)*	Billie Holiday, Produced by Michael Brooks
1980	Best Pop Instrumental Performance	*One on One*	Bob James & Earl Klugh
	Best Rhythm & Blues Vocal Performance, Female	"Never Knew Love Like This Before"	Stephanie Mills
	Best Rhythm & Blues Vocal Performance, Male	*Give Me the Night*	George Benson
	Best Rhythm & Blues Performance by a Group	"Shining Star"	The Manhattans
	Best Rhythm & Blues Instrumental Performance	"Off Broadway"	George Benson
	Best Soul Gospel Performance, Contemporary	*Rejoice*	Shirley Caesar
	Best Soul Gospel Performance, Traditional	*Lord, Let Me Be an Instrument*	James Cleveland & the Charles Fold Singers
	Best Ethnic or Traditional Recording	*Rare Blues*	Dr. Isaiah Ross & Others
	Best Recording for Children	*In Harmony/A Sesame Street Record*	Al Jarreau, George Benson, and others
	Best Jazz Vocal Performance, Female	*A Perfect Match/Ella & Basie*	Ella Fitzgerald
	Best Jazz Vocal Performance, Male	"Moody's Mood"	George Benson
	Best Jazz Instrumental Performance, Big Band	*On the Road*	Count Basie & Orchestra
	Best Instrumental Arrangement	"Dinorah, Dinorah"	Quincy Jones & Jerry Hey
	Best Classical Vocal Soloist Performance	*Prima Donna, Vol. 5*	Leontyne Price
1981	Best Pop Vocal Performance, Female	*Lena Horne: The Lady and Her Music Live on Broadway*	Lena Horne
	Best Pop Vocal Performance, Male	*Breakin' Away*	Al Jarreau
	Best Rhythm & Blues Performance, Female	"Hold On, I'm Comin' "	Aretha Franklin
	Best Rhythm & Blues Performance, Male	"One Hundred Ways"	James Ingram
	Best Rhythm & Blues Performance by a Group	*The Dude*	Quincy Jones
	Best Jazz Fusion Performance, Vocal or Instrumental	*Winelight*	Grover Washington, Jr.
	Best Soul Gospel Performance, Contemporary	*Don't Give Up*	Andrae Crouch
	Best Soul Gospel Performance, Traditional	*The Lord Will Make a Way*	Al Green
	Best Ethnic or Traditional Recording	*There Must Be a Better World Somewhere*	B.B. King
	Best Comedy Recording	*Rev. Du Rite*	Richard Pryor
	Best Cast Show Album	*Lena Horne: The Lady and Her Music Live on Broadway*	Producer: Quincy Jones
	Best Jazz Vocal Performance, Female	*Digital III at Montreux*	Ella Fitzgerald
	Best Jazz Vocal Performance, Male	"Blue Rondo à la Turk"	Al Jarreau
	Best Jazz Instrumental Performance, Soloist	*Bye Bye Blackbird*	John Coltrane
	Best Arrangement on an Instrumental Recording	"Velas"	Quincy Jones
	Best Instrumental Arrangement—Accompanying Vocals	"Ai No Corrida"	Quincy Jones
	Producer of the Year		Quincy Jones
1982	Best Pop Vocal Performance, Male	"Truly"	Lionel Richie
	Best Rhythm & Blues Performance, Male	"Sexual Healing"	Marvin Gaye
	Best Rhythm & Blues Performance by a Group with Vocals	"Let It Whip"	Dazz Band
		"Wanna Be With You"	Earth, Wind & Fire
	Best Rhythm & Blues Performance	"Sexual Healing"	Marvin Gaye
	Best Soul Gospel Performance, Contemporary	*Higher Plane*	Al Green
	Best Soul Gospel Performance, Traditional	*Precious Lord*	Al Green
	Best Traditional Blues Recording	*Alright Again*	Clarence Gatemouth Brown
	Best Ethnic or Traditional Folk Recording	*Queen Ida and the Bon Temps Zydeco Band on Tour*	Queen Ida
	Best Comedy Recording	*Live on the Sunset Strip*	Richard Pryor
	Best Jazz Instrumental Performance, Soloist	*We Want Miles*	Miles Davis
	Best Jazz Instrumental Performance, Big Band	*Warm Breeze*	Count Basie & Orchestra
	Best Classical Vocal Soloist Performance	*Leontyne Price Sings Verdi*	Leontyne Price
1983	Record of the Year	"Beat It"	Michael Jackson
	Album of the Year	*Thriller*	Michael Jackson
	Best Pop Vocal Performance, Female	"Flashdance (What a Feeling)"	Irene Cara
	Best Pop Vocal Performance, Male	*Thriller*	Michael Jackson
	Best Pop Instrumental Performance	"Being With You"	George Benson
	Best Rock Vocal Performance, Male	"Beat It"	Michael Jackson
	Best Rhythm & Blues Performance, Female	*Chaka Khan*	Chaka Khan
	Best Rhythm & Blues Performance, Male	"Billie Jean"	Michael Jackson

[continued]

Grammy Award winners [CONTINUED]

Year	Category	Performance	Performer
	Best Rhythm & Blues Performance by a Group or Duo	"Ain't Nobody"	Rufus & Chaka Khan
	Best Rhythm & Blues Instrumental Performance	"Rockit"	Herbie Hancock
	Best Gospel Performance by Duo or Group	"More Than Wonderful"	Larnelle Harris
	Best Soul Gospel Performance, Female	*We Sing Praises*	Sandra Crouch
	Best Soul Gospel Performance, Male	*I'll Rise Again*	Al Green
	Best Instrumental Performance	"He's a Rebel"	Donna Summer
	Best Traditional Blues Recording	*Blues 'n' Jazz*	B.B. King
	Best Ethnic or Traditional Folk Recording	*I'm Here*	Clifton Chenier & His Red Hot Louisiana Band
	Best Recording for Children	*E.T. The Extra-Terrestrial*	Michael Jackson, Quincy Jones
	Best Comedy Recording	*Eddie Murphy, Comedian*	Eddie Murphy
	Best Spoken Word or Nonmusical Recording	*Copland: A Lincoln Portrait*	William Warfield
	Best Jazz Vocal Performance, Female	*The Best Is Yet to Come*	Ella Fitzgerald
	Best Jazz Instrumental Performance, Soloist	*Think of One*	Wynton Marsalis
	Best Vocal Arrangement for Two or More Voices	"Be Bop Medley"	Arif Hardin & Chaka Khan
	Producer of the Year		Quincy Jones & Michael Jackson
	Best Classical Vocal Soloist Performance	*Leontyne Price & Marilyn Horne in Concert*	Leontyne Price & Marilyn Horne
1984	Record of the Year	"What's Love Got to Do With It?"	Tina Turner
	Album of the Year	*Can't Slow Down*	Lionel Richie
	Best Pop Vocal Performance, Female	"What's Love Got to Do with It?"	Tina Turner
	Best Pop Performance by a Group	"Jump (for My Love)"	Pointer Sisters
	Best Pop Instrumental Performance	"Ghostbusters"	Ray Parker, Jr.
	Best Rock Vocal Performance, Female	"Better Be Good to Me"	Tina Turner
	Best Rock Performance by Duo or Group	*Purple Rain*	Prince & the Revolution
	Best Rhythm & Blues Performance, Female	"I Feel for You"	Chaka Khan
	Best Rhythm & Blues Performance, Male	"Caribbean Queen"	Billy Ocean
	Best Rhythm & Blues Performance, Group	"Yah Mo B There"	James Ingram
	Best Rhythm & Blues Instrumental Performance	*Sound-System*	Herbie Hancock
	Best Soul Gospel Performance, Female	*Sailin'*	Shirley Caesar
	Best Soul Gospel Performance, Male	"Always Remember"	Andrae Crouch
	Best Soul Gospel Performance by Duo or Group	"Sailin' on the Sea of Your Love"	Shirley Caesar & Al Green
	Best Inspirational Performance	"Forgive Me"	Donna Summer
	Best Ethnic or Traditional Folk Recording	*Elizabeth Cotton Live!*	Elizabeth Cotton
	Best Reggae Recording	*Anthem*	Black Uhuru
	Best Album of Original Score for Film or TV	*Purple Rain*	Prince & the Revolution
	Best Video Album	*Making Michael Jackson's Thriller*	Michael Jackson
	Best Jazz Instrumental Performance, Soloist	*Hot House Flowers*	Wynton Marsalis
	Best Jazz Instrumental Performance, Big Band	*88 Basie Street*	Count Basie & Orchestra
	Best Arrangement on an Instrumental	"Grace (Gymnastics Theme)"	Quincy Jones
	Best Vocal Arrangement for Two or More Voices	"Automatic"	Pointer Sisters
	Producer of the Year		Lionel Richie
	Best Classical Performance	"Wynton Marsalis"	Wynton Marsalis
	Best Classical Vocal Soloist Performance	*Ravel: Songs of Maurice Ravel*	Jessye Norman
1985	Record of the Year	"We Are the World"	Producer: Quincy Jones
	Song of the Year	"We Are the World"	Michael Jackson & Lionel Richie
	Best New Artist		Sade
	Best Pop Vocal Performance, Female	"Saving All My Love for You"	Whitney Houston
	Best Rock Vocal Performance, Female	"One of the Living"	Tina Turner
	Best Rhythm & Blues Performance, Female	"Freeway of Love"	Aretha Franklin
	Best Rhythm & Blues Performance, Male	*In Square Circle*	Stevie Wonder
	Best Rhythm & Blues Performance, Group	"Nightshift"	The Commodores
	Best Jazz Vocal Performance, Male	"Another Night in Tunisia"	Jon Hendricks & Bobby McFerrin
	Best Jazz Instrumental Performance, Soloist	*Black Codes from the Underground*	Wynton Marsalis
	Best Jazz Instrumental Performance, Group	*Black Codes from the Underground*	Wynton Marsalis Group
	Best Gospel Performance, Male	"How Excellent Is Thy Name"	Larnelle Harris
	Best Gospel Performance, Group	"I've Just Seen Jesus"	Larnelle Harris
	Best Soul Gospel Performance, Female	"Martin"	Shirley Caesar
	Best Soul Gospel Performance, Male	"Bring Back the Days of Yea and Nay"	Marvin Winans
	Best Soul Gospel Performance, Group	*Tomorrow*	The Winans
	Best Inspirational Performance	"Come Sunday"	Jennifer Holliday
	Best Traditional Blues Recording	"My Guitar Sings the Blues"	B.B. King

[continued]

Grammy Award winners [CONTINUED]

Year	Category	Performance	Performer
	Best Ethnic or Traditional Folk Recording	"My Toot Toot"	Rockin' Sidney
	Best Reggae Recording	*Cliff Hanger*	Jimmy Cliff
	Best Comedy Recording	*Whoopi Goldberg*	Whoopi Goldberg
	Best Music Video, Short Form	"We Are the World"	Producer: Quincy Jones
	Best Vocal Arrangement for Two or More Voices	"Another Night in Tunisia"	Bobby McFerrin
1986	Song of the Year	"That's What Friends Are For"	Dionne Warwick, Gladys Knight & the Pips, Stevie Wonder
	Best Pop Performance by a Group	"That's What Friends Are For"	Warwick, and others
	Best Rock Vocal Performance, Female	"Back Where You Started"	Tina Turner
	Best Rhythm & Blues Performance, Female	*Rapture*	Anita Baker
	Best Rhythm & Blues Performance, Male	"Living in America"	James Brown
	Best Rhythm & Blues Performance, Group	"Kiss"	Prince & the Revolution
	Best Jazz Vocal Performance, Male	"'Round Midnight"	Bobby McFerrin
	Best Jazz Instrumental Performance, Soloist	*Tutu*	Miles Davis
	Best Jazz instrumental Performance, Group	*J Mood*	Wynton Marsalis
	Best Gospel Performance, Male	*Triumph*	Philip Bailey
	Best Gospel Performance by a Duo or Group	"They Say"	Sandi Patti & Deniece Williams
	Best Soul Gospel Performance, Female	"I Surrender All"	Deniece Williams
	Best Soul Performance, Male	"Going Away"	Al Green
	Best Soul Gospel Performance by a Duo or Group	*Let My People Go*	The Winans
	Best Traditional Blues Recording	*Showdown!*	Albert Collins, Robert Cray & Johnny Copeland
	Best Reggae Recording	*Babylon the Bandit*	Steel Pulse
	Best Comedy Recording	*Those of You With or Without Children, You'll Understand*	Bill Cosby
1987	Best Classical Vocal Soloist Performance	*Kathleen Battle Sings Mozart*	Kathleen Battle
	Song of the Year	"Somewhere Out There"	James Ingram & Linda Ronstadt
	Best New Artist		Jody Watley
	Best Pop Vocal Performance, Female	"I Wanna Dance with Somebody"	Whitney Houston
	Best New Age Performance	*Yusef Lateef's Little Symphony*	Yusef Lateef
	Best Rhythm & Blues Vocal Performance, Female	*Aretha*	Aretha Franklin
	Best Rhythm & Blues Vocal Performance, Male	"Just to See Her"	Smokey Robinson
	Best Rhythm & Blues Performance by a Duo or Group	"I Knew You Were Waiting"	Aretha Franklin & George Michael
	Best Jazz Vocal Performance	"What Is This Thing Called Love?"	Bobby McFerrin
	Best Jazz Instrumental Performance, Group	*Marsalis Standard Time—Vol. 1*	Wynton Marsalis
	Best Jazz Instrumental Performance, Big Band	*Digital Duke*	Duke Ellington Orchestra
	Best Gospel Performance, Female	"I Believe in You"	Deniece Williams
	Best Gospel Performance, Male	*The Father Hath Provided*	Larnelle Harris
	Best Soul Gospel Performance, Female	"For Always"	CeCe Winans
	Best Soul Gospel Performance, Male	"Everything's Gonna Be Alright"	Al Green
	Best Soul Gospel Performance by a Duo or Group	"Ain't No Need to Worry"	The Winans & Anita Baker
	Best Traditional Blues Recording	*Houseparty New Orleans Style*	Professor Longhair
	Best Contemporary Blues Recording	*Strong Persuader*	The Robert Cray Band
	Best Traditional Folk Recording	*Shaka Zulu*	Ladysmith Black Mambazo
	Best Reggae Recording	*No Nuclear War*	Peter Tosh
	Best Recording for Children	*The Elephant's Child*	Producer: Bobby McFerrin
	Best Instrumental Composition	"Call Street Blues"	Herbie Hancock
	Best Historical Album	*Thelonious Monk—The Riverside Recording*	Thelonious Monk
1988	Best Classical Vocal Soloist Performance	*Kathleen Battle—Salzburg Recital*	Kathleen Battle
	Record of the Year	"Don't Worry, Be Happy"	Bobby McFerrin
	Song of the Year	"Don't Worry, Be Happy"	Bobby McFerrin
	Best New Artist		Tracy Chapman
	Best Pop Vocal Performance, Female	"Fast Car"	Tracy Chapman
	Best Pop Vocal Performance, Male	"Don't Worry, Be Happy"	Bobby McFerrin
	Best Rock Vocal Performance, Female	*Tina Live in Europe*	Tina Turner
	Best Rhythm & Blues Vocal Performance, Female	"Giving You the Best That I Got"	Anita Baker
	Best Rhythm & Blues Vocal Performance, Male	*Introducing the Hardline According to Terence Trent D'Arby*	Terence Trent D'Arby
	Best Rhythm & Blues Performance by a Duo or Group	"Love Overboard"	Gladys Knight & the Pips
	Best Rap Performance	"Parents Just Don't Understand"	D.J. Jazzy Jeff & The Fresh Prince
	Best Jazz Vocal Performance, Male	"Brothers"	Bobby McFerrin
	Best Jazz Vocal Performance, Duo or Group	"Spread Love"	Take 6

[continued]

Grammy Award winners [CONTINUED]

Year	Category	Performance	Performer
	Best Jazz Instrumental Performance, Group	*Blues for Coltrane*	McCoy Tyner, Pharoah Sanders, David Murray, Cecil McBee, & Roy Haynes
	Best Gospel Performance, Male	*Christmas*	Larnelle Harris
	Best Soul Gospel Performance, Female	*One Lord, One Faith, One Baptism*	Aretha Franklin
	Best Soul Gospel Performance by a Duo or Group	*Take Six*	Take 6
	Best Traditional Blues Recording	*Hidden Charms*	Willie Dixon
	Best Contemporary Blues Recording	"Don't Be Afraid of the Dark"	The Robert Cray Band
	Best Contemporary Folk Recording	*Tracy Chapman*	Tracy Chapman
	Best Reggae Recording	*Conscious Party*	Ziggy Marley & The Melody Makers
	Best Spoken Word Recording	*Speech by Rev. Jesse Jackson*	Rev. Jesse Jackson
1989	Best Pop Vocal Performance by a Duo or Group	"Don't Know Much"	Linda Ronstadt & Aaron Neville
	Best Pop Instrumental	"Healing Chant"	Neville Brothers
	Best Rhythm & Blues Vocal Performance, Female	*Giving You the Best That I Got*	Anita Baker
	Best Rhythm & Blues Vocal Performance, Male	"Every Little Step"	Bobby Brown
	Best Rhythm & Blues Performance by a Duo or Group	"Back to Life"	Soul II Soul
	Best Rhythm & Blues Instrumental Performance	"African Dance"	Soul II Soul
	Best Rap Performance	"Bust a Move"	Young MC
	Best Jazz Instrumental Performance, Soloist	*Aura*	Miles Davis
	Best Jazz Instrumental Performance, Big Band	*Aura*	Miles Davis
	Best Traditional Blues Recording	"I'm in the Mood"	John Lee Hooker
	Best Gospel Vocal Performance, Female	"Don't Cry"	CeCe Winans
	Best Gospel Vocal Performance, Male	"Meantime"	BeBe Winans
	Best Gospel Vocal Performance by a Duo or Group	"The Savior Is Waiting"	Take 6
	Best Soul Gospel Vocal Performance	"As Long As We're Together"	Al Green
	Best Soul Gospel Vocal Performance by a Group	"Let Brotherly Love Continue"	Daniel Winans & Choir
	Best Reggae Recording	*One Bright Day*	Ziggy Marley & The Melody Makers
	Best Music Video—Short Form	*Leave Me Alone*	Michael Jackson
	Best Music Video—Long Form	*Rhythm Nation*	Janet Jackson
	Best Historical Album	*Chuck Berry—The Chess Set*	
1990	Best New Artist		Mariah Carey
	Album of the Year	*Back on the Block*	Quincy Jones
	Best Pop Vocal Performance, Female	"Vision of Love"	Mariah Carey
	Best Pop Vocal Performance by a Duo or Group	"All My Life"	Linda Ronstadt & Aaron Neville
	Best Rhythm & Blues Vocal Performance, Female	*Compositions*	Anita Baker
	Best Rhythm & Blues Vocal Performance, Male	"Here and Now"	Luther Vandross
	Best Rhythm & Blues Performance by a Duo or Group	"I'll Be Good to You"	Ray Charles & Chaka Khan
	Best Rap Solo Performance	"U Can't Touch This"	M.C. Hammer
	Best Rap Performance by a Duo or Group	"Back on the Block"	Ice-T, Melle Mel, Big Daddy Kane, Cool Moe Dee, Quincy Jones
	Best Jazz Fusion Performance	"Birdland"	Quincy Jones
	Best Jazz Vocal Performance, Female	*All That Jazz*	Ella Fitzgerald
	Best Jazz Instrumental Performance, Soloist	*The Legendary Oscar Peterson Trio Live at the Blue Note*	Oscar Peterson
	Best Jazz Instrumental Performance, Group	*The Legendary Oscar Peterson Trio Live at the Blue Note*	Oscar Peterson Trio
	Best Jazz Instrumental Performance, Big Band	"Basie's Bag"	Frank Foster
	Best Traditional Soul Gospel Album	*So Many 2 Say*	Take 6
	Best Traditional Blues Recording	*Live at San Quentin*	B.B. King
	Best Music Video—Long Form	*Please Hammer, Don't Hurt 'Em*	M.C. Hammer
	Best Arrangement on an Instrumental	"Birdland"	Quincy Jones
	Best Instrumental Arrangement—Accompanying Vocals	"The Places You Find Love"	Quincy Jones
	Producer of the Year		Quincy Jones
	Best Historical Album	*Robert Johnson: The Complete Recordings*	
	Record of the Year	"Unforgettable"	Natalie Cole
1991	Album of the Year	*Unforgettable*	Natalie Cole
	Best Traditional Pop Performance	"Unforgettable"	Natalie Cole
	Best Rhythm & Blues Vocal Performance, Female	*Burnin'*	Patti LaBelle
	Best Rhythm & Blues Vocal Performance, Male	*Power of Love*	Luther Vandross
	Best Rhythm & Blues Performance by a Duo or Group	*Cooley High Harmony*	Boyz II Men

[continued]

Grammy Award winners [CONTINUED]

Year	Category	Performance	Performer
	Best Rap Performance	"Mama Said Knock You Out"	L.L. Cool J.
	Best Rap Performance by a Duo or Group	"Summertime"	D.J. Jazzy Jeff & The Fresh Prince
	Best Jazz Vocal Performance	*He Is Christmas*	Take 6
	Best Jazz Instrumental Performance, Group	*Saturday Night at the Blue Note*	Oscar Peterson Trio
	Best Large Jazz Ensemble	*Live at the Royal Festival Hall*	Dizzy Gillespie & the U.N. Orchestra
	Best Traditional Soul Gospel Album	*Pray for Me*	Mighty Clouds of Joy
	Best Contemporary Soul Gospel Album	*Different Lifestyles*	BeBe & CeCe Winans
	Best Gospel Album by a Choir	*The Evolution of Gospel*	Sounds of Blackness
	Best Traditional Blues Album	*Live at the Apollo*	B.B. King
	Best Contemporary Blues Album	*Damn Right, I've Got the Blues*	Buddy Guy
	Best Reggae Album	*As Raw As Ever*	Shabba Ranks
	Best Historical Album	*Billie Holiday: The Complete Decca Recordings*	Billie Holiday
1992	Best New Artist		Arrested Development
	Best Pop Performance by a Duo or Group	"Beauty and the Beast"	Celine Dion & Peabo Bryson
	Best Rhythm & Blues Vocal Performance, Female	*The Woman I Am*	Chaka Khan
	Best Rhythm & Blues Vocal Performance, Male	*Heaven and Earth*	Al Jarreau
	Best Rhythm & Blues Performance by a Duo or Group	"End of the Road"	Boyz II Men
	Best Rhythm & Blues Instrumental Performance	*Doo-Bop*	Miles Davis
	Best Rap Solo Performance	"Baby Got Back"	Sir Mix-A-Lot
	Best Rap Performance by a Duo or Group	"Tennessee"	Arrested Development
	Best Jazz Vocal Performance/Album	"'Round Midnight"	Bobbie McFerrin
	Best Jazz Instrumental Solo Performance	"Lush Life"	Joe Henderson
	Best Jazz Instrumental Performance, Individual or Group	*I Heard You Twice the First Time*	Branford Marsalis
	Best Large Jazz Ensemble	*The Turning Point*	McCoy Tyner Big Band
	Best Traditional Soul Gospel Album	*He's Working It Out for You*	Shirley Caesar
	Best Gospel Album by a Choir	*Edwin Hawkins Music—Live in L.A.*	Edwin Hawkins
	Best Reggae Album	*X-Tra Naked*	Shabba Ranks
	Best Spoken Word Album	*What You Can Do to Avoid AIDS*	Earvin "Magic" Johnson
	Best Instrumental Composition	*Harlem Renaissance Suite*	Benny Carter
	Best Instrumental Arrangement	"Here's to Life"	Johnny Mandel
	Producer of the Year		L.A. Reid & Babyface
	Best Historical Album	*The Complete Capitol Recordings of the Nat "King" Cole Trio*	
	Best Classical Vocal Performance	"Kathleen Battle at Carnegie Hall"	Kathleen Battle
1993	Best New Artist		Toni Braxton
	Album of the Year	*The Bodyguard*	Whitney Houston
	Record of the Year	"I Will Always Love You"	Whitney Houston
	Best Pop Vocal Performance, Female	"I Will Always Love You"	Whitney Houston
	Best Pop Instrumental	"Barcelona Mona"	Branford Marsalis & Bruce Hornsby
	Best Pop Performance by a Duo or Group	"A Whole New World"	Peabo Bryson & Regina Bell
	Best Rhythm & Blues Song	"That's the Way Love Goes"	Janet Jackson
	Best Rhythm & Blues Vocal Performance, Female	"Another Sad Love Song"	Toni Braxton
	Best Rhythm & Blues Vocal Performance, Male	"A Song for You"	Ray Charles
	Best Rhythm & Blues Performance by a Duo or Group	"No Ordinary Love"	Sade
	Best Jazz Vocal Performance/Album	*Take A Look*	Natalie Cole
	Best Jazz Instrumental Solo	*Miles Ahead*	Joe Henderson
	Best Jazz Instrumental Album, Individual or Group	*So Near, So Far (For Miles)*	Joe Henderson
	Best Large Jazz Ensemble	*Miles & Quincy Live at Montreux*	Miles Davis & Quincy Jones
	Best Rap Solo Performance	"Let Me Ride"	Dr. Dre
	Best Rap Performance by a Duo or Group	"Rebirth of Slick"	Digable Planets
	Best Traditional Blues Album	*Blues Summit*	B.B. King
	Best Contemporary Blues Album	*Feels Like Rain*	Buddy Guy
	Best Traditional Soul Gospel Album	*Stand Still*	Shirley Caesar
	Best Contemporary Soul Gospel Album	*All Out*	The Winans
	Best Gospel Album by a Choir or Chorus	*Live...We Come Rejoicing*	Brooklyn Tabernacle Choir
	Best Reggae Album	*Bad Boys*	Inner Circle
1994	Best Spoken Word Album	*On the Pulse of Morning*	Maya Angelou
	Best Historical Album	*The Complete Billie Holiday on Verve 1945–59*	
	Best Rhythm & Blues Album	*II*	Boyz II Men
	Best Rhythm & Blues Vocal Performance, Female	"Breathe Again"	Toni Braxton
	Best Rhythm & Blues Vocal Performance, Male	"When Can I See You"	Babyface
	Best Rhythm & Blues Performance by a Duo or Group	"I'll Make Love to You"	Boyz II Men

[continued]

Grammy Award winners [CONTINUED]

Year	Category	Performance	Performer
	Best Jazz Vocal Performance/Album	*Mystery Lady—Songs of Billie Holiday*	Etta James
	Best Jazz Instrumental Solo	"Prelude to A Kiss"	Benny Carter
	Best Jazz Instrumental Album, Individual or Group	*A Tribute to Miles*	Ron Carter, Herbie Hancock, Wallace Roney, Wayne Shorter & Tony Williams
	Best Large Jazz Ensemble	"Journey"	McCoy Tyner
	Best Rap Solo Performance	"U.N.I.T.Y."	Queen Latifah
	Best Rap Performance by a Duo or Group	"None of Your Business"	Salt-N-Pepa
	Best Traditional Blues Album	*Chill Out*	John Lee Hooker
	Best Contemporary Blues Album	*Father Father*	Pops Staples
	Best Pop/Contemporary Gospel Album	*Mercy*	Andrae Crouch
	Best Traditional Soul Gospel Album	*Songs of the Church—Live in Memphis*	Albertina Walker
	Best Contemporary Soul Gospel Album	*Join the Band*	Take 6
	Best Gospel Album by a Choir or Chorus	*Live in Atlanta at Morehouse College*	Love Fellowship Crusade Choir and Through God's Eyes Thompson Community Singers
	Best Reggae Album	*Crucial! Roots Classics*	Bunny Wailer
	Best Historical Album	*The Complete Ella Fitzgerald Songbooks on Verve*	
1995	Best New Artist		Hootie & the Blowfish
	Song of the Year	"Kiss from a Rose"	Seal
	Record of the Year	"Kiss from a Rose"	Seal
	Best Pop Performance by a Duo or Group	"Let Her Cry"	Hootie & The Blowfish
	Best Rhythm & Blues Album	*CrazySexyCool*	TLC
	Best Rhythm & Blues Vocal Performance, Female	"I Apologize"	Anita Baker
	Best Rhythm & Blues Vocal Performance, Male	"For Your Love"	Stevie Wonder
	Best Rhythm & Blues Performance by a Duo or Group	"Creep"	TLC
	Best Jazz Vocal Performance/Album	*An Evening With Lena Horne*	Lena Horne
	Best Jazz Instrumental Album, Individual or Group	"Infinity"	McCoy Tyner Trio & Michael Brecker
	Best Rap Album	*Poverty's Paradise*	Naughty by Nature
	Best Rap Solo Performance	"Gangsta's Paradise"	Coolio
	Best Rap Performance by a Duo or Group	"I'll Be There for You/You're All I Need"	Method Man & Mary J. Blige
	Best Traditional Blues Album	*Deep in the Blues*	James Cotton
	Best Contemporary Blues Album	*Slippin' In*	Buddy Guy
	Best Traditional Soul Gospel Album	*Shirley Caesar Live—He Will Come*	Shirley Caesar
	Best Contemporary Soul Gospel Album	*Alone in His Presence*	CeCe Winan
	Best Gospel Album by a Choir or Chorus	*Praise Him…Live!*	Brooklyn Tabernacle Choir
	Best Reggae Album	*Boombastic*	Shaggy
	Best Spoken Word Album	*Phenomenal Women*	Maya Angelou
	Producer of the Year		Babyface
	Best Music Video, Short Form	"Scream"	Michael Jackson & Janet Jackson
1996	Best Pop Vocal Performance, Male	"Kiss from a Rose"	Seal
	Best Rock Song	"Give Me One Reason"	Tracy Chapman
	Best Pop Vocal Performance, Female	"Unbreak My Heart"	Toni Braxton
	Best Rhythm & Blues Album	*Words*	Tony Rich Project
	Best Rhythm & Blues Vocal Performance, Female	"You're Makin' Me High"	Toni Braxton
	Best Rhythm & Blues Vocal Performance, Male	"Your Secret Love"	Luther Vandross
	Best Rhythm & Blues Performance by a Duo or Group	"Killing Me Softly"	Fugees
	Best Jazz Performance/Album	*New Moon Daughter*	Cassandra Wilson
	Best Large Jazz Ensemble	*Live at Manchester Craftsmen's Guild*	Grover Mitchell
	Best Rap Album	*The Score*	The Fugees
	Best Rap Solo Performance	"Hey Lover"	L.L. Cool J
	Best Rap Performance by a Duo or Group	"The Crossroads"	Bone Thugs-N-Harmony
	Best Traditional Blues Album	*Don't Look Back*	John Lee Hooker
	Best Contemporary Blues Album	*Just Like You*	Keb' Mo'
	Best Pop/Contemporary Gospel Album	*Tribute—The Songs of Andrae Crouch*	Andrae Crouch
	Best Traditional Soul Gospel Album	*Face to Face*	Cissy Houston
	Best Contemporary Soul Gospel Album	*Whatcha Lookin' 4*	Kirk Franklin
	Best Gospel Album by a Choir or Chorus	*Just A Word*	Shirley Caesar's Outreach Convention Choir
	Best Reggae Album	*Hall of Fame—A Tribute to Bob Marley's 50th Anniversary*	Bunny Wailer
	Best Historical Album	*The Complete Columbia Studio Recordings*	
	Producer of the Year		Babyface

[continued]

Grammy Award winners [CONTINUED]

Year	Category	Performance	Performer
1997	Best Pop Performance by a Duo or Group	"Virtual Insanity	Jamiroquai
	Best Rhythm & Blues Album	*Baduizm*	Erykah Badu
	Best Rhythm & Blues Vocal Performance, Female	"On & On"	Erykah Badu
	Best Rhythm & Blues Vocal Performance, Male	"I Believe I Can Fly"	R. Kelly
	Best Rhythm & Blues Performance by a Duo or Group	"No Diggity"	Blackstreet
	Best Dance Recording	"Carry On "	Donna Summer & Giorgio Moroder
	Best Rap Album	*No Way Out*	P. Diddy
	Best Rap Solo Performance	"Men in Black"	Will Smith
	Best Rap Performance by a Duo or Group	"I'll Be Missing You"	P. Diddy, Faith Evans & 112
	Best Traditional Blues Album	*Chill Out*	John Lee Hooker
	Best Contemporary Blues Album	*Señor Blues*	Taj Mahal
	Best Traditional Soul Gospel Album	*I Couldn't Hear Nobody Pray*	Fairfield Four
	Best Contemporary Soul Gospel Album	*Brothers*	Take 6
	Best Gospel Album by a Choir or Chorus	*God's Property from Kirk Franklin's Nu Nation*	God's Property
	Best Jazz Performance/Album	*Dear Ella*	Dee Dee Bridgewater
	Best Jazz Instrumental Solo Performance	"Stardust"	Doc Cheatham & Nicholas Payton
	Best Large Jazz Ensemble Performance	*Joe Henderson Big Band*	Joe Henderson Big Band
	Best Reggae Album	*Fallen Is Babylon*	Ziggy Marley & The Melody Makers
	Best Spoken Comedy Album	*Roll With the New*	Chris Rock
	Producer of the Year		Babyface
	Best Music Video, Short Form	"Got Till It's Gone"	Janet Jackson
1998	Best New Artist		Lauryn Hill
	Album of the Year	*The Miseducation of Lauryn Hill*	Lauryn Hill
	Best Rhythm & Blues Album	*The Miseducation of Lauryn Hill*	Lauryn Hill
	Best Rhythm & Blues Vocal Performance, Female	"Doo Wop (That Thing)"	Lauryn Hill
	Best Rhythm & Blues Vocal Performance, Male	"St. Louis Blues"	Stevie Wonder
	Best Rhythm & Blues Performance by a Duo or Group	"The Boy is Mine"	Brandy & Monica
	Best Traditional Rhythm & Blues Performance	*Live! One Night Only*	Patti LaBelle
	Best Rhythm & Blues Song	"Doo Wop (That Thing)"	Lauryn Hill
	Best Rock Vocal Performance, Male	"Fly Away"	Lenny Kravitz
	Best Jazz Performance/Album	*I Remember Miles*	Shirley Horn
	Best Jazz Instrumental Album, Individual or Group	*Gershwin's World*	Herbie Hancock
	Best Instrumental Arrangement Accompanying Vocals	"St. Louis Blues"	Herbie Hancock
	Best Large Jazz Ensemble	*Count Plays Duke*	Grover Mitchell/Count Basie Orchestra
	Best Rap Album	*Volume 2…Hard Knock Life*	Jay-Z
	Best Rap Solo Performance	"Gettin' Jiggy Wit It"	Will Smith
	Best Traditional Blues Album	*Any Place I'm Going*	Otis Rush
	Best Contemporary Blues Album	*Slow Down*	Keb' Mo'
	Best Pop/Contemporary Gospel Album	*This Is My Song*	Deniece Williams
	Best Traditional Soul Gospel Album	*He Leadeth Me*	Cissy Houston
	Best Contemporary Soul Gospel Album	*The Nu Nation Project*	Kirk Franklin
	Best Gospel Album by a Choir or Chorus	*Reflections*	O'Landa Draper & The Associates Choir
	Best Reggae Album	*Friends*	Sly & Robbie
1999	Best Rhythm & Blues Vocal Performance, Female	"It's Not Right But It's Okay"	Whitney Houston
	Best Rhythm & Blues Album	*Fanmail*	TLC
	Best Rhythm & Blues Vocal Performance, Male	"Staying Power"	Barry White
	Best Rhythm & Blues Performance by a Duo or Group	"No Scrubs"	TLC
	Best Traditional Rhythm & Blues Performance	*Staying Power*	Barry White
	Best Rhythm & Blues Song	"No Scrubs"	TLC
	Best Rock Vocal Performance, Male	"American Woman"	Lenny Kravitz
	Best Jazz Instrumental Solo Performance	"In Walked Wayne"	Wayne Shorter
	Best Rap Performance by a Duo or Group	"You Got Me"	The Roots & Erykah Badu
	Best Traditional Blues Album	*Blues on the Bayou*	B.B. King
	Best Contemporary Blues Album	*Take Your Shoes Off*	The Robert Cray Band
	Best Traditional Soul Gospel Album	*Christmas With Shirley Caesar*	Shirley Caesar
	Best Contemporary Soul Gospel Album	*Mountain High…Valley Low*	Yolanda Adams
	Best Gospel Album by a Choir or Chorus	*High and Lifted Up*	Brooklyn Tabernacle Choir
	Best Reggae Album	*Calling Rastafari*	Burning Spear
	Best Spoken Word Album	*The Autobiography of Martin Luther King, Jr.*	LeVar Burton

[continued]

Grammy Award winners [CONTINUED]

Year	Category	Performance	Performer
	Best Spoken Comedy Album	*Bigger and Blacker*	Chris Rock
	Best Historical Album	*The Duke Ellington Centennial Edition—The Complete RCA Victor Recordings (1927–73)*	
	Best Music Video, Long Form	*Band of Gypsies—Live at Filmore East*	Jimi Hendrix
2000	Best Pop Vocal Performance, Female	"I Try"	Macy Gray
	Best Pop Collaboration with Vocals	"Is You Is, Or Is You Ain't (My Baby)"	B.B. King & Dr. John
	Best Rhythm & Blues Album	*Voodoo*	D'Angelo
	Best Rhythm & Blues Vocal Performance, Female	"He Wasn't Man Enough"	Toni Braxton
	Best Rhythm & Blues Vocal Performance, Male	"Untitled (How Does It Feel)"	D'Angelo
	Best Rhythm & Blues Performance by a Duo or Group	"Say My Name"	Destiny's Child
	Best Rhythm & Blues Song	"Say My Name"	Destiny's Child
	Best Rock Vocal Performance, Male	"Again"	Lenny Kravitz
	Best Traditional Rhythm & Blues Performance	*Ear-Resistable*	The Temptations
	Best Jazz Performance/Album	*In the Moment—Live in Concert*	Dianne Reeves
	Best Jazz Instrumental Album, Individual or Group	*Contemporary Jazz*	Branford Marsalis Quartet
	Best Traditional Blues Album	*Riding With the King*	B.B. King & Eric Clapton
	Best Dance Recording	"Who Let the Dogs Out"	Baha Men
	Best Contemporary Blues Album	*Shoutin' in Key*	Taj Mahal & the Phantom Blues Band
	Best Rap Performance by a Duo or Group	"Forgot About Dre"	Dr. Dre & Eminem
	Best Pop/Contemporary Gospel Album	*CeCe Winans*	CeCe Winans
	Best Traditional Soul Gospel Album	*You Can Make It*	Shirley Caesar
	Best Contemporary Soul Gospel Album	*Thankful*	Mary Mary
	Best Gospel Album by a Choir or Chorus	*Live…God Is Working*	Brooklyn Tabernacle Choir
	Best Reggae Album	*Art and Life*	Beenie Man
	Best Spoken Word Album	*The Measure of A Man*	Sidney Poitier
	Best Historical Album	*Louis Armstrong: The Complete Hot Five and Hot Seven Recodings*	
	Producer of the Year		Dr. Dre
2001	Best Rhythm & Blues Album	*Songs in A Minor*	Alicia Keys
	Best Rhythm & Blues Vocal Performance, Female	"Fallin'"	Alicia Keys
	Best Rhythm & Blues Vocal Performance, Male	"U Remind Me"	Usher
	Best Rhythm & Blues Performance by a Duo or Group	"Survivor"	Destiny's Child
	Best Traditional Rhythm & Blues Vocal Album	*At Last*	Gladys Knight
	Best Jazz Vocal Album	*The Calling*	Dianne Reeves
	Best Jazz Instrumental Album, Individual or Group	*This Is What I Do*	Sonny Rollins
	Best Rap Album	*Stankonia*	Outkast
	Best Rap Solo Performance	"Get Ur Freak On"	Missy Elliott
	Best Rap Performance by a Duo or Group	"Ms. Jackson"	Outkast
	Best Contemporary Blues Album	*Feels Like Rain*	Buddy Guy
	Best Traditional Soul Gospel Album	*Spirit of the Century*	Blind Boys of Alabama
	Best Contemporary Soul Gospel Album	*The Experience*	Yolanda Adams
	Best Gospel Album by a Choir or Chorus	*Love is Live!*	LFT Church Choir
	Best Reggae Album	*Halfway Tree*	Damian Marleyfor
	Best Spoken Word Album	*Q: The Autobiography of Quincy Jones*	Quincy Jones
	Song of the Year	"Fallin'"	Alicia Keys
	Best Dance Recording	"All for You"	Janet Jackson, Jimmy Jam, Terry Lewis, Steve Hoge
	Best Rap/Song Collaboration	"Let Me Blow Ya Mind"	Eve & Gwen Stefani
	Best Pop Vocal Album	*Lovers Rock*	Sade
	Best Rock Vocal Performance, Male	"Dig In"	Lenny Kravitz
	Best Historical Album	*Lady Day: The Complete Billie Holiday on Columbia, 1933–44*	
2002	Best Pop Performance by a Duo or Group	"Beauty and the Beast"	Celine Dion & Peabo Bryson
	Best Rhythm & Blues Album	*Voyage to India*	India.Arie
	Best Rhythm & Blues Vocal Performance, Female	"He Don't Think I Know"	Mary J. Blige
	Best Rhythm & Blues Vocal Performance, Male	"U Don't Have to Call"	Usher
	Best Rhythm & Blues Performance by a Duo or Group	"Love's in Need of Love Today"	Stevie Wonder & Take 6
	Best Traditional Rhythm & Blues Performance	"What's Goin' On"	Chaka Khan & The Funk Brothers
	Best Contemporary Rhythm & Blues Album	*Ashanti*	Ashanti
	Best Jazz Instrumental Solo Performance	"My Ship"	Herbie Hancock
	Best Jazz Instrumental Album, Individual or Group	*Directions in Music*	Michael Brecker, Herbie Hancock & Roy Hargrove
	Best Urban/Alternative Performance	"Little Things"	India.Arie
	Best Rap Solo Performance, Female	"Scream aka Itchin'"	Missy Elliott
	Best Rap Solo Performance, Male	"Hot in Herre"	Nelly
	Best Rap Performance by a Duo or Group	"The Whole World"	Outkast & Killer Mike
	Best Traditional Blues Album	*A Christmas Celebration of Hope*	B.B. King

[continued]

Grammy Award winners [CONTINUED]

Year	Category	Performance	Performer
	Best Contemporary Blues Album	*Don't Give Up on Me*	Solomon Burke
	Best Traditional Soul Gospel Album	*Higher Ground*	Blind Boys of Alabama
	Best Contemporary Soul Gospel Album	*Sidebars*	Eartha
	Best Gospel Album by a Choir or Chorus	*Be Glad*	Brooklyn Tabernacle Choir
	Best Reggae Album	*Jamaican E.T.*	Lee "Scratch" Perry
	Best Spoken Word Album	*A Song Flung Up to Heaven*	Maya Angelou
	Best Historical Album	*Scream' and Hollerin' the Blues: The Worlds of Charley Patton*	
	Best Pop Instrumental Performance	"Auld Lang Syne"	B.B. King
	Best Rhythm and Blues Song	"Love of My Life (An Ode to Hip Hop)"	Erykah Badee
	Best Rap/Sung Collaboration	"Dilemma"	Nelly & Kelly Rowlands
2003	Best New Album	*Speakerboxx/The Love Below*	Outkast
	Song of the Year	"Dance with My Father"	Luther Vandross
	Best Pop Collaboration with Vocals	"Whenever I Say Your Name"	Sting & Mary J. Blige
	Best Rhythm & Blues Album	*Dance With My Father*	Luther Vandross
	Best Contemporary Rhythm & Blues Album	*Dangerously in Love*	Beyoncé
	Best Rhythm & Blues Vocal Performance, Female	"Dangerously in Love 2"	Beyoncé
	Best Rhythm & Blues Vocal Performance, Male	"Dance with My Father"	Luther Vandross
	Best Rhythm & Blues Performance by a Duo or Group	"The Closer I Get to You"	Beyoncé & Luther Vandross
	Best Traditional Rhythm & Blues Vocal Performance	"Wonderful"	Aretha Franklin
	Best Urban/Alternative Performance	"Hey Ya!"	Outkast
	Best Rap Album	*Speakerboxx/The Love Below*	Outkast
	Best Rhythm and Blues Song	"Crazy in Love"	Beyoncé Knowles, Jay-Z, Rich Harrison
	Best Rap Solo Performance, Female	"Work It"	Missy Elliott
	Best Rap Performance by a Duo or Group	"Shake Ya Tailfeather"	Nelly, P. Diddy, Murphy Lee
	Best Rap/Sung Collaboration	"Crazy in Love"	Beyoncé & Jay Z
	Best Traditional Blues Album	*Blues Singer*	Buddy Guy
	Best Contemporary Blues Album	*Let's Roll*	Etta James
	Best Jazz Performance/Album	*A Little Moonlight*	Dianne Reeves
	Best Jazz Instrumental Album, Individual or Group	*Alegría*	Wayne Shorter
	Best Traditional Soul Gospel Album	*Go Tell It on the Mountain*	Blind Boys of Alabama
	Best Contemporary Soul Gospel Album	*...Again*	Donnie McClurkin
	Best Gospel Choir or Chorus Album	*A Wing and a Prayer*	Bishop T.D. Jakes & The Potter's House Mass Choir
	Best Reggae Album	*Dutty Rock*	Sean Paul
	Best Historical Album	*Martin Scorsese Presents the Blues: A Musical Journey*	
	Producer of the Year		The Neptunes
	Best Music Video, Long Form	*Legend*	Sam Cooke
	Best Instrumental Composition	*Sacajawea*	Wayne Shorter
2004	Album of the Year	*Genius Loves Company*	Ray Charles & Various Artists
	Record of the Year	"Here We Go Again"	Norah Jones & Ray Charles
	Best Pop Vocal Album	*Genius Loves Company*	Ray Charles & Various Artists
	Best Rhythm & Blues Album	*The Diary of Alicia Keys*	Alicia Keys
	Best Rhythm & Blues Vocal Performance, Female	"If I Ain't Got You"	Alicia Keys
	Best Rhythm & Blues Vocal Performance, Male	"Call My Name"	Prince
	Best Rhythm & Blues Performance by a Duo or Group	"My Boo"	Usher & Alicia Keys
	Best Traditional Blues Album	*Blues to the Bone*	Etta James
	Best Contemporary Blues Album	*Keep It Simple*	Keb' Mo'
	Best Traditional Rhythm & Blues Performance	"Musicology"	Prince
	Best Contemporary Rhythm & Blues Album	*Confessions*	Usher
	Best Jazz Performance/Album	*R.S.V.P. (Rare Songs, Very Personal)*	Nancy Wilson
	Best Jazz Instrumental Solo Performance	"Speak Like A Child"	Herbie Hancock
	Best Jazz Instrumental Album, Individual or Group	*Illuminations*	McCoy Tyner with Gary Bartz, Terence Blanchard, Christian McBride & Lewis Nash
	Best Rap Album	*The College Dropout*	Kanye West
	Best Rap Solo Performance, Male	"99 Problems"	Jay-Z
	Best Rap Performance by a Duo or Group	"Let's Get It Started"	Black Eyed Peas
	Best Rap/Song Collaboration	"Yeah!"	Usher, Lil Jon, Ludacris
	Best Rap Song	"Jesus Walks"	Kanye West, Che Smith, Miri Ben Ari

[continued]

Grammy Award winners [CONTINUED]

Year	Category	Performance	Performer
	Best Urban/Alternative Performance	"Cross My Mind"	Jill Scott
	Best Pop Instrumental Performance	"11ᵗʰ Commandment"	Ben Harper
	Best Pop Collaboration with Vocals	"Here We Go Again"	Ray Charles & Norah Jones
	Best Gospel Performance	"Heaven Help Us All"	Ray Charles & Gladys Knight
	Best Traditional Soul Gospel Album	*There Will Be A Light*	Ben Harper & Blind Boys of Alabama
	Best Contemporary Soul Gospel Album	*Nothing Without You*	Smokie Norful
	Best Gospel Album by a Choir or Chorus	*Live…This Is Your House*	Brooklyn Tabernacle Choir
	Best Reggae Album	*True Love*	Toots & the Maytals
	Best Historical Album	*Night Train to Nashville: Music City Rhythm and Blues, 1945–70*	
	Best Instrumental Arrangement	*Past, Present and Future*	Slide Hampton

FIGURE 5.1

Death rates in the U.S. by selected causes, 1960–2002*

Cause of death	Total					Black				
	1960	**1970**	**1980**	**1989**	**2002**	**1960**	**1970**	**1980**	**1989**	**2002**
Total	760.9	714.3	585.8	523.0	847.3	1,073.3	1,044.0	842.5	783.1	768.4
Diseases of the heart	286.2	253.6	202.0	155.9	241.7	334.5	307.6	255.7	216.4	205.6
Malignant neoplasms (cancer)	125.8	129.9	132.8	133.0	93.2	142.3	156.7	172.1	172.7	165.9
Cerebrovascular diseases[1]	79.7	66.3	40.8	28.0	56.4	18.6	140.2	114.5	68.5	49.0
Accidents and adverse effects	49.9	53.7	42.3	33.8	37.0	66.4	74.4	51.2	42.7	33.1
Homicide and legal intervention	—	9.1	10.8	9.4	6.2	—	46.1	40.6	35.7	22.3
Diabetes	13.6	14.1	10.1	11.5	25.4	22.0	26.5	20.3	23.7	33.6
Pneumonia, influenza[2]	28.0	22.1	12.9	13.7	22.8	56.4	40.4	19.2	19.8	15.6
Chronic lower respiratory diseases[3]	—	—	15.9	19.4	43.3	—	—	12.5	16.6	20.7
Cirrhosis and chronic liver disease	10.5	14.7	12.2	8.9	9.5	11.7	24.8	21.6	13.9	6.9
Suicide	—	11.8	11.4	11.3	11.0	—	6.1	6.4	7.1	5.1

* Deaths classified according to the revision of the International Classification of Diseases in use at that time; rates are per 100,000 for residential, age–adjusted population.

(1) Primarily strokes.

(2) 1960s figures for pneumonia and influenza

(3) Such as emphysema or asthma

— = data not available on a comparable basis with later years.

SOURCES: *National Abstract* (1984, 1992); U.S. National Center for Health Statistics, *Vital Statistics of the United States, 2004–2005.*

FIGURE 5.2

HIV/AIDS deaths in the U.S., 1987–2002*

Year	Black male	Black female	White male	White female	Total all races
1987	26.2	4.6	8.7	0.6	11.5
1990	46.3	10.1	15.7	1.1	18.5
1993	74.5	17.6	20.0	1.9	29.3
1995	89.0	24.4	20.4	2.5	27.3
1997	40.9	13.7	5.9	1.0	9.6
1998	33.2	12.0	4.5	0.8	7.6
1999	36.1	13.1	4.9	1.0	8.2
2000	35.1	13.2	4.6	1.0	7.9
2002	7.4	2.5	3.0	1.6	3.9

* Per 100,000 population.

SOURCES: *Black Americans: A Statistical Sourcebook* (2001) and *Statistical Abstract, 2004–2005.*

FIGURE 5.3

Birthrate, 1917–2002*

Year	Total	Black[+]
1917	28.5	32.9
1920	27.7	35.0
1930	21.3	27.5
1940	19.4	26.7
1950	24.1	33.3
1960	23.7	32.1
1970	18.4	25.3
1980	15.9	22.1
1990	16.7	22.4
2000	14.4	17.0
2001	14.1	16.3
2002	13.9	15.7

* Total live births per 1,000 population for specified group.
[+] Figures through 1960 are for total nonwhite births.

SOURCES: *Historical Statistics of the United States; Statistical Abstract, 1992*; U.S. National Center for Health Statistics data, 2005.

FIGURE 5.5

Life expectancy at birth, 1900–2000

Year	Total*	Black and other nonwhite**[+]
1900	47.3	33.0
1910	50.0	35.6
1920	54.1	45.3
1930	59.7	48.1
1940	62.9	53.1
1950	68.2	60.8
1960	69.7	63.6
1970	70.8	64.1
1980	73.7	68.1
1990	75.4	70.3
2000	77.0	71.7

* In years
[+] Figures through 1960 are for all nonwhites.

SOURCES: *Historical Statistics of the United States, Colonial Times to 1970*, part 1, p. 55; *Statistical Abstract, 1992*; *Statistical Abstract, 2004*.

FIGURE 5.4

Top ten countries in Central & South America and the Caribbean with the highest prevalence of HIV/AIDS cases, by percent of population, 2003

Number	Country	Total population	% Infected
1.	Haiti	7.6 million	5.6
2.	Trinidad & Tobago	1.1 million	3.2
3.	Bahamas	300,000	3.0
4.	Guyana	749,000	2.5
5.	Belize	273,000	2.4
6.	Honduras	6.9 million	1.8
7.	Dominican Republic	8.7 million	1.7
	Suriname	440,000	1.7
8.	Barbados	280,000	1.5
9.	Jamaica	2.7 million	1.2

FIGURE 6.1

Presidential Medal of Freedom honorees

1963	Marian Anderson, singer
	Ralph J. Bunche, scholar, diplomat—with distinction
1964	Lena F. Edwards, physician, humanitarian
	Leontyne Price, singer
	A. Philip Randolph, trade unionist
1969	Ralph Ellison, writer
	Roy Wilkins, civil rights leader
	Whitney M. Young, social worker
	Edward Kennedy "Duke" Ellington, pianist, composer
1976	Jesse Owens, athlete, humanitarian
1977	Martin Luther King, Jr., civil rights leader (posthumously)
1980	Andrew Young, public servant
	Clarence M. Mitchell, Jr., lawyer, civil rights activist
1981	James H. "Eubie" Blake, ragtime pianist and composer
	Andrew Young, public servant
1983	James Edward Cheek, educator, scholar
	Mabel Mercer, singer
1984	Jack Roosevelt Robinson, sportsman, baseball player (posthumously)
1985	William "Count" Basie, jazz pianist
	Jerome H. Holland, educator and ambassador, president of American Red Cross (posthumously)
1988	Pearl Bailey, entertainer
1991	Colin L. Powell, general, U.S. Army
	Leon Howard Sullivan, civil rights leader
1992	Ella Fitzgerald, singer
1993	Arthur Ashe, tennis player (posthumously)
	Thurgood Marshall, jurist (posthumously)
	Colin L. Powell, general, U.S. Army
1994	Dorothy Height, humanitarian
	Barbara Jordan, orator
1995	John Hope Franklin, educator, author
	William T. Coleman, Jr., lawyer, government official
	A. Leon Higginbotham, Jr., jurist
1996	James L. Farmer, civil rights leader
	John H. Johnson, publisher
	Rosa Parks, civil rights activist
2000	Marian Wright Edelman, humanitarian
	Jesse Jackson, religious and social leader
2002	Bill Cosby, entertainer
2003	Roberto Clemente, baseball player (posthumously)

FIGURE 6.2

Pulitzer Prize winners

Year	Recipient	Category
1950	Gwendolyn Brooks	Poetry
1969	Moneta Sleet, Jr.	Photography
1970	Charles Gordone	Drama
1975	Ovie Carter	International Reporting
	Matthew Lewis	Feature Photography
1976	Scott Joplin (posthumous)	Special Awards and Citations—Music
1977	Alex Haley	Special Awards and Citations—Letters
	Acel Moore	Local Investigative Specialized Reporting
1978	James Alan McPherson	Fiction
1982	Charles Fuller	Drama
	John H. White	Feature Photography
1983	Alice Walker	Fiction
1984	Kenneth Cooper	Local Investigative Specialized Reporting
	Norman Lockman	Local Investigative Specialized Reporting
1985	Dennis Bell	International Reporting
	Ozier Muhammad	International Reporting
1986	Michel duCille	Spot News Photography
1987	Michel duCille	Feature Photography
	Rita Dove	Poetry
1988	August Wilson	Drama
	Toni Morrison	Fiction
	Dean Baquet	Investigative Reporting
1989	Clarence Page	Commentary
1990	Rita Dove	Poetry
1994	Yusef Komunyakaa	Poetry
	David Levering Lewis	Biography
	William Raspberry	Commentary
	Isabel Wilkerson	Feature Writing
1995	Leon Dash	Explanatory Journalism
	Margo Jefferson	Criticism
1996	E.R. Shipp	Commentary
	George Walker	Music
1997	Wynton Marsalis	Music
1998	Clarence J. Williams	Feature Writing
1999	Angelo B. Henderson	Feature Writing
2001	David Levering Lewis	Biography
2002	Suzan Lori-Parks	Drama
2003	Colbert I. King	Commentary
2004	Edward P. Jones	Fiction
	Leonard Pitts, Jr.	Commentary

FIGURE 6.3

African Americans on U.S. postage stamps*	
Name	**Date appeared**
Thirteenth Amendment	1940
Booker T. Washington	1940; 1956
George Washington Carver	1948; 1998
Emancipation Proclamation	1963
Frederick Douglass	1967
Peter Salem	1968
W.C. Handy	1969
Henry O. Tanner	1973
Paul Laurence Dunbar	1975
Salem Poor	1975
Harriet Tubman	1978; 1995
Martin Luther King, Jr.	1979; 1999
Benjamin Banneker	1980
Whitney M. Young, Jr.	1981
Charles Drew	1981
Ralph J. Bunche	1982
Jackie Robinson	1982
Scott Joplin	1983
Carter G. Woodson	1984
Roberto Clemente	1984; 2000
Mary McLeod Bethune	1985
Sojourner Truth	1986
Duke Ellington	1986
Matthew A. Henson	1986
Jean Baptiste Pointe DuSable	1987
James Weldon Johnson	1988
A. Philip Randolph	1989
Ida B. Wells	1990
Jesse Owens	1990; 1998
Jan E. Matzeliger	1991; 1998
W. E. B. Du Bois	1992
Percy Lavon Julian	1993
Joe Louis	1993
Otis Redding	1993
Clyde McPhatter	1993
Dinah Washington	1993
Porgy and Bess	1993
Allison Davis	1994
Bill Pickett	1994
Jim Beckwourth	1994
Bessie Smith	1994
Billie Holiday	1994
Buffalo Soldier	1994
Jimmy Rushing	1994
Muddy Waters	1994
Robert Johnson	1994
Ma Rainey	1994
Howlin' Wolf	1994
Ethel Waters	1994
Olympic Games and Sports	1994
Nat "King" Cole	1994
Louis Armstrong	1995
Eubie Blake	1995
Bessie Coleman	1995
John Coltrane	1995
Frederick Douglass	1995
Erroll Garner	1995
Coleman Hawkins	1995
John Henry	1996
James P. Johnson	1995
Charles Mingus	1995
Thelonious Monk	1995
Jelly Roll Morton	1995
Charlie Parker	1995
Count Basie	1996
[continued]	

African Americans on U.S. postage stamps* [CONTINUED]	
Name	**Date appeared**
Ernest E. Just	1996
Benjamin O. Davis, Sr.	1997
Mahalia Jackson	1998
Jazz Flourishes	1998
Leadbelly	1998
Roberta Martin	1998
Sister Rosetta Tharpe	1998
Madam C.J. Walker	1998
Clara Ward	1998
Josh White	1998
Desegregating Public Schools	1999
Malcolm X	1999
Josh Gibson	2000
Patricia Roberts Harris	2000
Satchel Paige	2000
Jackie Robinson	2000
Roy Wilkins	2001
Langston Hughes	2002
Ethel L. Payne	2002
Zora Neale Hurston	2003
Thurgood Marshall	2003
Alvin Ailey	2004
James Baldwin	2004
Kwanzaa	2004
Paul Robeson	2004
Wilma Rudolph	2004
Sickle Cell Disease Awareness	2004
Arthur Ashe	2005
Marian Anderson	2005
Brown v. Board of Education	2005
Civil Rights Act of 1964	2005
Freedom Riders	2005
Little Rock Nine	2005
Lunch Counter Sit-Ins	2005
Montgomery Bus Boycott	2005
Selma March	2005
Executive Order 9981	2005
March on Washington	2005
Voting Rights Act of 1965	2005

* Includes people as well as important events in African American history.

FIGURE 6.4

Nobel Prize winners

Year	Winner	Birth–Death	Country	Category
1950	Ralph J. Bunche	(8/7/04–12/9/71)	United States	Peace
1964	Martin Luther King, Jr.	(1/15/29–4/4/68)	United States	Peace
1979	Arthur W. Lewis	(1/23/15–6/15/91)	St. Lucia	Economic Sciences
1992	Derek Alton Walcott	(1/23/30–)	St. Lucia	Literature
1993	Toni Morrison	(2/18/31–)	United States	Literature

FIGURE 7.1

| Occupations in the U.S., 1890–2000[1] | | | | | |

Year	Occupations	Total	Black		
			Both sexes	Male	Female
1890	All occupations	22,735,661	3,073,161	2,101,379	971,782
	Agriculture, fisheries & mining	9,013,336	1,757,403	1,329,594	427,809
	Professional services	944,333	33,991	25,170	8,821
	Domestic & personal services	4,360,577	963,080	457,091	505,989
	Trade & transportation	3,326,122	145,717	143,371	2,346
	Manufacturing & mech. industries	5,091,293	172,970	146,153	582,001
1900	All occupations	29,287,070	3,992,337	2,675,497	1,316,840
	Agriculture, fisheries & mining	10,438,219	2,143,154	1,561,153	582,001
	Professional services	1,264,536	47,219	31,625	15,594
	Domestic & personal services	5,693,778	1,317,859	635,933	681,926
	Trade & transportation	4,778,233	208,989	204,852	4,137
	Manufacturing & mech. industries	7,112,304	275,116	241,934	33,182
1910	All occupations	28,167,336	5,192,535	3,178,554	2,013,981
	Agriculture, forestry & husbandry	12,659,203	3,893,375	1,842,238	1,051,137
	Extraction of minerals	964,824	61,629	61,048	81
	Manufacturing & mech. industries	10,658,881	631,377	563,410	67,967
	Transportation	2,637,671	255,969	254,683	1,286
	Trade	3,614,670	119,491	112,464	7,027
	Public service (N.E.C)*	459,291	22,382	22,033	349
	Professional service	1,663,569	67,245	37,600	29,645
	Domestic & personal service	3,772,194	1,122,231	268,874	853,357
	Clerical occupation	1,737,053	19,336	16,204	3,132
1920	All occupations	41,617,248	4,824,151	3,252,862	1,571,289
	Agriculture, forestry & husbandry	10,953,158	2,178,888	1,566,627	612,261
	Extraction of minerals	1,090,223	73,229	72,892	337
	Manufacturing & mech. industries	12,818,524	886,810	781,827	104,983
	Transportation	3,063,582	312,421	308,896	3,525
	Trade	4,242,979	140,467	129,309	11,158
	Public service (N.E.C.)*	770,460	50,552	49,586	966
	Professional service	2,143,889	80,183	41,056	39,127
	Domestic & personal service	3,404,892	1,064,590	273,959	790,631
	Clerical occupation	3,126,541	37,011	28,710	8,301
1930	All occupations	48,829,920	5,503,535	3,662,893	1,840,642
	Agriculture	10,471,998	1,987,839	1,492,555	1,840,642
	Forestry & fishing	250,469	31,732	31,652	80
	Extraction of minerals	984,323	74,972	74,919	53
	Manufacturing & mech. industries	14,110,652	1,024,656	923,586	101,070
	Transportation & communication	3,843,147	397,645	395,437	2,208
	Trade	6,081,467	183,809	169,241	14,568
	Public service (N.E.C.)*	856,205	50,203	49,273	930
	Professional service	3,253,884	135,925	72,898	63,027
	Domestic & professional service	4,952,451	1,576,205	423,645	1,152,560
	Clerical occupation	4,025,324	40,529	29,687	10,862

[continued]

Occupations in the U.S., 1890–2000[1] [CONTINUED]

Year	Occupations	Total	Black Both sexes	Black Male	Black Female
1940	All occupations**	44,000,963	4,479,068	2,936,795	1,542,273
	Professional & semi-pro workers	3,345,048	119,200	53,312	65,888
	Farmers & farm managers	5,143,614	666,695	620,479	46,216
	Proprietors, managers, & officials, except farm	3,749,287	48,154	37,240	10,914
	Clerical, sales & kindred workers	7,517,630	79,332	58,557	20,765
	Craftsmen, foremen & kindred workers	5,055,722	132,110	129,736	2,374
	Operatives and kindred workers	8,252,277	464,195	368,005	96,190
	Domestic service workers	2,111,314	1,003,508	85,566	917,942
	Service workers, except domestic	3,458,334	522,229	362,424	159,805
	Farm laborers & foremen	1,924,890	780,312	581,763	198,549
	Laborers, except farm and mine	3,064,128	636,600	623,641	12,959
	Occupation not reported	378,719	26,743	16,072	10,671
1950	All occupations	56,225,340	5,832,450	3,787,560	2,044,890
	Prof., tech., & kindred workers	4,909,241	179,370	75,090	104,280
	Farmers and farm managers	4,306,253	503,970	471,180	32,790
	Managers, officials, & proprietors, except farm	5,017,465	97,080	71,130	25,950
	Clerical & kindred workers	6,894,374	197,610	116,760	80,850
	Sales workers	3,926,510	68,460	42,030	26,430
	Craftsmen, foremen & kindred workers	7,772,560	310,830	297,540	13,290
	Operatives & kindred workers	11,146,220	1,092,750	792,060	300,690
	Private household workers (PHW)	1,407,466	571,950	38,700	533,250
	Service workers, except PHW	4,287,703	877,440	498,180	379,260
	Farm laborers & foremen	2,399,794	529,920	377,460	152,460
	Laborers, except farm and mine	3,417,232	936,120	904,230	31,890
	Occupations not reported	740,522	166,950	103,200	63,750
1960	All occupations***	64,646,563	6,622,658	4,004,770	2,617,888
	Prof., tech., & kindred workers	7,223,241	352,298	155,774	196,524
	Farmers & farm managers	2,508,172			
	Managers, officials & proprietors, including farm	5,407,890	315,152	267,855	196,524
	Clerical & kindred workers	9,303,231	433,090	206,269	226,821
	Sales workers	4,643,784	108,316	62,274	46,042
	Craftsmen, foremen & kindred workers	8,753,468	424,817	407,343	17,474
	Operatives & kindred workers	11,920,442	1,278,134	941,073	337,061
	Service workers, including PHW	7,171,837	2,015,683	580,090	1,435,593
	Laborers, including farm	4,532,950	1,154,253	1,052,092	102,161
	Occupation not reported	3,181,548	540,915	332,000	208,915
1970	All occupations	76,805,171	7,403,056	4,069,397	3,33,659
	Prof., tech. & kindred workers	11,451,868	616,321	237,733	378,588
	Managers & administrators, except farm	6,386,977	166,187	119,562	46,625
	Sales workers	5,432,778	165,767	80,686	85,081
	Clerical & kindred workers	13,782,783	1,021,589	330,492	691,097
	Craftsmen & kindred workers	10,638,804	674,849	626,709	48,140
	Operatives, except transport	10,515,834	1,333,099	798,945	534,154
	Transport equipment operatives	2,954,932	416,146	403,209	12,937
	Laborers, except farm	3,430,637	688,212	639,840	48,140
	Farmers and farm managers	1,426,742	42,001	36,928	5,073
	Farm laborers & farm foremen	962,077	181,465	144,266	37,199
	Service workers, except PHW	8,653,987	1,483,993	633,538	850,455
	Private household workers	1,167,752	613,427	17,489	595,938

[continued]

Occupations in the U.S., 1890–2000[1] [CONTINUED]

Year	Occupations	Total	Black Both sexes	Black Male	Black Female
1980	All occupations	97,639,355	9,334,048	4,674,871	4,659,177
	Managerial & prof. specialty occupations	22,151,648	1,317,080	546,271	770,809
	Tech. sales & admin. support occupations	29,593,506	2,352,079	712,342	1,639,737
	Service occupations	12,269,425	2,156,194	792,530	1,363,664
	Farming, forestry & fishing occupations	2,811,258	182,190	156,822	25,368
	Precision product, craft & repair	12,594,175	834,947	726,192	108,755
	Operators, fabricators & laborers	17,859,343	2,491,558	1,740,714	750,844
1990	All occupations	127,041,599	12,775,917	6,102,232	6,673,685
	Managerial & prof. specialty occupations	31,226,845	2,156,676	821,977	1,334,699
	Tech. sales & admin. support occupations	38,525,740	3,723,838	1,130,062	2,593,776
	Service occupations	16,567,557	2,886,289	1,179,182	1,707,107
	Farming, forestry & fishing occupations	7,673,495	203,383	175,111	28,272
	Precision product, craft, & repair occupations	14,031,300	1,051,714	889,906	161,808
	Operators, fabricators & laborers	18,976,662	2,754,017	1,905,994	848,023
2000	Total employed population, 16 years and over	129,721,512	13,001,795	n.a.	n.a.
	Management, prof., and related occupations	43,646,731	10,998,976	n.a.	n.a.
	Service occupations	19,276,947	4,240,928	n.a.	n.a.
	Sales and office occupations	34,621,390	9,451,639	n.a.	n.a.
	Farming, fishing, and forestry occupations	951,810	38,072	n.a.	n.a.
	Construction, extractions, and maintenance occupations	12,256,138	796,649	n.a.	n.a.
	Production, transportation, and material moving occupations	18,968,496	3,528,140	n.a.	n.a.

(1) Methods of improving classification have been implemented by the Bureau of the Census over the years, making comparison of data difficult. A large-scale reworking of the classification system was put in place in 1940 (a partial key is included for that year). In some cases there were changes in title with no change in content. In others there were no changes in title but changes in content. Complete information on changes in occupational classification can be obtained from the Bureau of the Census and, for the 1940 census, from Alba M. Edwards, *Population: Comparative Occupation Statistics for the United States, 1870 to 1940* (Washington D.C., 1943).

*   N.E.C.=Not Elsewhere Classified

** Key to 1940 Census:

"Operatives and kindred workers" includes apprentices, attendants, brakemen, chauffeurs, conductors, motormen, power-station operators, mechanical workers in manufacturing plants, etc.

"Laborers, except farm and mine" workers includes fishermen and oystermen, longshoremen, lumbermen, laborers (not specified) in manufacturing plants, etc.

"Proprietors, managers, and officials, except farm" workers includes proprietors and managers of transportation and communication utilities, eating and drinking establishments, wholesale companies, advertising and insurance agencies, etc., and postmasters and miscellaneous government officials.

"Clerical, sales, and kindred workers" includes baggagemen, bookkeepers, mail carriers, office-machine operators, telegraph operators, canvassers and solicitors, clerks in stores, and salesmen and saleswomen.

"Craftsmen, foremen, and kindred workers" includes bakers, blacksmiths, boilermakers, carpenters, electricians, and foremen in industry.

"Professional and semiprofessional" workers includes actors, architects, authors, chemists, clergymen, dentists, engineers, lawyers, musicians, pharmacists, teachers, trained nurses, surveyors, etc.

"Service workers, except domestic" workers includes barbers, beauticians and manicurists, charwomen, janitors, cooks, waiters, etc.

***Data for 1960 are based on a 5 percent sample.

SOURCE: U.S. Census data, 1890–2000.

FIGURE 8.1

African-American mayors of U.S. cities with populations over 50,000, 1967–2005[1]

City	Mayor	Term
Alexandria, Va.	William D. Euille	2003—
Ann Arbor, Mich.	Albert Wheeler	1975–1978
Atlanta, Ga.	Maynard H. Jackson	1973–1982
	Andrew J. Young	1982–1990
	Maynard H. Jackson	1990–1993
	Bill Campbell	1994–2002
	Shirley Franklin	2002—
Baltimore, Md.	Clarence H. "Dru" Burns	1986–1987
	Kurt L. Schmoke	1987–1999
Berkeley, Calif.	Warren H. Widener	1971–1979
	Eugene "Gus" Newport	1979–1986
Birmingham, Ala.	Richard Arrington, Jr.	1979–1983
	Bernard Kincaid	1999—
Boulder, Colo.	Penfield W. Tate III	1974–1976
Cambridge, Mass.	Kenneth S. Reeves	1992–1995
Camden, N.J.	Melvin R. Primas, Jr.	1981–1990
	Aaron Thompson	1990–1993
	Arnold Webster	1993–1997
	Gwendolyn A. Faison	2000—
Carson, Calif.[2]	Clarence A. Bridgers	1975–1976
	Thomas G. Mills	1982–1986
Chandler, Ariz.	Coy Payne	1990–1994
Charlotte, N.C.	Harvey B. Gantt	1983–1987
Chesapeake, Va.		1990–2004
Chicago, Ill.	Harold Washington	1983–1987
	Eugene Sawyer	1987–1991
Cincinnati, Ohio	Theodore M. Berry	1972–1975
	John K. Blackwell	1979–1980
	Dwight Tillery	1991–1993
Cleveland, Ohio	Carl B. Stokes	1967–1971
	Michael R. White	1989–2000
Columbus, Ohio	Michael B. Coleman	1999—
Compton, Calif.	Douglas F. Dollarhide	1969–1973
	Doris A. Davis	1973–1977
	Lionel Cade	1977–1981
	Walter R. Tucker III	1981–1992
	Bernice Wood (interim appt.)	1992–1993
	Omar Bradley	1993–2001
	Eric Perrodin	2001—
Dayton, Ohio	James H. McGee	1970–1982
	Richard Clay Dixon	1989–1993
	Rhine McLin	2002—
Denver, Colo.	Wellington E. Webb	1991–2003
Detroit, Mich.	Coleman A. Young	1974–1993
	Dennis Archer	1993–2002
	Kwame Kilpatrick	2002—
Durham, N.C.	William V. Bell	2001—
East Orange, N.J.	William S. Hart, Sr.	1970–1978
	Thomas H. Cooke	1978–1985
	John Hatcher, Jr.	1985–1989
	Cardell Cooper	1990–1997
	Robert Bowser	1998—

[continued]

African-American mayors of U.S. cities with populations over 50,000, 1967–2005[1] [CONTINUED]

City	Mayor	Term
East St. Louis, Ill.	James E. Williams, Sr.	1971–1975
	William E. Mason	1975–1979
	Carl E. Officer	1979–1991
	Gordon D. Bush	1991–n.d.
Evanston, Ill.	Lorraine H. Morton	1993—
Fayetteville, N.C.	Marshall B. Pitts, Jr.	2001—
Flint, Mich.	James A. Sharp	1984–1987
	Stanley Woodrow	1991–2002
Gary, Ind.	Richard G. Hatcher	1967–1988
	Thomas Barnes	1988–1992
Grand Rapids, Mich.	Lyman S. Parks	1973–1975
Hampton, Va.	Mamie E. Locke	2000–2004
Hartford, Conn.	Thirman L. Milner	1981–1987
	Carrie Perry	1987–1993
Inglewood, Calif.	Edward Vincent	1983–1995
	Roosevelt S. Dorn	1997—
Irvington, N.J.	Michael Steele	1990–1994
	Wayne Smith	2002—
Jackson, Miss.	Harvey Johnson	1997—
Jersey City, N.J.	Glenn D. Cunningham	2001–2004
Kalamazoo, Mich.	Robert Jones	1997—
Kansas City, Mo.	Emanuel Cleaver II	1991–1999
Little Rock, Ark.	Charles Bussey	1981–1982
	Lottie Shakelford	1987–1988
Los Angeles, Calif.	Thomas Bradley	1973–1993
Macon, Ga.	Jack Ellis	1999—
Memphis, Tenn.	Willie Herenton	1991—
Miami Gardens, Fla.	Shirley Gibson	2003—
Minneapolis, Minn.	Sharon Sayles Belton	1994–2001
Monroe, La.	James Mayo	2001—
Mt. Vernon, N.Y.	Ronald A. Blackwood	1985–n.d.
	Ernest D. Davis	1995—
New Haven, Conn.	John C. Daniels, Jr.	1990
New Orleans, La.	Ernest N. "Dutch" Morial	1978–1986
	Sidney Barthelemy	1986–1994
	C. Ray Nagin	2002—
New York, N.Y.	David Dinkins	1990–1994
Newark, N.J.	Kenneth A. Gibson	1970–1986
	Sharpe James	1986—
Newport News, Va.	Jessie M. Rattley	1986–1990
North Miami, Fla.	Josaphat "Joe" Celestin	2001–2005
Oceanside, Calif.	Terry Johnson	2000–2004
Oakland, Calif.	Lionel J. Wilson	1977–1990
	Elihu M. Harris	1992–1999
Pasadena, Calif.	Loretta Thompson–Glickman	1982–1984
Philadelphia, Pa.	Wilson Goode	1983–1991
	John F. Street	2000—
Pompano Beach, Fla.	Pat Larkins	1985–1989

[continued]

African-American mayors of U.S. cities with populations over 50,000, 1967–2005[1] [CONTINUED]

City	Mayor	Term
Pontiac, Mich.	Wallace E. Holland	1974–1986
	Walter L. Moore	1986–1989
	Wallace E. Holland	1989–1993
	Charles Harrisson	1994–n.d.
	Willie Payne	2002—
Portsmouth, Va.	James W. Holley	1984–1987, 1996—
Raleigh, N.C.	Clarence Lightner	1973–1975
Richmond, Calif.	Booker T. Anderson	1969–1975
	George Livingston	1985–n.d.
	Irma Anderson	2001—
Richmond, Va.	Henry L. Marsh III	1977–1982
	Roy A. West	1982–1988
	Walter T. Kenney	1990–1994
	Rudolph C. McCollum, Jr.	2001–2004
Roanoke, Va.	Noel C. Taylor	1975–1992
Rochester, N.Y.	William Johnson	1993–2003
Rockford, Ill.	Charles E. Box	1989–n.a.
Saginaw, Mich.	S. Joe Stephens	1977–1979
	Lawrence D. Crawford	1983–1987
	Henry Nickelberry	1989–1993
	Gary Loster	1994–2001
	Wilmer Jones–Ham	2001—
Santa Monica, Calif.	Nathaniel Trives	1975–1979
Savannah, Ga.	Otis Johnson	2004—
Seattle, Wash.	Norman B. Rice	1990—
Southfield, Mich.	Brenda L. Lawrence	2001—
Spokane, Wash.	James Chase	1982–1985
St. Louis, Mo.	Freeman Bosley, Jr.	1993–1997
Tallahassee, Fla.[2]	James R. Ford	1972, 1976, 1982
	Jack McLean	1986–n.d.
	Dorothy J. (Lee) Inman	1989, 1993
Toledo, Ohio	Jack Ford	2001—
Trenton, N.J.	Douglas H. Palmer	1990—
Washington, D.C.[3]	Walter E. Washington	1974–1979
	Marion S. Barry, Jr.	1979–1990
	Sharon Pratt Kelly	1990–1994
	Anthony A. Williams	1999—
West Palm Beach, Fla.	Eva W. Mack	1982–1984
	Samuel A. Thomas	1986–1987
	James Poole	1989–1991
Wichita, Kans.	Price Woodard	1970–1971
Wilmington, Del.	James H. Sills, Jr.	1993–2001
	James M. Baker	2001—

(1) As of July 2005

(2) City council members of these cities each serve mayoral terms of one year at a time

(3) Washington, D.C., began holding mayoral elections in 1974

FIGURE 8.2

Black heads of state in the Americas and the Caribbean, 2005

Country	Head of state	Appointed/elected
The Caribbean		
Anguilla	Osbourne Fleming	March 3, 2000
Antigua and Barbuda	Winston Baldwin Spencer	March 24, 2004
Aruba	Nelson O. Oduber	October 30, 2001
Barbados	Owen Seymour Arthur	September 7, 1994
The Bahamas	Perry Christie	May 3, 2002
Bermuda	William Alexander Scott	July 24, 2003
British Virgin Islands	D. Orlando Smith	June 17, 2003
Dominica	Roosevelt Skerrit	January 8, 2004
Grenada	Keith Mitchell	June 22, 1995
Guadeloupe	Jacques Gillot	March 26, 2001
Jamaica	Percival James Patterson	March 30, 1992
Montserrat	John Osborne	April 5, 2001
Netherlands Antilles	Etienne Ys	June 3, 2004
St. Kitts and Nevis	Denzil Douglas	July 6, 1995
Trinidad and Tobago	Patrick Manning	December 24, 2001
Turks and Caicos	Michael Eugene Misick	August 15, 2003
U.S. Virgin Islands	Charles Wesley Turnbull	January 5, 1999
South America		
Guyana	Samuel Hinds	December 1997
Suriname	Runaldo Ronald Venetiaan	August 12, 2000

SOURCE: CIA World Factbook.

FIGURE 8.3

African-Americans in the U.S. Congress, 1870–2005

Name	Term
U.S. Senate	
Hiram R. Revel (R-MS)	1870–1871
Blanche K. Bruce (R-MS)	1875–1881
Edward W. Brooke (R-MA)	1967–1979
Carol Mosley Braun (D-IL)	1993–1999
Barack Obama (D-IL)	2005—
U.S. House of Representatives	
Joseph H. Rainey (R-SC)	1870–1879
Jefferson F. Long (R-GA)	1870–1871
Robert B. Elliott (R-SC)	1871–1874
Robert C. DeLarge (R-SC)	1871–1873
Benjamin S. Turner (R-AL)	1871–1873
Josiah T. Walls (R-FL)	1871–1873; 1873–1875; 1875–1876
Richard H. Cain (R-SC)	1873–1875; 1877–1879
John R. Lynch (R-MS)	1873–1877; 1882–1883
James T. Rapier (R-AL)	1873–1875
Alonzo J. Ransier (R-SC)	1873–1875
Jeremiah Haralson (R-AL)	1875–1877
John A. Hyman (R-NC)	1875–1877
Charles E. Nash (R-LA)	1875–1877
Robert Smalls (R-SC)	1875–1879
James E. O'Hara (R-NC)	1883–1887
Henry P. Cheatham (R-NC)	1889–1893
John M. Langston (R-VA)	1890–1891
Thomas E. Miller (R-SC)	1890–1891
George W. Murray (R-SC)	1893–1895; 1896–1897
George H. White (R-NC)	1897–1901
Oscar DePriest (R-IL)	1929–1935
Arthur W. Mitchell (D-IL)	1935–1943
William L. Dawson (D-IL)	1943–1970
Adam C. Powell, Jr. (D-NY)	1945–1967; 1969–1971
Charles C. Diggs, Jr. (D-MI)	1955–1980
Robert N.C. Nix (D-PA)	1958–1979
Augustus F. Hawkins (D-CA)	1963–1991
John Conyers, Jr. (D-MI)	1965—
William L. Clay (D-MO)	1969–2001
Louis Stokes (D-OH)	1969–1999
Shirley A. Chisholm (D-NY)	1969–1983
George H. Collins (D-IL)	1970–1972
Ronald V. Dellums (D-CA)	1971–1998
Ralph H. Metcalfe (D-IL)	1971–1979
Parren H. Mitchell (D-MD)	1971–1987
Charles B. Rangel (D-NY)	1971—
Walter E. Fauntroy (D-DC)*	1971–1991
Yvonne B. Burke (D-CA)	1973–1979
Cardiss Collins (D-IL)	1973–1997
Barbara C. Jordan (D-TX)	1973–1979
Andrew J. Young (D-GA)	1973–1977
Harold E. Ford (D-TN)	1975–1997
Bennett M. Stewart (D-IL)	1979–1981
Julian C. Dixon (D-CA)	1979–2000
William H. Gray (D-PA)	1979–1991
Mickey Leland (D-TX)	1979–1989
Melvin Evans (R-V.I.)*	1979–1981
George W. Crockett, Jr. (D-MI)	1980–1991
Mervyn M. Dymally (D-CA)	1981–1993
Gus Savage (D-IL)	1981–1993
Harold Washington (D-IL)	1981–1983
Katie B. Hall (D-IN)	1982–1985
Major R. Owens (D-NY)	1983—
[continued]	

African-Americans in the U.S. Congress, 1870–2005
[CONTINUED]

Name	Term
Edolphus Towns (D-NY)	1983—
Alan Wheat (D-MO)	1983–1995
Charles A. Hayes (D-IL)	1983–1993
Alton R. Waldon, Jr. (D-NY)	1986–1987
Mike Espy (D-MS)	1987–1993
Floyd H. Flake (D-NY)	1987–1997
John Lewis (D-GA)	1987—
Kweisi Mfume (D-MD)	1987–1996
Donald M. Payne (D-NJ)	1989—
Craig A. Washington (D-TX)	1989–1995
Barbara R. Collins (D-MI)	1991–1997
Gary A. Franks (R-CT)	1991–1997
William J. Jefferson (D-LA)	1991—
Eleanor H. Norton (D-DC)*	1991—
Maxine Waters (D-CA)	1991—
Lucian E. Blackwell (D-PA)	1991–1995
Eva M. Clayton (D-NC)	1992–2003
Sanford Bishop (D-GA)	1993—
Corrine Brown (D-FL)	1993—
James E. Clyburn (D-SC)	1993—
Cleo Fields (D-LA)	1993–1997
Alcee L. Hastings (D-FL)	1993—
Earl F. Hilliard (D-AL)	1993–2003
Eddie B. Johnson (D-TX)	1993—
Cynthia McKinney (D-GA)	1993–2003
Carrie Meek (D-FL)	1993–2003
Mel Reynolds (D-IL)	1993–1995
Bobby L. Rush (D-IL)	1993—
Robert C. Scott (D-VA)	1993—
Walter R. Tucker III (D-CA)	1993–1995
Melvin Watt (D-NC)	1993—
Albert R. Wynn (D-MD)	1993—
Bennie G. Thompson (D-MS)	1993—
Chaka Fattah (D-PA)	1995—
Victor O. Frazer (D-Virgin Islands)	1995–1997
Jesse L. Jackson, Jr. (D-IL)	1995—
Sheila Jackson Lee (D-TX)	1995—
J.C. Watts, Jr. (R-OK)	1995–2003
Elijah E. Cummings (D-MD)	1996—
Juanita Millender-McDonald (D-CA)	1996—
Julia M. Carson (D-IN)	1997—
Danny K. Davis (D-IL)	1997—
Harold E. Ford, Jr. (D-TN)	1997—
Carolyn Cheeks Kilpatrick (D-MI)	1997—
Barbara Lee (D-CA)	1998—
Gregory Meeks (D-NY)	1998—
Stephanie Tubbs Jones (D-OH)	1999—
Diane E. Watson (D-CA)	2001—
Artur Davis (D-AL)	2003—
Kendrick Meek (D-FL)	2003—
Denise L. Majette (D-GA)	2003—
David Scott (D-GA)	2003–2005
Frank W. Ballance (D-NC)	2004—
G.K. Butterfield (D-NC)	2004—
Emanuel Cleaver II (D-MO)	2005—
Al Green (D-TX)	2005—
Gwen Moore (D-WI)	2005—

* Indicates members of Congress with restricted voting.

FIGURE 9.1

Households, total number, average size, 1890–2004

Year	Total	Black[1]	Total	Black
1890	12,960	1,411	4.93	5.32
1900	15,964	1,834	4.76	4.83
1910	20,256	2,173	4.54	4.54
1920	24,352	2,431	4.34	4.31
1930	29,905	2,804	4.11	4.27
1940	34,949	3,142	3.67	4.12
1950	43,554	3,822	3.33	3.82
1960	52,799	4,779	3.33	3.54
1970	63,401	6,180	3.14	3.06
1980	80,390	8,382	2.75	3.06
1990	93,347	10,486	2.63	n.a.
2000	104,705	12,849	2.62	n.a.
2004	112,000	13,629	2.57	2.64

* A household consists of all persons who occupy a housing unit, which is a house, apartment, or other group of rooms occupied or intended as separate living quarters.

(1) For years prior to 2003 multiple race reporting was not available to CPS respondents. The category shown as "Black" refers to Black Alone.

SOURCE: *Statistical Abstracts, 1992: Historical Statistics of the United States, Colonial Times to 1970; The Social and Economic Status of the Black Population in the United States: An Historical View, 1790–1978*; U.S. Bureau of the Census, 1980; U.S. Bureau of the Census, 2005.

FIGURE 9.2

Black population by selected countries, 2003

Country	Total population	% Black
Argentina	38.7 million	3*
Barbados	280 thousand	90
Bahamas	300 thousand	85
Bermuda	64.5 thousand	58
Brazil	182.0 million	44
Canada	32.2 million	2
Cuba	11.3 million	11
Colombia	44.5 million	4**
Dominican Republic	8.7 million	11
Grenada	89.3 thousand	82
Guatemala	13.9 million	2*
Haiti	7.6 million	95
Honduras	6.7 million	2
Jamaica	2.7 million	90.9
Mexico	104.9 million	1*
Peru	27.9 million	1*
United States	290.3 million	12.9
Uruguay	3.4 million	4
Venezuela	24.7 million	1*
Virgin Islands	124.8 thousand	78

* Of mixed race, including black.

** Another 14 percent is mulatto (Spanish/African) and 3 percent zambo (Amerindian/African).

FIGURE 9.3

African-American population by state, 1790–2000

State	1790 Total population	Slave population	Free black population	% Black	1800 Total population	Slave population	Free black population	% Black
Alabama	—	—	—	—	—	—	—	—
Alaska	—	—	—	—	—	—	—	—
Arizona	—	—	—	—	—	—	—	—
Arkansas	—	—	—	—	—	—	—	—
California	—	—	—	—	—	—	—	—
Colorado	—	—	—	—	—	—	—	—
Connecticut	237,946	2,648	2,771	2.28	251,002	951	5,330	2.50
Delaware	59,096	8,887	3,899	21.64	64,273	6,153	8,268	22.44
Florida	—	—	—	—	—	—	—	—
Georgia	82,548	29,264	398	35.93	162,686	59,406	1,019	37.14
Hawaii	—	—	—	—	—	—	—	—
Idaho	—	—	—	—	—	—	—	—
Illinois	—	—	—	—	—	—	—	—
Indiana	—	—	—	—	5,641	135	163	5.28
Iowa	—	—	—	—	—	—	—	—
Kansas	—	—	—	—	—	—	—	—
Kentucky	73,677	12,430	114	17.03	220,955	40,393	739	18.59
Louisiana	—	—	—	—	—	—	—	—
Maine	96,540	0	536	0.56	151,719	0	818	0.54
Maryland	319,728	103,036	8,043	34.74	341,548	105,635	19,587	36.66
Massachusetts	378,787	0	5,369	1.42	422,845	0	6,452	1.53
Michigan	—	—	—	—	—	—	—	—
Minnesota	—	—	—	—	—	—	—	—
Mississippi	—	—	—	—	8,850	3,489	182	41.48
Missouri	—	—	—	—	—	—	—	—
Montana	—	—	—	—	—	—	—	—
Nebraska	—	—	—	—	—	—	—	—
Nevada	—	—	—	—	—	—	—	—
New Hampshire	141,885	157	630	0.55	183,858	8	852	0.47
New Jersey	184,139	11,423	2,762	7.70	211,149	12,422	4,402	7.97
New Mexico	—	—	—	—	—	—	—	—
New York	340,120	21,193	4,682	7.61	589,051	20,903	10,417	5.32
North Carolina	393,751	100,783	5,041	26.88	478,103	133,296	7,043	29.35
North Dakota[1]	—	—	—	—	—	—	—	—
Ohio	—	—	—	—	45,365	0	337	0.74
Oklahoma	—	—	—	—	—	—	—	—
Oregon	—	—	—	—	—	—	—	—
Pennsylvania	434,373	3,707	6,531	2.36	602,365	1,706	14,564	2.70
Rhode Island	68,825	958	3,484	6.45	69,122	380	3,304	5.33
South Carolina	249,073	107,094	1,801	43.72	345,591	146,151	3,185	43.21
South Dakota[1]	—	—	—	—	—	—	—	—
Tennessee	35,691	3,417	361	10.59	105,602	13,584	309	13.16
Texas	—	—	—	—	—	—	—	—
Utah	—	—	—	—	—	—	—	—
Vermont	85,425	0	269	0.31	154,465	0	557	0.36
Virginia	747,610	292,627	12,866	40.86	880,200	345,796	20,124	41.57
Washington	—	—	—	—	—	—	—	—
Washington, D.C.	—	—	—	—	14,093	3,244	783	28.57
West Virginia[2]	—	—	—	—	—	—	—	—
Wisconsin	—	—	—	—	—	—	—	—
Wyoming	—	—	—	—	—	—	—	—
[continued]								

African-American population by state, 1790–2000 [CONTINUED]

State	1810				1820			
	Total population	Slave population	Free black population	% Black	Total population	Slave population	Free black population	% Black
Alabama	—	—	—	—	127,901	41,879	571	33.19
Alaska	—	—	—	—	—	—	—	—
Arizona	—	—	—	—	—	—	—	—
Arkansas	1,062	—	—	—	14,273	1,617	59	11.74
California	—	—	—	—	—	—	—	—
Colorado	—	—	—	—	—	—	—	—
Connecticut	261,942	310	6,453	2.58	275,248	97	7,870	2.89
Delaware	72,674	4,177	13,136	23.82	72,749	4,509	12,958	24.01
Florida	—	—	—	—	—	—	—	—
Georgia	252,433	105,218	1,801	42.40	340,989	149,656	1,763	44.41
Hawaii	—	—	—	—	—	—	—	—
Idaho	—	—	—	—	—	—	—	—
Illinois	12,282	168	613	6.36	55,211	917	457	2.49
Indiana	24,520	237	393	2.57	147,178	190	1,230	0.96
Iowa	—	—	—	—	—	—	—	—
Kansas	—	—	—	—	—	—	—	—
Kentucky	406,511	80,561	1,713	20.24	564,317	126,732	2,759	22.95
Louisiana	76,556	34,660	7,585	55.18	153,407	69,064	10,476	51.85
Maine	228,705	0	969	0.42	298,335	0	929	0.31
Maryland	380,546	111,502	33,927	38.22	407,350	107,397	39,730	36.12
Massachusetts	472,040	0	6,737	1.43	523,287	0	6,740	1.29
Michigan	4,762	24	120	3.02	8,896	0	174	1.96
Minnesota	—	—	—	—	—	—	—	—
Mississippi	40,352	17,088	240	42.94	75,448	32,814	458	44.10
Missouri	19,783	3,011	607	18.29	66,586	10,222	347	15.87
Montana	—	—	—	—	—	—	—	—
Nebraska	—	—	—	—	—	—	—	—
Nevada	—	—	—	—	—	—	—	—
New Hampshire	214,460	0	970	0.45	244,161	0	786	0.32
New Jersey	245,562	10,851	7,843	7.61	277,575	7,557	12,460	7.21
New Mexico	—	—	—	—	—	—	—	—
New York	959,049	15,017	25,333	4.21	1,372,812	10,088	29,279	2.87
North Carolina	555,500	168,824	10,266	32.24	638,829	204,917	14,712	34.38
North Dakota[1]	—	—	—	—	—	—	—	—
Ohio	230,760	0	1,899	0.82	581,434	0	4,723	0.81
Oklahoma	—	—	—	—	—	—	—	—
Oregon	—	—	—	—	—	—	—	—
Pennsylvania	810,091	795	22,492	2.87	1,049,458	211	30,202	2.90
Rhode Island	76,931	108	3,609	4.83	83,059	48	3,554	4.34
South Carolina	415,115	196,365	4,554	48.40	502,741	204,917	14,712	43.69
South Dakota[1]	—	—	—	—	—	—	—	—
Tennessee	261,727	44,535	1,317	17.52	422,823	80,107	2,737	19.59
Texas	—	—	—	—	—	—	—	—
Utah	—	—	—	—	—	—	—	—
Vermont	217,895	0	750	0.34	235,981	0	903	0.38
Virginia	974,600	392,516	30,570	43.41	1,065,366	425,148	36,883	43.37
Washington	—	—	—	—	—	—	—	—
Washington, D.C.	24,023	5,395	2,549	33.07	33,039	6,377	4,048	31.55
West Virginia[2]	—	—	—	—	—	—	—	—
Wisconsin	—	—	—	—	—	—	—	—
Wyoming	—	—	—	—	—	—	—	—
[continued]								

African-American population by state, 1790–2000 [CONTINUED]

State	1830				1840			
	Total population	Slave population	Free black population	% Black	Total population	Slave population	Free black population	% Black
Alabama	309,527	117,549	1,572	38.48	590,756	253,532	2,039	43.26
Alaska	—	—	—	—	—	—	—	—
Arizona	—	—	—	—	—	—	—	—
Arkansas	30,388	4,576	141	15.52	97,574	19,935	465	20.91
California	—	—	—	—	—	—	—	—
Colorado	—	—	—	—	—	—	—	—
Connecticut	297,675	25	8,047	2.71	309,978	17	8,105	2.62
Delaware	76,748	3,292	15,855	24.95	78,085	2,605	16,919	25.00
Florida	34,730	15,501	844	47.06	54,477	25,717	817	48.71
Georgia	516,823	217,531	2,486	42.57	691,392	280,944	2,753	41.03
Hawaii	—	—	—	—	—	—	—	—
Idaho	—	—	—	—	—	—	—	—
Illinois	157,445	747	1,637	1.51	476,183	331	3,598	0.83
Indiana	343,031	3	3,629	1.06	685,866	3	7,165	1.05
Iowa	—	—	—	—	43,112	16	172	0.44
Kansas	—	—	—	—	—	—	—	—
Kentucky	687,917	165,213	4,917	24.73	779,828	182,258	7,317	24.31
Louisiana	215,739	109,588	16,710	58.54	352,411	168,452	25,502	55.04
Maine	399,455	2	1,190	0.30	501,793	0	1,355	0.27
Maryland	447,040	102,994	52,938	34.88	470,019	89,737	62,078	32.30
Massachusetts	610,408	1	7,048	1.15	737,699	0	8,669	1.18
Michigan	31,639	32	261	0.93	212,267	0	707	0.33
Minnesota	—	—	—	—	—	—	—	—
Mississippi	136,621	65,659	519	48.44	375,651	195,211	1,366	52.33
Missouri	140,455	25,091	569	18.27	383,702	58,240	1,574	15.59
Montana	—	—	—	—	—	—	—	—
Nebraska	—	—	—	—	—	—	—	—
Nevada	—	—	—	—	—	—	—	—
New Hampshire	269,328	3	604	0.23	284,574	1	537	0.19
New Jersey	320,823	2,254	18,303	6.41	373,306	674	21,044	5.82
New Mexico	—	—	—	—	—	—	—	—
New York	1,918,608	75	44,870	2.34	2,428,921	4	50,027	2.06
North Carolina	737,987	245,601	19,543	35.93	753,419	245,817	22,732	35.64
North Dakota	—	—	—	—	—	—	—	—
Ohio	937,903	6	9,568	1.02	1,519,467	3	17,342	1.14
Oklahoma	—	—	—	—	—	—	—	—
Oregon	—	—	—	—	—	—	—	—
Pennsylvania	1,348,233	403	37,930	2.84	1,724,033	64	47,854	2.78
Rhode Island	97,799	17	3,561	3.68	108,830	5	3,238	2.98
South Carolina	581,185	315,401	7,921	55.63	594,398	327,038	8,276	56.41
South Dakota[1]	—	—	—	—	—	—	—	—
Tennessee	681,904	141,603	4,555	21.43	829,210	183,059	5,524	22.74
Texas	—	—	—	—	—	—	—	—
Utah	—	—	—	—	—	—	—	—
Vermont	280,652	0	881	0.31	291,948	0	730	0.25
Virginia	1,211,405	469,757	47,348	42.69	1,239,797	448,987	49,842	40.23
Washington	—	—	—	—	—	—	—	—
Washington, D.C.	39,834	6,119	6,152	30.81	43,712	4,694	8,361	29.87
West Virginia[2]	—	—	—	—	—	—	—	—
Wisconsin	—	—	—	—	30,945	11	185	0.63
Wyoming	—	—	—	—	—	—	—	—
[continued]								

African-American population by state, 1790–2000 [CONTINUED]

State	1850 Total population	1850 Slave population	1850 Free black population	1850 % Black	1860 Total population	1860 Slave population	1860 Free black population	1860 % Black
Alabama	771,623	342,844	2,265	44.73	946,201	435,080	2,690	45.40
Alaska	—	—	—	—	—	—	—	—
Arizona	—	—	—	—	—	—	—	—
Arkansas	209,897	47,100	608	22.73	435,450	111,115	144	25.55
California	92,597	0	962	1.04	379,994	0	4,086	1.08
Colorado	—	—	—	—	34,277	0	46	0.13
Connecticut	370,792	0	7,693	2.07	460,147	0	8,627	1.87
Delaware	91,532	2,290	18,073	22.25	112,216	1,798	19,829	19.27
Florida	87,445	39,310	932	46.02	140,424	61,745	932	44.63
Georgia	906,185	381,682	2,931	42.44	1,057,286	462,198	3,500	44.05
Hawaii	—	—	—	—	—	—	—	—
Idaho	—	—	—	—	—	—	—	—
Illinois	851,470	0	5,436	0.64	1,711,951	0	7,628	0.45
Indiana	988,416	0	11,262	1.14	1,350,428	0	11,428	0.85
Iowa	192,214	0	333	0.17	674,913	0	1,069	0.16
Kansas	—	—	—	—	107,206	2	625	0.58
Kentucky	982,405	210,981	10,011	22.49	1,155,684	225,483	10,684	20.44
Louisiana	517,762	244,809	17,462	50.65	708,002	331,726	18,647	49.49
Maine	583,169	0	1,356	0.23	628,279	0	1,327	0.21
Maryland	583,034	90,368	74,723	28.32	687,049	87,189	83,942	24.91
Massachusetts	994,514	0	9,064	0.91	1,231,066	0	9,602	0.78
Michigan	397,654	0	2,583	0.65	749,113	—	6,799	0.91
Minnesota	6,077	0	39	—	172,023	0	259	0.15
Mississippi	606,526	309,878	930	51.24	791,305	436,631	773	55.28
Missouri	682,044	87,422	2,618	13.20	1,182,012	114,931	3,572	10.03
Montana	—	—	—	—	—	—	—	—
Nebraska	—	—	—	—	28,841	15	67	0.28
Nevada	—	—	—	—	6,857	0	45	0.66
New Hampshire	317,976	0	520	0.16	326,073	0	494	0.15
New Jersey	489,555	236	23,810	4.91	672,035	18	25,318	3.77
New Mexico	61,547	0	22	—	93,516	0	85	0.09
New York	3,097,394	0	49,069	1.58	3,880,735	0	49,005	1.26
North Carolina	869,039	288,548	27,463	36.36	992,622	331,059	30,463	36.42
North Dakota[1]	—	—	—	—	4,837	—	—	—
Ohio	1,980,329	0	25,279	1.28	2,339,511	0	36,673	1.57
Oklahoma	—	—	—	—	—	—	—	—
Oregon	13,294	0	207	—	52,465	0	128	0.24
Pennsylvania	2,311,786	0	53,626	2.32	2,906,215	0	56,949	1.96
Rhode Island	147,545	0	3,670	2.49	174,620	0	3,952	2.26
South Carolina	668,507	384,984	8,960	58.93	703,708	402,406	9,914	58.59
South Dakota[1]	—	—	—	—	—	—	—	—
Tennessee	1,002,717	239,459	6,422	24.52	1,109,801	275,719	7,300	25.50
Texas	212,592	58,161	397	27.54	604,215	182,566	355	30.27
Utah	11,380	26	24	0.44	40,273	29	30	0.15
Vermont	314,120	0	718	0.23	315,098	0	709	0.23
Virginia	1,421,661	472,528	54,333	37.06	1,596,318	490,865	58,042	34.39
Washington	—	—	—	—	11,594	0	30	0.26
Washington, D.C.	51,687	3,687	10,059	26.59	75,080	3,185	11,131	19.07
West Virginia[2]	—	—	—	—	—	—	—	—
Wisconsin	305,391	0	635	0.21	775,881	0	1,171	0.15
Wyoming	—	—	—	—	—	—	—	—

[continued]

African-American population by state, 1790–2000 [CONTINUED]

State	1870 Total population	1870 Black population	1870 % Black	1880 Total population	1880 Black population	1880 % Black
Alabama	996,992	475,510	47.69	1,262,505	600,103	47.53
Alaska	—	—	—	33,000	—	—
Arizona	9,658	26	0.27	40,440	155	0.38
Arkansas	484,471	122,169	25.22	802,525	210,666	26.25
California	560,247	4,272	0.76	864,694	6,018	0.70
Colorado	39,864	456	1.14	194,327	2,435	1.25
Connecticut	537,454	9,668	1.80	622,700	11,547	1.85
Delaware	125,015	22,794	18.23	146,608	26,442	18.04
Florida	187,748	91,689	48.84	269,493	126,690	47.01
Georgia	1,184,109	545,142	46.04	1,542,180	725,133	47.02
Hawaii	—	—	—	—	—	—
Idaho	14,999	60	0.40	32,610	53	0.16
Illinois	2,539,891	28,762	1.13	3,077,871	46,368	1.51
Indiana	1,680,637	24,560	1.46	1,978,301	39,228	1.98
Iowa	1,194,020	5,762	0.48	1,624,615	9,516	0.59
Kansas	364,399	17,108	4.69	996,096	43,107	4.33
Kentucky	1,321,011	222,210	16.82	1,648,690	271,451	16.46
Louisiana	726,915	364,210	50.10	939,946	483,655	51.46
Maine	626,915	1,606	0.26	648,936	1,451	0.22
Maryland	780,894	175,391	22.46	934,943	210,230	22.49
Massachusetts	1,457,351	13,947	0.96	1,783,085	18,697	1.05
Michigan	1,184,059	11,849	1.00	1,636,937	15,100	0.92
Minnesota	439,706	759	0.17	780,773	1,564	0.20
Mississippi	827,922	444,201	53.65	1,131,597	650,291	57.47
Missouri	1,721,295	118,071	6.86	2,168,380	145,350	6.70
Montana	20,595	183	0.89	39,159	346	0.88
Nebraska	122,993	789	0.64	452,402	2,385	0.53
Nevada	42,491	357	0.84	62,266	488	0.78
New Hampshire	318,300	580	0.18	346,991	685	0.20
New Jersey	906,096	30,658	3.38	1,131,116	38,856	3.43
New Mexico	91,874	172	0.19	119,565	1,015	0.85
New York	4,382,759	52,081	1.19	5,082,871	65,104	1.28
North Carolina	1,071,361	391,650	36.56	1,399,750	531,277	37.96
North Dakota[1]	14,181	94	0.66	135,177	401	0.30
Ohio	2,665,260	63,213	2.37	3,198,062	79,900	2.50
Oklahoma	—	—	—	—	—	—
Oregon	90,923	346	0.38	174,768	487	0.28
Pennsylvania	3,521,951	65,294	1.85	4,282,891	85,535	2.00
Rhode Island	217,353	4,980	2.29	276,531	6,488	2.35
South Carolina	705,606	415,814	58.93	995,577	604,332	60.70
South Dakota[1]	—	—	—	—	—	—
Tennessee	1,258,520	322,331	25.61	1,542,359	403,151	26.14
Texas	818,579	253,475	30.97	1,591,749	393,384	24.71
Utah	86,786	118	0.14	143,963	232	0.16
Vermont	330,551	924	0.28	332,286	1,057	0.32
Virginia	1,225,163	512,841	41.86	1,512,565	631,616	41.76
Washington	23,955	207	0.86	75,116	325	0.43
Washington, D.C.	131,700	43,404	32.96	177,624	59,596	33.55
West Virginia[2]	442,014	17,980	4.07	618,457	25,886	4.19
Wisconsin	1,054,670	2,113	0.20	1,315,497	2,702	0.21
Wyoming	9,118	183	2.01	20,789	298	1.43

[continued]

African-American population by state, 1790–2000 [CONTINUED]

State	1890 Total population	1890 Black population	1890 % Black	1900 Total population	1900 Black population	1900 % Black
Alabama	1,513,401	678,489	44.83	1,828,697	827,307	45.24
Alaska	32,000	—	—	64,000	—	—
Arizona	88,243	1,357	1.54	122,931	1,848	1.50
Arkansas	1,128,211	309,117	27.40	1,311,564	366,856	27.97
California	1,213,398	11,322	0.93	1,485,053	11,045	0.74
Colorado	413,249	6,215	1.50	539,700	8,570	1.59
Connecticut	746,258	12,302	1.65	908,420	15,226	1.68
Delaware	168,493	28,386	16.85	184,735	30,697	16.62
Florida	391,422	166,180	42.46	528,542	230,730	43.65
Georgia	1,837,353	858,815	46.74	2,216,331	1,034,813	46.69
Hawaii	—	—	—	154,000	—	—
Idaho	88,548	201	0.23	161,722	293	0.18
Illinois	3,826,352	57,028	1.49	4,821,550	85,078	1.76
Indiana	2,192,404	45,215	2.06	2,516,462	57,505	2.29
Iowa	1,912,297	10,685	0.56	2,231,853	12,693	0.57
Kansas	1,428,108	49,710	3.48	1,470,495	52,003	3.54
Kentucky	1,858,635	268,071	14.42	2,147,174	284,706	13.26
Louisiana	1,118,588	559,193	49.99	1,381,625	650,804	47.10
Maine	661,086	1,190	0.18	694,466	1,319	0.19
Maryland	1,042,390	215,657	20.69	1,188,044	235,064	19.79
Massachusetts	2,238,947	22,144	0.99	2,805,346	31,974	1.14
Michigan	2,093,890	15,223	0.73	2,420,982	15,816	0.65
Minnesota	1,310,283	3,683	0.28	1,751,394	4,959	0.28
Mississippi	1,289,600	742,559	57.58	1,551,270	907,630	58.51
Missouri	2,679,185	150,184	5.61	3,106,665	161,234	5.19
Montana	142,924	1,490	1.04	243,329	1,523	0.63
Nebraska	1,062,656	8,913	0.84	1,066,300	6,269	0.59
Nevada	47,355	242	0.51	42,335	134	0.32
New Hampshire	376,530	614	0.16	411,588	662	0.16
New Jersey	1,444,933	47,637	3.30	1,883,669	69,844	3.71
New Mexico	160,282	1,956	1.22	195,310	1,610	0.82
New York	6,003,174	70,092	1.17	7,268,894	99,232	1.37
North Carolina	1,617,949	561,018	34.67	1,893,810	624,469	32.97
North Dakota[1]	190,983	373	0.20	319,146	286	0.09
Ohio	3,672,329	87,113	2.37	4,157,545	96,901	2.33
Oklahoma	258,657	21,609	8.35	790,391	55,684	7.05
Oregon	317,704	1,186	0.37	413,536	1,105	0.27
Pennsylvania	5,258,113	107,596	2.05	6,302,115	156,845	2.49
Rhode Island	345,506	7,393	2.14	428,556	9,092	2.12
South Carolina	1,151,149	688,934	59.85	1,340,316	782,321	58.37
South Dakota[1]	348,600	541	0.16	401,570	465	0.12
Tennessee	1,767,518	430,678	24.37	2,020,616	480,243	23.77
Texas	2,235,527	488,171	21.84	3,048,710	620,722	20.36
Utah	210,779	588	0.28	276,749	672	0.24
Vermont	332,422	937	0.28	343,641	826	0.24
Virginia	1,655,980	635,438	38.37	1,854,184	660,722	35.63
Washington	357,232	1,602	0.45	518,103	2,514	0.49
Washington, D.C.	230,392	75,572	32.80	278,718	86,702	31.11
West Virginia[2]	762,794	32,690	4.29	958,800	43,499	4.54
Wisconsin	1,693,330	2,444	0.14	2,069,042	2,542	0.12
Wyoming	62,555	922	1.47	92,531	940	1.02

[continued]

African-American population by state, 1790–2000 [CONTINUED]

State	1910 Total population	1910 Black population	1910 % Black	1920 Total population	1920 Black population	1920 % Black
Alabama	2,138,093	908,282	42.48	2,348,174	900,652	38.36
Alaska	64,000	—	—	55,036		
Arizona	204,354	2,009	0.98	334,162	8,005	2.40
Arkansas	1,574,449	442,891	28.13	1,752,204	472,220	26.95
California	2,377,549	21,645	0.91	3,426,861	38,763	1.13
Colorado	799,024	11,453	1.43	939,629	11,318	1.20
Connecticut	1,114,756	15,174	1.36	1,380,631	21,046	1.52
Delaware	202,322	31,181	51.14	223,003	30,335	13.60
Florida	752,619	308,669	40.01	968,470	329,487	34.02
Georgia	2,609,121	1,176,987	45.11	2,895,832	1,206,365	41.66
Hawaii	192,000	1,000	0.52	255,912	—	—
Idaho	325,594	651	0.20	431,866	920	0.21
Illinois	5,638,591	109,049	1.93	6,485,280	182,274	2.81
Indiana	2,700,876	60,320	2.23	2,930,390	80,810	2.76
Iowa	2,224,771	14,973	0.67	2,404,021	19,005	0.79
Kansas	1,690,949	54,030	3.20	1,769,257	57,925	3.27
Kentucky	2,289,905	261,656	11.43	2,416,630	235,938	9.76
Louisiana	1,656,388	713,874	43.10	1,798,509	700,257	38.94
Maine	742,371	1,363	0.18	768,014	1,310	0.17
Maryland	1,295,346	232,250	17.93	1,449,661	244,479	16.86
Massachusetts	3,366,416	38,055	1.13	3,852,356	45,466	1.18
Michigan	2,810,173	17,115	0.61	3,668,412	60,082	1.64
Minnesota	2,075,708	7,084	0.34	2,387,125	8,809	0.37
Mississippi	1,797,114	1,009,487	56.17	1,790,618	935,184	52.23
Missouri	3,293,355	157,452	4.78	3,404,055	178,241	5.24
Montana	376,053	1,834	0.49	548,889	1,658	0.30
Nebraska	1,192,214	7,689	0.64	1,276,372	13,242	1.02
Nevada	81,875	513	0.63	77,407	346	0.45
New Hampshire	430,572	564	0.13	443,083	621	0.14
New Jersey	2,537,167	89,760	3.54	3,155,900	117,132	3.71
New Mexico	327,301	1,628	0.50	360,350	5,733	1.59
New York	9,113,614	134,191	1.47	10,385,227	198,483	1.91
North Carolina	2,206,287	697,843	31.63	2,559,123	763,407	29.83
North Dakota[1]	577,056	617	0.11	646,872	467	0.07
Ohio	4,767,121	111,452	2.34	5,759,394	186,187	3.23
Oklahoma	1,657,155	137,612	8.30	2,028,283	149,408	7.37
Oregon	672,765	1,492	0.22	783,389	2,144	0.27
Pennsylvania	7,665,111	193,919	2.53	8,720,017	284,568	3.26
Rhode Island	542,610	9,529	1.76	604,397	10,036	1.66
South Carolina	1,515,400	835,843	55.16	1,683,724	864,719	51.36
South Dakota[1]	583,888	817	0.14	636,547	832	0.13
Tennessee	2,184,789	473,088	21.65	2,337,885	451,758	19.32
Texas	3,896,542	690,049	17.71	4,663,228	741,694	15.91
Utah	373,351	1,144	0.31	449,396	1,446	0.32
Vermont	355,956	1,621	0.46	352,428	572	0.16
Virginia	2,061,612	671,096	32.55	2,309,187	690,017	29.88
Washington	1,141,990	6,058	0.53	1,356,621	6,883	0.51
Washington, D.C.	331,069	94,446	28.53	437,571	109,966	25.13
West Virginia[2]	1,221,119	64,173	5.26	1,463,701	86,345	5.90
Wisconsin	2,333,860	2,900	0.12	2,632,067	5,201	0.20
Wyoming	145,965	2,235	1.53	194,402	1,375	0.71

[continued]

African-American population by state, 1790–2000 [CONTINUED]

State	1930 Total population	1930 Black population	1930 % Black	1940 Total population	1940 Black population	1940 % Black
Alabama	2,646,248	944,834	35.70	2,832,961	983,290	34.71
Alaska	59,278	—	—	72,524	141	0.19
Arizona	435,573	10,749	2.47	499,261	14,993	3.00
Arkansas	1,854,482	478,463	25.80	1,949,387	482,578	24.76
California	5,677,251	81,048	1.43	6,907,387	124,306	1.80
Colorado	1,035,791	11,828	1.14	1,123,296	12,176	1.08
Connecticut	1,606,903	29,354	1.83	1,709,242	32,992	1.93
Delaware	238,380	32,602	13.68	266,505	35,876	13.46
Florida	1,468,211	431,828	29.41	1,897,414	514,198	27.10
Georgia	2,908,506	1,071,125	36.83	3,123,723	1,084,927	34.73
Hawaii	368,336	—	—	423,330	255	0.06
Idaho	445,032	668	0.15	524,873	595	0.11
Illinois	7,630,654	328,972	4.31	7,897,241	387,446	4.91
Indiana	3,238,503	111,982	3.46	3,427,796	121,916	3.56
Iowa	2,470,939	17,380	0.70	2,538,268	16,694	0.66
Kansas	1,880,999	66,344	3.53	1,801,028	65,138	3.62
Kentucky	2,614,589	226,040	8.65	2,845,627	214,031	7.52
Louisiana	2,101,593	766,326	36.94	2,363,880	849,303	35.93
Maine	797,423	1,096	0.14	847,226	1,304	0.15
Maryland	1,631,526	276,379	16.94	1,821,244	301,931	16.58
Massachusetts	4,249,614	52,365	1.23	4,316,721	55,391	1.28
Michigan	4,842,325	169,453	3.50	5,256,106	208,345	3.96
Minnesota	2,563,953	9,445	0.37	2,792,300	9,928	0.36
Mississippi	2,009,821	1,009,718	50.24	2,183,796	1,074,578	49.21
Missouri	3,629,367	223,840	6.17	3,784,664	244,386	6.46
Montana	537,606	1,256	0.23	559,456	1,120	0.20
Nebraska	1,377,963	13,752	1.00	1,315,834	14,171	1.08
Nevada	91,058	516	0.57	110,247	664	0.60
New Hampshire	465,293	790	0.17	491,524	414	0.08
New Jersey	4,041,334	208,828	5.17	4,160,165	226,973	5.46
New Mexico	423,317	2,850	0.67	531,818	4,672	0.88
New York	12,588,066	412,814	3.28	13,479,142	571,221	4.24
North Carolina	3,170,276	918,647	28.98	3,571,623	981,298	24.47
North Dakota[1]	680,845	377	0.06	641,935	201	0.03
Ohio	6,646,697	309,304	4.65	6,907,612	339,461	4.91
Oklahoma	2,396,040	172,198	7.19	2,336,434	168,849	7.23
Oregon	953,786	2,234	0.23	1,089,684	2,565	0.24
Pennsylvania	9,631,350	431,257	4.48	9,900,180	470,172	4.75
Rhode Island	687,497	9,913	1.44	713,346	11,024	1.55
South Carolina	1,738,765	793,681	45.65	1,899,804	814,164	42.86
South Dakota[1]	692,849	646	0.09	642,961	474	0.07
Tennessee	2,616,556	477,646	18.25	2,915,841	508,736	17.45
Texas	5,824,715	854,964	14.68	6,414,824	924,391	14.14
Utah	507,847	1,108	0.22	550,310	1,235	0.22
Vermont	359,611	568	0.16	359,231	384	0.11
Virginia	2,421,851	650,165	26.85	2,677,773	661,449	24.70
Washington	1,563,396	6,840	0.44	1,736,191	7,424	0.43
Washington, D.C.	486,869	132,068	27.13	663,091	187,266	28.24
West Virginia[2]	1,729,205	114,893	6.64	1,901,974	117,754	6.19
Wisconsin	2,939,006	10,739	0.37	3,137,587	12,158	0.39
Wyoming	225,565	1,250	0.55	250,742	956	0.38

[continued]

African-American population by state, 1790–2000 [CONTINUED]

State	1950 Total population	1950 Black population	% Black	1960 Total population	1960 Black population	% Black
Alabama	3,061,743	979,617	32.00	3,266,740	980,271	30.01
Alaska	128,643	—	—	226,167	6,771	2.99
Arizona	749,587	25,974	3.47	1,302,161	43,403	3.33
Arkansas	1,909,511	426,639	22.34	1,786,272	388,787	21.77
California	10,586,223	462,172	4.37	15,717,204	883,861	5.62
Colorado	1,325,089	20,177	1.52	1,753,947	39,992	2.28
Connecticut	2,007,280	53,472	2.66	2,535,234	107,449	4.24
Delaware	318,085	43,598	13.71	446,292	60,688	13.60
Florida	2,771,305	603,101	21.76	4,951,560	880,186	17.78
Georgia	3,444,578	1,062,762	30.85	3,943,116	1,122,596	28.47
Hawaii	499,794	2,651	0.53	632,772	4,943	0.78
Idaho	588,637	1,050	0.18	667,191	1,502	0.23
Illinois	8,712,176	645,980	7.41	10,081,158	1,037,470	10.29
Indiana	3,934,224	174,168	4.43	4,662,498	269,275	5.78
Iowa	2,621,073	19,692	0.75	2,757,537	25,354	0.92
Kansas	1,905,299	73,158	3.84	2,178,611	91,445	4.20
Kentucky	2,944,806	201,921	6.86	3,038,156	215,949	7.11
Louisiana	2,683,516	882,428	32.88	3,257,022	1,039,207	31.91
Maine	913,774	1,221	0.13	969,265	3,318	0.34
Maryland	2,343,001	385,972	16.47	3,100,689	518,410	16.72
Massachusetts	4,690,514	73,171	1.56	3,148,582	111,842	2.17
Michigan	6,371,766	442,296	6.94	7,823,194	717,581	9.17
Minnesota	2,982,483	14,022	0.47	3,413,864	22,263	0.65
Mississippi	2,178,914	986,494	45.27	2,178,141	915,743	42.04
Missouri	3,954,653	297,088	7.51	4,319,813	390,853	9.05
Montana	591,024	1,232	0.21	674,767	1,467	0.22
Nebraska	1,325,510	19,234	1.45	1,411,330	29,262	2.07
Nevada	160,083	4,302	2.69	285,278	13,484	4.73
New Hampshire	533,242	731	0.14	606,921	1,903	0.31
New Jersey	4,835,329	318,565	6.59	6,066,782	514,875	8.49
New Mexico	681,187	8,408	1.23	951,023	17,063	1.79
New York	14,830,192	918,191	6.19	16,782,304	1,417,511	8.45
North Carolina	4,061,929	1,047,353	25.78	4,556,155	1,116,021	24.49
North Dakota[1]	619,636	257	0.04	632,446	777	0.12
Ohio	7,946,627	513,072	6.46	9,706,397	786,097	8.10
Oklahoma	2,233,351	145,503	6.52	2,328,284	153,084	6.57
Oregon	1,521,341	11,529	0.76	1,768,687	18,133	1.03
Pennsylvania	10,498,012	638,485	6.08	11,319,366	852,750	7.53
Rhode Island	791,896	13,903	1.76	859,488	18,332	2.13
South Carolina	2,117,027	822,077	38.83	2,382,594	829,291	34.81
South Dakota[1]	652,740	727	0.11	680,514	1,114	0.16
Tennessee	3,291,718	530,603	16.12	3,567,089	586,876	16.45
Texas	7,711,194	977,458	12.68	9,579,677	1,187,125	12.39
Utah	688,862	2,729	0.40	890,627	4,148	0.47
Vermont	377,747	443	0.12	389,881	519	0.13
Virginia	3,318,680	734,211	22.12	3,966,949	816,258	20.58
Washington	2,378,963	30,691	1.29	2,853,214	48,738	1.71
Washington, D.C.	802,178	280,803	35.01	763,956	411,737	53.90
West Virginia[2]	2,005,552	114,867	5.73	1,860,421	89,378	4.80
Wisconsin	3,434,575	28,182	0.82	3,951,777	74,546	1.89
Wyoming	290,529	2,557	0.88	330,066	2,183	0.66

[continued]

African-American population by state, 1790–2000 [CONTINUED]

State	1970			1980		
	Total population	Black population	% Black	Total population	Black population	% Black
Alabama	3,444,165	903,467	26.23	3,893,888	996,283	25.59
Alaska	300,382	8,911	2.97	401,851	13,748	3.42
Arizona	1,770,900	53,334	3.01	2,718,215	74,159	2.73
Arkansas	1,923,295	352,445	18.33	2,286,435	373,025	16.31
California	19,953,134	1,400,143	7.02	23,667,902	1,818,660	7.68
Colorado	2,207,259	66,411	3.01	2,889,964	101,695	3.52
Connecticut	3,031,709	181,177	5.98	3,107,576	216,641	6.97
Delaware	548,104	78,276	14.28	594,338	96,157	16.18
Florida	6,789,443	1,041,651	15.34	9,746,324	1,343,134	13.78
Georgia	4,589,575	1,187,149	25.87	5,463,105	1,464,435	26.81
Hawaii	768,561	7,573	0.99	964,691	17,687	1.83
Idaho	712,567	2,130	0.30	943,935	2,711	0.29
Illinois	11,113,976	1,425,674	12.83	11,427,518	1,674,467	14.65
Indiana	5,193,669	357,464	6.88	5,490,224	414,489	7.55
Iowa	2,824,376	32,596	1.15	2,913,808	42,228	1.45
Kansas	2,246,578	106,977	4.76	2,363,679	126,356	5.35
Kentucky	3,218,706	230,793	7.17	3,660,777	359,289	9.81
Louisiana	3,641,306	1,086,832	29.85	4,205,900	1,238,472	29.45
Maine	992,048	2,800	0.28	1,124,660	3,381	0.30
Maryland	3,922,399	699,479	17.83	4,216,975	957,418	22.70
Massachusetts	5,689,170	175,817	3.09	5,737,037	221,029	3.85
Michigan	8,875,083	991,066	11.17	9,262,078	1,197,177	12.93
Minnesota	3,804,971	34,868	0.92	4,075,970	52,325	1.28
Mississippi	2,216,912	815,770	36.80	2,520,637	887,111	35.19
Missouri	4,676,501	480,172	10.27	4,916,686	513,385	10.44
Montana	694,409	1,995	0.29	786,690	1,738	0.22
Nebraska	1,483,493	39,911	2.69	1,569,825	47,946	3.05
Nevada	488,738	27,762	5.68	800,493	51,203	6.40
New Hampshire	737,681	2,505	0.34	920,610	4,324	0.47
New Jersey	7,168,164	770,292	10.75	7,364,823	924,909	12.56
New Mexico	1,016,000	19,555	1.92	1,302,894	23,071	1.77
New York	18,236,967	2,168,949	11.89	17,558,072	2,405,818	13.70
North Carolina	5,082,059	1,126,478	22.17	5,881,766	1,319,054	22.43
North Dakota[1]	617,761	2,494	0.40	652,717	2,471	0.38
Ohio	10,651,987	970,477	9.11	10,797,630	1,076,742	9.97
Oklahoma	2,559,229	171,892	6.72	3,025,290	204,810	6.77
Oregon	2,091,385	26,308	1.26	2,633,105	37,454	1.42
Pennsylvania	11,793,909	1,016,514	8.62	11,893,895	1,045,318	8.79
Rhode Island	946,725	25,338	2.68	947,154	27,361	2.89
South Carolina	2,590,516	789,041	30.46	3,121,820	947,969	30.37
South Dakota[1]	665,507	1,627	0.24	690,768	2,152	0.31
Tennessee	3,923,687	621,261	15.83	4,591,120	724,808	15.79
Texas	11,196,730	1,399,005	12.49	14,229,191	1,704,741	11.98
Utah	1,059,273	6,617	0.62	1,461,037	9,691	0.66
Vermont	444,330	761	0.17	511,456	1,188	0.23
Virginia	4,648,494	861,368	18.53	5,346,818	1,008,665	18.86
Washington	3,409,169	71,308	2.09	4,132,156	105,604	2.56
Washington, D.C.	756,510	537,712	71.08	638,333	448,370	70.24
West Virginia[2]	1,744,237	67,342	3.86	1,949,664	65,041	3.34
Wisconsin	4,417,731	128,224	2.90	4,705,767	183,169	3.89
Wyoming	332,416	2,568	0.77	469,557	3,270	0.70

[continued]

African-American population by state, 1790–2000 [CONTINUED]

State	1990 Total population	1990 Black population	% Black	2000 Total population	2000 Black population	% Black
Alabama	4,040,587	1,020,705	25.26	4,447,100	1,155,930	26.0
Alaska	550,043	22,451	4.08	626,932	21,787	3.5
Arizona	3,665,228	110,524	3.02	5,130,632	158,873	3.1
Arkansas	2,350,725	373,912	15.91	2,673,400	418,950	15.7
California	29,760,021	2,208,801	7.42	33,871,648	2,263,882	6.7
Colorado	3,294,394	133,146	4.04	4,301,261	165,063	3.8
Connecticut	3,287,116	274,269	8.34	3,405,565	309,843	9.1
Delaware	666,168	112,460	16.88	783,600	150,666	19.2
Florida	12,937,926	1,759,534	13.60	15,982,378	2,335,505	14.6
Georgia	6,478,216	1,746,565	26.96	8,186,453	2,349,542	28.7
Hawaii	1,108,229	27,195	2.45	1,211,537	22,003	1.8
Idaho	1,006,749	3,370	0.33	1,293,953	5,456	0.4
Illinois	11,430,602	1,694,273	14.82	12,419,293	1,876,875	15.1
Indiana	5,554,159	432,092	7.79	6,080,485	510,034	8.4
Iowa	2,776,755	48,090	1.73	2,296,324	61,853	2.1
Kansas	2,477,574	143,076	5.77	2,688,418	154,198	5.7
Kentucky	3,685,296	262,907	7.13	4,041,769	295,994	7.3
Louisiana	4,219,973	1,299,281	30.79	4,468,976	1,451,944	32.5
Maine	1,227,928	5,138	0.42	1,274,923	6,760	0.5
Maryland	4,781,468	1,190,000	24.89	5,296,486	1,477,411	27.9
Massachusetts	6,016,425	300,130	4.99	6,349,097	343,454	5.4
Michigan	9,295,297	1,291,706	13.90	9,938,444	1,412,742	14.2
Minnesota	4,375,099	94,944	2.17	4,919,479	171,731	3.5
Mississippi	2,573,216	915,057	35.56	2,844,658	1,033,809	36.3
Missouri	5,117,073	548,208	10.71	5,595,211	629,391	11.2
Montana	799,065	2,381	0.30	902,195	2,692	0.3
Nebraska	1,578,385	57,404	3.64	1,711,263	68,541	4.0
Nevada	1,201,833	78,771	6.55	1,998,257	135,477	6.8
New Hampshire	1,109,252	7,198	0.65	1,235,786	9,035	0.7
New Jersey	7,730,188	1,036,825	13.41	8,414,350	1,141,821	13.6
New Mexico	1,515,069	30,210	1.99	1,819,046	34,343	1.9
New York	17,990,455	2,859,055	15.89	18,976,457	3,014,385	15.9
North Carolina	6,628,637	1,456,323	21.97	8,049,313	1,737,545	21.6
North Dakota[1]	638,800	3,524	0.55	642,200	3,916	0.6
Ohio	10,847,115	1,154,826	10.65	11,353,140	1,301,307	11.5
Oklahoma	3,145,585	23,301	0.74	3,450,654	260,968	7.6
Oregon	2,842,321	46,178	1.62	3,421,399	55,662	1.6
Pennsylvania	11,881,643	1,089,795	9.17	12,281,054	1,224,612	10.0
Rhode Island	1,003,464	38,861	3.87	1,048,319	46,908	4.5
South Carolina	3,468,703	1,039,884	29.98	4,012,012	1,185,216	29.5
South Dakota[1]	696,004	3,258	0.47	754,844	4,685	0.6
Tennessee	4,877,185	778,035	15.95	5,689,283	932,809	16.4
Texas	16,986,510	2,021,632	11.90	20,851,820	2,404,566	11.5
Utah	1,722,850	11,576	0.67	2,233,169	17,657	0.8
Vermont	562,758	1,951	0.35	608,827	3,063	0.5
Virginia	6,187,358	1,162,994	18.80	7,078,515	1,390,293	19.6
Washington	4,866,692	149,801	3.08	5,894,121	190,267	3.2
Washington, D.C.	606,900	399,604	65.84	572,059	343,312	60.0
West Virginia[2]	1,793,477	56,295	3.14	1,808,344	57,232	3.2
Wisconsin	4,891,769	244,539	5.00	5,363,675	304,460	5.7
Wyoming	453,588	3,606	0.79	493,782	3,722	0.8

(1) Figures for North Dakota represent whole of Dakota Territory until 1890. North and South Dakota became states in 1889.
(2) West Virginia was originally part of Virginia. It became a separate state in 1863.

FIGURE 9.4

African-American population during the colonial period, according to the U.S. Census

Year	Total population[1]	Black population	%
Connecticut			
1756	130,612	3,657	2.80
1774	197,842	6,529	3.30
Georgia			
1753	2,261	1,600	70.77
1756	6,355	1,856	29.21
Maryland			
1701	22,258	2,849	12.80
1704	34,912	4,475	12.82
1710	42,741	7,945	18.59
1712	46,151	8,408	18.22
1762	164,007	49,694	30.30
Massachusetts			
1764	245,698	6,880	2.80[2]
New Hampshire			
1767	52,720	633	1.20
1773	73,097	674	0.92
1775	81,300	650	0.80
New Jersey[3]			
1726	32,442	2,595	8.00
1737–38	46,676	3,981	8.53
1745	61,403	4,606	7.50
New Orleans[4]			
1721	372	94	25.27
1771	3,190	1,387	43.48
New York			
1698	18,067	2,168	12.00[5]
1703	20,665	2,258	10.93
1712–14	22,608	2,425	10.73
1723	40,564	6,171	15.21
1731	50,286	7,231	14.38
1737	60,437	8,941	14.79
1746	61,589	9,107	14.79
1749	73,348	10,592	14.44
1756	96,590	13,348	13.82
1771	168,007	19,825	11.80
Rhode Island			
1708	7,181	424	5.90
1730	17,935	1,648	9.19
1774	59,607	5,067	8.50
South Carolina			
1708	9,580	5,499	57.40[6]
Virginia			
1624	1,275	22	1.73

(1) The terms "black," "Negro," and "slave" were often used interchangeably by colonial census-takers, so accurate figures on free blacks and slaves are not available.

(2) Includes 0.7% Indians.

(3) West Jersey, 1726–74.

(4) Not a British colony; no census data available for Louisiana.

(5) Includes 2.3% Indians.

(6) Includes 14.5% Indians.

FIGURE 9.5

African-American population in selected cities, 1790

City	Total population	Black population	%
Charleston, SC	16,359	8,270	50.5
New York, NY	33,131	3,470	10.5
New Orleans, LA[1]	4,516	2,451	54.3
Philadelphia, PA	28,522	2,078	7.3
Petersburg, VA	3,761	1,744	46.4
Baltimore, MD	13,503	1,578	11.7
Norfolk, VA	2,959	1,355	45.8
Boston, MA	18,038	761	4.2
Newport, RI	6,716	640	9.5
Albany, NY	3,498	598	17.1
Providence, RI	6.380	475	7.4
Brooklyn, NY	1,603	419	26.1

(1) Figures for New Orleans, then owned by Spain, from 1791.

SOURCE: U.S. Census, 1790; Randall M. Miller and John David Smith, eds., *Dictionary of Afro-American Slavery.*

FIGURE 9.6

Black population for selected cities of Canada, Central America, South America, and the Caribbean, 2004

City	Total population	% Black population
1. Buenos Aires, Argentina	12.0 million	2*
2. São Paolo, Brazil	10.9 million	2*
3. Mexico City, Mexico	8.7 million	1*
4. Lima, Peru	8.3 million	0.6*
5. Bogotá, Colombia	11.3 million	3*
6. Toronto, Canada	5.2 million	6.6
7. Caracas, Venezuela	5.1 million	0.5*
7. Havana, Cuba	2.1 million	8*
8. Santo Domingo	2.1 million	9.5*
9. Port au Prince, Haiti	950,000	97*
10. Kingston, Jamaica	600,000	92*

* Figures are estimates extrapolated from the black population for the entire country.

FIGURE 9.7

African-American population of the United States, 1790–2000

Decade	Total population	Total black population	Slave population	Free population	% Black
1790	3,929,214	757,208	697,624	59,557	19.27
1800	5,308,483	1,002,037	893,602	108,435	18.88
1810	7,239,881	1,377,808	1,191,362	186,446	19.03
1820	9,638,453	1,771,656	1,538,022	233,634	18.38
1830	12,866,020	2,328,612	2,009,043	319,599	18.10
1840	17,069,453	2,873,648	2,487,355	386,293	16.84
1850	23,191,876	3,638,808	3,204,313	434,495	15.69
1860	31,443,321	4,441,830	3,953,760	488,070	14.13
1870	38,558,371	4,880,009			12.66
1880	50,155,783	6,580,793			13.12
1890	62,947,714	7,488,676			11.90
1900	75,991,575	8,883,994			11.62
1910	91,972,266	9,827,763			10.69
1920	105,710,620	10,463,131			9.90
1930	122,775,046	11,891,143			9.69
1940	131,669,275	12,865,518			9.77
1950	150,697,361	15,042,286			9.98
1960	179,323,175	18,871,831			10.52
1970	203,211,920	22,580,289			11.11
1980	226,546,000	26,495,000			11.70
1990	248,710,000	29,986,000			12.06
2000	281,421,906	34,658,190			12.32

FIGURE 9.8

Families, total number, average size, status of head, U.S., 1940–1991

Year	Single parent families (in thousands)*		Average size		% Husband-wife		% Male head		% Female head	
	Total	Black	Total	Black	Total	Black	Total	Black	Total	Black
1940	32,166	2,699[1]	3.76	—	83.8	77.1	4.9	5.0	11.2	17.9
1950	39,303	3,432[2]	3.54	—	87.6	77.7	3.0	4.7	9.4	17.6
1960	45,111	3,950	3.67	—	87.2	74.1	2.8	4.1	10.0	21.7
1970	51,586	4,774	3.58	4.13	86.8	68.1	2.4	3.7	10.8	28.3
1980	59,550	6,184	3.29	3.67	82.5	55.5	2.9	4.1	14.6	40.3
1990	66,090	7,470	3.17	3.46	79.2	50.2	4.4	6.0	16.5	43.8
1991	66,322	7,471	3.18	3.51	78.6	47.8	4.4	6.3	17.0	45.9
2003	75,596	4,165	n.a.	n.a.	80.1	n.a.	5.0	n.a.	14.5	n.a.
2004	76,217	4,040	3.19	2.90	n.a.	n.a.	4.2	n.a.	12.3	n.a.

*   "Family" refers to a group of two or more persons related by blood, marriage, or adoption and residing together in a household.

(1) Data revised to exclude one-person families.

(2) Data include families of other nonwhite races.

SOURCES: *Statistical Abstract, 1992*; *Historical Statistics of the United States, Colonial Times to 1970*; *The Social and Economic Status of the Black Population in the United States: An Historical View, 1790–1978*; U.S. Bureau of the Census, 2005 and earlier years.

FIGURE 9.9

Top ten U.S. cities of African-American population, 1820–2000

City	Total population	Black population	%	City	Total population	Black population	%
1820				**1940**			
1. Baltimore	62,738	14,192	22.62	1. New York	7,454,995	458,444	6.15
2. Charleston	24,780	14,127	57.01	2. Chicago	3,396,808	277,731	8.18
3. District of Columbia	33,039	10,425	31.55	3. Philadelphia	1,931,334	251,880	13.04
4. New York	123,706	10,086	8.15	4. District of Columbia	663,091	187,226	28.24
5. Philadelphia	63,802	8,785	13.77	5. Baltimore	859,100	165,843	19.30
6. New Orleans	14,175	8,515	60.07	6. Detroit	1,623,452	149,119	9.19
7. Richmond	12,067	5,622	46.59	7. New Orleans	494,537	149,034	30.14
8. Savannah	7,523	3,657	48.61	8. Memphis	292,942	121,498	41.48
9. St. Louis	10,049	2,035	20.25	9. Birmingham	267,583	108,938	40.71
10. Boston	42,536	1,737	4.08	10. St. Louis	816,048	108,765	13.33
1860				**1960**			
1. Baltimore	212,418	27,898	13.13	1. New York	7,781,984	1,087,931	13.98
2. New Orleans	168,675	24,074	14.27	2. Chicago	3,550,404	812,637	22.89
3. Philadelphia	562,529	22,185	3.94	3. Philadelphia	2,002,512	529,240	26.43
4. Charleston	40,522	17,146	42.31	4. Detroit	1,670,144	482,223	28.87
5. District of Columbia	75,080	14,316	19.07	5. District of Columbia	763,956	411,737	53.90
6. Richmond	37,910	14,275	37.65	6. Los Angeles	2,479,015	334,916	13.51
7. New York	805,658	12,472	1.55	7. Baltimore	939,024	325,589	34.67
8. Savannah	22,292	8,417	37.76	8. New Orleans	627,525	233,514	37.21
9. Mobile	29,258	8,404	28.72	9. Houston	938,219	215,037	22.92
10. Donaldsonville, La.	11,484	4,544	65.69	10. St. Louis	750,026	214,377	28.58
1900				**1990**			
1. District of Columbia	278,718	86,702	31.11	1. New York	7,322,564	2,102,512	28.17
2. Baltimore	508,957	79,258	15.57	2. Chicago	2,783,726	1,087,711	39.07
3. New Orleans	287,104	77,714	27.07	3. Detroit	1,027,974	777,916	75.67
4. Philadelphia	1,293,697	62,613	4.84	4. Philadelphia	1,585,577	631,936	39.86
5. New York	3,437,202	60,666	1.76	5. Los Angeles	3,485,398	487,674	13.99
6. Memphis	102,320	49,910	48.78	6. Houston	1,630,553	457,990	28.09
7. Louisville	204,731	39,139	19.12	7. Baltimore	736,014	435,768	59.21
8. Atlanta	89,872	35,727	39.75	8. District of Columbia	606,900	399,604	65.84
9. St. Louis	575,238	35,516	6.17	9. Memphis	610,337	334,737	54.84
10. Richmond	85,050	32,230	37.90	10. New Orleans	496,938	307,728	61.92
1920				**2000**			
1. New York	5,620,048	152,467	2.71	1. New York	8,008,278	2,129,762	26.6
2. Philadelphia	1,823,799	134,229	7.30	2. Chicago	2,898,016	1,065,009	36.8
3. District of Columbia	437,571	109,966	25.13	3. Detroit	951,270	775,772	81.6
4. Chicago	2,701,705	109,458	4.05	4. Philadelphia	1,517,550	655,824	43.2
5. Baltimore	733,826	103,322	14.08	5. Houston	1,953,631	494,496	25.3
6. New Orleans	387,219	100,930	26.07	6. Los Angeles	3,694,820	415,195	11.2
7. Birmingham	178,806	70,230	39.28	7. Baltimore	651,154	418,951	64.3
8. St. Louis	772,897	69,854	9.04	8. Memphis	650,100	399,208	61.4
9. Atlanta	200,616	62,796	31.30	9. District of Columbia	572,059	343,312	60.0
10. Memphis	162,351	61,181	37.68	10. New Orleans	484,674	325,947	67.3

SOURCE: U.S. Bureau of the Census, 2005, and earlier reports.

FIGURE 9.10

African-American population by U.S. region, 1790–2000

	Region	Total population of region	Black population of region	% of U.S. black population in region	% of regional population black
1790	Northeast	1,968,040	67,120	8.86	3.41
	Midwest	0	0	0.00	0.00
	Southeast	1,961,174	690,061	91.13	35.19
	South Central	0	0	—	—
	Mountain	0	0	—	—
	Pacific	0	0	—	—
1800	Northeast	2,635,576	83,066	8.29	3.15
	Midwest	51,006	635	0.06	1.24
	Southeast	2,621,901	918,336	91.65	35.03
	South Central	0	0	—	—
	Mountain	0	0	—	—
	Pacific	0	0	—	—
1810	Northeast	3,486,675	102,237	7.42	2.93
	Midwest	292,107	7,072	0.51	2.42
	Southeast	3,383,481	1,226,254	89.00	36.24
	South Central	77,618	42,245	3.07	54.43
	Mountain	0	0	—	—
	Pacific	0	0	—	—
1820	Northeast	4,359,916	110,724	6.25	2.54
	Midwest	859,305	18,260	1.03	2.12
	Southeast	4,251,552	1,515,784	85.56	35.65
	South Central	167,680	81,216	4.58	48.44
	Mountain	0	0	—	—
	Pacific	0	0	—	—
1830	Northeast	5,542,381	125,214	5.38	2.26
	Midwest	1,610,473	41,543	1.78	2.58
	Southeast	5,461,721	2,030,870	87.21	37.18
	South Central	246,127	131,015	5.63	53.23
	Mountain	0	0	—	—
	Pacific	0	0	—	—
1840	Northeast	6,761,082	142,324	4.95	2.11
	Midwest	3,351,542	89,347	3.11	2.67
	Southeast	6,500,744	2,427,623	84.48	37.34
	South Central	449,985	214,354	7.46	47.64
	Mountain	0	0	—	—
	Pacific	0	0	—	—
1850	Northeast	8,626,851	149,762	4.12	1.74
	Midwest	5,403,595	135,607	3.73	2.51
	Southeast	8,042,361	2,983,661	82.00	37.10
	South Central	940,251	368,537	10.13	39.20
	Mountain	72,927	72	0.00	0.10
	Pacific	105,891	1,169	0.03	1.10
1860	Northeast	10,594,268	156,001	3.51	1.47
	Midwest	9,096,716	184,239	4.15	2.03
	Southeast	9,385,694	3,452,558	77.73	36.79
	South Central	1,747,667	644,553	14.51	36.88
	Mountain	174,923	235	0.01	0.13
	Pacific	444,063	4,244	0.10	0.96
1870	Northeast	12,298,730	179,738	3.68	1.46
	Midwest	12,981,111	273,080	5.60	2.10
	Southeast	10,258,055	3,680,957	75.43	35.88
	South Central	2,029,965	739,854	15.16	36.45
	Mountain	315,385	1,555	0.03	0.49
	Pacific	675,125	4,825	0.10	0.71
1880	Northeast	14,507,407	229,417	3.49	1.58
	Midwest	17,364,111	385,621	5.86	2.22
	Southeast	13,182,348	4,866,198	73.95	36.91
	South Central	3,334,220	1,087,705	16.53	32.62
	Mountain	653,119	5,022	0.08	0.77
	Pacific	1,147,578	6,830	0.10	0.60

[continued]

African-American population by U.S. region, 1790–2000 [CONTINUED]

	Region	Total population of region	Black population of region	% of U.S. black population in region	% of regional population black
1890	Northeast	17,406,969	269,906	3.60	1.55
	Midwest	22,410,417	431,112	5.76	1.92
	Southeast	15,287,076	5,382,487	71.88	35.21
	South Central	4,740,983	1,378,090	18.40	29.07
	Mountain	1,213,935	12,971	0.17	1.07
	Pacific	1,920,334	14,110	0.19	0.73
1900	Northeast	21,046,695	385,020	4.36	1.83
	Midwest	26,333,004	495,751	5.61	1.88
	Southeast	17,991,237	6,228,903	70.51	l34.62
	South Central	6,532,290	1,694,066	19.18	25.93
	Mountain	1,674,607	15,590	0.18	0.93
	Pacific	2,634,692	14,664	0.17	0.56
1910	Northeast	25,868,573	484,176	4.93	1.87
	Midwest	29,888,542	543,498	5.53	1.82
	Southeast	20,604,796	6,765,001	68.84	32.83
	South Central	8,784,534	1,984,426	20.19	22.59
	Mountain	2,633,517	21,467	0.22	0.82
	Pacific	4,448,304	30,195	0.31	0.68
1920	Northeast	29,662,053	679,234	6.49	2.29
	Midwest	34,019,792	793,075	7.58	2.33
	Southeast	22,883,579	6,848,652	65.46	29.93
	South Central	10,242,224	2,063,579	19.72	20.15
	Mountain	3,336,101	30,801	0.29	0.92
	Pacific	5,877,819	47,790	0.46	0.81
1930	Northeast	34,427,091	1,146,985	9.65	3.33
	Midwest	38,594,100	1,262,234	10.62	3.27
	Southeast	25,680,803	7,079,626	59.54	27.57
	South Central	12,176,830	2,281,951	19.19	18.74
	Mountain	3,701,789	30,225	0.25	0.82
	Pacific	8,622,047	90,122	0.76	1.05
1940	Northeast	35,976,777	1,369,875	10.65	3.81
	Midwest	40,143,332	1,420,318	11.04	3.54
	Southeast	28,601,376	7,479,498	58.13	26.15
	South Central	13,064,525	2,425,121	18.85	18.56
	Mountain	4,150,003	36,411	0.28	0.88
	Pacific	10,229,116	134,691	1.05	1.32
1950	Northeast	39,477,986	2,018,182	13.42	5.11
	Midwest	44,460,762	2,227,876	14.81	5.01
	Southeast	32,659,516	7,793,379	51.81	23.86
	South Central	14,537,572	2,432,028	16.17	16.73
	Mountain	5,074,998	66,429	0.44	1.31
	Pacific	15,114,964	507,043	3.37	3.35
1960	Northeast	44,677,823	3,028,499	16.05	6.78
	Midwest	51,619,139	3,446,037	18.26	6.68
	Southeast	38,021,858	8,543,404	45.27	22.47
	South Central	16,951,255	2,768,203	14.67	16.33
	Mountain	6,855,060	123,242	0.65	1.80
	Pacific*	21,198,044	962,446	5.10	4.54
1970	Northeast	49,040,703	4,344,153	19.24	8.86
	Midwest	56,571,633	4,571,550	20.25	8.08
	Southeast	43,474,807	8,959,787	39.68	20.61
	South Central	19,320,560	3,010,174	13.33	15.58
	Mountain	8,281,562	180,382	0.80	2.18
	Pacific	26,522,631	1,514,243	6.71	5.71
1980	Northeast	49,165,283	4,849,969	18.18	9.86
	Midwest	58,886,670	5,332,907	19.99	9.06
	Southeast	51,625,566	10,617,734	39.79	20.57
	South Central	23,746,816	3,521,048	13.20	14.83
	Mountain	11,372,785	267,538	1.00	2.35
	Pacific	31,799,705	1,993,153	7.47	6.27

[continued]

African-American population by U.S. region, 1790–2000 [CONTINUED]

	Region	Total population of region	Black population of region	% of U.S. black population in region	% of regional population black
1990	Northeast	50,809,229	5,613,222	18.72	11.05
	Midwest	59,668,632	5,715,940	19.06	9.58
	Southeast	58,725,137	11,900,363	39.69	20.26
	South Central	26,702,793	3,718,126	12.40	13.92
	Mountain	13,658,776	373,584	1.25	2.74
	Pacific	39,127,306	2,454,426	8.19	6.27
2000	Northeast	53,594,000	6,100,000	11.4	17.6
	Midwest	64,393,000	6,500,000	10.0	18.8
	South	100,237,000	18,982,000	18.9	54.8
	West	63,198,000	3,077,000	4.9	8.9

Geographic Distribution 1790–1990:
Northeast: Connecticut, Maine, Massachusetts, New Hampshire, New Jersey, New York, Pennsylvania, Rhode Island, Vermont
Midwest: Illinois, Indiana, Iowa, Kansas, Michigan, Minnesota, Missouri, Nebraska, North Dakota, Ohio, South Dakota, Wisconsin, Virginia, West Virginia
South Central: Arkansas, Louisiana, Oklahoma, Texas
Southeast: Alabama, Delaware, Washington, D.C., Florida, Georgia, Kentucky, Maryland, Mississippi, North Carolina, South Carolina, Tennessee.
Mountain: Arizona, Colorado, Idaho, Montana, Nevada, New Mexico, Utah, Wyoming
Pacific: Alaska, California, Hawaii, Oregon, Washington

Geographic Distribution, 2000:
Northeast: Connecticut, Maine, Massachusetts, New Hampshire, New Jersey, New York, Pennsylvania, Rhode Island, Vermont.
Midwest: Illinois, Indiana, Iowa, Kansas, Michigan, Minnesota, Missouri, Nebraska, North Dakota, Ohio, South Dakota, Wisconsin.
South: Alabama, Arkansas, Delaware, District of Columbia, Florida, Georgia, Kentucky, Louisiana, Maryland, Mississippi, North Carolina, Oklahoma, South Carolina, Tennessee, Texas, Virginia, West Virginia.
West: Alaska, Arizona, California, Colorado, Hawaii, Idaho, Montana, Nevada, New Mexico, Oregon, Utah, Washington, Wyoming.

* Includes Alaska and Hawaii for first time.

SOURCE: U.S. Bureau of the Census Release, 1991, 2000; and *Statistical Abstract, 1990.*

FIGURE 10.1

Estimated membership of predominantly black denominations in the U.S., 1947–1993

Denomination (year of founding)	1950–1975			1976–1993		
	Year	Churches	Members	Year	Churches	Members
African Orthodox Churches						
African Orthodox Church (1921)	1957	24	6,000	1971*	—	10,000
African Orthodox Church of the West (1984)	—	—	—	1985	2	200
Baptist Bodies						
Black Primitive Baptists (1877)	1970	43	3,000	—	—	—
Fundamental Baptist Fellowship Association (1962)	1970	10	—	—	—	—
National Baptist Convention of America (1915)	1956	1,398	2,668,799	1987	2,500	3,500,000
National Baptist Convention of the United States of America, Inc. (1895)	1958	26,000	5,500,000	1991	30,000	7,800,000
National Baptist Evangelical Life and Soul Saving Assembly of the United States of America (1920)	1951	264	57,674	—	—	—
National Primitive Baptist Convention of the United States of America (1907)	1975	606	250,000	1991	—	250,000
Progressive National Baptist Convention, Inc. (1961)	—	—	—	1991	1,400	2,500,000
United Free-Will Baptist Church (1901)	—	—	—	1992	836	100,000
Black Hebrews						
Church of God and Saints of Christ (1896)	—	—	—	1991	217	38,127
House of Judah (1965)	—	—	—	1985	1	80
Original Hebrew Israelite Nation (1960)	—	—	—	1980	—	3,000
Yahweh's Temple (1947)	1973	—	10,000	—	—	—
Catholic Bodies						
American Catholic Church (Syro–Antiochean) (1930s)	1961	40	4,663	1979	3	501
Sacred Heart Catholic Church (1980)	—	—	—	1983	3	50
The Coptic Orthodox Church	—	—	—	1992	55	260,000
International Council Of Community Churches (1946)	—	—	—	1988	300	250,000
Kodesh Church of Immanuel (1829)	—	—	—	1980	5	326
Methodist Bodies						
African Methodist Episcopal Church (1816)	1951	5,878	1,666,301	1991	8,000	3,500,000
African Methodist Episcopal Zion Church (1821)	1959	4,083	770,000	1991	3,000	1,200,000
African Union First Colored Methodist Protestant Church (1866)	—	—	—	1988	35	6,500
Christian Methodist Episcopal Church (1870)	1961	2,523	444,493	1988	—	788,922
Free Christian Zion Church of Christ (1905)	1956	742	22,260	—	—	—
Reformed Methodist Union Episcopal Church (1885)	1970	21	5,000	1980	33	3,800
Reformed Zion Union Apostolic Church (1869)	1960	50	16,000	—	—	—
Mount Hebron Apostolic Temple of Our Lord Jesus of the Apostolic Faith (1963)	—	—	—	1980	9	3,000
[continued]						

Estimated membership of predominantly black denominations in the U.S., 1947–1993 [CONTINUED]

Denomination (year of founding)	1950–1975			1976–1993		
	Year	Churches	Members	Year	Churches	Members
Muslim Bodies						
Muslims	—	—	—	1993	—	1,000,000
Nation of Islam (Farrakhan) (1978)	—	—	—	1989	—	20,000
Pentecostal Bodies						
Alpha and Omega Pentecostal Church of God of America, Inc. (1945)	1970	3	400	1990	—	800
Apostolic Assemblies of Christ, Inc. (1970)	—	—	—	1980	23	3,500
Apostolic Church of Christ (1969)	1980*	6	300	1900	10	600
Apostolic Church of Christ in God	—	—	—	1980	13	2,150
Apostolic Faith Mission Church of God (1906)	—	—	—	1989	18	6,200
Apostolic Overcoming Holy Church of God (1920)	1956	300	75,000	1988	200	12,000
The Bible Church of Christ	—	—	—	1991	6	6,812
Bible Way Church of Our Lord Jesus Christ World Wide (1957)	1970	350	30,000	1991	300	250,000
Christ's Sanctified Holy Church (Louisiana) (1904)	1957	30	600	—	—	—
Church of Christ (Holiness) U.S.A. (1907)	1965	159	9,289	1990	189	12,890
Church of God in Christ (1906)	1965	4,500	425,000	1991	15,300	5,477,875
Church of God in Christ, Congregational (1932)	1970	33	—	—	—	—
Church of God in Christ, International (1969)	1971	1,041	501,000	1982	300	200,000
Church of God (Sanctified Church) (1901)	1975	60	5,000	1991	69	6,000
Church of the Living God (Christian Workers for Fellowship) (1889)	—	—	—	1985	170	42,000
Church of Living God, the Pillar and Ground of Truth (1903)	—	—	—	1988	100	2,000
Church of the Lord Jesus Christ of the Apostolic Faith (1919)	1954	155	30,000	1993	457	81,000
Churches of God, Holiness (1914)	1967	42	165,000	—	—	—
Commandment Keepers Congregation of the Living God (1924)	1970	—	3,000	—	—	—
Fire-Baptized Holiness Church of God of the Americas (1908)	1958	53	998	1991	49	695
Highway Christian Church of Christ (1929)	1980*	13	3,000	1991	—	900
House of God, Which Is the Church of the Living God, the Pillar and Ground of Truth, Inc. (1919)	1956	107	2,350	1970*	103	25,800
Latter House of the Lord for All People and the Church of the Mountain, Apostolic Faith (1936)	1947	—	4,000	—	—	—
Mount Sinai Holy Church (1924)	1968	92	2,000	1991	125	10,000
Original Glorious Church of God in Christ Apostolic Faith (1921)	—	—	—	1980	55	25,000
Original United Holy Church International (1977)	—	—	—	1985	210	15,000
Pentecostal Assemblies of the World (1906)	1960	550	4,500	1989	1,005	500,000
Pentecostal Churches of Apostolic Faith (1957)	—	—	—	1991	128	151,000
Shiloh Apostolic Temple (1953)	—	—	—	1985	33	7,500
Sought Out Church of God in Christ	1949	4	60	—	—	—
Triumph the Church and Kingdom of God in Christ (1902)	1972	475	54,307	—	—	—
United Church of Jesus Christ (Apostolic) (1945)	—	—	—	1985	75	100,000
United Holy Church of America (1886)	1960	470	28,890	1970*	470	50,000
United Way of the Cross Churches of Christ of the Apostolic Faith	1980*	14	1,100	1990	14	1,002
Universal Christian Spiritual Faith and Churches for All Nations (1952)	1965	60	40,816	—	—	—
Way of the Cross Church of Christ (1927)	1980	48	50,000	1987	68	60,000

[continued]

Estimated membership of predominantly black denominations in the U.S., 1947–1993 [CONTINUED]

Denomination (year of founding)	1950–1975			1976–1993		
	Year	Churches	Members	Year	Churches	Members
Presbyterian Bodies Second Cumberland Presbyterian Church in the United States (1874)	1959	221	30,000	—	—	—

* Most recent data available

SOURCE: "Black Americans and the Churches," in *Religions of America* (New York, 1975); *Black Americans Information Directory (1990–91)* (New York, 1990); *Directory of African American Religious Bodies: A Compendium by the Howard University School of Divinity* (Washington, D.C., 1991); "The Negro in American Religious Life," in *The American Negro Reference Book* (Englewood Cliffs, N.J., 1970); *Statistical Record of Black America* (Detroit, 1990); *Yearbook of American and Canadian Churches: 1993* (Nashville, Tenn., 1992); *Yearbook of American and Canadian Churches: 1992* (Nashville, Tenn., 1991); *Yearbook of American and Canadian Churches: 1973* (Nashville, Tenn., 1973). Membership figures provided by denominations themselves, which use different criteria to determine them.

FIGURE 10.2

Membership of racially mixed denominations in the U.S., 1890, 1916, and 1936

Denomination	1890		1916		1936	
	Black members	Total members	Black members	Total members	Black members	Total members
Adventist Bodies Advent Christian	—	25,816	317	30,597	—	26,258
Seventh-Day	—	28,991	2,553	79,355	6,367	133,254
Baptist Bodies Northern Convention	35,221	800,025	53,842	1,232,135	45,821	1,329,044
Congregational Church	6,908	512,771	13,209	791,274	20,437	976,388
Disciples of Christ	18,578	641,051	11,478	1,226,028	21,950	1,196,315
Lutheran Bodies Synodical Conference	211	357,153	1,525	777,701	8,985	1,463,482
Methodist Bodies Methodist Episcopal	246,249	2,240,354	320,025	3,717,785	193,761	3,509,763
Methodist Protestant	3,183	141,989	2,869	186,908	2,321	148,288
Moravian Bodies Moravian Church (Unitas Fratrum)	—	11,781	419	26,373	628	30,904
Presbyterian Bodies Presbyterian Church in the United States of America	14,961	788,224	31,957	1,611,251	279	449,045
Presbyterian Church in the United States	1,568	179,721	1,429	357,769	2,971	1,797,927
Protestant Episcopal Church	2,977	532,054	23,775	1,092,821	29,738	1,735,335
Reformed Episcopal Church	1,723	8,455	3,017	11,050	2,434	7,656
Roman Catholic Church	17,079	6,231,417	51,688	15,721,815	137,684	19,914,937
Salvation Army	—	8,741	—	35,954	436	103,038

SOURCES: *Report on Statistics of Churches of the United States at the Eleventh Census: 1890* (Washington, D.C., 1894); *Religious Bodies: 1916* (Washington, D.C., 1919); *Religious Bodies: 1936* (Washington, D.C., 1941).

FIGURE 10.3

Membership of racially mixed denominations in the U.S., 1963–1992

Denomination	Year	Black membership	Total membership
American Baptist Convention	1964	200,000	1,559,103
	1990	496,000	1,535,971
Christian Churches	1964	80,000	1,920,760
(Disciples of Christ)	1992	61,000	1,039,692
Congregational Christian	1964	38,000	110,000
Churches	1992	9,000	75,000
Lutheran Church-	1991	15,147	2,609,025
Missouri Synod			
Mennonite Church	1992	3,476	114,307
Protestant Episcopal Church	1963	73,867	3,340,759
	1990	250,000	2,446,050
Reformed Episcopal Church	1992	3,184	6,042
Roman Catholic Church	1964	722,609	45,640,619
	1990	2,000,000	58,568,015
Seventh-Day Adventists	1964	167,892	370,688
	1990	280,000	717,446
United Church of Christ	1964	21,859	2,056,696
	1989	62,048	1,662,568
United Methodist Church	1964	373,327	10,304,184
	1992	257,436	8,853,455
United Presbyterian Church	1964	6,000	3,302,839
in the United States of	1990	65,000	3,788,009
America			

FIGURE 11.1

African-American members of the National Baseball Hall of Fame, Cooperstown, N.Y.

Year inducted	Member	Born-Died
1962	Jack R. Robinson	1919–1972
1969	Roy Campanella	1921–1993
1971	Leroy R. "Satchel" Paige*	1906–1982
1972	Joshua Gibson*	1911–1947
	Walter F. "Buck" Leonard*	1907–1997
1973	Roberto W. Clemente	1934–1972
	Monford "Monte" Irvin*	1919—
1974	James T. "Cool Papa" Bell*	1903–1991
1975	William J. "Judy" Johnson*	1900–1989
1976	Oscar M. Charleston*	1896–1954
1977	Ernest Banks	1931—
	Martin Dihigo*	1905–1971
1979	Willie H. Mays	1931—
1981	Andrew "Rube" Foster*	1878–1930
	Robert Gibson	1935—
1982	Henry L. Aaron	1934—
	Frank Robinson	1935—
1983	Juan A. Marichal	1937—
1985	Louis C. Brock	1939—
1986	Willie L. McCovey	1938—
1987	Raymond E. Dandridge*	1913—
	Billy Williams	1938—
1988	Wilver D. Stargell	1940—
1990	Joe L. Morgan	1943—
1991	Rodney C. Carew	1945—
	Ferguson A. Jenkins	1943—
1993	Reginald M. Jackson	1946—
1995	Leon Day*	1916–1995
1996	Bill Foster*	1904–1978
1997	Willie Wells*	1906–1989
1998	Larry Doby	1924–2003
	Wilber "Bullet" Joe Rogan*	1889–1967
1999	Orlando Cepeda	1937—
	Joe Williams*	1886–1951
2000	Tony Pérez	1942—
	Turkey Stearnes*	1901–1979
2001	Kirby Puckett	1961—
	Hilton Smith*	1907–1983
	Dave Winfield	1951—
2002	Ozzie Smith	1954—
2003	Eddie Murray	1956—

* Members of the Negro League.

FIGURE 11.2

African-American members of the National Track & Field Hall of Fame, Indianapolis, Ind.

Year inducted	Member	Born-Died
1974	Ralph Boston	1939—
	Lee Calhoun	1933–1989
	Harrison Dillard	1923—
	Rafer Johnson	1935—
	Jesse Owens	1913–1980
	Mal Whitfield	1924—
	Wilma Rudolph	1940—
1975	Alice Coachman (Davis)	1932—
	Edward Hurt	1900–1989
	Ralph Metcalfe	1910–1978
1976	Mae Faggs (Starrs)	1932—
	Bob Hayes	1942–2002
	Hayes Jones	1938—
1977	Bob Beamon	1946—
	Andy Stanfield	1927–1985
1978	Tommie Smith	1944—
	John Woodruff	1915—
1979	Jim Hines	1946—
	Dehart Hubbard	1903–1976
	Edith McGuire (DuVall)	1944—
1980	Dave Albritton	1913–1944
	Wyomia Tyus Tillman	1945—
1981	Willye White	1939—
1982	Willie Davenport	1943–2002
	Eddie Tolan	1908–1967
1983	Lee Evans	1947—
	Mildred McDaniel (Singleton)	1933–2004
	LeRoy Walker	1918—
1984	Madeline Manning (Mims)	1948—
	Joseph Yancey	1910–1991
1985	John Thomas	1941—
1986	Barney Ewell	1918–1996
1987	Eulace Peacock	1914–996
	Martha Watson	1946—
1988	Greg Bell	1928—
	Barbara Ferrell (Edmonson)	1947—
1989	Milt Campbell	1933—
	Nell Jackson	1929–1988
	Ed Temple	1927—
1990	Charles Dumas	1937–2004
1992	Charles Greene	1944—
	Charlie Jenkins	1934—
	Archie Williams	1915–1993
1993	Rod Milburn	1950–1997
	Stan Wright	1921–1998
1994	Cornelius Johnson	1913–1946
	Edwin Moses	1955—
1995	Valerie Brisco-Hooks	1960—
	Florence Griffith-Joyner	1959—
1996	Cleve Abbott	1894–1955
[continued]		

African-American members of the National Track & Field Hall of Fame, Indianapolis, Ind. [CONTINUED]

Year inducted	Member	Born-Died
1997	Evelyn Ashford	1957–
	Henry Carr	1942–
	Renaldo Nehemiah	1959–
1999	Willie Banks	1956–
	Larry Ellis	1929–1998
2000	John Borican	1913–1943
	Chandra Cheeseborough	1959–
2001	Carl Lewis	1961–
	Larry Myricks	1956–
2002	Gwen Torrence	1965–
2003	John Carlos	1945–
	Larry James	1947–

FIGURE 11.3

African-American Olympic medalists

1904: St. Louis, Missouri, USA

George C. Poage	bronze	400-m hurdles
	bronze	200-m hurdles

1908: London, England

John Baxter Taylor	gold	4 x 400-m relay

1924: Paris, France

Edward Gourdin	silver	long jump
William DeHart Hubbard	gold	long jump
Earl Johnson	bronze	10,000-m cross country

1932: Los Angeles, Calif.

Edward Gordon	gold	long jump
Ralph Metcalfe	silver	100-m dash
	bronze	200-m dash
Eddie Tolan	gold	100-m dash
	gold	200-m dash

1936: Berlin, Germany

David Albritton	silver	high jump
Cornelius Johnson	gold	high jump
James Luvalle	bronze	400-m dash
Ralph Metcalfe	gold	4 x 100-m relay
	silver	100-m dash
Jesse Owens	gold	100-m dash
	gold	200-m dash
	gold	long jump
	gold	4 x 100-m relay
Fritz Pollard, Jr.	bronze	110-m hurdles
Mack Robinson	silver	200-m dash
Archie Williams	gold	400-m run
Jackie Wilson	silver	boxing (bantam weight)
John Woodruff	gold	800-m run

1948: London, England

Women

Alice Coachman	gold	high jump
Audrey Patterson	bronze	200-m dash

Men

Don Barksdale	gold	basketball
John Davis	gold	weightlifting (heavyweight)
Harrison Dillard	gold	100-m dash
	gold	4 x 100-m relay
Norwood Ewell	gold	4 x 100-m relay
	silver	100-m dash
Horace Herring	silver	boxing (welter weight)
Willie Steele	gold	long jump
Mal Whitfield	gold	800-m run
Lorenzo Wright	gold	4 x 100-m relay

1952: Helsinki, Finland

Women

Mae Faggs	gold	4 x 100-m relay
Catherine Hardy	gold	4 x 100-m relay
Barbara Jones	gold	4 x 100-m relay

Men

Charles Adkins	gold	boxing (light welterweight)

[continued]

African-American Olympic medalists [CONTINUED]

Jerome Biffle	gold	long jump
James Bradford	silver	weightlifting (heavyweight)
Nathan Brooks	gold	boxing (flyweight)
Milton Campbell	silver	decathalon
John Davis	gold	weightlifting (heavyweight)
Harrison Dillard	gold	110-m hurdles
	gold	4 x 100-m relay
Meredith Gourdine	silver	long jump
Norvel Lee	gold	boxing (light heavyweight)
Ollie Matson	silver	4 x 400-m relay
	bronze	400-m dash
Floyd Patterson	gold	boxing (middle-weight)
Edward Hayes Sanders	gold	boxing (heavy-weight)
Andrew Stanfield	gold	200-m dash
	gold	4 x 100-m relay
Mal Whitfield	gold	800-m run
	silver	4 x 400-m relay

1956: Melbourne, Australia

Women

Isabelle Danielles	bronze	4 x 100-m relay
Mae Faggs	bronze	4 x 100-m relay
Margaret Matthews	bronze	4 x 100-m relay
Mildred McDaniel	gold	high jump
Wilma Rudolph	bronze	4 x 100-m relay
Willye White	silver	long jump

Men

Greg Bell	gold	long jump
James Boyd	gold	boxing (light heavyweight)
Carl Cain	gold	basketball
Lee Calhoun	gold	110-m hurdles
Milton Campbell	gold	decathalon
Josh Culbreath	bronze	400-m hurdles
Charles Dumas	gold	high jump
Charles Jenkins	gold	4 x 400-m relay
	gold	400-m dash
Rafer Johnson	silver	decathalon
K.C. Jones	gold	basketball
Lou Jones	gold	4 x 400-m relay
Leamon King	gold	4 x 100-m relay
Ira Murchison	gold	4 x 100-m relay
Bill Russell	gold	basketball
Andrew Stanfield	silver	200-m dash
Jose Torres	silver	boxing (light middleweight)

1960: Rome, Italy

Women

Earline Brown	bronze	shot put
Martha Hudson	gold	4 x 100-m relay
Barbara Jones	gold	4 x 100-m relay
Wilma Rudolph	gold	100-m dash
	gold	200-m dash
	gold	4 x 100-m relay
Lucinda Williams	gold	4 x 100-m relay

[continued]

African-American Olympic medalists [CONTINUED]

Men

Cassius Clay (Muhammad Ali)	gold	boxing (light-heavyweight)
Walt Bellamy	gold	basketball
Bob Boozer	gold	basketball
Ralph Boston	gold	long jump
James Bradford	silver	weightlifting (heavyweight)
Lee Calhoun	gold	110-m hurdles
Lester Carney	silver	200-m dash
Edward Crook	gold	boxing (middle-weight)
Quincey Daniels	bronze	boxing (light welterweight)
Otis Davis	gold	400-m dash
	gold	4 x 400-m relay
Rafer Johnson	gold	decathalon
Hayes Jones	bronze	110-m hurdles
Willie May	silver	110-m hurdles
Wilbert McClure	gold	boxing (light middleweight)
Irvin Roberson	silver	long jump
Oscar Robertson	gold	basketball
John Thomas	bronze	high jump

1964: Tokyo, Japan

Women

Edith McGuire	gold	200-m dash
	silver	4 x 100-m relay
	silver	100-m dash
Wyomia Tyus	gold	100-m dash
	silver	4 x 100-m relay
Marilyn White	silver	4 x 100-m relay
Willye White	silver	4 x 100-m relay

Men

Jim Barnes	gold	basketball
Ralph Boston	silver	long jump
Charles Brown	bronze	boxing (feather-weight)
Joe Caldwell	gold	basketball
Henry Carr	gold	200-m dash
	gold	4 x 400-m relay
Paul Drayton	gold	4 x 100-m relay
	silver	200-m dash
Joseph "Joe" Frazier	gold	boxing (heavy-weight)
Ronald Harris	bronze	boxing (light-weight)
Bob Hayes	gold	100-m dash
	gold	4 x 100-m relay
Walt Hazzard	gold	basketball
Luke Jackson	gold	basketball
Hayes Jones	gold	110-m hurdles
John Rambo	bronze	high jump
Richard Stebbins	gold	4 x 100-m relay
John Thomas	silver	high jump
Ulis Williams	gold	4 x 400-m relay
George Wilson	gold	basketball

[continued]

African-American Olympic medalists [CONTINUED]

1968: Mexico City, Mexico
Women

Margaret Bailes	gold	4 x 100-m relay
Barbara Ferrell	gold	4 x 100-m relay
	silver	100-m dash
Madeline Manning	gold	800-m run
Mildrette Netter	gold	4 x 100-m relay
Wyomia Tyus	gold	100-m dash
	gold	4 x 100-m relay

Men

John Lee Baldwin	bronze	boxing (light middleweight)
Bob Beamon	gold	long jump
Ralph Boston	bronze	long jump
John Carlos	bronze	200-m dash
Edward Caruthers	silver	high jump
Willie Davenport	gold	110-m hurdles
Lee Evans	gold	400-m dash
	gold	4 x 400-m relay
George Foreman	gold	boxing (heavyweight)
Calvin Fowles	gold	basketball
Ron Freeman	gold	4 x 400-m relay
	bronze	400-m dash
Charles Greene	gold	4 x 100-m relay
	bronze	100-m dash
Ervin Hall	silver	110-m hurdles
Ronald Harris	gold	boxing (lightweight)
Spencer Haywood	gold	basketball
James Hines	gold	100-m dash
	gold	4 x 100-m relay
Larry James	gold	4 x 400-m relay
	silver	400-m dash
Alfred Jones	bronze	boxing (middleweight)
James King	gold	basketball
Harlan Marbley	bronze	boxing (light flyweight)
Vincent Mathews	gold	4 x 400-m relay
Melvin Pender	gold	4 x 100-m relay
Albert Robinson	silver	boxing (featherweight)
Charlie Scott	gold	basketball
Ronnie Smith	gold	4 x 100-m relay
Tommie Smith	gold	200-m dash
James Wallington	bronze	boxing (light welterweight)
Jo Jo White	gold	basketball

1972: Munich, West Germany
Women

Mable Ferguson	silver	4 x 400-m relay
Madeline Manning	silver	4 x 400-m relay
Cheryl Toussaint	silver	4 x 400-m relay

Men

Mike Bantom	silver	basketball

[continued]

African-American Olympic medalists [CONTINUED]

Larry Black	gold	4 x 100-m relay
	silver	200-m dash
Jim Brewer	silver	basketball
Ricardo Carreras	bronze	boxing (bantamweight)
Wayne Collett	silver	400-m dash
James Forbes	silver	basketball
Eddie Hart	gold	4 x 100-m relay
Tom Henderson	silver	basketball
Marvin L. Johnson	bronze	boxing (middleweight)
Dwight Jones	silver	basketball
Vincent Mathews	gold	400-m dash
Rod Milburn	gold	110-m hurdles
Ed Ratleff	silver	basketball
Arnie Robinson	bronze	long jump
Ray Seales	gold	boxing (light-welterweight)
Robert Taylor	gold	4 x 100-m relay
	silver	100-m dash
Gerald Tinker	gold	4 x 100-m relay
Randy Williams	gold	long jump

1976: Montreal, Canada
Women

Rosalyn Bryant	silver	4 x 400-m relay
Anita DeFrantz	bronze	rowing (eights with coxswain)
Lusia Harris	silver	basketball
Sheila Ingram	silver	4 x 400-m relay
Pamela Jiles	silver	4 x 400-m relay
Charlotte Lewis	silver	basketball
Gail Marquis	silver	basketball
Patricia Roberts	silver	basketball
Deborah Sapenter	silver	4 x 400-m relay

Men

David Lee Armstrong	silver	boxing (featherweight)
Benny Brown	gold	4 x 400-m relay
Quinn Buckner	gold	basketball
James Butts	silver	triple jump
Kenny Carr	gold	basketball
Allen Coage	bronze	judo
Adrian Dantley	gold	basketball
Willie Davenport	bronze	110-m hurdles
Howard Davis	gold	boxing (lightweight)
Dwayne Evans	bronze	200-m dash
Phil Ford	gold	basketball
Herman Frazier	gold	4 x 400-m relay
	bronze	400-m dash
Harvey Glance	gold	4 x 100-m relay
Millard Hampton	gold	4 x 100-m relay
	silver	200-m dash
Phil Hubbard	gold	basketball
John Jones	gold	4 x 100-m relay

[continued]

African-American Olympic medalists [CONTINUED]

Lloyd Keaser	silver	wrestling (freestyle)
"Sugar" Ray Leonard	gold	boxing (light-welterweight)
Scott May	gold	basketball
Charles Michael Mooney	silver	boxing (bantam-weight)
Edwin Moses	gold	400-m hurdles
Fred Newhouse	gold	4 x 400-m relay
	silver	400-m dash
Maxie Parks	gold	4 x 400-m relay
Leo Randolph	gold	boxing (flyweight)
Arnie Robinson	gold	long jump
Steve Riddick	gold	4 x 100-m relay
Steve Sheppard	gold	basketball
Leon Spinks	gold	boxing (light-heavyweight)
Michael Spinks	gold	boxing (middle-weight)
Johnny Tate	bronze	boxing (heavy-weight)
Randy Williams	silver	long jump

1984: Los Angeles, California, USA

Women

Evelyn Ashford	gold	100-m dash
	gold	4 x 100-m relay
Jeanette Bolden	gold	4 x 100-m relay
Cathy Boswell	gold	basketball
Valerie Brisco-Hooks	gold	200-m dash
	gold	400-m dash
	gold	4 x 400-m relay
Alice Brown	gold	4 x 100-m relay
	silver	100-m dash
Judi Brown	silver	400-m hurdles
Rita Crockett	silver	volleyball
Chandra Cheeseborough	gold	4 x 100-m relay
	gold	4 x 400-m relay
	silver	400-m dash
Teresa Edwards	gold	basketball
Benita Fitzgerald-Brown	gold	100-m hurdles
Florence Griffith	silver	200-m dash
Sherri Howard	gold	4 x 400-m relay
Flo Hyman	silver	volleyball
Jackie Joyner	silver	heptathlon
Janice Lawrence	gold	basketball
Lillie Leatherwood	gold	4 x 400-m relay
Rose Magers	silver	volleyball
Pam McGee	gold	basketball
Cheryl Miller	gold	basketball
Kim Turner	bronze	100-m hurdles
Lynette Woodard	gold	basketball

Men

Ray Armstead	gold	4 x 400-m relay
Alonzo Babers	gold	400-m dash
	gold	4 x 400-m relay
Kirk Baptiste	silver	200-m dash
Tyrell Biggs	gold	boxing (super heavyweight)

[continued]

African-American Olympic medalists [CONTINUED]

Mark Breland	gold	boxing (welter-weight)
Ron Brown	gold	4 x 100-m relay
Mike Conley	silver	triple jump
Patrick Ewing	gold	basketball
Vern Fleming	gold	basketball
Greg Foster	silver	110-m hurdles
Greg Gibson	silver	wrestling (Greco-Roman)
Sam Graddy	gold	4 x 100-m relay
	silver	100-m dash
Danny Harris	silver	400-m hurdles
Virgil Eugene Hill	silver	boxing (middle-weight)
Evander Holyfield	bronze	boxing (light heavyweight)
Earl Jones	bronze	800-m run
Michael Jordan	gold	basketball
Al Joyner	gold	triple jump
Roger Kingdom	gold	110-m hurdles
Carl Lewis	gold	100-m dash
	gold	200-m dash
	gold	long jump
	gold	4 x 100-m relay
Edward Liddie	bronze	judo
Steve McCroy	gold	boxing (flyweight)
Antonio McKay	gold	4 x 400-m relay
	bronze	400-m dash
Edwin Moses	gold	400-m hurdles
Sunder Nix	gold	4 x 400-m relay
Jerry Page	gold	boxing (light welterweight)
Sam Perkins	gold	basketball
Alvin Robertson	gold	basketball
Calvin Smith	gold	4 x 400-m relay
Frank Tate	gold	boxing (light middleweight)
Meldrick Taylor	gold	boxing (feather-weight)
Henry Tillman	gold	boxing (heavy-weight)
Waymon Tisdale	gold	basketball
Nelson Vails	gold	cycling
Peter Westbrook	bronze	fencing (saber)
Pernell Whitaker	gold	boxing (light-weight)
Leon Wood	gold	basketball

1988: Seoul, Korea

Women

Evelyn Ashford	gold	4 x 100-m relay
Valerie Brisco	silver	4 x 400-m relay
Alice Brown	gold	4 x 100-m relay
Cynthia Brown	gold	basketball
Victoria Bullett	gold	basketball
Diane Dixon	silver	4 x 400-m relay
Sheila Echols	gold	4 x 100-m relay
Teresa Edwards	gold	basketball
Bridgette Gordon	gold	basketball

[continued]

African-American Olympic medalists [CONTINUED]

Florence Griffith-Joyner	gold	100-m dash
	gold	200-m dash
	gold	4 x 100-m relay
	silver	4 x 400-m relay
Denean Howard-Hill	silver	4 x 400-m relay
Jackie Joyner-Kersee	gold	heptathlon
	gold	long jump
Katrian McClain	gold	basketball
Teresa Weatherspoon	gold	basketball

Men

Willie Anderson	silver	basketball
Stacey Augman	silver	basketball
Anthony Campbell	bronze	110-m hurdles
Vernell Coles	silver	basketball
Joe Deloach	gold	200-m dash
Romallis Ellis	bronze	boxing (light-weight)
Danny Everett	gold	4 x 400-m relay
Kenneth Gould	bronze	boxing (welter-weight)
Hersey Hawkins	silver	basketball
Roy L. Jones II	silver	boxing (light middleweight)
Robert Kingdom	gold	110-m hurdles
Carl Lewis	gold	100-m dash
	gold	long jump
	silver	200-m dash
Steve Lewis	gold	400-m dash
	gold	4 x 400-m relay
Danny Manning	silver	basketball
Andrew Maynard	gold	boxing (light heavyweight)
Kennedy McKinney	gold	boxing (bantam-weight)
Ray Mercer	gold	boxing (heavy-weight)
Edwin Moses	bronze	400-m hurdles
Andre Phillips	gold	400-m hurdles
Mike Powell	silver	long jump
Herman "J.R." Reid	silver	basketball
Harold "Butch" Reynolds	gold	4 x 400-m relay
	silver	400-m dash
Mitchell Richmond	silver	basketball
David Robinson	silver	basketball
Charles D. Smith	silver	basketball
Charles E. Smith	silver	basketball

1988: Calgary, Canada

Debi Thomas	bronze	figure skating

1992: Barcelona, Spain

Women

Evelyn Ashford	gold	4 x 100-m relay
Victoria Bullett	bronze	basketball
Dedra Charles	bronze	basketball
Tara Cross-Battle	bronze	volleyball
Clarissa Davis	bronze	basketball
Gail Devers	gold	100-m dash
Medina Dixon	bronze	basketball
Sandra Farmer-Patrick	silver	400-m hurdles
Carlette Guidry	gold	4 x 100-m relay
Tammie Jackson	bronze	basketball
Carolyn Jones	bronze	basketball
Esther Jones	gold	4 x 100-m relay
Jackie Joyner-Kersee	gold	heptathlon

[continued]

African-American Olympic medalists [CONTINUED]

Natasha Kaiser	bronze	long jump
	silver	4 x 400-m relay
Ruth T. Lawanson	bronze	volleyball
Lavona Martin	silver	100-m hurdles
Katrina McClain	bronze	basketball
Jearl Miles	silver	4 x 400-m relay
Elaina Oden	bronze	volleyball
Kimberly Yvette Oden	bronze	volleyball
Vickie Orr	bronze	basketball
Tonya "Tee" Sanders	bronze	volleyball
Rochelle Stevens	silver	4 x 400-m relay
Gwen Torrence	gold	200-m dash
	gold	4 x 100-m relay
	silver	4 x 400-m relay
Janeene Vickers	bronze	basketball
Teresa Weatherspoon	bronze	basketball

Men

Tim Austin	bronze	boxing (flyweight)
Charles Barkley	gold	basketball
Mike Bates	bronze	200-m dash
Chris Byrd	silver	boxing (middle-weight)
Leroy Burrell	gold	4 x 100-m relay
Chris Campbell	bronze	wrestling (freestyle)
Mike Conley	gold	triple jump
Tony Dees	silver	110-m hurdles
Clyde Drexler	gold	basketball
Patrick Ewing	gold	basketball
Johnny Gray	bronze	800-m run
Joe Greene	bronze	long jump
Kevin Jackson	gold	wrestling (freestyle)
Michael Johnson	gold	4 x 400-m relay
Earvin "Magic" Johnson	gold	basketball
Michael Johnson	gold	4 x 400-m relay
Carl Lewis	gold	4 x 100-m relay
	gold	long jump
Steve Lewis	gold	4 x 400-m relay
	silver	400-m dash
Karl Malone	gold	basketball
Mike Marsh	gold	200-m dash
	gold	4 x 100-m relay
Dennis Mitchell	gold	4 x 100-m relay
	bronze	100-m dash
Kenny Monday	silver	wrestling (freestyle)
Scottie Pippen	gold	basketball
Mike Powell	silver	long jump
David Robinson	gold	basketball
Charles Simpkins	silver	triple jump
Rodney Smith	bronze	wrestling (Greco-Roman)
Quincy Watts	gold	400-m dash
	gold	4 x 400-m relay
Andrew Yalmon	gold	4 x 400-m relay
Kevin Young	gold	400-m hurdles

1996: Atlanta, Georgia, USA

Women

Kim Batten	silver	400-m hurdles
Ruthie Bolton	gold	basketball
Tonya Buford-Bailey	bronze	400-m hurdles
Chryste Gaines	gold	4 x 100-m relay
Dominique Dawes	bronze	gymnastics (floor exercise)
	gold	gymnastics (team)

[continued]

African-American Olympic medalists [CONTINUED]

Gail Deavers	gold	100-m dash
	gold	4 x 100-m relay
Teresa Edwards	gold	basketball
Kim Graham	gold	4 x 400-m relay
Jackie Joyner-Kersee	bronze	long jump
Venus Lacey	gold	basketball
Lisa Leslie	gold	basketball
Maicel Malone	gold	4 x 400-m relay
Katrina McClain	gold	Ibasketball
Nikki McCray	gold	basketball
Carla McGhee	gold	basketball
Jearl Miles	gold	4 x 400-m relay
Inger Miller	gold	4 x 100-m relay
Brianna Scurry	gold	soccer
Dawn Staley	gold	basketball
Rochelle Stevens	gold	4 x 400-m relay
Sheryl Swoopes	gold	basketball
Gwen Torrence	bronze	100-m dash
	gold	4 x 100-m relay
Linetta Wilson	gold	4 x 400-m relay

Men

Derrick Adkins	gold	400-m hurdles
Kurt Angle	gold	wrestling (freestyle)
Charles Austin	gold	high jump
Charles Barkley	gold	basketball
Terrance Cauthen	bronze	boxing (light-weight)
Mike Crear	silver	110-m hurdles
Calvin Davis	bronze	400-m hurdles
Jon Drummond	silver	4 x 100-m relay
Joe Greene	broze	long jump
Anfernee Hardaway	gold	basketball
Tim Harden	silver	4 x 100-m relay
Alvin Harrison	gold	4 x 400-m relay
Kenny Harrison	gold	triple jump
Grant Hill	gold	basketball
Allen Johnson	gold	110-m hurdles
Michael Johnson	gold	200-m dash
Carl Lewis	gold	long jump
Jair Lynch	silver	gymnastics (parallel bars)
Karl Malone	gold	basketball
Michael Marsh	silver	4 x 100-m relay
Anthuan Maybank	gold	4 x 400-m relay
Floyd Mayweather	bronze	boxing (feather-weight)
Reggie Miller	gold	basketball
Derek Mills	gold	4 x 400-m relay
Dennis Mitchell	silver	4 x 100-relay
Tim Montgomery	silver	4 x 100-m relay
Hakeem Olajuwon	gold	basketball
Dan O'Brien	gold	decathlon
Shaquille O'Neal	gold	basketball
Gary Payton	gold	basketball
Scottie Pippen	gold	basketball
Mitch Richmond	gold	basketball
David Reid	gold	boxing (light middleweight)
David Robinson	gold	basketball
Jason Rouser	gold	4 x 400-m relay
LaMont Smith	gold	4 x 400-m relay

[continued]

African-American Olympic medalists [CONTINUED]

Antonio Tarver	bronze	boxing (light heavyweight)
Roshii Wells	bronze	boxing (middle-weight)

2000: Sydney, Australia

Women

Ruthie Bolton	gold	basketball
LaTasha Colander-Richardson	gold	4 x 400-m relay
Teresa Edwards	gold	basketball
Torrie Edwards	bronze	4 x 100-m relay
Chryste Gaines	bronze	4 x 100-m relay
Yolanda Griffith	gold	basketball
Monique Hennagan	gold	4 x 400-m relay
Chamique Holdsclaw	gold	basketball
Marion Jones	gold	100-m dash
	gold	200-m dash
	gold	4 x 400-m relay
	bronze	4 x 100-m relay
	bronze	long jump
Lisa Leslie	gold	basketball
Katrina McClain	gold	basketball
Nikki McCray	gold	basketball
Jearl Miles-Clark	gold	4 x 400-m relay
DeLisha Milton	gold	basketball
Melissa Morrison	bronze	100-m hurdles
Nanceen Perry	bronze	4 x 100-m relay
Brianna Scurry	silver	soccer
Danielle Slaton	silver	soccer
Dawn Staley	gold	basketball
Sheryl Swoopes	gold	basketball
Natalie Williams	gold	basketball

Men

Shareef Abdur-Rahim	gold	basketball
Ray Allen	gold	basketball
Vin Baker	gold	basketball
Dain Blanton	gold	beach volleyball
Vince Carter	gold	basketball
Mike Crear	bronze	110-m hurdles
Jonathan Drummond	gold	4 x 100-m relay
Kevin Garnett	gold	basketball
Maurice Greene	gold	100-m dash
	gold	4 x 100-m relay
Tim Hardaway	gold	basketball
Alvin Harrison	silver	400-m dash
Calvin Harrison	gold	4 x 400-m relay
	gold	4 x 400-m relay
Allan Houston	gold	basketball
Chris Huffins	bronze	decathlon
Lawrence Johnson	silver	pole vault
Michael Johnson	gold	400-m dash
	gold	4 x 400-m relay
Jason Kidd	gold	basketball
Brian Lewis	gold	4 x 100-m relay
Antonio McDyess	gold	basketball
Alonzo Mourning	gold	basketball
Gary Payton	gold	basketball
Antonio Pettigrew	gold	4 x 400-m relay
Steve Smith	gold	basketball
Angelo Taylor	gold	400-m hurdles
Jermain Taylor	bronze	boxing (light middleweight)

[continued]

African-American Olympic medalists [CONTINUED]

Terence Trammell	silver	110-m hurdles
Clarence Vinson	broze	boxing (bantam-weight)
Bernard Williams III	gold	4 x 100-m relay
Ricardo Williams	silver	boxing (light welterweight)

2004: Athens, Greece

Women

Swin Cash	gold	basketball
Tamika Catchings	gold	basketball
Crystal Cox	gold	4 x 400-m relay
Allyson Felix	silver	200-m dash
Yolanda Griffith	gold	basketball
Joanna Hayes	gold	100-m hurdles
Monique Henderson	gold	4 x 400-m relay
Monique Hennagan	gold	4 x 400-m relay
Angela Hucles	gold	soccer
Shannon Johnson	gold	basketball
Lisa Leslie	gold	basketball
Melissa Morrison	bronze	100-m hurdles
Sanya Richards	gold	4 x 400-m relay
Ruth Riley	gold	basketball
Moushaumi Robinson	gold	4 x 400-m relay
Brianna Scurry	gold	soccer
Dawn Staley	gold	basketball
Sheryl Swoopes	gold	basketball
Tina Thompson	gold	basketball
DeeDee Trotter	gold	4 x 400-m relay
Lauryn Williams	silver	100-m dash

Men

Carmelo Anthony	bronze	basketball
Carlos Boozer	bronze	basketball
Derrick Brew	gold	4 x 400-m relay
Shawn Crawford	gold	200-m dash
	silver	4 x 100-m relay
Andre Dirrell	bronxe	boxing (middle-weight)
Tim Duncan	bronze	basketball
Justin Gatlin	gold	100-m dash
	bronze	200-m dash
	silver	4 x 100-m relay
Maurice Greene	bronze	100-m dash
Otis Harris	silver	400-m dash
Allen Iverson	bronze	basketball
Lebron James	bronze	basketball
Richard Jefferson	bronze	basketball
Stephon Marbury	bronze	basketball
Shawn Marion	bronze	basketball
Lamar Odom	bronze	basketball
Emeka Okafor	bronze	basketball
Amaré Stoudemire	bronze	basketball
Terence Trammell	silver	110-m hurdles
Dwyane Wade	bronze	basketball
Andre Ward	gold	boxing (light heavyweight)
Bernard Williams	silver	200-m dash

FIGURE 11.4

First African-American players on Major League Baseball teams

Player	Date	Team
Jackie Robinson	4/47	Brooklyn Dodgers
Larry Doby	4/47	Cleveland Indians
Henry Thompson	7/47	St. Louis Browns
Henry Thompson	7/49	New York Giants
Sam Jethroe	4/50	Boston Braves
Sam Hairston	7/51	Chicago White Sox
Bob Trice	9/53	Philadelphia Athletics
Gene Baker	9/53	Chicago Cubs
Curt Roberts	4/54	Pittsburgh Pirates
Tom Alston	4/54	St. Louis Cardinals
Nino Escalera	4/54	Cincinnati Reds
Carlos Paula	9/54	Washington Senators
Elston Howard	4/55	New York Yankees
John Kennedy	4/57	Philadelphia Phillies
Ossie Virgil	6/58	Detroit Tigers
Pumpsie Green	7/59	Boston Red Sox

FIGURE 11.5

West Indies Cricket ("Windies") Board* Sticky Wicket West Indies Cricket Hall of Fame

Name	Country
Sir Vivian Richards	Antigua
Andy Roberts	Antigua
Michael Holding	Jamaica
Curtly Ambrose	Antigua
Lance Gibbs	Guyana
George Headley	Panama
Michael Holding	Jamaica
Brian Lara	Trinidad
Clive Lloyd	Guyana
Malcolm Marshall	Barbados
Sir Garfield Sobers	Barbados
Courtney Walsh	Jamaica
Sir Everton Weekes	Barbados

*   Barbados, Guyana, Jamaica, Leeward Islands, Trinidad & Tobago, Winward Islands.

FIGURE 11.6

African-American members of the Naismith Memorial Basketball Hall of Fame, Springfield, Mass.

Year inducted	Member	Born-Died
1963	New York Renaissance (team)	
1971	Robert L. "Bob" Douglas*	1884–1979
1974	William F. "Bill" Russell	1934–
1976	Elgin Baylor	1934–
	Charles T. "Tarzan" Cooper	1907–1980
1978	Wilton N. "Wilt" Chamberlain	1936–1999
	John B. McLendon, Jr.*	1915–1999
1979	Oscar P. "Big O" Robertson	1938–
1982	Clarence E. "Bighouse" Gaines*	1923–2005
	Harold E. "Hal" Greer	1936–
	Willis Reed, Jr.	1942–
1983	Samuel "Sam" Jones	1933–
1984	Nate Thurmond	1941–
1987	Walter "Walt" Frazier, Jr.	1945–
1988	Wesley S. "Wes" Unseld	1946–
1989	William "Pops" Gates	1917–1999
	K.C. Jones	1932–
	Leonard R. "Lenny" Wilkens+	1937–
1990	Earl "The Pearl" Monroe	1944–
	David "Dave" Bing	1943–
	Elvin E. Hayes	1945–
1991	Nathaniel "Nate" Archibald	1948–
1992	Connie "The Hawk" Hawkins	1942–
	Robert J. "Bob" Lanier	1948–
	Lusia Harris Stewart	1955–
1993	Walt Bellamy	1939–
	Julius W. "Dr. J" Erving II	1950–
	Calvin J. Murphy	1948–
1995	Kareem Abdul-Jabbar	1947–
	Cheryl Miller	1964–
1996	George Gervin	1952–
	David Thompson	1954–
1997	Alex English	1954–
1998	Marques Haynes	1926–
	Leonard "Lenny" Wilkens+	1937
1999	John Thompson*	1941–
2000	Robert "Bob" McAdoo	1951–
	Isiah Thomas	1961–
2001	John Chaney*	1932–
	Moses Malone	1955–
2002	The Harlem Globetrotters (team)	
	Earvin "Magic" Johnson	1959–
2003	Meadowlark Lemon	1935–
	Earl Lloyd	1928–
	Robert Parish	1953–
	James Worthy	1961–
2004	Clyde Drexler	1962–
	Maurice Stokes	1933–1970
	Lynette Woodard	1959–

* Coach
\+ Inducted as a player and a coach.

SOURCE: www.hoophall.com/index.htm

FIGURE 11.7

Negro League batting champions

Year	Player, Team	Average
Negro National League I		
1920	Cris Torriente, CAG	.411
1921	Charles Blackwell, STL	.448
1922	Heavy Johnson, KC	.389
1923	Cris Torriente, CAG	.412
1924	Dobie Moore, KC	.453
1925	Edgar Wesley, DET	.416
1926	Mule Suttles, STL	.418
1927	Red Parnell, BIR	.426
1928	Pythian Russ, CAG	.406
Negro National League		
1929	Mule Suttles, STL	.372
1930	Willie Wells, STL	.403
1931	Nat Rogers, MEM	.424
Negro National League II		
1933	Oscar Charleston, PIT	.372
1934	Jud Wilson, HG	.361
1935	Turkey Stearnes, CAG	.430
1936	Lazaro Salazar, NYC	.367
1937	Bill Wright, HG	.410
1938	Ray Dandridge, NWK	.404
1939	Bill Wright, BAL	.402
1940	Buck Leonard, HG	.383
1941	Monte Irvin, NWK	.463
1942	Willie Wells, NWK	.344
	Josh Gibson, HG	.344
1943	Josh Gibson, HG	.474
1944	Frank Austin, PHI	.390
1945	Josh Gibson, HG	.393
1946	Monte Irvin, NWK	.389
1947	Luis Marquez, HG	.417
1948	Buck Leonard, HG	.395
Eastern Colored League		
1923	Jud Wilson, BB	.373
1924	Pop Lloyd, BG	.433
1925	Oscar Charleston, BG	.445
1926	Robert Hudspeth, LG	.365
1927	Clarence Jenkins, BG	.398
1928	Pop Lloyd, LG	.564
Negro American League		
1929	Chino Smith, LG	.454
1930	John Beckwith, NY/BB	.480
1931	George Scales, NY/HG	.393
East-West League		
1932	Bill Perkins, CLE	.352
Negro American League		
1937	Willard Brown, KC	.371
1938	Willard Brown, KC	.356
1939	Willard Brown, KC	.336
1940	Chester Williams, MEM	.473
1941	Lyman Bostock, CAG	.488
1942	Ducky Davenport, BBB	.381
1943	Lester Lockett, BBB	.408
1944	Sam Jethroe, CLE	.353
1945	Sam Jethroe, CLE	.393
1946	Buck O'Neil, KC	.350
1947	John Ritchie, CAG	.381
1948	Artie Wilson, BBB	.402

FIGURE 11.8

Negro league teams*	
Negro National League I	(1920–1931)
Birmingham Black Barons	(1925,1927–1930)
Chicago American Giants	(1920–1931)
Chicago Giants	(1920–1921)
Columbus Buckeyes	(1921)
Cuban Stars	(1920, 1922)
Cleveland Browns	(1924)
Cleveland Cubs	(1931)
Cleveland Elites	(1926)
Cleveland Hornets	(1927)
Cleveland Tate Stars	(1922)
Dayton Marcos	(1920, 1926)
Detroit Stars	(1920–1931)
Indianapolis ABCs	(1920–1926, 1931)
Kansas City Monarchs	(1920–1931)
Louisville White Sox	(1931)
Memphis Red Sox	(1924–1925, 1927–1930)
Milwaukee Bears	(1923)
Nashville Elite Giants	(1930)
Pittsburgh Keystones	(1922)
St. Louis Giants	(1920–1921)
Toledo Tigers	(1923)
Eastern Colored League/	(1923–1928)
American Negro League	(1929)
Bacharach Giants [Atlantic City]	(1923–1929)
Baltimore Black Sox	(1923–1929)
Brooklyn Royal Giants	(1923–1927)
Cuban Stars (East)	(1923–1929)
Harrisburg [Pa.] Giants	(1924–1927)
Hilldale [Philadelphia]	(1923–1927, 1929)
Homestead Grays	(1929)
Lincoln Giants [New York]	(1923–1926, 1928–1929)
Newark Stars	(1926)
Philadelphia Tigers	(1928)
Washington Potomacs	(1924)
Negro Southern League	(1920–1932)
Cole's American Giants (Chicago)	
Columbus (Ohio) Turfs	
Indianapolis ABCs	
Louisville Black Caps	
Memphis Red Sox	
Monroe Monarchs	
Montgomery Grey Sox	
Nashville Elite Giants	
East-West League	(Spring 1932)
Baltimore Black Sox	
Cleveland Stars	
Cuban Stars	
Hilldale [Philadelphia]	
Homestead [Pa.] Grays	
Newark Browns	
[continued]	

Negro league teams* [CONTINUED]	
Negro National League II	(1933–1948)
Bacharach Giants [Atlantic City]	(1934)
Baltimore Black Sox	(1933–1934)
Baltimore Elite Giants	(1938–1948)
Brooklyn Eagles	(1935)
Cleveland Giants	(1933)
Cleveland Red Sox	(1934)
Cole's American Giants [Chicago]	(1933–1935)
Columbus Blue Birds	(1933)
Columbus Elite Giants	(1935)
Detroit Stars	(1933)
Harrisburg-St.Louis Stars	(1943)
Homestead Grays[1]	(1935–1948)
Nashville Elite Giants	(1933–1934)
Newark Dodgers	(1934–1935)
Newark Eagles	(1936–1948)
New York Black Yankees	(1936–1948)
New York Cubans	(1935–1936, 1939–1948)
Philadelphia Stars	(1934–1948)
Pittsburgh Crawfords	(1933–1938)
Washington Black Senators	(1938)
Washington Elite Giants	(1936–1937)
Negro-American League	(1937–1950)
Atlanta Black Crackers	(1938)
Baltimore Elite Giants	(1949–1950)
Birmingham Black Barons	(1937–1938, 1940–1950)
Chicago American Giants	(1937–1950)
Cleveland Buckeyes	(1943–1948, 1950)
Cincinnati Buckeyes	(1942)
Cincinnati Tigers	(1937)
Cleveland Bears	(1939–1940)
Detroit Stars	(1937)
Houston Eagles	(1949–1950)
Indianapolis ABCs	(1938–1939)
Indianapolis Athletics	(1937)
Indianapolis Clowns[2]	(1943–1950)
Indianapolis Crawfords	(1940)
Jacksonville Red Caps	(1938, 1941–1942)
Kansas City Monarchs	(1937–1941, 1943–1950)
New York Cubans	(1949–1950)
Philadelphia Stars	(1949–1950)
St. Louis Stars	(1937, 1939, 1941)
Toledo Crawfords	(1939)

* Home cities have been identified where known.
(1) Sometimes referred to as Washington Homestead Grays.
(2) Cincinnati Clowns (1943); Cincinnati-Indianapolis Clowns (1944).

FIGURE 11.9

African-American members of the Pro Football Hall of Fame, Canton, Ohio

Year inducted	Member	Born-Died
1967	Emlen Tunnell	1925–1975
1968	Marion Motley	1920–1999
1969	Fletcher Joseph "Joe" Perry	1927–
1971	James N. Brown*	1936–
	Gene Upshaw	1945–
1972	Ollie Matson	1930–
1973	James Thomas Parker	1934–2005
1974	Richard "Night Train" Lane	1928–2002
1975	Roosevelt Brown	1932–2004
	Lenny Moore	1933–
1976	Len Ford	1926–1972
1977	Gale Sayers	1943–
	Bill Willis	1921–
1980	Herb Adderley	1939–
	David "Deacon" Jones	1938–
1981	Willie Davis	1934–
1983	Bobby Bell	1940–
	Bobby Mitchell	1935–
	Paul Warfield	1942–
1984	Willie Brown	1940–
	Charles Robert "Charley" Taylor	1942–
1985	Orenthal James "O.J." Simpson	1947–
	Willie Lanier	1945–
1986	Ken Houston	1944–
1987	Charles Edward "Mean Joe" Greene	1946–
	John Henry Johnson	1929–
1988	Alan Page	1945–
1989	Mel Blount	1948–
	Art Shell	1946–
	Willie Wood	1936–
1990	Buck Buchanan	1940–1992
	Franco Harris	1950–
1991	Earl Campbell	1955–
1992	Lem Barney	1945–
	John Mackey	1941–
1993	Larry Little	1945–
	Walter Payton	1954–1999
1994	Tony Dorse	1919–2003
	Jimmy Johnson	1938–
	Leroy Kelly	1942–
1995	Lee Roy Selmon	1954–
	Kellen Winslow	1957–
1996	Charlie Joiner	1947–
	Mel Renfro	1941–
1997	Mike Haynes	1953–
1998	Mike Singletary	1958–
	Dwight Stephenson	1957–
1999	Eric Dickerson	1960–
	Ozzie Newsome	1956–
	Lawrence Taylor	1959–
2000	Ronnie Lott	1959–
2001	Jackie Slater	1954–
	Lynn Swann	1952–
2002	John Stallworth	1952–
2003	Marcus Allen	1960–
	Elvin Bethea	1946–
	James Lofton	1956–
2004	Carl Eller	1942–
	Barry Sanders	1968–
2005	Fritz Pollard	1894–1986

* James Brown was inducted into the Lacrosse Hall of Fame, Baltimore, Md., in 1957. As of 2005 he was the only African-American member of the Lacrosse Hall of Fame.

SOURCE: www.profootballhof.com

TEXT ACKNOWLEDGMENTS

King, Johannes. Excerpts from **"Guerilla Warfare: A Bush Negro View."** In *Maroon Societies: Rebel Slave Communities in the Americas.* Second Edition. Edited by Richard Price. The Johns Hopkins University Press, 1979. From Johannes King, Skrekiboekoe, Manuscript, 1885. This fragment is a rather free translation (by Richard and Sally Price) of parts of the original Sranan text, which may be found in Ursy M. Lichtveld and Jan Voorhoeve (eds.) "Suriname" 1958, pp. 90–119. First edition published by Anchor Press/Doubleday, 1973. Copyright © 1973 by Richard Price. Second edition published by The Johns Hopkins University Press, by arrangement with Doubleday and Company, Inc. Copyright © 1979 by Doubleday, a division of Random House, Inc. Reproduced by permission of Doubleday, a division of Random House, Inc., and the author.

King, Martin Luther, Jr. **"I Have a Dream"** (**speech**). From *A Testament of Hope: The Essential Writings of Martin Luther King, Jr.* Harper & Row, Publishers, 1986. Copyright © 1963 Martin Luther King Jr., copyright renewed 1991 Coretta Scott King. Reprinted by arrangement with the Estate of Martin Luther King Jr., c/o Writers House as agent for the proprietor, New York, N.Y.

King, Martin Luther, Jr. **"Letter from a Birmingham Jail."** From *Approaches to Peace.* Oxford University Press, 1963. Copyright © 1963 Martin Luther King Jr., copyright renewed 1991 Coretta Scott King. Reprinted by arrangement with the Estate of Martin Luther King Jr., c/o Writers House as agent for the proprietor, New York, N.Y.

Lamming, George. **"The African Presence."** From *The Pleasures of Exile.* Allison & Busby Limited, 1984. First published by Michael Joseph in 1960. Copyright © 1960, 1984 by George Lamming. Reproduced by permission.

McKay, Claude. **"If We Must Die."** In *The Book of American Negro Poetry.* Edited by James Weldon Johnson. Harcourt, Brace & World, Inc. Copyright © 1922, 1931 by Harcourt, Brace & World, Inc. Copyright © 1950 by Grace Johnson. Copyright © 1958 by Mrs. Grace Nail Johnson. All rights reserved. Courtesy of the Literary Representative for the Works of Claude McKay, Schomburg Center for Research in Black Culture, The New York Public Library, Astor, Lenox, and Tilden Foundations.

Rodney, Walter. **"Black Power—Its Relevance to the West Indies."** From *The Groundings with My Brothers.* Copyright © 1969. Reprinted by permission of Bogle L'Ouverture Publishers Ltd.

"We Shall Overcome." Musical and lyrical adaptation by Zilphia Horton, Frank Hamilton, Guy Carawan, and Pete Seeger. Inspired by African American Gospel Singing, members of the Food and Tobacco Workers Union, Charleston, S.C., and the southern Civil Rights Movement. TRO Copyright © 1960 and 1963 Ludlow Music, Inc., New York, N.Y. International Copyright Secured. Made in U.S.A. All rights reserved including public performance for profit. Reproduced by permission.

X, Malcolm. **"The Ballot or the Bullet"** (**speech**). From *Malcolm X Speaks: Selected Speeches and Statements,* edited by George Breitman. Copyright 1965, 1989 by Betty Shabazz and Pathfinder Press. Reprinted by permission.

Index

Page references in bold indicate main entries and italics indicate photos or illustrations. A page reference followed by a lowercase f or t indicates a figure or table.

Agriculture
   Africanisms, 39–40
   Agricultural Adjustment
     Administration (AAA), 943
   Black-Indian relations, 262
   Burke, Lilly Mae, 358
   Burke, Rudolph Augustus, 359–
     360
   Canada, 385
   Caribbean, 1627, 1628
   Carver, George Washington, 422
   Colored Farmers Alliance, 500
   Farm Worker Program, 748–750
   labor and labor unions, 1252
   Rapier, James Thomas, 1383–
     1384
   Rebouças, André, 1892
   Social Security Act, 947–948
   St. Kitts, 840
   Tuskegee University training,
     2218
Aguiar, Célia, 1776
Aguiar, Jayme de, 273
Aguinaldo, Emilio, 1449
Agüro, Salvador Garcia, 412
Ahmadiyyah movement, 1129
Ahrens, Lynn, 1551
Ai, 1792
Aidoo, Ama Ata, 536
AIDS (acquired immune deficiency
  syndrome), **58–63,** *61*
   Ashe, Arthur, 155
   Caribbean, 1489
   Caribbean art, 1034
   Johnson, Earvin "Magic," 1181
   lesbians, 1279–1280
   Rainbow/PUSH Coalition, 1877
   United States, 1491
Aid to Families with Dependent
  Children (AFDC), 1619
Ailey, Alvin, **63–65,** *64*
   ballet, 182
   Dance Theater of Harlem, 577
   diasporic dance, 575
   homosexuality, 913
   theatrical dance, 2189
   and Williams, Mary Lou, 2307
Ailey Camps program, 65
Aïnouz, Karim, 773
Ain't I a Woman (hooks), 761
"Ain't I a Woman?" (speech), 759,
  2209, 2210
Air, 250
Air Force, U.S.
   black airmen, 1452
   Davis, Benjamin O., Jr., 584–585
Aiyetoro, Adjoa, 1926
Akan, 1981, 2057
Akers, Doris, 931

Akram, Wali, 1129
Akumphrah, John, 629
Alabá, João, 1999, 2197
Alabama
   African Methodist Episcopal
     Church, 42
   International Labor Defense,
     2023–2024
   Lowndes County Freedom
     Organization, 1345–1346
Alabama Association of Women's
  Clubs, 2268
Alabama Christian Movement for
  Human rights, 2033
Al-Amin, Jamil Abdullah, **65–66**
   Islam, 1129
    speaking style, 1883–1884
    Student Nonviolent Coordinating
     Committee, 2151–2152
Alberdi, Juan Bautista, 827
Albert, Donnie Ray, 1684
Alberto, Carlos, 2092
Albizu Campos, Pedro, **66–68,** 1798
Albritton, David, 2140
*The Alchemy of Race and Rights: A
  Diary of a Law Professor*
  (Williams), 2307
Alcindor, Lew. *See* Abdul-Jabbar,
  Kareem
al-Din, Nasr, 733
Aldridge, Amanda, 91
Aldridge, Ira, 38, *68,* **68–69,** 1548
Aldridge, Madeline, 1687
Alexander, Clifford L., Jr., **69**
Alexander, James Woodie, 930
Alexander, Kelly, Sr., 1598
Alexander, Raymond Pace, **70,** 71,
  1107
Alexander, Roberta, 1684
Alexander, Sadie Tanner Mossell,
  70–71, *71*
Alexander, W. J., 1963
Alexander, Will, 621, 1792
Alexander, William, 627, 783
Alexander IV, Pope, 424
Alexander's Magazine, 1212
Alexandria, Lorez, 1171
Alexis, Jacques-Stéphen, 1314, 2324
Alfred Stieglitz Collection of
  Modern Art, 801
Algebra Project, 1493
Algeria, 1434
Ali (film), 2090
Ali, Bardu, 803
Ali, Duse Muhammad, 1640, 1719
Ali, Laila, 321
Ali, Muhammad, **71–74,** *72*
   boxing, 319–321

   Foreman, George, match with,
     856
   Frazier, Joe, match with, 871
   Islam, 2142
   Moore, Archie, match with, 1478
   Olympics, 1680
   poetry, 1883
   Smith, Will, portrayal by, 2090
   Vietnam War, 109
Ali, Rashied, 501
Alienated American (newspaper),
  1204
"Alien Huddle" (Puryear), *1852*
All-America Football Conference,
  852
Allan, Harold, **74–75**
Allen, Betty, 1684
Allen, Debbie, **75–76**
Allen, George, 1353
Allen, Geri, 1166
Allen, James Latimer, 1779
Allen, Lillian, 661
Allen, Macon Bolling, **76**
Allen, Marshall, 2154
Allen, Rance, 933
Allen, Richard, **76–78,** *77*
   African Methodist Episcopal
     Church, 41, 44, 460
   African Methodist Episcopal Zion
     Church, 46
   anticolonizationism, 1718
   and Coker, Daniel, 495
   evangelicalism, 1459
   and Forten, James, 857
   Free African Society, 1564
   General Conference of the AME
     Church, 1847
   gospel music, 928
   insurance companies, 1094
   and Jones, Absalom, 1189, 1190
   Lee, Jarena, appeal of, 1913
   *The Life Experience and Gospel
    Labors of the Rt. Rev. Richard
    Allen,* 2389–2396
   nationalism, 1612
   Negro spirituals, 1523
   Protestantism, 1844
   religion, 1912
Allen, Samuel
   black-owned publishing houses,
     1330
   Négritude, 1634
   poetry, 1791
Allen, Wanda Jean, 1279
Allen, William Barclay, 2228
Allen, William Francis, 2135
Allensworth, Allen, 285
Allensworth, California, 284–285
Allen University, 41

missions, 1913
National Baptist Convention,
    U.S.A., Inc., 1605
Primitive Baptists, 1836–1837
slaves, 726–727
women, 1914
Baquaqua, Mahommah, 1127
Baraka, Amiri, **197–198**
    African American Review, 1312
    anti-colonial movement, 109
    Black Arts movement, 247, 250,
        252, 1766
    Brooks, Gwendolyn, influence
        on, 335
    and Brown, Sterling Allen, 345
    Bullins, Ed, influence on, 354
    cultural criticism, 1114
    cultural nationalism, 1113
    experimental theater, 739
    film, 785
    and Gibson, Kenneth, 1409
    Haywood, Harry, influence of,
        1031
    Hughes, Langston, influence of,
        648
    Kawaida, 1228
    literary criticism, 1304
    literary magazines, 1311
    literature, 1329
    Madhubuti, Haki R., influence
        on, 1360
    masking, 645
    and Mayfield, Julian, 1408
    Million Man March, criticism of
        the, 1453
    poetry, 1790, 1791, 1792
    Savoy Ballroom, 2014
    Wilson, August, influence of,
        2312
Barbadoes, James G., **198**
Barbados
    archival collections, 132
    Barbados Labour Party, 198–200
    Barrow, Errol, 202
    Barrow, Nita, 203–204
    emancipation, *698*
    food and cuisine, 840
    Grantley, Adams, 15–17
    Moore, Richard Benjamin, 1479
    nursing, 1663
    Sobers, Garfield, 2091
    University of the West Indies,
        2231–2233
    Walcott, Frank, 2251–2252
Barbados Labour Party, **198–200**
    Adams, Grantley, 16–17
    Barrow, Errol, 202
Barbados Progressive League. *See*
    Barbados Labour Party

Barbados Workers' Union, 2251
Barber, J. Max, 1308
Barber, Jesse Belmont, 1833
Barbershops, 713, 969–970
Barbosa Gomes, Joaquim Benedito,
    200, **200–201**
Barcellos, Alcebiades. *See* Bide
Barco, Henry E., 848
Bardolph, Richard, 242
Barefoot in the Park (television
    show), 2173
Bare-knuckle fighting, 315–316
Bar-Kays, 1535, 1536
Barker, Thurman, 156
Barkley, Charles, 223
Barksdale, Don, 1679
Barksdale, Richard, 1304
Barnes, Albert, 1002
Barnes, Frank, 1591
Barnes, Steven, 1331
Barnes, Thomas V., 1029
Barnet, Miguel, 1471
Barnett, Claude A., 781
Barnett, Marguerite Ross, **201–202**
Barnett, Richard "Dick," 221
Barnett, Ross, 1426
Barnett-Aden Gallery, 152
Barney, Lem, 854
Barrelhouses, 1529
Barrett, Janie Porter, 2103
Barrett Sisters, 933, 1532
Barrios, Pilar, 1798
Barrios, Ventura, 1798
Barroso, Ary, 2001
Barrow, Errol, **202–203**
Barrow, Joseph Louis. *See* Louis, Joe
Barrow, Luis de, 773
Barrow, Nita, **203–204,** 1663, 1821
Barry, Marion, **204–205,** 2151
Barth, John, 1358
Barthé, Richmond, **205–206,** 1507,
    1701
Barthelemy, Sidney, 1410
Bartholomew, Dave, 1944
Barthwell, Sydney, 719
Bartleman, Frank, 1752
Baryshnikov, Mikhail, 1159
Bascom, William, 2008
Baseball and baseball players, **206–
216,** *208, 210, 213*
    Aaron, Hank, 1–2
    Courier (newspaper), 1209
    Gibson, Josh, 916
    Major League baseball, first
        African-American players
        (table), 2582
    Mays, Willie, 1413

Negro League batting champions
    (table), 2583
Negro League teams (table), 2584
Paige, Satchel, 1694–1695
race and sports, 2138
Robinson, Jackie, 1966–1967
Baseball Hall of Fame, 211, 2575
    (table)
Basie, William James "Count," **216–
217**
    Apollo Theater, 114
    big bands, 1163, 1530
    blues, 300
    and Calloway, Cab, 379
    and Holiday, Billie, 1057
    jazz, 1162–1163, 1167
    and Jones, Quincy, 1194
    and Mabley, Jackie "Moms,"
        1355
    Nat "King" Cole Show, 2172
    1950s, 1164
    radio, 1169
    recordings, 1894
    Savoy Ballroom, 2014
    and Scott, Hazel, 2022
    swing, 1160, 2099
    and Tharpe, "Sister" Rosetta,
        2185
    and Williams, Joe, 1170
Basilica do Bom Jesus de
    Matozinhos, 1294, *1294*
Basilio, Carmen, 1969
Basketball and basketball players,
    217–223, *219, 221*
    Abdul-Jabbar, Kareem, 4–5
    Chamberlain, Wilt, 441–442
    Hall of Fame inductees (table),
        2583
    Harlem Globetrotters, 997–998
    Johnson, Earvin "Magic," 1180–
        1181
    Jordan, Michael, 1199–1200,
        2143
    Renaissance Big Five, 1924
Basketball Association of America,
    220
Basket names, 1573
Basketry, 805–806
Baskette, Jimmy, 503
Basquiat, Jean-Michel, 147, **223–224**
    murals, 1508
    performance art, 1766
    works, 1708
Bass, Harry W., 1292
Bass, Kingsley B. *See* Bullins, Ed
Basso, Hamilton, 1735
Bass playing, 1547
Bastide, Roger
    African diaspora, 36

revolts and maroon community
locations, *1979, 1983, 1987,
1990*

Seventh-day Adventists, 1846

slave narratives, 2053–2054

slavery, historiography of, 2066–2068

soccer, 2092–2093

women, 332

See also Anglophone Caribbean;
British Caribbean; Specific
countries

Caribbean, education in the, **677–680**

Caribbean, emancipation in the, **697–701**

Caribbean, film in the, **770–778**

Caribbean, Islam in the, **1132–1134**

Caribbean, Maroon societies in the, **1385–1391**

Caribbean, media in the, **1420–1423**

Caribbean, mortality and morbidity in the, **1488–1490**

Caribbean, natural resources of the, **1626–1631**

Caribbean, nursing in the, **1662–1664**

Caribbean, runaway slaves in the, **1978–1985**

Caribbean, urban poverty in the, **2235–2237**

Caribbean, women traders of the, **2320–2322**, *2321*

Caribbean, women writers of the, **2322–2327**

Caribbean Americans, 994

Caribbean Artists Movement, 1321

Caribbean Basin Initiative, 1121, 1421

Caribbean-Canada Trade Agreement (CARIBCAN), 1121

Caribbean Commission, **401–402**

Caribbean Community and
Common Market (CARICOM), **402–405**, *403*

Barrow, Errol, 202

Barrow, Nita, 204

Burnham, Forbes, 364–365

creation of, 1121

Manley, Norman, 1375

member nations, *403*

ministers, *404*

Patterson, Percival James, 1741

People's National Congress, 1754–1755

Teshea, Isabel, 2182

Caribbean Contemporary Arts, 145

Caribbean Court of Justice, 403

Caribbean culture

Carneiro, Edison, 412–413

Dunham, Katherine, 664–665

folklore, 96–97

McBurnie, Beryl, 1413–1414

musical theater, 1551

Sherlock, Philip, 2032

Caribbean Examination Council, 165

Caribbean federation, 324

Caribbean Federation Act, 2284

Caribbean filmmakers, **794–798**

Caribbean folklore, 821–829

Caribbean Free Trade Area
(CARIFTA)

Anglophone Caribbean, 1121

Barrow, Errol, 202

Burnham, Forbes, 364

Caribbean Community and
Common Market, 402

People's National Congress, 1754

Caribbean healing and the arts, **1032–1035**

Caribbean immigrants, 632

Caribbean Labour Congress, 1370

Caribbean League, 2282

Caribbean liberation theology, 156

Caribbean literature, **1319–1322**

Marson, Una, 1397–1398

reggae aesthetics, 1907–1909

Caribbean Media Corporation, 1422–1423

Caribbean Pentecostalism, **1748–1751**

Caribbean politics, **1818–1823**

Caribbean Regional Alliance, 411

Caribbean representations of
blackness, **1928–1932**

Caribbean Research Council, 401, 2299

Caribbean Single Market and
Economy (CSME), 1121

Caribbean theater, **408–411**, 1042–1753

Caribbean Voices (show), 1320, 1397, 2324

Caribbean Women's Association, 1173

Caribbean writers, **405–407**

Carib Indians, 254

Caricatures

Ecuador, 1931

Jim Crow, 1176

minstrel shows, 574, 1456–1457

ragtime, 1872

white stage portrayals of African
Americans, 644

CARICOM. *See* Caribbean
Community and Common Market
(CARICOM)

CARICOM Single Market and
Economy, 402–403

CARIFESTA, 1755

CARIFTA. *See* Caribbean Free Trade
Area (CARIFTA)

Carlos, John, *2143*

Ali, Muhammad, influence of, 72–73

Olympics, 1681

sports, 2142–2143

Carlos, Laurie, 651, 741

Carlos I, King, 425

Carmichael, Frank, 1080

Carmichael, Hoagy, 448

Carmichael, Stokely, **411–412**, *412*

"Black is Beautiful," 971

Black Panther Party, 267

Black Power movement, 268, *269*, 2190

and Brown, Sterling Allen, 345

civil rights movement, 476

and Farrakhan, Louis, 751

Haywood, Harry, influence of, 1031

Lowndes County Freedom
Organization, 1345

Meredith, James H., on the
shooting of, 1426

Student Nonviolent Coordinating
Committee, 1285, 2151–2152

"Toward Black Liberation,"
2483–2489

Williams, Henry Sylvester,
influence of, 2305

Carnegie, Andrew, 801, 2264

Carnegie, Charles, 101

Carnegie Corporation, 277, 1770, 2012

Carnegie Hall, 736–737

Carneiro, Edison, 98, **412–414**, 2204

Carnera, Primo, 1341

Carney, Harry, 695

Carney, William H., **414**, 1284

Carnival, **414–418**, *415, 417*

calypso, 381

clubs, 1542–1544

Congos of Panama, 521

festivals, 766–767

film, 773

Francisco, Slinger, 862

groups, 274

samba, 2000–2001

Caroling Dusk (Cullen), *568*

Carpenter, Thelma, 2173

Carpenters and Joiners
International, 1256

Chess Records, 2168
Cheswell, Wentworth, 1807
Chevannes, Barry, 99, 1939
Cheyney State College, 534
A Chibata, 273
Chic, 1536, 1897
Chica da Silva, **452–453**
Chicago, Illinois
　AfriCobra, 1707
　baseball, 208
　Binga State Bank, *714*
　Black Arts movement, 249, 250,
　　252
　boogie-woogie, 1529
　Du Sable, Jean Baptiste Pointe,
　　667
　gospel music, 1916
　jazz, 1161–1162
　King, Martin Luther, Jr., 1242
　labor and labor unions, 1254
　Moorish Science Temple
　　movement, 1128
　OBAC Writers' Workshop, 1671–
　　1672
　painting and sculpture, 1704
　Provident Hospital and Nurses
　　Training School, 1665, 1666
　race relations, 1179
　radio, 1869
　Spiritual church movement, 2131
　Washington, Harold, 2267–2268
Chicago, Judy, 740, 1761
Chicago Bee (newspaper), 1689
Chicago Bulls, 222, 1199–1200
Chicago Defender (newspaper), **453–454**
　Abbott, Robert Sengstacke, 4
　Brazilian press, 273
　entrepreneurship, 717
　journalism, 1207–1208, 1207–
　　1209, 1211
Chicago Eight, 2026
"Chicago Freedom Movement,"
　2126
Chicago Metropolitan Mutual
　Association, 1096
Chicago riot of 1919, 2277
Chicago School of sociology, 277,
　756
Chicago Tribune (newspaper), 1349
Child, Lydia Maria, 1150, 1283,
　1977
Child Abuse Prevention Training
　Program, 2270
Childers, Lulu V., 1603
Childes, John Brown, 1108
Child psychiatry, 1271
Children
　AIDS, *61*

coartación, 492
Ebony Jr. (magazine), 1213
　Jack and Jill of America, 1135
　Johnson, Joshua, art of, 1185,
　　1187
　mortality, 1488
　of slaveholders, 631
　slaves, *2061*
　television programming for, 2178
Children's books
　Davis, Ossie, 588
　Feelings, Thomas, 757–758
　Jordan, June, 1198
Children's Defense Fund, 676
Children's issues
　Edelman, Marian Wright, 676
　Hope, Lugenia Burns, 1064
Children's literature, **455–457**
Childress, Alice, **457**
　American Negro Theatre, 86
　Communist Party of the United
　　States, 514
　literature, 1329
Childress, Alvin, 2170
Childs, Frank, 1181
Childs, Matt, 115
Chile
　food and cuisine, 841
　Pentecostalism, 1749
Chilembwe, John, 1719
Chi-Lites, 1535, 1896, 1945
Chimboté meeting, 1285
Chin, Staceyann, 1311, 1321
China (musician), 2000
Ching, Madam, 2150
Chisholm, Shirley, **457–458**, *458*
　Caribbean heritage, 604
　Gary Convention, 907
　politics, 1814, 1822
Chocolate, Kid, 319
Chocolate Dandies (show), 2187
Cholmondeley, H. M. E., 1754
Chomsky, Noam, 1258
Chong, Albert, 144, 1781
Choreography and choreographers
　Alvin Ailey American Dance
　　Theater, 64
　Black Arts movement, 251
　diasporic dance, 575–576
　Dove, Ulysses, 642
　Dunham, Katherine, 664–666
　Holder, Geoffrey, 1056
　Mitchell, Arthur, 1464–1465
　Motown, 2100
　theatrical dance, 2189
　Walker, Aida Overton, 2253
Choreopoems, 2028
Choro, 1999

*The Chosen Place, The Timeless
　People* (Marshall), 1394
Christensen, Carlos Hugo, 777–778
Christian, Barbara, 1114, 1306, 1332
Christian, Jodie, 156, 157, 249–250
Christiana Revolt, **458–459**
Christian denominations,
　independent, **459–463**
Christian Endeavour Union, 1475
Christianity
　biocentrism, 2338–2339
　Central African religion, 435–438
　Cone, James H., 519–520
　emancipation, 1913
　Ethiopianism, 52
　ethnic origins, 732–733
　folk religion, 837–838
　free villages, 884
　George, David, 913–914
　Grimké, Francis James, 956–957
　Hart sisters, 1026–1027
　iconography, 612
　and Judaism, 1222
　liberation theology, 1285–1287
　missionary movements, 1459–
　　1462
　nationalism, 1612
　Negro spirituals, 1522–1524
　Obeah, 1672–1673
　and Orisha, 1688
　Pan-Africanism, 1718
　slave religion, 2058–2059
　slavery, 1910–1912
　social gospel, 2102–2103
　spirituals, 813–814
　theology, black, 2189–2191
　See also Specific denominations
Christianity in film, **463–467**
*Christianity, Islam, and the Negro
　Race* (Blyden), 1129
Christian Methodist Episcopal
　(CME) Church, **467–468**
　and African Methodist Episcopal
　　Zion Church, 49
　founding, 1913
　as independent denomination,
　　461
　membership, 1915
　merger possibilities, 1917
Christian Recorder (periodical), **468–469**
Christian voluntary societies, 2103
Christie, Fred, 386
Christie v. York (1936), 386
Christmas, 766–767
Christmas, Walter, 153, 1018
Christocentric black theology, 1115
Christophe, Henri, 115, 134, **469–470**

Clarke, Lewis G., **485**
Clarke, Richard V., 153
Clarke, Shirley, 785
Clarke, William Alexander. *See* Bustamante, Alexander
Clark Sisters, 933, 1533, 1753
Clarkson, Thomas, 566
Clarkson Benevolent Society, 1564
The Clash, 618
Class, socioeconomic
    academic achievement, 689
    anthropology, 99
    black middle class, 265–266
    Brazilian film, 772
    Cuban film, 776–777
    domestic workers, 631–632
    Harrison, Hubert Henry, 1026
    identity and race, 1088
    middle class blacks, 265–266
    migration, 1447
    and racial bias, 2114–2115
    racism, 2104
    skin color, 2047
    sociological aspects, 2117
    Spiritual church movement, 2132
Class Act tap, 2166
Classical dance, 577–578
Classical music, 1558–1560
Classical Pentecostalism, 1748–1749
Classical scholarship, 2302–2303
Classical singing. *See* Opera
Classification
    black studies, 275–276
    historiography, 1111
    race, 100, 1859–1860, 1864, 2137
    racial identity, 1091–1092
Claxton, Jimmy, 208
Clay, Cassius, Jr. *See* Ali, Muhammad
Clay, Fannie, 1965
Clay, William Lacy, **486**
Clay pipes, 117
Clayton, Mark, 853
Clayton, Willie, 305
Claytor, Mary Pullins, 1105
Claytor, William Waldron Schieffelin, 1406
Cleage, Albert B., Jr., **486–487**, 1721–1722
Clear Channel, 1871
Cleaver, Arizona, 2123
Cleaver, Eldridge, **487–488**, *488*
    Black Arts Alliance, 354
    Black Panther (newspaper), 1212
    Black Panther Party, 266–268, 1812
    and Newton, Huey P., 1650
Clef Club, 736, 737, 1000, 1875
Clement, Rufus E., 666

Clemmons, Ithiel, 1753
Cleo Parker Robinson Dance Ensemble, 251
Cleopatra Jones (film), 294
Clergy
    Aristide, Jean-Bertrand, 135–136
    Brawley, Edward McKnight, 327
    Butts, Calvin, 374–375
    Cain, Richard Harvey, 378
    Cardozo, Francis L., 398–399
    Carey, Lott, 400–401
    Cleage, Albert B., Jr., 486–487
    Coker, Daniel, 495
    Coppin, Levi Jenkins, 534–535
    Father Divine, 753
    Flake, Floyd H., 803
    Franklin, C. L., 864–865
    Garnet, Henry Highland, 899–900
    Gomes, Peter John, 924
    Green, Al, 950–951
    Griggs, Sutton Elbert, 952–953
    Grimké, Francis James, *956*, 956–957
    Hancock, Gordon Blaine, 989
    Henson, Josiah, 1040
    Hood, James Walker, 1060–1061
    Hooks, Benjamin L., 1062
    Jackson, Jesse, 1137–1139
    Jackson, Joseph Harrison, 1140–1141
    Jones, Absalom, 1189–1190
    Liele, George, 1288–1289
    Martin, John Sella, 1398
    Mays, Benjamin E., 1411–1412
    Michaux, Elder, 1429–1430
    Murray, Pauli, 1510–1511
    Payne, Daniel Alexander, 1743–1744
    Pennington, James W. C., 1747–1748
    Proctor, Henry Hugh, 1841–1842
    Revels, Hiram Rhoades, 1938
    Rier, Carl P., 1948
    Scholes, Theophilus, 2015
    Sharpton, Al, 2030
    Shuttlesworth, Fred L., 2033
    social gospel, 2103
    Southern Christian Leadership Conference, 2125
    Sullivan, Leon Howard, 2152–2153
    Thurman, Howard, 2194–2195
    Turner, Henry McNeal, 2213–2214
    Twilight, Alexander, 2219
    Walker, Wyatt Tee, 2261–2262
    Ward, Samuel Ringgold, 2263

    Wesley, Charles Harris, 2277–2278
    Williams, George Washington, 2303–2304
    Williams, Peter, Jr., 2308
    Wright, Theodore Sedgwick, 2337–2338
    Yoruba religion, 2346
    See also Preachers
Cleveland, James, **488–489**
    Baptists, 195
    contemporary gospel, 1533
    and Dorsey, Thomas A., 635
    and Franklin, Aretha, 863
    gospel music, 932, 1532
    and Tharpe, "Sister" Rosetta, 2185
Cleveland, Joseph R., 160
Cleveland, Ohio
    rally of 1965, *1241*
    Stokes, Carl Burton, 2148–2149
Cleveland Call and Post (newspaper), 1210
Cleveland Indians, *213*
Cliff, Jimmy, 796, *797*, 1906
Cliff, Michelle, 406, 1321, 2324
Clifton, Louise, 455
Clifton, Lucille, 1330, 1791
Clifton, Nat "Sweetwater," 220, 998
Clijsters, Kim, 2311
Climate, Caribbean, 1627
Clinton, Bill
    affirmative action, 20
    apology to Hawaiians, 1927
    and Aristide, Jean-Bertrand, 136
    and Brown, Ronald H., 344
    Commission on Civil Rights, U.S., 2229
    Elders, Joycelyn, appointment of, 692
    environmental justice, 725
    Flipper, Henry O., presidential pardon of, 804
    and Franklin, Aretha, 864
    Initiative on Race, 866
    and Jackson, Jesse, 1139
    and Jordan, Vernon, 1201
    and Mfume, Kweisi, 522
    Mitchell, Arthur, award for, 1465
    Powell, Colin, Presidential Medal of Freedom for, 1828
    and Sister Souljah, 1898
    and Waters, Maxine Moore, 2271
Clinton, George
    funk music, 1535
    funk-style rap, 1884
    performance art, 1766
Clinton, Joseph J., 49
Clinton Junior College, 46

Cullen, Countee, **566–569,** *567, 1014*
    Damas, Léon-Gontran, influence
       on, 1313
    Du Bois, W. E. B., support of,
       1299
    Harlem Renaissance, 1720
    "Heritage" (poem), 2450–2451
    homosexuality, 911
    literary magazines, 1309
    literature, 1327
    Manhattan's Civil Club event,
       1002
    Négritude, 1634
    Opportunity: Journal of Negro Life
       (magazine), 1687
    photographic portrait of, 1779
    Phylon (journal), 1781
    poetry, 1789, 1790
    politics, 1016
    texts used in music, 1527
    and West, Dorothy, 2279
Cullen, Frederick, 567
Cullen, Ida, 150
Culp, Robert, 2173
Culpepper, Daunte, 854
Cults of affliction, 436
Cultural continuity, 611, 616
Cultural criticism
    blaxploitation films, 295
    Communist Party of the United
       States, 513
    Crouch, Stanley, 563
    gay men, 913
    intellectual life, 1113–1114
Cultural-ecological theory, 1675–
    1676
Cultural inferiority, 2111
Cultural nationalism
    Baraka, Amiri, 197–198
    Black Arts movement, 248
    Black Power movement, 271
    Black World/Negro Digest, 287–
       288
    Harlem Renaissance, 1009
    intellectual life, 1112, 1113
    Johnson, Charles Richard, 1178
    Karenga, Maulana, 1227–1228
    Kawaida, 1228–1229
    Kwanza, 1249–1250
    literature, 1330
    names and naming, 1574
    Pan-Africanism, 1718, 1720
    racial nomenclature, 1575
Cultural relativism, 1106
Cultural syncretism, 1981
Cultural Training Center of Jamaica.
    See Edna Manley College for the
    Visual and Performing Arts
Cultural Wellness Center, 1565

Culture
    approaches to, 610–611
    Communist Party of the United
       States, 514
    critical mixed-race studies, 558–
       560
    double consciousness, 1088–1089
    English, African-American, 710
    ethnic origins, 735–736
    Federal Writers' Project, 756
    folklife and folklore studies, 1106
    gardens and yard art, 896–898
    gay men, 912–913
    Gullah, 961
    Hurston, Zora Neale, 1083
    Nettleford, Rex, 1643
    as sociological concept, 2112
    See also Assimilation and
      acculturation; Cultural
      nationalism; Harlem
      Renaissance
Culture, Blues in African-American,
    302–305
Culture, jazz in African-American,
    1167–1169
Culture (music group), 1906
Culture building, 812–813
Culture of poverty, 689
Cultures, diasporic, **610–617**
Cumberbatch, Charles, 756
Cumbia, 1516
Cumbo, Marion, 1559, 1639
Cummings, Blondell, 1764, 1767
Cummings, Floyd, 871
Cummings, Harry Sythe, 1803
Cumper, Pat, 409
Cunard, Nancy, 1017
Cundall, Frank, 1368
Cuney, Waring, 756
Cuney-Hare, Maude, 1113–1114
Cunningham, Arthur, 1559
Cunningham, Merce, 642
Cunningham, Randall, 854
Curators
    Hutson, Jean Blackwell, 1085
    Willis, Deborah, 2311–2312
Curbeam, Robert L., 161
Curled hair, 966
Current events, 1515
Curriculum development, 164–165
Curry, George, 1215
Curtin, Benjamin Robbins, 654
Curtin, Philip, 600
Curtis, Austin M., 878
Curtis, Isaac, 853
Curtis, King, 1942
Cushing, Richard, 1806–1807
Cushman, Charlotte, 1283
Customs, 776

Cuvier, Georges, 1860, 2018
Cuyjet, Marion, 1158
CWA (Civil Works Administration),
    945
Cypress Hill, 1519
Cypriano, Tania, 774

D

Dabney, Ford, 1550
Dabney, Stephanie, 577
Da Brat, 1886, 1899
Da Costa, Mathieu, 383
Daddy Grace, 1916
Dafora, Asadata, 251, 575, 1972
Daguerre, Jacques-Mandé, 1778
D'Aguiar, Fred, 1321
D'Aguiar, Peter, 1754
D'Aguilar, T., 1153
Dahomey, 734
Daily Creole (newspaper), 1205
Daily Gleaner (newspaper), 1423
Daily News (newspaper), 1218
Dalby, David, 38, 709
Daley, Christopher, 410
Daley, Henry, 1368
Dalton-James, Edith, **571–572**
Daly, Marie Maynard, 2020
Daly, Mary, 1286
Damas, Léon
    literature of, 1313
    Négritude, 1633
    performance art, 1763
    "race men," 1402
D'Amato, Constantine "Cus," 633,
    1740
DaMatta, Roberto, 2001
Dameron, Tadd, 586, 917
Damoison, David, 1777
Dance, Daryl Cumber, 832
Dance, diasporic, **572–576,** *575*
Dance, social, **2094–2102**
Dance, theatrical, **2186–2189**
Dance and dancers
    Allen, Debbie, 75–76
    Baker, Josephine, 175–177, *176*
    ballet, 181–182
    Bell, Arthur, 180
    Black Arts movement, 251
    breakdancing, 328
    Brown, James, 342
    Bubbles, John, 353
    Carnival, 415
    Central African religion, 436, 437
    Colombia, 1516
    Davis, Sammy, Jr., 588–590, *589*
    divination and spirit possession,
      623

Employment *continued*
  National Council of Negro
    Women, 1608
  National Negro Labor Council,
    1615–1617
  National Urban League, 1617–
    1618
  nursing, 1663
  Opportunities Industrialization
    Centers of America, 2152
  Rainbow/PUSH Coalition, 1876–
    1877
  seniority systems, 23–24
  skin color, 2044
  sociological aspects, 2118, 2119
  workplace discrimination, 943
  See also Fair employment
Empowerment Project, 778
Encyclopedia of the Negro project,
  1337
Endorsements
  Jordan, Michael, 2143
  Williams, Venus and Serena,
    2310
Energy, U.S. Department of
  O'Leary, Hazel Rollins, 1676–
    1677
  Powell, Colin, 1828
Enforcement, desegregation, 1570,
  1593–1594
Engineering, 683, 1127
England. *See* United Kingdom
English, African-American, **708–711**
  Bailey, Beryl Loftman, 172
  and creoles, 551
  Labov, William, 1257–1258
  literacy education, 1295–1297
  Turner, Lorenzo Dow, 2215
English-based creole language, 546–
  547
English Canadian writers, 387–390
Enlightenment
  masculinity, 1400
  racial theories, 1859
Enlightenment doctrine, 1099
Ennis, Ethel, 1171
Enriquez, Carlos, 141
Enslavement and ethnic origins,
  733–734
Ensley, Elizabeth, 2318
Entertainment
  dandyism, 259
  De Passe, Suzanne, 607
  entrepreneurs, 717, 721
  Harlem, 992
Entine, John, 2144

Entrepreneurship and entrepreneurs,
711–725
  Black Enterprise (magazine),
    1214–1215
  Black Entertainment Television,
    259–260
  Combs, Sean, 502
  computer science and industry,
    620
  Franks, Gary, 867
  Gordy, Berry, 926–927
  hair and beauty culture, 970
  insurance companies, 1094
  Johnson, John H., 1213
  Simmons, Russell, 2035
  Smith, Barbara, 2085–2086
  Spaulding, Charles Clinton,
    2127–2128
  Walker, Madam C. J., 2259–2260
Environmental issues
  Caribbean, 1628–1629
  NAACP Legal Defense and
    Educational Fund, 1571
Environmental racism, **725–726**
Enwezor, Okwui, 1777
Ephemerides, 186–187
Epic Records, 1148
Epidemiological transition, 1489
Episcopalians, **726–729**
  Harris, Barbara Clementine, 1022
  Holly, James T., 1060
  Jones, Absalom, 1189–1190
Episcopal Society of Cultural and
  Racial Unity, 728
EPMD, 1885
Epps, Omar, 790
Epstein, Dena J., 1560
Equal Employment Opportunity
  Commission
  Alexander, Clifford L., Jr., 69
  creation of, 19
  Thomas, Clarence, 2193
"Equality of Educational
  Opportunity" (Coleman and
  Campbell), 2116–2117
"Equality Under Law" campaign,
  NAACP, 1592
Equal protection
  affirmative action, 23
  Brownsville incident, 349
  education, 683
  Fourteenth Amendment, 860–861
  Sweatt v. Painter (1950), 2156–
    2157
Equiano, Olaudah, **729**, *791*
  autobiography, 166, 2374–2377
  ethnic origins, 734
  literature, 1324
  masculinity, 1400

  Pan-Africanism, 1717
Erazo, Rafael, 1799
Eric B and Rakim, 1051, 1885
Erosion, 1628
Ervin, Booker, 1455
Erving, Julius, 722
The Escape; or a Leap for Freedom
  (Brown), 645
Escape routes, Underground
  Railroad, *2225*
Esmeraldas, Ecuador, 613–616, 1982
Esmeraldas Ambassadors (painting),
  613, 614
Espinet, Ramabai, 1321
Essence (magazine), 1214, 2319
Essence Communications, 721, 1219
Essex County Anti-Slavery Society,
  1923
Essien, Ivy, 1153
Estácio samba, 2001
Estado Novo, 273–274
Esteban, 261
Estebanico, 2061
Estenoz, Evaristo, 1731–1732, 1798
Estes, Simon, 1526, 1685
Estimé, Dumarsais, 668, **729–730**
Ethics, 2215–2216
Ethiopia
  Christian iconography, 612
  Christian tradition of, 52
  James, C. L. R., 1156
Ethiopia (drama), 647
Ethiopia, Italian invasion of
  anti-colonial movement, 107
  black Americans opposition to,
    270
  Committee for the Defense of
    Ethiopia, 473
  Communist Party of the United
    States, 512
  Courier coverage, 1208
  François, Elma, 863
  Garvey, Marcus, 905
  National Association for the
    Advancement of Colored
    People, 1588
  National Negro Congress, 1614
  Universal Negro Improvement
    Association, 2231
Ethiopia Awakening (Fuller), *887*,
  889
Ethiopian Church of South Africa,
  43
"Ethiopian Delineation," 1456
Ethiopian Hebrew Rabbinical
  College, 1222
Ethiopianism
  intellectual life, 1099
  and Judaism, 1222

Federated Workers Union, 863

Fedon, Julien, 1819

"Feed, clothe and house the nation" program, 1755–1756

Feelings, Muriel, 757

Feelings, Thomas, 510, **757–758**

Fellowship Church for All Peoples, 2194

Fellowship of Reconciliation (FOR)
    Bevel, James, 238
    and Congress of Racial Equality (CORE), 524
    Farmer, James, 747
    Rustin, Bayard, 1993–1994

Feminism
    African Methodist Episcopal Church, 45
    art, 146–147
    Black Arts movement, 252
    "Black Feminist Statement" (Combahee River Collective), 2493–2498
    black women's studies, 278–279
    Communist Party of the United States, 514
    critical race theory, 561
    Douglass, Frederick, 639, 641
    drama, 650–651
    hip-hop, 1538
    intellectual life, 1117–1118
    Jeffers, Audrey, 1173
    lesbians, 1279
    liberation theology, 1286
    literary criticism, 1307
    literature, 1331
    Lorde, Audre, 1340
    Marson, Una, 1397–1398
    Norton, Eleanor Holmes, 1659
    political ideology, 1795–1796
    politics, 1808
    Reed, Ishmael, criticism of, 1904
    religion, 1918–1919
    Ringgold, Faith, 1950
    Smith, Barbara, 2085
    Smith, Vincent, 1707
    theology, black, 2191
    Tubman, Harriet, 2210–2212, *2211*
    vaudeville blues, 1529

Feminist Arts program, 1761

Feminist performance art, 739–740

Feminist theory and criticism, **758–762**

Ferebee, Dorothy Boulding, 1608

Ferguson, Charles, 551

Ferguson, Herman, 1940–1941

Ferguson, Leland, 117

Fernandes, Ari Cândido, 771

Fernandes, Florestan, 100, 1866

Fernandes, João, 453

Fernandes, Maria Dezonne Pacheco, 771

Fernandes, Silvio. *See* Brancura

Fernández, Ariel, 1520

Fernandez, Joseito, 776

Fernandez, Lorena, 777

Ferrand, Carlos, 778

Ferraz, Aydano Couto, 412

Ferré, Rosario, 2326, 2327

Ferreira, Jovino, 2197

Ferrer, Ibrahim, 776

Ferri, Enrico, 98

Ferris, William H.
    and Crummell, Alexander, 564
    Negro World, 1640
    Pan-Africanism, 1719
    textiles, 2185

Fertilizin theory, 1224

Festa da Penha, 1543

Festivals, **762–768**
    Caribbean theater, 408
    Carnival, 414–417
    Festa da Penha, 1543
    Gullah Festival, *962,* 963
    Maroons, 1390
    Negro Election Day, 1806
    Penha celebrations, 1543
    as performance art, 1763–1764, 1765

Field, Frederick V., 539–540

Field calls, 1524

Fields, Barbara J., 1054

Fields, Johnny L., 930

Fields, Julia, 1792

Fields, Mary, 1277

Fields, W. C., 2297

Fife makers, 807

Fifteenth Amendment, **768–770,** *769,* 1851

Fifth Pan-African Congress, 1720

50 Cent, 1900

"Fight for Freedom Fund" campaign, NAACP, 1592

The Fights of All (newspaper), 1204

Figure dances, 2095

Filho, Alfredo Viana. *See* Pixinguinha

Filho, Antônio Marques, 771

Filho, José Cajado, 771

Fillmore, Millard, 458

Film, **770–792**
    Academy Award winners (table), 2522
    blaxploitation, 292–297
    breakdancing, 328
    English, African-American, 710
    ethnography, 1555–1556
    fraternities, 869

Freeman, Morgan, 883

gay men, 913

hip-hop, 1992

Johnson, Noble and George, 1188–1189

Jones, Quincy, scores by, 1194

Los Angeles school of filmmakers, 792–794

popular culture, 1825

Prince, 1838–1839

rap, 1885

Robinson, Bill "Bojangles," 1966

Ross, Diana, 1974

Sambo stereotype, 1936

Simmons, Russell, 2035

stereotypes, 1588, 2290

tap dance, 2166

urban cinema, 2233–2235

Van Peebles, Melvin, 2240–2241

Wonder, Stevie, film scores by, 2328

See also Documentary film

Film, Christianity in, **463–467**

Filmmakers, **794–798**
    Burnett, Charles, 362–363
    Dash, Julie, 580
    Lee, Spike, 1273–1275
    lesbians, 1279
    Micheaux, Oscar, 1430–1432
    Palcy, Euzhan, 1710–1711
    Peck, Raoul, 1744
    Poitier, Sidney, 1793–1794
    popular culture, 1825
    Riggs, Marlon, 1949
    Van Peebles, Melvin, 2240–2241
    See also Blaxploitation films; Directors; Documentary film

Film producers
    Simmons, Russell, 2035
    Singleton, John, 2041

Finance
    entrepreneurs, 722
    Freedman's Bank, 876–878
    Nethersole, Noel Newton, 1641–1642

Finance Act, 1963

Finch, William, 1803

Fine, Alvin, 2194

Finney, Michael, 1937

Firefighters Local Union No. 1784 v. Stotts (1984), 23

Fire!! (magazine)
    condemnation of, 1012
    history, 1310
    Hurston, Zora Neale, 1083
    Thurman, Wallace, 2195

The Fire Next Time (Baldwin), 178–179

Firespitters, 536

Frazier, Edward Franklin *continued*
  National Association for the
    Advancement of Colored
    People, 1587
  socioeconomic class divisions,
    1447
  sociology of race relations, 2113
  and Williams, Eric, 1014
Frazier, James, 1603
Frazier, Joe, *871*, **871–872**
  Ali, Muhammad, match with, 73
  boxing, 320
  Foreman, George, match with,
    856
  Olympics, 1680
Frazier, Skipper Lee, 1870
Frazier, Thurston, 932
Frazier-Lyde, Jacqui, 321
Fred Anderson Quintet, 250
Frederick Douglass Company, 780
Frederick Douglass' Paper
  (newspaper), **872**
Fredrickson, George, 1055
Free African societies
  African Methodist Episcopal
    (AME) Church, 460
  Allen, Richard, 41, 77
  founding, 1564
  insurance companies, 1094
  intellectual life, 1099
  Jones, Absalom, 1189
  philanthropy, 1768, 1769
Free blacks, **872–876**, *873*
  Freeman, Elizabeth, 882–883
  free villages, 884–885
  Haitian Revolution, reaction to
    the, 979
  Jamaica, 1201–1202
  Latin America, 493
  magazines, 1308
  mutual aid societies, 1768–1769
  Negro spirituals, 1523
  politics, 1802–1803, 1805–1810
  pressure politics, 1807–1808
Freed, Alan, 1869, 1895
Freedman's Bank, **876–878**
Freedman's Savings and Trust
  Company. *See* Freedman's Bank
Freedmen
  black codes, 255–257
  Bureau of Refugees, Freedmen,
    and Abandoned Lands, 356–357
  Dred Scott v. Sandford (1857),
    653–654
  See also Emancipation
Freedmen's aid societies, 707–708
Freedmen's Bureau. *See* Bureau of
  Refugees, Freedmen, and
  Abandoned Lands

Freedmen's Bureau Act, 675, 1925
Freedmen's Hospital, **878–879**
Freedom (newspaper), 1407
Freedom celebrations, 765
Freedom Farm Corporation, 983
"Freedom Fulfillment" conference,
  1592–1593
Freedom in diasporic cultures, 614–
  616, 616
Freedom Now Party, 1812
"Freedom of choice" educational
  plans, 684
Freedom Rides, **879–880**
  Baker, Ella, 760
  Chaney, James Earl, 444–445
  civil rights movement, 475
  Congress of Racial Equality
    (CORE), 526–527
  Farmer, James, 748
  Lewis, John, 1284
  Nash, Diane, 1578
  Student Nonviolent Coordinating
    Committee (SNCC), 2151
  Sutton, Percy Ellis, 2156
Freedom Schools, 881
Freedom's Journal (newspaper), **880**
  Cornish, Samuel E., 535
  founding, 1204
  intellectual life, 1099
  Russwurm, John Brown, 1992
  Underground Railroad, 1991
  Varick, James, 2242
  Walker, David, 2255
  Williams, Peter, Jr., 2308
*Freedom's Odyssey: African American
  History Essays from* Phylon, 1781
Freedom songs, 1533–1534
Freedom's People (radio show), 1868
Freedom Summer, **880–882**, *881*
  Chaney, James Earl, 444–445
  civil rights movement, 475–476
  Congress of Racial Equality
    (CORE), 527
  Mississippi Freedom Democratic
    Party, 1463
  Moses, Robert Parris, 1493
Freedom to the Free (Commission
  on Civil Rights), 2228
Freeeman, Carla, 101
Freehold Negro, 1520
Free jazz, 1164–1165, 1530
Free Katanga Committee, 2343
Freelon, Allan Randall, 1840
Freelon, Nnenna, 1171
Freeman, Al, Jr., 2175
Freeman, Alan, 561
Freeman, Brian, 651
Freeman, Chico, 157
Freeman, Elizabeth, **882–883**

Freeman, Harry Lawrence, 1685
Freeman, Henry, 86
Freeman, Monica J., 629
Freeman, Morgan, **883–884**
Freeman (newspaper), 858
Freeman, Roland, 1781
Freeman, Ron, 1681
Freeman's Commission, Episcopal
  Church, 727
Freemasons, 867–868
Free Soil Party, 1809
Free Speech (newspaper), 2275–2276
Freestyle exhibition, 149
Free trade, 2285
Free Trade Area of the Americas
  (FTAA), 1121
Free villages, **884–885**
Freewill Baptists, 193
Freire, Paulo, 581, 1296
Freitas, Ricardo, 1940
Frelinghuysen University, 533
French-based creole languages, 548
French Canadian writers, 390–392
French colonialism
  Caribbean education, 677–678
  emancipation, 697–699
  free blacks, 874
  Haitian Revolution, 974–980
  slave codes, 2049–2050
French Guiana
  arts, 1380–1384
  food and cuisine, 843
  maroon communities, 1983–1984
French Guiana, literature of, **1312–
  1314**
French Revolution
  and Haitian Revolution, 977–979
  Tailor's Revolt, 2159
Frente Negra Brasileira, 273, **885–
  887**, 1577, 1798
Frescoes, 1505
Fresh, Doug E., 1537
Fresh (film), 710
Fresh Prince, 1538, 1885
Freyre, Gilberto
  African Muslim influence, 1562
  ethnic origins, 731
  intra-class racism, 772
  race relations, 1866
  Sambodrome, 2002
  sociology of slavery, 100
Friday (film), 2234
Frido, 142
Friedel-Crafts reaction, 380
Friendly, Fred, 1211
Frierson, Andrew, 1685
Frilot, Shari, 629
Fritz, Marie, 456
Frobenius, Leo, 438, 1634, 1720

Genealogy, 980

General Association of the Western States and Territories, 192

General Conference of the AME Church, 1847

General Education Board, 1769–1770

General Social Survey of the National Opinion Research Center, 2119

General State Convention, 192

Generations (television show), 2175

Genetics and race, 1860–1861, 1864–1866, 2018–2019

Genovese, Eugene D., 1054

Gentry, Herbert, 1706

Geography and geology, Caribbean, 1627

George, Bryant, 1833

George, David, **913–914**
 Baptists, 190, 191
 Canadian writing, 388
 missionary movement, 1461
 Protestantism, 1844

George, Henry, 858

George, Nelson
 high-brow *vs.* working class music, 1894
 intellectual life, 1114
 music, 1897
 music collections, 1555

George Foreman Youth and Community Center, 856

Georgetown University, 222

Georgia, 191

Georgia Writer's Project, 809

Gerard, Gil, 913

Gerima, Haile
 films of, 786, 788, 790
 Los Angeles school of filmmakers, 792–794, 1825

Germany
 Berlin Olympics, 1679, 1690
 Louis/Schmeling boxing match, 319, *320*, 1341
 race and sports, 2140–2141

Gerrymandering, 1804

Gershwin, George
 and Europe, James Reese, 737
 Lincoln Theatre, 1292
 "Swanee" (song), 1934

Getino, Octavio, 793

Geto Boys, 1538, 1539, 1899

Gettys, Charles, 1827

Getz, Stan, 1164, 1455

Geulio, Vargas, 886

Ghana
 anti-colonial movement, 109
 Du Bois, W. E. B., 660

Ghettos
 de Jesus, Carolina Maria, 595
 Great Migration, 1445–1446
 Harlem, 995
 murals, 1508
 urban poverty in the Caribbean, 2235–2237

Gibbes, Emily V., 1833

Gibbons, Rawle, 409

Gibbs, Ernest, Jr., 509

Gibbs, Marla, 2177

Gibbs, Mifflin, 1803

GI Bill, 121

Gibson, Althea, 87, **914–916,** 2180

Gibson, Bob, 214, 998

Gibson, Donald, 1332

Gibson, Jack, 1869, 1895

Gibson, Josh, 209–211, **916,** 1694

Gibson, Kenneth, 1409

Gibson, William F., 1598, 1599

Giddings, Paula, 1055, 1118

Gideon's Band, 1826

Gikuyu, 1404

Gil, Gilberto, 773

Gilbert, Ane Hart, **1026–1027**

Gilchrist, Carlton "Cookie," 853

Giles, Harriet E., 2128

Gilkes, Cheryl, 1919, 1920

Gilkes, Michael, 409

Gill, Robert, 1108

Gillespie, Dizzy, *917,* **917–918**
 bebop, 1163, 1530
 and Calloway, Cab, 379
 and Coltrane, John, 501
 Cuban film, 776
 and Fitzgerald, Ella, 803
 Harlem, 992
 intellectual life, 1116
 jazz and culture, 1167
 and Jones, Quincy, 1194
 Latin music influence, 1166
 and Mingus, Charles, 1455
 and Parker, Charlie, 1725
 and Pozo, Chano, 3
 and Roach, Max, 1960
 and Williams, Mary Lou, 2307

Gillespie, Ezekiel, 42

Gilliam, Angela, 100

Gilliam, Dorothy, 1211, 1215

Gilliam, Joe, 854

Gilliam, Leah, 1647

Gilliam, Sam, 147, 1708, 1841

Gilmore, John, 2154

Gilpin, Charles, 1004, 1259

Gilroy, Paul
 African diasporic identity, 1928
 literary criticism, 1307

Giovanni, Nikki, **918–919**
 Black Arts movement, 252

black-owned publishing houses, 1330

blues, 303

Broadside Press, 331

poetry, 1791, 1884

sororities, 2124

Giovanni's Room (Baldwin), 178

Giral, Sergio, 775, 795

Girl groups, 1895

Girl's Institute at Tuskegee, 2269

Giroux, Henry, 1296

Gist, Eloyce King Patrick, 464

Gist, James, 464

Givens, Ernest, 854

Givens, Robin, 2221, 2298

Gladstone, WIlliam, 800

Glass, Ron, 2174

Glasspole, Florizel, **919–921**

Glaude, Eddie S., Jr., 1054

Glave, E. J., 433

Glave, Thomas, 406

Glazer, Nathan, 21

Gliddon, George R., 1860

Glissant, Edouard, **921,** 1317, 2202–2203

Glissant, Gabriel, 795

Globalization
 anthropological aspects, 101–102
 urban poverty in the Caribbean, 2235–2236
 women traders, 2321–2322

Globe (newspaper), 858

Globetrotters, Harlem. *See* Harlem Globetrotters

Gloster, Hugh, 1302, 1484, 1781

Gloucester, John, 1832

Glover, Danny, 787, **921–922**

Glover, George Washington, 1558

Glover, Keith, 304

Glover, Rebecca, 1847

Glover, Savion, **922**
 Black and Blue (musical revue), 2189
 diasporic dance, 575
 tap dance, 2167

Gluford, Guion S. "Guy," 159

Gnawa, 1434

Gobineau, Comte de, 2137

Gobineau, Joseph-Arthur de, 1314

"God is a Negro" (Turner), **2441–2442**

Godreau, Miguel, 64

Goetz, Bernhard, 529

Goff, James, 1751

Go-go music, 1536

Goings, Russell, 1214

Goins, Gregoria Fraser, 1558

Goldberg, Bert and Jack, 783

Goldberg, David Theo, 2120

Liberia *continued*
    Garvey, Marcus, 905
    Libretto for the Republic of Liberia
        (Tolson), 2199
    missionary movement, 1461–
        1462
    Russwurm, John Brown, 1992–
        1993
    Turner, Henry McNeal, 2214
Libertarianism, 22
Liberty Deferred (drama), 647
Liberty League of Negro-Americans,
    107
Liberty Life Insurance Building,
    Chicago, IL, *1095*
Liberty Party, 900, 1808–1809
Liberty Street Presbyterian Church,
    899
Libraries, 1100
Library of Congress, 1390
Libretto for the Republic of Liberia
    (Tolson), 2199
Lieber, Judith, 1950
Lieberman, Joseph, *1659*
Lieberson, Stanley, 2118
Liele, George, **1288–1289**
    Baptists, 191, 193
    missionary movement, 1461
    Protestantism, 1844
Lieutenant governors, 1815–1816
Life (magazine), 1726–1727
*The Life and Times of Frederick
    Douglass*, 1479
Life expectancy, 1490–1491
*The Life Experience and Gospel
    Labors of the Rt. Rev. Richard Allen*
    (Allen), **2389–2396**
"Life in Mississippi" (Hamer
    interview), 2477–2482
Life insurance companies. *See*
    Insurance companies
*The Life of Josiah Henson, Formerly
    a Slave, Now an Inhabitant of
    Canada, as Narrated by Himself*
    (Henson), 1040
A Life of Langston Hughes
    (Rampersad), 1305
Lifetime achievement awards, 1165
Lift Every Voice and Sing (hymnal),
    728
Liga Metropolitana de Desportos
    Terrestres, 2139–s2140
Liggins, Joe, 1534
Lighbourne, Robert, **1289**
*Light and Truth; Collected from the
    Bible and Ancient and Modern
    History* (Lewis), 1100
Lightfoot, Elba
    Harlem Artists Guild, 1507

Savage, Augusta, study with,
    1703
Lightfoot, Sara Lawrence, 1118
Light-skinned blacks. *See* Skin color
Ligon, Glenn, 146, **1289–1291,** *1290*
Ligon, Willie Joe, 932
Lil' Bow Wow, 1899
Lil Jon, 1887
Lil' Kim, 502, 1886
Lillard, Joe, 848, 850
Lil Romeo, 1886
Lil' Wayne, 1899
Lim, Genny, 1651
Lima, Peru, 1174–1175
Linacre, Thomas, 1424
Lincoln, Abbey, **1291**
    jazz, 1167, 1171
    and Roach, Max, 1959
Lincoln, Abraham
    abolition, 12
    emancipation, 702–703
    Emancipation Proclamation,
        2413–2414
    The Liberator (newspaper), 1288
    slavery, 2072
    Thirteenth Amendment, 2192
Lincoln, C. Eric, 246, 1621
Lincoln, Lord, 2286
Lincoln, Mary Todd, 1229, 1325
Lincoln Company, 780
Lincoln Film Company, 1430–1431
Lincoln Institutes Moses, 617
Lincoln Motion Pictures, 1188–1189
Lincoln's Dream (film), 779–780
Lincoln Theatre, 993, **1291–1292**
Lincoln University, **1292–1293**
Lindo, Archie, 1397
Lindsay, John, 1547
Lindsay, Vachel, 1301
Lindsey, Melvin, 1871
Lindsey, Richard, 1703–1704
Lindy hop, 574, 2014–2015, 2098–
    2099
Line dances, 2100
Lines Ballet, 1767
Linguistics. *See* Language and
    linguistics
Link, Arthur, 1220
Linnaeus, Carolus, 1864, 2018
Lion, Jules, 1697, 1778, 1839
Lippmann, Walter, 1932
Lisboa, Antônio Francisco, **1293–
    1295**
Lisk-Carew, Alphonso, 1775
Liston, Melba, 1557
Liston, Sonny, 72, 1740
Literacy
    churches' support of, 1099
    newspapers, 1207

post-Reconstruction era, 674,
    1102
Literacy education, **1295–1297**
Literacy tests, 939
Literary contests, 1687
Literary criticism, **1297–1307**
    of *Cane* (Toomer), 2200
    Condé, Maryse, 518–519
    Giovanni, Nikki, work of, 919
    Hurston, Zora Neale, works of,
        1084
    intellectual life, 1113–1114
    Madhubuti, Haki R., 1360–1361
    Négritude, 1634
    Opportunity: Journal of Negro Life
        (magazine), 1687
    Thurman, Wallace, 2195–2196
Literary magazines, 287–288, **1307–
    1312**
Literary movements
    antebellum era, 1100
    Les Cenelles, 1100
Literary societies
    free blacks, 875
    intellectual life, 1100
Literature, **1312–1333**
    Black World/Negro Digest, 287–
        288
    blues, 303–304
    Brawley, Benjamin Griffith, 326–
        327
    Brown, Sterling Allen, 345–346
    English, African-American, 710
    gay and lesbian, 912
    jazz in, 1166
    passing, 1732–1736
Literature, children's, **455–457**
Lithography, 253, 1839–1841
Little, Floyd, 851
Little, Larry, 852, 853
Little, Louise, 1640
Little, Mary Lou Allison Gardner,
    2123
"Little Bea," 2014
Little Benny and the Masters, 1536
Little Carib Theatre, 408, 1414
Little Eva, 1895
Littlefield, Daniel C., 1054
Littlejohn, David, 1298
Little Milton, 304
Little Richard, **1333–1334**
    dandyism, 259
    funk, influence on, 1946
    gospel music, 932
    Pioneer Awards, 1946
    rhythm and blues, 1534, 1944
Little Rock Nine, 225, 1594
Little Saints in Praise, 1533
Little Theatre Movement, 234, 408

Masculinity, **1398–1406**
  art, 146
  Colón Man, 499–500
  in film, 793
Mase, 502, 1900
Maseko, Andreis, 2093
Mashiani, Jan, 1678
Masilela, Ntongela, 792
Masking, 645, 767–768
Maslow, Sophie, 1464
Mason, Charles Harrison
  Church of God in Christ, 462
  gospel music, 928, 929
  Holiness movement, 1058
  Pentecostalism, 1752, 1753
  religion, 1915
Mason, Charlotte Osgood, 1083,
  1300
Mason, L. M., 928
Masons
  diasporic textiles, symbolism in,
    2184
  Dickson, Moses, 617–618
  fraternal orders, 867–868
  free blacks, 875
  Hall, Prince, 981
  Jones, Absalom, 1190
  Marrant, John, 1391
  philanthropy, 1768
Mason Temple COGIC, 462
Massachusetts
  archaeology, 117
  education, 681
  Freeman, Elizabeth, 882–883
  fugitive slave laws, 366
  slave trade ban, 981
Massachusetts Anti-Slavery Society,
  639, 1923
Massachusetts General Colored
  Association, 2255
Massachusetts Institute of
  Technology, 118
Massachusetts Racial Protective
  Association (MRPA), 2206
Massey, Douglas, 2104, 2119
Massey, Walter, 1484, 2020
Massiah, Louis, 628
Massing, Michael, 1216
Master P, 1052, 1539, 1886, 1899
Masters, Edgar Lee, 1301
Masters Golf Tournament, 1090,
  2331, 2332
Mastin, Will, 588–589
Matawai maroons, 1983
Material culture, 116–117, 815
Maternal mortality, 1490
Mathematical Association of
  America, 1406

Mathematics and mathematicians,
  1104, **1406–1407**
Mather, Cotton, *2055*
Mathews, Michael, 652
Mathias, John Royce. *See* Mathis,
  Johnny
Mathis, Johnny, **1407**
Matjáu clan, 615
Matney, Bill, 1215
Matrifocal kinship, 99–100
Matrilineage
  diasporic cultures, 615, 616
  maroons, 1981
Matson, Ollie, 850, 852
Matsuda, Mari, 561, 2038
Mattachine Society, 1278
Matthew, Wentworth Arthur, 1222
Matthews, Artie, 1528, 1874
Matthews, Dom Basil, 2299
Matthews, Howard "Dixie," 850
Matthews, Inez, 1684
Matthews, Victoria Earle
  social gospel, 2103
  social work, 2107
  Woman's Era (newspaper), 2318
Matthews, Vince, 1681
Matthias, Robert, 2209
Maturana, Francisco, 2092
Matzeliger, Jan, 1126, 1738
Mau Mau movement, 1719
Maxim, Hiram, 1264
Maxim, Joey, 1477, 1969
Maxwell, Marina Omowale, 408
Maxwell v. Bishop (1970), 1570
May, Brother Joe, 930
May, Debbie, 1556
"Maybelline" (song), 235
Mayersville, Mississippi, 286
Mayfair Mansions, 1430
Mayfield, Curtis
  blaxploitation films, 1896
  funk, 1946
  and Marley, Bob, 1380
  rhythm and blues, 1943
Mayfield, Julian, 1018, **1407–1408**
Mayhew, Richard, 2331
Maynard, Andrew, 1681
Maynard, Robert, 1211, 1215
Maynor, Dorothy
  arranged spirituals, 1526
  music collections, 1559
  opera, 1684
Mayors, **1408–1411**, 2549–2550
  (table)
  Barry, Marion, 204–205
  black candidates, 1816
  Blackwell, Unita, 286
  Bradley, Tom, 323
  Brown, Willie, 347

  Dinkins, David, 622, 996
  Evers, Charles, 737–738
  Hatcher, Richard Gordon, 1028–
    1029
  Jackson, Maynard Holbrook, Jr.,
    1144–1145
  Jordon, Edward, 1201–1202
  King, Iris, 1238
  politics, 1805
  Stokes, Carl Burton, 2148–2149
  Washington, Harold, 2267–2268
  Wilder, Lawrence Douglas, 2294–
    2295
  Young, Andrew, 2346–2347
  Young, Coleman, 2348–2349
Mayor's Commission on Conditions
  in Harlem, 994
Mays, Benjamin E.
  Durham Manifesto, 666, **1411–
    1412**
  intellectual life, 1115
  religion, 1919
Mays, Willie, **1413**
Mayweather, Floyd, 1276
Mazzini, Giuseppe, 2015
Mbuy-Beya, Bernadette, 1287
McBurnie, Beryl, **1413–1414**
McCabe, Edwin, 281–282
McCain, James, 526
McCall, Steve, 156, 157, 250
McCann, Les, 1531
McCard, H. Stanton, 86
McCarran Act, 540
McCarthy era
  Afro-American (newspaper), 1209
  anti-colonial movement, 108
  Civil Rights Congress, 471
  Communist Party of the United
    States, 513
  Horne, Lena, 1065
  Hudson, Hosea, 1077
  Hughes, Langston, 1079
  Hunton, Alphaeus, 1073
  Scott, Hazel, 2022
McCartney, Paul, 1039, 1897
McCarty, CeCee, 714
McCarty, Oseola, 80
McCauley, Robbie, 651, 1764, 1766
McClaskey, John, 47
McClendon, Lloyd, 215
McClennan, Tommy, 300
McCleskey v. Kemp (1987), 1571
McClure, Cubena, 2123
McCoy, Albert B., 1832
McCoy, Cecil A., 2127
McCoy, Elijah, *1123*, 1126, 1738,
  1739
McCoy, "Kansas" Joe, 307
McCoy, Memphis Minnie, 643

Meek, Carrie, **1425–1426**

Meeks, James, 1877–1878

Mehlinger, Louis, 155

Meier, August
   biography, 242, 243
   black studies, 277
   emigrationist politics, 1809
   historiography, 1054

Meirelles, Fernando, 773

Melle Mel, 1538, 1885

Melo, Roberto, 968

Melville, Herman, 1563

Melvin, Harold, 1536, 1896, 1945

Membership intake, fraternity, 869

Memeses, Guillermo, 778

Memories of the World Program,
   130, 133

"Memphis Blues" (song), 299, 302

Memphis Free Speech (newspapers),
   1206

Memphis Jug Band, 1546

Memphis Minnie, 300, 307–308,
   2167

Memphis Slim, 1178

Memphis sound, 1896

Mena, Zulia, 1801

Menace II Society (film), 2234

Menchú, Rigoberta, 1820, 1822

Mencken, H. L., 1786

Mendel, Gregor, 2018

Mendez, Jose, 2138

Menelik II, 889

The Men of Brewster Place (Naylor),
   1631–1632

Menzies, William, 1751

Meoyer, Louis, 118

Mercer, Mabel, 1558

Merchant marines, 1503–1504

Mercury Records, 1194

Meredith, James H., **1426–1427**
   civil rights movement, 475
   March against Fear, 2190
   National Association for the
     Advancement of Colored
     People, 1595–1596

Meredith, William, 1191

Meredith v. Fair (1962), 1495

Merengue, *1518*

Mergers and acquisitions
   Dillard University, 621
   insurance companies, 1097

Meriwether, Louise, 1019

Merrick, John
   entrepreneurship, 716
   hair and beauty culture, 970
   insurance companies, 1094, 1095
   North Carolina Mutual Life
     Insurance Company, 1656

Merrill, James G., 800

Merriman, Claude, 1754

"Message to the Grass Roots"
   (Malcolm X), 1365

The Messenger (magazine), *1206*,
1427
   Domingo, W. A., 633
   founding of, 1879
   history, 1310
   Huiswoud, Otto, 1080
   intellectual life, 1108
   launching, 1212
   Owen, Chandler, 1689
   Schuyler, George S., 2017
   Thurman, Wallace, 2195

Mestizaje, 1929–1930

Mestre, Armando, 80

Metalwork 1793-1880 (exhibition),
   2314

Metcalfe, Ralph, **1428**, 1679, 2140,
   2267

Métellus, Jean, 1315

Metheny, Pat, 498

Methodist Church
   Hart sisters, 1026–1027
   Holiness movement, 1057–1058
   slavery, 726–727

Methodist Episcopal Church
   African Methodist Episcopal Zion
     Church, 49
   Christian Methodist Episcopal
     (CME) Church, 467
   independent denominations,
     460–461
   Wilberforce University, 2292

Methodist Episcopal General
   Conference, 1460

Methodist Pentecostal Church, 1749

Methodists
   independent churches, 460–461
   institutional history, 1913
   merger, 1917

Method Man and Redman, 1900

Metoyer, Marie, 713–714

Metranix, Alfred, 99

Metro Broadcasting, Inc. v. FCC
   (1990), 28

Metropolitan Museum, 2240

Metropolitan Opera
   Anderson, Marian, 90–91
   Battle, Kathleen, 225
   Collins, Janet, 182
   Norman, Jessye, 1655
   opera, 1684
   Price, Leontyne, 1835

Mexakinz, 1519

Mexican mural movement, 2330

Mexico
   ethnic origins, 731
   film, 777

Garrido, Juan, 901–902

hip-hop, 1519

maroon communities, 1982

murals, 1505

music, 1517

resistance heroes, 824

San Lorenzo de los Negros,
   2005–2006

Mexico City Olympic Games, 1681

Meyerowitz, Jan, 1079

MFDP. *See* Mississippi Freedom
   Democratic Party (MFDP)

MFSB, 1536

Mfume, Kweisi, **1428–1429**, *1429*,
1599
   Congressional Black Caucus, 522
   liberal integrationism, 1795
   National Association for the
     Advancement of Colored
     People, 1599

Miami riot, 1953

Mia X, 1899

Michael, George, 1898

Michaux, Elder, **1429–1430**

Micheaux, Oscar, 463–464, 781, 783,
   786, 792, **1430–1432**

Middle class, **265–266**
   Afrocubanismo, 57
   Brazil, 1931
   de Jesus, Carolina Maria, 595
   film, 782
   intellectual life, 1112–1113
   migration, 1447
   Morris Knibb, Mary, 1486
   religion, 1919–1920
   sociology of race relations, 2114–
     2115
   wealth, racial differences in, 674

Middle Passage (Johnson), 1179

Midwifery, **1432–1433**

Mighty Clouds of Joy, 932

"The Mighty Sparrow," **862**

Migrant workers, 1438–1439

Migration, **1433–1449**
   African diaspora, 34–35
   archaeology, 117
   black towns, 281–285
   Caribbean art, 144
   Colón Man, 499–500
   economic conditions, 675
   entrepreneurs, 718–719
   Haiti, 668
   intellectual life, 1112
   Islam, 1128
   Missouri Compromise, 2071–
     2072
   National League for the
     Protection of Colored Women,
     1613–1614

Migration *continued*
  resettlement movement, 270
  Singleton, Benjamin "Pap," 2040
  Tanner, Benjamin T., opposition
    by, 43–44
  western, 675
  See also Emigrationism;
    Immigration
Migration of the Negro (art series),
  1269, 1270
Milai, Sammy, 510
Milam, J. W., 2198
Les Milandes, 177
Milburn, Amos
  club blues, 1534
  recordings, 1894
  rhythm and blues, 1944
Milburn, Rodney, 1681
Miles, Bertrand, 1780
Miles, Buddy, 1039
Miles, William, 467–468, 629, 786
Miley, Bubber
  and Ellington, Duke, 693, 694
  and Smith, Mamie, 2089
  trumpet, 1547
Milholland, John E., 1582
Mili, Gjon, 783
Militancy
  Briggs, Cyril, 329
  radio, 1870
  Revolutionary Action Movement,
    1940–1941
  Student Nonviolent Coordinating
    Committee, 2151–2152
Military, **1449–1453**
  Almeida Bosque, Juan, 79–81
  Bandera, Quintín, 185–186
  bases, 440–441
  and Christophe, Henri, 469–470
  Davis, Benjamin O., Jr., 584–585
  Delany, Martin R., 597
  Dessalines, Jean-Jacques, 608
  Dreke, Víctor, 655
  expansion, 599
  fair employment, 337, 1376
  James, Daniel "Chappie," 1157
  Luperón, Gregorio, 1347
  Maceo, Antonio, 1355–1356
  Moncada, Guillermo, 1469
  NAACP's antisegregation
    activism, 2289
  Nanny of the Maroons, 1576
  Poor, Salem, 1823
  Powell, Colin, 1827–1828
  Revolutionary War, 1806–1807
  Romaine-la-Prophétesse, 1972–
    1973
  Toussaint-Louverture, 2202–2203
  Trotter, James Monroe, 2205

  See also Armed forces
    desegregation; Union Army
    recruitment
Militia, black, 874
Mill, John Stuart, 1021, 1480
Millen, Herbert, 1292
Millenarianism, 230
Miller, Bebe, 1764
Miller, Cheryl, 222
Miller, Douglas, 933
Miller, Erroll, 1108
Miller, Flournoy
  and Blake, Eubie, 290
  Harlem, 993
  Harlem Renaissance, 1003
  Shuffle Along (show), 1550, 2097
  theatrical dance, 2186–2187
Miller, Glenn, 1163
Miller, Kelly
  and Briggs, Cyril, 329
  Howard University, 1073
  intellectual life, 1116
  literary criticism, 1299
  Negro National Anthem, 1637
  racial theories, criticism of, 1865
  skin color, 2044
Miller, Lewis, 311
Miller, May, 646
Miller, Norma, 2014, 2188
Miller, Paul D., 742, 1648
Miller, Portia Simpson. *See* Simpson
  Miller, Portia
Miller, Rice, 301
Miller, William, 46
Milliken v. Bradley (1974), 686
Millinder, Lucky, 1944, 2185
Millington, Andrew, 797
Million Man March, **1453–1454,**
  1454
  Chavis, Benjamin Franklin, Jr.,
    450
  Davis, Angela, criticism by, 584
  Farrakhan, Louis, 751
  feminist criticism of, 761
  Nation of Islam, 1624
  Rowan, Carl T., criticism by,
    1976
Million Youth March, 997
Mills, Florence
  Harlem, 993
  Lincoln Theatre, 1291
  Shuffle Along (show), 1550
  theatrical dance, 2187
Mills, Lev, 1840
Mills, Stephanie, 1839
Mills Brothers, 1894, 1943
Milner, Ron, 250, 649
Milton, Roy, 1534
Milwaukee Bucks, 5

Minerals, 1630–1631
Mingus, Charles, **1454–1456**
  avant-garde jazz, 1164
  bebop, 1163
  Black Arts movement, 250
  blues, 300
  hard bop, 1164
  lifetime achievement award, 1165
  and Parker, Charlie, 1725
Minimum wage, 943, 948–949
Mining the Museum (exhibition),
  1709, 2314
Miniseries, television, 607, 2175
Ministers. *See* Clergy
Minnelli, Liza, 590
Minns, Al, 2014
Minor, Robert, 1003
Minority as sociological concept,
  2112
Minority business programs, 1144–
  1145
Minority set-asides, 18, 27–28, 2229
Minstrel shows, **1456–1459**
  breaking of standard of, 574
  comedians, 502
  dandyism, 258
  folk music, 835
  Jim Crow, 1176
  musical instruments, 1546
  Nelson, John, 1298
  as performance art, 1765–1766
  poster, *1458*
  Sambo stereotype, 645, 1935
  sheet music, *1457*
  tap dance, 2164–2165
  theatrical dance, 2186
  Walker, George William, 2257–
    2258
  Williams, Bert, 2296–2297
Minton's Playhouse, 1470
Mintz, Sidney
  Afrocentrism, 53
  anthropology, 97–98, 101
  common orientations, 812
  creole languages, 549
Minus, Marion, 1310
Miracles (music group), 1945
Miranda, Francisco, 977
Mirnyi, Max, 2310
Mirror of Liberty (magazine), 1212,
  1977
Miscegenation, 772, 775–776
Missionaries
  African Civilization Society,
    33–34
  African Methodist Episcopal
    Church, 460
  African Methodist Episcopal Zion
    Church, 48, 49

See also Rainbow/PUSH
Coalition
Operation Restore Democracy, 136
Opportunities Industrialization
Centers of America, 2152
Opportunity: Journal of Negro Life
(magazine), *1309*, **1687**
awards ceremonies, 1008–1011
history, 1309, 1310, 1311
Johnson, Charles Spurgeon,
1179–1180
launching, 1212
literary contests, 646
See also National Urban League
Oppositional culture, 1675–1676,
2105
Oppression, psychological aspects of,
2115
The Oprah Winfrey Show
(television), 1091, *2176*, 2317
Oral history
blues musicians, 1556
Caribbean theater, 410
jazz musicians, 1557
musicians, 1555, 1558
slaves, 2050
Oral theater, 1168
Oratory
antebellum era, 1101
Douglass, Frederick, 638–641
Franklin, C. L., 865
Martin, John Sella, 1398
Proctor, Henry Hugh, 1841
Ward, Samuel Ringgold, 2263
Orbison, Roy, 1944
Orchestral jazz, 737
Order of the Eastern Star, 868
Ordination
African Methodist Episcopal
Church, 44
African Methodist Episcopal Zion
Church, 49
Baptists, 194
Episcopalians, 727–728
Protestantism, 1846–1847
women, 1913, 2214
Oregon, 1166
Orfeo (opera), 1682
Organic Act, 1028
Organisation of Eastern Caribbean
States, 446
Organization of African Unity, 1716,
1721
Organization of Afro-American
United, 1366
Organization of Black American
Culture, 249, 1671–1672
Organization of Petroleum
Exporting Countries, 1372

Organization of Women Writers of
Africa, 536
Organized crime, 1660
Organized labor. *See* Labor and
labor unions
Original Celtics, 218
Original Dixieland Jazz Band, 1161
Original Gospel Harmonettes, 930,
931
Original Hebrew Israelite Nation,
1223
Origin tales, 816–817
Orioles, 1534, 1895
Orisha, 392–393, 622–625, **1688–
1689,** 2343–2346
Ormes, Jackie, 510
*Oroonoko, or the Royal Slave, a True
History* (Behn), 1399
Orozco, José Clemente, 1505
Orser, Charles E., 117
Orthodox Muslim community, 1132
Orthography, 973
Ortiz, Fernando
Afrocubanismo, 3
anthropology, 96, 98
doll collection, 200915
Orville, Xavier, 1317
Ory, Kid
and Armstrong, Louis, 139
blues, 306
jazz, 1160, 1161
New Orleans jazz, 1530
Osbey, Brenda Marie, 1792
Osby, Greg, 1166, 1531
Oscarito, 772
Oscars. *See* Academy Awards
Osman, 1561, 1562
Osoborn, Robert, 1202
Osofsky, Gilbert, 756
Osório, Carloa, 1777
Otelo, Grande, 772, 773
Othello (Shakespeare), 1399
Otis, Harrison Gray, 2257
Otis, Johnny, 1158, 1534, 1942
Ottley, Roi, 756
Otto, John Solomon, 116
Oubré, Hayward, 2330
Ouditt, Steve, 144
Ououloguem, Yambo, 1634
*Our Nig; or, Sketches from the Life of
a Free Black. . .* (Wilson), 2315
Our Women and Children
(magazine), 2319
"Our Women Getting into the
Larger Life" (document), **2452**
Our World (magazine), 1213, 2082
The Outcasts (television show), 2174
Outerbridge, Mary, 2180

OutKast, *259*
black dandies, 259
hip-hop, 1052
Parks, Rosa, lawsuit by, 1729
rap, 1539, 1887
recording industry, 1899, 1900
"The Outlaw" (Johnson), 828
Outlawry legislation, 1988
The Outlet (magazine), 1036, 2195
Ové, Horace, 797
Overr, Oscar O., 285
Overrepresentation of African
Americans
criminal justice system, 555–556
military, 1452–1453
Overstreet, Harry, 124, 125
Overstreet, Joe, 249
Overton, Anthony, 716, 970
Overton Hygienic Manufacturing
Company, 970
Ovesey, Lionel, 2115
Ovington, Mary White
on Garvey, Marcus, 1007
National Association for the
Advancement of Colored
People, 1581–1583, 1587, 1588
Niagara Movement, 1653
Owen, Chandler, **1689**
Harlem, 992
Harrison, Hubert Henry,
influence of, 1025
The Messenger (magazine), 1080,
1212, 1879
National Association for the
Advancement of Colored
People, 1585
New Negro, 1649
socialism, 1811
Owen, Randolph and Chandler,
1112
Owens, Dana Elaine. *See* Queen
Latifah
Owens, Jesse, *1678*, **1689–1691**, *1690*
Berlin Olympic Games, 2140
experiments on, 2137
Olympics, 1679
Owens, Leslie Howard, 127, 1054
Owens, Ricky, 2179
Owens, Robert, 1559
Own style baskets, 806
Oxford University, 1963
Oyewole, Abiodun, 1264
Oyo, 734

P

Pace, Harry
Black Swan Records, 1894

film, 785
Harlem, 995
journalism, 1214
photography, *1726,* 1780
Parks, John, 1159
Parks, Rosa, *1472,* **1728–1729**
  and Abernathy, Ralph David, 7
  children's literature, 456
  Citizenship Schools, 1042
  civil rights movement, 474
  Montgomery bus boycott, 1471–
    1472
  Montgomery Improvement
    Association, 1474
  Nixon, Edgar Daniel, 1654
  and Robinson, Jo Ann Gibson,
    1968
  sororities, 2124
Parks, Suzan-Lori, **1729–1730**
  drama, 651
  experimental theater, 742
  literature, 1332
Parks Sausage Company, 720, 724
Parliament, 1535
Parliament (musical group), 1884
Parliament members, 1892–1893
Parra, Pim de la, 774
Parsons, Lucy, **1730–1731**
Parsons, Talcott, 482
Partido Autoctono Negro
  (Uruguay). *See* Black
  Autochthonous Party (Uruguay)
Partido Independiente de Color
  (Cuba), **1731–1732,** 1798
Partido Revolucionario Dominicano.
  See Dominican Revolutionary
  Party
Partlow, Roy, 212
Party rap, 1537, 1885
Passing, **1732–1737**
  Chesnutt, Charles W., 451
  Craft, Ellen, 542, *543*
  identity and race, 1091
  Piper, Adrian, 1784
  See also Skin color
Passing (Larsen), 1014
Pastinha, Vicente Ferreira, 398
Patchwork, 1383
Patents and inventions, 1123–1126,
  1737–1740
Paternalism, 632
Paton, Alan, 2194
Patrick, Pat, 2154
Patriotism
  Owens, Jesse, 1690–1691
  Spaulding, Charles Clinton, 2128
Patterson, Andrew, 849
Patterson, Floyd, **1740**
  and Ali, Muhammad, 72

boxing, 317
  Moore, Archie, match with, 1477
  Olympics, 1680
Patterson, Frederick D., 2218
Patterson, Haywood, 2023–2024
Patterson, J. O., 1753
Patterson, John, 879
Patterson, Louise Thompson, 512–
  514, *513, 514,* 540
Patterson, Orlando, 1045, 1321
Patterson, Percival James "P. J.,"
  1740–1742
  and Manning, Patrick, 1376
  People's National Party, 1761
Patterson, Raymond, 1791
Patterson, William, 471, 514, **1742–
  1743**
Patterson, Willis, 1526
Patterson v. McLean Credit Union
  (1989), 477
Pattillo, Walter A., 500
Patton, Charley
  blues, 299
  recordings, 1894
  rural blues, 1529
Patton, Mel, 1679
Patton v. Mississippi (1947), 1396
Paul, Susan, 241
Paul, Thomas, 14, 798
Pauling, Linus, 2034
Paul Quinn College, 41
Payne, Charles, 1054
Payne, Daniel Alexander, **1743–1744**
  African Methodist Episcopal
    Church, 41, 42
  The Anglo-African (magazine),
    92, 1308
  autobiography, 166
  religion, 1913
  religious music, 1523
  Wilberforce University, 2292
Payne, Harrison G., 44
Payne, John, 564
Payne, William A., 285
Payner, John B., 1811
Payola, 1869–1870
Payton, Benjamin F., 2219
Payton, Phillip A., Jr., 717, 991, 999
Payton, Walter, 852, 853
Peabody, Ephraim, 1324
Peabody Fund, 1769
Peace and Freedom Party, 1812
Peacekeeping forces, 356
Peace Missions, 753, 1770–1771,
  1916
Peale, Charles Wilson, 1186, 1697
Peale Charles Polk, 1697
Pearson, Conrad, 2127
Peary, Robert E., 1040–1041

Peau Noire, Masques Blancs (Black
  Skin, White Masks), **2453–2456**
Peck, James, 526, 879
Peck, Raoul, 774, **1744**
Péean, Stanley, 390
Peeples, Nat, 213, 214
Peer, Ralph, 1893
Pegler, Westbrook, 211
Pegues, A. W., 1604
Pelé, **1744–1746,** *1745, 1746,* 2092,
  2093
Pelham, Robert, 1738
"Pelo telefone" (song), 1999–2000,
  2197
Pemberton, James, 566
Peña, Alberto, 57
Penal Code of 1890 (Brazil), 1542–
  1543
Pender, Paul, 1969
Pendergrass, Teddy, 1945
Pendleton, Clarence, Jr., 2228
Penguins (music group), 1895, 1943
Penha celebrations, 1543
Penn Center on Saint Helena Island,
  South Carolina, 963
Penniman, Richard. *See* Little
  Richard
Pennington, James W. C., **1747–
  1748**
  Afrocentrism, 52
  historiography, 1052
  Presbyterianism, 1832
  slave narratives, 2052
  social gospel, 2103
Pennsylvania
  Lincoln University, 1292–1293
  Moravian Church, 1482–1483
Pennsylvania Abolition Society,
  1377–1378
Pennsylvania Academy of the Fine
  Arts, 2161
Pennsylvania Society for the
  Abolition of Slavery, 2146
Penny, Rob, 2312
Pentecostalism, **1748–1753,** *1751–
  1753*
  anthropology, 99
  Catholicism and, 430
  gospel music, 929, 1531
  history, 461–462
  Holiness movement, 1058
  missionary movement, 1462
  northern churches, 1915–1916
  Seymour, William Joseph, 1846
  Smith, Lucy, 1914
Peoples, Theo, 2179
People's Charter of 1956, 1758
People's Communication Network,
  1647

People's Convention (Jamaica), 1151

People's Education Movement, 1757

People's National Congress
(Guyana), **1754–1756**
Burnham, Forbes, 363–364
Carter, John, 419
Carter, Martin, 420
Gaskin, Winifred, 908
Hoyte, Desmond, 1075–1076
King, Sydney, 1246
Phillips-Gay, Jane, 1774

Peoples National Movement
(Trinidad and Tobago), 1156,
1756–1758
Chambers, George, 442
Constantine, Learie, 529–530
February Revolt, 755
Manning, Patrick, 1376–1377
Robinson, A. N. R., 1963–1964
Solomon, Patrick, 2122
Teshea, Isabel, 2182
and West Indies Federal Labour
Party, 2281–2282
Williams, Eric, 2299, 2300–2301

People's National Party (Jamaica),
1758–1761
Blake, Vivian, 291
Burke, Rudolph Augustus, 360
Bustamante, Alexander, 370
Cooke, Howard, 531
Dalton-James, Edith, 572
Domingo, W. A., 633
Glasspole, Florizel, 920
Hill, Ken, 1043–1044
and Jamaica Progressive League,
1153, 1154
King, Iris, 1238–1239
Leon, Rose, 1275
Mais, Roger, 1362
Manley, Michael, 1369–1372
Manley, Norman, 1373–1376
Nethersole, Noel Newton, 1642
Patterson, Percival James "P. J.,"
1740–1742
Simpson Miller, Portia, 2039

People's Political Party (Jamaica),
1151

People's Political Party (St.
Vincent), 1202–1203

People's Progressive Party (Guyana),
1245–1246
Benn, Brindley, 233
Burnham, Forbes, 363–364
Carter, Martin, 420
Chase, Ashton, 449
Rodney, Walter, 1970
women, 1820
See also People's National
Congress (Guyana)

People's Reform Party (Guyana),
339

People's Revolutionary Army
(Grenada), 1644

People's United Party (Belize), 1833

People United to Serve Humanity.
See Operation PUSH; Rainbow/
PUSH Coalition

Pepsi-Cola soccer clinics, 1746–1747

Perciliana, Tia, 1541

Percussion instruments, 1546–1547

Percy, Earl, 315

Perdomo, Willie, 1311–1312

Perdue, Charles L., 756

Pereira, Geraldo, 1544, 2001

Pereira dos Santos, Nelson, 772

Perfectionists, 2209

Performance art, **1761–1768**
feminist, 739–740
maroons, 1383–1384
Piper, Adrian, 1784–1785
Smith, Anna Deavere, 651, 2084–
2085

Performing Arts Training Center,
665–666

Perkins, Benjamin J., 864

Perkins, Samuel H., 1989

Perkinson, Coleridge-Taylor, 1559

Perl, Arnold, 1274

Permed hair, 966

Pérola Negra, Jovelina, 2002

Perón, Eva, 1821

Perón, Maria, 1821

Perry, Bruce, 243

Perry, Carrie, 1410

Perry, Edward, 716

Perry, Herman, 717, 1096

Perry, Joe, 849, 852

Perry, Julia, 1559, 1603

Perry, Lee "Scratch," 1906

Perry, Lincoln. *See* Stepin Fetchit

Perry, Pettis, 514

Perry, Ronald, 577

Perse, Saint-John, 1316

Persian Gulf War, 599

Personal-care industry. *See* Hair and
beauty culture

Persson, Gene, 785

Peru
demography, 605
food and cuisine, 841
Jesús, Úrsula de, 1174–1175
San Martín de Porras, 2006–2007

Pete, Peaches, and Duke, 2166

Peter, Carla, 1307

Peters, Albert, 1723–1724

Peters, DeWitt, 141, 142

Peters, Margaret "Pete," 87, 2180

Peters, Matilda Roumania "Repeat,"
87, 2180

Petersburg, Virginia, 1142

Peterson, Carla, 1914

Pétion, Alexandre, 134, 469, 977

Petit marronage, 2067–2068

Petro-Lemba, 2057

Petry, Ann, 455, 995, 1328

Pettey, Charles Calvin, 49

Pettiaugers, 806

Pettie, Fannie, 2123

Pharmacists, 240

Phelps, Anthony, 390, 1315

Phelps-Stokes Fund, 1770

Phi Beta Sigma, 869

Philadelphia, Pennsylvania
American Moral Reform Society,
83–84, 93
Antebellum Convention
movement, 93
Forten, James, 857
Jones, Absalom, 1189–1190
mutual aid societies, 1564

Philadelphia Dance Company, 251

Philadelphia Free African Society, 77

Philadelphia Library of Colored
Persons, 2288

The Philadelphia Negro (Du Bois),
276, 658, 1104, 2108

Philadelphia Pythians, 206

Philadelphia Tribune (newspaper),
1205

Philadelphia Vigilance Committee,
1851

Philadelphia Warriors, 441

Philanthropy and foundations,
1768–1773
art, 1508
Cosby, Bill, 538
Fisk University, 801
Harlem Renaissance, 1008–1010
Jack and Jill of America, 1135
LaBelle, Patti, 1251
Simmons, Russell, 2035
social work, 2107
Toussaint, Pierre, 2201
Tuskegee University funding,
2218
Winfrey, Oprah, 2317

Philbrick, Edward, 1826

Philips, Esther, 1170

Phillip, Marlene Nourbese, 389, 406,
1321

Phillips, Caryl, 1321, **1773–1774**

Phillips, Charles H., 468

Phillips, Dewey, 1869

Phillips, Henry, 2103

Phillips, Jane, 1330

Phillips, Lisa, 147

Politics and politicians *continued*
    Williams, Hosea Lorenzo, 2305–
        2306
    Woodford Square, 2328–2330
    Young, Andrew, 2346–2347
    Young, Coleman, 2348–2349
    See also Political activism;
        Political parties
Polk, Charles Peale, 1186
Polk, P. H., 1780
Pollard, Frederick Douglass "Fritz,"
    847
Pollard, Fritz, Jr., 849, 850, 2140
Pollard, Ingrid, 144
Pollard, Leslie, 848
Pollard, Sam, 628
Pollard, Velm, 1320
Pollock, Jackson, 596
Pollution, 725–726
Polygenism, 1859–1860, 1864
Polyrhythms, 573
Pomare, Eleo, 251, 2189
Pomo Afro Homos, 651, 1767
Po' Monkeys, 305
Ponder, Henry, 801
Pontecorvo, Gillo, 774
Poole, Robert. *See* Elijah
    Muhammad
Poor, Salem, **1823**
Poor people
    National Welfare Rights
        Organization, 1619–1620
    religion, 1920
    See also Poverty
Poor People's Campaign, 1242,
    1823–1824
    Abernathy, Ralph David, 6
    Franklin, C. L., 865
    National Urban League, 1618
    Southern Christian Leadership
        Conference, 2126
Poor Righteous Teachers, 1885
Pope, Eddie, 2093
Pope.L, William, 1764, *1765*, 1767
Popenoe, Paul, 1865
Popkin, Harry and Leo, 783
Poplack, Shana, 550, 709
Popoff, Rovana, 1927
Popping (dance), 2101
Popular culture, 710, **1824–1826**
Popular dance. *See* Social dance
Popular Front, 512–513
Popular music
    Afrocubanismo, 56
    collections, 2555
    folk music, influence on, 836
    Jackson family, 1148
    Mathis, Johnny, 1407
Popular sovereignty, 2071

Population
    of African Americans by state,
        1890, *832*
    blacks as percentage of total U.S.
        population, *603*
    Canada, 385, 387
    distribution of African Americans
        in 1874, *1441*
    free black and slave populations,
        1860, *480*
    free blacks, 873
    and the Great Migration, 1440–
        1448
    Harlem, 991, 999
    Louisiana census of 1860, *2064*
    Ohio black codes, 255
    statistical data, 2553–2570
    See also Demography
Populism
    Colored Farmers Alliance, 500
    and lynching, 1351
Populist Afrocentrism, 53–54
Porgy (play), 1011
Porgy and Bess (show), 1558
Poro Company, 717, 970
Porres, Martin of, 426
Portal Aro, 275
Portela, Paulo da, 2001
Porter, Alfred Haynes, 2218
Porter, Charles Ethan, 1699
Porter, David, 1029
Porter, James, 150, 1254, 1702
Porter, William S., 779
Portocarrero, René, 141
Portrait of Daniel Coker (Johnson),
    1185, *1186*
*Portrait of Mr. and Mrs. James
    McCormick and Their Children*
    (Johnson), *1187*
Portraits
    Huie, Albert, 1079
    Johnson, Joshua, 1185–1187
    Muslims, 1561
    Savage, Augusta, 2011–2012
    VanDerZee, James, 2239, 2240
Port Royal Experiment, 707, **1826–
    1827**
Portuguese colonialism
    coartación, 490–493
    Palmares, 1713–1716
    Querino, Manuel, 1856–1857
    riots and popular protests, 1956–
        1957
    slave codes, 2048–2049
    Tailor's Revolt, 2159–2160
Portuguese slave trade
    African diaspora migration, 1434
    diasporic cultures, 612
    ethnic origins, 730–731, 735

overview, 2074–2076, 2079
slavery, 2062
smuggling, 2080
Portuondo, Omara, 776
Posey, Pearlie, 2185
Positive image movies, 296
Positive K, 1537, 1538
Post, Amy, 1150
Post civil rights era
    historiography, 1054
    sociology, 2115, 2116–2121
Postage Stamps, African Americans
    on, 2542
Postell, Tom, 1790
Post emancipation era
    Caribbean education, 677–680
    education, 680–682
    folk medicine, 833–834
    slave narratives, 2052
Post emancipation folklore, 815–816
Postmodern drama, 651
Postnational art, 143
Poston, Ted, 1210
Poston, Tom, 756
Post World War I era, 107
Post World War II era
    film, 784–785
    Harlem, 995
    middle class blacks, 265–266
    nursing, 1667–1669
    sociology of race relations, 2114
Potawotomi, 667
Potter, Lou, 628
Potter, Tommy, 1725
Pottery
    archaeology, 116–117
    crafting, 807–809
Pottinger, David, 1368
Poussaint, Alvin, 246, 295
Pouyat, Buddy, 410
Poverty, **2235–2237**
    Brazilian film, 773
    de Jesus, Carolina Maria, 595
    sociological aspects, 2118–2119
    Wilson, William Julius, 2316
Povich, Shirley, 211
Powell, Adam Clayton, Jr.
    Abyssinian Baptist Church, 14–15
    The American Experience
        (documentary series), 2178
    Council on African Affairs, 540
    election to House of
        Representatives, 1447
    Harlem, 994, 995
    National Negro Congress, 1614
    politics, 1804
    Rangel, Charles Bernard, defeat
        by, 1882
    and Scott, Hazel, 2022

Stout, Jefferson, 1610
Stout, Reneé, 1709, **2150**, 2185
Stovey, George, 207
Stowe, Harriet Beecher
    Dred: A Tale of the Great Dismal Swamp, 1563, 1989
    and Henson, Josiah, 1040
    and Jacobs, Harriet Ann, 1150
    literature of, 1324
    slave narratives, influence of, 2051
    and Webb, Frank J., 2273
Stowers, William Haslip, 389
Straight College. *See* Dillard University
Straightening, hair, 966, 970–971
Straight Out of Brooklyn (film), 788–789, 2234
Stratford, John, 470
Straw, Petrine Archer, 1368
Strayhorn, Billy, 695, 913
Street, John, 1410, 1411
Street, Richard, 2179
Street, Wendell Douglas, 790
Street cries, 1524
Street sweepers, 409–410
Streisand, Barbra, 1407, 1793
Stribling, T. S., 1004, 1006
Strickland, Arvarh, 1054
Strickland, Susanna, 1838
Stride, 1160, 1874–1875
Strikes. *See* Labor and labor unions
Stringed instruments, 1545–1546
Stringer, C. Vivian, 222
Strip quilts, 810
Strode, Woodrow "Woody," 848–850, 852
Strong, A. C., 688
"Strong Men" (poem), **2451–2452**
Stryker, Roy, 1726
Stuart, Gilbert, 1696
Stuart, O. J. E., 1124
Stubblefield, John, 157
Stubbs Thomas, Marion T., 1135
Stuckey, Sterling
    African beliefs, retention of, 1910
    Afrocentrism, 51, 53
    historiography, 1054
Student activism
    Anti-Apartheid movement, 104–105
    Baker, Ella, 760
    black studies, 277
    civil rights movement, 475
    Congress of Racial Equality (CORE), 526
    Freedom Rides, 879–880
    Freedom Summer, 880–882, 881
    Haiti, 1314

Lucy Foster, Autherine, 1346–1347
Nash, Diane, 1578
National Association for the Advancement of Colored People, 1595
Shakur, Assata, 2027
Shuttlesworth, Fred L., 2033
See also Student Nonviolent Coordinating Committee (SNCC)
Student Central Committee, 1578
Student Nonviolent Coordinating Committee (SNCC), **2150–2152**
    Al-Amin, Jamil Abdullah, 66
    Baker, Ella, 760
    Baker, Ella J., 175
    Barry, Marion, 204
    Bevel, James, 238–239
    Black Power movement, 268
    Blackwell, Unita, 286
    Bond, Julian, 312
    Carmichael, Stokely, 411
    civil rights movement, 475–476
    Davis, Angela, 584
    Freedom Rides, 879
    Freedom Summer, 880–881
    Hamer, Fannie Lou, 982
    King, Martin Luther, Jr., 1240
    Lewis, John, 1284–1285
    Lowndes County Freedom Organization, 1345
    Mississippi Freedom Democratic Party, 1462–1464
    Moses, Robert Parris, 1492–1493
    Nash, Diane, 1578
    Norton, Eleanor Holmes, 1658
    photographers, 1781
    religion, 1918
    Third World Women's Alliance, 2191–2192
Student Performance Group, 65
Students for a Democratic Society, 104
Studies, reports and surveys
    "The African Abroad, or the African Diaspora" (International Congress of African Historians), 36–37
    "The Anglo-American Caribbean Commission: Its Problems and Prospects" (Williams), 2299
    Baldus Study, 1570–1571
    baseball, 215
    black studies scholarship, 278
    children's literature, 455
    The Death of White Sociology (Ladner), 2117
    Deep South (Davis), 583, 643–644

"Equality of Educational Opportunity" (Coleman and Campbell), 2116–2117
Freedom to the Free (Commission on Civil Rights), 2228
Kerner Report, 1210–1211, 1232
literature, 1332
Moyne Commission report, 2771
National Urban League, 1618
"The Negro Family: The Case for National Action" (Moynihan), 2116
"The Negro in Chicago: A Study in Race Relations and a Race Riot" (Chicago Commission on Race Relations), 1179
The Negro's Church (Mays), 1412
The Negro's God as Reflected in His Literature (Mays), 1412
race relations studies, foundation funded, 1770
A Red Record: Tabulated Statistics and Alleged Causes of Lynchings in the United States (Wells-Barnett), 2276
"The Social Stratification of English in New York City" (Labov), 1257
sociology of race, *2111,* 2112–2113, 2116–2120
Thirty Years of Lynching in the United States, 1889-1918 (NAACP), 1584
"To Secure These Rights," 71, 1590
"Toxic Wastes and Race in the United States" (Commission for Racial Justice), 725
The Tragedy of Lynching (Raper), 1350
The Truly Disadvantaged: The Inner City, the Underclass, and Public Policy (Wilson), 2118–2119
See also An American Dilemma: The Negro Problem and Modern Democracy (Myrdal)
Studies in a Dying Colonialism (Fanon), 746
Studin, Charles H., 1585
Studio Museum, 152, 591, 996
Studios, film, 780
Studios, movie, 293
Stull, David Lee, 125
Stull, Donald L., 125
Stump and Stumpy, 2166
Stylistics, 1896, 1945–1946
Stylus (magazine), 1309
Suarez y Romero, Anselmo, 775

Tuskegee University *continued*
Scott, Emmett J., 2021
Washington, Booker T., 2264–2266
Washington, Margaret Murray, 2269
Work, Monroe Nathan, 2334
Tutt, H., 1549
Twain, Mark, 1563, 1699, 1733
Twelve Knights of Tabor, 617, 868
Twelvetrees, Harper, 1398
Twelve Tribes of Israel, 1890
Twelve Years a Slave: Narrative of Solomon Northrup (Northrup), 1657
Twentieth Century
African diasporic photography, 1775–1776
lynching, 1352–1353
women and politics, 1820–1821
25th Infantry, 348–349
Twilight, Alexander, 1806–1807, **2219**
Twine, Frances Winddane, 100
The Twist (dance), 1895, 2100
Two Black Crows (radio show), 1868
2 Fast 2 Furious (film), 2234
2 Live Crew, 1538, 1899
"Two Tracks" (Simpson), *148*
Two Trains Running (Wilson), 2313
227 (television show), 2177
Tyers, Will, 1893
Tyler, Viola, 2123
Tympani Five, 1894
Tyner, McCoy, 501, 1531
Tynes, Margaret, 1684
Typologies. *See* Classification
Tyson, Andre, 65
Tyson, Cicely, *2169*, **2220**
East Side/West Side, 2172
television, 2173, 2175
Tyson, Mike, 318, 321, 758, **2220–2222**, *2221*
Tyson, Ron, 2179
Tyus, Wyomia, 1680

U

U. Roy, 660
Ueberroth, Peter, 1413
Uggams, Leslie, 2173–2174
Ullman, Victor, 242
Ulmer, James "Blood," 498
Ulysse, Gina, 101
Umar ibn Said, 1561, 1562
Umbanda
Brazilian film, 772

divination and spirit possession, 624–625
jongo, 1196
Umbra Workshop
Black Arts movement, 248
poetry, 1791
Reed, Ishmael, 1903
Umidfica, 968
"Uncle Jack," 191, 1460
Uncle Remus stories
Africanisms, 39
folklore, 814
Sambo stereotype, 1935–1936
Uncles, Charles Randolph, 428
Uncle Tom's Cabin (show), 1457, 1548
Uncle Tom's Cabin (Stowe)
Baldwin's criticism of, 177–178
Henson, Josiah, 1040
Walker, Kara, art of, 2258
Underclass communities, 2118–2119
Underground Railroad, **2223–2226**
African Methodist Episcopal (AME) Zion Church, 461
The American Experience (documentary series), 2178
archaeology, 117
Big Quarterly, 765
Brown, William Wells, 346
Canada, 385
diasporic textiles, symbolism in, 2184
Dickson, Moses, 617
escape routes, *2225*
Garnet, Henry Highland, 899
Henson, Josiah, 1040
Langston, John Mercer, 1262
philanthropy, 1768
Ruggles, David, 1977
runaway slaves, 1991
Still, William, 2146–2147
Tubman, Harriet, 2211
See also Runaway slaves
Underhill, Edward, 1482
Under the Bamboo Tree (Cole, Johnson and Johnson), *1872*, 1872–1873
Under the Oaks (Bannister), 189
Underwood, Blair, 466, 2035, 2175
Underwriting, insurance, 1096–1097
Unemployment
Great Depression, 941
rates by race, 673–674
sociological aspects, 2118, 2119
UNESCO
archival projects, 130, 133
Brazilian race relations, 1866
Centre d'Art, 141
Maroon societies, 1390

Statement on Race, 1860
Unified Black Movement. *See* Movimento Negro Unificado
Unilateral Declaration of Independence, 2005
Union American Methodist Episcopal Church, 50–51
Union Army
abolitionists, 12–13
African Methodist Episcopal Church, 41–42
black soldiers, *481*, 1449
black troops, 414
Civil War, 479–481, *481*
emancipation, 702–703, 706–997
recruitment, *639*, 640
Trotter, James Monroe, 2205
Tubman, Harriet, 481, 2211
Union Army recruitment, *639*
abolitionists, 12–13
African Methodist Episcopal Church, 41–42
Cary, Mary Ann Shadd, 423
Douglass, Frederick, 640, 1802
Langston, John Mercer, 1262
Remond, Charles Lenox, 1923
Turner, Henry McNeal, 1845
Union Association, 1912
Union Central Relief Association, 1094
Union League of America, **2226–2227**
Union Missionary Society, 2338
Union of Afro-Brazilian Sects of Bahia, 413
Union of Black Clergy, 1022
Union of Black Episcopalians, 728
Union Transportation Company, 716
United American Freewill Baptists, 193
United Church of Christ's Commission for Racial Justice, 450
United Colored Democracy, 994, 1016
United Democratic Party, 1754
United Force, 1754
United Front (Trinidad and Tobago), 2122
United Fruit Enterprise, 828
United House of Prayer for All People of the Church on the Rock of the Apostolic Faith, 936
United Jewish Organizations v. Carey (1977), 23
United Kingdom
abolition, 7–8, 2064
African Civilization Society, 33–34

music of, 1547
and Parker, Charlie, 1163
Williams, Cottie, 694
Williams, Daniel Hale, 878
Williams, Danny, 1320, 2222
Williams, Darnell, 2175
Williams, Delores, 1286, 1919, 2191
Williams, Donald, 577
Williams, Doug, 854
Williams, Dudley, 64
Williams, Eric, **2298–2302,** *2299*
    African diaspora, 36
    anti-colonial movement, 109
    Associates in Negro Folk
        Education, 1114
    Chaguaramas, 441
    February Revolt, 755
    and Harris, Abram Lincoln, Jr.,
        1021
    *The Journal of African American
        History,* 1220
    Little Carib Theatre, 1414
    Manning, Patrick, appointment
        of, 1376
    and McBurnie, Beryl, 1414
    People's National Movement,
        1156, 1756–1758
    "race men," 1402
    and Robinson, A. N. R., 1963,
        1964
    slavery studies, 2065
    Teshea, Isabel, support of, 24
    West Indies Federal Labour
        Party, 2281–2282
    West Indies Federation, 17, 2284
    Woodford Square, 2328–2330
Williams, Eugene, 2023
Williams, Fannie Barrier, 1649,
    2108, **2302,** 2318
Williams, Francis, **2302–2303**
Williams, George Washington,
    2303–2304
    African diaspora, 36
    black studies, 276
    historiography, 1052
    history, 1325
    intellectual life, 1110
    Pan-Africanism, 1718–1719
Williams, Gerald, 249
Williams, Harold T., 377
Williams, Henry Sylvester, 1719–
    1720, **2304–2305**
Williams, Hosea Lorenzo, **2305–
    2306**
Williams, Jay "Inky," 849
Williams, Joe, 1170
Williams, John, 2306
Williams, John A., 242, 1330
Williams, Kenny, 1306

Williams, Lillian, 1054
Williams, Lorraine, 158, 1221
Williams, Marion, 932, 1532
Williams, Martin, 2189
Williams, Mary Lou, **2306–2307**
    and Gillespie, Dizzy, 918
    jazz, 1166, 1167
    music collections, 1557
Williams, Mayo "Ink," 1894
Williams, Nat D., 1869
Williams, Otis, 2179
Williams, Patricia Joyce, 561, 1116,
    2307–2308
Williams, Pat Ward, 146, 1781
Williams, Paul, 1534, 2179
Williams, Paulette. *See* Shange,
    Ntozake
Williams, Paul Revere, 121
Williams, Peter, Jr., **2308**
    African Free School, 38
    and Crummell, Alexander, 563
Williams, Peter, Sr., 712
    African colonization, 1718
    African Methodist Episcopal Zion
        Church, 47, 461
    Pan-Africanism, 1717
Williams, Prince, 193
Williams, Ranny, 408
Williams, Reggie, 222
Williams, Rhonda Y., 1055
Williams, Robert Franklin, **2308–
    2309**
    anti-colonial movement, 109
    critical race theory, 561
    and Mayfield, Julian, 1408
    National Association for the
        Advancement of Colored
        People, 1595
    and Newton, Huey P., 1650
    Revolutionary Action Movement,
        1940–1941
Williams, Rubberlegs, 586
Williams, Russell, 2014
Williams, Serena, 2181
Williams, Sherley Anne
    *Afro-American Literature: The
        Reconstruction of Instruction,*
        1304
    literature, 1331
    poetry, 1792
Williams, Smallwood, 1752, 1753
Williams, "Smokey Joe," 208
Williams, Spencer, 464, 2170
Williams, Todd, 1392
Williams, Tony, 587, 1391
Williams, Tonya Lee, 2175
Williams, Vanessa, 2047
Williams, Venus, 2181

Williams, Venus and Serena, 2144,
    2309, **2309–2311**
Williams, Walter, 1105, 1840
Williams, William T., 1707
Williams and Walker, 2257
Williams Brothers, 933
Williams-Jones, Pearl, 1533
Williamson, Fred, 2173
Williamson, Joel, 1054, 1351
Williamson, John Lee, 301
Williamson, Sonny Boy, 301, 1530,
    2167
Williamsy, Joe, 1171
Willingham, Tyrone, 851
Willis, Bill, 849, 852
Willis, Deborah, 1831, **2311–2312**
Willis, Nathaniel Parker, 1150
Willkie, Wendell, 2290
Will Mastin Trio, 588–589
Wills, Maury, 214, 628
Willson, Charles, 1561
Wilmington, Delaware, 764–765
Wilmington Ten, 450, 1344
Wilmore, Gayraud S., 2191
Wilson, Anthony, 1811
Wilson, August, **2312–2314**
    blues, 304
    literature, 1332
    realism, 651
Wilson, Billy, 179
Wilson, Cassandra, 1166, 1172, *1172*
Wilson, David, 1657
Wilson, Delroy, 1906
Wilson, Demond, 2176
Wilson, Dooley, 2170
Wilson, Dreck Spurlock, 126
Wilson, Ellis, 1704
Wilson, Flip, 504, **2314**
Wilson, Frank T., 1833
Wilson, Fred, 148, 1709, **2314–2315**
Wilson, Harriet E. Adams, **2315–
    2316**
Wilson, Henry M., 33–34
Wilson, Jackie
    Apollo Theater, 114
    Pioneer Awards, 1946
    rhythm and blues, 1943
Wilson, Joe Lee, 1171
Wilson, John, 1875
Wilson, John Louis, 121, 1110
Wilson, Margaret, 1597, 1598
Wilson, Mary, 1974, 1975, 2155
Wilson, Nancy, 1170, 1355
Wilson, Peter, 20, 99, 101
Wilson, Teddy, 783, 1160, 1163
Wilson, W. Rollo, 1208
Wilson, William Julius, **2316**
    North Star (newspaper), 1658